Errata

Page 18: Labels for illustrations in right-hand margin should read *Adult Great Shearwater* and *Adult Wilson's Storm Petrel*.

Page 32: Label for top illustration in right-hand margin should read *Adult Black Stork*.

Page 38: Captions 1 and 2 should be transposed.

Page 46: Replace distribution map for *Lesser Spotted Eagle* with

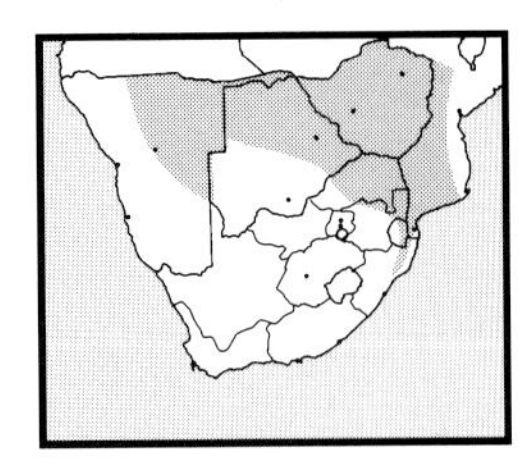

Page 70: Replace captions and grid with
1. Adult Crested Francolin 2. Male Coqui Francolin 3. Adult Greywing Francolin 4. Adult Redwing Francolin 5. Adult Orange River Francolin 6. Adult Shelley's Francolin

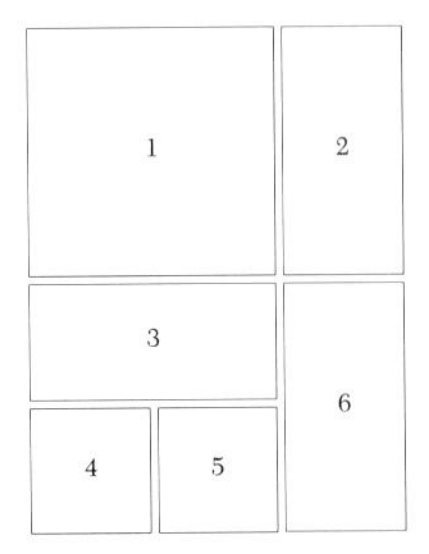

Page 82: Caption 5 should read:
5. *Female African Finfoot*.

Page 92: Caption 4 should read:
4. *Adult Grey Plover (non-breeding)*.

Page 110: Replace distribution map for *Hartlaub's Gull* with

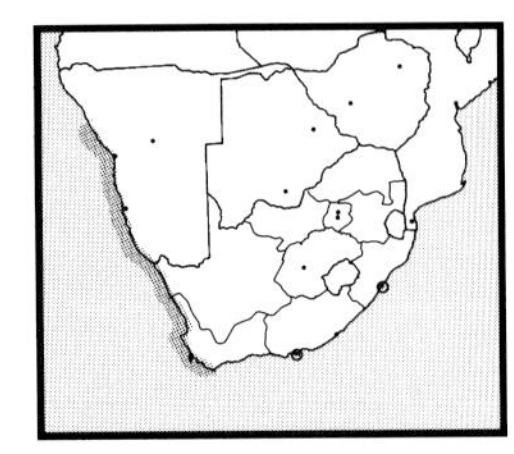

Page 130: Caption 4 should read:
4. *Immature Thickbilled Cuckoo*.

Page 174: Caption 3 should read:
3. *Adult Fawncoloured Lark*.
Replace grid with

Page 185: Photograph numbered 6 is upside down.

Page 193: Photographs numbered 2 and 4 should be rotated 90° anti-clockwise.

Page 196: Replace distribution map for *Yellowspotted Nicator* with

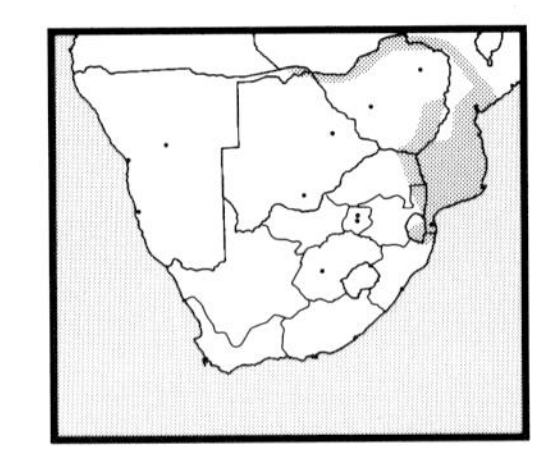

Page 218: Captions 1 and 2 should be transposed.

Page 221: Photograph numbered 5 should be rotated 90° anti-clockwise.

Page 236: Captions 3, 4 and 9 should read:
3. *Male Fiscal Flycatcher*
4. *Female Fiscal Flycatcher*
9. *Female Paradise Flycatcher*

Page 263: Photograph numbered 8 should be rotated 90° anti-clockwise.

Southern African

BIRDS

A Photographic Guide

SASOL

Southern African BIRDS

A Photographic Guide

IAN SINCLAIR ◆ IAN DAVIDSON

STRUIK

Dedication

To Jackie, in millions Ian Sinclair
To Ginger, with love and affection Ian Davidson

Acknowledgments

From the origins of this book in a dim and distant past, I thank Eve Gracie, the power behind the guide and a constant source of enthusiasm at all levels. Mega thanks and micro grovelling to all those photographers who once again scoured their collections and made their images available for this work, which is all theirs. For the continual banter and source of humour throughout the project I humbly thank Tracey Hawthorne, Pippa Parker, Ilze Bezuidenhout, Lellyn Creamer, Kevin Shenton, Damian Gibbs and Jane Maliepaard. Very often sheer tenacity overcame the banter, and workloads vanished overnight. Arlene de Muijnk had the arduous and nightmarish task of collating over 8 000 images to be viewed for this work, and to her I am forever grateful. Jackie, a birding widow, and Daryn and Kiera, two birding orphans, have had the understanding to endure my long absences in the field and have been a constant source of encouragement and support.
Ian Sinclair

A big thank you to Ginger Brown for support and suggestions during the many hours spent working towards this book. To many others, too numerous to mention, with whom I have spent many enjoyable hours in the field gathering first-hand knowledge and expertise, my heartfelt thanks. To my parents, thanks for your support over the years. Ian Davidson

---

Struik Publishers (Pty) Ltd
(a member of the Struik Publishing Group (Pty) Ltd)
Cornelis Struik House
80 McKenzie Street
Cape Town 8001

Reg. No.: 54/00965/07

First published 1995

ISBN 1 86825 785 1

The colour illustrations appearing in this book were taken from *Sasol Birds of Southern Africa* (Struik 1993) and were painted by Peter Hayman, Norman Arlott and Simon Barlow (see page 304)

Publishing director Tracey Hawthorne
Editor Pippa Parker
Editorial assistant Jane Maliepaard
Designers Kevin Shenton and Damian Gibbs
Design assistant Lellyn Creamer
Photographic researcher Arlene de Muijnk
Typeset by Struik DTP, Cape Town
Reproduction by Hirt & Carter (Pty) Ltd, Cape Town
Printed and bound by Tien Wah Press (Pte) Ltd, Singapore

Also available in Afrikaans as
Suider-Afrikaanse Voëls: 'n Fotografiese Gids

Front cover main picture: Jackal Buzzard; insets left to right: Greater Doublecollared Sunbird, Pygmy Goose, Grey Heron. Spine: Knysna Lourie. Back cover insets top to bottom: Cape Vulture, Malachite Kingfisher, African Jacana. Half-title page: Bateleur. Title page: Lesser Flamingoes. Contents page: Yellow Weaver.

Contents

Sponsor's foreword

Southern Africa is blessed with an abundance of fauna and flora, including more than 900 species of bird. The variety and number of birds are often cited as a barometer of the state of health of the environment. We subscribe to this hypothesis and believe that an awareness and concern for our avifauna will eventually lead to active conservation of birds and our natural surroundings.

When *Sasol Birds of Southern Africa* was released a few years ago, we hoped to encourage birders and potential birders to become fully acquainted with the birds they see around them. That book, the most comprehensively illustrated field guide to the region's birds, has to a large degree achieved its goals.

We hope that this book, *Southern African Birds: A Photographic Guide,* will supplement the illustrations contained in the field guide and allow birders to fully appreciate the diversity and beauty of southern African bird life.

PAUL DU P. KRUGER
Managing Director and Deputy Chairman, Sasol Limited

Sasol and the environment

'Protecting the environment is an obligation, not a choice.'

Sasol believes the quality of the air, water and soil should be protected for the continued benefit of all ecosystems. In this way, the needs of the present and future generations will be met, enabling them to live in an environment of acceptable quality.

Sasol is committed to act responsibly towards the environment and to consider the effects of Sasol's operations on the environment when making decisions.

Introduction

Aims of this book

The main purpose of this book is to bring together more photographs than ever before of birds that occur in southern Africa. Since the publication of the second edition of Ian Sinclair's *Field Guide to the Birds of Southern Africa* (Struik, 1984) and *The Complete Book of Southern African Birds* (Struik Winchester, 1989), there has been an even greater interest in birds and subsequently an increase in the number of bird photographers. Encouraged by these two publications, bird photographers in southern Africa have together amassed an enormous wealth of bird photographs, including some of species never taken before and some of obscure and little-known plumage sequences. This book goes further than any other similar photographic reference guide by providing more than 1 000 colour photographs, showing a variety of plumages and sexual dimorphism necessary for identification.

In selecting which species to include in this guide, we eliminated the very rare and vagrant birds, and those that have been seen in the region only a handful of times – perhaps only once. We also omitted those species of which no photographs are available or which, to our knowledge, have never before been photographed. In a few instances, where a species is common but little photographed (usually because the bird is extremely furtive or spends much of its life on the wing), we have used colour illustrations to depict the species.

The arguments for and against using photographs instead of artwork to illustrate a field guide are many. It is an awesome task for any one artist to illustrate accurately all the different species in southern Africa, and no single artist should be expected to have the knowledge of so many different birds and their diverse range of plumages. By the same token, when it comes to photography, light conditions can influence the overall plumage colour and in some instances exaggerate colours. However, the value of the photograph lies in its portrayal of the shape and jizz of the bird, which is very often lacking in an illustrated field guide. Photographic bird guides in this large format are ideal for comparisons between male and female plumages or immatures where they differ significantly from each other. A photograph taken in good light with the crispness and sharpness of focus renders a true likeness of a bird not normally captured by an artist.

This work does not replace the traditionally illustrated field guide but ideally should be used in conjunction with one to identify a bird. No single field guide should be used to identify all the different birds in the region or the many different plumages and age groups that occur. In fact, every available book should be consulted; each will help in the process of identifying those sometimes very difficult groups. In those rare instances where a trick of light has altered a colour, highlighted an unimportant colour or obscured some small detail, the observer, by comparing the species with artwork or other photographs, will immediately recognize this. In the field it is only on rare occasions that a bird will remain motionless for any length of time, enabling an observer to scrutinize it and absorb every detail. Birds in flight are sometimes moving so rapidly that important details are a blur, but several of the photographs chosen here highlight important features and details (not often seen on birds in flight) in action shots.

The numerous photographs reproduced in this volume were selected from a range of more than 8 000. A fair number have never been published before and go a long way towards illustrating the very high standard of bird photography in southern Africa. A few were sourced from established professionals whose work is well known and the envy of photographers worldwide. Many, however, were selected from the files of amateur photographers, whose tenacity and patience have been the making of high-quality photographs. These individuals have travelled the length and breadth of the region, from the high reaches of the Drakensberg to the endless swamps of the Okavango, from the windswept plains of the west coast to the escarpment edges of the east. Special journeys to the most remote regions to capture, for example, the image of an obscure cisticola were cheerfully undertaken, and in some instances months were spent trying to get that impossible shot of an elusive and furtive bird.

Very few of the photographs between these covers were taken of birds involved in any breeding activity; today's conservation-conscious photographer avoids unnecessary disturbance of birds at their nests. The action and flight shots are, in any case, much more interesting than scenes of a bird incubating an egg or feeding its young. Indeed, for identification purposes, a bird away from the nest is of much more value than one that may be partly obscured because it is sitting on its eggs.

About this book

The area covered by this book is the southern African subregion, that is, Africa south of the Kunene River in the west and the Zambezi River in the east, and including the islands off the coasts of Namibia, South Africa and Mozambique. The distribution maps supplied for each species are enlarged versions of those used in *Sasol Birds of Southern Africa*, and are the most up-to-date maps available for the region. Each bird is ascribed both its English and scientific names and its Roberts number. The overall length of the bird is also given; where this is exaggerated by an extremely long tail, details of this are given separately, and if there is a notable difference in size between the male and the female, or between breeding and non-breeding plumages, this is also indicated.

The main text provides information on how to identify each bird, its preferred habitat, any behavioural characteristics where these are pertinent to identification, and for many of the species a phonetic rendition of the call or song. The main aim of this book is to convey those field characters that help to identify the bird as quickly as possible. This guide does not describe in detail irrelevant plumage colours, but concentrates rather on those marks or combinations of marks that make a particular species unique. These characters are also compared with those of closely related or similar birds.

The arrangement of photographs on the plates allows for easy comparison of like species or of different plumage stages of the same species where the differences are marked. To aid the reader, a simple block design alongside the text indicates (in conjunction with captions) the position of the different species on the plate. In addition to the full-colour photographs of each species, colour illustrations have in some instances been included on the text page to highlight features or plumages not captured by the photographs.

The order in which the birds are presented is based on the classification adopted by the Southern African Ornithological Society, except in a few cases where species have been juggled around to aid identification and allow for the direct comparison of similar species.

Bird habitats

The habitat in which a bird lives is very often, but not always, a clue to its identity: it is highly unlikely, for example, that we would see albatrosses flying around the highest peaks in the Drakensberg or encounter a rockjumper far out to sea. Each species has its own unique set of environmental requirements; some birds may display a very limited habitat choice, for example, several forest species remain within their limited habitat and never venture from it; other birds, however, will move happily between different habitats.

Most habitats in southern Africa have been altered by man to some extent and in some cases this has been beneficial to the bird population of a particular area. Those areas still in pristine or near-pristine condition are very distinct and support bird species peculiar to them. For example, a stroll through a miombo woodland would reveal species like the Spotted Creeper, the Whitebreasted Cuckooshrike and the Violetbacked Sunbird, none of which would be encountered on a similar stroll through, say, a highland evergreen forest.

The major habitats found in southern Africa include lagoons, estuaries, dams, lakes and pans; the seashore; the oceans (Atlantic and Indian); marshlands and rivers; grasslands and cultivated lands; forests; savanna; fynbos; and desert and semi-desert. The habitat map provided on the opposite page indicates the boundaries of the main terrestrial regions found in southern Africa.

Lagoons, estuaries, dams, lakes and pans

Estuaries, lagoons, lakes, dams and pans are wide-open areas harbouring large numbers of waterfowl and shorebirds; a muddy estuary at low tide can hold thousands of migrant wading birds. Lakes, pans and man-made dams are important in the numbers of waterfowl they sustain and if islands are present they are doubly important as breeding areas. Seasonally flooded pans or depressions, often with a high saline content, also support large numbers of birds, including many migrant or nomadic species.

Seashore

The seashore habitat includes the beaches, rocky shorelines, cliffs and bluffs along the high- and low-tide mark. These locations do not hold a vast array of species but many gulls and terns use this zone for roosting, sometimes in very large numbers. A few of our endemic birds are confined to this habitat and at times come under severe pressure from the disturbance caused by, for example, vehicular traffic, sunbathers and fishermen.

Oceans

The ocean habitat encompasses the immediate adjacent Indian and Atlantic oceans around our coasts. The Indian Ocean has a warm-water current, and the Atlantic a cold-water current, which to some extent influence the kinds of birds that occur over their surfaces. True seabirds occurring over the oceans include albatrosses, shearwaters and petrels, which usually stay very far out to sea, pass close by near-jutting promontories or headlands, or are storm-driven ashore. Most of the birds occurring in our oceanic waters visit the southern African subregion on journeys from the South Pole (albatrosses) or the North Pole (skuas, gulls and petrels).

Marshlands and rivers

Marshlands and rivers comprise wide and varied habitats, very important for the large numbers of species they support. Some marshes are seasonally flooded and during droughts may go for years in a dry state, whereas others are large and permanent wetlands; the vegetation varies depending on the type of marsh. Stands of tall reeds or impenetrable beds of papyrus tend to dominate some, while others have rank grass growth but are wet and provide cover and protection to the warblers, rails and crakes that frequent them. Rivers may have adjoining marshy areas or tall stands of forests bordering them, important in that this vegetation provides refuge to a wide range of sometimes very rare or specialized birds.

Grasslands (including montane grasslands) and cultivated lands

The grasslands in the region are one of the fastest diminishing habitats, and very few such areas remain. They support important bird communities such as bustards, cranes, larks and pipits, many of which are endemic. The planting over of these grasslands with exotic trees for the timber industry has created plantations stretching to the horizon but these emerald woods harbour very few birds and are mostly silent green deserts; the same applies to the endless sugarcane fields, to which very few bird species have adapted. Montane grasslands include the higher reaches of South Africa and Zimbabwe where many interesting species, some endemic, are found above the tree line and in the valleys.

Forests

Forests cover a very small proportion of southern Africa, occurring as a series of scattered islands along the eastern side of the subcontinent where the rainfall is highest, but are rich in bird species. They encompass natural wooded areas, and can be divided into two distinct types: evergreen montane forests and coastal forests, confined to low-lying areas along the eastern coastal plain. Lowland forests have a distinctly different flora to that of the montane forests, and are generally richer in bird species.

Habitat map

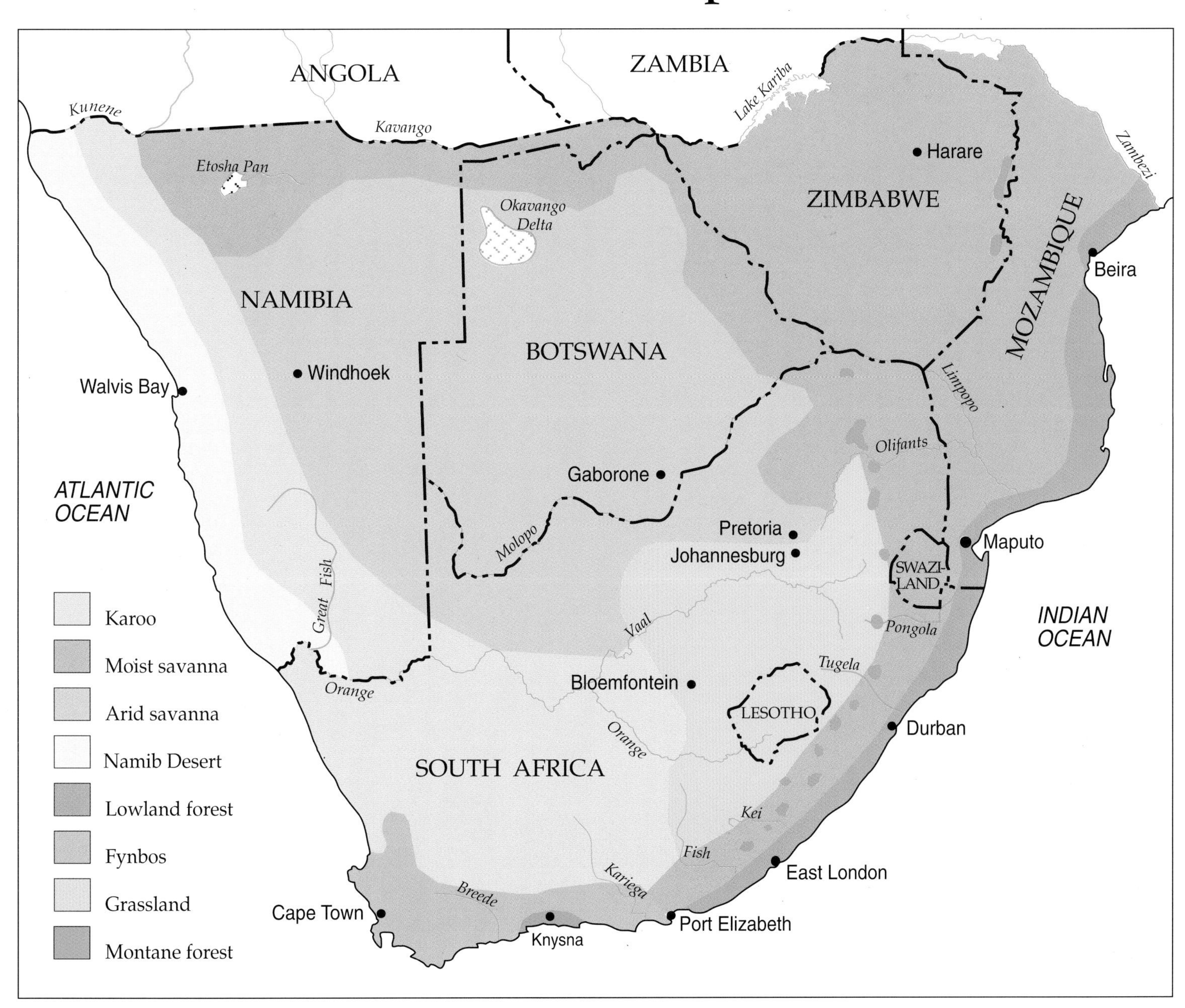

Savanna

This habitat, often referred to as bushveld, embraces a range of wooded country, from the tall, broad-leaved miombo woodland of Zimbabwe and northern Mozambique to the arid thornveld of the Kalahari. Its essential feature is deciduous trees with an understorey of grass, irrespective of tree type or spacing of the trees. Usually the term 'woodland' is used if the trees form a closed canopy, and 'parkland' if the trees are scattered. There are two distinct divisions within this biome: arid savanna and moist savanna. Arid savanna dominates the western half of the savanna biome and has the greatest diversity of bird species. Moist savanna, dominated by broad-leaved tree species, forms the eastern and northern parts of the region.

Fynbos

The fynbos habitat is famous for its immense number of plant species, including hundreds of species of *Protea*, *Erica* and *Restio*. Although it lacks a great diversity of birds, those that do occur in this unusual habitat are mostly unique and endemic.

Desert and semi-desert (Namib Desert and Karoo)

This habitat is the vast low-rainfall area in the west of the region, in which the highest incidence of endemism occurs. Bird populations are small and one can travel long distances through sparse vegetation without glimpsing a single bird. The rainfall is unpredictable and, consequently, many of the species occurring here are nomadic.

Bird topography

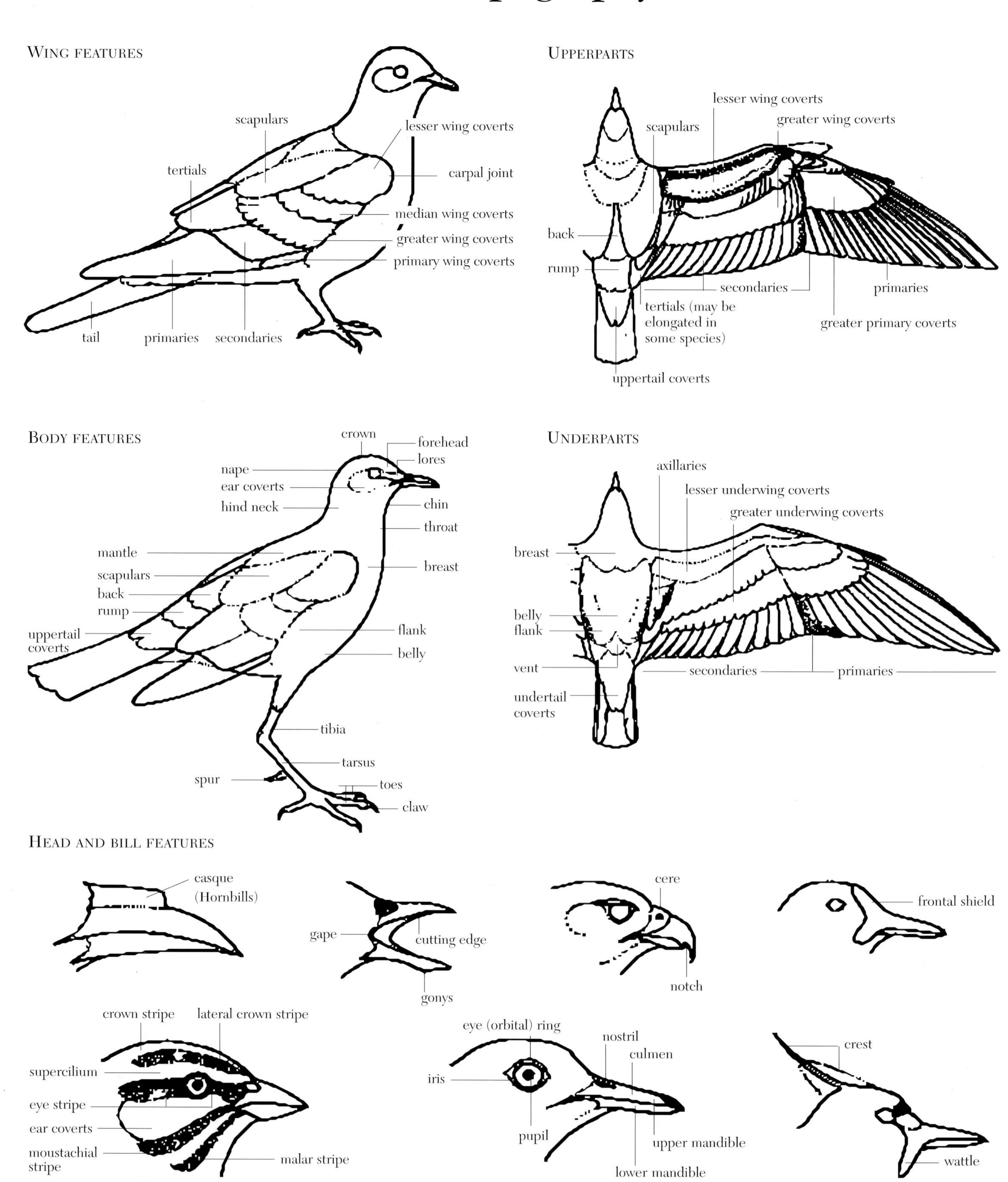

Glossary of terms

Accidental. A vagrant or stray species not normally found within the region under discussion.

Albinism. A loss of body pigments resulting in red eyes, legs and bill.

Allopatric. Mutually exclusive geographically; that is, the ranges of two or more species do not overlap.

Arboreal. Tree dwelling.

Breeding endemic. A species which breeds only in a particular region but undertakes movements or migrations during the non-breeding season such that a measurable proportion of the population leaves the region.

Caruncle. A fleshy outgrowth on the heads of certain birds.

Colonial. Associating in close proximity, while roosting, feeding or nesting.

Commensal. Living with or near another species, without being interdependent.

Corvid. Of the crow family.

Crepuscular. Active at dawn and dusk.

Cryptic. Pertaining to camouflage coloration.

Diurnal. Active during daylight hours.

Eclipse plumage. Dull plumage attained, for example, by male ducks during a transitional moult, after the breeding season and before they acquire brighter plumage.

Endemic. A species whose breeding and non-breeding ranges are confined to a particular region.

Feral. Relating to populations of domesticated species that have reverted to a free existence.

Flight feathers. The longest feathers on the wings and tail.

Flush. To put to flight.

Form. A colour variant within a species; such variation may or may not be linked to subspecific status.

Fulvous. Reddish yellow or tawny.

Gular. Of or relating to the throat.

Immature. A bird that has moulted from juvenile plumage but has not attained adult plumage. Can also include juvenile plumage, and for the purposes of this work generally does so.

Irruption. A rapid expansion of a species' normal range.

Juvenile. The first full-feathered plumage of a young bird.

Jizz. Acronym for General Impression, Size, Shape. Used to refer to a bird's characteristic behaviour and shape.

Lek. A communal display ground where males congregate for the sole purpose of courtship.

Leucism. A partial loss of feather pigment; normal body colours retained.

Melanism. An increase in the amount of black or brown pigment, melanin, which masks other colours causing a bird to appear all black or brown.

Migrant. A species which undertakes long-distance flights between its breeding and non-breeding areas.

Mirrors. The white spots on the primaries of gulls.

Montane. Pertaining to mountains.

Near endemic. A species whose range is largely restricted to a region but extends slightly outside the region's borders. This book includes mostly species whose ranges extend into the arid regions of southwestern Angola.

Nocturnal. Active at night.

Non-passerine. Not belonging to the order Passeriformes.

Overwintering. A bird, normally a migrant, which remains in the subregion instead of migrating to its breeding grounds.

Passerine. A bird belonging to the order Passeriformes.

Palearctic. All of Europe, Africa north of the Sahara, and temperate Asia north of the Himalayas.

Pelagic. Ocean dwelling.

Polyandrous. Pertaining to a mating system where individual females mate with more than one male; often the nest is attended by a single parent, normally the male. Occurs, for example, in the Painted Snipe.

Race. A geographical population of a species; a subspecies.

Range. A bird's distribution.

Raptor. A bird of prey.

Resident. A species not prone to migration, remaining in the same area all year.

Rictal bristles. The bristles around the basal opening of the bill, or gape.

'Ringneck' doves. Pertaining to doves with a black nape band.

Rufous. Reddish brown.

Sub-adult. A bird intermediate in age and plumage between immature and adult (*see* 'Immature').

Sympatric. Occurring together in the same geographical area.

Territory. The area a bird establishes and then defends from others.

Vagrant. Rare and accidental to the region under discussion.

Abbreviations

The abbreviation at the end of each species entry indicates the status of a bird within the region.
R = *resident*, S = *summer visitor*, W = *winter visitor*, P = *passage visitor*, I = *intra-African migrant*, E = *endemic*, and NE = *near endemic*.

Abbreviations appearing at the end of each species account are also explained at the bottom of each page.
Other abbrevaitions used include:
m = *male*, f = *female*, cm = *centimetres*

Penguins Family Spheniscidae

These flightless marine birds have powerful, rigid flippers that are used for rapid underwater swimming. Ashore they waddle with a clumsy, side-to-side gait or hop. The stiff, dense feathers are shed in a complete annual moult during which the bird comes ashore for a period of three to four weeks.

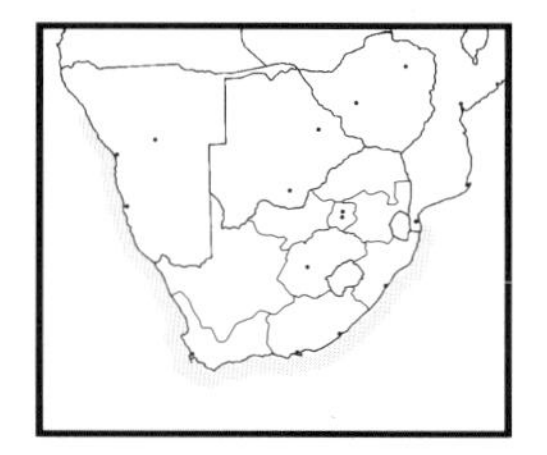

Jackass Penguin *Spheniscus demersus* (3) 60 cm

The black and white head pattern of the adult is diagnostic and is visible from a great distance. On land and on hot days the bare skin above the eye turns a bright pinkish red, indicating that the bird is overheating. The black spotting on the white underparts is variable. Juveniles are dark blue-grey above and have shorter, stubbier bills than do adults. Jackass Penguins are nocturnal when ashore; their loud, donkey-like braying builds up to a crescendo just after nightfall. They swim rapidly underwater and can 'porpoise', clearing the water by heights of up to almost a metre. They are found in large colonies on offshore islands and on a few mainland localities, and small groups can be seen swimming offshore at the Cape. R, E

Grebes Family Podicipedidae

Small to medium-sized diving birds with lobed toes (not webbed feet), larger species show a straight, pointed bill and all species develop richer, more elaborate head feathering when breeding. They feed on aquatic insects and fish. The nest are mounds of rotting vegetation placed on floating matter or among reeds. The young have striking head patterns and are often seen riding on their swimming parent's back.

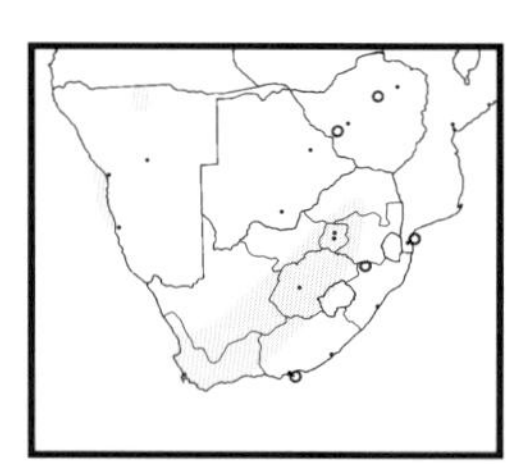

Great Crested Grebe *Podiceps cristatus* (6) 50 cm

Breeding adults are unmistakable, showing a rufous-fringed white face with a black cap and ear tufts. Immature and non-breeding birds lack the rufous and black colouring, and have a longer, thinner and whiter neck than the immature Reed Cormorant (see page 24) with which they might be confused. In flight these birds show broad expanses of white on both the leading and the trailing edges of the wing. Immatures might be confused with non-breeding or immature Blacknecked Grebes but are very much larger and have a longer, thinner neck. Displaying birds face each other on the water and, with the head frills fanned out, constantly flick their heads from side to side. They utter grunts and growls during display but are otherwise silent. Great Crested Grebes occur on large expanses of cold, fresh water. R

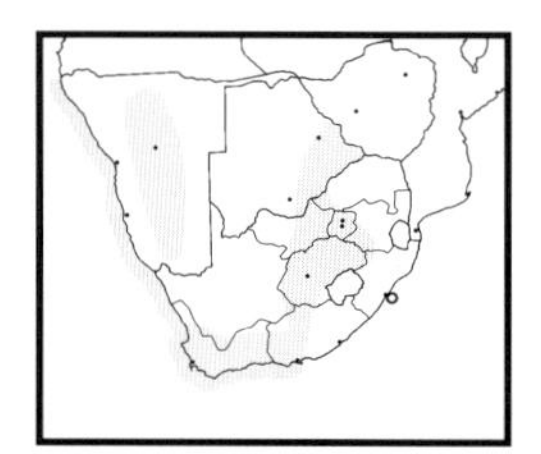

Blacknecked Grebe *Podiceps nigricollis* (7) 28 cm

The breeding bird appears dark overall from a distance but at closer range the chestnut flanks and the golden tufts fanning out from behind the eye are evident; so too are the bright, cherry-red eye and slightly upturned bill. Non-breeding and immature birds could be confused with the similar Dabchick but are larger, have a clear white throat and cheeks, and are dark grey on the front of the neck. In flight the large expanse of white on the primaries and secondaries is clearly evident. Blacknecked Grebes are mostly silent, except for the various trills and whistles uttered when they are breeding. Large flocks gather on saline lakes, especially around saltworks and on the inshore waters of the Namibian coast. R

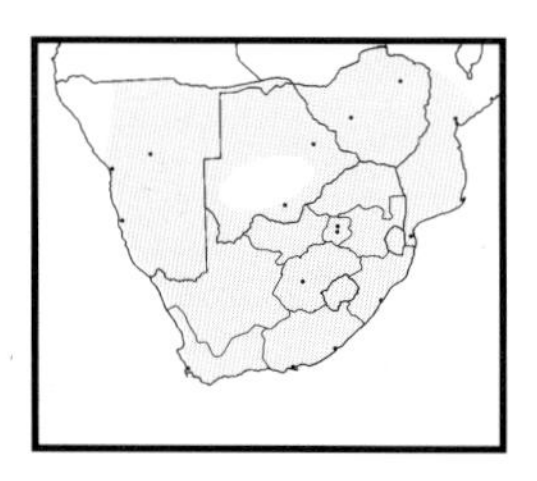

Dabchick (Little Grebe) *Tachybaptus ruficollis* (8) 20 cm

This is a small, rotund, very dark waterbird with a very pale yellow gape. In breeding plumage it shows a dark rusty throat and foreneck. Non-breeding and immature birds are drabber brown with a paler gape and may be confused with the non-breeding Blacknecked Grebe but are browner, not grey, overall, have a darker throat and cheeks, and are much smaller. The pale vent area is very often fluffed up, especially on cold days. Dabchicks are gregarious, forming small groups in the non-breeding period, but become very furtive when breeding. Their clear, loud, descending trill is very often the first indication of their presence. They may be encountered on any stretch of fresh water. R

Adult Great Crested Grebe

Adult Blacknecked Grebe (non-breeding)

Adult Dabchick (non-breeding)

1. Immature Jackass Penguin
2. Adult Great Crested Grebe
3. Adult Jackass Penguin with young
4. Adult Blacknecked Grebe (breeding)
5. Adult Dabchick (breeding)
6. Adult Dabchick (non-breeding)

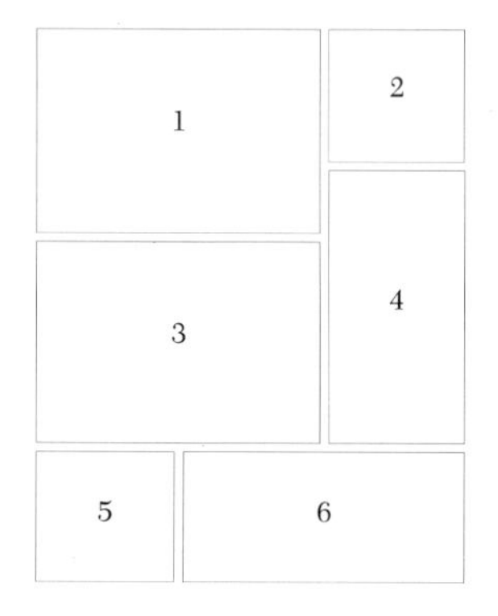

R *resident* • E *endemic*

Albatrosses Family Diomedeidae

These huge, long-winged seabirds come ashore only to breed, chiefly in the southern hemisphere. Closely related to the shearwaters (see page 16) and tiny storm petrels (see page 20), they share the peculiar feature of separate, raised tubular nostrils. Large numbers occur over trawling grounds in the southwest of the region.

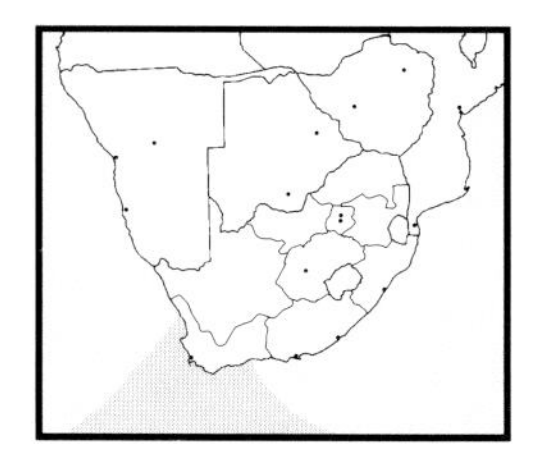

Royal Albatross *Diomedea epomophora* (9) 122 cm

The Royal Albatross and the Wandering Albatross are very difficult to tell apart in adult plumage except at very close range when the black cutting edge to the bill and black eye-ring of the Royal Albatross can clearly be seen. The northern race, *sandfordi*, is distinguishable from the Wandering Albatross by the broad, irregular black border to the underwing from the carpals to the wingtips. Immature Royal Albatrosses do not have the striking chocolate-brown plumage of immature Wandering Albatrosses, nor do they show the intermediate mottled brown and white plumages. Royal Albatrosses are found far offshore in the Benguela Current, rarely venturing over shallow waters. W, P

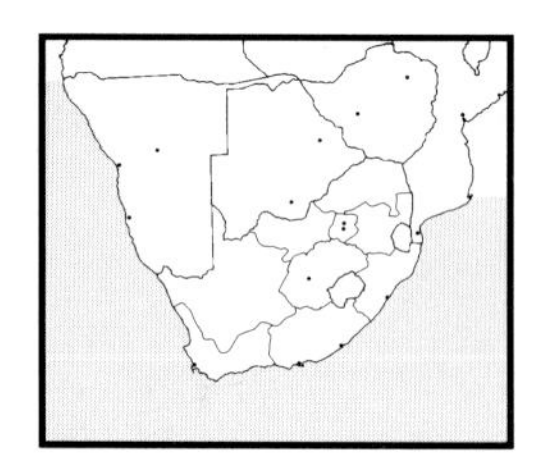

Wandering Albatross *Diomedea exulans* (10) 125 cm

Both the Royal Albatross and the Wandering Albatross, known collectively as the 'great' albatrosses, can be told apart from the smaller albatross species by their white backs and their much greater wingspans. The immature Wandering Albatross in its first year has a dark chocolate-brown plumage relieved only by a white face and underwing. Over a period of five years it progressively becomes whiter through various stages of mottled brown and white. In these immature plumages it cannot be confused with the Royal Albatross as the latter does not show this immature plumage sequence. Adult birds can safely be distinguished from adult Royal Albatrosses only at close range when the bill and eye characters can be seen, the Wandering Albatross lacking the black edges to the bill and the black eye-ring of the Royal Albatross. This, the longest-winged bird in the world, has powerful and dynamic soaring abilities: it hugs the contours of enormous waves and sweeps to great heights, covering long distances over the ocean. It very rarely ventures inshore, preferring to stay above deeper waters. The call is a harsh, nasal 'waaaak'. W, P

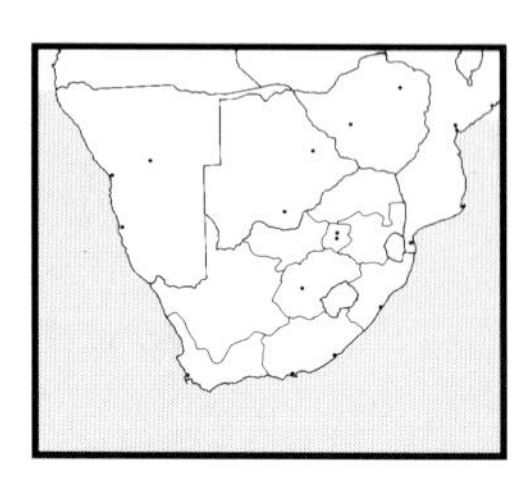

Shy Albatross *Diomedea cauta* (11) 98 cm

Although only slightly smaller than the 'great' albatrosses, this species differs by having an all-dark back uniform with the upperwings. At long range when only the underparts are seen, however, it could easily be mistaken for a Royal Albatross or a Wandering Albatross; at closer range, a small black 'thumbprint' at the base of the wing is noticeable. The back and upperwings are paler in this species than they are in the other dark-mantled albatrosses. They have a pale grey wash to the head with a vaguely contrasting white crown and a greenish bill with a yellow tip. Immature birds have a smudged greyish head and collar, and a dark-tipped grey bill. Resembling the immature Blackbrowed Albatross, the immature Shy Albatross is distinguished by its much larger size and its underwing pattern, which (as in adult birds) is totally white with a narrow black border. The call is a deep and harsh 'waaaek', given only when the birds fight for food scraps. S, W, P

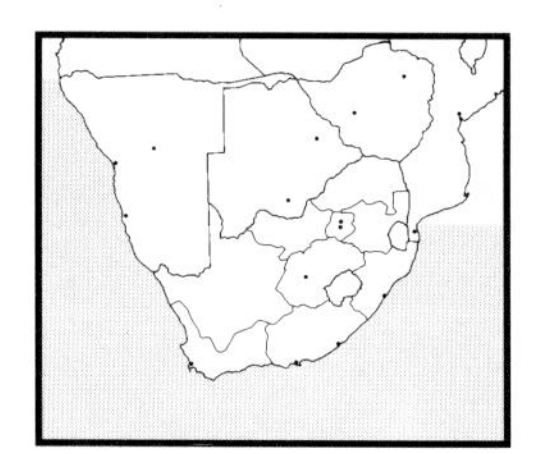

Blackbrowed Albatross *Diomedea melanophris* (12) 90 cm

This species is much smaller than the 'great' albatrosses and differs further by having a black back uniform with the upperwings. It can be distinguished from the Kelp Gull (see page 110) by its much larger size and stiff-winged, gliding flight. Adults have a diagnostic pink-tipped yellow bill, a black lozenge-shaped mark around the eye and a black line running from in front of to behind the eye. The underwing of the adult is white with a broad black border and at long range this differentiates it from the adult Yellownosed Albatross (see page 16). The immature at rest on the water can easily be mistaken for the larger immature Shy Albatross but when put to flight shows a dusky, not white, underwing. The underwing flight pattern of the immature Blackbrowed Albatross is very similar to that of the immature Greyheaded Albatross (see page 16) but the latter species has an all-dark, not dark-tipped, bill. The Blackbrowed Albatross utters a throaty 'whaaa' and squawks. S, W, P

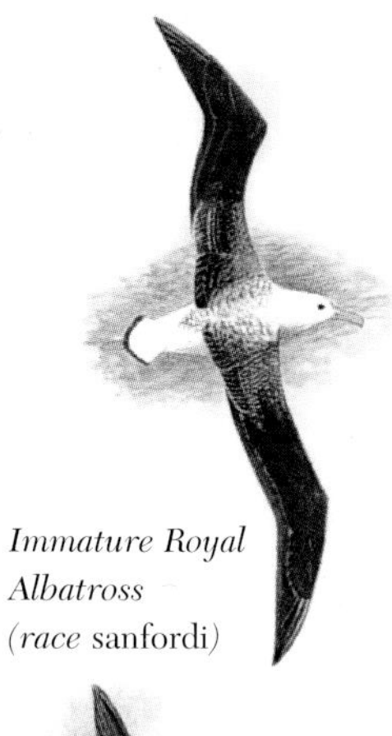

Immature Royal Albatross (race sanfordi*)*

Immature Wandering Albatross

Immature Blackbrowed Albatross

1. Adult Royal Albatross
2. Immature Wandering Albatross
3. Adult Royal Albatross
4. Adult Wandering Albatross with chick
5. Immature Blackbrowed Albatross
6. Immature Wandering Albatross
7. Adult Wandering Albatross
8. Adult Blackbrowed Albatross
9. Immature Shy Albatross
10. Immature Shy Albatross

1	2	
3	4	
5	6	7
8	9	10

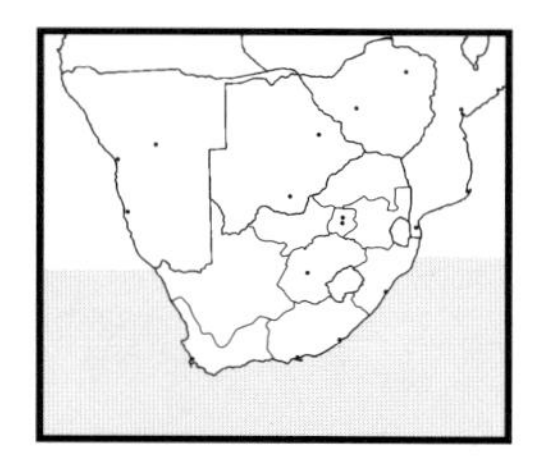

Greyheaded Albatross *Diomedea chrysostoma* (13) 89 cm

The deep blue-grey head combined with the broad black borders of the underwings render the adult unmistakable. At closer range the dark bill shows very obvious yellow stripes along the ridges of the upper and lower mandibles. Immatures and adults in worn plumage sometimes have a white, not grey, head and could then be confused with the immature Blackbrowed Albatross (see page 14). Adult Greyheaded Albatrosses differ, however, by having a dark, not yellow, bill and immatures have a dark grey, not dark-tipped, bill. The birds breed on sub-Antarctic islands during summer, and typically utter grunts and squawks when fighting over food. W, P

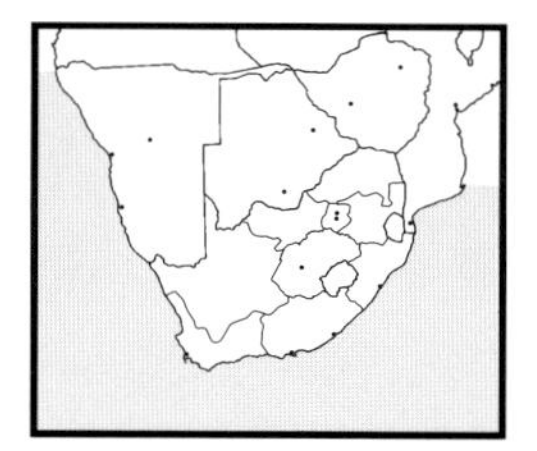

Yellownosed Albatross *Diomedea chlororhynchos* (14) 80 cm

Smaller than both the Blackbrowed Albatross (see page 14) and the Greyheaded Albatross, this species is also much more slender, with a longer-necked and thinner-billed appearance. Adults in newly moulted plumage show a distinct grey head, some more so than others, and this could lead to confusion with the Greyheaded Albatross. However, the underwing of the Yellownosed Albatross shows much more white and has a narrow, not broad, black border. Immatures differ from adults in having an all-black bill and a white head. This small albatross has the stiff-winged, soaring flight typical of its family but will readily fly with regular wing-flapping in calm conditions, quite unlike the larger albatrosses. The usual albatross 'waaak' or 'woooaak' notes are given when the birds fight over offal in a boat's wake. S, W, P

Immature Greyheaded Albatross

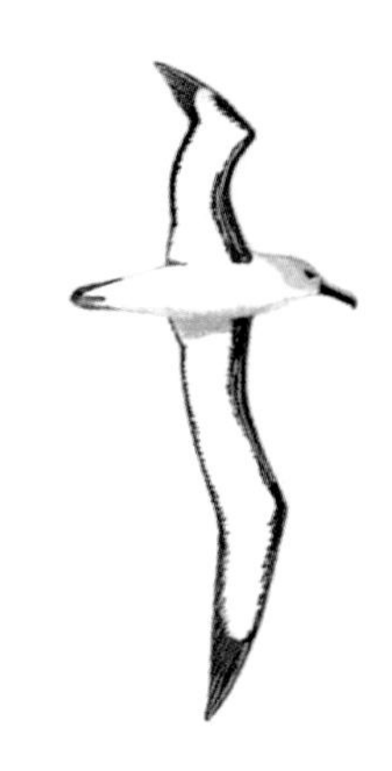

Adult Yellownosed Albatross

Shearwaters and petrels Family Procellariidae

The genera vary in size from the small prions to the huge giant petrels. The *Puffinus* group differs from the *Pterodroma* group by having long and slender, not short and stubby, bills and by their wings which are straight and stiffly held, not angled and flexed at the wrist. All the species are tube-nosed. Individual species have characteristic flight actions which aid identifiaction. The sexes are usually alike and most species do not show an obvious immature plumage.

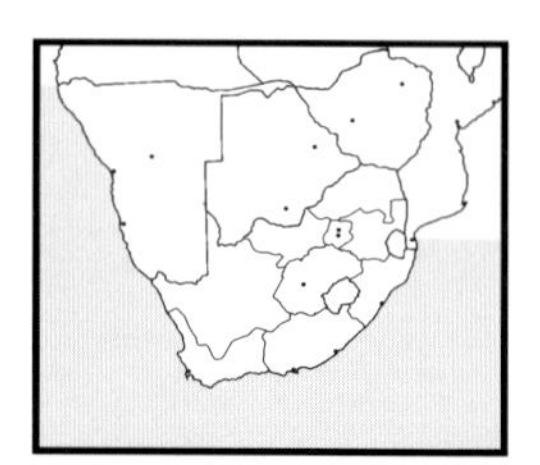

Southern Giant Petrel *Macronectes giganteus* (17) 90 cm

The Southern Giant Petrel is instantly recognizable in its pale phase, which is all white with random black spotting; this phase does not occur in the Northern Giant Petrel. The dark phase of the Southern Giant Petrel can be reliably differentiated from the Northern Giant Petrel only when the bill colour is seen: this species has a pink to olive bill with a greenish tip, which appears uniform in colour. The adult body plumage of the Southern Giant Petrel is very variable and similar to that of the Northern Giant Petrel, but its head is mostly very pale grey or white and does not impart a capped appearance. This bird has the same lumbering flight as the Northern Giant Petrel and a similar voice. Both species if trapped or threatened eject an accurate stream of evil-smelling fluid. Southern Giant Petrels patrol close inshore, sometimes just beyond the breakers, searching for offal or beached dead seals. They utter harsh grunts when fighting over food. S, W, P

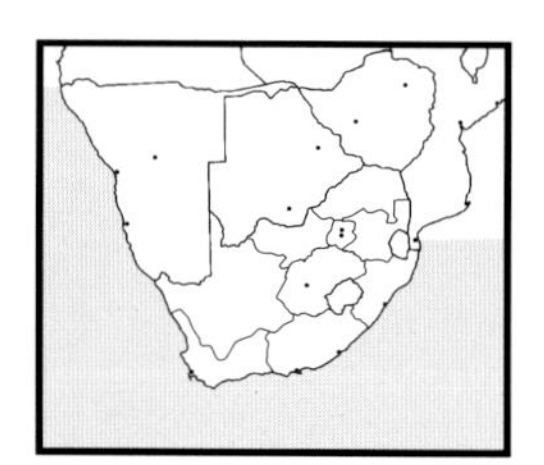

Northern Giant Petrel *Macronectes halli* (18) 90 cm

A very large, albatross-sized petrel with an enormous bill, the Northern Giant Petrel may be confused only with the Southern Giant Petrel in both immature and adult plumages. Although this species does not have the white phase of the Southern Giant Petrel, the plumage in both species is so variable that the only positive means of identification are the bill characters, which can be seen only at close range. The Northern Giant Petrel has a pinkish to olive-coloured bill with a reddish-brown tip, imparting a dark-tipped bill appearance in the field. Adults have a greyish body with darker wings, and a paler head which often gives a capped appearance that is lacking in the Southern Giant Petrel. In flight, both species have a slow, lumbering gait with a distinct 'hunchbacked' look, the heavy bill being held below the body line. Immatures are a dark chocolate-brown and grow progressively paler with age. Northern Giant Petrels are mostly silent but do hiss and grunt when fighting over food. They are much less common on our coasts than are Southern Giant Petrels. S, W, P

1. Adult Greyheaded Albatross
2. Adult Yellownosed Albatross
3. Adult Greyheaded Albatross
4. Adult Southern Giant Petrel
5. Immature Yellownosed Albatross
6. Immature Southern Giant Petrel
7. Adult Southern Giant Petrel (dark phase and pale phase)
8. Adult Northern Giant Petrel

1	2
3	4
5	6
7	8

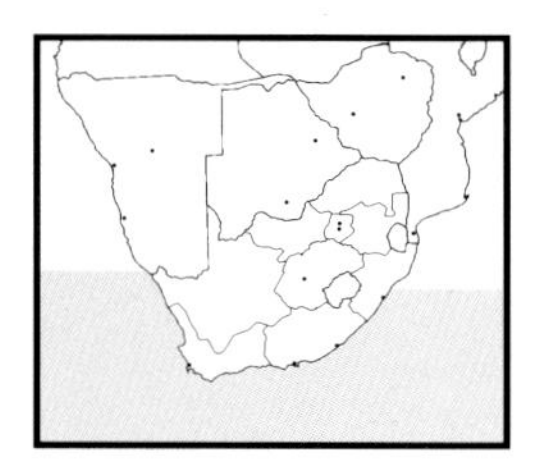

Antarctic Fulmar *Fulmarus glacialoides* (19) 48 cm

This grey and white bird could easily be overlooked as a gull were it not for its stiff-winged, soaring and gliding flight. A very pale grey seabird, it is most conspicuous when seen among the dark brown and grey petrels that occur in southern African waters. The combination of totally white underparts and head, pale grey upperwings and the white primary base make this bird unmistakable. At close range the pinkish bill can be seen to have a dark tip. The Antarctic Fulmar is more aerial than other similarly sized petrels and can stay aloft in the wake of a ship for long periods. A high-pitched cackle is given when the birds are fighting over food. W

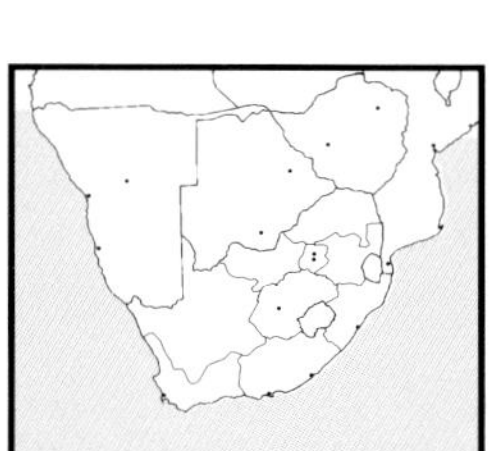

Pintado Petrel *Daption capense* (21) 40 cm

The contrasting pied plumage, combined with the twisting, buoyant flight of this species, makes it one of the easiest seabirds to identify. At rest on the ocean it swims very high in the water, almost phalarope-like, with its breast down and its tail up. It will dive from the surface or plunge from insignificant heights. The call is an incessant, high-pitched tittering given when the birds fight over food. Small to large flocks typically follow ships to scavenge in their wakes. W, P

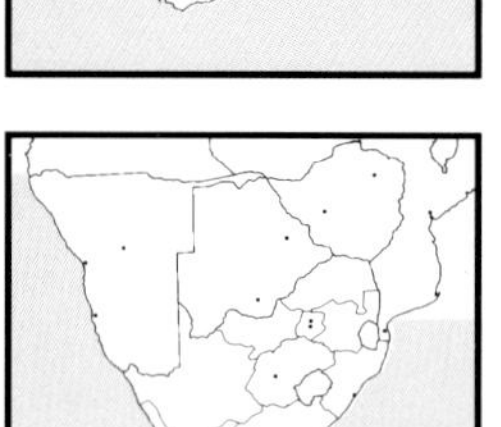

Greatwinged Petrel *Pterodroma macroptera* (23) 42 cm

Similar in size and colour to the Sooty Shearwater (see page 20), this species differs by having an all-dark, not silvery, underwing, and in its flight action: the Greatwinged Petrel has very angled wings, not straight and stiffly held, and it soars and sweeps in arcs over the ocean rather than gliding between stiff wing beats. The head of the Greatwinged Petrel appears disproportionately large in relation to the rest of its body, and the bill is held angled at 45 degrees. These birds are silent in our area. S, W, P

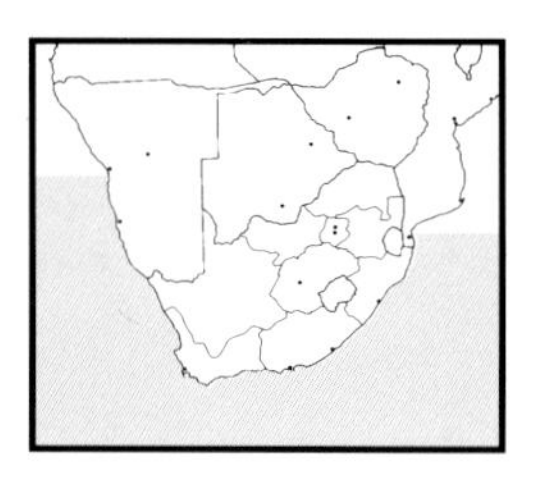

Softplumaged Petrel *Pterodroma mollis* (24) 35 cm

This small, fragile-looking petrel is identified by its dark brown upperparts, white underparts with contrasting dark underwings and narrow breast band. In good light a faint, open 'M' pattern is evident across the upperwings and back. Its flight is dynamic, especially so in windy conditions, and entails sweeping arcs high above the sea with sudden plummets to a wave front. Unlike other petrels and shearwaters, the wings of this bird are not held stiffly and outstretched but are sharply angular with the carpals bent and held forwards in line with the head. The Softplumaged Petrel occurs in a very rare dark phase which could be confused with the all-dark-brown Greatwinged Petrel, but the latter species is much larger and has a grizzled face. The Softplumaged Petrel is not known to call in our waters. W, P

Broadbilled Prion *Pachyptila vittata* (29) 30 cm

Members of the prion group are notoriously difficult to identify at sea. The Broadbilled Prion and the Fairy Prion can be separated safely only by the amount of black in the tail and by the bill and head colour. The Broadbilled Prion is the larger of the two and has a heavy-headed appearance which is enhanced by its large black, not blue, bill. The greyish-blue on the head is darker than that on the head of the Fairy Prion and extends on to the shoulders; the Broadbilled Prion also shows a distinct broad, dark line through the eye, and the black on the tail is confined to the tip. The flight is buoyant and erratic, the bird twisting and turning over the waves but not reaching any great height above the sea. When feeding, it 'hydroplanes', jutting its head underwater and flying along over the surface as it paddles with its dangling feet. It is silent in southern African waters. W, P

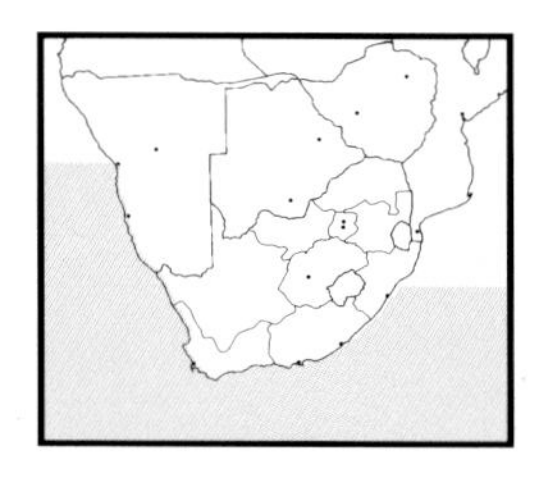

Fairy Prion *Pachyptila turtur* (31) 24 cm

Noticeably smaller than the Broadbilled Prion, the Fairy Prion is also much paler and tends to be blue, rather than grey, in colour. The head is more compact and neater, and the bill is smaller and is blue, not black. The head colour is very pale blue, at times appearing white, with a faint blue line through the eye. The diagnostic feature is the tail, the black in which extends for about a third of the way up, unlike that of the Broadbilled Prion, which shows just a narrow black tip. The flight of the Fairy Prion is similar to that of other prions although when feeding this species tends to pick food from the ocean's surface rather than 'hydroplaning'. Fairy Prions are silent in southern African waters. W, P

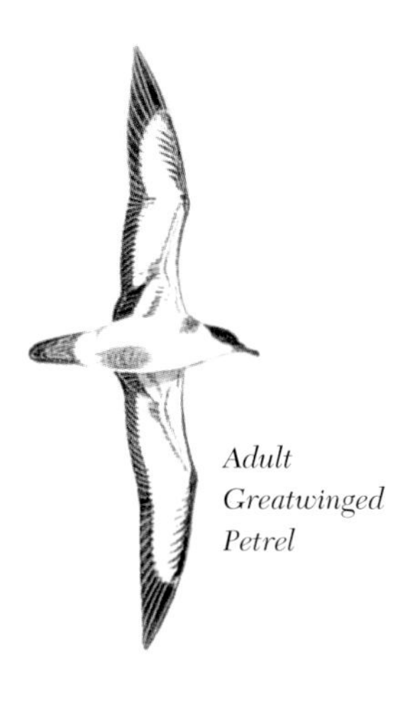

Adult Greatwinged Petrel

Adult Softplumaged Petrel

1. Adult Antarctic Fulmar
2. Adult Pintado Petrel
3. Adult Pintado Petrel
4. Adult Softplumaged Petrel
5. Adult Broadbilled Prion
6. Adult Greatwinged Petrel
7. Adult Softplumaged Petrel
8. Adult Fairy Prion
9. Adult Fairy Prion

1	2	3
4	5	6
7	8	
9		

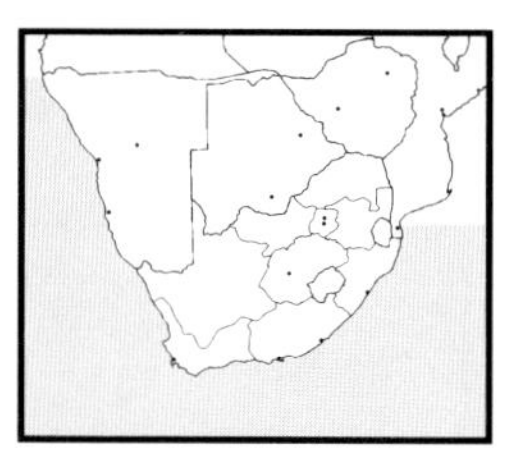

Whitechinned Petrel *Procellaria aequinoctialis* (32) 54 cm

This, the largest of the petrels and shearwaters in the region, is easily identified by its all-dark-brown plumage, its large size and its large, pale-coloured bill. The white on the chin, very variable in extent, can be seen at close range. The flight action is powerful with slow wing beats and long, stiff-winged glides. Its call is a high-pitched and rapidly repeated 'tee-tee-tee'. This bird is often seen close inshore and habitually follows boats. S, W, P

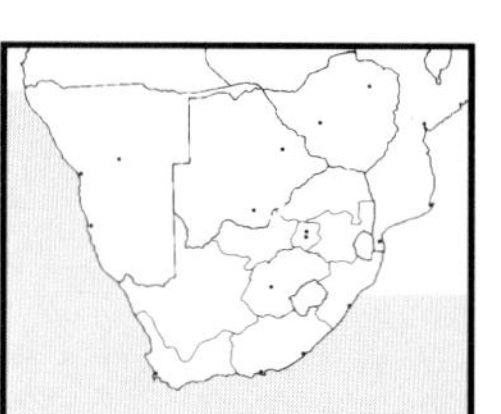

Cory's Shearwater *Calonectris diomedea* (34) 45 cm

This medium-sized, brown and white shearwater can be distinguished from the similar Great Shearwater by its brownish-grey, not dark grey, upperparts, its white collar and dark patch on the belly, and by having little or no white on the rump. The bill is pale with a dusky tip. The flight action is slow and ponderous on bowed and angled wings, with short glides, and the bird usually flies close to the water. It congregates in small flocks and is most often seen roosting on rafts among Whitechinned Petrels. It does not habitually follow ships but will scavenge behind trawlers. Cory's Shearwater is silent in southern Africa. S, P

Adult Great Shearwater

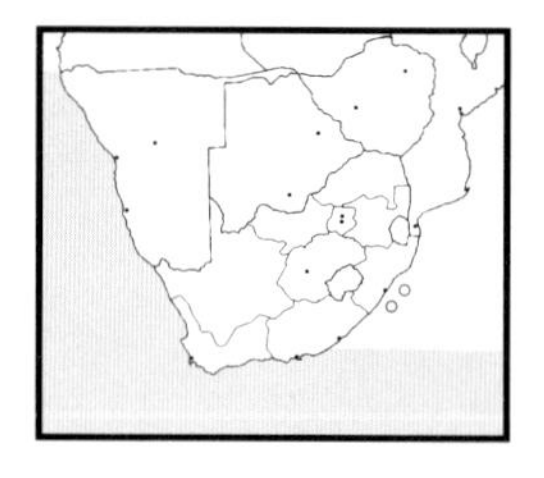

Great Shearwater *Puffinus gravis* (35) 46 cm

Similar in size to Cory's Shearwater, the Great Shearwater differs by having a more contrasting black and white appearance, a distinct cap contrasting with white cheeks, a narrow white hind collar, a broad white base to the uppertail, white underwings bisected by a variable black diagonal bar, and a diagnostic black patch on the belly and lower abdomen. In flight it is more dynamic than Cory's Shearwater, flying with more rapid wing beats and longer, higher and faster glides. It occurs in sometimes sizeable flocks and is a regular scavenger on the trawling grounds off the western Cape. It is silent in our area. S, W, P

Adult Wilson's Storm Petrel

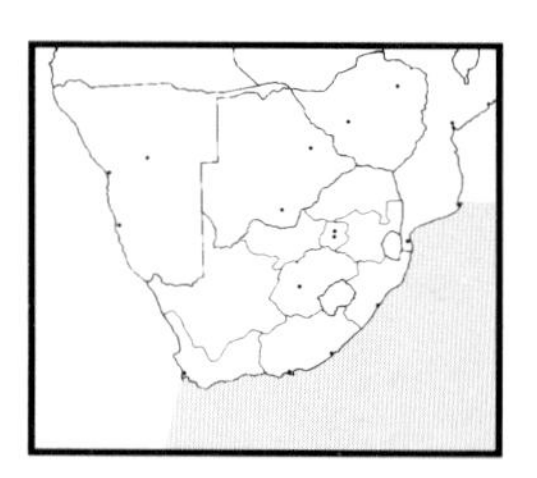

Fleshfooted Shearwater *Puffinus carneipes* (36) 49 cm

This is an all-brown, medium-sized bird which has diagnostic whitish-pink legs and feet. It can easily be distinguished from the Whitechinned Petrel by its smaller size, more rapid flight and dark-tipped pinkish, not uniformly pale, bill; from the Sooty Shearwater by its dark, not silvery, underwing; and from the Greatwinged Petrel by its larger size and very different flight action. The Fleshfooted Shearwater is silent in southern African waters. S, W, P

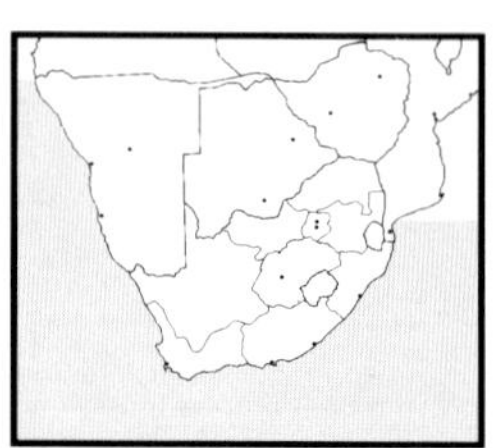

Sooty Shearwater *Puffinus griseus* (37) 46 cm

The Sooty Shearwater appears in some lights to be a dark sooty-brown in colour and in others to be a dark sooty-grey. The white centre to the underwing is diagnostic. The long slender bill and its mode of flight differentiate this species from the Greatwinged Petrel, and its smaller size and pale, not dark, underwing from the Whitechinned Petrel. It most resembles the Fleshfooted Shearwater in size and colour but lacks that bird's pale bill and pink-coloured legs and feet. The flight action involves rapid wing beats interspersed with long and short glides low over the water. Its wings are held unusually straight and stiffly and have a very marked backswept appearance. This bird is silent at sea. S, W, P

1. Adult Whitechinned Petrel
2. Adult Cory's Shearwater
3. Adult Cory's Shearwater
4. Adult Great Shearwater
5. Adult Fleshfooted Shearwater
6. Adult Great Shearwater
7. Adult Sooty Shearwater
8. Adult Wilson's Storm Petrel

Storm petrels Family Oceanitidae

The smallest members of the tube-nosed group of pelagic seabirds, storm petrels are very swallow- or swift-like in appearance, tending to intersperse their gliding with hovering and fluttering over the water, and often dabbling their feet. In continuous flight they stay very close to the surface of the water, and during prolonged bad weather and food shortages may venture close inshore.

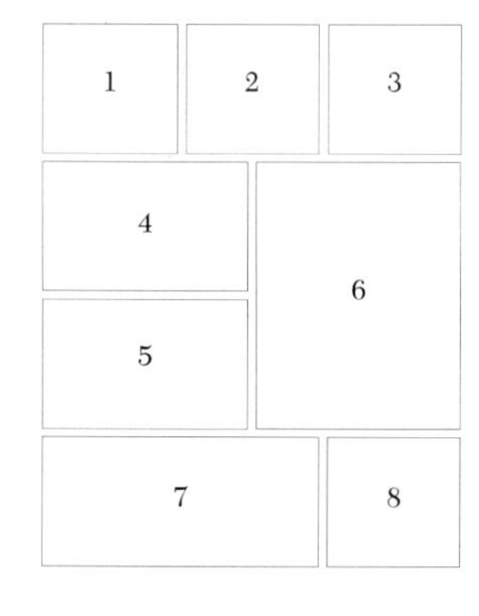

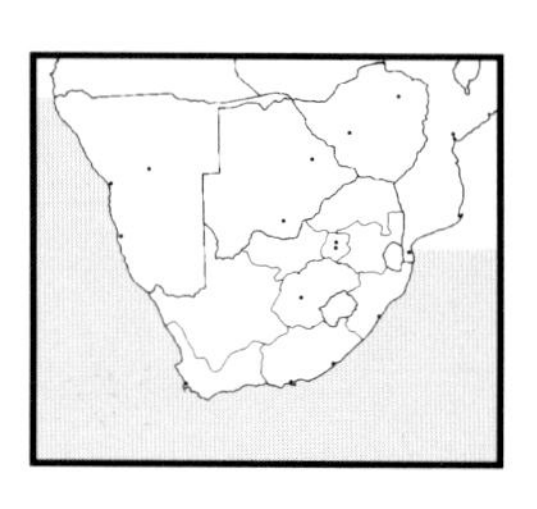

Wilson's Storm Petrel *Oceanites oceanicus* (44) 18 cm

Wilson's Storm Petrel can be distinguished from others in the family by its wing shape and flight action, which is powerful with wing flapping, short bursts of gliding and constant changes of direction. The upperwings have a pale greyish-buff bar across the secondary coverts, which appears as a pale crescent when viewed from above. Its long legs dangle in the water when it hovers, and it 'walks' or treadles the water's surface with a bounding action, swaying from side to side. It is silent at sea. S, W, P

Tropicbirds Family Phaethontidae

Mainly white, medium-sized seabirds, tropicbirds are identifiable by the combination of bill and tail streamer colour, and by the amount of black in the wings. The sexes are alike. Immatures are heavily streaked and barred, and lack the long tail streamers of the adults.

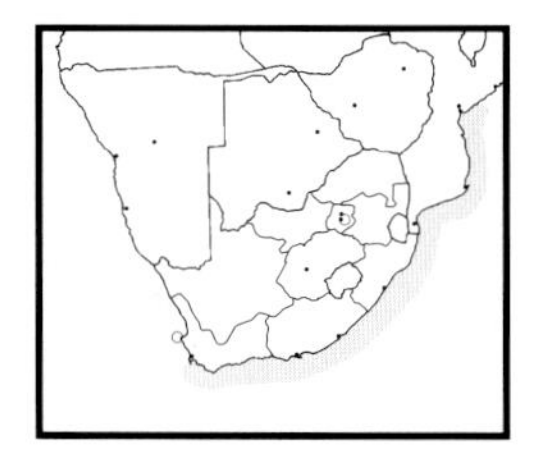

Redtailed Tropicbird *Phaethon rubricauda* (47) 50 cm

Adults are instantly recognizable by their all-white plumage, bright red bill and long red central tail feathers. The white plumage has a pinkish blush, seen at close range. This bird is larger, more robust and dumpier than the Whitetailed Tropicbird. Immatures are very heavily barred above, larger than the similar immature Whitetailed Tropicbird and have a nearly all-black bill. The Redtailed Tropicbird utters a raucous 'waaaagh' when agitated. P

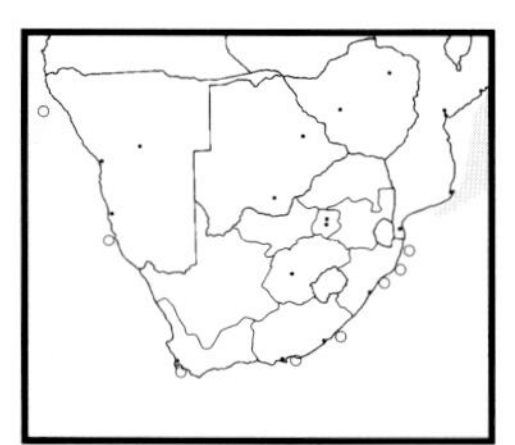

Whitetailed Tropicbird *Phaethon lepturus* (48) 44 cm

This species has diagnostic black patches on its upperwings, long white central tail feathers and a bright yellow bill. Immatures differ from the immature Redtailed Tropicbird by their smaller size, daintier proportions and dark-tipped pale-yellow, not black, bill; they also have solid black (not greyish) tips to the wings. The bird's fast-action level flight is buoyant and more graceful than that of the Redtailed Tropicbird. It is silent at sea. P

Immature Redtailed Tropicbird

Pelicans Family Pelecanidae

Pelicans are large, heavily built birds with grey, black and white plumage. The exceptionally long bill has a distensible pouch which is used to scoop fish. Pelicans are found in both salt- and freshwater localities.

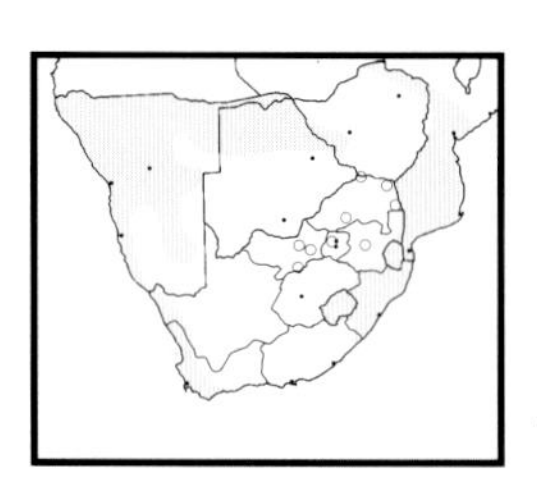

Eastern White Pelican *Pelecanus onocrotalus* (49) 180 cm

The Eastern White Pelican may be confused only with the much smaller Pinkbacked Pelican. However, it is white, not grey, and has a pinkish-yellow, not grey, face and a pouch that is yellowish-orange, not grey. Immatures are more difficult to separate from immature Pinkbacked Pelicans but are much larger, very much darker overall, especially on the upperparts, and have a diagnostic yellowish, not grey, pouch. Eastern White Pelicans feed in groups, not solitarily as do Pinkbacked Pelicans. They are found on estuaries and open stretches of fresh water, and at colonies give a deep 'mooing' sound. R

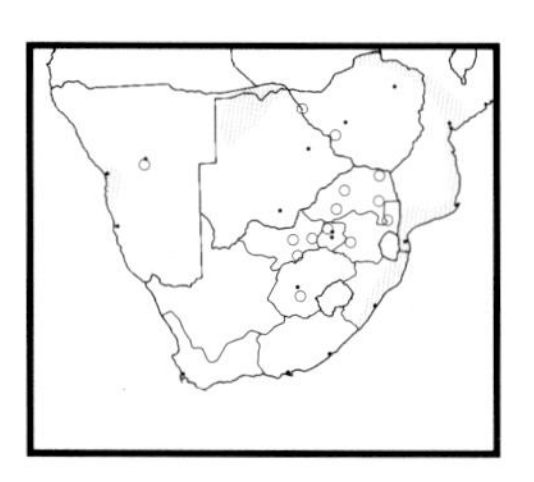

Pinkbacked Pelican *Pelecanus rufescens* (50) 140 cm

When seen alongside the Eastern White Pelican this species is easily identified by its much smaller appearance and its greyish, not white, coloration. In flight the underwing pattern is uniform grey. Immatures are paler than immature Eastern White Pelicans, much smaller in size, and have a greyish, not yellowish, pouch. The breeding bird has a noticeable crest and the facial skin and pouch become yellowish. Except for grunts at breeding colonies, the bird is silent. R

Immature Pinkbacked Pelican

1. Adult Redtailed Tropicbird
2. Immature Whitetailed Tropicbird
3. Adult Whitetailed Tropicbird
4. Adult Eastern White Pelican
5. Immature and adult Eastern White Pelicans
6. Adult Pinkbacked Pelican
7. Immature Cape Gannet
8. Immature Pinkbacked Pelican
9. Adult Cape Gannet

Gannets Family Sulidae

Large white, or white and brown, seabirds with cigar-shaped bodies and hefty, pointed bills, gannets are inshore or open-ocean feeders. They breed in colonies on islands and cliffs.

Cape Gannet *Morus capensis* (53) 85 cm

In flight the overall impression of the Cape Gannet is of a long, pointed, white bird with black flight and tail feathers. The massive pointed bill and yellowish-creamy head, seen best at close range, are diagnostic. Immatures are large, all-brown birds, darker above and covered with small white speckles. At sea, these birds often fly in skeins, high or low over the water. The call at sea and in breeding colonies is a loud 'warrra-warrra-warrra'. R, BE

P *passage visitor* • BE *breeding endemic* • R *resident*

Cormorants Family Phalacrocoracidae

Cormorants are black, or black and white, duck-like birds with long necks and tails. They forage on inland and in marine coastal waters, diving below the surface to catch fish with their long, hooked bills.

Immature Crowned Cormorant

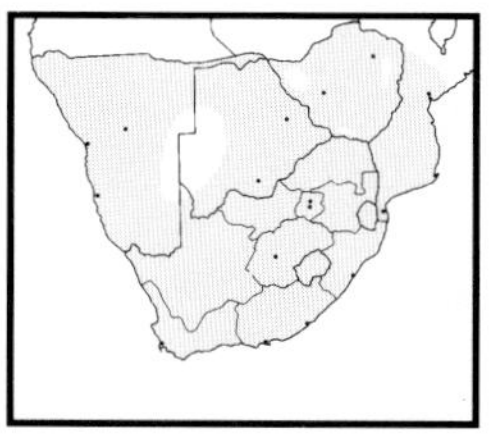

Whitebreasted Cormorant *Phalacrocorax carbo* (55) 90 cm

The largest of all the cormorants, it is recognizable by its all-white throat and breast. For a short period while breeding it shows a large white flank patch and white flecking on the head. Immatures have an all-white throat, breast and belly and are larger and more robust than the similar immature Reed Cormorant, and have a shorter tail. In display the bird throws back its head and flicks its wings to expose the white flank patches. It utters a deep growling at the nest. R

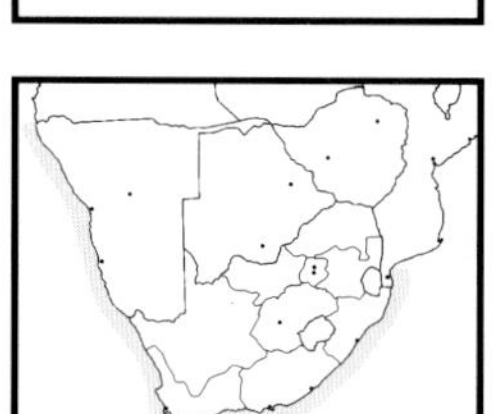

Cape Cormorant *Phalacrocorax capensis* (56) 65 cm

When seen singly, this medium-sized cormorant might be confused with either the Bank or the Crowned cormorants. Smaller than the Bank Cormorant, it also has a flatter crown and a more snake-like head with an orange to yellow gular area. Immatures lack the bright gular but differ from immature Bank Cormorants by their thinner, more kinked neck and flat forehead. Much larger than the Crowned, the Cape Cormorant lacks a forehead crest. Immatures are larger than immature Crowned Cormorants, have a shorter tail and a flatter forehead and crown. The call is a 'gaaa' or 'gheee' given when breeding. R, BE

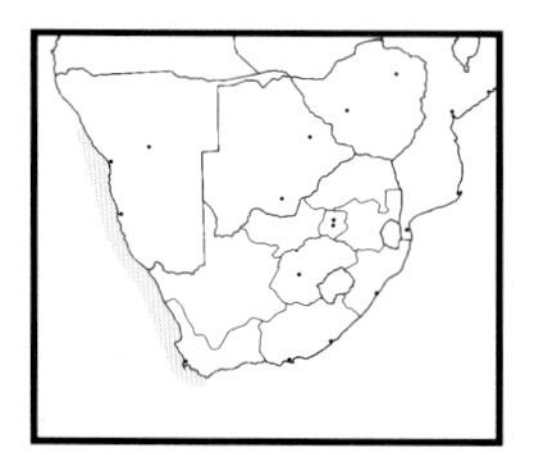

Bank Cormorant *Phalacrocorax neglectus* (57) 76 cm

This species is larger than the Cape and Crowned cormorants, and smaller than the Whitebreasted Cormorant. It differs further from the Cape and Crowned cormorants by the lack of colour on the gular. The immature Cape Cormorant could cause confusion but is smaller and has a more snake-like head. The adult Bank Cormorant has the classic bump on the forehead: a small, rounded, erectile crest. The call is a wheezy 'weeee'. E

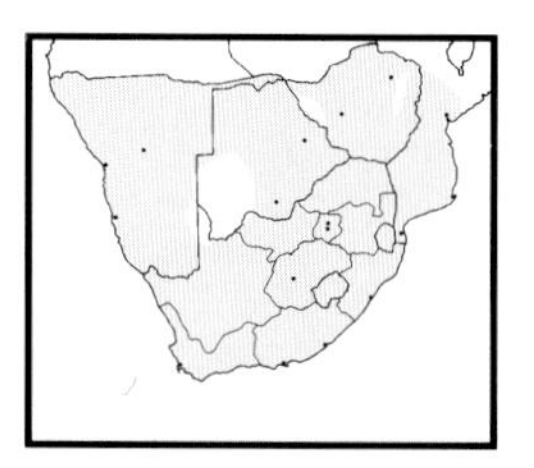

Reed Cormorant *Phalacrocorax africanus* (58) 52 cm

This small freshwater cormorant could be confused only with the Crowned Cormorant, a marine bird, but as the two never overlap in habitat any small cormorant on fresh water would be this species. Immatures resemble immature Whitebreasted Cormorants but are much smaller, more slender and have a longer tail. Reed Cormorants are often found on narrow rivers, far away from large open stretches of water. They are silent except when breeding. R

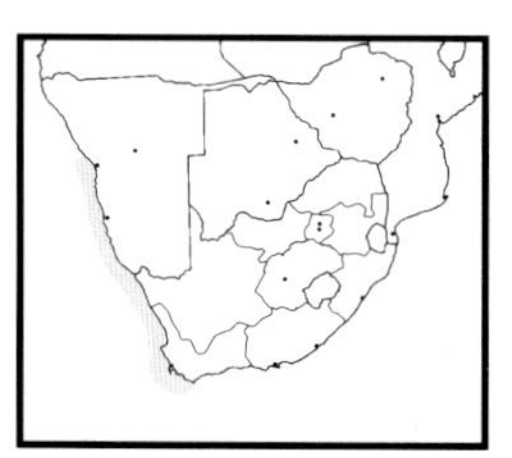

Crowned Cormorant *Phalacrocorax coronatus* (59) 50 cm

This, the smallest marine cormorant, differs from the larger Cape Cormorant by having a yellow-orange gular region, extending around and over the eye, and by its obvious forehead crest. When breeding, the bare face and gular area turns reddish. Immatures differ from immature Cape Cormorants by their smaller size and more angular-shaped forehead, the longer tail and white underparts. Habitat preference (cold-water areas of the west coast) excludes confusion with the very similar Reed Cormorant. The bird is silent except when breeding. E

1. Adult Whitebreasted Cormorant
2. Immature Whitebreasted Cormorant
3. Adult Cape Cormorant
4. Adult Bank Cormorant
5. Immature Cape Cormorant
6. Adult Crowned Cormorant
7. Immature Darter
8. Adult Reed Cormorant
9. Immature Reed Cormorant
10. Adult Darter

1	2	5
3	4	5
6	8	9
7	8	10

Darters Family Anhingidae

Medium-sized birds with very thin, long necks and elongated tails, Darters swim with the body submerged and only the slender neck and head visible, resembling swimming snakes – hence the colloquial name 'snakebird'.

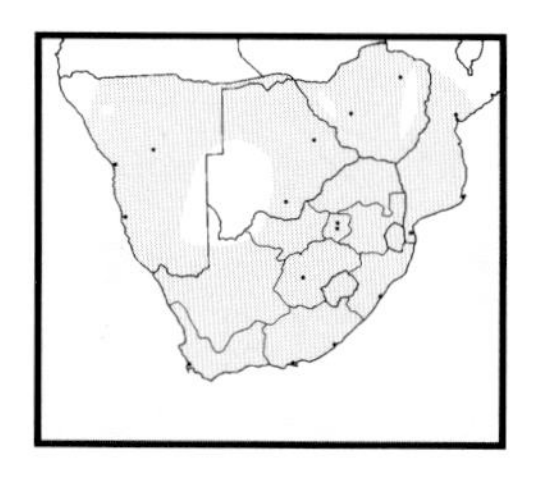

Darter *Anhinga melanogaster* (60) 80 cm

The Darter resembles the cormorants but has a long pointed, not hooked, bill. The dark crown and hindneck are separated from the rust-coloured throat by a white line. When perched, the neck shows a noticeable kink and the long tail is evident. Immatures lack the rust-coloured throat and are dark above and buff below. Solitary feeders on open stretches of fresh water, Darters congregate at roosts and breeding colonies. The call is a distinctive croaking. R

R *resident* • BE *breeding endemic* • E *endemic*

Herons, egrets and bitterns Family Ardeidae

This is a family of variably sized birds with long legs, long necks and powerful, dagger-like beaks. Most species are aquatic, and prey on fish, frogs and aquatic insects. The white-plumaged species in the family are generally referred to as egrets. Bitterns are the most secretive, being cryptically marked and skulking by nature.

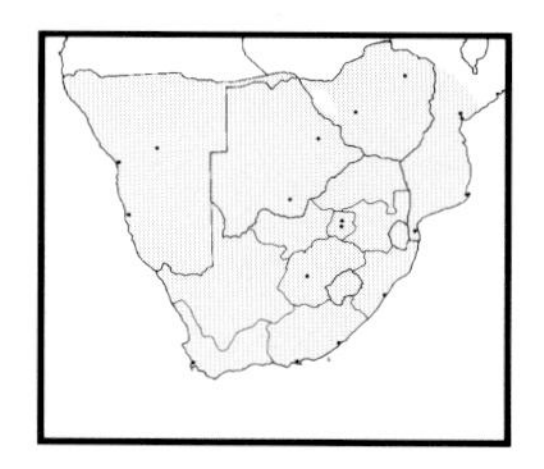

Grey Heron *Ardea cinerea* (62) 100 cm

The Grey Heron is slightly larger than Blackheaded Heron, and differs further by having an obvious yellow bill, and a pale grey head with a dark stripe through the eye ending in a wispy black plume. The immature Grey Heron is very similar to the immature Blackheaded Heron but has a dark cap and a pale, not dark, vent and thighs. This is the common large heron seen around water. In flight the underwings are uniformly grey, not contrasting white and dark as in the Blackheaded heron. The flight call is 'kruaank'. R

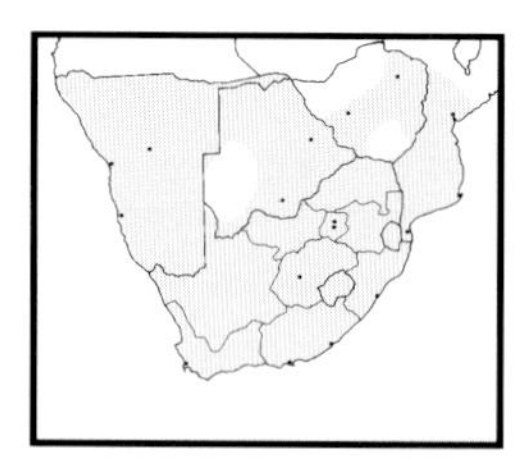

Blackheaded Heron *Ardea melanocephala* (63) 96 cm

This and the Grey Heron could be confused but the black cap and hindneck of the Blackheaded Heron are diagnostic. The immature Blackheaded Heron may be told apart from the very similar immature Grey Heron by its dark grey cap which is uniform with the nape and not confined to the crown only, and by its grey, not white, vent and thighs. In flight the Blackheaded Heron may immediately be separated from the Grey Heron by the bright white wing linings which contrast with the darker primaries and secondaries. The call is a harsh 'aaaark'. This is the heron most often seen striding across pastures, often very far from water. It is normally seen alone except when roosting and breeding when it may gather in hundreds. R

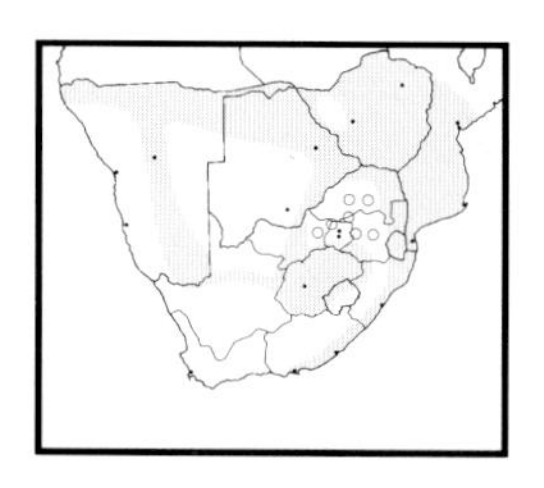

Goliath Heron *Ardea goliath* (64) 140 cm

This enormous wading bird is easily recognized by its size alone, standing nearly two metres tall. In flight, the rich chestnut wing linings and underparts render it unmistakable. The very much smaller Purple Heron might be mistaken for this species only if seen at long range, otherwise size should rule out any confusion. The call is a low, loud 'kwaaark'. It is usually a solitary feeder and wades out over deeper water than do other herons, remaining motionless for long periods. It is not normally found far from water. R

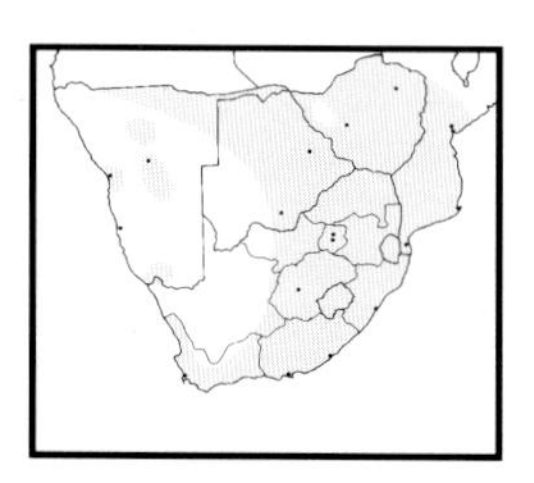

Purple Heron *Ardea purpurea* (65) 91 cm

Superficially resembling the Goliath Heron, the Purple Heron is more than one-third smaller than that species, in flight has more rapid wing beats and is altogether much more slender and streamlined. The rufous head and neck are striped and streaked black. Immatures lack the grey nape and mantle of the adult birds, are less streaked on the neck and have far less black on the crown. The call is a typical heron-like 'kwaark'. Solitary unless breeding, the Purple Heron keeps to denser stands of reeds and is more secretive than are other large herons. R

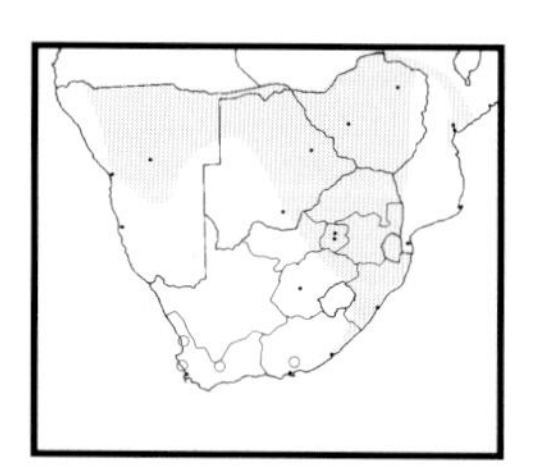

Black Egret *Egretta ardesiaca* (69) 66 cm

This all-dark egret could be confused with the Slaty Egret but has dark, not yellow, legs and lacks any rufous on the throat. Its feeding behaviour is diagnostic and an easy clue to its identity: when wading through water the bird stops suddenly and quickly spreads its wings over its head to form a dome. The breast, nape and mantle plumes, obvious on this species, are lacking in the Slaty Egret. The call is a deep 'kraak'. Usually found in small groups or singly, under optimum conditions the Black Egret can occur in flocks of hundreds. R

Slaty Egret *Egretta vinaceigula* (70) 60 cm

The Slaty Egret differs from the similarly coloured Black Egret by having a rufous throat and yellowish-green legs and toes; it does not wing-canopy feed like the Black Egret. Its shape and jizz resemble those of the Little Egret (see page 28), although it does not dash around as much as that bird. It utters a typically heron-like, sharp 'kaark, kaark, kaark'. Solitary when feeding, several birds might be found in the same area together, however. Slaty Egrets occur in large roosts and breeding colonies. R

Immature Purple Heron

Adult Slaty Egret

1. Immature Blackheaded Heron
2. Adult Grey Heron
3. Adult Blackheaded Heron
4. Immature Grey Heron
5. Adult Goliath Heron
6. Immature Purple Heron
7. Adult Purple Heron
8. Immature Goliath Heron
9. Adult Black Egret
10. Adult Black Egret
11. Adult Slaty Egret

1	2	5
3	4	
6	7	8
9	10	11

R *resident*

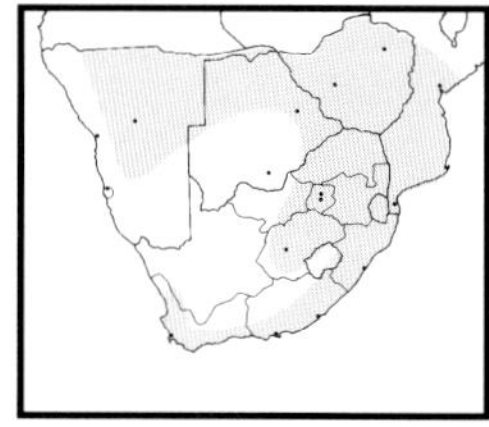
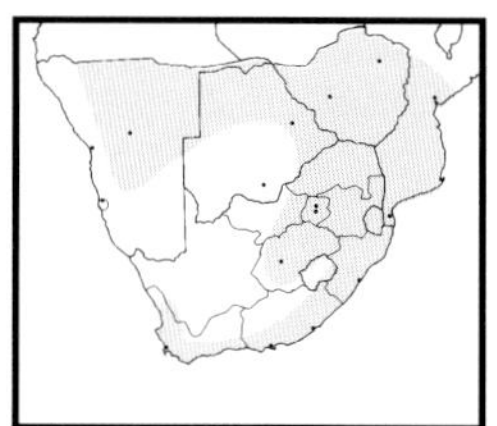

Great White Egret *Casmerodius albus* (66) 95 cm

This is the largest white egret of the region and may be confused only with the Yellowbilled Egret. For a short period during the breeding season the bird has a black bill and then can easily be told apart from the Yellowbilled Egret; at other times, when its bill is yellow, it can be separated by its larger overall size, and much longer and thinner neck, normally with a diagnostic 'S' kink in it. At closer range the gape can be seen to extend to behind the eye, imparting a particularly fierce expression. The call is a low, harsh 'waaark'. The Great White Egret feeds singly in shallow to thigh-deep water, and breeds and roosts in mixed groups of egrets and herons. R

Adult Great White Egret (non-breeding)

Yellowbilled Egret *Egretta intermedia* (68) 66 cm

Although this species is smaller than the similar Great White Egret, this can be used to distinguish the two only when they are seen together. Unlike the Great White Egret, the Yellowbilled Egret always has a yellow bill, but the main difference between the species lies in the latter having a shorter and thicker neck which is not held in a pronounced, kinked 'S' shape. The bird's gape, seen at close range, does not extend to behind the eye as it does in the Great White Egret, but ends just below the eye. The call of the Yellowbilled Egret is a similar 'waark' to that of other egrets and herons. Usually found in pairs or singly, the Yellowbilled Egret prefers to feed over flooded grasslands and not directly in water. R

Adult Great White Egret (breeding)

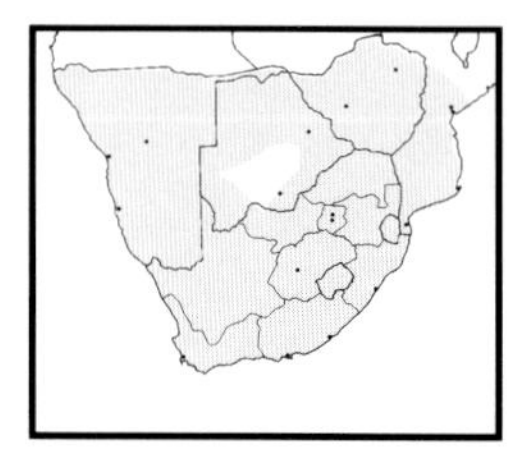

Little Egret *Egretta garzetta* (67) 65 cm

This small white egret has diagnostic black legs and yellow toes, a combination that renders it unmistakable. Its bill is black at all times and is long, thin and pointed. The Little Egret could be confused with the very much larger Great White Egret in breeding plumage, but the behaviour of the Little Egret differs from that of the Great White Egret, as it dashes to and fro in pursuit of prey when feeding, sometimes prancing with partly opened wings and then lunging forward with its thin bill. Its flight action is on quick wing beats with the head and neck drawn well into the shoulders. Its call is a hissing, bubbling noise and a short 'kaark'. R

Immature Greenbacked Heron

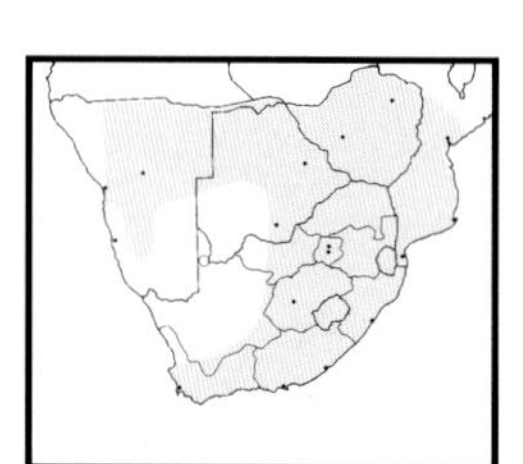

Cattle Egret *Bubulcus ibis* (71) 54 cm

Any small white egret seen in fields alongside livestock or game is almost certain to be this species. Away from this habitat and in roosts it can be told from the Little Egret by its squatter and more hunched appearance and by its yellow or orange bill. Its legs vary from dark brown to yellowish green, and are red at the start of the breeding season. It differs from the larger white egrets by its shape and, in breeding plumage, by having a buffy wash to the breast, back and crown. Its bill is short and deep-based, and its shaggy chin imparts a distinct jowled appearance. Its calls include heron-like 'kaaark' and 'pok-pok' notes. R

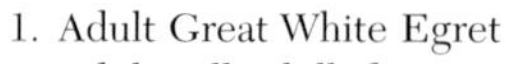

1. Adult Great White Egret
2. Adult Yellowbilled Egret
3. Adult Cattle Egret (non-breeding)
4. Adult Cattle Egret (breeding)
5. Adult Little Egret
6. Adult Squacco Heron (non-breeding)
7. Immature Greenbacked Heron
8. Adult Squacco Heron (breeding)
9. Adult Greenbacked Heron

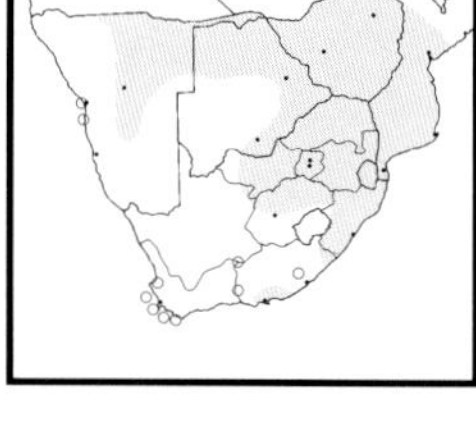
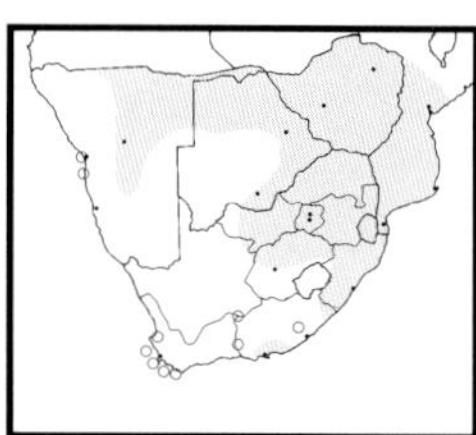

Squacco Heron *Ardeola ralloides* (72) 42 cm

Smaller than any other white heron, the Squacco Heron at rest appears mostly buffish or brownish. When the bird is flushed, however, the all-white wings and tail become visible. Immatures are very brown with broad dark streaks on the breast and mantle. The bill is blue with a dark tip when breeding; otherwise, it is a dark-tipped yellowish green. The flight of the Squacco Heron is distinctly jerky and wobbly, and less direct than that of other small herons. Its call is a duck-like 'kek-kek-kek'. Although a common bird, it tends to skulk in thicker stands of reeds, sitting motionless for long periods and usually venturing forth in twilight. R

1	2	
1	3	4
5	6	7
8	9	

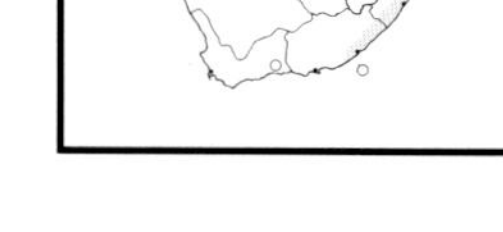

Greenbacked Heron *Butorides striatus* (74) 40 cm

This small, very dark heron is not likely to be confused with any other heron in the region. Its head is large and its bill is proportionately long and deep at the base. The legs and feet are bright orange-yellow. Immatures may be confused with immature Dwarf Bitterns (see page 30) but have a much paler back and buff spotting on the wing coverts. The call is a short, sharp 'baaek', given when the bird is flushed. Greenbacked Herons skulk in riverside tangles, mangroves and freshwater dams overhung with trees, but fish in the open in coastal rock pools and on coral reefs. R

R *resident*

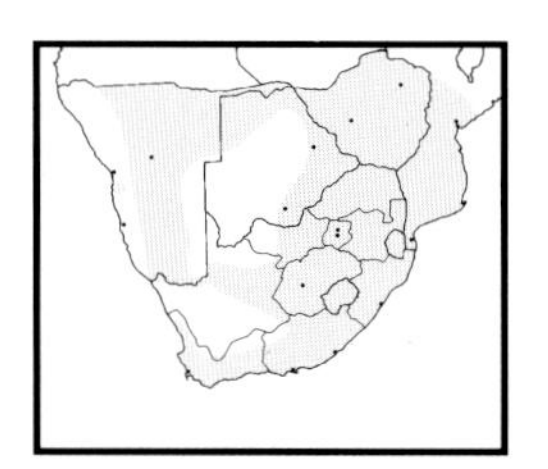

Blackcrowned Night Heron *Nycticorax nycticorax* (76) 56 cm

The Blackcrowned Night Heron is a small but squat and bulky, very pale grey and black bird with bright yellow legs and a long, white, wispy nape plume. Immatures might be mistaken for Bitterns but are browner, have very large buff or white spots on the upperparts and in flight have more rapid wing beats. Blackcrowned Night Herons spend most of the day roosting, usually in tree tangles and thickets. They venture forth at sunset to feed. Their call is a frog-like 'kwok'. They occur in sometimes large roosts. R

Immature Whitebacked Night Heron

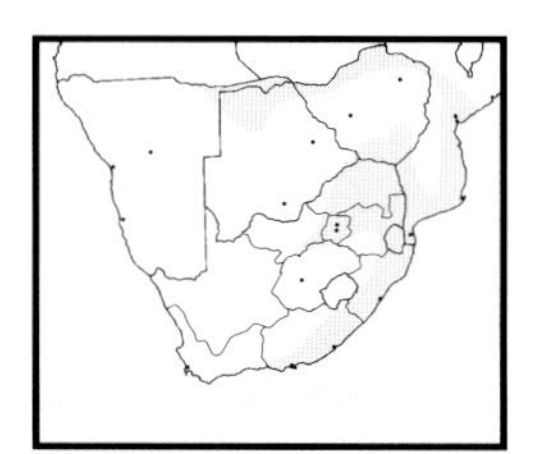

Whitebacked Night Heron *Gorsachius leuconotus* (77) 53 cm

This large-headed, small heron is instantly recognizable by its black head with very large, almost owl-like eyes surrounded by white. The reddish brown on the breast and neck contrasts with the darker back; the white triangle on the back is rarely visible except in flight. Immatures are similar to the immature Blackcrowned Night Heron but have large white spots on the back and show a paler version of the adult head markings. The alarm call is a short, sharp 'kaark'. A rarer and much more solitary bird than the gregarious Blackcrowned Night Heron, the Whitebacked Night Heron roosts in thick tangles overhanging water, mostly on rivers. R

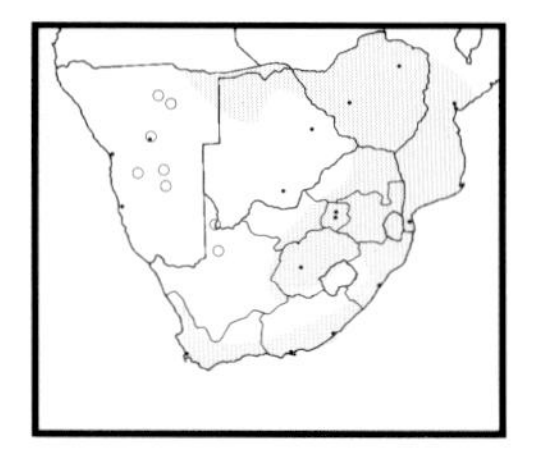

Little Bittern *Ixobrychus minutus* (78) 36 cm

This tiny heron is easily identified by its pale, buffy forewings which contrast with the black flight feathers. The females and immatures are more heavily striped than the males and may be told apart from the immature Greenbacked Heron (see page 28) by their green, not yellow, legs and toes and by having pale forewings. The call, a short 'rao' bark, is uttered every few seconds during the breeding season. Most often seen in flight when flushed from reedbeds or when males display in the early mornings over their territories, Little Bitterns otherwise skulk in dense reedbeds, venturing forth only after dark. R, S

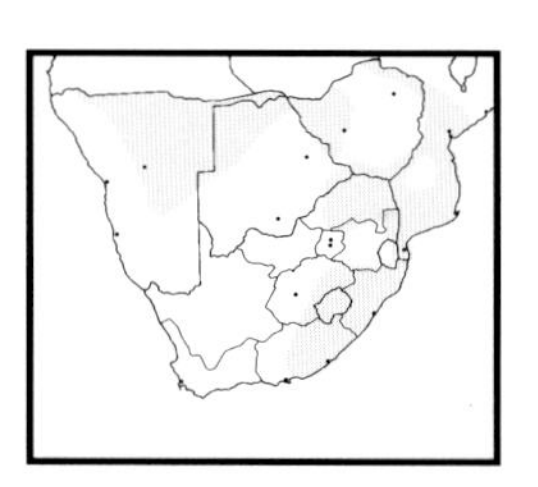

Dwarf Bittern *Ixobrychus sturmii* (79) 25 cm

This is the smallest of our herons and is easily identified by its dark upperparts and heavily streaked, creamy underparts. Because of its tiny size and skulking behaviour, however, the Dwarf Bittern may be mistaken for a rail. Immatures may be confused with the immature Greenbacked Heron (see page 28) but are very much smaller and darker overall and have less spotting on the upperparts. The call is a short 'kwaark', given when alarmed. Dwarf Bitterns roost in trees and thickets in seasonally flooded areas. I

Bittern *Botaurus stellaris* (80) 64 cm

The warm brown and buffy plumage overlaid with blackish streaks and stripes makes this stocky heron easily identifiable. When seen in flight during the twilight hours it is very owl-like; it could also be confused with an immature Blackcrowned Night Heron but is paler and more streaked on the upperparts. It clambers around reedbeds and when disturbed freezes with its bill pointing upwards. This bird is more often heard than seen and the male's booming 'uh-pooombh' call carries a long way over the marshes in which it dwells. R

1. Immature Blackcrowned Night Heron
2. Adult Whitebacked Night Heron
3. Adult Blackcrowned Night Heron
4. Immature Whitebacked Night Heron
5. Immature male Little Bittern
6. Adult Bittern
7. Adult Dwarf Bittern
8. Adult Hamerkop
9. Female Little Bittern

1	2	
3	4	5
6	7	9
	8	

Hamerkop Family Scopidae

A strange-looking, medium-sized, brown bird with a dorsoventrally compressed bill and shaggy, elongated nape feathers, the Hamerkop is neither a stork nor a heron, but shows characters of both. It builds an enormous domed nest of mud, sticks and grass in a tree.

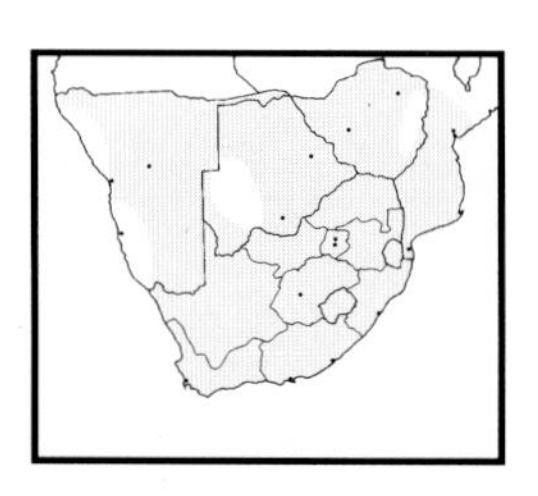

Hamerkop *Scopus umbretta* (81) 56 cm

This large brown wading bird is truly unmistakable; the profile of its head with its shaggy crest accounts for its common name ('hammerhead'). In flight it has the appearance of a bird of prey; even the tail is noticeably barred when viewed from below. However, any doubt about its identity is removed when the head and long legs are visible. Hamerkops are usually found in pairs or small displaying groups and are very often seen patrolling roads in the early morning, searching for road-kill amphibians. The flight call is a sharp 'kiep'. R

Storks Family Ciconiidae

Storks are large birds with long necks and long legs, relatively short tails, and broad wings. Most species have striking black and white plumage. Storks nest singly or semi-colonially in trees or on cliffs.

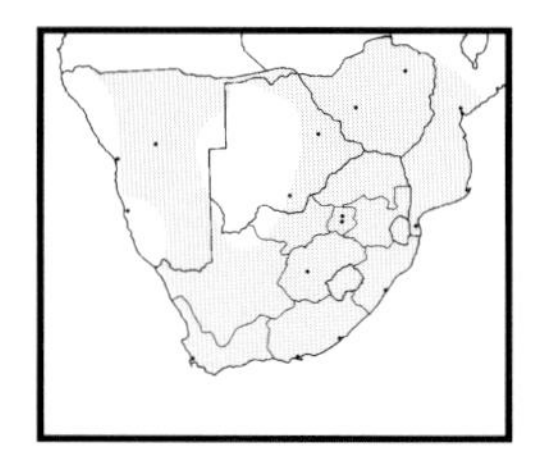

Black Stork *Ciconia nigra* (84) 97 cm

This large, glossy black stork may be confused only with the smaller Abdim's Stork from which it differs by having a black, not white, rump and lower back, and by its bright red, not dark, bill, legs and feet. Immatures are similar to the adults but are browner in colour and have greenish bills, legs and feet. In soaring flight the Black Stork shows a contrasting white belly, armpits and undertail with a black breast and head. Black Storks are usually solitary and occur near water; they are frequently found fishing in mountain streams and rivers, and also occur along the coast in estuaries and lagoons. They roost on cliffs. They are mostly silent, except at the nest when their loud whinnying call is uttered. R

Adult Abdim's Stork

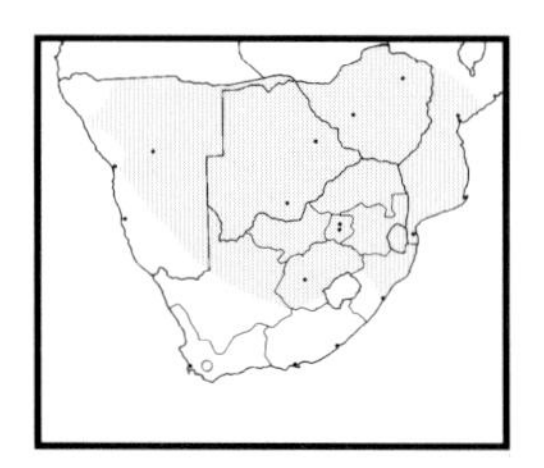

Abdim's Stork *Ciconia abdimii* (85) 76 cm

Abdim's Stork may be confused only with the larger Black Stork but has an obvious white rump and lower back which the Black Stork lacks. At rest, when the rump and lower back are not visible, it can be distinguished from the Black Stork by its dark, not bright red, bill, legs and feet. At close range the legs can be seen to be greyish olive with red joints and toes, and the base of the bill and the skin around the eyes to be red. Immatures are similar to the adults but are somewhat duller, lacking colour on the legs and face. The birds are mostly silent, except for soft, two-note whistles given at their roosts. They can be found in flocks of thousands, striding across the veld or tightly packed as they ride thermals high in the sky. S

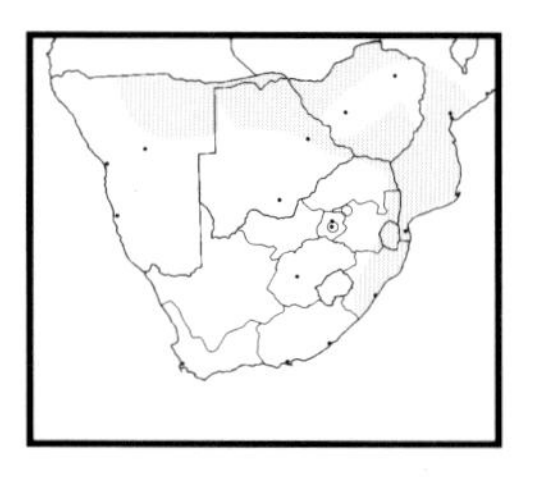

Woollynecked Stork *Ciconia episcopus* (86) 85 cm

This is the only dark stork that has a white neck. The combination of black body, white neck and belly, and dark legs and bill is diagnostic. Immatures have a pale bill and dark cap but still show the white neck. At close range the neck feathering can be seen to be ruffled, imparting a woolly appearance and accounting for the bird's common name. The call is a harsh croaking but the bird is usually silent. It is associated mainly with water or is found in fields close by. Woollynecked Storks sometimes occur in small groups but mostly are found in pairs or singly. R

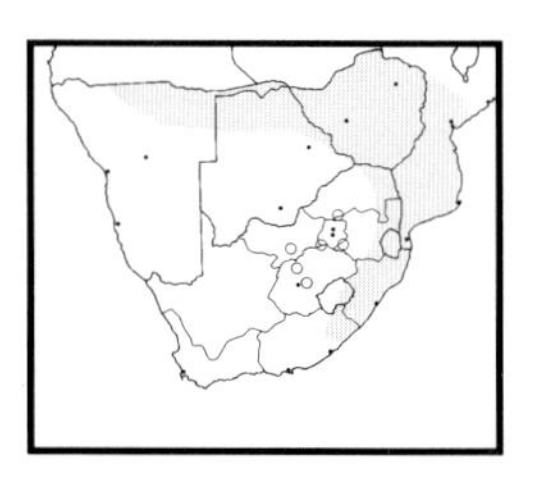

Openbilled Stork *Anastomus lamelligerus* (87) 94 cm

The Openbilled Stork is the only all-black stork in the region. From a distance its bill looks massive and deep; only at closer range can the wide, nutcracker-like gap that gives it its name be seen. This gap enables the bird to manoeuvre the bivalves on which it feeds. The plumage is a glossy purplish black, having an oily appearance with bronze highlights. The feathers on the mantle and breast are elongate. Immatures resemble the adults but lack the opening in the bill, which develops gradually with maturity. The call is a deep cackling, given at roosts and at breeding colonies, but is not often heard. Openbilled Storks are always associated with water and may occur in large congregations, especially if food is abundant. R

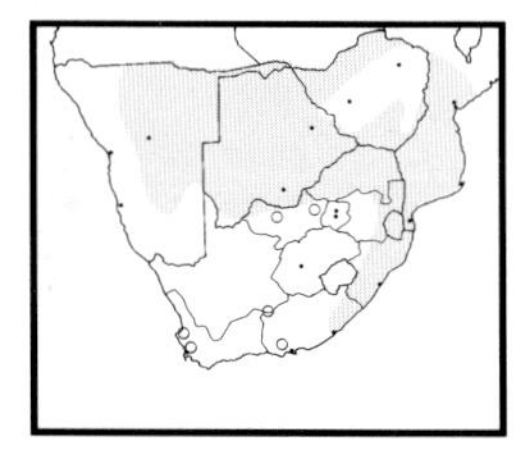

Marabou Stork *Leptoptilos crumeniferus* (89) 150 cm

A contender with the Wandering Albatross (see page 14) for having the longest wingspan of any bird in the world, the enormous size of this bird combined with its massive bill and naked head and throat pouch make it easy to identify. In flight, its black wings contrast with the white body, and the head is tucked into the shoulders; at this time it is very vulture-like but can be distinguished by its pointed bill and long legs. It defecates on its legs to regulate its body temperature and this renders the limbs white; their true colour is a dark bluish black. The bubbling and hissing call is given only at the nest or when squabbling over food; it claps its bill in display. Marabou Storks are found mainly in large game reserves where they scavenge at carcasses. They are frequently seen riding thermals with vultures. R

1. Adult Black Stork
2. Adult Abdim's Stork
3. Sub-adult Woollynecked Stork
4. Adult Marabou Stork
5. Adult Woollynecked Stork
6. Adult Openbilled Stork

1	2
3	2
3	4
5	6

R *resident* • S *summer visitor*

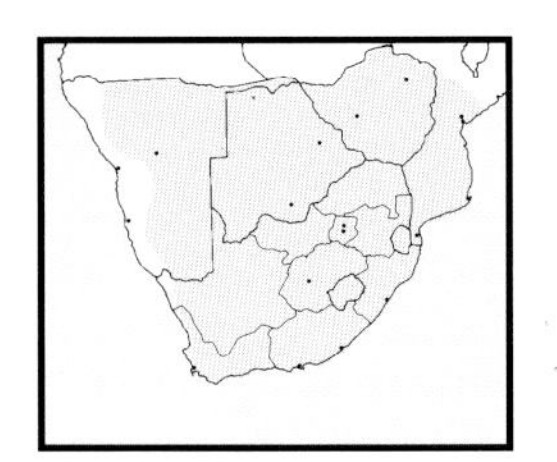

White Stork *Ciconia ciconia* (83) 102 cm

In flight the White Stork may be confused with the Yellowbilled Stork but can be distinguished from that bird by its all-white, not black, tail and shorter, straight, red (not long, decurved, yellow) bill. The red legs of this species more frequently appear white, a discoloration caused by the birds' defecating on their limbs in order to cool off. Immatures have a darker bill and legs than in the adult, and white plumage tinged with brown. White Storks are often encountered in large flocks riding thermals or in agricultural lands. They are mostly silent away from the nest but sometimes utter a soft, whinnying noise and indulge in loud bill clappering. R, S

Adult White Stork

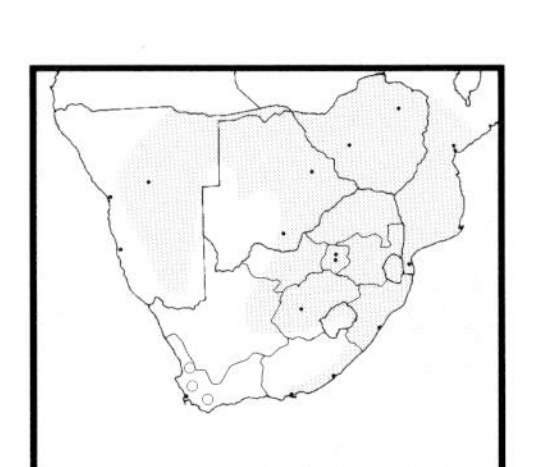

Yellowbilled Stork *Mycteria ibis* (90) 95 cm

The long, slightly decurved, yellow bill of this white stork is diagnostic. In flight at long range it may be confused with the White Stork but has an all-black, not white, tail. During the breeding season, the breast plumage and upperparts take on a pinkish tinge and the naked face turns a bright orange-red. Immatures are greyish versions of the adults and have an ivory-coloured bill. In breeding colonies the Yellowbilled Stork utters loud squeaks and hisses, although at other times it is usually silent; it also snaps and clatters the bill. This stork is associated with water, where it wades, often in company with egrets and herons, feeling for food with its submerged bill. R, S

Adult Yellowbilled Stork

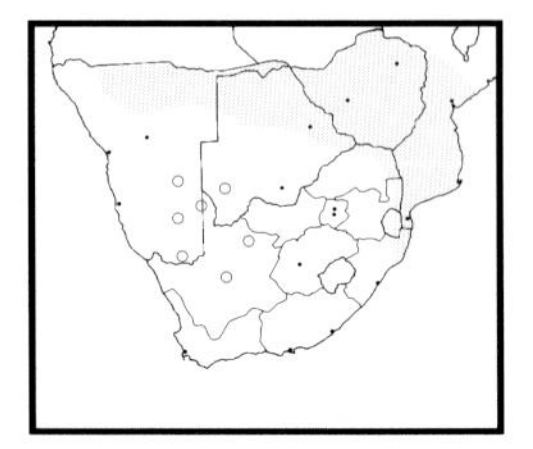

Saddlebilled Stork *Ephippiorhynchus senegalensis* (88) 145 cm

Approaching the Marabou Stork (see page 32) in size, this attractive black and white stork with its bizarrely coloured bill is unmistakable. Females may be told apart from males by their bright yellow, not dark, eyes. In flight the Saddlebilled Stork has a diagnostic wing pattern of all white with a broad black panel along the centre. Immatures lack the bright bill colours and have darker underwings with a pale centre. The call is a soft 'waark', and is often accompanied by loud bill clappering. Saddlebilled Storks are usually found in pairs or with an immature. They hold very large territories and are normally found within this area throughout the year. R

Flamingos Family Phoenicopteridae

Flamingos are unmistakable, extraordinarily long-legged and long-necked, pink-coloured aquatic birds with short, heavy, decurved bills. They feed by partly submerging and inverting the bill in water and filtering out algae and micro-organisms through fine sieves in the bill. Gregarious, flamingos sometimes occur in huge numbers. They are highly nomadic birds.

Immature Lesser Flamingo

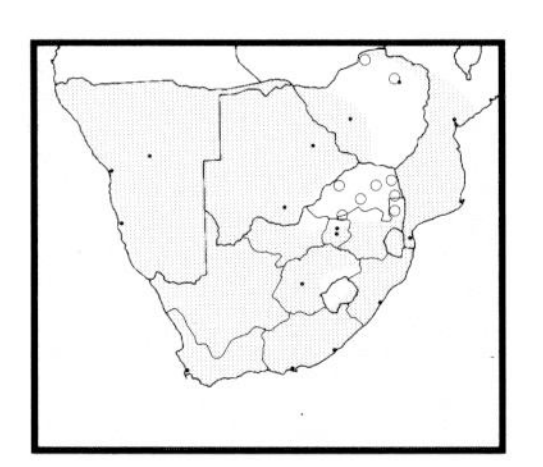

Greater Flamingo *Phoenicopterus ruber* (96) 127 cm

This species may easily be told apart from the Lesser Flamingo by its larger size and all-pink bill with a black tip; it is also never as uniformly deep pink in colour as the Lesser Flamingo. Immatures resemble adults but are dirty grey and white with a black-tipped greyish bill. The call is a very goose-like honking, and is given especially in flight. The Greater Flamingo flies with its neck outstretched and slightly drooped; at this time, the brilliant red patches in the forewings can be seen. It often flies in skeins. This flamingo is associated with water, in estuaries, lakes and saltpans. R

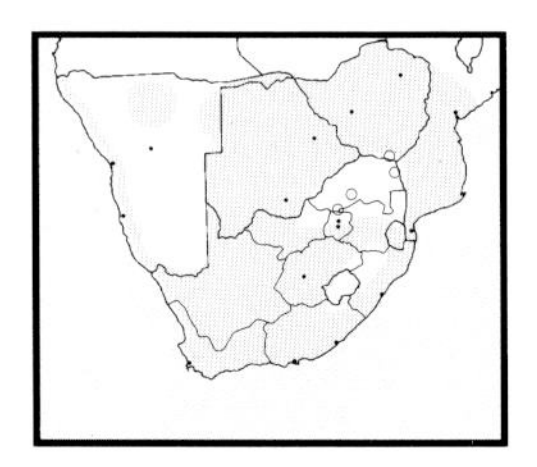

Lesser Flamingo *Phoenicopterus minor* (97) 100 cm

Although noticeably smaller and shorter than the Greater Flamingo when the two species are seen side by side, the diagnostic difference is the bill colour. In this species the bill is a deep red, appearing black at a distance, whereas the Greater Flamingo has a dark-tipped, flesh-coloured bill. The Lesser Flamingo is generally more uniformly deeper pink in colour than the Greater Flamingo, although its head, neck and body plumage are very variable. Immature Lesser Flamingos are very similar to immature Greater Flamingos but have an all-dark bill, whereas the bill of the immature Greater Flamingo is grey, tipped with black. The bird's call is a goose-like honking, very similar to that of the Greater Flamingo but higher pitched. A common bird, it sometimes gathers in mixed flocks of thousands with Greater Flamingos. R

1. Immature White Stork
2. Adult White Stork
3. Adult Yellowbilled Stork
4. Immature Yellowbilled Stork
5. Female Saddlebilled Stork
6. Adult Greater Flamingo
7. Adult Lesser Flamingo
8. Adult Greater Flamingos
9. Immature Lesser Flamingos

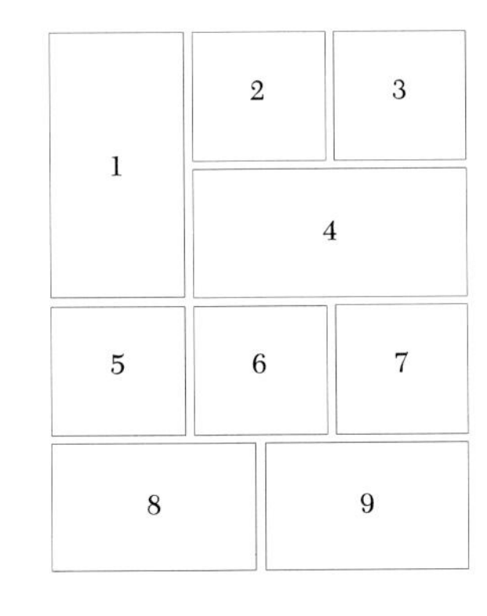

R *resident* • S *summer visitor*

Ibises and spoonbills Family Threskiornithidae

These are medium-sized birds with elongated, decurved or flattened bills, long legs and variable plumage coloration. They feed by probing in shallow water, mud or grass.

Adult Sacred Ibis (breeding)

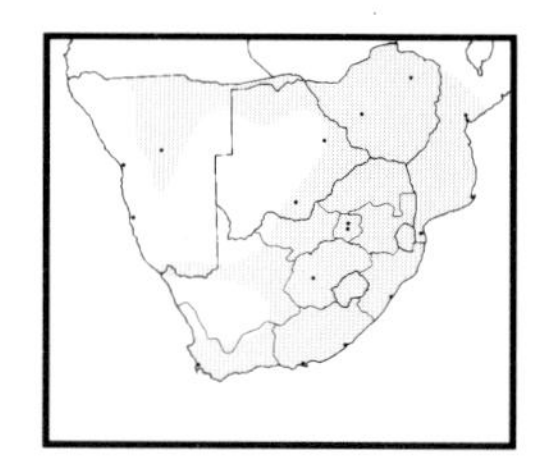

Sacred Ibis *Threskiornis aethiopicus* (91) 90 cm

The Sacred Ibis is instantly recognizable by its black, unfeathered head and long, decurved, black bill. Its body is white but very often stained, and the tertials are bluish black and shaggy, giving the bird a ragged hind end. In flight the Sacred Ibis shows a narrow black border to the wings, and in breeding plumage it shows a bright scarlet line on the underwing and buffy thighs. Immatures are similar to adults but lack the shaggy tertial plumes and have a feathered neck and throat. Sacred Ibises call only at breeding colonies and roosts, giving a mixture of wheezes and croaks. They gather in large numbers to roost and sometimes when feeding, but regularly forage alone or in pairs. They typically fly to roost in skeins. The Sacred Ibis occurs over agricultural lands, wetlands and on offshore islands. R

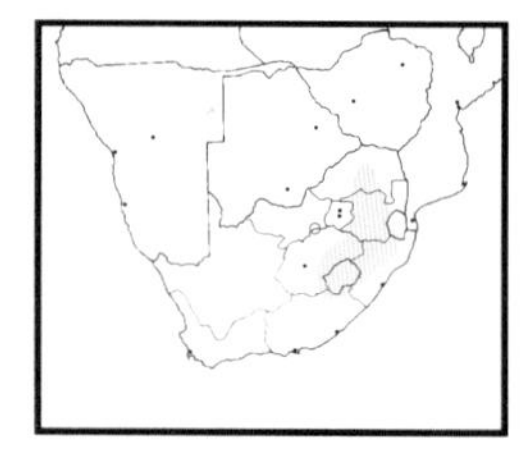

Southern Bald Ibis *Geronticus calvus* (92) 78 cm

Although from a distance the Southern Bald Ibis appears all black with a conspicuous white head, red crown and long, decurved, red bill, from close range its plumage can be seen to be an iridescent greenish black with a coppery sheen on the wing coverts. The unfeathered white head and red 'skull cap' are irregularly scratched and scored. Immatures lack the head and bill colouring and their plumage is matt black. In flight the wings are long and pointed; the flight action is duck-like, with rapid wing beats. The Southern Bald Ibis calls at the nest, uttering a wheezy 'keeaaw-klaup-klaup'. It occurs in small groups in upland pastures, damp meadows and burnt veld, and roosts and breeds on cliffs. E

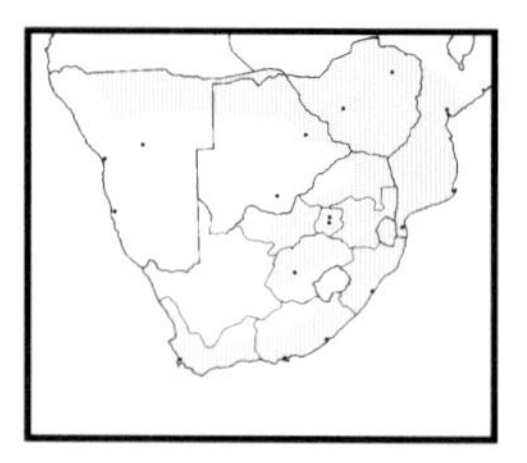

Glossy Ibis *Plegadis falcinellus* (93) 65 cm

Although the Glossy Ibis may be confused with the Hadeda Ibis, it is much smaller, more slender and appears all black at a distance. When seen at close range the glossy bronze shimmer on the head and body and especially on the wing coverts is very evident. Immatures are dull versions of the adults. The Glossy Ibis is a very long-legged bird and the only ibis to be habitually associated with water, wading and probing with its bill in shallows and emergent vegetation. In flight it appears very slender and thin-necked, much more so than other dark ibises. The birds are usually silent but call at the nest, giving only soft croaks and grunts. R

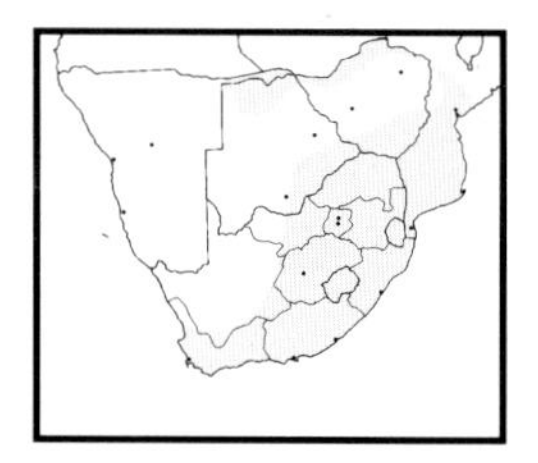

Hadeda Ibis *Bostrychia hagedash* (94) 76 cm

Most often heard as it flies to and from its roosts, when the distinctive and loud 'ha-ha-ha-da-da' calls are given, the drab, greyish-brown Hadeda Ibis would appear to have no distinctive features. At close range, however, the birds can be seen to have a distinct glossy bronze patch on the wing coverts, a pale, curved stripe from the base of the bill to behind the eye and a deep red stripe running along the upper mandible. Immatures are dowdy versions of the adults. In flight the wings appear rounded and broad and are held very bowed, and the birds fly with quick, jerky wing beats interspersed with slower flaps and glides. The habitat choice of this bird is diverse, including woodland, savanna, open grasslands and farmlands. R

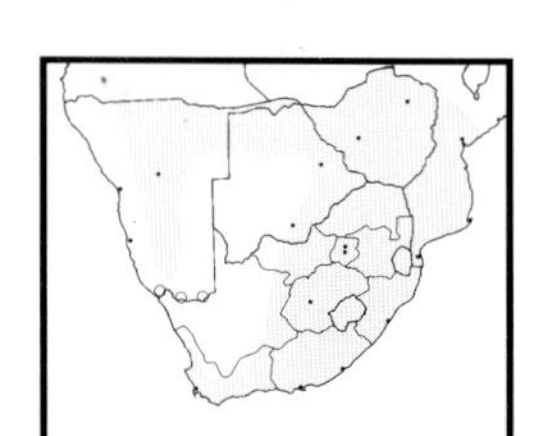

African Spoonbill *Platalea alba* (95) 90 cm

This all-white, long-legged wading bird with its distinctively shaped bill is instantly recognizable. Immatures differ from adults by having dark, not red, legs and a beige-coloured, not grey and red, bill. Adults when breeding show a bright red, unfeathered mask. The call is a low 'kaark' and the bird also emits hisses and grunts at the nest and clappers its bill. It wades in shallow water while sweeping its bill from side to side, sifting food items. In flight the bill is held straight and the neck outstretched but slightly dropped, and the bird flies with quick wing beats but also soars often. African Spoonbills congregate in large numbers when breeding, and feed in loose groups or singly. R

1. Adult Sacred Ibis
2. Immature Sacred Ibis
3. Adult Glossy Ibis
4. Adult Bald Ibis
5. Immature Glossy Ibis
6. Adult Hadeda Ibis
7. Immature Bald Ibis
8. Adult African Spoonbill

1	2
3	4
5	6
7	8

R *resident* • E *endemic*

Ducks and geese Family Anatidae

Ducks and geese are aquatic birds that occupy a range of freshwater habitats and spend most of their time swimming on open water. They are variable in social habits (some are gregarious, others solitary), feeding behaviour (some dive for food, others surface feed or graze) and breeding behaviour (some nest on the ground or over water, others in trees). The flight is fast and direct with the neck held outstretched.

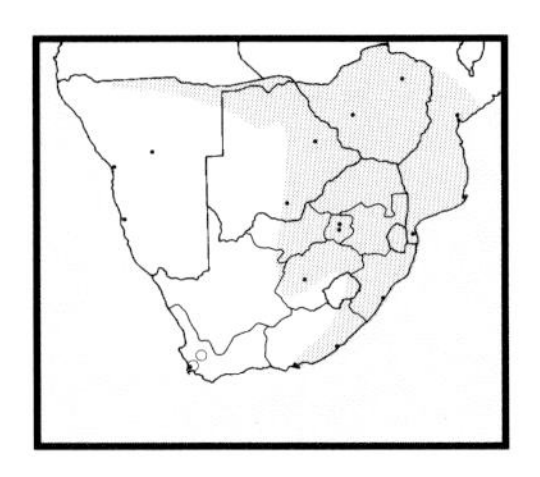

Whitefaced Duck *Dendrocygna viduata* (99) 48 cm

The white face and throat of this duck are diagnostic but because these are very often mud-stained the duck's distinctive posture is the easiest means of identification: it has a very upright stance and when standing the neck appears extremely long and slender. South African Shelduck females also have a white face but are much larger and have an all-chestnut body. Immatures may be confused with the immature Fulvous Duck but are distinguished by the dark, not white, rump. The call is a three-whistled 'wheeet-wee-weeeo'. R

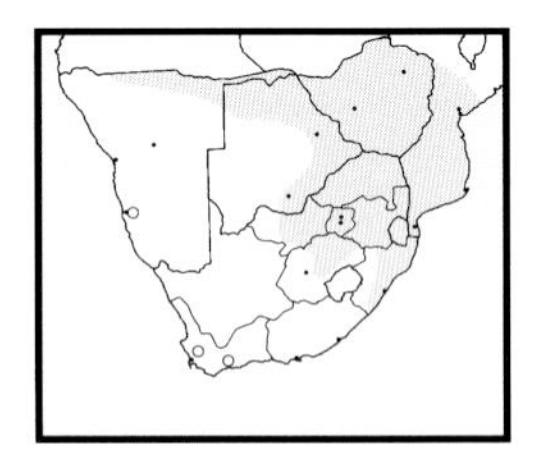

Fulvous Duck *Dendrocygna bicolor* (100) 46 cm

This rich tawny-coloured duck, with a dark line down its neck, large white stripes on its flanks and a dark brown back, is easily identified. Immatures differ from the immature Whitefaced Duck by having a white, not dark, rump. The call is a coarser whistle than that of the Whitefaced Duck and is only two-noted, 'tsu-tchwee'. More active at night, the Fulvous Duck prefers to rest up in daylight. It occurs mostly in small groups but large numbers may gather on floodplains when conditions are right. R

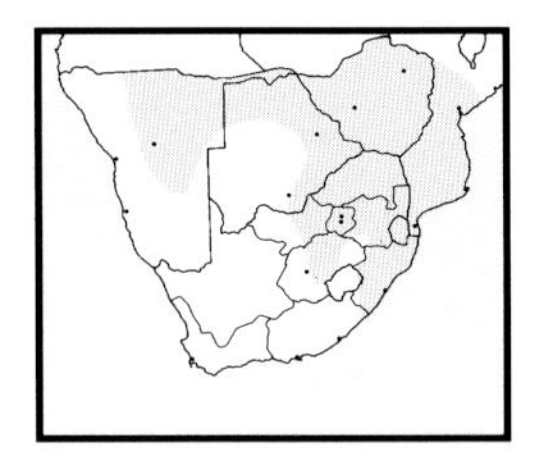

Knobbilled Duck *Sarkidiornis melanotos* (115) 73 cm

The male of this large black and white duck has a peculiar fleshy black knob on top of its bill which enlarges at the height of the breeding season. The female is smaller than the male and lacks the knob. The plumage of both sexes appears black but is in fact a glossy blue and green. In flight the upperwings and underwings are unmarked. The call is a subdued, whistled hiss. The Knobbilled Duck is frequently seen well away from water, flying over woodland and forests or perched high in dead trees. It occurs in large flocks during the dry season. R

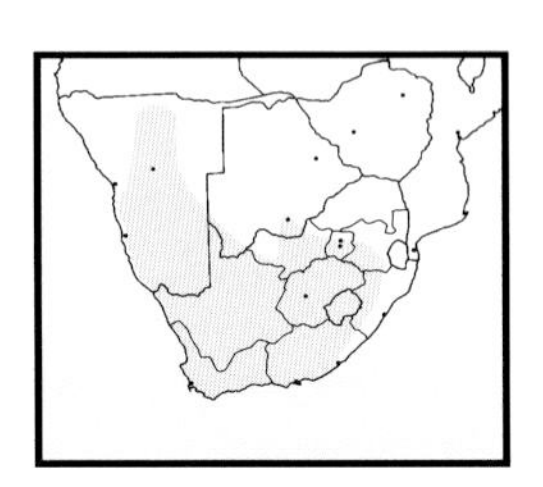

South African Shelduck *Tadorna cana* (103) 64 cm

This large chestnut or russet-coloured duck is easily recognizable, the male having a grey head and neck and the female a white head with a brown neck. In flight the upperwing pattern resembles that of the Egyptian Goose but the South African Shelduck lacks the black line separating the white wing coverts. The call consists of various honks and hisses. This species of arid regions congregates in large flocks on open water when good rains prevail; at other times it forms strong pair-bonds and breeds far from water down aardvark tunnels. E

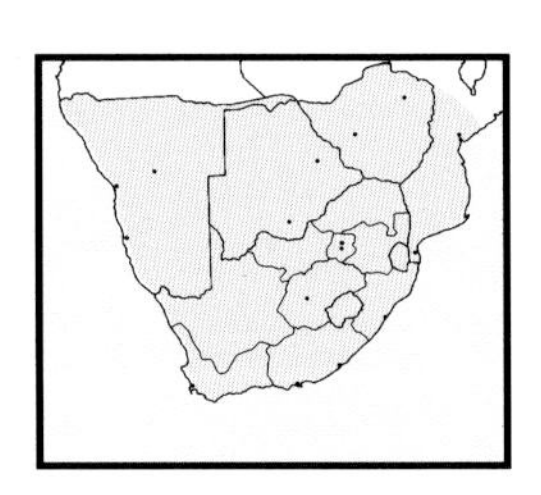

Egyptian Goose *Alopochen aegyptiacus* (102) 70 cm

This large goose-like duck is one of the region's most familiar waterbirds and may be found on virtually any stretch of water; it frequently also feeds in fields. It is easily recognized by its dark spectacles, buffy grey body, dark breast patch and long legs. The sexes are similar; immatures are duller versions of the adults and lack the dark breast patch. In flight the bird shows large white forewings, resembling those of the smaller South African Shelduck but the black line running through the white wing panel distinguishes it. The male's call is a hissing and the female's a mixture of honking notes; both sexes give rapid, repeated honks on taking to the wing. R

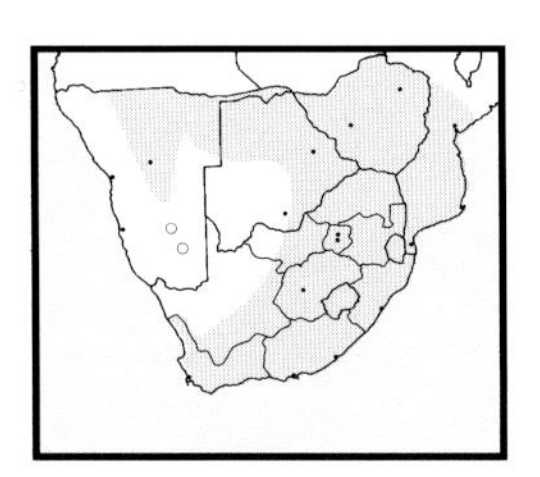

Spurwinged Goose *Plectropterus gambensis* (116) 100 cm

This is the largest waterfowl in the region and is a duck, not a true goose. It is easily recognized by its apparently black (actually iridescent greenish-black) plumage, its red bill and legs, and by the varying quantities of white on its head. In flight it shows white wing linings and white leading edges to the upperwings. Immatures have a browner cast to the plumage and less extensive unfeathered skin on the face. The call is a weak, wheezy 'chik-we', given in flight. Large flocks gather on wide, open bodies of water to moult, but this bird otherwise occurs in small groups and in pairs. R

Adult Whitefaced Duck

Adult Fulvous Duck

Female South African Shelduck

Adult Egyptian Goose

1. Adult Whitefaced Ducks
2. Immature Whitefaced Ducks
3. Adult Fulvous Duck
4. Male Knobbilled Duck
5. Female South African Shelduck
6. Male South African Shelduck
7. Female Knobbilled Duck
8. Adult Egyptian Goose
9. Adult Spurwinged Goose
10. Adult Spurwinged Goose
11. Adult Spurwinged Goose

1	2	3
4	5	6
7		8
9	10	11

R *resident* • E *endemic*

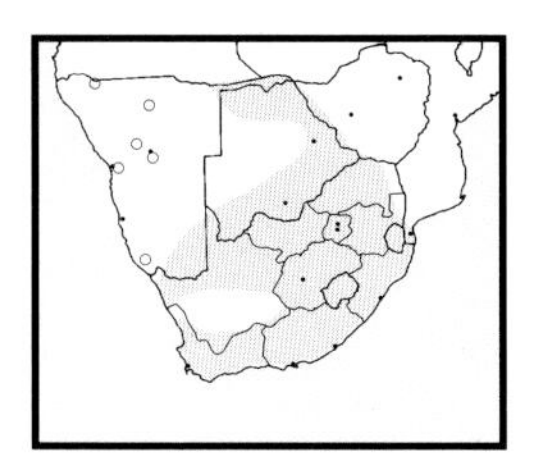

Yellowbilled Duck *Anas undulata* (104) 54 cm

This fairly drab, mottled brown and buff duck with its diagnostic yellow and black bill may be confused with the African Black Duck at a distance but never appears as dark as that species and sits much higher in the water. In flight the Yellowbilled Duck shows white wing linings and an iridescent bluish-green speculum edged with white and black. The sexes are similar and both have bright orange feet. Immatures are duller versions of the adults. The call of the male is a rasping hiss; that of the female is the classic 'quack-quack' duck sound. They feed by dabbling and upending but dive only when threatened. Yellowbilled Ducks are common in most freshwater areas and on open estuaries, and often occur in flocks. R

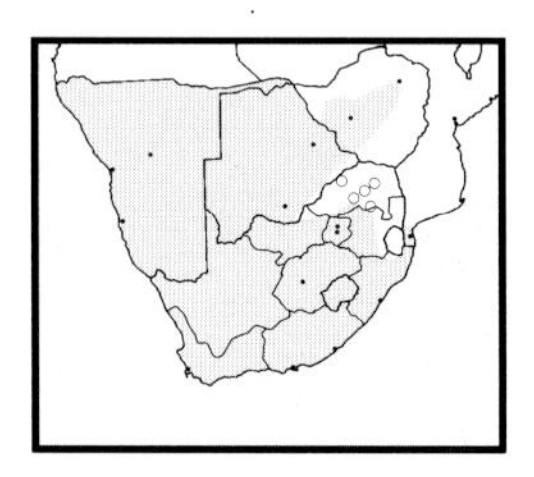

African Black Duck *Anas sparsa* (105) 56 cm

The all-dull-black plumage, relieved only by white spots on the upperparts and tail, render this duck unmistakable. Although it may be confused with the Yellowbilled Duck, its plumage is never as pale as that of that species and the African Black Duck has an all-black, not yellow and black, bill. In flight it shows white wing linings and an iridescent purplish speculum bordered by black and white. The sexes are similar, although the female is smaller than the male, and both have bright orange legs and feet. Immatures are paler than the adults and have a whitish belly. The African Black Duck swims very low in the water and is more slender and elongate than the Yellowbilled Duck. The call consists of the usual 'quack-quack' duck sounds as well as hisses. Confined to river systems, these birds rarely venture out on to open stretches of water. They are seen either singly or in small family parties but never in large flocks. R

Cape Teal *Anas capensis* (106) 46 cm

This grey and brown mottled duck has a pinkish bill and a finely speckled head and breast. The base of the bill is solid black and the eye is a bright cherry-red. The flight pattern reveals a small green speculum bordered by a large area of white, more so than in any other small duck. This species can be told apart from the Redbilled Teal by its pale grey head which lacks a dark cap. The call is a soft, thin whistle, usually given in flight, and it also utters short, clicking or snickering notes. The Cape Teal prefers drier regions and is commonly found on saline waters although it does readily frequent other water systems. It occurs in small to large flocks, and sometimes in mixed flocks, with greater concentrations occurring outside the breeding season. R

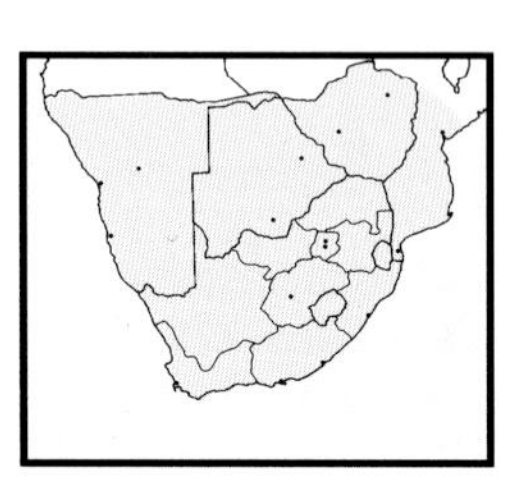

Redbilled Teal *Anas erythrorhyncha* (108) 48 cm

The Redbilled Teal is likely to be confused only with the Cape Teal, which has a pinkish, not red, bill, but the plumage of this species is mottled brown and buff, not grey. It differs further by having a dark brown cap which the Cape Teal lacks. The smaller Hottentot Teal also has a dark cap but has a blue, not red, bill and a dark smudge on the cheek which this species lacks. In flight the Redbilled Teal shows a pale buffy and white speculum bisected by a black stripe. Immature Redbilled Teals are duller versions of the adults. The male's call is a soft whistle and the female's a muffled quack. The birds are found on virtually all freshwater systems and newly flooded areas, in small groups and sometimes in hundreds during the dry season. R

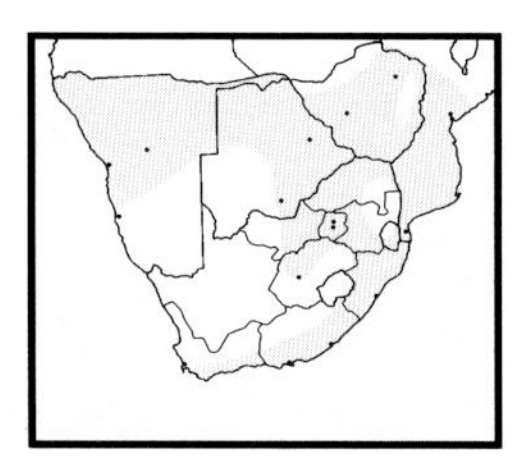

Hottentot Teal *Anas hottentota* (107) 35 cm

This very small duck superficially resembles the larger Redbilled Teal but differs by having a blue, not red, bill and by showing a distinctive brown smudge on its creamy cheeks. Immatures are duller versions of the adults. In flight it shows an obvious white trailing edge to the green speculum and contrasting black and white underwings. The flight is very rapid and jinky, and small flocks of these birds can be seen to turn and twist as they fly over marshes. The male's call is a clicking sound; the female quacks softly and utters a jumbled mixture of whistles and grunts. The Hottentot Teal loafs in quiet backwaters in small groups but congregates in hundreds during the dry season or if sufficient food is available. R

Adult Cape Teal

Adult Redbilled Teal

1. Adult Yellowbilled Duck
2. Adult Cape Teal
3. Adult Redbilled Teal
4. Adult Hottentot Teal
5. Male (front) and female (rear) African Black Ducks

1	2
3	4
5	

R *resident*

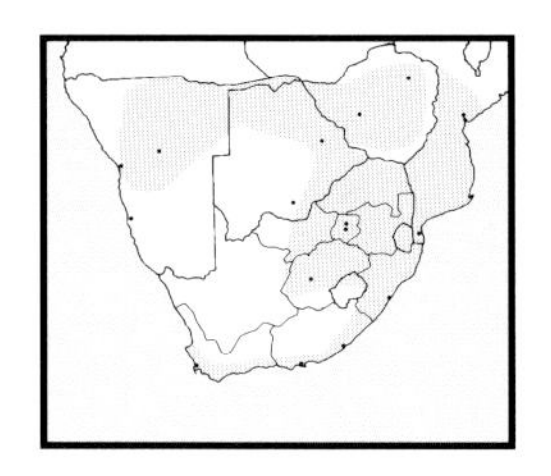

Whitebacked Duck *Thalassornis leuconotus* (101) 43 cm

This drab duck has a buff and brown mottled plumage, an orange neck and a white spot at the base of its bill; the white back is visible only in flight. The sexes are similar. Immatures have a reduced amount of white on the back and lack the white spot at the base of the bill. Take-off is long and laboured, and in flight the feet project well beyond the short tail. This squat and dumpy duck, with its large head and humped back, sits very low in the water, usually among floating vegetation where it is well camouflaged. The call is a low-pitched whistle, rising on the second syllable. The Whitebacked Duck occurs in pairs and small groups but never in large numbers and is usually quiet, unobtrusive and may easily be overlooked. R

Adult Whitebacked Duck

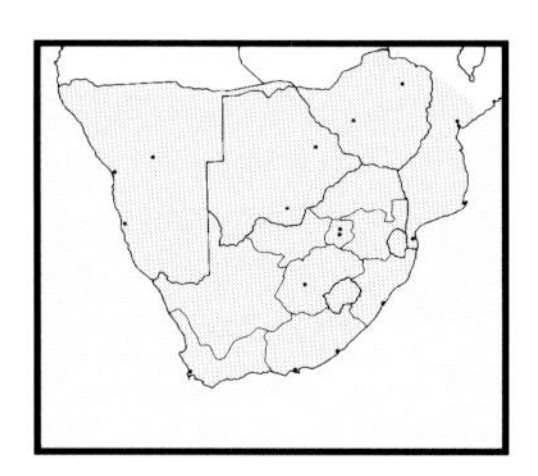

Southern Pochard *Netta erythrophthalma* (113) 50 cm

This small, all-dark duck at a distance appears black but at close range may be seen to be blackish brown with a glossy sheen and a bright red eye. Its blue bill may cause confusion with the Maccoa Duck but that species has a russet-coloured body and a black head. The female is a much paler brown and has white on the throat encircling the cheeks, creating a white crescent, and has white feathering at the bill base. Immatures resemble the females but lack the white crescent. The flight pattern shows a very obvious white wing bar. The Southern Pochard runs along the surface of the water before take-off and the flight action is rapid and direct. This bird, which sits low in the water with its tail submerged, dives frequently for food. It has a head-bobbing display, and is mostly silent although sometimes will give a purring call and a few soft quacks. R

Male Pygmy Goose

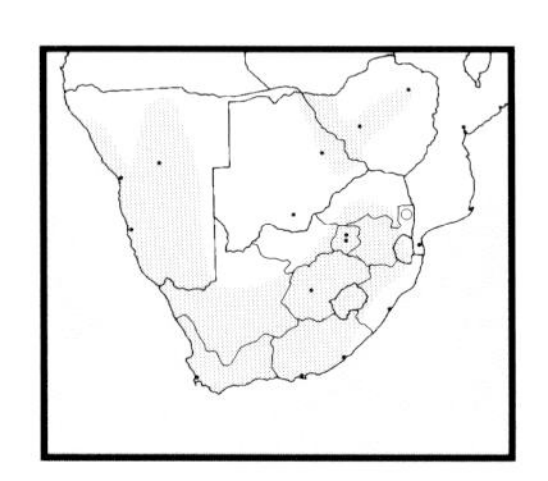

Maccoa Duck *Oxyura maccoa* (117) 46 cm

The chestnut body of the male Maccoa Duck, its large black head and cobalt-blue bill render it unmistakable. The Southern Pochard, for which it may be mistaken, has a paler blue bill and is dark all over. The female Maccoa Duck is drab, with the same squat body shape as the male and pale cheeks with a dark bar running through each. The female may be confused with the female Southern Pochard but the latter has a vertical pale crescent behind the eye and not horizontal striping across the cheeks. Immatures and males in eclipse resemble the female. These ducks swim very low in the water and frequently hold their stiff tails cocked at 45 degrees. The Maccoa Duck is very reluctant to fly and needs a long run across the water to achieve this. The call is a peculiar nasal trill. R

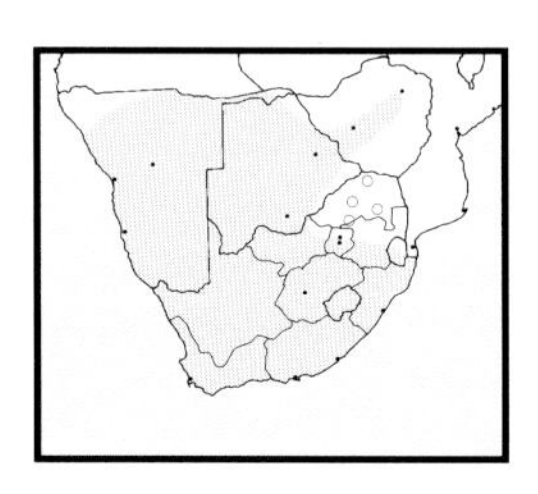

Cape Shoveller *Anas smithii* (112) 53 cm

This drab, mottled duck has an obviously large, black bill which when seen front-on is flattened laterally. The male has a much paler head and neck than the female and shows greater contrast between its plumage and the all-black bill. Both sexes have bright yellow legs and feet. Immature birds resemble the females. In flight the lilac-blue forewings are conspicuous and the white wing linings flash as they flip from side to side. The bird's speculum is an iridescent greenish blue. The call consists of a typically duck-like 'quack-quack' and a raspy hiss. The Cape Shoveller is resident in wide and varied freshwater habitats and coastal lagoons and estuaries. E

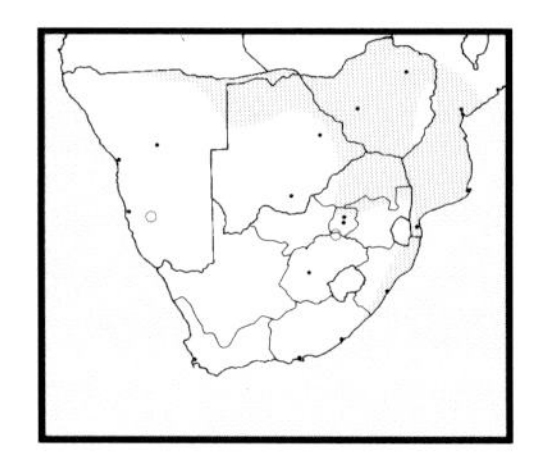

Pygmy Goose *Nettapus auritus* (114) 33 cm

The smallest waterfowl of the region, this bird's distinctive orange-coloured body, green back and glossy green head patch, yellow bill and white face make it an easy duck to identify. The female lacks the glossy green head patch of the male bird; immatures resemble the females. In flight the Pygmy Goose shows a conspicuous white wing patch. Its flight action is very fast, with blurred wing beats. It hides among floating vegetation, especially water-lilies, where it is very well camouflaged. The call is a short, two-noted whistle. These birds occur in small groups and pairs but not usually in large flocks. They are often seen far from water in woodland areas where they nest in tree cavities. R

1. Adult Whitebacked Duck
2. Male Southern Pochard
3. Male Maccoa Duck
4. Female Southern Pochard
5. Male Cape Shoveller
6. Female Maccoa Duck
7. Male Maccoa Duck
8. Female Cape Shoveller
9. Male Pygmy Goose
10. Female Pygmy Goose

1	2	
3	4	5
6	7	8
9	10	

R *resident* • E *endemic*

Raptors Family Accipitridae

This diverse assemblage includes most of the birds of prey. Vultures have unfeathered heads (to varying degrees) and are scavengers. Eagles have feathered legs (which distinguish them from snake eagles and buzzards), and are known for their soaring flight and hunting prowess. Buzzards have unfeathered legs and very variable plumages. The smaller goshawks and sparrowhawks have rounded wings and long tails, yellow or red eyes and, in some cases, very long toes designed for gripping prey. They hunt using a dash-and-seize technique. Harriers have long, narrow wings and tails and are distinctive in flight as they glide low over the ground, head down, with the wings held in a shallow 'V'.

Adult Cape Vulture

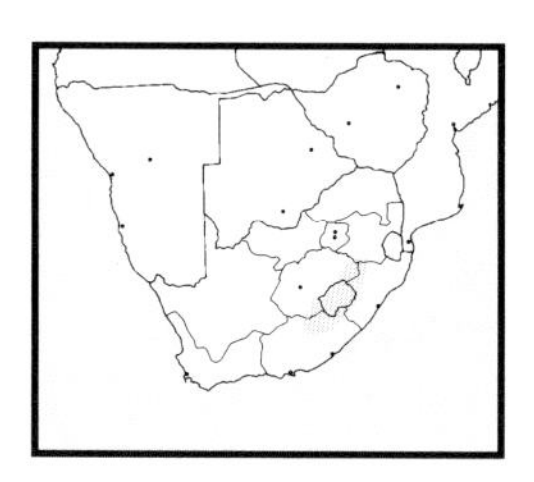

Bearded Vulture *Gypaetus barbatus* (119) 110 cm

This huge, dark, falcon-like bird with its three-metre wingspan and large wedge-shaped tail is most often seen soaring on mountain air currents. When perched the obvious 'goatee' beard, bright yellow eye and red eye-ring may be discerned. It is a specialist feeder, taking mostly bone fragments from carcasses or breaking bones by dropping them on to large, flat boulders known as ossuaries. It usually occurs singly in association with high mountains. Normally silent, when displaying it whistles a shrill 'feeeee'. R

Adult Whitebacked Vulture

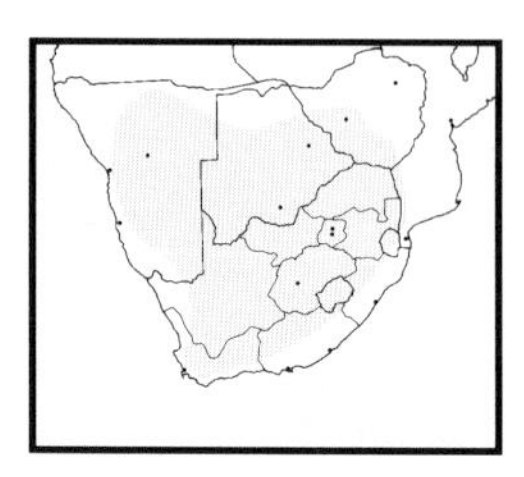

Cape Vulture *Gyps coprotheres* (122) 115 cm

The Cape Vulture has a blue throat and facial disc and a yellowish eye; immatures have a pink throat and facial disc and their eye colour changes from dark brown to tan as they mature. When perched the Cape Vulture can be distinguished from the Whitebacked Vulture by the black spot on the greater wing covert. It is most often found in hilly terrain but may occur in wooded savannas, and nests on high cliffs in very large colonies. It utters loud cackles and squeaks at the nest and at carcasses. E

Adult Lappetfaced Vulture

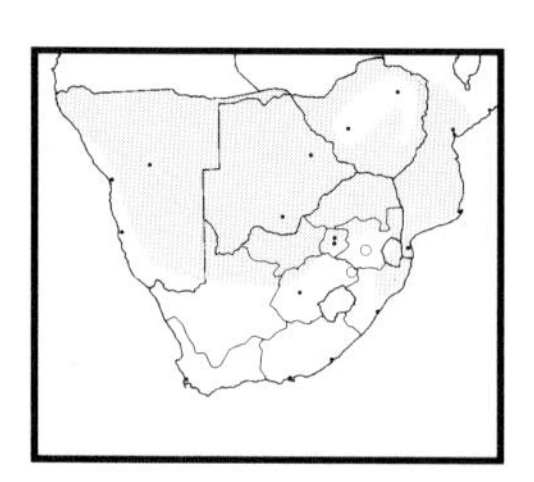

Whitebacked Vulture *Gyps africanus* (123) 95 cm

This species is a little smaller than the Cape Vulture which it resembles superficially, especially in flight when the size is difficult to assess. It is a dirtier brown than the Cape Vulture, has dark facial skin, and a dark brown, not yellowish, eye. The white rump contrasts with the rest of the upperparts. Immatures are similar to adults but their upperwing coverts and belly feathers have a central white streak imparting a heavily streaked appearance. Whitebacked Vultures nest at the top of large trees, sometimes in loose colonies, and occur in thornveld savannas. R

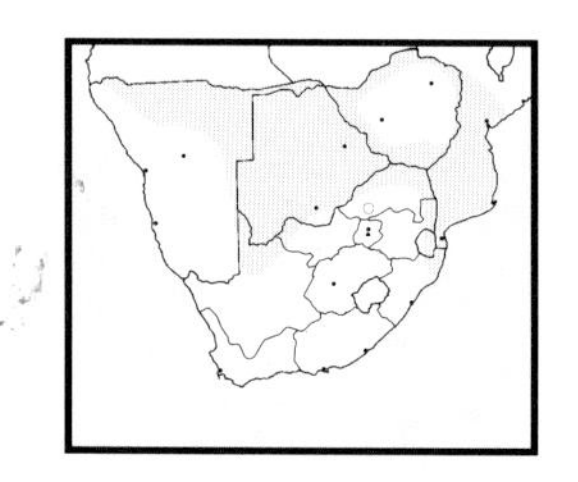

Whiteheaded Vulture *Trigonoceps occipitalis* (125) 80 cm

The head of this vulture, angular in shape, is a mixture of pastel colours: pale pink facial skin, orange bill and pale blue cere. In flight it is the only dark vulture with pale secondaries: white in the female and greyish brown in the male. Immatures are similar to immature Lappetfaced and Hooded vultures but have a narrow white line between the flight feathers and underwing coverts. Occurring singly or in pairs in thornveld and savanna, Whiteheaded Vultures are normally silent. R

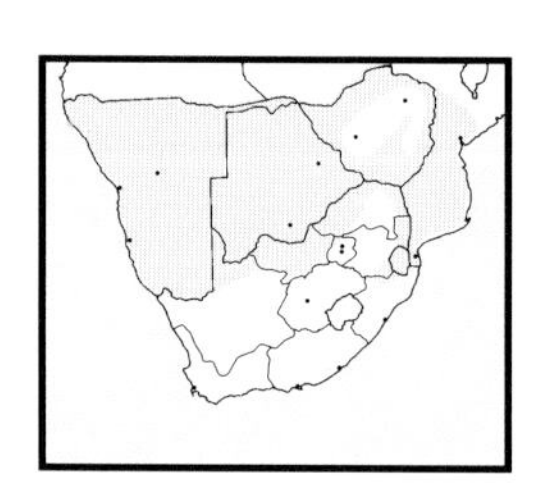

Lappetfaced Vulture *Torgos tracheliotus* (124) 100 cm

The bare red skin on the face and throat of the Lappetfaced Vulture and its very large size should render it unmistakable. The white thighs and white bar along the leading edge of the underwing are diagnostic in flight. Immatures are all dark brown and may be mistaken for Hooded Vultures but size and head shape should separate the two. An aggressive yet usually silent bird at carcasses, it also takes prey such as guineafowl, mongooses and hares. It occurs alone or in pairs in a range of habitats from savanna to desert. R

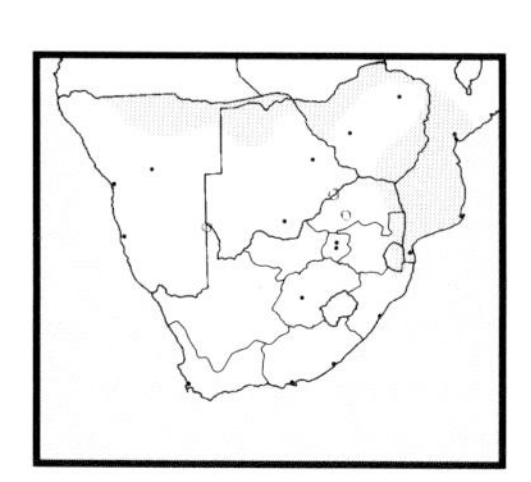

Hooded Vulture *Necrosyrtes monachus* (121) 70 cm

Adult birds have a naked crown and foreneck which turn pink to scarlet when the bird is excited. In flight the underwing is all black and the head is tiny in comparison with the rest of the body. Confusion may arise with the immature Lappetfaced Vulture but that bird is twice the size and has a much larger head. Normally silent, with some quiet, whistling noises given at the nest, it is solitary. It nests in trees below the canopy and occurs in open woodland and savanna. R

1. Adult Bearded Vulture
2. Adult Cape Vulture
3. Adult Whitebacked Vulture
4. Adult Whitebacked Vulture
5. Adult Cape Vulture
6. Adult Whiteheaded Vulture
7. Adult Whiteheaded Vulture
8. Adult Lappetfaced Vulture (left) with immature Whiteheaded Vulture (right)
9. Adult Hooded Vulture

R *resident* • E *endemic*

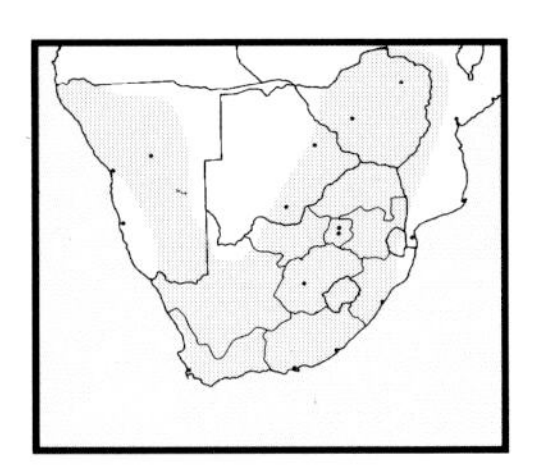

Black Eagle *Aquila verreauxii* (131) 75-95 cm

This all-black eagle should be unmistakable: in flight it shows a large, white rump, and the trailing edge of the wing is bulbous midway, narrowing at the body with a white wing panel at the base of the primaries. Immatures are mottled light and dark brown and have a rufous crown or nape which contrasts with the dark facial disc. Black Eagles feed mostly on dassies and are therefore associated with rocky ridges to high mountain ranges. Territorial and usually silent, it is often seen in pairs, or in a pair with an immature. The nest is a large stick structure built on a ledge or cliff face and is added to each time it is used. R

Immature Black Eagle

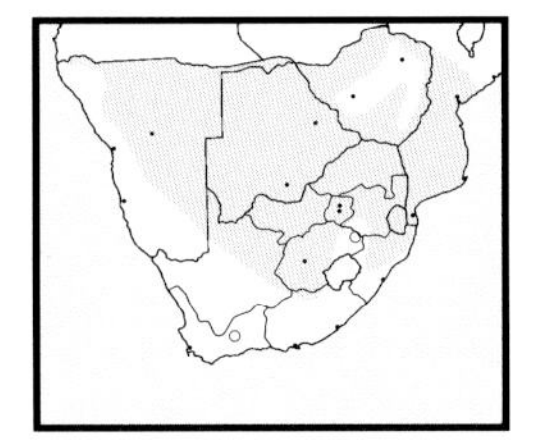

Tawny Eagle *Aquila rapax* (132) 65-80 cm

An untidy, rather 'baggy-trousered' bird, the Tawny Eagle can be distinguished from the similar-sized migrant Steppe Eagle by its gape length which extends only to the centre of the eye, not beyond. These eagles are generally tawny to rusty brown in colour, although 'blonde' morphs do occur. First-year birds may appear almost white with rusty heads due to feather wear. In flight the Tawny Eagle is uniform rusty brown above and below, including the underwing coverts, which are lighter than the flight feathers. The base of the first few primaries is paler than the remainder of the wing, showing as a pale panel. Immature birds present a pale, narrow 'U'-shaped rump in flight and may appear white-headed. Normally silent, Tawny Eagles occasionally give a bark-like 'koh' call. They favour thornveld habitat. R

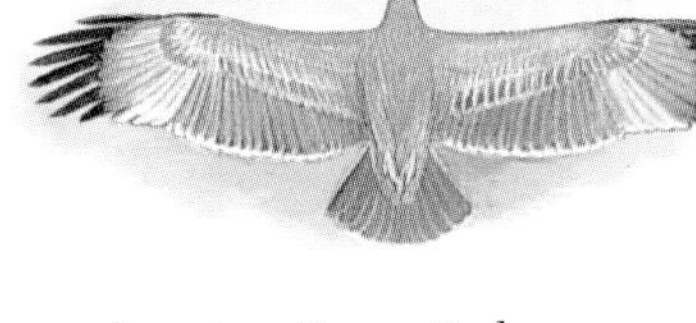

Immature Tawny Eagle

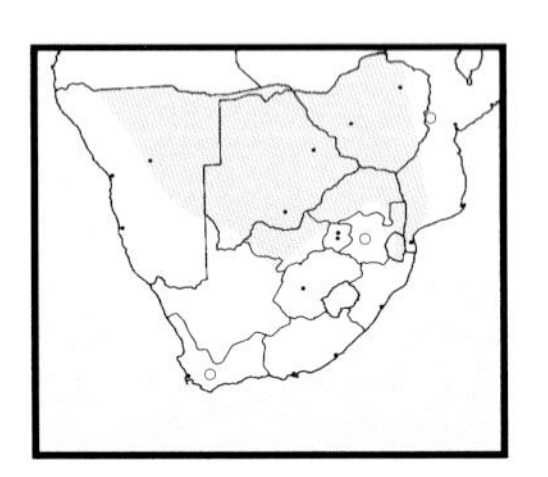

Steppe Eagle *Aquila nipalensis* (133) 65-80 cm

The Steppe Eagle could be confused with the Tawny Eagle but is usually more chocolate-brown in colour, and in southern Africa most records are sightings of immature individuals. The head and bill shape is flatter and more elongate than that of the Tawny Eagle, and the gape, seen at close range only, is long and extends beyond the middle of the eye. In flight, immature birds show a broad 'U'-shaped rump above, and from below the edge of the underwing coverts shows as a broad white band. Adult birds are dark with a dark rump but tend to show well-barred flight and tail feathers. Normally silent, Steppe Eagles occur in woodland and open savannas. S

Immature Steppe Eagle

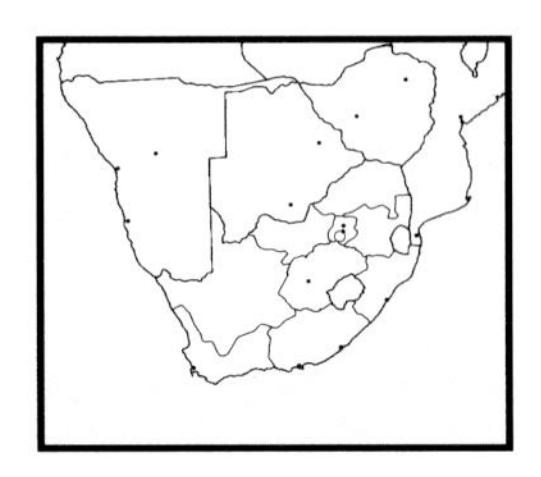

Lesser Spotted Eagle *Aquila pomarina* (134) 61-66 cm

This dark brown eagle has a short, rounded tail and a dirty-white vent. In flight there is some contrast between the underwing coverts and the flight feathers, the coverts being marginally darker. The flight profile is quite distinct with the wings drooping towards the tips, giving a bowed appearance. Immatures show a narrower white rump than do immature Steppe Eagles. Adults are dark brown with numerous small white spots in the plumage. The Lesser Spotted Eagle tends to associate with well-wooded terrain and is often seen at termite eruptions. It is usually silent in Africa. As is the case with the Steppe Eagle, it is mainly the immature birds that move this far south. S

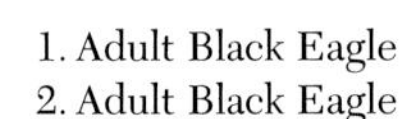

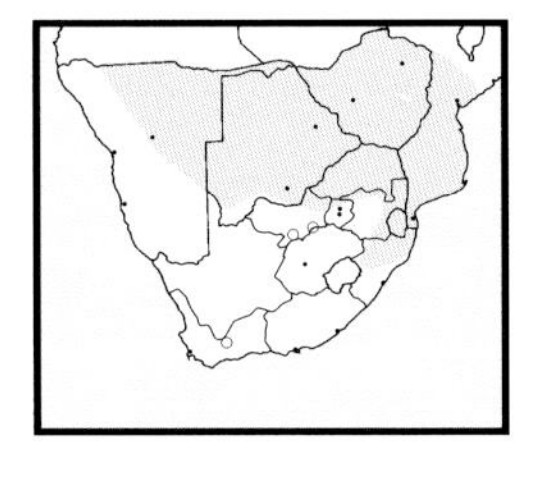

Wahlberg's Eagle *Aquila wahlbergi* (135) 55-60 cm

Wahlberg's Eagle occurs in a range of colour morphs, from leucistic to melanistic. In flight it has a characteristic flat profile and narrow, parallel-edged wings; the tail is square-ended and is normally held closed; the head peers earthwards, the large yellow cere giving the impression of a yellow bill and sometimes leading to confusion with the Yellowbilled Kite. This species can be distinguished from the Booted Eagle by its lack of white shoulder patches (noticeable in flight) and in having a pale patch on the forehead. It occurs in well-wooded savannas. A drawn-out, whistled 'kleeeu' is given when the bird soars and yelping noises are uttered at the nest. Wahlberg's Eagles return to the same territory year after year. I

1. Adult Black Eagle
2. Adult Black Eagle
3. Adult Tawny Eagle
4. Adult Steppe Eagle
5. Adult Steppe Eagle
6. Adult Tawny Eagle
7. Adult Wahlberg's Eagle
8. Adult Wahlberg's Eagle (pale form)
9. Adult Lesser Spotted Eagle
10. Adult Booted Eagle
11. Adult Booted Eagle

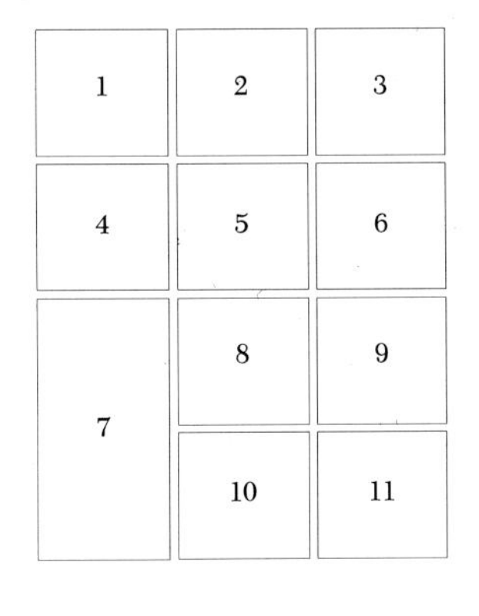

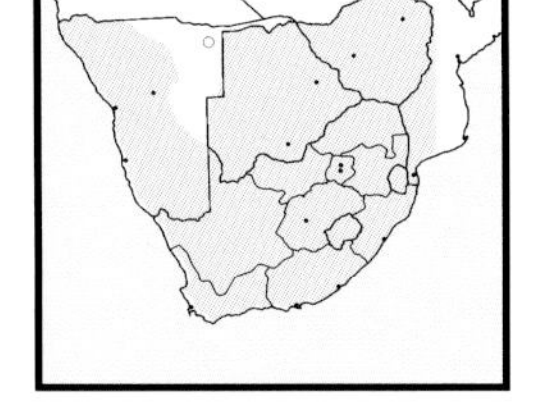

Booted Eagle *Hieraaetus pennatus* (136) 46-53 cm

The pale morph which predominates differs from dark morphs in having whitish, not dark brown, underparts. In flight it appears similar to Wahlberg's Eagle but the profile is not as flat, the trailing edge of the wing is more bulbous and the tail is slightly spread and graduating from silvery grey at the vent to dark at the tip. A characteristic feature of both morphs is the white patch at the shoulder, visible in flight. Booted Eagles utter a high-pitched territorial whistle. They occur in mountainous terrain, Karoo edge and woodland savanna. I, S

R *resident* • S *summer visitor* • I *intra-African migrant*

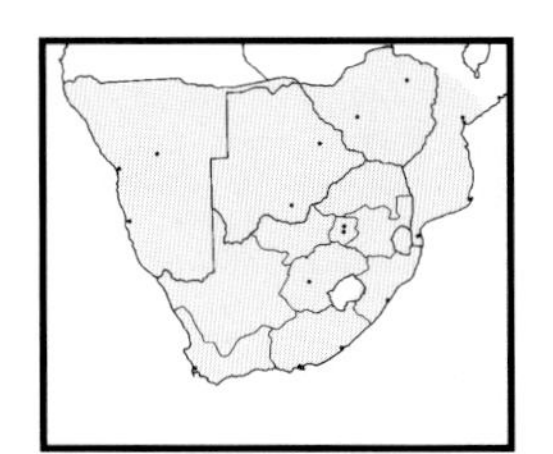

Martial Eagle *Polemaetus bellicosus* (140) 78-83 cm

The Martial Eagle and the Crowned Eagle are the largest African eagles, with females (which are larger than males) weighing up to six kilograms. From a distance the Martial Eagle could be mistaken for a Blackbreasted Snake Eagle (see page 50), but it has feathered, not unfeathered, legs, a markedly larger head and a much larger bill; in flight its wing shape differs and its underwing can be seen to be all grey, not barred white and black. Immatures are creamy-white with no black markings on the head and the underwing coverts are all white. Martial Eagles hunt from a perch but may also hunt on the wing and are occasionally seen hovering in windy conditions. They occur in woodland savanna, especially where large trees predominate. Often silent, they may give a whistling 'kleeou' in display. Gamebirds, leguaans and small antelope are an important part of their diet. R

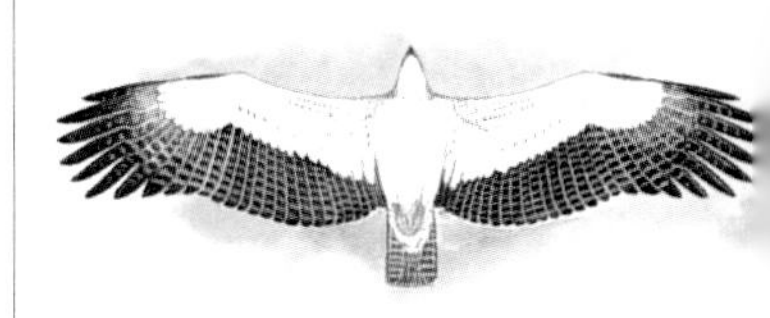

Immature Martial Eagle

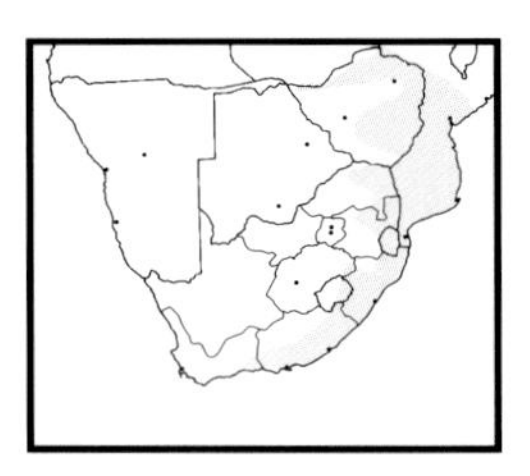

Crowned Eagle *Stephanoaetus coronatus* (141) 80-90 cm

This very colourful eagle with its well-barred underparts is comparable in size to the Martial Eagle. A very vocal species, it is often seen in display when, high above the forest, it gives its continuous, penetrating 'kewee-kewee-kewee-kewee-kewee' call. Immatures are less colourful than the adults and resemble immature Martial Eagles but can be distinguished from that species by their heavily barred underwings and blotchy buff underwing coverts and underbody. Crowned Eagles wait quietly for hours for an unsuspecting antelope, guineafowl or monkey to pass below their perch, then drop to paralyse and kill with their extremely powerful talons. They occur in temperate forests and heavily wooded terrain. R

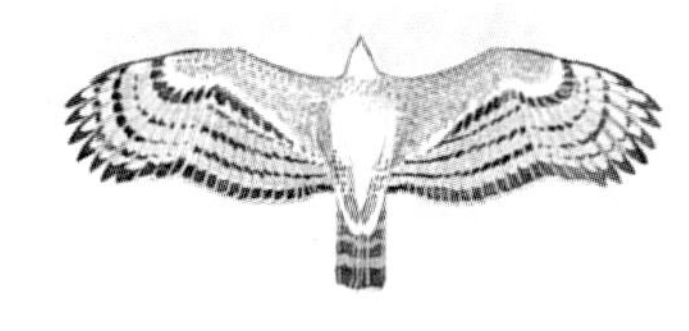

Immature Crowned Eagle

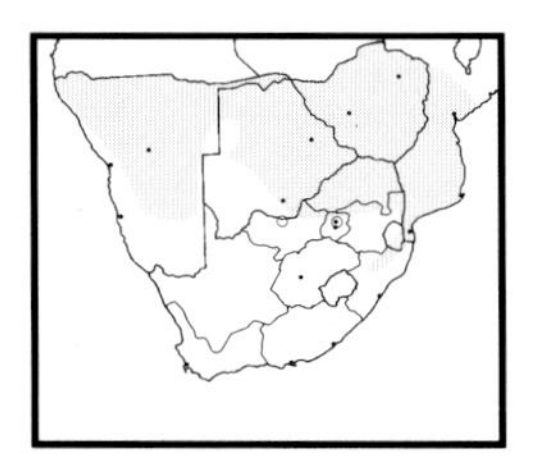

African Hawk Eagle *Hieraaetus spilogaster* (137) 66-74 cm

African Hawk Eagles are generally dark above and light below. In flight the underwing is white except for some dark blotching on the coverts and a very broad, black trailing edge to the wing and to the well-rounded tail. This trailing edge and the unbarred, creamy-white flight and tail feathers differentiate it from Ayres' Eagle. The sexes are similar but the female is larger than the male. Immatures are russet-brown and have a long, rounded tail and broad wings with a convex trailing edge; the flight feathers and tail are seen to be silvery-grey in flight with some faint barring. Immatures have feathered legs, which differentiates them from immature snake eagles and from the immature Gymnogene (see page 50). The African Hawk Eagle is invariably seen soaring in pairs and prefers well-wooded savannas in hilly terrain. It is seldom vocal but may cry 'klee klee klee' in flight. R

Ayres' Eagle *Hieraaetus ayresii* (138) 45-55 cm

This long-tailed raptor is smaller and has a narrower wing shape than does the African Hawk Eagle for which it might be mistaken. It occurs in denser woodland and forest edges, and is normally seen singly rather than in pairs. Adults are much darker in colour than the African Hawk Eagle, with heavy blotching on the breast, belly, legs and entire underwing which is also heavily barred. The sexes are similar but the female is larger than the male. A distinctive feature of Ayres' Eagle is the white patch at the junction of the leading edge of the wing and the body, a character it shares with the Booted Eagle (see page 46). Immatures are similar to immature African Hawk Eagles but are smaller, have narrow wings, strongly barred flight and tail feathers, and a lighter body and underwing coverts. Usually silent, in display it gives a rapid piping call. R

Longcrested Eagle *Lophaetus occipitalis* (139) 52-58 cm

This eagle's comically long crest, dark brown plumage and piercing yellow eyes render it unmistakable. In flight it shows white windows at the base of the primaries and the tail is well barred with a broad subterminal band. Males have white leggings and a longer crest than the females; females have brown or brown and white mottled leggings. Immatures are similar to the adults but have a shorter crest and a greyish eye. The Longcrested Eagle is common in well-wooded country (including exotic plantations) near wetlands, and normally occurs singly. It hunts from a perch and has a fondness for vlei rats. From a distance the short, sharp wing beats and white wing 'windows' help to identify this species. The call is a high-pitched scream, 'kee-ah', given during display flight and when perched. R

1. Immature Martial Eagle
2. Adult Longcrested Eagle
3. Adult Martial Eagle
4. Adult Crowned Eagle
5. Adult Longcrested Eagle
6. Adult African Hawk Eagle with young
7. Immature Martial Eagle
8. Immature Ayres' Eagle
9. Adult Ayres' Eagle

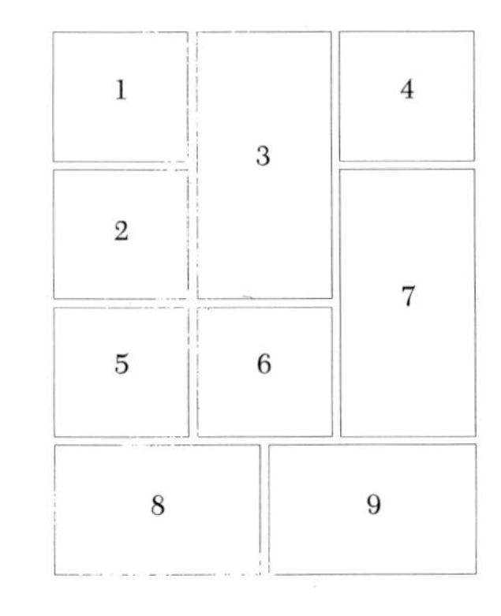

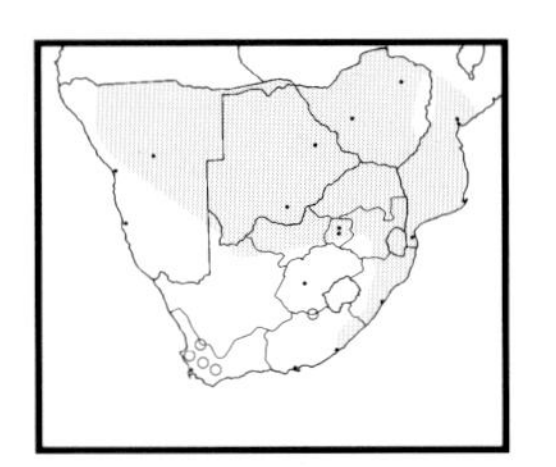

Brown Snake Eagle *Circaetus cinereus* (142) 70-76 cm

This large brown eagle is typified, as are all the snake eagles, by its bright yellow eyes and naked legs. In flight the underwing of the adult can be seen to have dark brown underwing coverts and silvery-grey flight feathers. The tail is narrowly barred white on brown. Brown Snake Eagles are commonly seen perched, characteristically bolt upright, on the tops of trees and telegraph poles. They hunt in thornveld and broad-leaved woodland. They prey on larger snakes than do Blackbreasted Snake Eagles but also take monitor lizards. The prey is taken back to a perch before being eaten. The call, when uttered, is a drawn-out 'hok-hok-hok-hok'. R

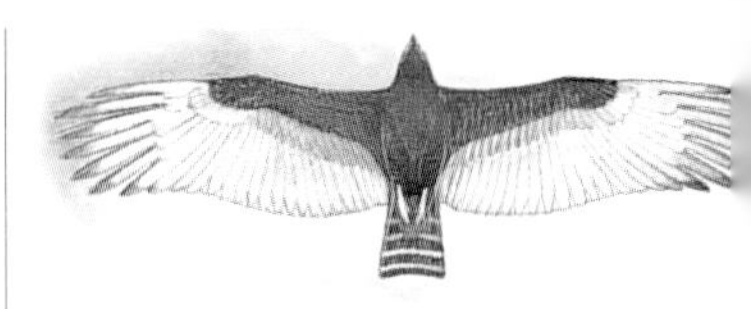

Adult Brown Snake Eagle

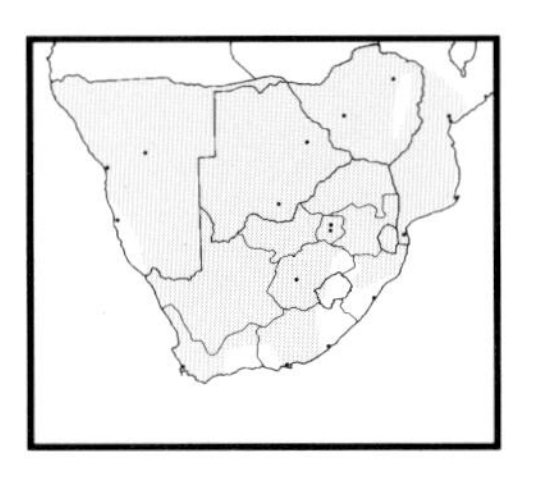

Blackbreasted Snake Eagle *Circaetus gallicus* (143) 63-68 cm

When visible, the creamy-white unfeathered legs will eliminate confusion between this species and the otherwise similar Martial Eagle (see page 48). In flight the Blackbreasted Snake Eagle shows all-white underwing coverts with bands of black on white on the flight feathers; Martial Eagles have all-grey underwings and no bars. The sexes are similar although the female is larger than the male. Immature snake eagles are difficult to separate from one another. This snake eagle characteristically hunts on the wing and can be identified from a distance by its hunting technique: gliding, it comes round into the wind and hangs in the air, giving only the occasional wing flap and scanning the terrain for prey; on sighting prey it folds its wings and hurtles earthwards in a dive. It occurs in open woodland to semi-desert areas with scattered trees, and calls when flying – a medley of fluty whistles and yapping sounds. R

Immature Blackbreasted Snake Eagle

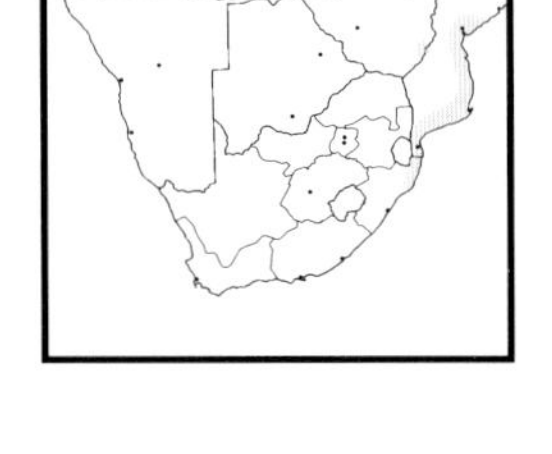

Southern Banded Snake Eagle *Circaetus fasciolatus* (144) 55-60 cm

This species and the Western Banded Snake Eagle are smaller and greyer than both the Brown Snake Eagle and the Blackbreasted Snake Eagle. The Southern Banded Snake Eagle can be told apart from the similar Western Banded Snake Eagle by the tail pattern of four dark bands separated by three whitish bars, not one broad white band. The lower chest and belly are broadly barred, rather like those of a Cuckoo Hawk (see page 56). The sexes are similar and immatures are dark brown above and pale below, with dark streaks on the face, throat and upper breast. The Southern Banded Snake Eagle hunts from a perch, from which it utters a high-pitched 'ko-ko-ko-keow'. It frequents coastal evergreen forests and flooded woodland. R

Western Banded Snake Eagle *Circaetus cinerascens* (145) 45-60 cm

This species is similar to the Southern Banded Snake Eagle, with a yellowish cere and base of the bill, but has a less extensively banded belly; the tail is black and has a broad white band through its middle. In flight the underwing is similar to that of the Southern Banded Snake Eagle, both being narrowly barred. Immatures of this species, which are paler than the adults, are also similar to immature Southern Banded Snake Eagles. However, it is unlikely that confusion between the Western Banded Snake Eagle and the Southern Banded Snake Eagle should arise as their ranges do not overlap. The Western Banded Snake Eagle hunts from a perch and tends to inhabit woodlands subject to flooding, as well as riverine woodland. Its call is a loud, resonant 'kok-kok-kok-kok-kok'. R

1. Immature Brown Snake Eagle
2. Adult Southern Banded Snake Eagle
3. Adult Blackbreasted Snake Eagle
4. Adult Gymnogene
5. Adult Western Banded Snake Eagle
6. Immature Gymnogene
7. Adult Gymnogene

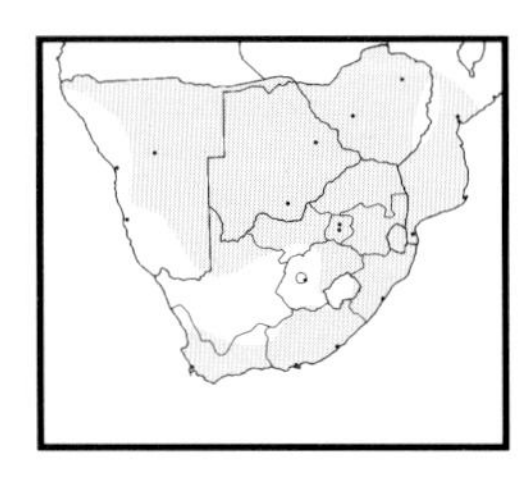

Gymnogene *Polyboroides typus* (169) 60-66 cm

The clown of the raptors, the Gymnogene is often seen hanging upside down from a bough of a tree flapping its wings or scrambling along branches and sticking its legs into holes. Adults are dark grey with yellow legs and feet, and yellow facial skin which flushes to pink when the bird is excited. In flight the underside is all grey with a broad black band along the trailing edge of the wing and black primaries; the tail is black with a broad grey bar across the middle. Immatures are a mottled rusty-brown in colour; the underwing coverts are rusty-brown and the flight feathers are barred; the tail is brown with four darker brown, broad bars; the facial skin is a dirty yellowish grey. The Gymnogene has a double-jointed 'knee' which enables it to bend its legs forwards and backwards, facilitating the extraction of prey from holes. It prefers wooded habitats along rivers, and is also found in forests and broad-leaved woodland. It is silent, except in the breeding season when it utters a whistled 'suuu-eee-ooo'. R

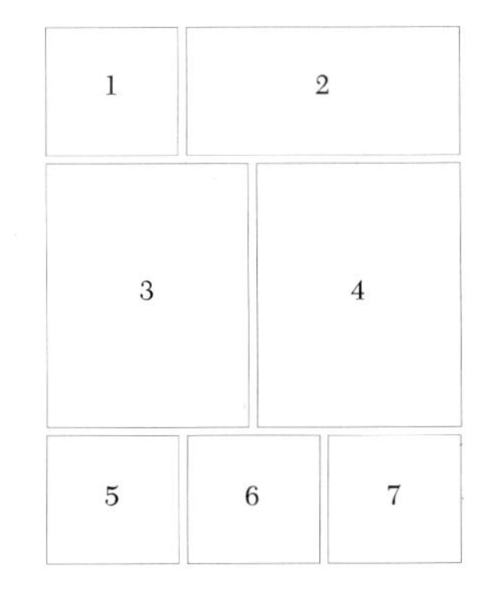

R *resident*

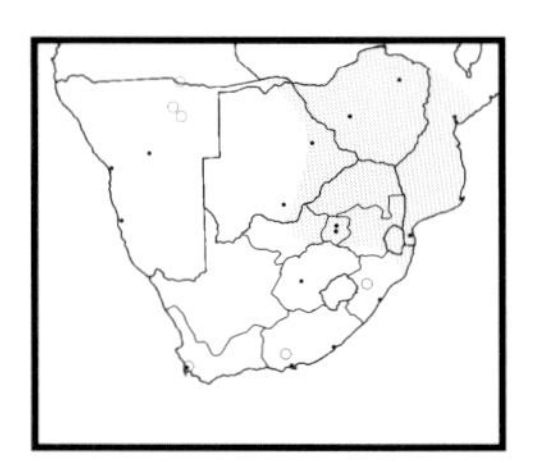

Honey Buzzard *Pernis apivorus* (130) 56 cm

Similar to the Steppe Buzzard in flight, the Honey Buzzard can be distinguished by the two broad bars (sometimes indistinct) near the base of the tail and the broader terminal tail band. It is also slimmer and has a smaller head. At close range the bright yellow eye of the adult and the scaly feathers seen around the facial area are diagnostic. The immature lacks the tail bars and has a dark brown eye which could lead to confusion with adult Steppe Buzzards, but its small head, slender appearance and flight action should help to identify it. The Honey Buzzard rarely glides, flying strongly with very deep wing beats. A shy, secretive species, it searches the ground in mature woodlands for colonies of the bees and wasps on which it feeds. It is normally silent in Africa. S

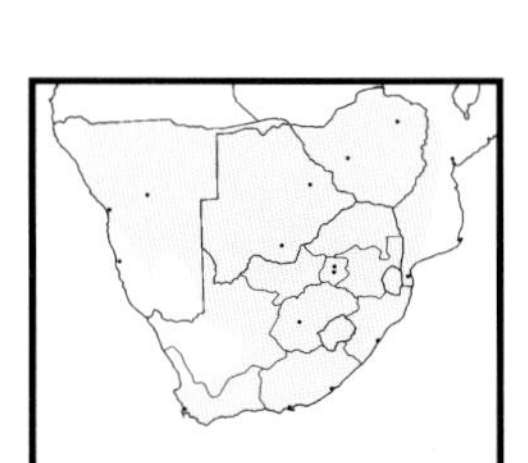

Steppe Buzzard *Buteo buteo* (149) 45-50 cm

Buteo species are characterized by having only their upper legs feathered. Further, adult birds have dark brown eyes and immatures have light biscuit-coloured eyes. Steppe Buzzards show variable plumage coloration in shades of brown, rufous and grey, being plain above and blotched to barred below, and usually showing a white breast band. Adults have the uppertail tinged with russet, lightly and finely barred above with a distinct, broad subterminal bar. Immatures are similar in colour to the adults but have a typically light biscuit-coloured eye and the tail is finely barred black on brown above with a broad subterminal bar. On migration these birds seek out thermals and glide between them. This mode of flight separates Steppe Buzzards from the similar Honey Buzzards, which have a very active flight action. Steppe Buzzards occur in all types of habitats and are frequently seen perched on telegraph poles. They are normally silent in Africa. S.

Forest Buzzard *Buteo trizonatus* (150) 45-50 cm

Between September and April when Steppe Buzzards visit the region, confusion may arise between these two species. The Forest Buzzard tends to be paler on the underbody and underwing than the Steppe Buzzard with tear-drop streaks, not bars, on the underparts; the tail banding is similar in adults and immatures and resembles that of the immature Steppe Buzzard, but the tail coloration of the adult Forest Buzzard is more yellow than russet. Adults typically have dark eyes and immatures light biscuit-coloured eyes. The Forest Buzzard is confined in our region to temperate forests and forest edges and has adapted to exotic pine and eucalyptus plantations in some areas. The call is a gull-like 'pee-ooo'. R

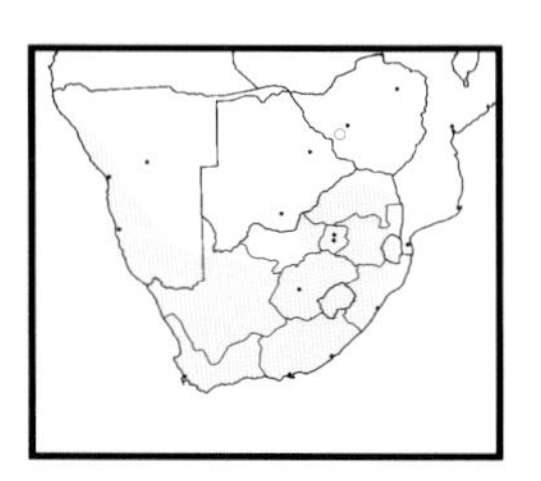

Jackal Buzzard *Buteo rufofuscus* (152) 45-53 cm

The Jackal Buzzard generally has a black head and throat, and a rufous breast of variable intensity, sometimes being almost white. In flight the underwing coverts are seen to be black and the flight feathers white with a broad, dark trailing edge. The tail is rufous. Immatures are more difficult to identify, resembling a large Steppe Buzzard, but can be distinguished by their general rusty-coloured appearance, larger, broader wings and pale, finely barred tail without a subterminal band. The Jackal Buzzard is commonly seen perched on telegraph poles, an ideal vantage point from which to launch an attack on unsuspecting prey. The birds are generally found in mountain ranges and adjacent grassland. The call is a drawn-out yelp, 'weeaah-ka-ka-ka', much like the yelp of a Blackbacked Jackal. E

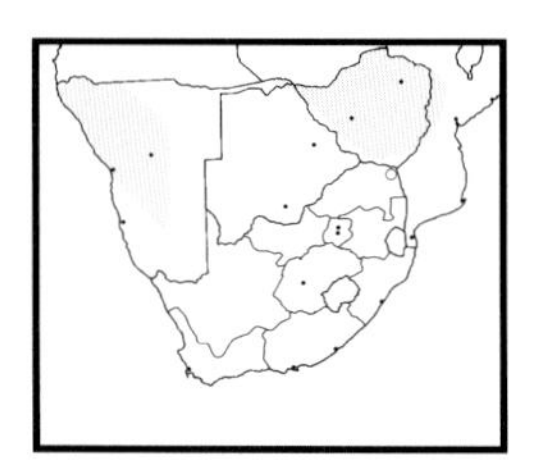

Augur Buzzard *Buteo augur* (153) 45-53 cm

The adult Augur Buzzard has an all-white throat and belly, as well as all-white underwing coverts and flight feathers, and a broad, dark margin to the trailing edge of the wing. A melanistic morph with an all-black breast, black underwing coverts, pale flight feathers and a broad band along the trailing edge of the wing also occurs. Both morphs have rufous tails. The adult bird may be confused with adult pale-breasted morphs of the Jackal Buzzard, but the underwing-covert plumage of the two species differs in flight. Immatures have a narrowly barred tail and are separable from the similar-looking adult Steppe Buzzard on eye colour and size. It is very difficult, however, to separate immature Jackal Buzzards and Augur Buzzards in the field. Augur Buzzards occur in woodland, savanna and desert. They generally hunt from a perch, and utter a harsh 'kow-kow-kow-kow' in display. R

Adult Jackal Buzzard

Male Augur Buzzard

1. Adult Honey Buzzard
2. Adult Jackal Buzzard
3. Adult Jackal Buzzard
4. Immature Jackal Buzzard
5. Adult Forest Buzzard
6. Adult Steppe Buzzard
7. Immature Augur Buzzard
8. Adult Steppe Buzzard

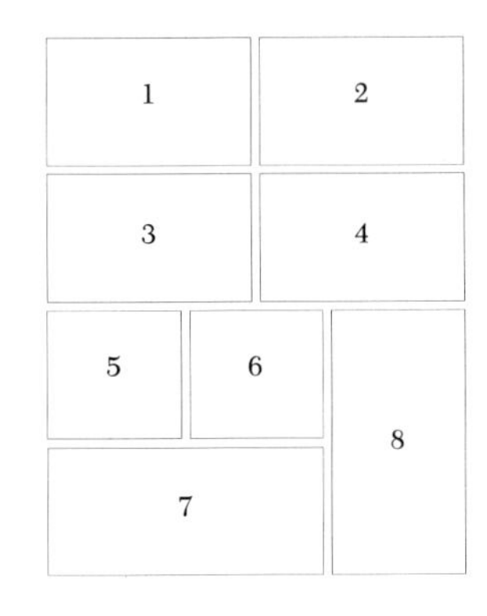

S *summer visitor* • R *resident* • E *endemic*

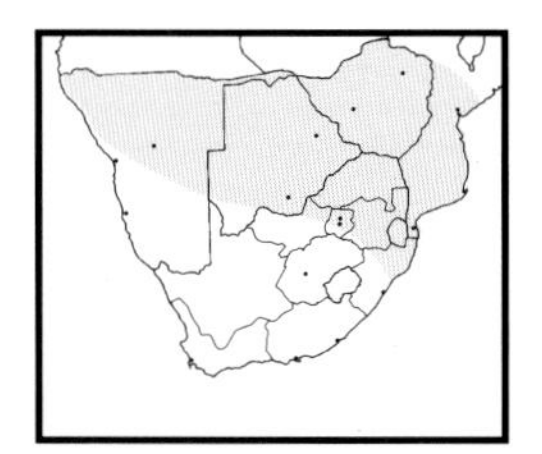

Black Kite *Milvus migrans* (126a) 56 cm

The adult Black Kite can be separated from the adult Yellowbilled Kite by its black bill and greyish head; also, the tail is not as deeply forked as that of the Yellowbilled Kite. Although similar in size to a Steppe Buzzard (see page 52), the Black Kite has a much longer tail which in flight is twisted from side to side, and its longer, narrower wings are angled backwards. It superficially resembles the African Marsh Harrier (see page 60) but that species has a square-ended tail and flies with its wings held above the body in a stiff flight action; the Black Kite has a floppy flight action. The immature Black Kite is similar to the immature Yellowbilled Kite and is difficult to distinguish as both have black bills and shallowly forked tails. The Black Kite occurs in a diversity of habitats, from forest edge to savanna and semi-desert; it is often found in flocks at termite emergences. Its call is a high-pitched, whinnying 'kleeeeeuu'. S

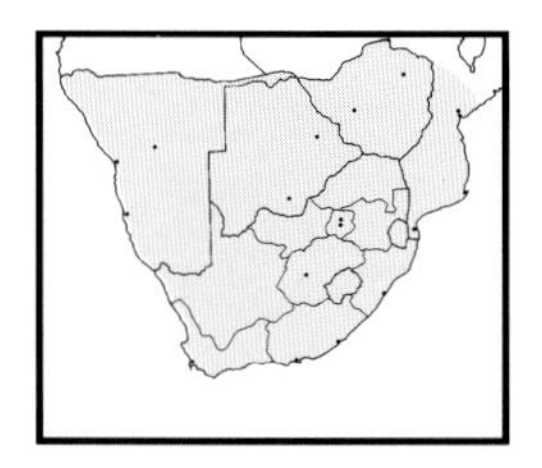

Yellowbilled Kite *Milvus aegyptius* (126b) 56 cm

The Yellowbilled Kite may be confused with the Black Kite from which it differs by its bright yellow bill, more deeply forked tail and brown, not grey, crown; immatures, however, are virtually inseparable from immature Black Kites as both species have black bills. The adult Yellowbilled Kite can be distinguished from the similar African Marsh Harrier (see page 60) by its tail shape (forked, not square ended) and by its flight action (stiff in the African Marsh Harrier). The Yellowbilled Kite is an agile scavenger with a floppy flight action; it twists its tail from side to side in flight as does the Black Kite. It is commonly seen near human habitation, and its call is similar to that of the Black Kite, a high-pitched, whinnying 'kleeeeeuu'. I

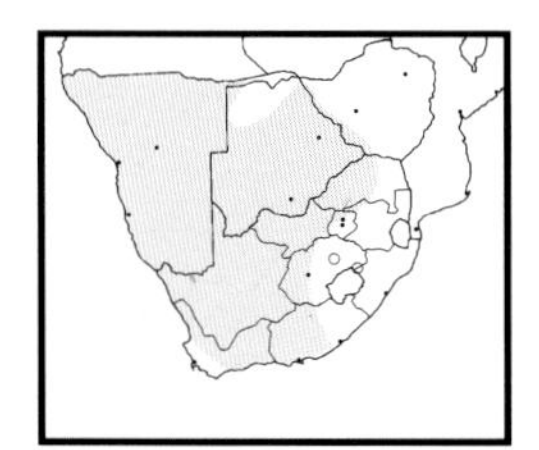

Pale Chanting Goshawk *Melierax canorus* (162) 54-63 cm

When perched, this species and the Dark Chanting Goshawk are difficult to tell apart. The Pale Chanting Goshawk has a white rump and the secondaries show white on the upperwing; the Dark Chanting Goshawk shows an apparently dark rump and an all-dark upperwing in flight. Immatures can be separated only at close range by the markings on the rump feathers: white horizontal bars on a dark feather in the Pale Chanting Goshawk, and white arrow-shaped markings on a dark feather in the Dark Chanting Goshawk. Pale Chanting Goshawks show some similarity to Gabar Goshawks (see page 58) but are much larger and have a plain, dark grey tail, not bands of black on grey. The call, a melodious, chanting 'kleeeu, kleeeu, klu klu klu' repeated a number of times, is virtually identical to that of the Dark Chanting Goshawk. These are the common roadside hawks of arid areas and also favour thornveld habitat. NE

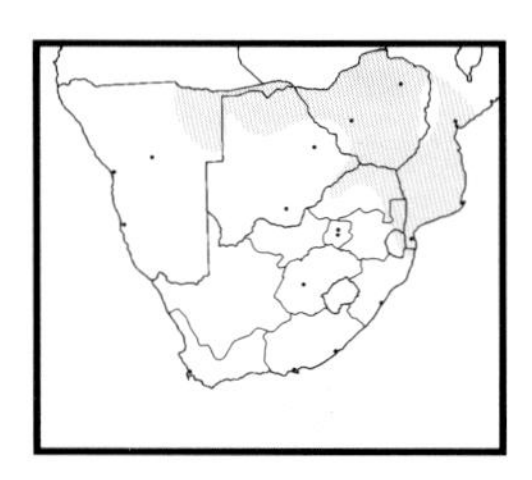

Dark Chanting Goshawk *Melierax metabates* (163) 50-56 cm

Similar to the Pale Chanting Goshawk, this species is slightly smaller than that bird and is usually darker. In flight and from a distance the feathers of the upper rump appear dark; at close range they can be seen to be grey and finely barred with white. Immatures can also be separated from immature Pale Chanting Goshawks by this feature but also have a darker brown breast than immature Pale Chanting Goshawks. The Dark Chanting Goshawk prefers more heavily wooded country than does the Pale Chanting Goshawk. It is usually seen singly or in pairs. Out of the breeding season the bird is silent but it becomes quite vocal when breeding with call that is virtually identical to that of the Pale Chanting Goshawk. R

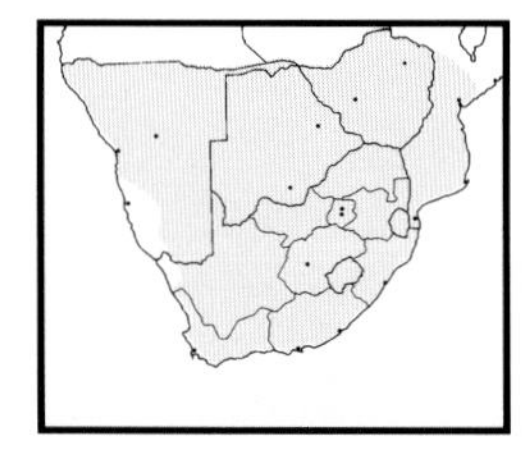

Blackshouldered Kite *Elanus caeruleus* (127) 33 cm

The adult Blackshouldered Kite is all grey with black shoulder patches, a white tail and a burgundy-red eye. Characteristically it cocks its tail up and down when perched. Immatures are mottled grey and brown with a dirty-yellow eye. At a distance the adult bird may be confused with the Pallid Harrier (see page 60) which has a similar underwing pattern, but it differs from that species by its smaller size, black shoulder patches on the upperwing and by its characteristic hunting technique: this small, pointed-winged raptor is frequently seen hovering with fast wing beats along roadsides and over fields in search of food while the Pallid Harrier flies low over the ground, relying on the element of surprise in hunting. The Blackshouldered Kite is normally seen singly but outside the breeding season may roost in large groups of up to 40 individuals. It utters a high-pitched whistle 'peeeu', a soft 'weep' and a rasping 'wee-ah'. R

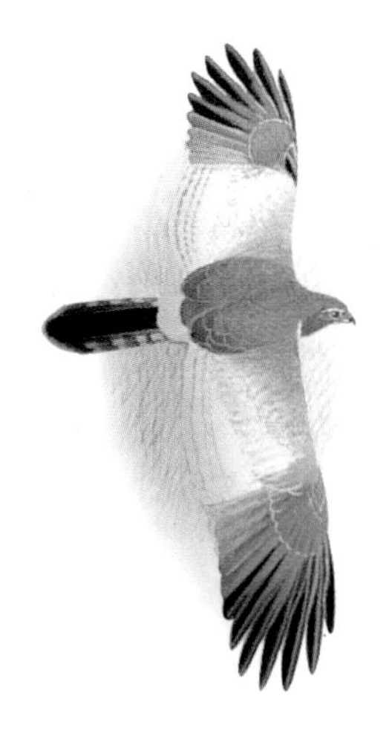

Adult Pale Chanting Goshawk

Adult Dark Chanting Goshawk

1. Adult Black Kite
2. Adult Yellowbilled Kite
3. Adult Pale Chanting Goshawk
4. Adult Dark Chanting Goshawk
5. Immature Blackshouldered Kite
6. Adult Blackshouldered Kite
7. Adult Blackshouldered Kite

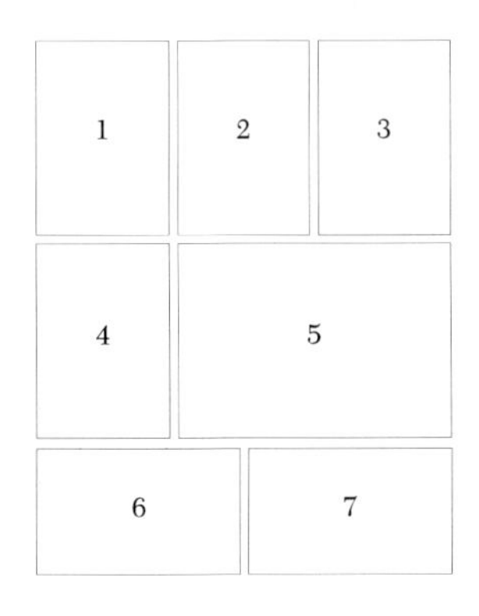

S *summer visitor* • R *resident* • NE *near endemic*

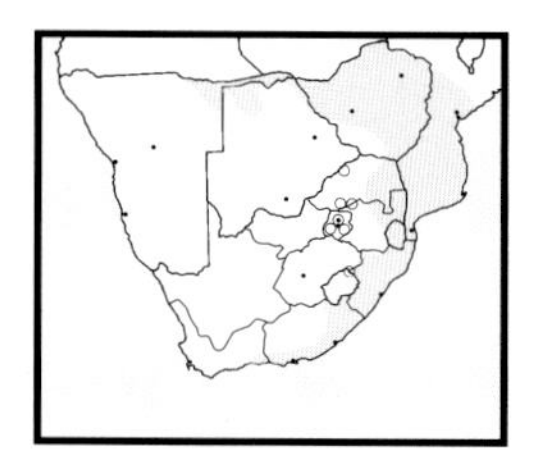

Cuckoo Hawk *Aviceda cuculoides* (128) 40 cm

Superficially and sometimes when seen head-on, the adult Cuckoo Hawk resembles the African Cuckoo (see page 130). It may also be confused with a male African Goshawk but shows a slight head crest, a yellow (in the female) to red (in the male) eye, a grey throat and wide russet bars on the white belly. In flight it appears long tailed with long, broad, pointed (not rounded as in the African Goshawk) wings; the underwing coverts are barred russet-brown, which might lead to confusion with some of the accipiters (the African Goshawk and Little Sparrowhawk in particular) but those of the accipiters are plain tawny, fawn or russet, sometimes with some fine barring and spotting. Immatures are brown, resembling young Little Sparrowhawks (see page 58) or African Goshawks, but have a short crest, are larger, longer winged and less blotched on the underside and belly, and have less distinct barring on the flight feathers. The Cuckoo Hawk occurs in mature woodland and forest edges. It is noisy when nest building and during aerial displays, giving a far-carrying, whistling 'teeeeooo' call. R

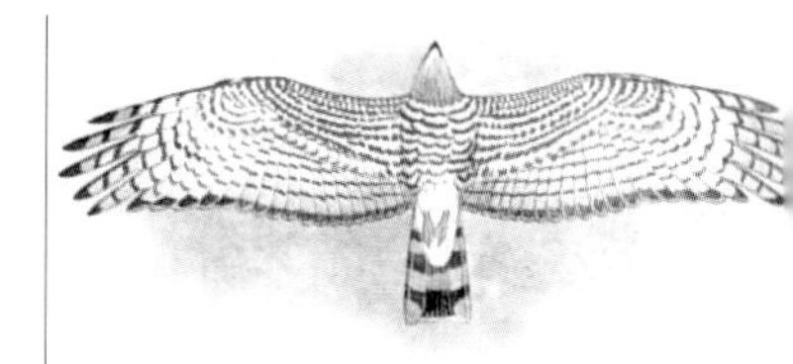

Adult Cuckoo Hawk

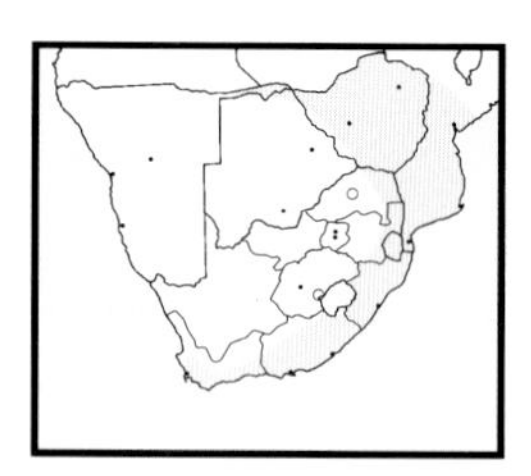

African Goshawk *Accipiter tachiro* (160) 36-39 cm

The sexes of this species are highly dimorphic. Female African Goshawks are much larger than the males, and are brown above, barred brown on white on the belly and have a broadly barred tail. Males are grey on the back and crown with narrow, russet bars on the chest and belly; the tail shows two white spots, as does that of the Little Sparrowhawk (see page 58). Both sexes have a yellow eye and a grey cere but immatures, which are all brown with a heavily spotted breast, have a brown eye. The Little Sparrowhawk can be distinguished from this species by its much smaller size and yellow, not grey, cere. Found in most well-wooded and forested habitat, and sometimes seen in well-wooded suburbia, the African Goshawk is most often recorded when seen in display, circling high above the canopy and giving its characteristic 'kek-kek-kek-kek' call. R

Adult Male African Goshawk

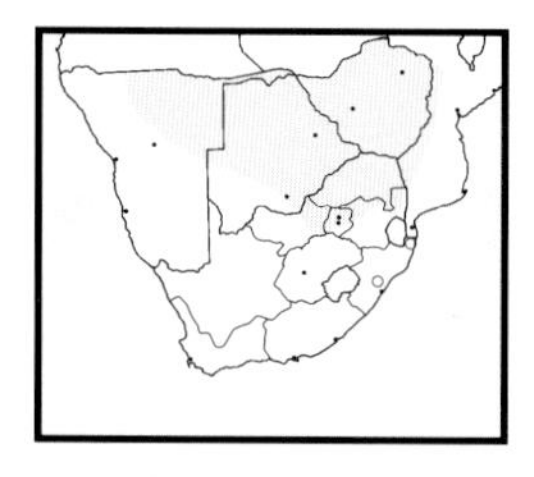

Ovambo Sparrowhawk *Accipiter ovampensis* (156) 33-40 cm

The female Ovambo Sparrowhawk is larger than the male; both sexes have a wine-red eye, a yellow to pinkish cere and yellowish to orange legs. The upper tail is grey with four broad dark bars, the feather shafts of the grey parts being white. In flight adults are grey above and show a narrow white rump. They can be distinguished from the Little Banded Goshawk (see page 58) by their barred, not plain, tail and grey-barred, not rufous-barred, chest. A rare melanistic morph, all black except for white vertical flecks in the tail, occurs and is separable from the melanistic form of the Gabar Goshawk (see page 58) by having orange, not black-flecked pink, legs. Immatures appear in two morphs, a pale form with a white head and a flecked white breast, and a rufous form with a russet head and streaked breast; both have a dirty-yellow eye. The rufous form resembles an immature Redbreasted Sparrowhawk but can be distinguished from that species by its yellowish-brown, not yellow, eye and darker brown, unmarked crown. The Ovambo Sparrowhawk prefers tall woodland but has adapted well to eucalyptus and poplar plantations. Perching in the sub-canopy, it preys on small birds. The call, a soft 'keeeep-keeeep', is given only when breeding. R

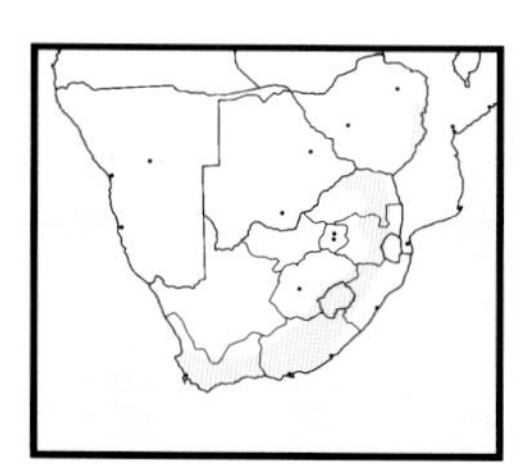

Redbreasted Sparrowhawk *Accipiter rufiventris* (155) 33-40 cm

The adult Redbreasted Sparrowhawk has an unmarked rufous chest with a pale throat, a white vent, grey back and a bright yellow eye. In flight it can be seen to be plain grey above and the white vent is seen to extend to the sides of the rump. The sexes are similar although females are larger than the males. Immatures are similar to immature rufous-morph Ovambo Sparrowhawks but have a yellow, not yellowish-brown, eye, and a darker, uniform cap. Normally solitary, the Redbreasted Sparrowhawk is usually seen calling in display, a series of 'kee-kee-kee-kee' notes. It is found in montane grasslands with isolated forest patches and has recently extended its distribution to eucalyptus and poplar plantations. R

1. Adult Cuckoo Hawk
2. Adult African Goshawk
3. Immature African Goshawk
4. Adult Ovambo Sparrowhawk
5. Immature Redbreasted Sparrowhawk
6. Male (standing) and female Redbreasted Sparrowhawk

R *resident*

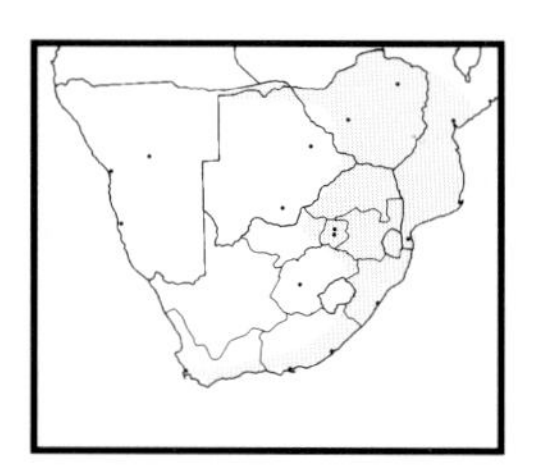

Black Sparrowhawk *Accipiter melanoleucus* (158) 46-58 cm

This large, black and white accipiter might be confused with an Augur Buzzard (see page 52) from a distance. The sexes are similar but the female is larger than the male. Immatures occur in two colour morphs, pale and rufous, both of which have a yellow eye. The pale immature morphs and the immature African Goshawk (see page 56) are similar but differ in size and in eye colour (brown in the immature African Goshawk). Rufous immature morphs resemble immature African Hawk Eagles (see page 48) but have heavier streaking on the rufous breast and belly, unfeathered tarsi and a tail with three or four broad, dark bands; the tail is narrowly barred in the immature African Hawk Eagle. The Black Sparrowhawk prefers wooded kloofs, forests and eucalyptus plantations. Usually silent, the male calls a 'keeup' and the female a repeated 'kek' when breeding. R

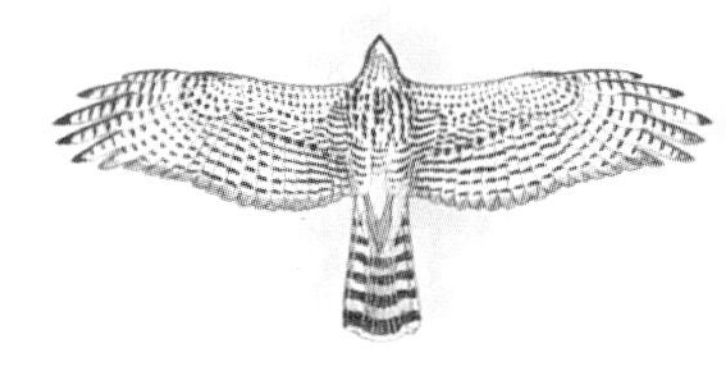

Immature female Little Sparrowhawk

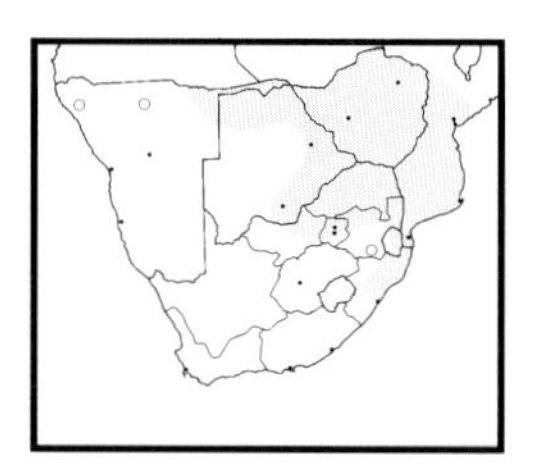

Lizard Buzzard *Kaupifalco monogrammicus* (154) 35-37 cm

The Lizard Buzzard is a larger bird than the similar Gabar Goshawk and has a pinkish-red cere, a wine-red eye and pinkish legs. The black streak through the middle of the otherwise white throat is diagnostic, as is the white rump and one white band (or, rarely, two bands) in the tail. Adults and immatures are almost identical. This pugnacious, stocky little raptor is often seen out in the open, usually singly, perched on the top of telegraph poles along the roadside. From this vantage point it swoops low over the ground to take rodents, lizards and grasshoppers. It occurs in woodlands, especially mature broad-leaved woodland. The call is a melodious, whistled 'klioo-klu-klu-klu-klu', given most frequently during the breeding season. R

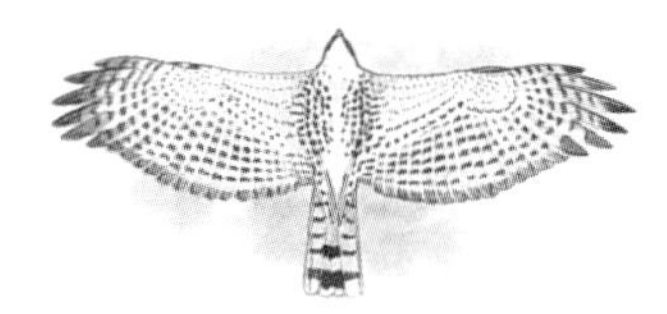

Immature female Little Banded Goshawk

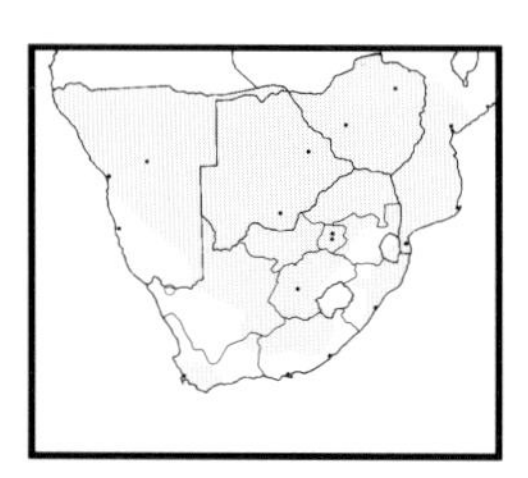

Gabar Goshawk *Micronisus gabar* (161) 30-34 cm

This frequently seen 'little grey guy' is distinctive in flight with its broad, white rump and tail showing four dark bars on grey. At rest it shows a deep red (appearing dark brown) eye, a pink to red cere and legs, a grey throat and a barred chest; the underwing is heavily barred. Immatures are brown above with a brown-streaked throat and an untidily barred belly but show a broad white rump in flight; the cere and legs are yellowish in colour. The melanistic morph of the Gabar Goshawk is all black, except for white barring in the flight feathers, and shows a pink to red cere, red legs flecked with black, and a dark rump. It may be confused with the melanistic form of the Ovambo Sparrowhawk (see page 56) but that species has orange legs and white vertical flecks in the tail. The Gabar Goshawk, normally seen singly in savanna habitats, especially thornveld and semi-arid ones, has a high-pitched, whistling 'kik-kik-kik-kik' call. R

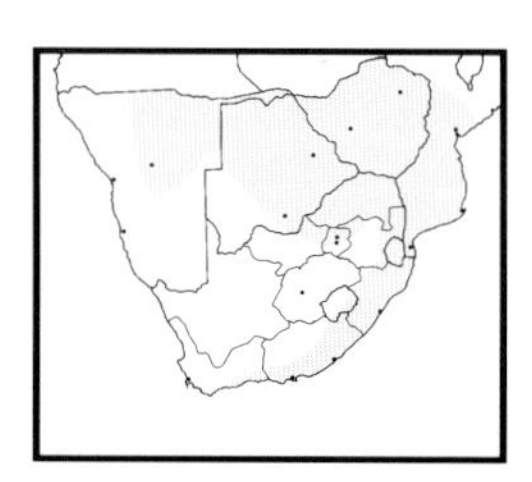

Little Sparrowhawk *Accipiter minullus* (157) 23-25 cm

This pugnacious little raptor is similar to the Little Banded Goshawk, having an all-grey back and tail, but can be told apart from that species by its two white central tail spots and bright yellow cere and eye. The African Goshawk (see page 56), which the adult Little Sparrowhawk resembles, has a grey cere and a dark, not white, rump. Immatures are brown, and show heavy brown blotches on cream on the chest and belly. In flight the Little Sparrowhawk is seen to have a narrow white rump. It inhabits a variety of wooded habitats, including exotic plantations such as eucalyptus and poplar. It has a soft 'kew kew kew' call and is usually solitary. R

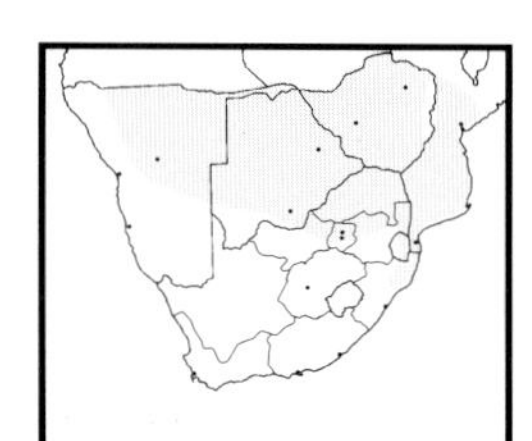

Little Banded Goshawk *Accipiter badius* (159) 28-30 cm

When perching, the Little Banded Goshawk can be seen to have a narrowly russet-barred belly, a deep orange to bright red eye, yellow legs and a plain, unmarked back and tail. In flight the plain grey rump and plain uppertail are visible. Immatures are brown, with an indistinctly and broadly barred tail; they have a yellow eye and a gingery-blotched belly with a plain white throat. The Little Banded Goshawk may be confused with the Ovambo Sparrowhawk (see page 56), but the heavy blotching, rather than streaking, on the breast, the unbarred tail and the yellow, not yellow-brown eye, distinguish it. These birds, which occur in thornveld, broad-leaved woodland and exotic plantations, hunt from perches and are sometimes seen on telegraph poles along roadsides. The male gives a high-pitched 'kleevil-kleeevil' call; the female's call is a softer 'tee-uuu'. R

1. Immature Black Sparrowhawk
2. Adult Lizard Buzzard
3. Adult Black Sparrowhawk
4. Adult Lizard Buzzard
5. Adult Gabar Goshawk
6. Juvenile Gabar Goshawk
7. Adult Gabar Goshawk
8. Adult Little Sparrowhawk
9. Immature Little Sparrowhawk
10. Immature Little Banded Goshawk

1	2	
3	4	5
	6	7
8	9	10

R *resident*

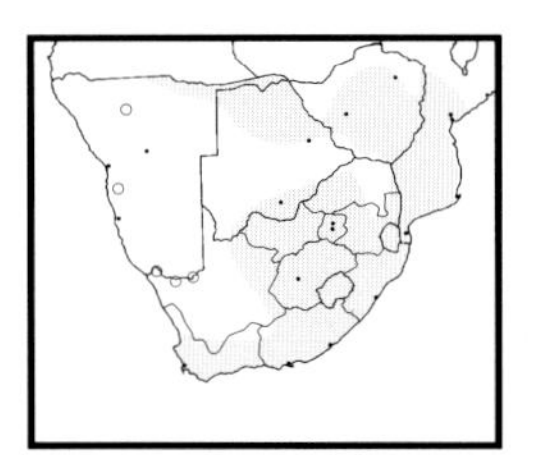

African Marsh Harrier *Circus ranivorus* (165) 45-50 cm

The adult African Marsh Harrier has a brown body and greyish-brown primaries and tail. The tail is not as grey as that of the European Marsh Harrier, and the leading edge of the wing is white. In flight the underwing and undertail are strongly barred, unlike the unbarred underwing of the European Marsh Harrier. The dark rump separates this species from the female Pallid Harrier and Montagu's Harrier, both of which have a white rump. Immatures have a broad white band across the chest, and a pale creamy head and leading edge to the wing. They may be confused with the female European Marsh Harrier but in flight can be told apart from that species by their barred, not unbarred, underwing and tail. A bird of marshlands and vleis, the African Marsh Harrier hunts by flying over the reeds and dropping down on to its prey. Except for a variety of chattering noises given at the nest during the breeding season, the bird is silent. R

Adult African Marsh Harrier

European Marsh Harrier *Circus aeruginosus* (164) 48-55 cm

The male European Marsh Harrier has a grey head, an unmarked grey tail and grey primaries and carpals. Females and immatures are browner than the male, with a pale, almost white, head, a white throat and a plain, unmarked tail; they can be distinguished from the female and immature African Marsh Harrier by their unbarred, not barred, underwing in flight and by the lack of a white chest band. European Marsh Harriers glide on raised wings, this action preceded by a series of six or seven flaps, and forage by flying low over reeds in an attempt to surprise their prey. They are confined to wetland habitats, and are silent in Africa. S

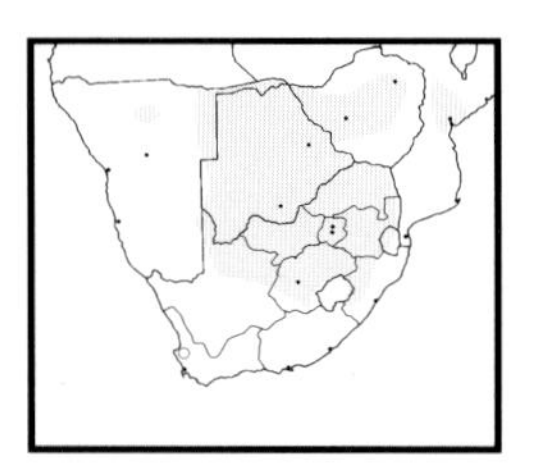

Montagu's Harrier *Circus pygargus* (166) 41-46 cm

The adult male Montagu's Harrier is dark grey above and white below with longitudinal brown centres to the belly feathers. In flight the edges of the upperwing coverts form a distinct black bar through the middle of the wing, and all the primaries are black, standing out sharply against the otherwise grey upperwing. The underwing is strongly barred. Females and immatures are brown with a white rump, and, as such, similar to the female and immature Pallid Harrier; subtle differences based on facial markings separate the females and immatures of the two species. A rare melanistic morph occurs, being all black with a yellow eye and yellow legs. Montagu's Harrier favours upland grasslands. It is silent in Africa. S

Immature Black Harrier

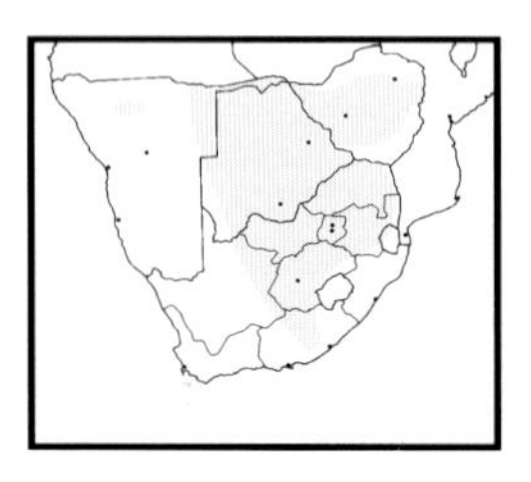

Pallid Harrier *Circus macrourus* (167) 38-46 cm

The male Pallid Harrier is generally light grey in colour, but slightly darker on the upperbody. In flight the upperwing is grey and unmarked except for a distinct black wedge at the wing tip formed by four or five, all-black primaries; the underwing is very pale and similarly unmarked except for the black primaries. Females and immatures are brown with a white rump and are not easily separated from female and immature Montagu's Harriers; a distinguishing feature is the white facial disc edged with a broad black crescent and with a dark line through the eye, a character that is either lacking or less distinct in Montagu's Harrier. The Pallid Harrier occurs in grassland and savanna, and is silent in Africa. S

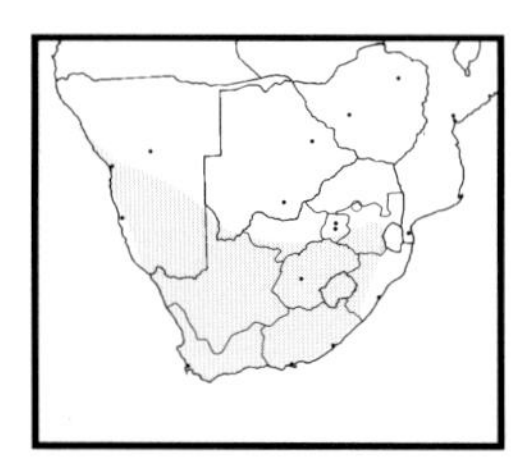

Black Harrier *Circus maurus* (168) 48-53 cm

The adult Black Harrier is unmistakable: it is one of the few predominantly black harriers in the world, with only the flight feathers and rump being white and the tail boldly striped black and white. It has a broad black trailing edge to the wing. Immatures resemble the immature and female Pallid Harrier and Montagu's Harrier (called 'ringtails'), but can be distinguished by the secondaries of the underwing which are barred black on white rather than on grey. This raptor forages mainly over semi-desert scrub, montane fynbos and grasslands. The call is a 'pi pi pi pi pi', often given in display; a harsh 'chak chak chak' may be uttered when the bird is alarmed. E

1. Male African Marsh Harrier
2. Female African Marsh Harrier
3. Male European Marsh Harrier
4. Adult Black Harrier
5. Female European Marsh Harrier
6. Male Montagu's Harrier
7. Male Pallid Harrier
8. Male Pallid Harrier

R *resident* • S *summer visitor* • E *endemic*

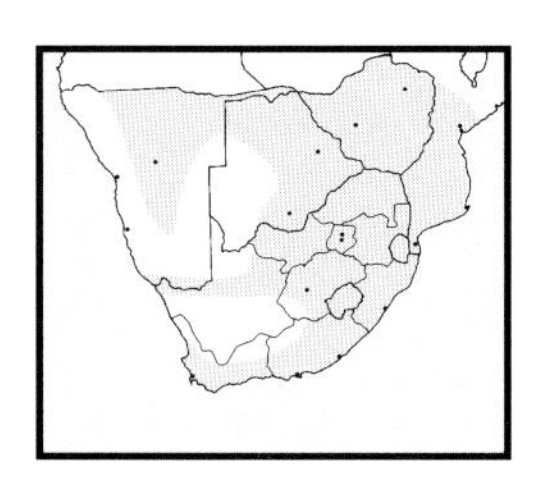

African Fish Eagle *Haliaeetus vocifer* (148) 63-73 cm

The adult African Fish Eagle is unmistakable with its white head, throat and tail, chestnut belly and underwing coverts, and black flight feathers. The sexes are alike but the female is larger than the male. In flight it appears as a large, broad-winged eagle with a short tail. Immatures are a mottled brown splashed with white, quite often showing a brown streak through the eye which may cause some confusion with the smaller, narrow-winged Osprey. The African Fish Eagle usually hunts from a perch and may call either from a perch or on the wing, throwing its head back as it does so; its evocative cry is probably the best known of any African bird. It frequents large rivers, dams and lakes, and sometimes estuaries and lagoons. R

Immature African Fish Eagle

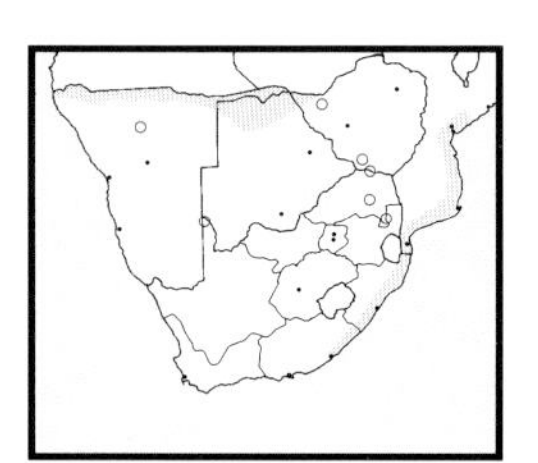

Palmnut Vulture *Gypohierax angolensis* (147) 60 cm

The adult Palmnut Vulture is all white with black secondaries (in flight the black tips to the otherwise white primaries can be seen), and a black tail with a broad white terminal band. The eye and bill are yellow, the facial skin is pink and featherless, and the cere is greyish. Immatures are reddish brown with greyish-yellow naked skin about the face; in flight their dark flight feathers contrast with their rusty-brown underwing coverts and body. Immatures may be mistaken for immature Gymnogenes (see page 50) but have no barring on the tail or underwing, and have a much larger bill and bluish-grey, not yellow, legs. When gliding, the Palmnut Vulture holds its wings in a shallow 'V'; the wing beats are shallow and rapid. It rarely calls, and feeds predominantly on palm fruits but also takes fish, crabs and land snails. The Palmnut Vulture occurs in coastal forest, mangroves and and in the vicinity of raffia palms. R

Sub-adult Palmnut Vulture

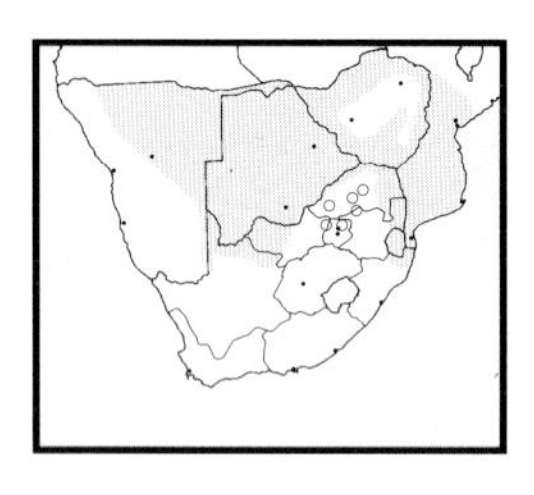

Bateleur *Terathopius ecaudatus* (146) 55-70 cm

This is the most easily recognized eagle, its black, white and chestnut colouring, peculiar wing shape, and very short tail rendering the bird unmistakable. It rarely flaps its wings in its daily wanderings about the sky; rather, it glides about, wings held in a steep 'V'-shape, rocking from side to side. It becomes sexually dimorphic after eight years when it reaches sexual maturity. Females show white secondaries, males black. Immatures have blue facial skin, and are otherwise brown, with a much longer tail than the adults. This species is more often seen scavenging at carcasses or road-kills than taking its own prey. It is solitary or seen in large groups, sometimes in association with Tawny Eagles (see page 46). Usually silent, it may emit a 'kow-oow'-like bark. It occurs in woodland savanna, including Kalahari thornveld, but in the east is confined to major conservation areas. R

Osprey Family Pandionidae

Resembling a medium-sized eagle, the Osprey preys exclusively on fish caught by plunge-diving in rivers, lakes, estuaries and shallow coastal waters. The feet are especially adapted for catching fish, having spiny soles and a reversible outer toe. The Osprey breeds singly, usually in large trees.

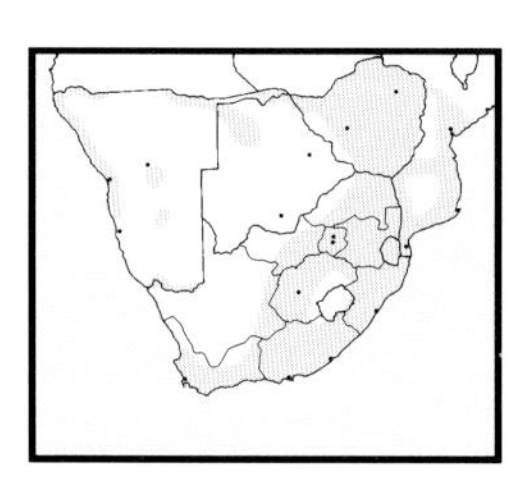

Osprey *Pandion haliaetus* (170) 55-69 cm

This small fish-eating raptor has a bouncy, gull-like flight. It is identifiable by its coloration: brown above and white below, with a brown line through the eye and a white crown. In flight it is narrow winged and long tailed; the underwing coverts are white except for the carpals which are black, as are the wingtips; the rest of the underwing and the tail are silvery-grey with some faint barring. Immatures resemble the adults and may be mistaken for an immature African Fish Eagle, but their mode of flight, smaller size, narrow wings and longish, dark grey tail should prevent confusion. The Osprey is silent in Africa. R, S, W

1. Adult African Fish Eagle
2. Immature African Fish Eagle
3. Adult African Fish Eagle
4. Adult Palmnut Vulture
5. Adult Osprey
6. Immature Bateleur
7. Male Bateleur

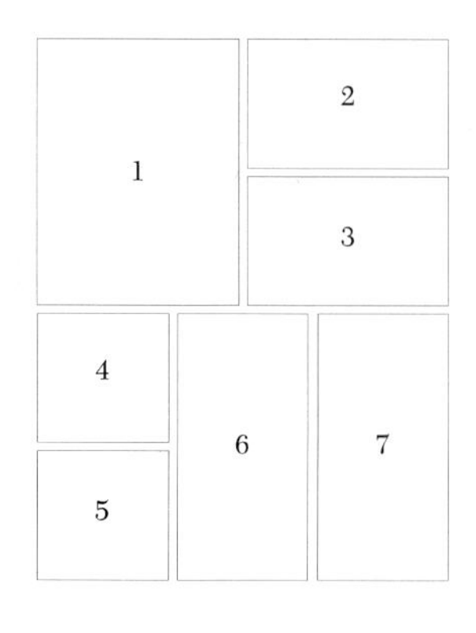

Falcons and kestrels Family Falconidae

Small to medium-sized birds, falcons and kestrels are swift, agile fliers on long, pointed wings. Some species are dynamic aerial hunters, stooping at great speeds to strike at their prey in mid-air. They are mostly diurnal, although some are crepuscular. The female is often much larger than the male.

Immature Peregrine Falcon

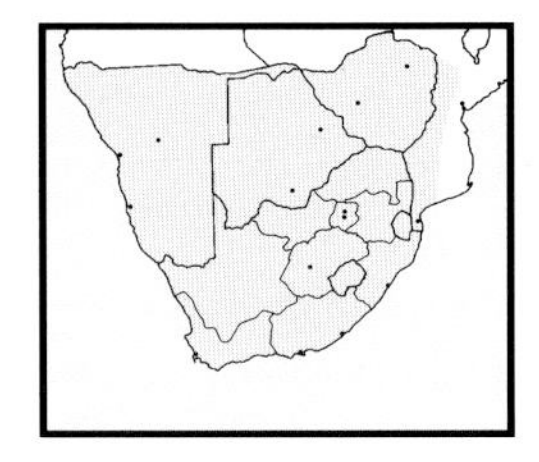

Peregrine Falcon *Falco peregrinus* (171) 34-38 cm

The black crown, heavy black moustachials (brown in immatures) and finely barred belly of the Peregrine Falcon distinguish it from the similar Lanner Falcon. The upperparts are generally dark bluish grey and the underparts are white barred blackish, except for the white chin and throat. Its stocky build, pointed wings and short tail make for an extremely powerful and fast-flying bird that has been recorded stooping at speeds of more than 200 kilometres per hour. Its ideal habitat is around high cliffs and steep gorges, but occasionally it occurs in cities and over grasslands hunting for prey . The call, a shrill 'kak kak kak', is given when alarmed; a whining 'chik-ik, chik-ik' is uttered when the bird is threatened. R, S

Immature Lanner Falcon

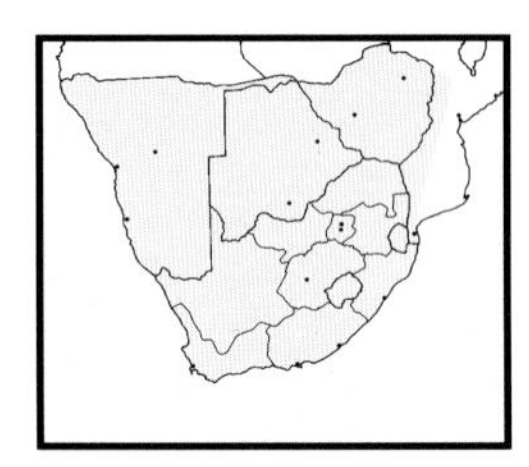

Lanner Falcon *Falco biarmicus* (172) 40-45 cm

This extremely successful and common species may be distinguished from the similar Peregrine Falcon by its rufous crown and plain suffused-pinkish underbody and underwing coverts. The upperparts are dark grey brown and although distinct the moustachial stripes are narrower than those of the Peregrine Falcon. Larger than resident Peregrine Falcons, the Lanner Falcon also has broader, less pointed wings and a longer tail. Immatures are heavily streaked dark brown on light brown and may be told apart from the similar immature Peregrine Falcon by their light rufous, not blackish-brown, crown; also, the dark underwing coverts contrast more with the flight feathers than is the case with the immature Peregrine Falcon. The Lanner Falcon feeds on a range of prey items from termites to large gamebirds and is likely to be encountered just about anywhere from mountains to open grasslands, and even in cities, although it tends to avoid forests. It utters a harsh 'kak-kak-kak' and piercing 'kree, kree' screams. R

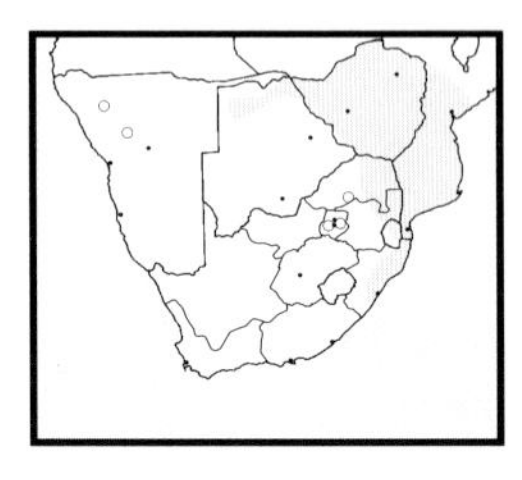

Bat Hawk *Macheiramphus alcinus* (129) 45 cm

This dark brown bird has a bright yellow eye, white feet, legs, thigh feathers and eyelids, and two small, eye-like, white patches on the nape. It could be mistaken for a Lanner Falcon or Peregrine Falcon in flight, but has a narrower body and longer, broader wings. Immatures resemble the adults but show a pale throat and breast. The Bat Hawk is found in thick woodlands, riverine forest and sometimes in eucalyptus plantations. It spends most of its day perched in thick foliage, becoming active usually for very short periods at dusk and at dawn; it is easily overlooked because of its crepuscular nature. It may hunt for longer periods on moonlit nights. It feeds mainly on bats but may also take quails which migrate at night. The call is a high-pitched whistle, sounding like that of a Dikkop (see page 102). R

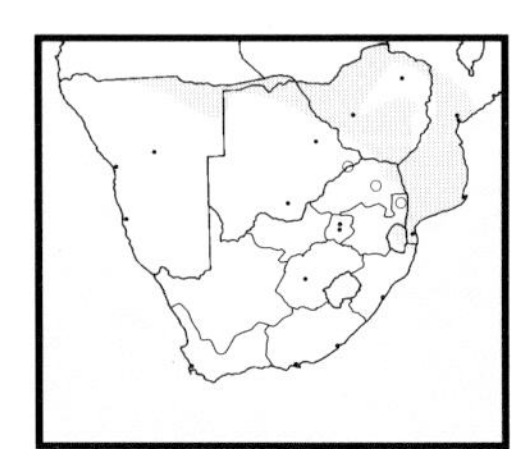

Dickinson's Kestrel *Falco dickinsoni* (185) 28-30 cm

Dickinson's Kestrel has a pale greyish-white head and rump which contrast with a darker slate-grey body. The bright yellow cere and eye-ring should render this species unmistakable. The tail is barred and in flight the rump appears conspicuously pale against the dark grey wings and tail. Immatures resemble the adults but are browner on the underparts with some white barring on the flanks. This falcon hunts from a perch, from a prominent dead branch or from the top of a dead palm trunk, from which it glides to the ground to take insects, crabs, bats, birds and rodents. A mewing 'ki-ki-ki-ki' call is uttered during the breeding season, otherwise the bird is silent. It prefers palm savanna but is also found in open woodland especially in baobab country. R

1. Immature Peregrine Falcon
2. Adult Peregrine Falcon
3. Adult Lanner Falcon
4. Immature Lanner Falcon
5. Adult Bat Hawk
6. Adult Bat Hawk
7. Adult Dickinson's Kestrel

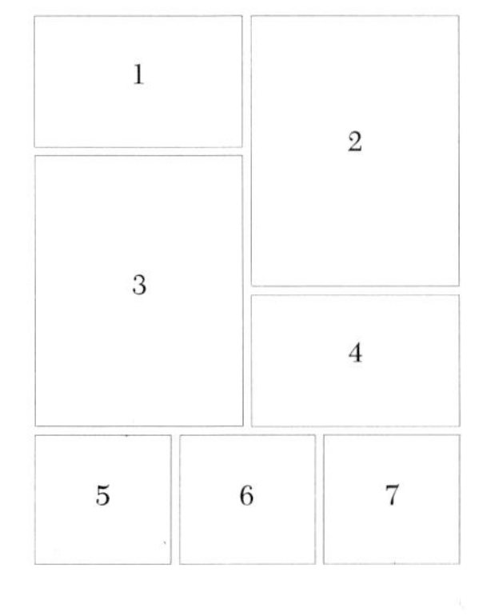

R *resident* • S *summer visitor*

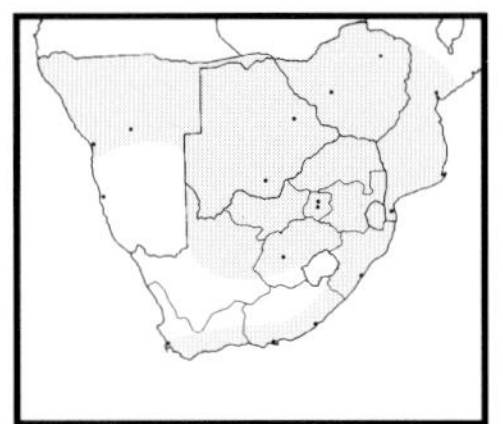
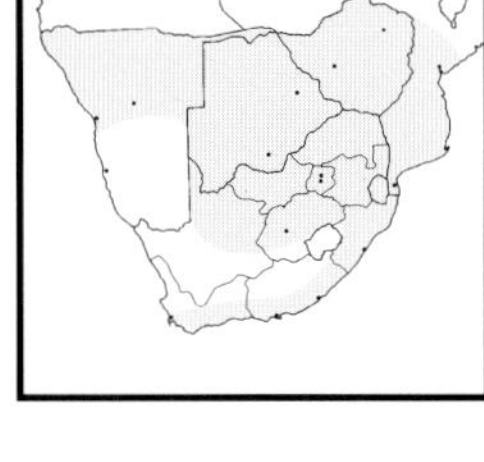

European Hobby *Falco subbuteo* (173) 28-35 cm

A larger and more robust bird than the African Hobby, the European Hobby may be identified by its long, pointed wings and short tail, heavily streaked underparts and rufous vent (in the adult). It is separable from the immature and female Eastern Redfooted Falcon (see page 68) and from the immature Western Redfooted Falcon (see page 68) by its more heavily streaked underparts, darker upperparts and plain grey, unbarred uppertail. Also, its strong active flight action is unlike the floppy, loose wing action of the 'redfoots'. Often crepuscular in nature when flying termites are emerging, it may at these times be mistaken for a Bat Hawk (see page 64) or an African Hobby. The European Hobby catches insects deftly with its talons, and feeds on the wing; it also takes small birds. It occurs in broad-leaved woodland and savannas and is often found along rivers and near open water but avoids forested and arid habitats. It is silent in Africa. S

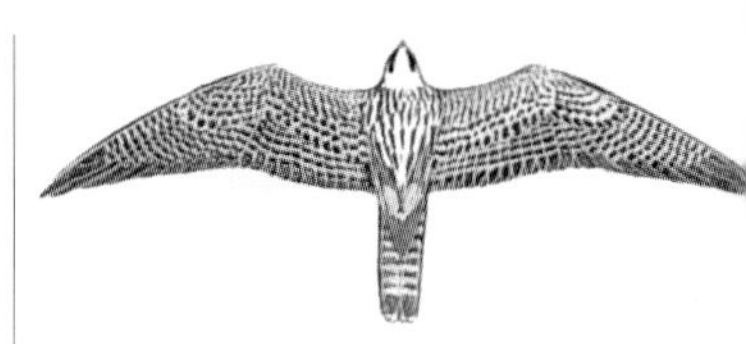

Adult European Hobby

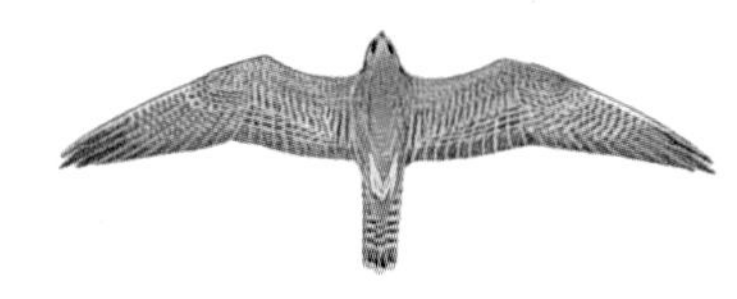

Adult African Hobby

African Hobby *Falco cuvierii* (174) 28-30 cm

The African Hobby feeds on the wing as do the European Hobby and the Bat Hawk (see page 64), for which it may be mistaken in poor light. The African Hobby has a rufous throat, belly and underwing which distinguish it from the otherwise similar Taita Falcon, which has a white throat; the similar European Hobby is white below with heavy breast streaking and a rufous vent (in the adult). Also, slightly smaller in size than the European Hobby, it is much swifter in flight with shallower, shorter wing beats. The African Hobby feeds at dusk, being attracted to flying termites after rain showers, and at dawn; like the European Hobby, it also takes small birds. It occurs in open broad-leaved woodland, large clearings and in well-watered savanna country. Its call is a high-pitched, shrieking 'kik-kik-kik-kik'. I

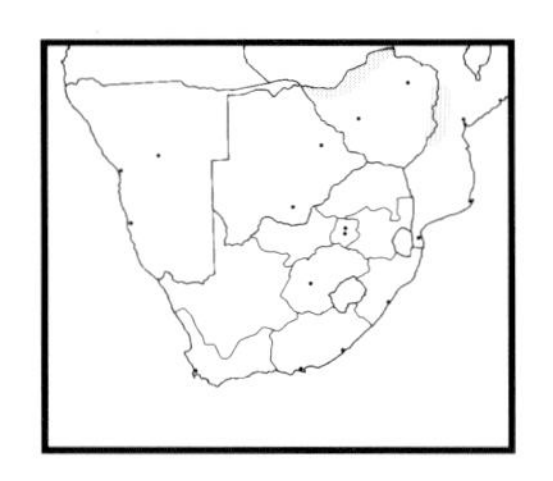

Taita Falcon *Falco fasciinucha* (176) 28-30 cm

A small, compact falcon, equivalent in size to and resembling the African Hobby in having rufous underparts, the Taita Falcon may be distinguished from that species by its dark moustachial streaks and dark crown, white throat, rufous forehead and two rufous nape patches. It is a very swift and agile flier with short, shallow, almost parrot-like wing beats, and feeds primarily on birds, including swifts. It occupies a very restricted range, confined to remote gorges and high cliffs in mountainous terrain. Its rarity may be attributable to the fact that it probably competes for nesting sites with the much larger and more aggressive Peregrine and Lanner falcons (see page 66). It utters a typical falcon shriek, a high-pitched 'kree-kree-kree' and 'kek-kek-kek-kek'. R

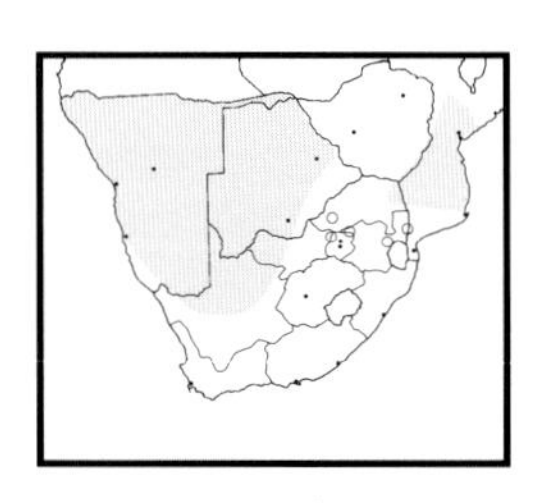

Rednecked Falcon *Falco chicquera* (178) 30-36 cm

This strikingly plumaged, fierce, bird-eating raptor is short winged and long tailed. The adults are distinctive with a chestnut crown, grey back and belly (both with fine black barring), and dark brown moustachial stripes on white cheeks. Immatures are similar to the adults apart from the belly which is finely barred dark brown on pale rufous, and the crown which is brown. In flight the Rednecked Falcon appears as an all-grey raptor with a broad black subterminal band to the tail and a brown to rufous crown. The call is a shrill 'ki-ki-ki-ki-ki' given during the breeding season around the nest site. This bird prefers drier regions, occurring in arid thornbush where it typically sits in the subcanopy of the thorn trees. R.

1. Adult European Hobby
2. Adult European Hobby
3. Adult Rednecked Falcon
4. Adult African Hobby
5. Male Pygmy Falcon
6. Female Taita Falcon
7. Female Pygmy Falcon

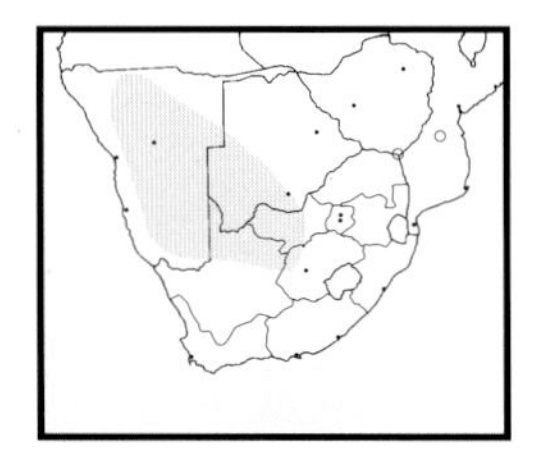

Pygmy Falcon *Polihierax semitorquatus* (186) 18-20 cm

This, our smallest falcon, is about the size of a shrike. The sexes are similar in size but the female is sexually dimorphic, having a russet back; males have a plain grey back. Immatures resemble the females but are duller. In flight, the white spots in the tail and wing are clearly visible. Pygmy Falcons are found in association with the nests of Sociable Weavers (see page 272), taking over nesting chambers for their own use. They perch upright on telegraph poles, dead branches and on the tops of small bushes and trees from where they hunt. The birds typically bob their heads up and down before swooping to the ground, and feed on insects, lizards and birds. Their flight is fast and direct with alternate flapping and gliding. Often seen in pairs, they are mostly restricted to the arid west in dry thornveld wherever Sociable Weavers occur. A noisy, high-pitched and penetrating 'ki-ki-ki-ki-ki' call is given. R

S *summer visitor* • I *intra-African migrant* • R *resident*

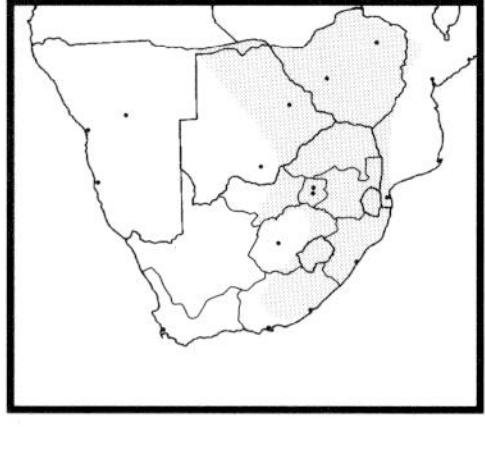
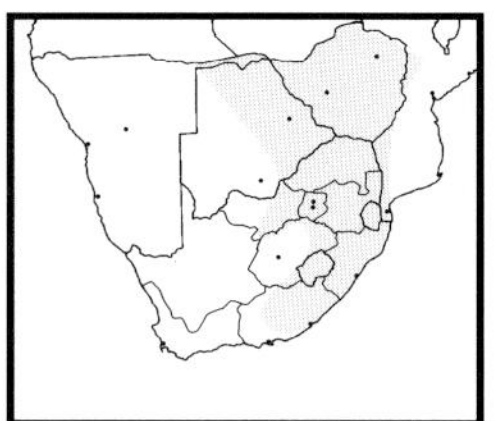

Eastern Redfooted Falcon *Falco amurensis* (180) 30 cm

The male Eastern Redfooted Falcon resembles the male Western Redfooted Falcon but can be told apart by its white, not grey, underwing coverts. Females, with their strongly barred underwings and white forehead, resemble European Hobbies (see page 66), but are blotched below with black on white, not streaked with black on buff; further, they have a grey, not black, crown, and poorly developed moustachial stripes. Immatures resemble the female but are streaked below, not barred and blotched, and above they are browner with buff feather edges, not grey with black bars. Eastern Redfooted Falcons are often seen with Western Redfooted Falcons in communal feeding flocks, hovering over open grasslands and agricultural land and searching for insects. They chatter shrilly at communal roosts at night. S

Female Eastern Redfooted Falcon

Western Redfooted Falcon *Falco vespertinus* (179) 30 cm

The male Western Redfooted Falcon is uniform dark grey above and below with a rufous vent and red legs; it resembles the male Eastern Redfooted Falcon but in flight shows all grey, not white, underwing coverts. Females are reddish brown below and on the crown and nape, and grey above with black barring. In flight the rufous underbody extends to the undercoverts but the flight feathers are barred with grey. Immatures are similar to the immature Eastern Redfooted Falcon but are more rufous in colour. They may be confused with immature Lesser Kestrels and Rock Kestrels but are darker and greyer above, especially on the tail; the black patch around the eye, heavy moustachial stripes and white face also separate them. Western Redfooted Falcons may be found in mixed flocks over open grasslands and agricultural land with Eastern Redfooted Falcons but are less commonly recorded than that species. They chatter shrilly at communal roosts at night. S

Female Western Redfooted Falcon

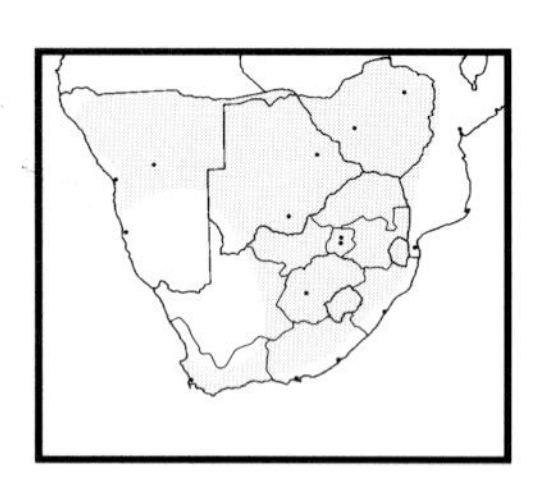

Lesser Kestrel *Falco naumanni* (183) 30 cm

The male Lesser Kestrel has an almost plain chestnut back and upperwing coverts with a broad grey margin separating these coverts from the flight feathers. In flight, the underwing is seen to be silvery grey and unmarked. Females and immatures have a light brown flecked back and wings, a grey rump and a brown barred tail. This species may be mistaken for the Rock Kestrel but at close quarters may be seen to have white, not black, talons and two elongated central tail feathers. Otherwise, the tail of both species is dark grey with a broad black subterminal band. A communal species, it occurs over grasslands and agricultural lands. It is silent except at roosts where it chatters shrilly. S

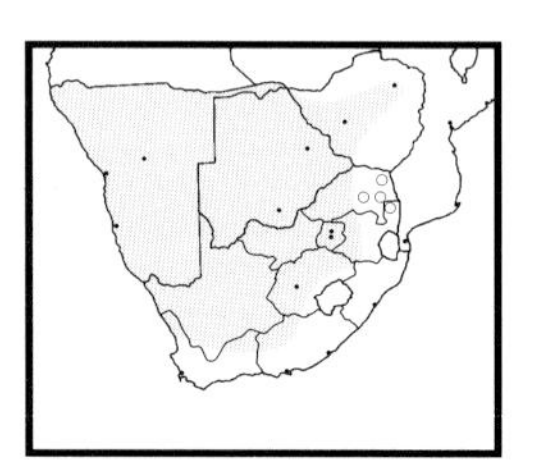

Greater Kestrel *Falco rupicoloides* (182) 36-40 cm

The Greater Kestrel with its pale yellow to white eye (in the adult) is unlike any of the other *Falco* species, all of which have dark brown eyes. It is light tawny to rufous overall with black bars above and on the flanks and is otherwise streaked below. The rump and tail are grey, barred with black and, in flight, the underwing is seen to be white. Immatures are streaked below and have a dark brown eye; the tail and rump are rufous barred with black. Immatures could be confused with immature Rock Kestrels but the latter are spotted, not streaked, below. Preferring open grassland, agricultural land and semi-desert, Greater Kestrels tend to hunt from a perch. They are normally silent except during display, when the shrill 'keek-keek-keek' is given. R

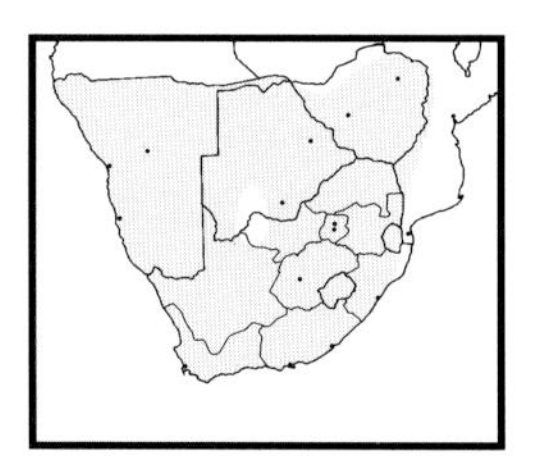

Rock Kestrel *Falco tinnunculus* (181) 33-39 cm

The male and female Rock Kestrel are similar. The female is a little duller than the male but both sexes have a grey head streaked with black, and are rufous above and below with a lightly spotted back; both have a grey-banded tail but this is more barred in the female than in the male (which may have an unbarred tail except for the broad subterminal band). Immatures lack the grey head and tail (although still show the barring) and are uniformly brown, well streaked with black. Rock Kestrels may be confused with male Lesser Kestrels but the flight feathers are barred, not plain, the back and upperwing are rufous spotted with black marks, not plain chestnut with a grey bar, and the head is black-streaked, not plain grey. The immature Rock Kestrel lacks the teardrop-shaped moustachial streaks of the female and immature Lesser Kestrel. Rock Kestrels call a shrill 'kee-kee-kee' or 'kik-kik-kik'. They prefer mountainous terrain and rocky ridges but have adapted to urban situations. R

1. Male Eastern Redfooted Falcon
2. Male Lesser Kestrel
3. Male Western Redfooted Falcon
4. Female Western Redfooted Falcon
5. Female Lesser Kestrel
6. Adult Greater Kestrel
7. Female Rock Kestrel
8. Male Rock Kestrel

1 3 4
2
5 7 8
6

S *summer visitor* • R *resident*

Francolins and quail Family Phasianidae

These ground-living gamebirds are mostly cryptically coloured and have characteristic call notes. They are variable in social habits, behaviour, roosting habits and sexual dimorphism. The nest is built on the ground.

Adult Coqui Francolin

Adult Greywing Francolin

Adult Redwing Francolin

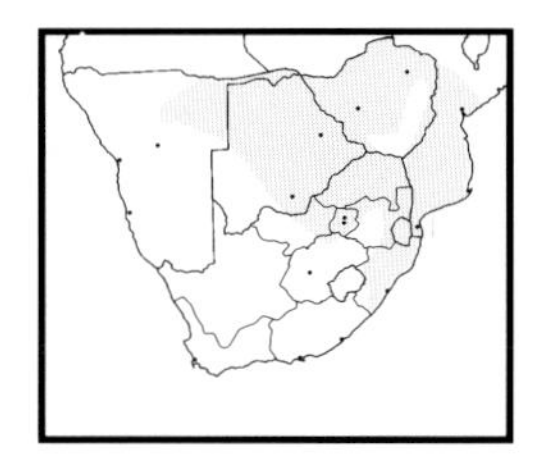

Coqui Francolin *Francolinus coqui* (188) 28 cm

More often heard than seen, this small francolin is very secretive. The male is instantly recognizable by its warm buffy head coloration with a darker crown and by its heavily barred underparts. Females might be confused with Shelley's Francolin but are smaller and more rotund, have a broad white eyebrow stripe and lack the bold chestnut striping on the belly and flanks. The call is a distinctive 'co-qui, co-qui', given in the early mornings from high ground. Coqui Francolins frequent grassland in open woodland and surrounding areas. R

Crested Francolin *Francolinus sephaena* (189) 33-35 cm

This small francolin has a distinct capped appearance and a broad white eyebrow stripe which, combined with its freckled neck and breast, distinguish it. When agitated it raises its crest and cocks its tail like a bantam, and is the only francolin to do so. The sexes are similar, and immatures resemble the adults. Usually seen in small groups, frequenting woodland and thick bush, the Crested Francolin calls regularly, mostly at dawn and dusk, in a duet that is rendered 'chee-chakla, chee-chakla'. R

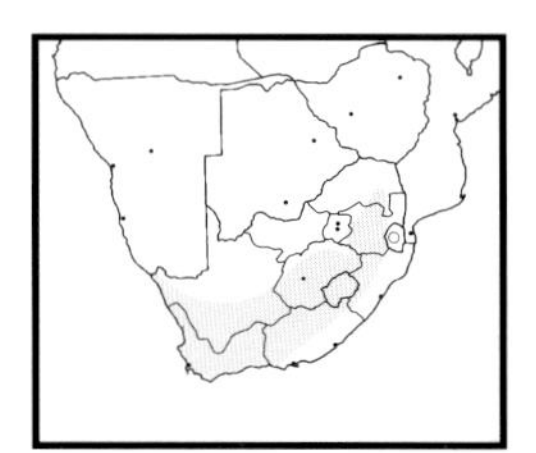

Greywing Francolin *Francolinus africanus* (190) 33 cm

This small grassland francolin may be confused with the Orange River Francolin, Shelley's Francolin, the Redwing Francolin and the female Coqui Francolin. Best distinguished by its characteristic call, careful scrutiny of the bird's plumage is necessary if it is silent. In general appearance this species is much greyer than the other francolins; in flight it has very little chestnut in the wings. Its throat is grizzled grey and white, unlike the other four species which have unmarked white throats. The call is a 'wip, ki-peroo', and in flight a series of 'pi' notes. The Greywing Francolin is found in coastal regions in the south and at very high altitudes in other regions. NE

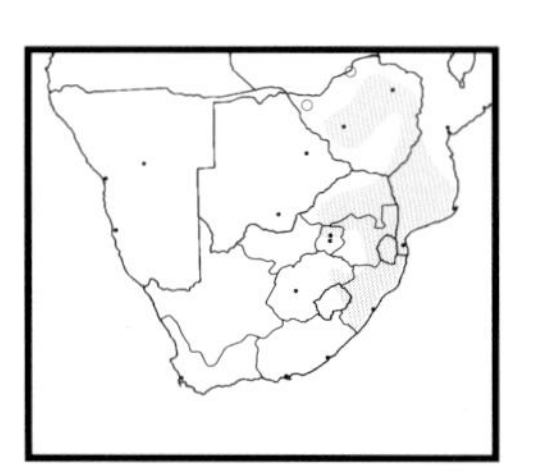

Shelley's Francolin *Francolinus shelleyi* (191) 33 cm

Shelley's Francolin differs from the Orange River, the Greywing and the Redwing francolins by the bold chestnut striping on its flanks adjacent to the contrasting black and white barring on the lower breast and belly; although Greywing Francolins have a similar pattern, their breast and belly lack the contrasting pattern of this species. The call, 'titit-teeteeo', is repeated often at dawn and dusk. Covies burst into flight and hurtle off low over the ground when startled, giving short 'ke-ke-ke-ke' calls. This bird occurs in various habitats but favours grassed stony ridges and savanna. R

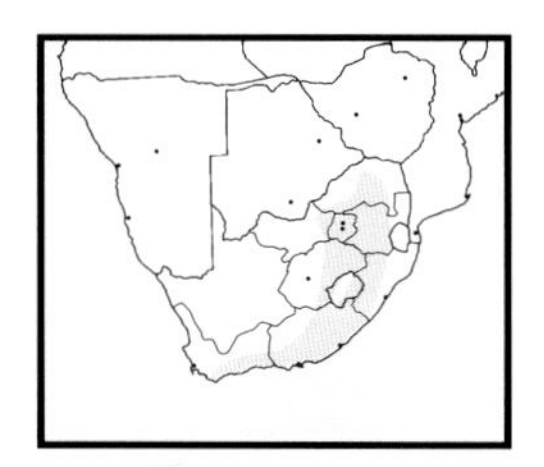

Redwing Francolin *Francolinus levaillantii* (192) 38 cm

The Redwing Francolin is distinguishable from the other small 'freckled' francolins by the vivid orange stripes on its head and neck. This is offset by a bold black and white necklace on the breast and sides of the neck, broader than in other similar francolins. This species shows very bright chestnut primaries and secondaries in flight. The sexes are similar, and the young are dowdy forms of the adults. The call is a ringing 'too-queequee', repeated at dawn. This bird frequents upland grasslands, bracken slopes and adjacent agricultural lands. R

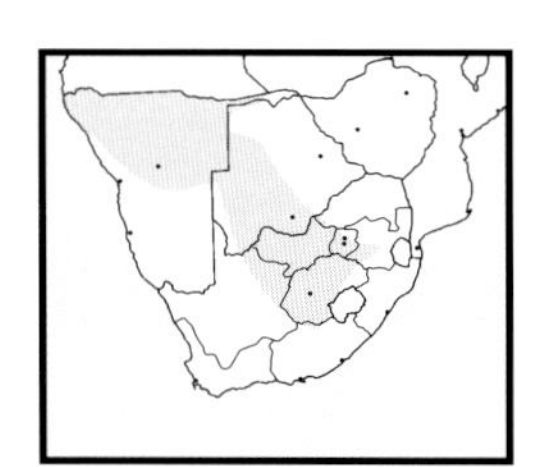

Orange River Francolin *Francolinus levaillantoides* (193) 35 cm

The most obvious identifying feature of the Orange River Francolin is its white throat bordered by a thin black or grizzled border which never broadens into a breast band. It also shows variable amounts of chestnut striping on the underparts, much more so than in other similar francolins. The sexes are similar and the immatures are dowdy versions of the adults. Very shy and not easily flushed, the Orange River Francolin prefers to creep away through long grass. The call is similar to that of Shelley's Francolin but the phrasing is faster, a higher-pitched 'kibitele'. It occurs in more arid areas than do the other smaller francolins of the region. E

1. Female Coqui Francolin
2. Adult Crested Francolin
3. Male Coqui Francolin
4. Adult Greywing Francolin
5. Adult Redwing Francolin
6. Adult Orange River Francolin
7. Adult Shelley's Francolin

1	3
2	
4	7
5 · 6	

R *resident* • NE *near endemic* • E *endemic*

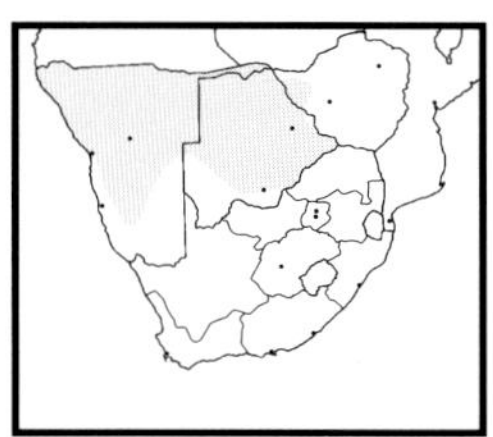

Redbilled Francolin *Francolinus adspersus* (194) 35-38 cm

The Redbilled Francolin might be confused with Swainson's Francolin but lacks any obvious unfeathered throat patches, and has red, not brown, legs and a distinctive patch of yellow skin around the eyes. It is best separated from the Natal Francolin by its red, not yellow, bill and by its yellow eye patches. The call is a raucous, crowing 'chaa-chaa-chek-chek', given at dawn and dusk. It occurs in dry bush country, especially along wooded, dry river beds, and feeds freely in the open, being less skulking than other francolins. NE

Immature Redbilled Francolin

Cape Francolin *Francolinus capensis* (195) 42 cm

The only large, dark francolin in the Cape region, this species is unlikely to be confused with any other francolin. At close range the plumage can be seen to be greyish brown, finely flecked, streaked and scalloped with buff and brown. Immatures show a darker crown which imparts a capped appearance. The call is a screeching 'cackalac-cackalac-cackalac'. Cape Francolins generally keep together in small groups or in pairs, but where there is an abundant supply of food they gather in larger numbers. They are found in dry karroid, fynbos and agricultural lands. E

Male Rednecked Francolin (subspecies swynnertoni*)*

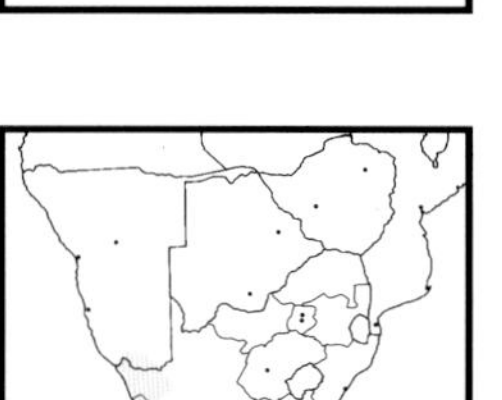

Natal Francolin *Francolinus natalensis* (196) 35 cm

This large, drably coloured francolin might be confused with the Rednecked Francolin because they both appear to have a red bill, legs and feet, but this species lacks the unfeathered red throat and eye patches as well as the black and white stripes on the underparts. It is generally brown above, and barred and speckled black and white below. Close up it can be seen that the bill is orange with a yellower base and the legs can be seen to be pinkish red. The bird's crowing is distinctive, a raucous and sometimes drawn-out 'graa-ch, che, che' which is given in a decidedly unmusical duet; the alarm call is a short, harsh 'chek-chek'. The Natal Francolin is found alongside well-wooded river courses and adjoining wooded grasslands. NE

Hartlaub's Francolin *Francolinus hartlaubi* (197) 26 cm

This tiny francolin, the smallest in the region, and about the same size as the female Coqui Francolin (see page 70), is easily overlooked. The male has an unusually large and decurved bill, a broad white eyebrow stripe and heavily streaked underparts. Females and immatures are greyish brown above and have uniformly rusty-coloured underparts, as well as the large bill of the male. The call is a fast, duetted 'wiitchta-vitcheo' and the bird has a 'wa-wa-ak-ak-ak' alarm call. Found on stony hillsides and rocky outcrops in mountainous regions where it rapidly hops over boulders and scuttles into crevices, it is normally difficult to see because of its skulking behaviour. NE

Rednecked Francolin *Francolinus afer* (198) 36 cm

This large, bright francolin is easily recognized by the bare red skin around its eyes and throat, its bright red legs and the variable black and white striping on its underparts. Swainson's Francolin has a similarly patterned head but has dark brown, not red, legs and uniform brown, not black and white, underparts. Different races occur in the region, which vary in the amount of white that they show on the face and underparts. Immatures are duller versions of the adults and lack the unfeathered skin around the eyes and throat. The bird's call is a harsh, crowing 'kwoor-kwoor-kwaaa', most often given at dawn and dusk, and increases in volume before trailing off. Rednecked Francolins are found in pairs or in small family parties in thick bush alongside rivers and adjacent woodland areas. R

1. Adult Redbilled Francolin
2. Adult Cape Francolin
3. Adult Natal Francolin
4. Adult Rednecked Francolin
5. Male Hartlaub's Francolin
6. Adult Swainson's Francolin

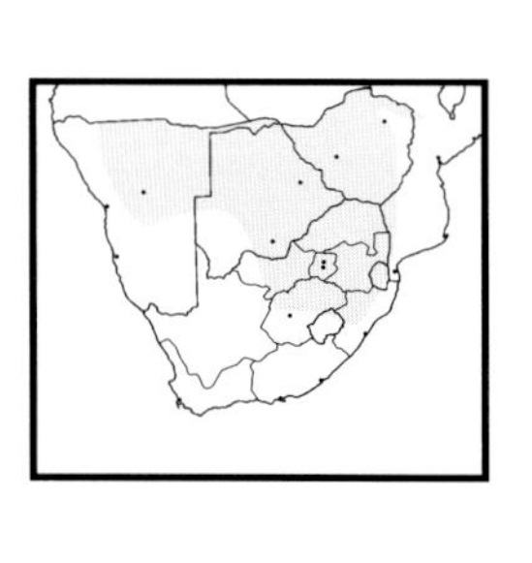

Swainson's Francolin *Francolinus swainsonii* (199) 38 cm

This large, brown and mostly unmarked francolin has a patch of unfeathered red skin around its eyes and on the throat. This feature it shares with the Rednecked Francolin but it can be distinguished from that species by its brown, not red, legs and uniform brown, not black and white striped, underparts. Immatures have very reduced amounts of red on the head. Swainson's Francolins can be seen in the early morning or evening on top of a fence post or termite mound, giving their raucous 'kraaee-kraaee-kraaee' crowing call. They favour dry thornveld and agricultural lands, where they may be seen in groups of three to five. R

NE *near endemic* • E *endemic* • R *resident*

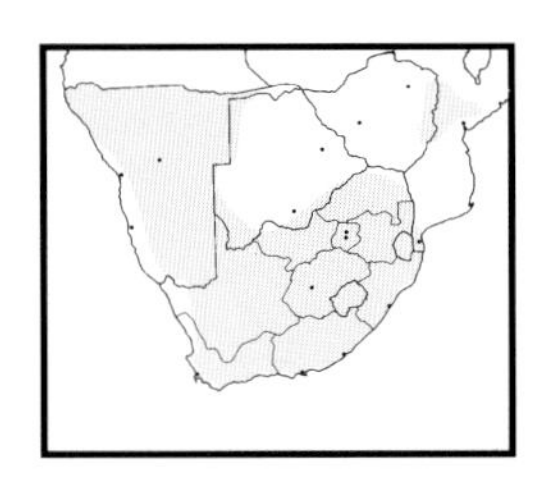

Common Quail *Coturnix coturnix* (200) 18 cm

It is unlikely that this species could be separated in flight from the female Harlequin Quail unless its much paler underparts were clearly visible. It is readily flushed from cover, typically bursting forth at one's feet. Its flight is a rapid whirr of wing beats and it jinks from side to side, giving a short glide before crashing into cover. Rarely seen on the ground, it crouches low in the grass and runs with speed. Its 'wit-tit-it' call is often the only evidence of its presence. R, S

Adult Common Quail

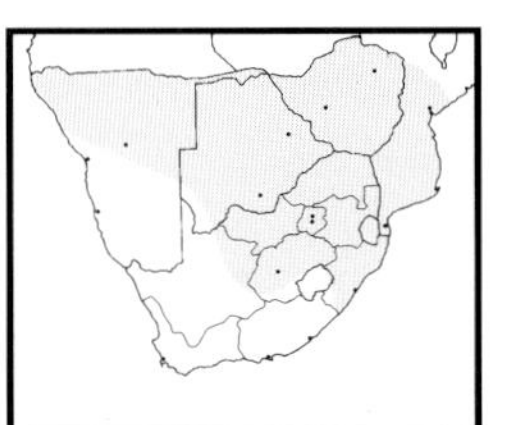

Harlequin Quail *Coturnix delegorguei* (201) 18 cm

The male Harlequin Quail has chestnut and black underparts which distinguish it; when flushed it appears very much darker than the Common Quail. The female is generally buffier and darker below than the female Common Quail but this is not easy to see. The call is similar to that of the Common Quail but is sharper and higher pitched. S

Buttonquail Family Turnicidae

Small, ground-living, quail-like birds, buttonquail are cryptically marked and exhibit reversed sexual dimorphism and reversed parental roles when breeding. They are nomadic, and are found in open habitats.

Adult Blackrumped Buttonquail

Blackrumped Buttonquail *Turnix hottentotta* (206) 14 cm

This species is difficult to tell apart from the Kurrichane Buttonquail unless seen under optimum conditions on the ground. The face, throat and breast are uniformly buffy, and the black and white scaling on the shoulders extends on to the flanks. It also has two buffy stripes down the back – lacking in the Kurrichane Buttonquail. In flight the lower back and rump are seen to contrast with the upperparts. The call is a low hooting. The Blackrumped Buttonquail, about which little is known, frequents mainly upland grasslands and damper areas than the Kurrichane Buttonquail. R, S

Adult Kurrichane Buttonquail

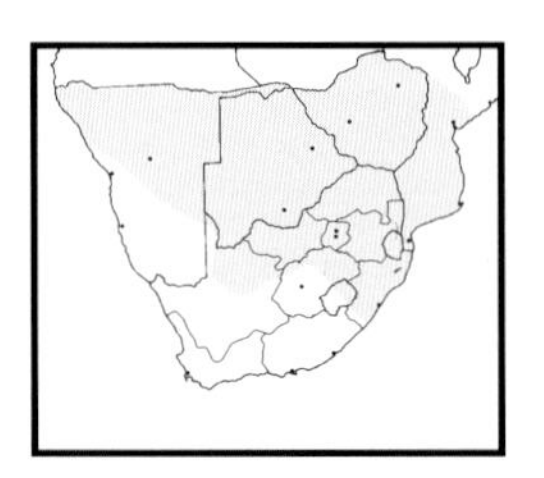

Kurrichane Buttonquail *Turnix sylvatica* (205) 14 cm

In flight this species shows very pale, buffish-grey forewings and a brown lower back and tail; on the ground, the bird's almost-white eye is very obvious, and the warm buffy wash across the breast, which is not uniform as in the Blackrumped Buttonquail, can be discerned. The call is a series of flufftail-like hoots, and sounds very similar to that of the Blackrumped Buttonquail. The Kurrichane Buttonquail prefers drier grasslands than the Blackrumped Buttonquail. R

Guineafowl Family Numididae

Guineafowl are distinctively plumaged ground-living gamebirds with prominent casques or feather tufts on the crown. The sexes are alike. Gregarious, they sometimes occur in large flocks.

Crested Guineafowl *Guttera pucherani* (204) 50 cm

The curly tuft of short feathers on the head of this gamebird imparts a comical and startled look. The plumage is black, finely speckled with pale blue and white. Crested Guineafowl occur in smaller groups than do Helmeted Guineafowl and are most often seen in pairs, quietly picking their way through the undergrowth. Calls consist of a 'chik-chil-chrr' alarm and a softer 'keet-keet' contact note. These birds keep to thicker wooded areas and do not venture out into grasslands as do Helmeted Guineafowl. R

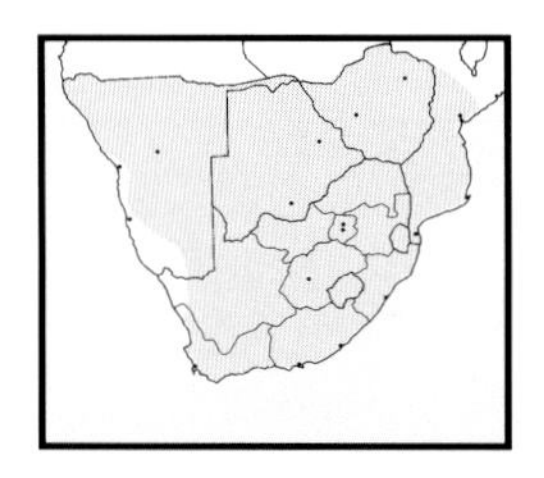

Helmeted Guineafowl *Numida meleagris* (203) 56 cm

The bright blue and red, unfeathered head with its horny crest, quite unlike the Crested Guineafowl's black tuft of curly feathers, renders this bird unmistakable. Probably one of our most familiar birds, the Helmeted Guineafowl can occur in very large flocks in the wild. The call, a far-carrying 'krrdii-krrddii-krrddii', is given mostly at dawn. The birds occur in grasslands, agricultural lands, thornveld and open woodland. R

1. Female Common Quail
2. Male Common Quail
3. Harlequin Quail chick
4. Male Harlequin Quail
5. Adult Crested Guineafowl
6. Adult Blackrumped Buttonquail
7. Adult Kurrichane Buttonquail
8. Adult Helmeted Guineafowl

1 2 3 4 5 6 7 8

R *resident* • S *summer visitor*

Cranes Family Gruidae

Very large, long-legged birds with relatively short bills, cranes inhabit wetlands and open grasslands and, when not breeding, aggregate in large flocks. All have complex dancing displays and some are extremely vocal.

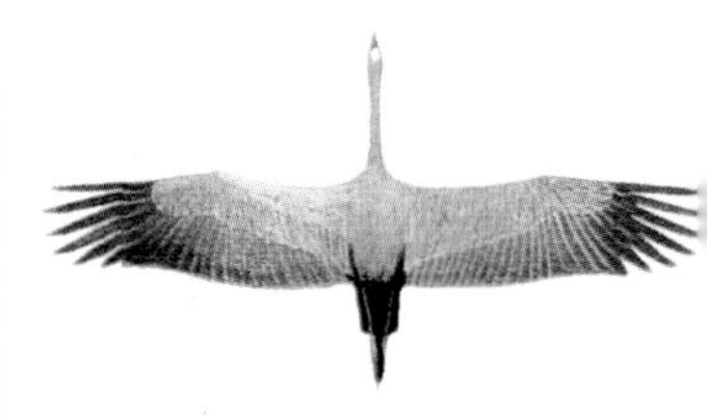

Adult Blue Crane

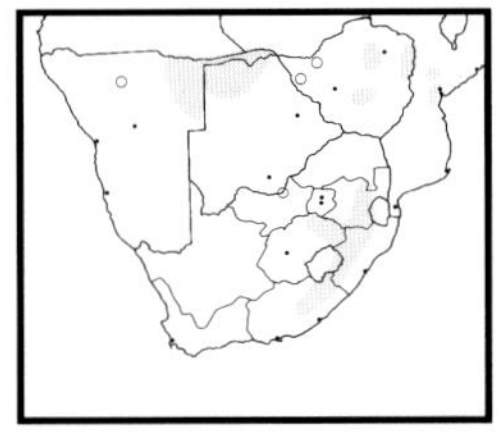

Wattled Crane *Grus carunculata* (207) 120 cm

This very large, stately crane is easily recognized by its enormous size, and by its white head and neck which contrast with its grey and black body. Closer views reveal crimson caruncles covering the face and the long, white-feathered wattles. Immatures are similar to adults but have less well-developed caruncles and wattles. The Wattled Crane is usually found in pairs or in small groups. Although normally silent, these birds may call a loud 'krannrk'. R

Adult Secretarybird

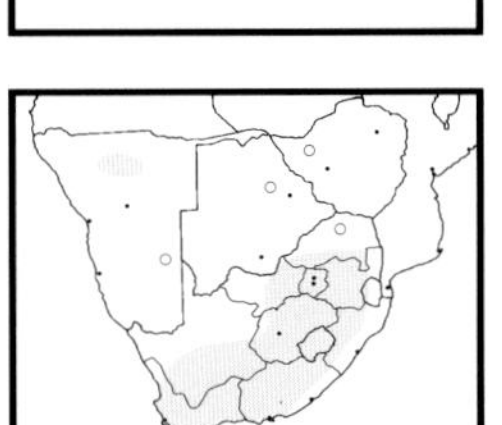

Blue Crane *Anthropoides paradiseus* (208) 100 cm

South Africa's national bird, the Blue Crane may from a distance be confused with the Wattled Crane but it has no white on the neck nor any black on the shoulders and wings. Not always associated with water, the Blue Crane is often found in wide-open arid areas. Although usually encountered in small groups or pairs, outside of the breeding season Blue Cranes may gather in very large flocks. The call is an echoing, nasal 'kraaaank'. E

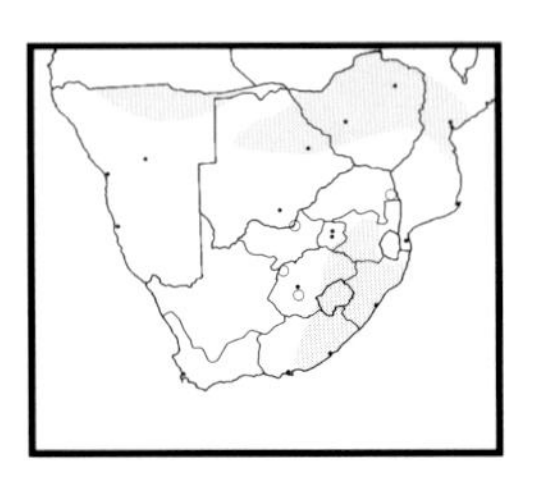

Southern Crowned Crane *Balearica regulorum* (209) 105 cm

The Southern Crowned Crane differs from the two other cranes in the region by having white upper- and underwing coverts, conspicuous in flight. At closer range the golden crest, white unfeathered face and scarlet wattles are obvious. Although they breed in marshes and swamps, they are often found far from water. The call of the Southern Crowned Crane is a two-syllabled 'huuum-huuum', given mostly in flight. R

Secretarybird Family Sagittariidae

This very large, long-legged and long-necked bird of prey takes large insects, reptiles and rodents, and all prey is caught on the ground. Secretarybirds nest singly, normally on top of a bush or tree.

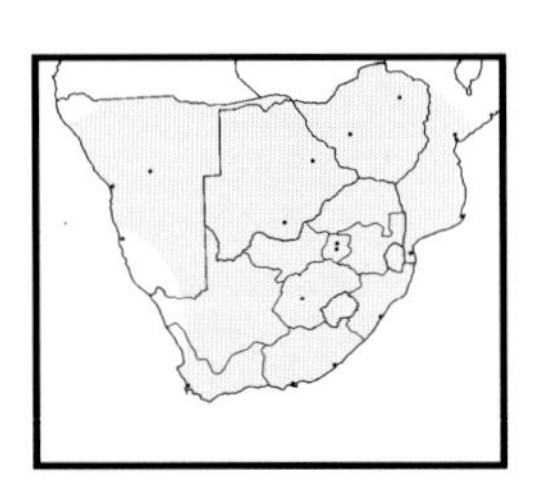

Secretarybird *Sagittarius serpentarius* (118) 140 cm

This bird could easily be mistaken at long range for a crane. Its black-feathered 'leggings' and black-tipped, wispy crest are conspicuous. In flight its short bill, long protruding legs, and elongated central tail feathers distinguish it. Seen mostly in pairs, the birds stride along purposefully, stopping to pick at food. Although mainly silent, they utter deep croaks when displaying. These birds are found in open grasslands and savanna. R

1. Adult Wattled Crane
2. Adult Blue Crane
3. Adult Southern Crowned Crane
4. Adult Secretarybird
5. Male Ostrich
6. Female Ostrich

Ostrich Family Struthionidae

This is the world's largest bird, and is flightless. It is unusual in lacking a preen gland and in having only two toes developed. Ostriches are polygamous, and several females may lay their eggs in one nest.

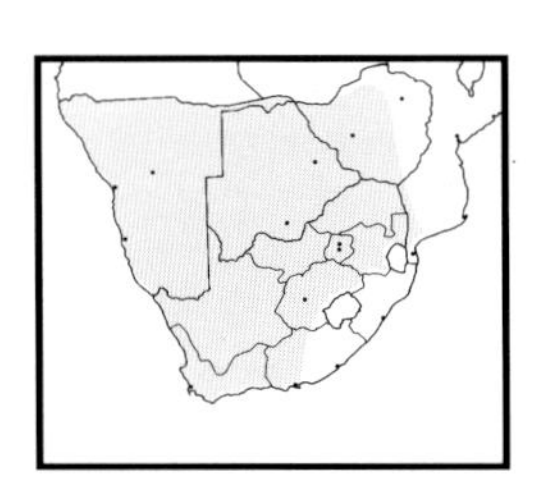

Ostrich *Struthio camelus* (1) Height 2 m

Male Ostriches are easily distinguished from the drab, brown females and immature males by their black body plumage, fluffy, glisteningly white wing plumes and rusty-red tail. They can reach running speeds of up to 60 kilometres per hour. Displaying males crouch on their tarsi and sway from side to side with their white wing plumes draped beyond the 'drumsticks'. The male's call is a booming 'huooom-huooom'. Juveniles seen unaccompanied might be confused with a korhaan or bustard (see pages 84-86) but their spiky mantle feathers, laterally flattened bill and thick legs should distinguish them. Most Ostriches in the region are from mixed feral stock. R

R *resident* • E *endemic*

Rails, crakes, flufftails, gallinules, moorhens and coots Family Rallidae

These small to medium-sized, ground-dwelling birds with long legs and toes have a very short tail which is often held erect and flicked up and down. Good swimmers, they generally inhabit marshes. Although most are reluctant to fly when disturbed, many species undertake long-distance migrations at night.

Adult African Crake

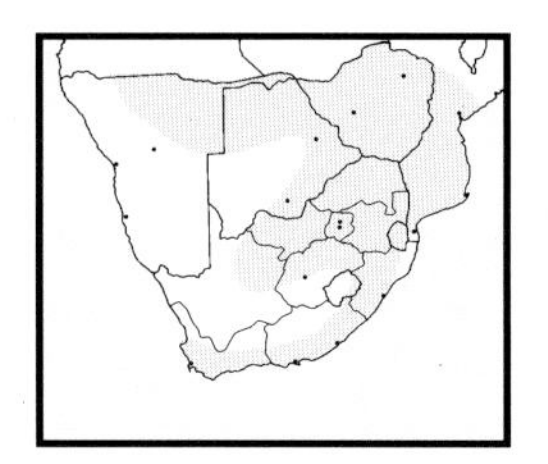

African Rail *Rallus caerulescens* (210) 37 cm

Like the African Crake, the female Striped Crake and Baillon's Crake, the African Rail has a grey throat and breast but is larger than each of those species and has a diagnostic long, red, decurved bill. Immatures are dull versions of the adults and have brown bills. The call is a high-pitched trilling 'trrre-teee-teee' and various other grunts and moans. African Rails are very vocal at night and venture into the open more readily at dawn and dusk. They frequent thick stands of reedbeds and sedges. R

Adult Spotted Crake

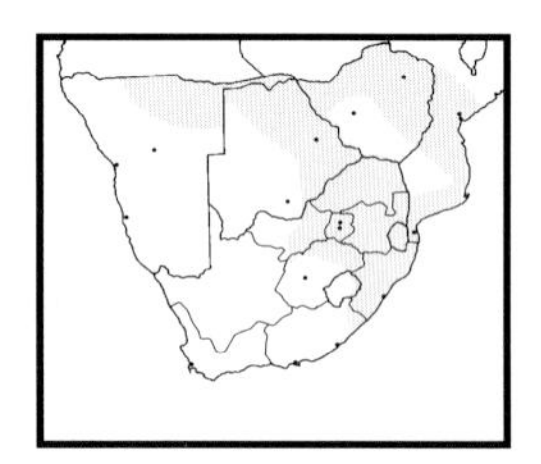

African Crake *Crex egregia* (212) 22 cm

This species may be confused only with the African Rail, from which it differs by being a paler mottled brown above, having more extensive black and white barring on the belly and flanks, and by its short and stubby bill. Immatures resemble the adults although they are browner in appearance. The African Crake's call is a series of hollow-sounding 'krrr-krrr-krrr' notes, and it also utters a short 'kek-kek-kek' in flight at night and from cover during overcast weather. When flushed from its damp grassland or vlei habitat, it rises at one's feet and flies a short distance with dangling legs and feet before crashing back into cover. I, S

Adult Striped Crake

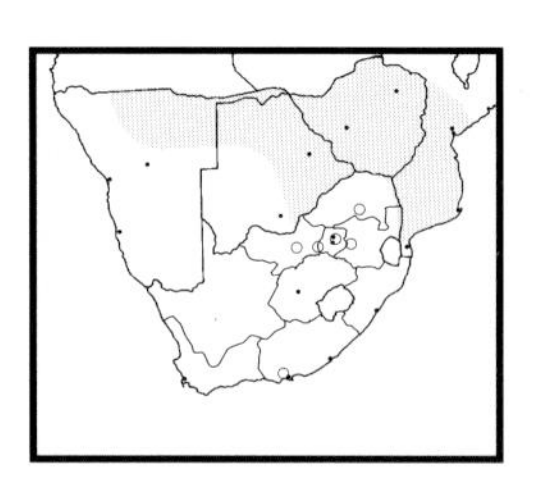

Spotted Crake *Porzana porzana* (214) 20 cm

This bird when put to flight might be confused with the Lesser Moorhen (see page 82) but is smaller and has a well-patterned, not uniform, back. Confusion may also arise with the African Crake, but the Spotted Crake is overall much paler in flight, and has a yellowish bill and a very conspicuous white leading edge to the wings; the barring on the flanks is also not as conspicuous as it is in the African Crake. Immatures resemble the adults. It is rarely seen unless flushed from its preferred habitat of flooded grasslands. The bird is silent in our region. S

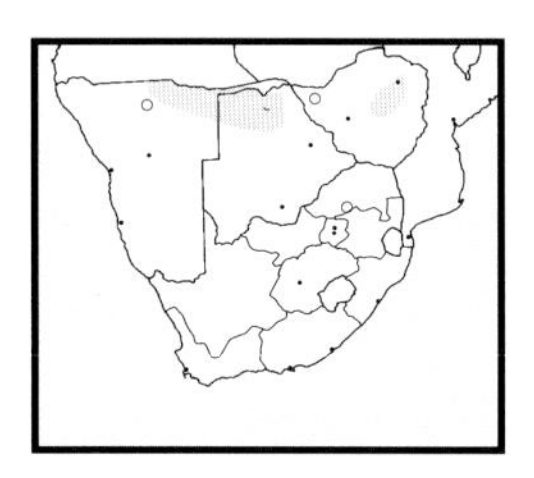

Striped Crake *Aenigmatolimnas marginalis* (216) 20 cm

When a Striped Crake is flushed the best field characters to look for are the warm brown to rusty undertail coverts and the conspicuous white stripes down its back. Males and immatures have brown breasts, female birds have grey breasts. The call is a rapid 'tik-tik-tik-tik-tik', run together in a long phrase; a low growling noise is given when the bird is disturbed in cover. It frequents flooded grasslands and pans. I

1. Adult African Rail
2. Adult African Crake
3. Adult Spotted Crake
4. Male Striped Crake
5. Adult Corncrake
6. Adult Baillon's Crake

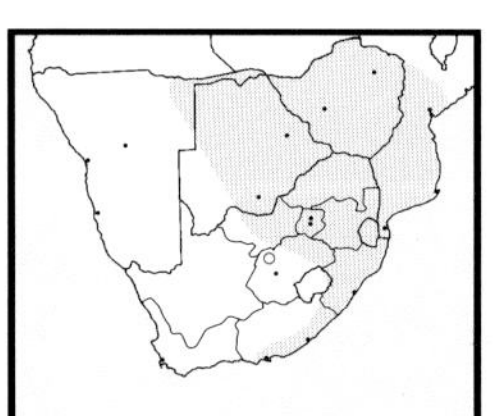

Corncrake *Crex crex* (211) 35 cm

The easiest of crakes to identify when flushed, the Corncrake is very pale overall, appearing sandy-brown, with conspicuous orange-chestnut wing coverts. The flight is rapid on whirring wings, reminiscent of that of a quail (see page 74), and the bird drops quickly back into cover. The sexes are alike and the immature resembles the adults. Silent when in Africa, the Corncrake occurs in open natural grassland habitats and is not associated directly with damp or flooded areas. S

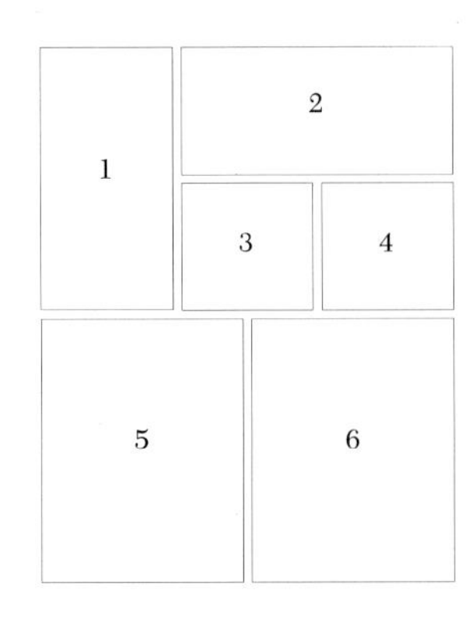

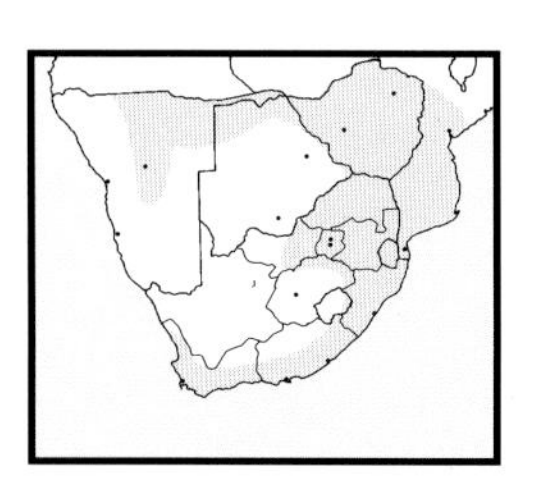

Baillon's Crake *Porzana pusilla* (215) 18 cm

This tiny crake resembles the African Crake but has very much reduced barring on the belly and flanks; it may further be differentiated by the white flecking and spots on the upperparts. The legs are pale olive. Immatures are faintly barred grey and white below. Calls are a soft 'qurrr-qurrrr' and various frog-like croaks. Not easily flushed, Baillon's Crake can be seen out in the open at dawn and dusk, or creeping through reeds as it clambers from stalk to stalk. It is found in a variety of freshwater and brackish wetlands. R

R *resident* • I *intra-African migrant* • S *summer visitor*

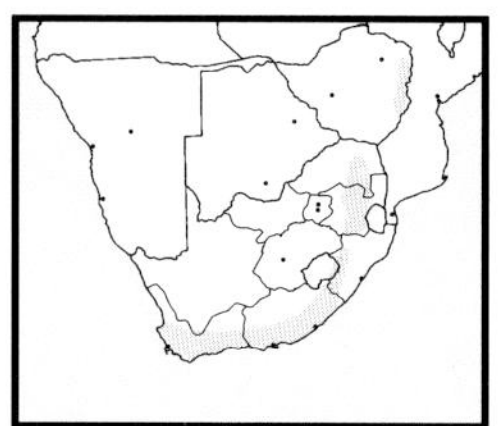

Striped Flufftail *Sarothrura affinis* (221) 15 cm

When the birds are seen on the ground, the all-chestnut tail (in both sexes) is diagnostic; the similar Redchested Flufftail has an all-dark tail. Habitat excludes confusion with the Buffspotted Flufftail. The female Striped Flufftail is drab brown above and paler below; the immature resembles the female. The call is a soft, long, low 'oooooop', lasting about two seconds and repeated at one-second intervals. The intensity and frequency of the call changes in the breeding season and varies with weather conditions. These birds are found in damp areas of montane grasslands, sometimes in marshes alongside the Redchested Flufftail, and are not easy to flush. R

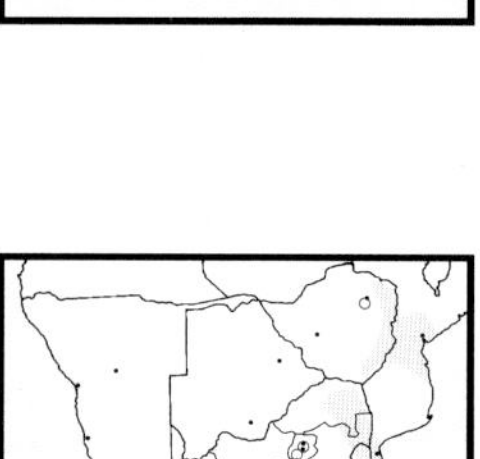

Buffspotted Flufftail *Sarothrura elegans* (218) 16 cm

The male Buffspotted Flufftail has the typical chestnut head of flufftails and this extends on to the breast and nape. The whole body is black, loudly spotted with golden-buff, and the tail is barred orange and black. The female is brown above and barred brown and buff below, with an orange and black barred tail, and the immature resembles the female. The call is a low, moaning hoot, lasting roughly four or five seconds, and is given on overcast days, at dusk and on rainy nights. The Buffspotted Flufftail is the only flufftail in the region to be found in thick tangles in bush and forests, where it is exceptionally well camouflaged; it sometimes occurs in well-wooded gardens. It creeps along with its tail often held cocked like that of a bantam. R

Redchested Flufftail *Sarothrura rufa* (217) 16 cm

Seen mostly when put to flight, the chestnut head and breast, and the all-black body, wings and tail of this species identify it. It may be confused with the slightly smaller Striped Flufftail, but can be distinguished from that species by its black, not chestnut, tail. The female differs from the female Striped Flufftail by lacking a chestnut tail and appearing all-dark-brown in flight. The call is a typical flufftail hooting, 'hooo-hooo-hooo', in ascending scale and often ending in a ringing 'tuwi-tuwi-tuwi'; it also gives 'gu-duk, gu-duk' grunting notes. The Redchested Flufftail frequents sedges and reedbeds in both small and large, more permanent marshes. R

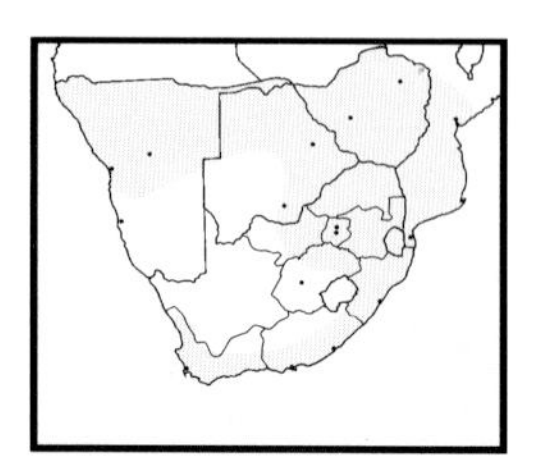

Black Crake *Amaurornis flavirostris* (213) 20 cm

This is the boldest of our small crakes; although more often heard than seen, it frequently ventures into the open. The all-smoky-black plumage, bright red legs and yellow bill render identification easy. Immatures are greyish brown with dark legs and a grey bill. The call, given from deep cover, is a loud, throaty 'chrooong-chrooong' and a rippling, trilling 'weeet-eet-eet'. The Black Crake frequents permanent marshes and large stands of reeds and sedges with adjoining floating vegetation over which it forages freely. When disturbed it runs for cover, but will fly when pressured. R

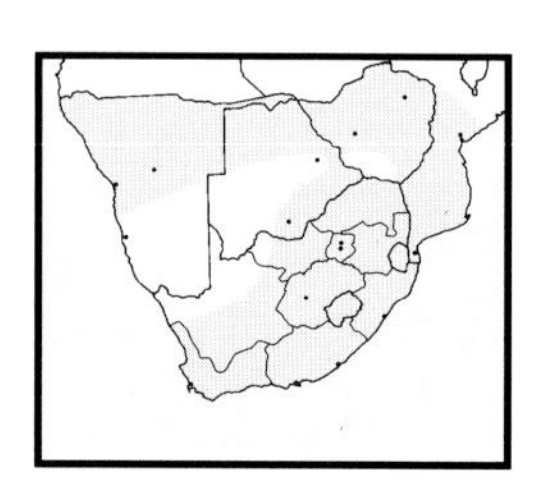

Purple Gallinule *Porphyrio porphyrio* (223) 46 cm

This large, purple, chicken-sized and chicken-shaped waterbird has a massive red bill, red legs and a white undertail. It is much larger than the Lesser Gallinule, which has a large blue, not red, frontal shield. The similar Moorhen (see page 82) is much smaller and is smoky grey-brown with yellow, not red, legs. The immature Purple Gallinule is much greyer than the adult and has no frontal shield. Calls include a wide range of shrieks, wails and booming notes. Normally fairly shy and secretive, the Purple Gallinule will forage in the open when undisturbed and walks along reed edges flicking its cocked tail and revealing the blaze of white below. R

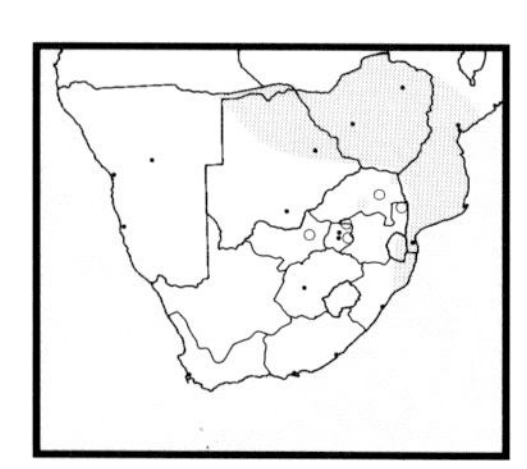

Lesser Gallinule *Porphyrio alleni* (224) 25 cm

This species might be confused with the very much larger Purple Gallinule but can be distinguished by its less massive bill and, when breeding, by its blue, not red, frontal shield. Non-breeding birds of both sexes have dull brown frontal shields. Immatures are buff below with a brown and buff mottled back and dark brown bill. The call comprises a series of rapidly repeated, sharp clicks: 'duk duk duk'. The Lesser Gallinule behaves in much the same way as the Purple Gallinule but is prone to climbing high up along reed stems to forage for seeds. During breeding the birds will fly over marshes, sometimes in pair pursuit, and forage freely in the open at twilight. I, S

Male Redchested Flufftail

Male Striped Flufftail

1. Female Striped Flufftail
2. Male Striped Flufftail
3. Male Buffspotted Flufftail
4. Male Redchested Flufftail
5. Female Redchested Flufftail
6. Adult Black Crake
7. Immature Black Crake
8. Adult Purple Gallinule
9. Adult Lesser Gallinule
10. Immature Purple Gallinule

1	2	3
4	5	
6	7	8
9	10	

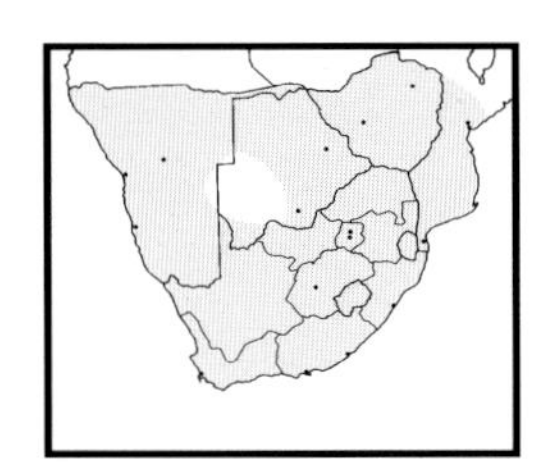

Moorhen *Gallinula chloropus* (226) 32 cm

The Moorhen is smoky black overall with a dark olive mantle and a horizontal white stripe on the flank. The bill and frontal shield are bright red with a small yellow tip and the legs are bright yellow with red 'garters'. Immatures are a smoky greyish brown with green legs. Calls are many and varied, the usual being a metallic 'krrlack'. The Moorhen is found in most freshwater and brackish wetlands where it forages in the open, constantly flicking its white undertail. R

Immature Moorhen

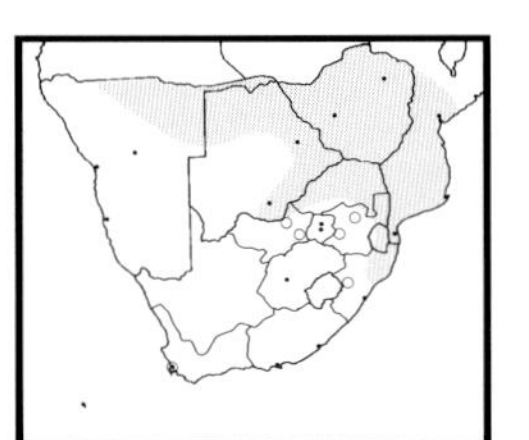

Lesser Moorhen *Gallinula angulata* (227) 24 cm

A smaller version of the Moorhen, and paler overall, the Lesser Moorhen differs mainly in the colour of the bill, which is yellow with a red stripe along the top ridge, and legs, which are green, not yellow. Immatures are buffier and paler than immature Moorhens and have pale yellow bills. The call is a series of hollow notes, 'do-do-do-do-do'. Much more secretive than the Moorhen, the Lesser Moorhen tends to skulk in its flooded grassland habitat. I, S

Immature Lesser Moorhen

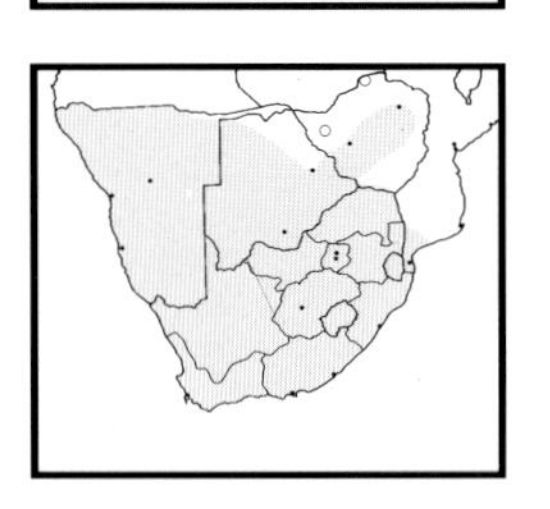

Redknobbed Coot *Fulica cristata* (228) 44 cm

The sooty-black plumage, relieved only by the white bill and frontal shield, identifies this waterbird. Immatures are grey versions of the adults and differ from immature Moorhens by having dark, not white, undertail coverts. When breeding the two red knobs on the frontal shield become swollen. Redknobbed Coots give a variety of calls, the most frequent being 'kowk kowk' or 'klaak klaak'. They swim around on open lakes and pans, frequently diving for food. R

Finfoots Family Heliornithidae

Superficially resembling cormorants (see page 24), finfoots can be separated by the heavy and pointed, not hooked, bill. The toes are lobed, not webbed. Shy and retiring, they are found along well-vegetated rivers.

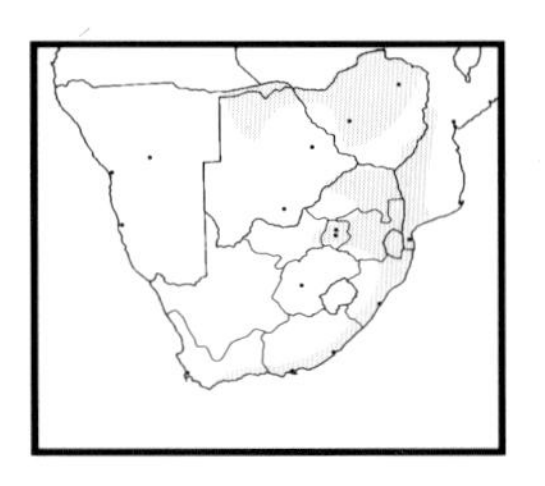

African Finfoot *Podica senegalensis* (229) 63 cm

The very long body shape, its usually low position in the water, and the backwards and forwards motion of the head and neck all suggest the Darter (see page 24) but the African Finfoot has a very much shorter and thicker neck. Males have a dark head, a red bill and a white line running behind the eye down the neck. Females and immatures have a paler head and neck, and a darker bill. When flushed, they paddle across the water, and the bright red legs and toes are clearly visible. The call is a short, frog-like 'krork'. R

Jacanas Family Jacanidae

This is a distinctive family of aquatic birds with extraordinarily long toes and toenails which enable them to walk on floating vegetation. Often gregarious in suitable habitat, they can be noisy and conspicuous.

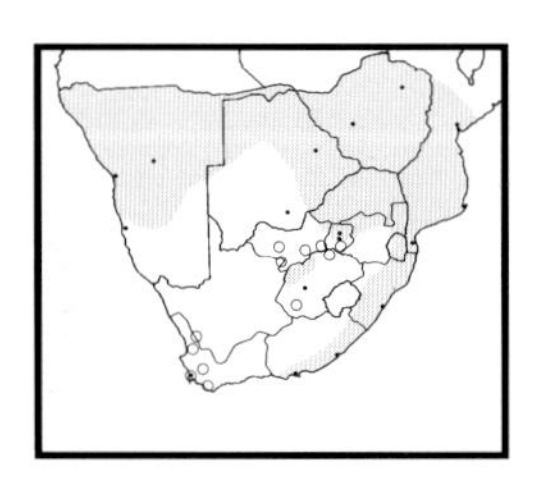

African Jacana *Actophilornis africanus* (240) 28 cm

The chestnut body and wings, white throat and upper breast, and blue frontal shield make identification of this waterbird easy. Immatures have white underparts and should not be confused with the immature Lesser Jacana which is very much smaller; when the young are the size of the Lesser Jacana they are still fluffy and unfeathered. In flight this bird shows its long toes and toenails, and does not show the contrasting upperwing pattern of the Lesser Jacana. Calls are a sharp 'krreek', a rasping 'krrrrk' and a barking 'yowk-yowk'. R

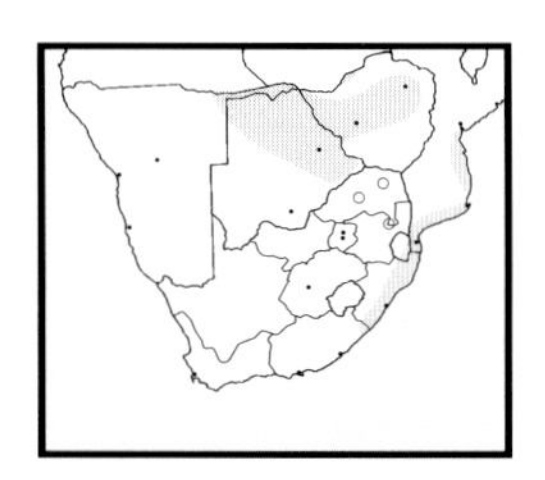

Lesser Jacana *Microparra capensis* (241) 15 cm

The Lesser Jacana can be told from the immature African Jacana by its lack of a frontal shield and the presence of chestnut shoulder patches. In flight the upperwings show an obvious contrasting pattern with the forewings, and the dark flight feathers have a white trailing edge. Mainly silent, the Lesser Jacana sometimes gives a soft 'pooop-pooop' or a high-pitched 'tititititititi'. It frequents river floodplains, lagoons and bays in wetlands. R

1. Adult Moorhen
2. Adult Lesser Moorhen
3. Adult Redknobbed Coot
4. Immature Redknobbed Coot
5. Male African Finfoot
6. Female African Finfoot
7. Immature African Jacana
8. Adult African Jacana
9. Adult Lesser Jacana

1	2	
3	4	
5	6	
7	8	9

R *resident* • I *intra-African migrant* • S *summer visitor*

Bustards Family Otididae

Medium to very large terrestrial birds, bustards have long, sometimes very slender necks, and long legs. They walk slowly, with the neck being swung back and forth as they proceed. Reluctant to take to flight, they tend to crouch or run when alarmed. In some species the male birds perform elaborate courtship displays; some species have a communal display ground or lek, where males congregate during the breeding season for the sole purpose of courtship.

Adult Stanley's Bustard

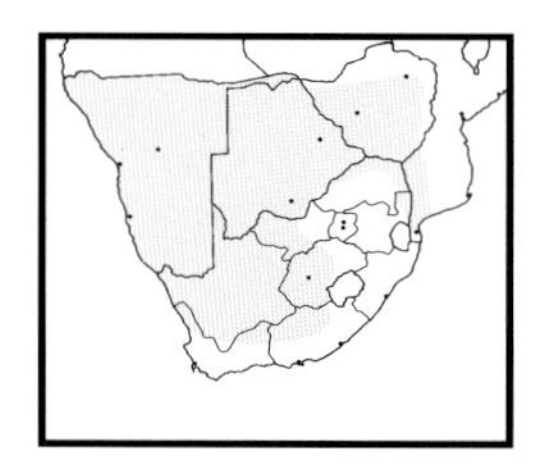

Kori Bustard *Ardeotis kori* (230) 135 cm

This is the largest bustard in the region. The male of this species is the world's heaviest flying bird; females are noticeably smaller than the males. In some parts of their range bee-eaters regularly hawk insects from the backs of these birds. Kori Bustards fly like enormous geese with powerful, uninterrupted wing beats and, unlike other large bustards, show no white in the wings. Displaying males inflate the throat sacs to show off the white underfeathers and cock their tails over the back. The call is a deep, booming 'oom-oom-oom'. Occurring on open grassy plains, in dry thornveld and semi-desert, the Kori Bustard is most frequently found in large game reserves. R

Adult Stanley's Bustard

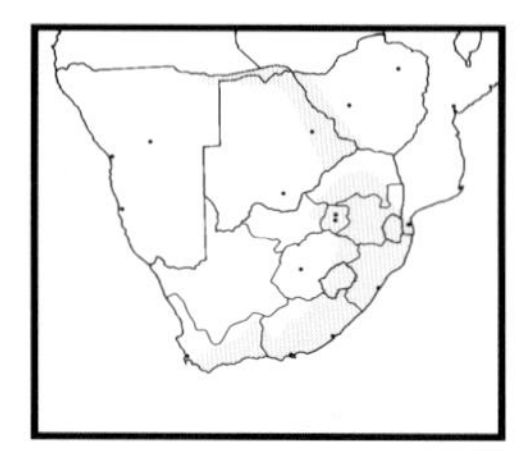

Stanley's Bustard *Neotis denhami* (231) 104 cm

Stanley's Bustard is most likely to be confused with the similar-sized Ludwig's Bustard. Both species show a considerable amount of chestnut on the nape and hindneck but the extent of grey and brown on the face and throat of Stanley's Bustard is never quite as dark as that of Ludwig's Bustard. This species also has black stripes on the crown which are lacking in Ludwig's Bustard. Further, in flight Stanley's Bustard shows much less white on the wings and when displaying inflates the throat to show a white, not grey, neck 'balloon'. Male Stanley's Bustards are considerably larger than the females. The call is a deep 'woodoomp' given in display, during which the male puffs out the neck feathers, drops the wings and cocks the tail. Stanley's Bustard frequents open grasslands in coastal and mountainous regions. R

Adult Ludwig's Bustard

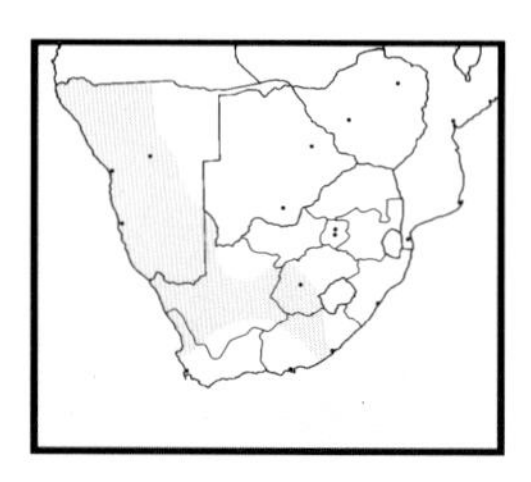

Ludwig's Bustard *Neotis ludwigii* (232) 90 cm

Likely to be confused only with the similar-sized Stanley's Bustard, this species can be told apart by its lack of black stripes on the crown and by its dark brown face, throat and foreneck. In flight it shows more extensive white patches in the wings. The female has a paler face and throat than the male. The displaying male inflates the throat to show a grey, not white, 'balloon'. The call is a far-carrying, booming sound, similar to that given by Stanley's Bustard. Ludwig's Bustard favours much drier regions than does Stanley's Bustard, and is frequently encountered in desert areas. E

Adult Ludwig's Bustard

Whitebellied Korhaan *Eupodotis cafra* (233) 52 cm

The Whitebellied Korhaan may be confused with the Blue Korhaan, but is distinguishable by the paler blue on its neck and breast and by its white belly and vent. The head markings on the male are a striking black and white with a black line running down the hindneck; the female has shadow markings of the male's head pattern; immatures lack the blue on the neck and are more buffy-brown. In flight this bird shows a contrasting blue breast abruptly demarcated from the white belly and creamy underwings. Its call is a typical korhaan croaking, given early in the morning. The Whitebellied Korhaan favours longer grasses than do other korhaans; it is found in open grasslands, and frequently in lightly wooded savanna. E

1. Adult Kori Bustard
2. Adult Stanley's Bustard
3. Adult Ludwig's Bustard
4. Adult Whitebellied Korhaan
5. Adult Blue Korhaan

Blue Korhaan *Eupodotis caerulescens* (234) 56 cm

The all-blue underparts separate this species from the Whitebellied Korhaan, and in flight it shows blue on the upperwings and underwings. Females and immatures have a russet marking on the sides of the face and are a dowdier blue below. In flight all plumages show flashes of white on the underwings. The call is a duetted croaking given in the early morning. Found in open grasslands, the Blue Korhaan occurs mostly in pairs or in small family parties and is extremely wary, crouching low when disturbed and readily flying off, uttering its croaking 'krok-kaa-krow' call. E

R *resident* • E *endemic*

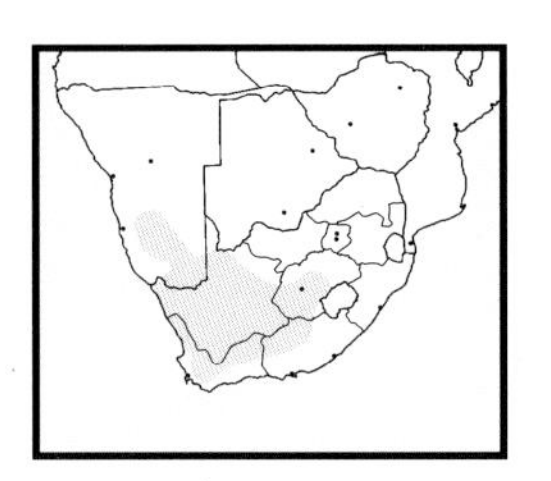

Karoo Korhaan *Eupodotis vigorsii* (235) 58 cm

This desert to semi-desert korhaan is so well camouflaged in its habitat that unless it moves it remains undetected. Its colouring is fairly uniform brown and grey above, slightly paler below, with black patches on the throat and neck. In flight it shows creamy or buffy panels on the upperwings and underwings. Immatures and females have fewer marks on the head and neck. The duetted croaking call is far carrying. Karoo Korhaans are seen mostly in pairs or in small groups. E

Rüppell's Korhaan *Eupodotis rueppellii* (236) 58 cm

This korhaan has greyish-buff upperparts; closer views reveal delicate bluish grey on the neck and complex black markings on the neck front, nape and head. It can be differentiated from the Karoo Korhaan by being much paler overall and by having more extensive markings on the head and neck. In flight Rüppell's Korhaan shows large expanses of creamy buff in the primaries and secondaries, bisected with black stripes. Females and immatures have reduced head and neck markings. The call is the typical duetted korhaan croaking. Occurring in small groups or pairs in true gravel desert and desert edge, these birds run or creep away from disturbance. When pushed they fly off, sometimes with twisting, dashing manoeuvres. E

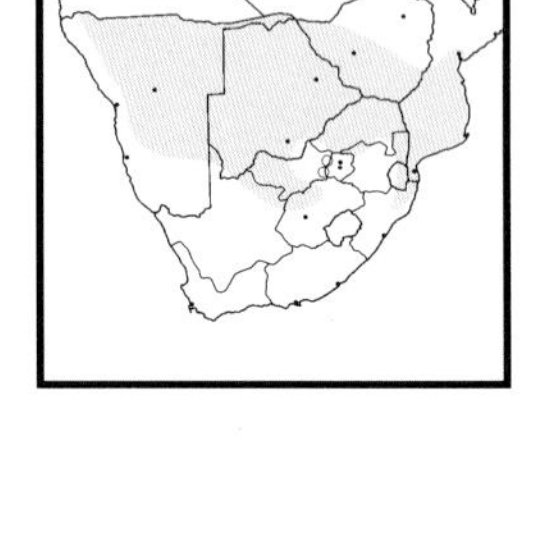

Redcrested Korhaan *Eupodotis ruficrista* (237) 50 cm

Most closely resembling the female Northern Black Korhaan, this species differs by having an obviously longer and thinner neck, chevron-shaped markings (not barring) on the back, and olive, not bright yellow, legs. The russet crest of the male Redcrested Korhaan is erected only in display. In flight it shows an all-black belly and underwings. Females resemble males but are dowdier and lack the grey on the throat and neck. The call is a loud, piercing 'chew-chew-chew-chew'. In display the male ascends over bush and tree tops only to suddenly fold its wings and legs and plummet in a ball to the ground. The Redcrested Korhaan frequents dry bushveld and open woodland. E

Blackbellied Korhaan *Eupodotis melanogaster* (238) 64 cm

The long-legged Blackbellied Korhaan superficially resembles the Redcrested Korhaan but is much larger, has a very long, thin neck and a diagnostic black line down the centre of the throat. Females bear a slight resemblance to female Whitebellied Korhaans (see page 84) in plumage coloration but are overall much more slender, with exceptionally long legs and neck. In flight the extensive white in the upperwings contrasting with the black and white underwings is characteristic. The male in display flight is graceful and buoyant, almost butterfly-like, giving slow-motion wing beats over its territory; males also fly directly upwards from the ground, twisting over suddenly and descending rapidly with wings stretched over the back. The call of the displaying male is a soft whistle followed by a 'plop' sound. R

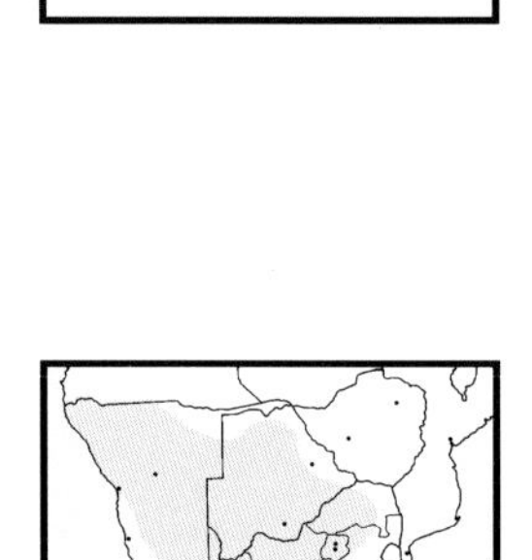

Northern Black Korhaan *Eupodotis afraoides* (239b) 52 cm

The exclusive range of this species and that of the very similar Southern Black Korhaan precludes any confusion between them. The female may be confused with the Redcrested Korhaan but is squatter, dumpier and shorter legged, has a shorter and thicker neck, with barring, not white chevrons, on the back, and bright yellow, not olive-coloured, legs. The male's call is a loud, raucous 'kerrack-kerrack-kerrack', often repeated and given from the ground or in display flight. Northern Black Korhaans occur in a variety of habitats, from open grasslands or semi-desert to lightly wooded savanna. E

Southern Black Korhaan *Eupodotis afra* (239a) 52 cm

The black underparts and bright yellow legs of this small korhaan make it easy to recognize. The main difference between the Southern Black Korhaan and the Northern Black Korhaan is the lack of a white patch in the primaries of this species. The calls (similar in both species) and display flight of both are spectacular, with the male rising to 50 metres or more and flying over its territory with slow-motion wing beats. Near the end of such display flights the bird gives ever-slower wing beats and dangles its legs, and with a series of circular wing flaps slowly descends to the ground. The male is solitary and the female is very secretive. Southern Black Korhaans frequent coastal fynbos. E

Male Blackbellied Korhaan

Adult Northern Black Korhaan (male upperwing)

Adult Southern Black Korhaan (male upperwing)

1. Adult Karoo Korhaan
2. Adult Rüppell's Korhaan
3. Male Redcrested Korhaan
4. Male Blackbellied Korhaan
5. Male Northern Black Korhaan
6. Female Redcrested Korhaan
7. Female Southern Black Korhaan
8. Female Blackbellied Korhaan
9. Female Northern Black Korhaan
10. Male Southern Black Korhaan

1 2 3
4 5 6
7
8 9 10

Oystercatchers Family Haematopodidae

Oystercatchers are large waders with long, straight, orange-red bills. The plumage is black or black and white. They forage mainly on open shorelines and in estuaries. All have highly ritualized and vocal displays.

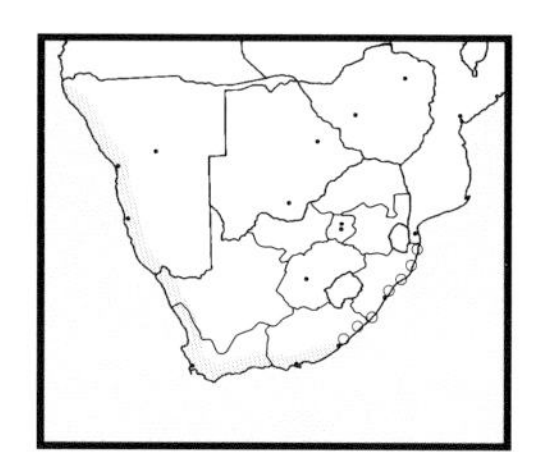

African Black Oystercatcher *Haematopus moquini* (244) 44 cm

This large shorebird with its red eye-ring and deep pink legs and toes is easily identifiable. The bill and legs of immatures are duller coloured. In flight they show no wing bars or distinctive patterns. Calls are a high-pitched 'kee-leeep, kleeeep' and a faster 'peeeka-peeeka' alarm note. They usually occur in small groups and pair off when breeding, but may otherwise gather in larger numbers. When breeding, small groups chase each other in tight circles, bills pointing down, and utter shrill 'beeeek' notes. E

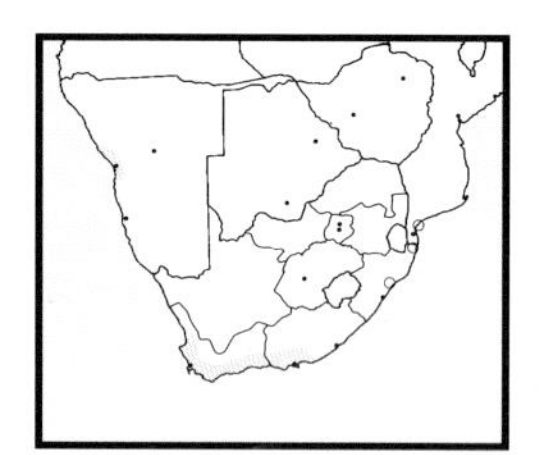

European Oystercatcher *Haematopus ostralegus* (243) 43 cm

Smaller and more slender than the African Black Oystercatcher, this pied oystercatcher is easily identified by its striking black and white plumage. The sexes are alike, and immatures and most non-breeding adults have a white throat crescent. In flight it shows a broad white wing bar, conspicuous white rump and black tip to the tail. This species is normally silent in Africa except when alarmed. S

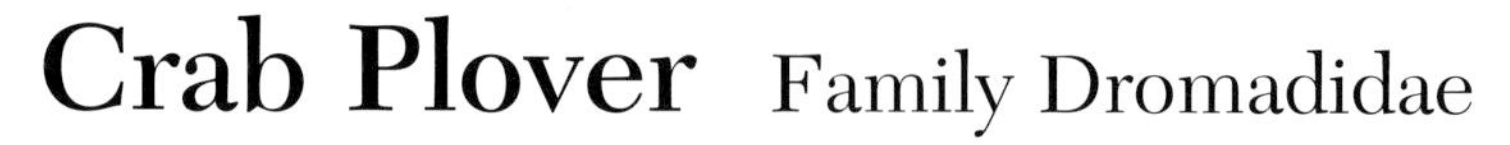

Crab Plover Family Dromadidae

A large wader with a characteristic heavy, black bill and very long, bluish-grey legs, the Crab Plover feeds on crabs, marine molluscs and worms. It breeds colonially in burrows abutting sandy beaches.

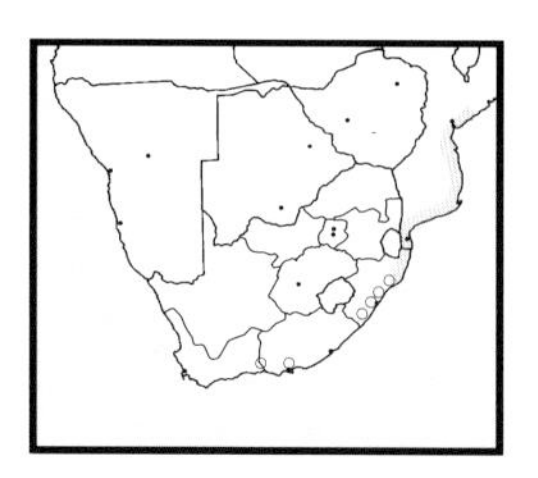

Crab Plover *Dromas ardeola* (296) 38 cm

This lanky shorebird is easily recognized by its black and white patterned plumage and very heavy, dagger-shaped bill. In flight the long legs project well beyond the tail. Immatures have a less well-developed bill and show greyish smudges on the head and wings. Although it has a loping gait when walking, it can run very swiftly in pursuit of prey. The call is a variety of metallic 'kwa-daa-dak' notes and its gives a 'kwa-da' flight call. The Crab Plover frequents sandy beaches and coastal estuaries. S

Avocets and stilts Family Recurvirostridae

These are medium-sized waders with very long legs and long, thin bills. They are found mainly at estuaries and inland waterbodies, including hypersaline pans. They prey predominantly on aquatic invertebrates.

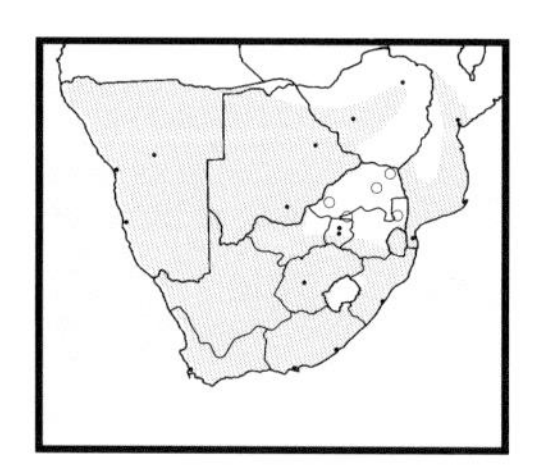

Avocet *Recurvirostra avosetta* (294) 42 cm

This is the only black and white wading bird with a thin, strongly upturned bill. The plumage, shining white with jet-black markings, and the long, blue-grey legs superficially resemble those of the Crab Plover but the bill of the Avocet rules out confusion. Immatures are dowdier, dirty-looking versions of the adults. The partly webbed feet enable the bird to swim freely. Very restless and nervy in flocks, Avocets will take flight on rapid wings, the flocks wheeling and turning before re-alighting. The call is an excited 'kluit-kluit-kluit'. R

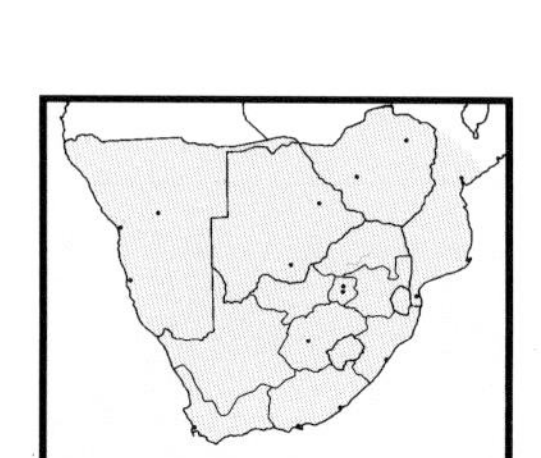

Blackwinged Stilt *Himantopus himantopus* (295) 38 cm

This species is almost impossible to misidentify: it has extremely long red legs, a long, very thin black bill, a shining white body and head, and contrasting black wings and a black back. Immatures have a brownish cast to the black back and dull red legs. Calls include a harsh, short 'klit-klit-klit' and a rougher 'kyik-kyik'. Usually seen singly or in small groups, the Blackwinged Stilt sometimes keeps company with Avocets. R

Adult Crab Plover

Adult Avocet

1. Adult African Black Oystercatcher
2. Adult European Oystercatcher
3. Immature Crab Plover
4. Adult Avocet
5. Adult Crab Plovers
6. Immature Blackwinged Stilt
7. Adult Blackwinged Stilt

1	2
	3
4	5
6	7

E *endemic* • S *summer visitor* • R *resident*

Plovers Family Charadriidae

Small to medium-sized waders with characteristically short bills and long legs, plovers inhabit a range of habitats, from open coasts and marshes to deserts, grassland, savannas and inland waterbodies.

Adult Ringed Plover (breeding)

Adult Threebanded Plover

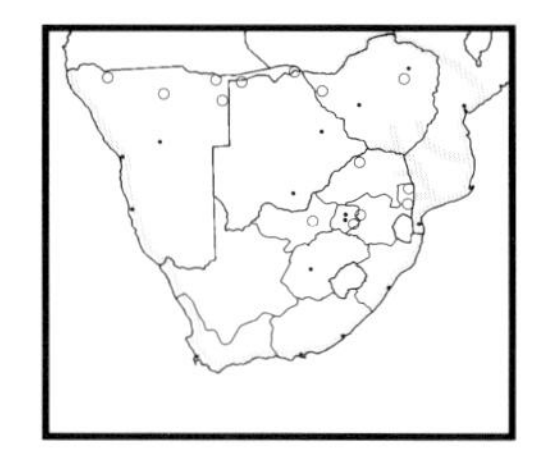

Whitefronted Plover *Charadrius marginatus* (246) 18 cm

This pallid little plover differs from the Sand Plover and Mongolian Plover by its smaller size and obvious white collar. Immatures are very similar to immature Kittlitz's Plovers (see page 92) but are best told apart by the lack of a broad buffy eyebrow stripe. Larger than the similar non-breeding Chestnutbanded Plover, the Whitefronted Plover is also browner above than that species and lacks the marked shoulder patches. Calls include a clear, sharp 'wiiit' and a 'tukut' alarm call. The Whitefronted Plover occurs mostly on sandy shorelines but frequents a diverse range of habitats. R

Chestnutbanded Plover *Charadrius pallidus* (247) 15 cm

The male Chestnutbanded Plover in breeding plumage is unmistakable with its narrow chestnut breast band, black bar on the forehead and narrow chestnut stripe running from the forehead to behind the eye to join with the breast band; the female has a shadow of the chestnut breast band. Immatures are similar to the immature Whitefronted Plover but are noticeably smaller and very much paler. The call is a single, short 'prrrp' or 'toooeet'. Occurring on salt pans, the Chestnutbanded Plover congregates in coastal areas, such as lagoons and estuaries, when not breeding. R

Mongolian Plover *Charadrius mongolus* (250) 19 cm

This species and the Sand Plover are difficult to tell apart. The Mongolian Plover has a less robust bill, shorter, generally darker legs and a more rotund appearance. In breeding plumage it has a much larger amount of chestnut on the breast band. In this plumage it might also be mistaken for a breeding Caspian Plover (see page 92) but has a more robust bill and a black mask. The call is a 'chittick-chittick', given mostly in flight. Mongolian Plovers frequent estuaries and coastal lagoons. S

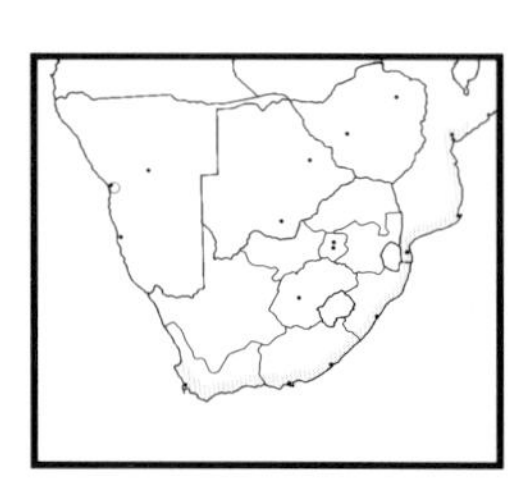

Sand Plover *Charadrius leschenaultii* (251) 22 cm

This species may be confused with the Mongolian Plover and the Caspian Plover (see page 92). It can best be told from the Mongolian Plover by its larger size, longer and paler legs and more robust, longer bill; and from the Caspian Plover it can be distinguished by its more robust bill, its broad white wing bar, the white sides to the tail and by the lack of a broad buffy eyebrow stripe. In breeding plumage the Sand Plover has a variable amount of chestnut on the breast band but this is always narrower than in the Mongolian Plover. Its call is a 'trriii' or 'trrrirrrt'. Sand Plovers feed on muddy flats on estuaries and gather to roost on sandbars at high tide. S

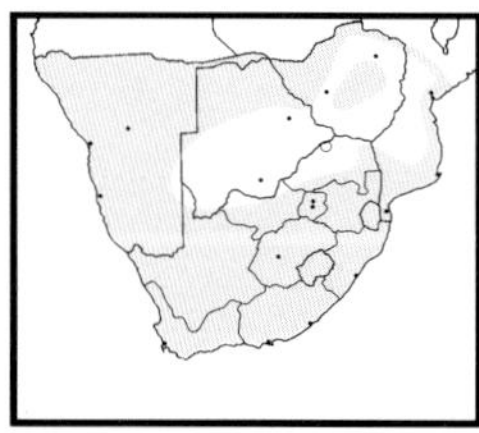

Ringed Plover *Charadrius hiaticula* (245) 16 cm

Resembling the Threebanded Plover but having only one black band, the Ringed Plover is smaller than both the Mongolian Plover and the Sand Plover and differs further by having yellow-orange legs and a more complete collar. Breeding adults have a complete black breast band, black head markings and a dark-tipped orange bill; immatures and non-breeding adults are duller overall and have incomplete brown breast bands. The call is a soft, fluty 'tooee'. Ringed Plovers forage over muddy or sandy stretches of shoreline on coastal and inland wetlands. S

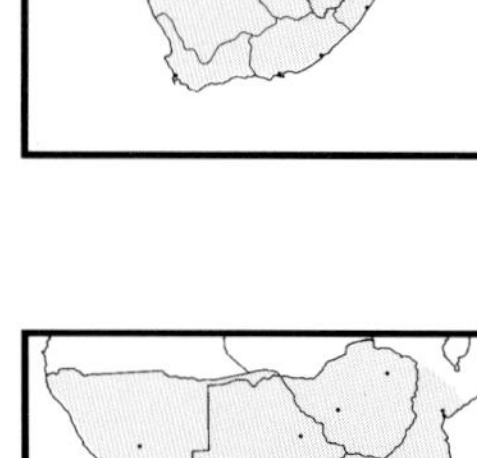

Threebanded Plover *Charadrius tricollaris* (249) 18 cm

A little larger than the Ringed Plover, the Threebanded Plover has two black breast bands, compared with the Ringed Plover's one. These, along with the grey cheeks, red eye-ring and red base to the bill, are diagnostic. The sexes are alike, and immatures are duller than the adults and lack the red eye-ring. The Threebanded Plover is widespread on waterbodies with sandy or stony margins but is less common on coastal mudflats. The call is a penetrating 'pi-peep', given in flight. R

1. Adult Whitefronted Plover (breeding)
2. Adult Chestnutbanded Plover
3. Adult Sand Plover (breeding)
4. Adult Mongolian Plover (breeding)
5. Adult Ringed Plover (non-breeding)
6. Adult Ringed Plover (breeding)
7. Adult Threebanded Plover

1	2
3	4
	5
6	7

R *resident* • S *summer visitor*

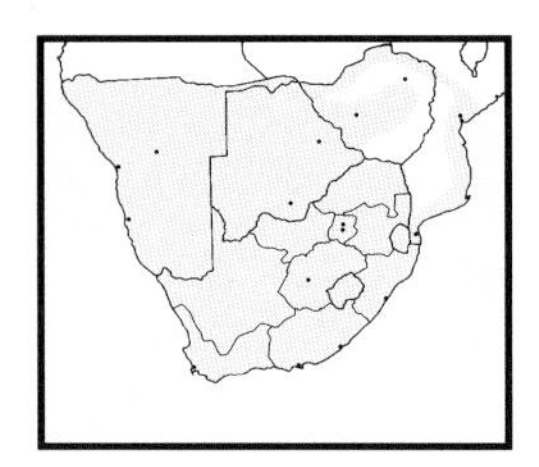

Kittlitz's Plover *Charadrius pecuarius* (248) 16 cm

In breeding plumage this small plover has a black bar crossing the forehead and continuing on to the shoulder; the bordering white line runs on to the nape and gives the bird a capped appearance. The head is less well marked in non-breeding plumage. The breast colour is variable, from pale creamy-buff to pale orange. The Whitefronted Plover (see page 90) sometimes also shows buffy underparts but lacks the striking head markings of this species. The call is a short, clipped and trilled 'kittip'. Favouring areas of short grass, Kittlitz's Plovers occur in dry habitats, often far from water, but are also found on wetlands and muddy estuaries. R

Grey Plover *Pluvialis squatarola* (254) 30 cm

In non-breeding plumage, this medium-sized shorebird has an overall greyish, mottled plumage with a greyish breast band and a vague, paler eyebrow stripe. In this plumage it might be mistaken for an American Golden Plover but it is larger than that species and has no trace of golden flecks on the mantle or wing coverts. If doubt arises, flush the bird and it should reveal jet-black ovals ('armpits') at the base of the underwing; it is the only plover to have this feature. In breeding plumage the Grey Plover has black underparts demarcated from the black and white spangled upperparts by a white border. The call is a clear 'teluuee', lower in pitch in the middle. The Grey Plover frequents coastal estuaries and rocky coasts, and is also encountered on inland wetland systems. S

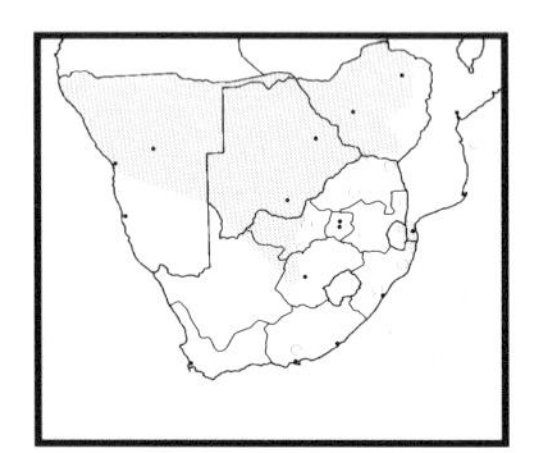

Caspian Plover *Charadrius asiaticus* (252) 22 cm

This species, the Sand Plover (see page 90) and the Mongolian Plover (see page 90) cause much confusion. Fortunately, the Caspian Plover can be distinguished by the fact that it habitually frequents arid to semi-arid areas, unlike the other two plovers. In breeding plumage the Caspian Plover is best identified by its whitish face with a broad, buff and white eyebrow stripe and by its lack of any black on the face. The orange breast band is extensive and is bordered below by a black band. The bill is fine and pointed, unlike the robust bills of the other two species. In non-breeding plumage it is nondescript except for the dun-brown breast band which is complete and for the broad buffy eyebrow stripe. In flight it is all dark above and has neither wing bars nor the pale outertail of the other two plovers. Usually silent, it does give a clear, whistled, 'tooeet' call. S

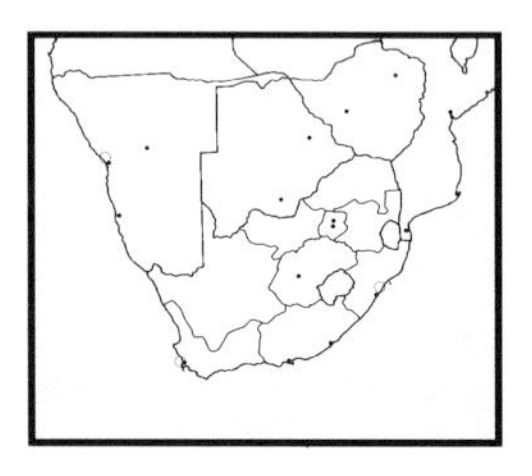

American Golden Plover *Pluvialis dominica* (253a) 25 cm

The American Golden Plover might be confused with the Pacific Golden Plover but is bulkier and more robust than that species, and has a bigger, angular head, and wings that project further beyond the end of the tail. It differs further by having a broad, conspicuous, buffy eyebrow stripe and a greyish wash across the breast; also, it does not have the same extent of golden flecks on the upperparts. Superficially it resembles the Grey Plover but is smaller and daintier, lacks the black 'armpits' of that species and has a dark, not pale, rump; it also has a longer-necked appearance. The call is variable, a single or double-noted whistle, 'oodle-oo'. The American Golden Plover occurs in dry, grassy areas and in coastal lagoons and estuaries. S

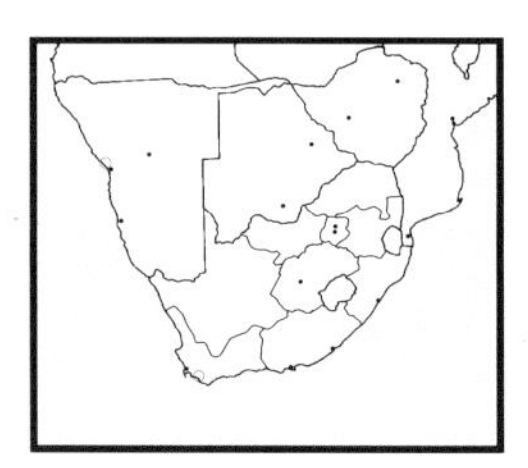

Pacific Golden Plover *Pluvialis fulva* (253b) 26 cm

Very like the American Golden Plover in many aspects, this species differs by being smaller, much more finely proportioned, longer-legged and more slender. Its eyebrow stripe is less distinct and it has very obvious golden spangling on the upperparts, much more so than in the American Golden Plover. In breeding plumage this species may easily be told apart by its all-black underparts and white, not black, vent and undertail coverts. The call is a 'chewick-chewick'. Pacific Golden Plovers prefer more grassy areas to wetlands. S

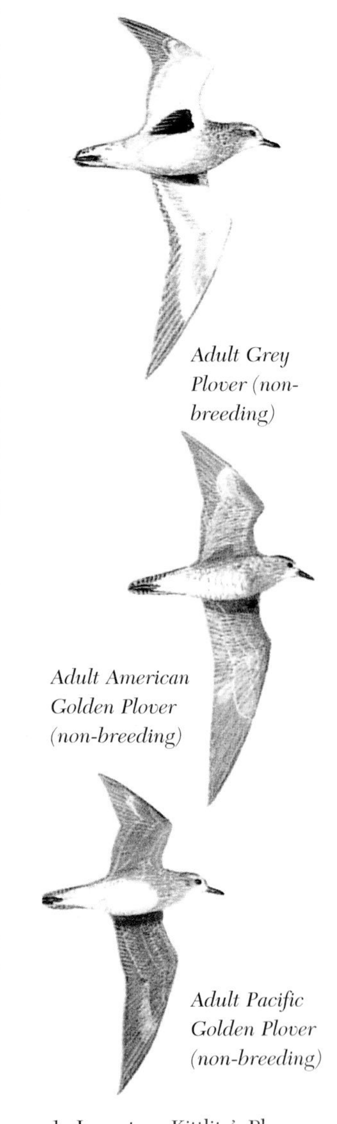

Adult Grey Plover (non-breeding)

Adult American Golden Plover (non-breeding)

Adult Pacific Golden Plover (non-breeding)

1. Immature Kittlitz's Plover
2. Adult Kittlitz's Plover (breeding)
3. Adult Kittlitz's Plover (non-breeding)
4. Adult Grey Plover (breeding)
5. Adult Caspian Plover (breeding)
6. Adult American Golden Plover (non-breeding)
7. Adult American Golden Plover (breeding)
8. Adult Pacific Golden Plover (non-breeding)

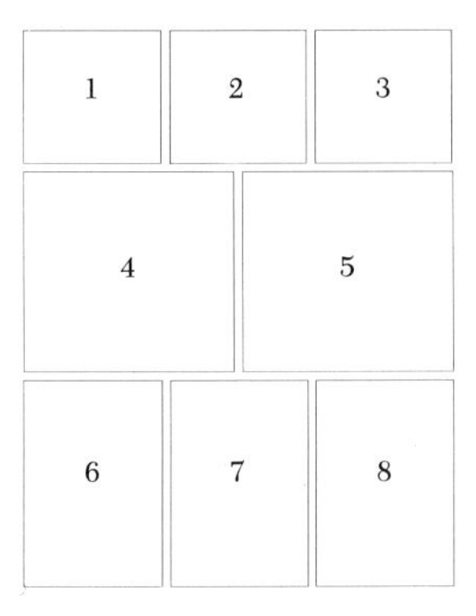

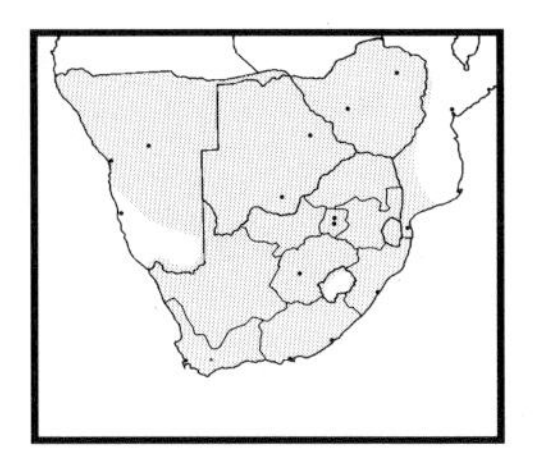

Crowned Plover *Vanellus coronatus* (255) 30 cm

This large, conspicuous plover has a diagnostic head pattern – a white line across the head demarcating a black cap – which is obvious in all plumages. The bill is dark-tipped pink and the legs dull pink in the adult and yellow in the immature. Brown overall with a distinct brown breast bordered by a narrow black band, the Crowned Plover shows black flight feathers in flight and a broad white bar running across the wing. The Wattled Plover has a similar wing pattern but lacks the head pattern, and has obvious yellow wattles and an entirely different call to that given by this species. Calls are a loud, piercing 'keeweet' and a grating 'kreeep'. Preferring arid to semi-arid areas and open grasslands, the Crowned Plover has adapted to suburbia and is often seen on grassy verges, golf courses and sports fields. R

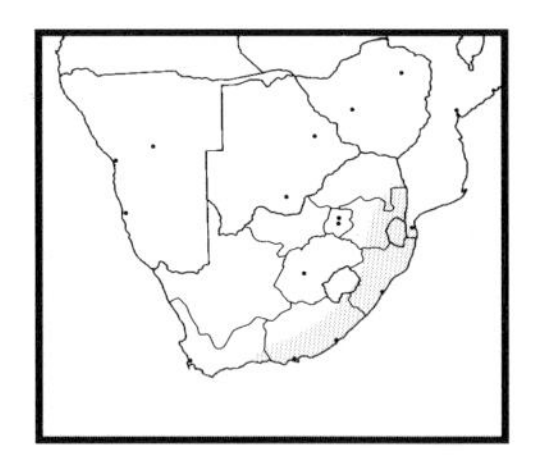

Blackwinged Plover *Vanellus melanopterus* (257) 27 cm

Very similar to the Lesser Blackwinged Plover, the Blackwinged Plover is larger and more robust, has a greater extent of white on the forehead, and dull pink, not dark, legs. Further, in flight it shows dark upperwings with a broad white bar across the centre, unlike the broad white trailing edge to the wings of the Lesser Blackwinged Plover; the underwing has much less white than is present in the underwing of the Lesser Blackwinged Plover. Immatures are browner and have ill-defined, paler edgings to the mantle. Calls are 'te-terreee' and a ringing 'kitti-kitti-kirrick'. Blackwinged Plovers frequent open grasslands and are not generally associated with water. R

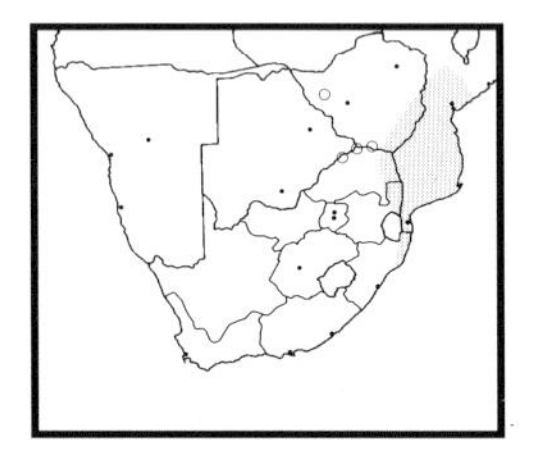

Lesser Blackwinged Plover *Vanellus lugubris* (256) 22 cm

This species may be told apart from the Blackwinged Plover by its darker overall colouring and the much smaller extent of white on the forehead. The legs are dark grey, not dull pink. The upperwing of the Lesser Blackwinged Plover shows a blazing white trailing edge and the underwing is white with dark primaries. Immatures are paler and have buff edgings to the mantle and wing feathers. The call is a distinctive, piping 'teeyoo-teeyoo'. The Lesser Blackwinged Plover frequents grassy regions in savanna and coastal grasslands, and shows a preference for burnt areas. R

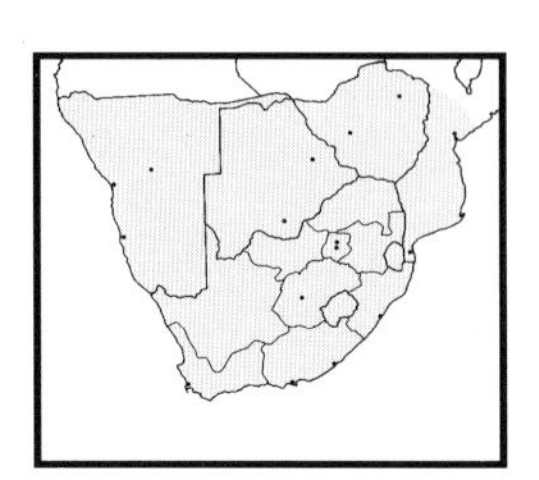

Blacksmith Plover *Vanellus armatus* (258) 30 cm

This large, black, white and grey wading bird would be difficult to misidentify, and its bold pattern makes it easily distinguishable in flight. The juveniles and immatures have greyish-brown feathering replacing the black and brown streaking on the crown of the adults, and can be more difficult to identify but are usually seen close to the adults. Calls include a ringing 'tink-tink-tink-tink' alarm and a long, screeching 'keeeeuur'. Very noisy and aggressive, these birds dive-bomb intruders in their territories. Although normally associated with water, the Blacksmith Plover also feeds over grasslands and grassy fields away from water. R

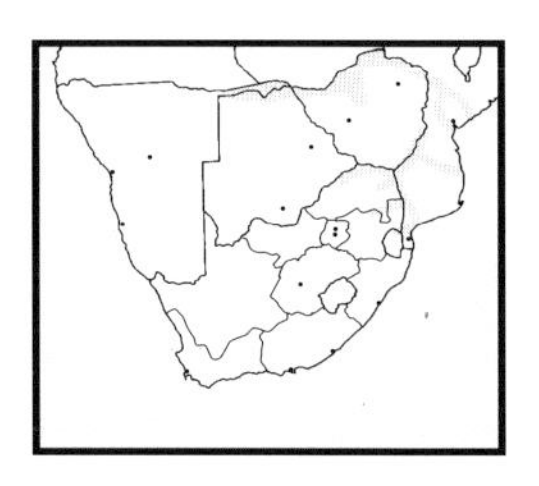

Whitecrowned Plover *Vanellus albiceps* (259) 30 cm

This and the Wattled Plover are the only two wading birds with long, pendulous, yellow wattles hanging from the base of the bill. The wattles of this species are extra long, and it has a grey head and neck and a white stripe running down the centre of the crown. It shows predominantly white underwings and upperwings with the latter having black secondary coverts. Immatures have smaller wattles, a brown, not grey, head, and mottled upperparts. The call is a sharp, penetrating, repeated 'peeek-peeek'. The Whitecrowned Plover frequents the islands and edges of larger river systems. R

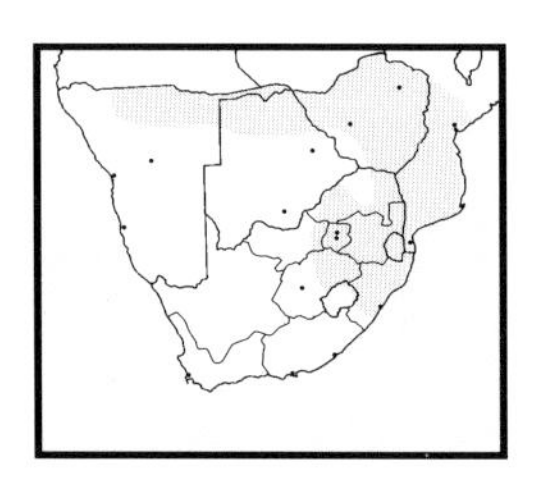

Wattled Plover *Vanellus senegallus* (260) 35 cm

The Wattled Plover is not normally found in the same habitat as the Whitecrowned Plover, which also has long yellow wattles. This species is larger and lacks the predominantly white wings of the Whitecrowned Plover. In flight the Wattled Plover could be confused with the Crowned Plover but lacks that bird's diagnostic head pattern, and is further distinguished by its yellow wattles. Immatures have tiny, undeveloped wattles, and are dowdier and mottled on the back. Calls are a sharp 'keep-keep', and a shriller 'keeeaap' given when dive-bombing an intruder. Very active at night, the Wattled Plover frequents damp grasslands and wetland fringes. R

Adult Blackwinged Plover

Adult Lesser Blackwinged Plover

1. Adult Crowned Plover
2. Adult Blackwinged Plover
3. Adult Lesser Blackwinged Plover
4. Adult Blacksmith Plover
5. Adult Whitecrowned Plover
6. Adult Wattled Plover

1	2
3	4
5	6

R *resident*

Sandpipers, snipes, godwits, stints, curlews and phalaropes Family Scolopacidae

Members of this highly diverse family range in size from large to small. All the species occurring in southern Africa, with the exception of the Ethiopian Snipe, breed in the northern hemisphere and migrate to southern Africa in the summertime. Marine and freshwater invertebrates are the principal food of all the species within the family.

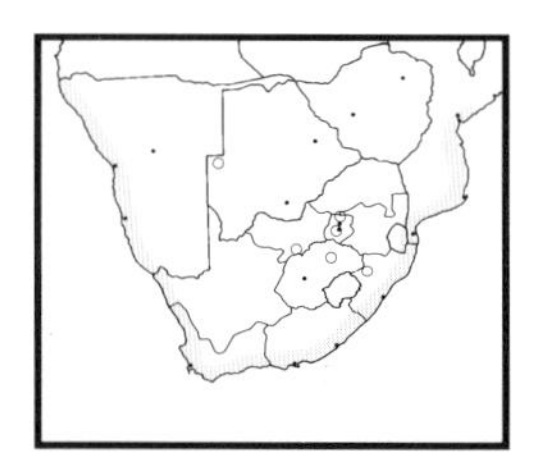

Terek Sandpiper *Xenus cinereus* (263) 23 cm

At a distance this small shorebird might be confused with the Curlew Sandpiper (see page 98) but at closer range it can be seen to have a long, upturned bill; it is the only small wader with this characteristic. It is generally paler than the Curlew Sandpiper, with a dark shoulder and conspicuous yellow-orange legs and feet. In flight it shows a thin white trailing edge to the wing and a pale grey rump and tail. Its gait is very hunched and horizontal and it 'teeters' like a Common Sandpiper. Continually on the move, it runs in a crouched position to pursue food items. Terek Sandpipers inhabit muddy estuaries, bays and coastal lagoons. The call is a fluty, uniformly pitched 'weet-weet-weet'. It forages solitarily but roosts in large flocks. S

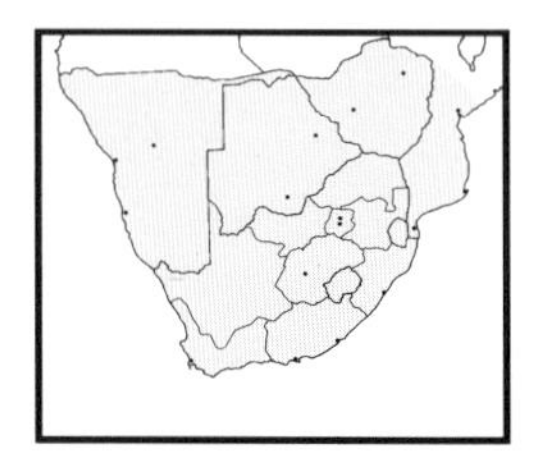

Common Sandpiper *Actitis hypoleucos* (264) 19 cm

The Common Sandpiper is a small, nondescript wader normally seen resting in a hunched position with its body rocking back and forth. A white crescent is present at the shoulder and in front of the wing. The sexes are alike, and immatures resemble the adults. The call is a high-pitched 'hee-deee-deee-deee', given mostly in flight. The Common Sandpiper is usually solitary unless roosting, when it gathers in small numbers. It occurs in a wide range of wetland habitats, including rivers, streams, dams, lakes, estuaries and coastal lagoons; it may also be seen around sewage works. S

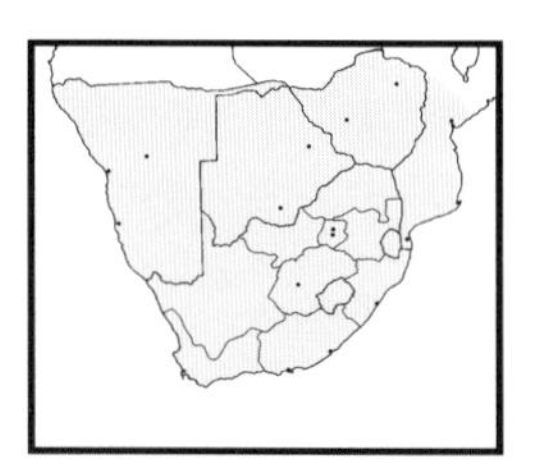

Wood Sandpiper *Tringa glareola* (266) 20 cm

In breeding plumage the Wood Sandpiper shows dark olive-brown upperparts with prominent pale spotting, also evident over the head and neck. The face, throat and breast are heavily spotted and streaked dark greyish-brown. Non-breeding birds are much duller and the spotting and streaking over the body, head and breast is less well defined. The sexes are alike and immatures resemble the adults but are warmer brown on the upperparts. The call is a diagnostic 'chiff-iff-iff', given when the bird is flushed. The Wood Sandpiper occurs in a wide range of wetland habitats, but favours muddy and grassy edges of freshwater ponds, and is relatively rare along the coast. It can occur in large congregations. S

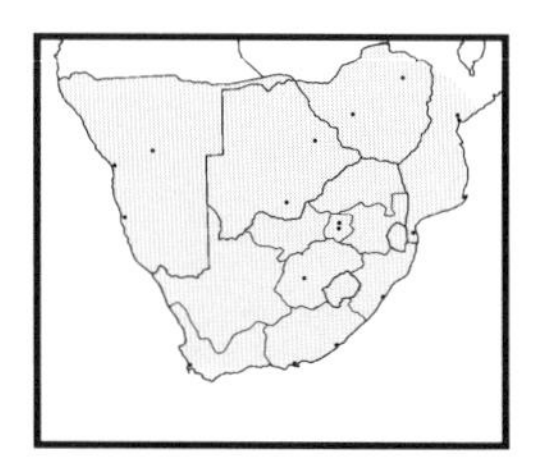

Marsh Sandpiper *Tringa stagnatilis* (269) 23 cm

This species is smaller and more slender than the similar Greenshank, and has a long, straight and very thin bill. It is paler and longer-legged than the Wood Sandpiper, and lacks pale spotting on the back. In flight it resembles a Greenshank but its feet project well beyond the end of the tail. In breeding plumage the Marsh Sandpiper has black markings on the upperparts, with the neck and breast streaked. Calls include a high-pitched 'chewk' or 'yeup' and a weaker 'tew tew tew'. These birds are solitary, or found in small groups, in a wide range of wetland habitats, both coastal and inland. S

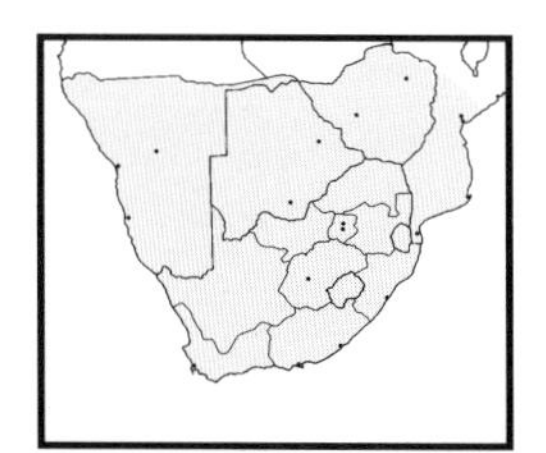

Greenshank *Tringa nebularia* (270) 32 cm

The Greenshank could be confused with the Marsh Sandpiper but is heavier-set with a long, fairly thick-based and slightly upturned bill. Smaller than the godwits (see page 100), the Greenshank is also greyer overall and has a shorter bill. The flight pattern is similar to that of the Marsh Sandpiper, with the white rump extending on to the back as a broad white wedge, but this species is broader winged and has a more powerful flight. The call is a loud, far-carrying 'chew chew chew'. Wide ranging in habitat, from coastal estuaries to virtually any stretch of fresh water, the Greenshank occurs singly or in small groups, and in large flocks if exceptional conditions prevail. S

Adult Marsh Sandpiper (worn plumage)

Adult Greenshank (non-breeding, worn plumage)

1. Adult Terek Sandpiper
2. Adult Wood Sandpiper
3. Adult Common Sandpiper
4. Adult Marsh Sandpiper
5. Adult Greenshank

1 2 3 4 5

S *summer visitor*

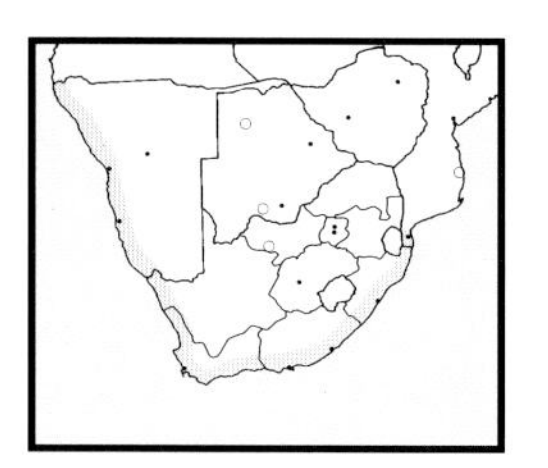

Knot *Calidris canutus* (271) 25 cm

The Knot is uniformly nondescript grey above and paler below. The bill is thick based and short, the legs proportionately short, and the bird's jizz is rotund, giving it a roly-poly running motion. It resembles the Grey Plover (see page 92) but is much smaller and shorter legged, and has a longer, thinner bill. In flight it shows a pale wing bar and a pale grey rump. In breeding plumage the Knot is brick-red below with a spangled back pattern, and then resembles the breeding Curlew Sandpiper but is very much larger and plumper. The call is a low, grunting 'knutt'. This gregarious bird occurs in coastal estuaries and lagoons, and rarely inland. S

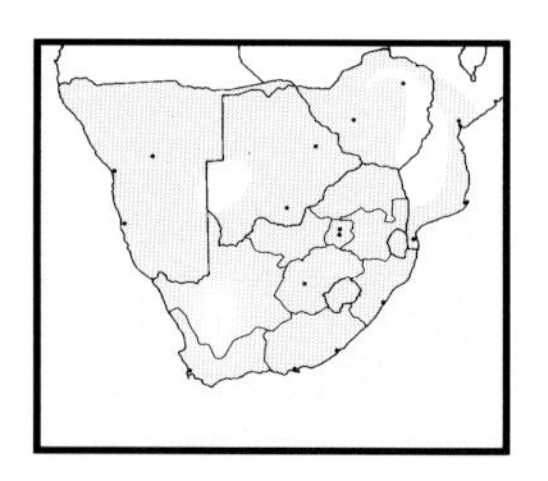

Curlew Sandpiper *Calidris ferruginea* (272) 19 cm

Larger than the Little Stint (see page 100) and smaller than the Knot, the Curlew Sandpiper differs from both by having a decurved bill and a white rump; the smaller Broadbilled Sandpiper and Pectoral Sandpiper also have decurved bills but both of those species lack the white rump. In breeding plumage the Curlew Sandpiper has brightly patterned upperparts and rufous underparts and the white rump becomes barred; in this plumage it can be distinguished from the similar-coloured Knot by its smaller size and its longer, decurved bill. The call is a short, trilled 'chrrrupp'. Sometimes occurring in flocks of thousands, the Curlew Sandpiper frequents coastal estuaries and, in smaller numbers, inland wetlands. S

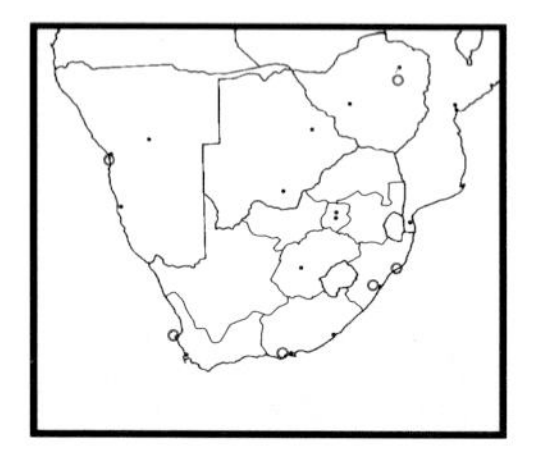

Broadbilled Sandpiper *Limicola falcinellus* (283) 17 cm

This small shorebird might be mistaken for a Curlew Sandpiper but is smaller and shorter legged, and has noticeable stripes on the head, and a dark, not white, rump in flight. It is very grey in general appearance with a dark shoulder. Its hunched jizz and short legs give it a roly-poly running motion, somewhat like a tiny Knot. The call is a short 'trrett', given in flight. Broadbilled Sandpipers occur singly or in small numbers, frequenting coastal estuaries and inland wetlands. S

Pectoral Sandpiper *Calidris melanotos* (279) 19 cm

Larger than the Curlew Sandpiper, the Pectoral Sandpiper is also browner with dark mantle feathers clearly edged with buff, so resembling a Ruff. The breast is heavily streaked and ends abruptly on the white belly; the head pattern imparts a capped appearance. The legs are olive to fleshy-yellow and the bill is slightly decurved and dark with a paler base. In flight it differs from the Curlew Sandpiper by its dark, not white, rump. The sexes are alike, and immatures resemble the adults. The call is a short, low, trilling 'prrrritt'. This solitary species is found mostly on freshwater wetlands and brackish pools, usually preferring the grassy margins. S

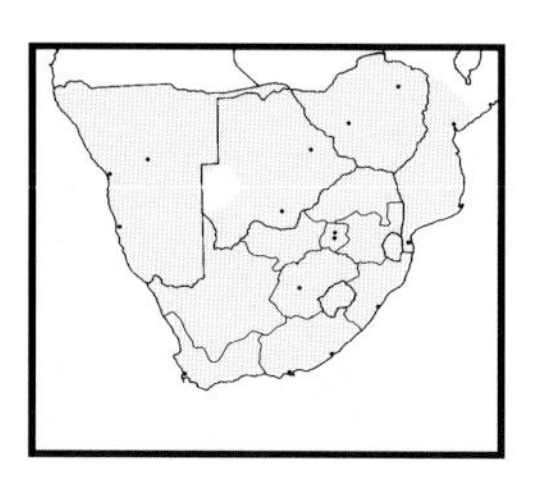

Ruff *Philomachus pugnax* (284) m=30 cm, f=24 cm

The Ruff differs from the *Tringa* waders in having its upperparts conspicuously 'scale'-patterned. The female Ruff is significantly smaller than the male and is very much more buff in colour. The male often shows a white head and breast. The stance is sometimes very upright, imparting a small-headed appearance. In flight, the Ruff shows a narrow white wing bar and two large white oval patches at the tail base. Males never show the full 'ruffed' breeding plumage in southern Africa. Immatures resemble the non-breeding adults. Usually silent, the Ruff occurs in most wetland habitats, from coastal estuaries to fresh waterbodies, often well inland. S

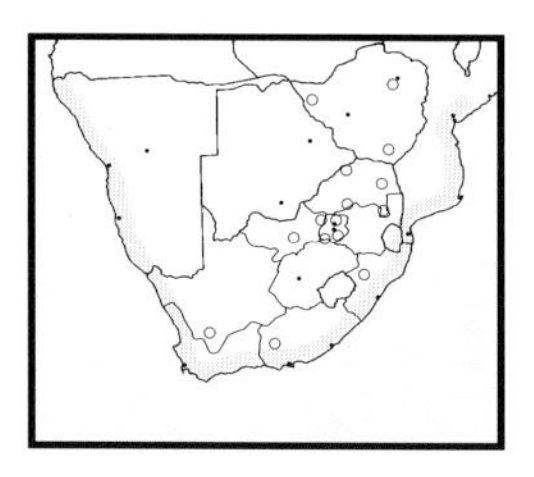

Turnstone *Arenaria interpres* (262) 23 cm

This small shorebird is unmistakable with its highly patterned back and wings. In breeding plumage the bright chestnut back, black and white 'frosted' head pattern and black breast pattern are diagnostic. Non-breeding adults and immatures lack the chestnut and black contrast but have the obvious dark breast pattern. In flight, the Turnstone shows a heavily patterned back and wings, with white stripes running down the back, and a black tail tip. The legs and feet are bright orange with darker joints. The bird takes its name from its habit of flicking over small stones with its bill in search of food. The call is a rattling 'chittick', given in flight. It frequents coastal estuaries, rocky shores and lagoons, normally in small flocks, but is not usually seen inland. S

Adult Knot (non-breeding)

Female Ruff (non-breeding)

Adult Turnstone (non-breeding)

1. Adult Knot (transitional)
2. Adult Curlew Sandpiper (non-breeding)
3. Adult Pectoral Sandpiper
4. Adult Broadbilled Sandpiper (non-breeding)*
5. Adult Curlew Sandpiper (breeding)
6. Male Ruff
7. Female Ruff
8. Adult Turnstone (non-breeding)
9. Adult Turnstone (breeding)

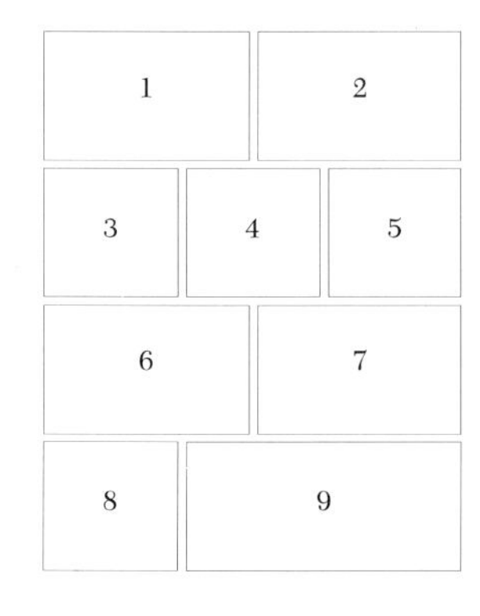

S *summer visitor*

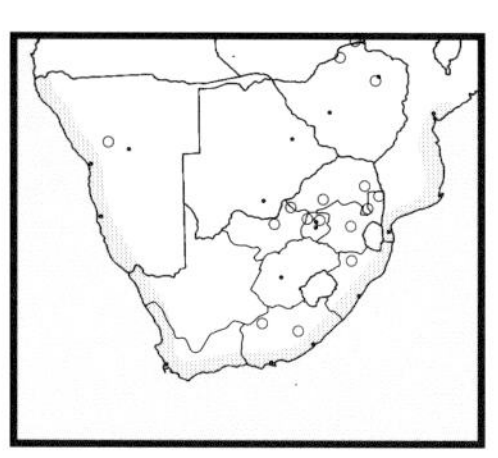

Sanderling *Calidris alba* (281) 19 cm

The very pale grey and white plumage and dark shoulder patch make this small shorebird easy to recognize. The bill is short, thick based and straight. The sexes are alike, and immatures resemble the non-breeding adults. The Sanderling's habit of chasing waves on open, sandy beaches is characteristic. In flight it has a very obvious broad white wing bar. The call is a short 'wick-wick-wick'. Usually occurring in small flocks on open sandy beaches, the Sanderling also gathers in large numbers on estuaries when roosting. S

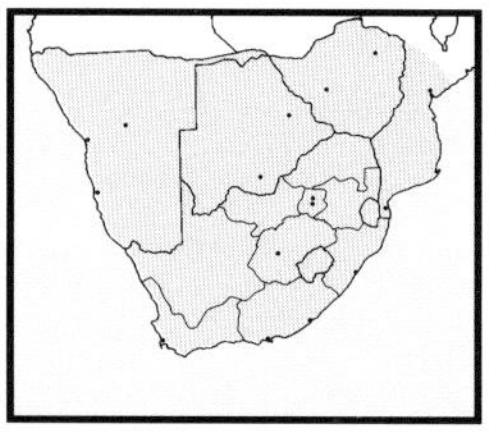

Little Stint *Calidris minuta* (274) 14 cm

This common small shorebird is easily confused with other tiny waders. It is much smaller than the Curlew Sandpiper (see page 98) and has a short, thin bill. The similar Sanderling is much larger than this species, paler grey overall, and has a dark shoulder. In flight the narrow white wing bar and white sides to the rump are obvious. The call is a soft 'schit-schit'. Occurring in flocks, sometimes comprising hundreds of birds, Little Stints forage with a rapid stabbing of the bill into mud in their coastal and freshwater wetland habitats. S

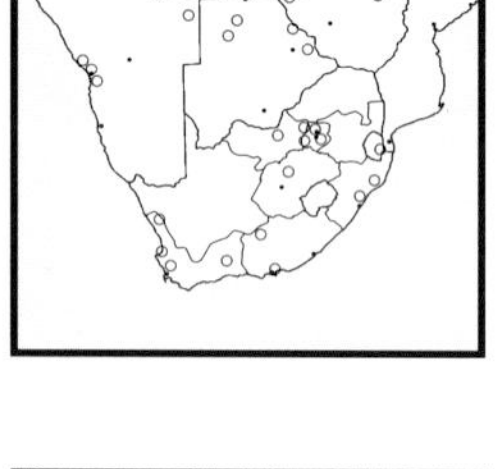

Blacktailed Godwit *Limosa limosa* (287) 40 cm

This large shorebird may be confused with the Bartailed Godwit at rest, but can be separated by its larger size, longer, straighter bill and more uniform grey, not brown-patterned, back. In flight it shows a broad white wing bar and a contrasting white rump with a broad black band on the tail tip. In breeding plumage it has deep chestnut underparts but these are not as extensive as in the Bartailed Godwit. The call is a repeated 'weeka-weeka', given especially in flight. It frequents large inland lakes, estuaries and coastal lagoons. S

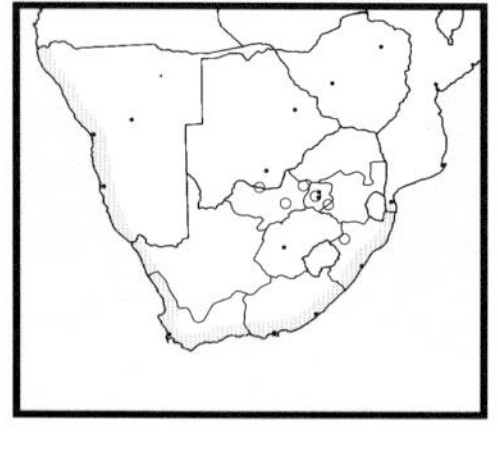

Bartailed Godwit *Limosa lapponica* (288) 38 cm

Much more common than the Blacktailed Godwit, this godwit differs by having a slightly shorter and more obviously upturned bill and a browner, more patterned back. It is most easily distinguished in flight, when it shows a barred tail but no wing bar as seen in the Blacktailed Godwit. The Whimbrel and the Curlew are vaguely similar to this species but have decurved bills. The call is a series of 'wik-wik' notes or a sharper 'kirrik'. Inhabiting coastal estuaries and lagoons, the Bartailed Godwit is unusual inland. S

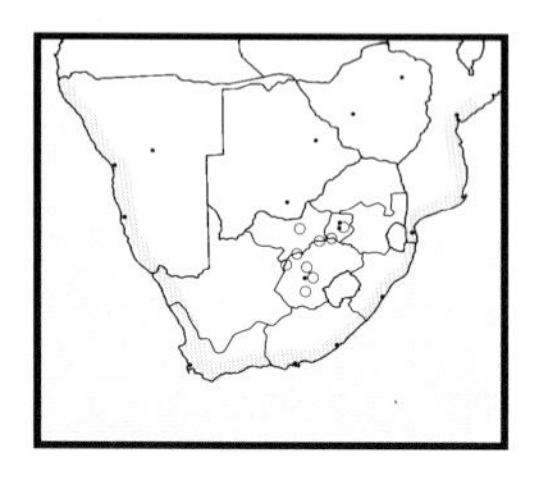

Curlew *Numenius arquata* (289) 55 cm

This large, imposing shorebird can be confused only with the smaller Whimbrel but has a much longer and more decurved bill and lacks stripes on the crown. Further, the overall colour is generally much paler, sometimes appearing a very pale biscuity-buff. When foraging on estuaries it can be seen to be longer legged and to have a longer, more slender profile than the Whimbrel. The call is a clearly whistled and drawn-out 'kuurl-eee'. The Curlew frequents large estuaries and coastal lagoons, and is rarely seen inland. S

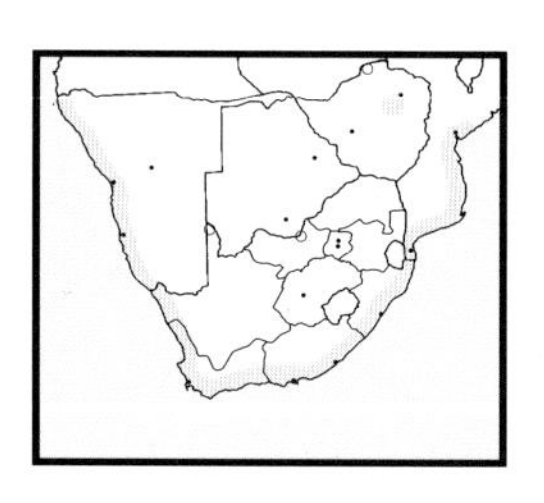

Whimbrel *Numenius phaeopus* (290) 43 cm

The Whimbrel with its decurved bill resembles the Curlew but has a diagnostic buff eyebrow stripe and clear black stripes on the crown, both of which are lacking in the Curlew; the overall impression is of a smaller, squatter, distinctly darker bird. In flight it also appears darker and shorter billed and has faster wing beats. The call is an even-pitched bubbling of about seven syllables. Whimbrels inhabit coastal regions such as estuaries, sandy beaches, rocky shorelines and lagoons, and are rarely seen inland. S

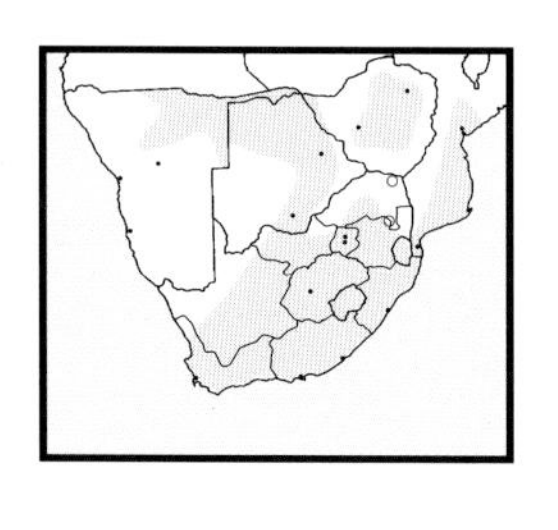

Ethiopian Snipe *Gallinago nigripennis* (286) 32 cm

The most commonly encountered snipe in the region, although not often seen foraging in the open, the Ethiopian Snipe usually flushes directly at one's feet. It might be confused with the Great Snipe (see page 102), but has much less white on the edging of the wings, very restricted barring on the flanks and a much faster, more erratic, zigzagging flight action; at rest it has slight, not heavy, barring on the flanks and a longer, much thinner bill. Calls include a short alarm note and a 'kek-kek-kek'. A 'drumming' display is performed in the evenings and on overcast days by birds stooping and fanning their tails with the wind vibrating the stiff outer retrices. Ethiopian Snipes are usually solitary. They frequent extensive marshes and wetland margins. R

Adult Blacktailed Godwit

Adult Bartailed Godwit

1. Adult Sanderling
2. Adult Little Stint
3. Adult Blacktailed Godwit (breeding)
4. Adult Blacktailed Godwit (non-breeding)
5. Female Bartailed Godwit (non-breeding)
6. Adult Curlew
7. Male Bartailed Godwit (breeding)
8. Adult Whimbrel
9. Adult Ethiopian Snipe

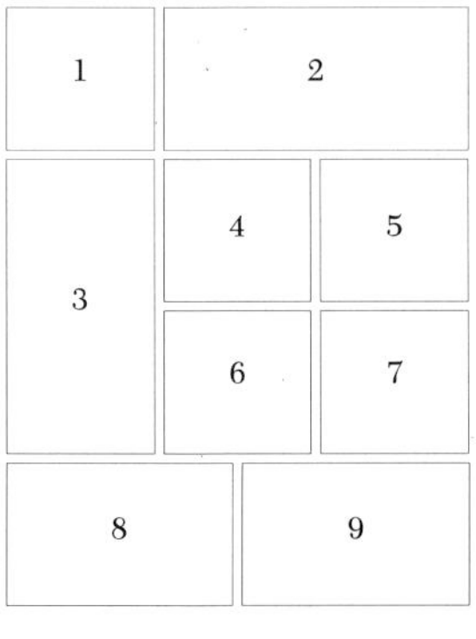

1 2
3 4 5
6 7
8 9

S *summer visitor* • R *resident*

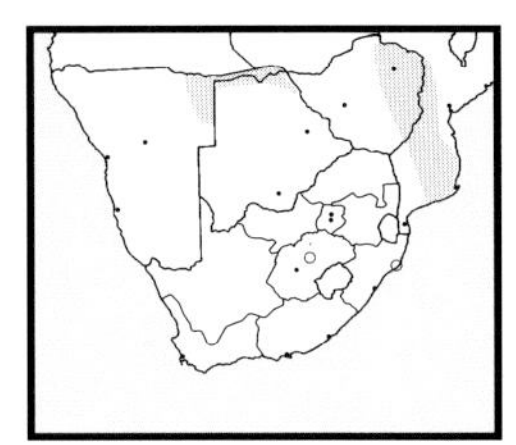

Great Snipe *Gallinago media* (285) 35 cm

Only slightly larger than very similar Ethiopian Snipe (see page 100), the Great Snipe is best distinguished by jizz alone. When flushed it has a much more sluggish mode of flight on more rounded wings and it lacks the dynamic flight action of the Ethiopian Snipe; the wing beats are more clipped and the direct flight much shorter. Also, the bill is shorter and thicker, and there is more obvious white on the wings and more extensive barring on the flanks. In flight the call is an 'ekkk-ekkk-ekkk' croak, very different to that of the Ethiopian Snipe. Great Snipes are usually solitary, and occur in marshes and along wetland margins. S

Grey Phalarope *Phalaropus fulicarius* (291) 18 cm

This small grey wader is usually seen swimming very high in the water, breast down and tail up. It may be confused with the Ruff (see page 98) and the Curlew Sandpiper (see page 98), but those birds are much larger and darker, have different bills and are never as buoyant as the phalaropes. The Grey Phalarope has a uniform grey back and a short, thick, pale-based bill. In breeding plumage, the chestnut underparts, white sides to the head and black crown are diagnostic. Usually silent, it may give a short 'wiit' flight note. It prefers coastal lagoons and inland wetlands but may also be found far out to sea. S

Male Painted Snipe

Adult Spotted Dikkop

Adult Water Dikkop

Painted Snipes Family Rostratulidae

Medium-sized waders with long bills, rounded wings and short tails, Painted Snipes frequent marshes and the fringes of reedbeds. They probe for food in soft mud. They have reversed sexual dimorphism and are polyandrous, all parental care being undertaken by the male.

Painted Snipe *Rostratula benghalensis* (242) 24-28 cm

This species' general appearance and much shorter bill separate it from the Great Snipe and Ethiopian Snipe (see page 100). Males and females have a white crescent that runs from the breast and curves over the shoulder. The male has a greyish head and the back pattern is mottled and streaked buff. The female is more brightly coloured, and has a chestnut-coloured head and a more uniform back. Very rail-like in flight, it shows wide, rounded wings and dangling legs. The female's call is a repeated 'wuk-oooooo', and the male's a short trill. In display, birds spread out their wings and lean forwards, increasing their size. R

Dikkops Family Burhinidae

Dikkops are large, cryptically coloured waders with large heads. Their large yellow eyes are indicative of their nocturnal habits. Generally quiet during the day, at night their mournful cries and whistles can be heard over great distances.

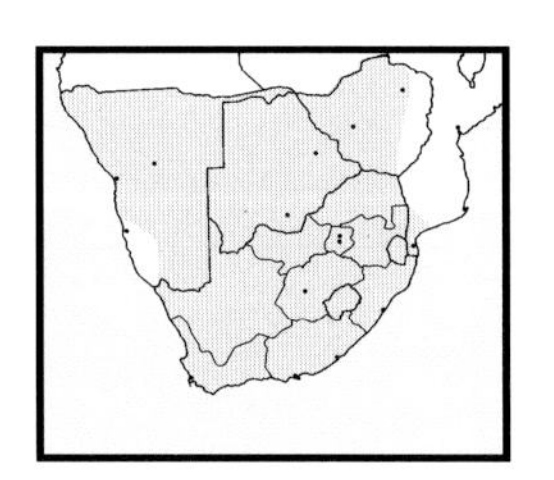

Spotted Dikkop *Burhinus capensis* (297) 44 cm

Very similar to the Water Dikkop, the Spotted Dikkop is a larger bird with heavier patterning above and mottled, not grey, wing panels. It lacks the white horizontal stripe across the wings when at rest. In flight it shows white spots on the primaries and no obvious wing bars. It hunches up and sleeps in the shade in the day, and when disturbed runs away with its neck tucked into its shoulders. It calls mostly at night, a series of mournful whistles. The Spotted Dikkop is not often associated with water and is found in arid and semi-arid regions. R

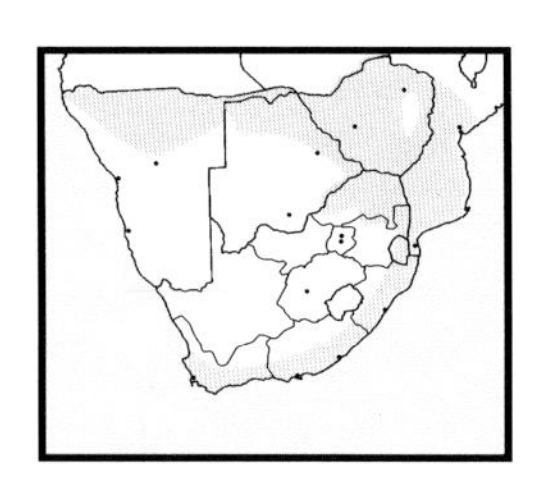

Water Dikkop *Burhinus vermiculatus* (298) 40 cm

Smaller and more compact than the Spotted Dikkop, the Water Dikkop has a generally paler appearance. It differs further by having its grey wing panel bordered by white bars (most obvious in flight). The upperparts are streaked, not mottled and spotted. The Water Dikkop hunches up and rests during the day in shade and cover or among rocks, usually close to water. Its call is uttered at dusk and at night, a whistled 'ti-ti-teeteee-ooo', slowing and dropping in pitch at the end. It is found in coastal wetlands, river systems and inland wetlands. R

1. Adult Great Snipe
2. Adult Grey Phalarope
3. Adult Spotted Dikkop
4. Female Painted Snipe
5. Adult Water Dikkop

Coursers and pratincoles Family Glareolidae

Coursers are waders which generally inhabit drier regions. Their long legs enable them to run swiftly and their cryptic back coloration blends well with their environment. In flight they show boldly patterned wings. Pratincoles are short-legged birds with long, pointed wings and black and white, forked tails. In flight they resemble huge swallows. Both groups have large eyes, indicative of their nocturnal and crepuscular habits. Insectivorous, they catch their prey in flight or on the ground.

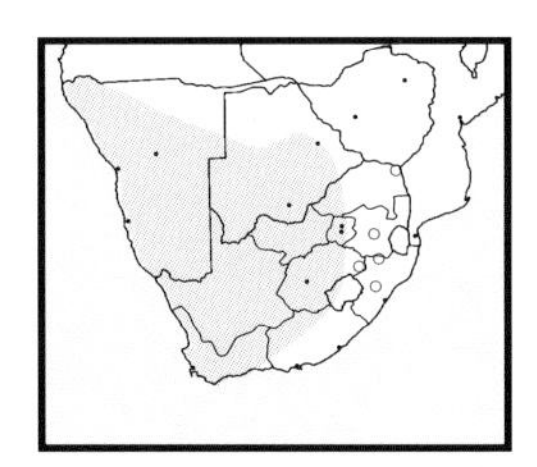

Burchell's Courser *Cursorius rufus* (299) 23 cm

Burchell's Courser might be confused with Temminck's Courser but is larger and usually paler overall, with diminished black markings on the head and a diagnostic blue-grey, not rufous, nape. In flight it further differs by showing a white trailing edge to the secondaries. It has a more upright stance, is longer legged and more slender in appearance than Temminck's Courser. The sexes are alike, and the immature is mottled above and has less well-defined breast markings. Usually silent, it grunts a short 'wark' when flushed. It favours dry, sparsely grassed areas, true desert and semi-arid regions. E

Temminck's Courser *Cursorius temminckii* (300) 20 cm

This is a smaller, darker version of Burchell's Courser, with a more conspicuous black stripe running from behind the eye and no blue-grey on the nape. The black eye-stripe meets on the nape and is narrowly bordered by a white line. Temminck's Courser also shows more extensive black and chestnut on the belly between the legs. In flight it has no white trailing edge to the wings, and its stance is more horizontal. The sexes are alike, and the immature is duller than the adults, with lightly speckled underparts and scalloped upperparts. The call is a grating, rolled 'keerkeer', given mostly in flight. Temminck's Courser favours moister habitats than does Burchell's Courser, and shows a preference for recently burnt areas. R

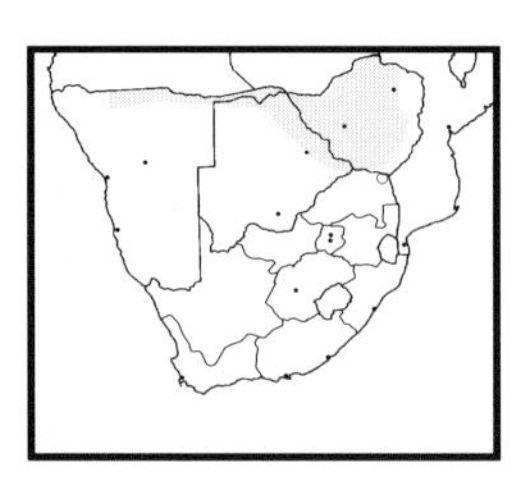

Threebanded Courser *Rhinoptilus cinctus* (302) 28 cm

The characteristic three bands of this species are positioned on both the neck and the throat, and the breast is streaked and bordered by further black and chestnut bands. This bird also has a broad white eyebrow stripe and chestnut-washed cheeks. The back is scaled and scalloped brown and buff, and the legs are greenish. In flight the wings are broad and rounded and the bird shows a contrasting white rump. The sexes are alike, and the immature resembles the adults. During the day this courser crouches, hidden in the shade of low bushes. When disturbed it slowly walks away with backward glances before springing to flight and alighting soon after. The call is a repeated 'kika-kika-kika'. It is found in dry mopane and acacia woodland. R

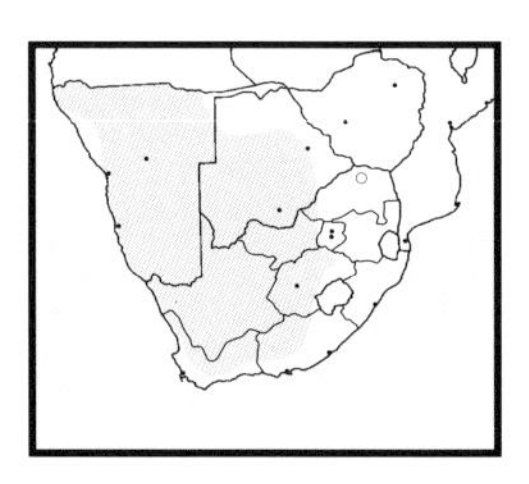

Doublebanded Courser *Smutsornis africanus* (301) 22 cm

Very much paler than the other coursers, the Doublebanded Courser has a very finely scaled back and two distinct, narrow black breast bands which are diagnostic. The legs are pale grey to white and the neck buffy to rust in colour. In flight this bird shows a contrasting chestnut wing panel, darker primaries, and an obvious white rump. The sexes are alike, and the immature has chestnut breast bands. The Doublebanded Courser tends to crouch in open, stony areas, favouring grassy plains and deserts which provide better camouflage. It runs swiftly before springing into jerky flight. The call includes a thin, rising and falling 'teeeu-weee' whistle and repeated 'kee-kee' notes. R

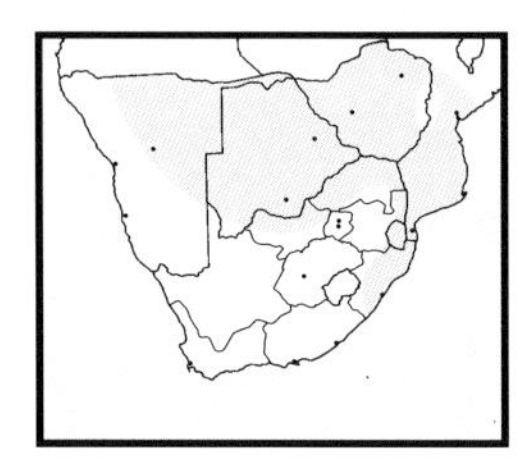

Bronzewinged Courser *Rhinoptilus chalcopterus* (303) 25 cm

This species has a distinctly large head, reminiscent of that of a dikkop (see page 102) . Most shorebird-like in profile, it is the largest courser and has uniform upperparts, unlike the scaled pattern of the Doublebanded Courser and Threebanded Courser. Its most obvious characters are the broad white markings above and behind the eyes, the single narrow black breast band and the dull red legs. The sexes are alike, and the immature has rufous-tipped feathers. The Bronzewinged Courser rests during the day, crouched up under the shade of thick bush and low shrubs. The call, given at night, is a ringing 'ki-kooi'. It is found in various woodlands and savanna. R, S

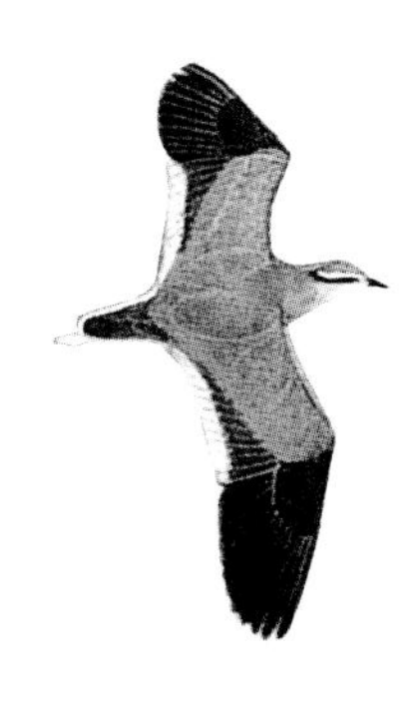

Adult Burchell's Courser

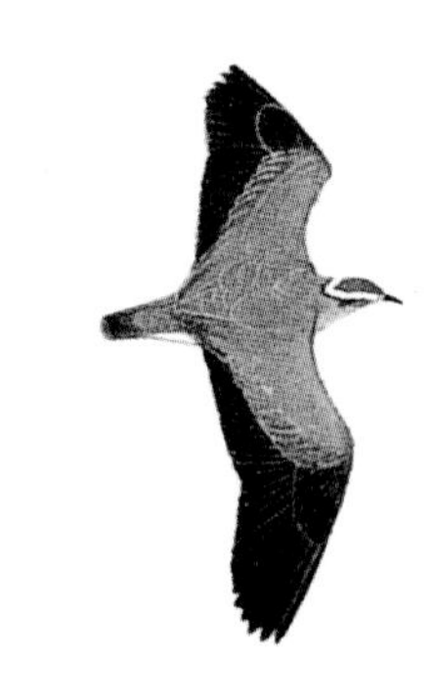

Adult Temminck's Courser

Adult Doublebanded Courser

1. Adult Burchell's Courser
2. Adult Temminck's Courser
3. Adult Threebanded Courser
4. Adult Doublebanded Courser
5. Adult Doublebanded Courser
6. Adult Bronzewinged Courser

1	2
1	3
4	6
5	6

E *endemic* • R *resident* • S *summer visitor*

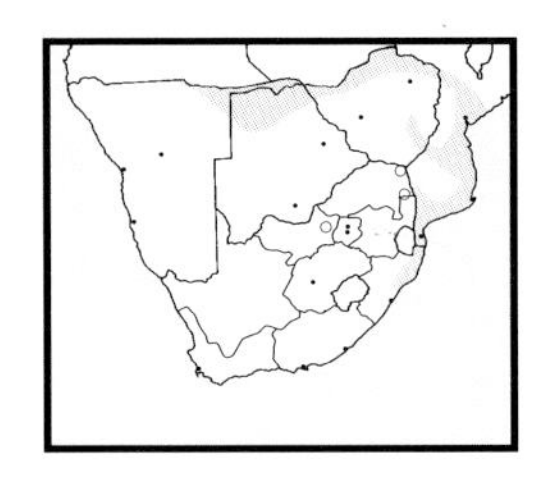

Redwinged Pratincole *Glareola pratincola* (304) 25 cm

This species differs from the Blackwinged Pratincole in having rusty-coloured, not black, wing linings but these can appear black when the bird is backlit by the sun. It is slightly paler on the upperparts and has a thin white trailing edge to the secondaries. Non-breeding adults lack a creamy-coloured throat, and immatures have a scaled back pattern. Redwinged Pratincoles can run fast and have an elegant flight. The call is a repeated 'kik-kik-kik'. They inhabit a variety of wetlands from coastal regions to temporary pans in arid areas, and are usually found in small colonies. Larger flocks may form outside the breeding season. I, S

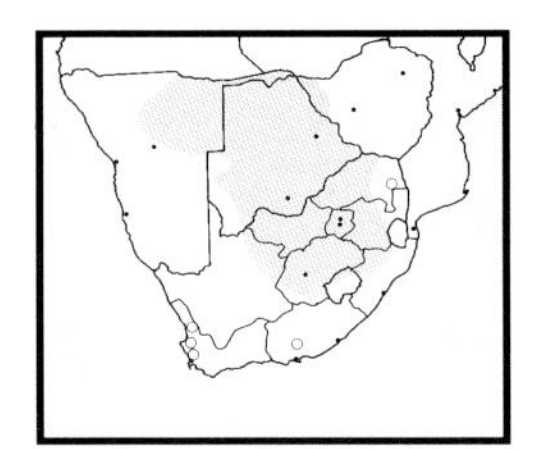

Blackwinged Pratincole *Glareola nordmanni* (305) 25 cm

Very similar to the Redwinged Pratincole, the Blackwinged Pratincole has a more contrasting black and white appearance, and the mantle and upperwing coverts are more uniform with the flight feathers. It differs further in having black, not rusty-coloured, wing linings, and lacks a white trailing edge to the secondaries. The call is a repeated, excited 'pik-pik'. Unlike the Redwinged Pratincole, this bird is often seen over agricultural lands in huge flocks wheeling around. S

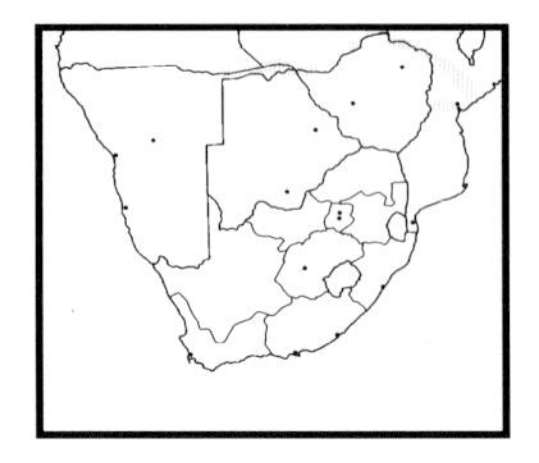

Rock Pratincole *Glareola nuchalis* (306) 18 cm

Almost always found on rivers near rocky areas, this bird at rest has a very distinct capped appearance; it appears tiny when crouching on rocks in mid-river. A white stripe runs from behind the eye on to the nape to form the white collar. The base of the bill and the legs are red. In flight it lacks the deeply forked tail of other pratincoles, and appears very buoyant. The darker upperwings, white rump and undertail, black tail tip and white stripe on the underwing are visible in flight. Immatures have scaly and mottled upperparts. The call is a loud, repeated, plover-like 'kik-kik'. S, R

Skimmers Family Rynchopidae

Skimmers are large, tern-like birds with fairly long, reddish bills. The bill is laterally compressed with an elongated lower mandible. Skimmers have a unique foraging behaviour, flying low over the water with the tip of the lower mandible inserted in the water to detect fish. They are found mostly along large rivers, where they roost and breed colonially on sandbars.

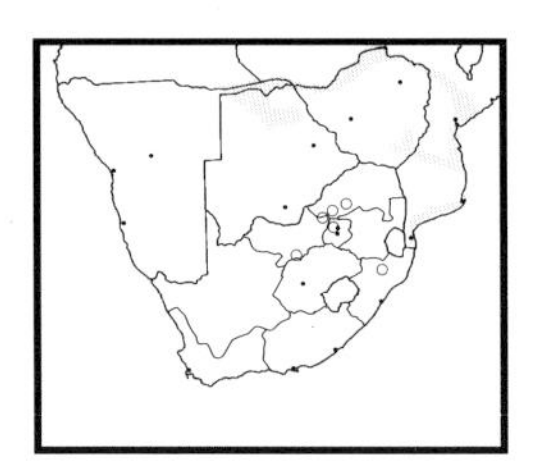

African Skimmer *Rynchops flavirostris* (343) 38 cm

The African Skimmer is sometimes confused with the Caspian Tern (see page 112) because both have large red bills. This species has black, not grey, upperparts and the bill is long and flattened laterally. The immature bird has a dark-tipped red bill and buffy edging to the feathers on the mantle and back. The African Skimmer's flight is extremely buoyant and graceful with slow-motion wing beats. It feeds mostly at dawn and dusk. I, S, R

Adult Redwinged Pratincole (non-breeding)

Adult Blackwinged Pratincole (non-breeding)

1. Adult Redwinged Pratincole (breeding)
2. Adult Redwinged Pratincole (non-breeding)
3. Adult Blackwinged Pratincole
4. Immature Blackwinged Pratincole
5. Adult African Skimmer
6. Adult Rock Pratincole
7. Adult African Skimmer

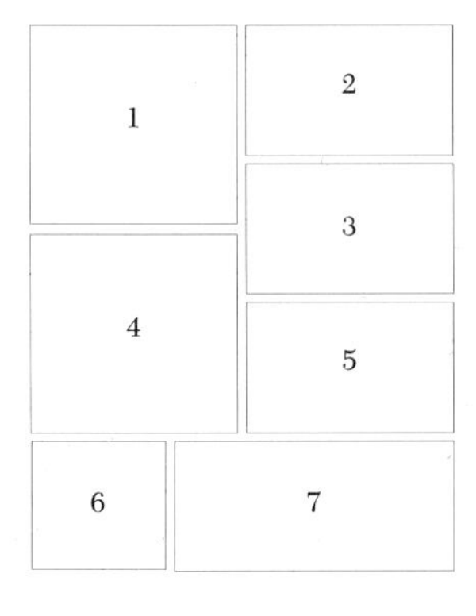

I *intra-African migrant* • S *summer visitor* • R *resident*

Skuas, gulls and terns Family Laridae

Predominantly grey and white birds, with distinct immature plumages, gulls are usually identifiable by their wing and head patterns, and bill and leg coloration. Fork-tailed, terns are on average smaller than gulls and have a more buoyant, agile flight on long, pointed wings; when breeding, many terns display brightly coloured bills and black caps. Skuas are brown-coloured, gull-like birds that obtain much of their food by pirating from gulls and terns, chasing their victims in flight with great agility.

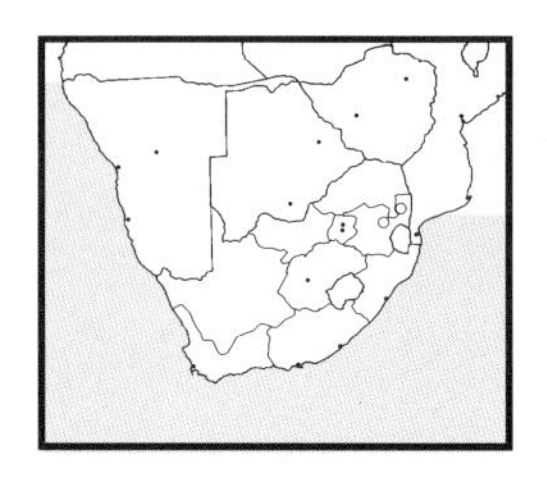

Arctic Skua *Stercorarius parasiticus* (307) 46 cm

The Arctic Skua is lighter in build than the similar Pomarine Skua and has more slender wings and pointed tail projections; it is larger-bodied than the Longtailed Skua, has a more powerful flight, is less buoyant and shows a greater extent of white at the base of the primaries. Immatures are very difficult to tell apart from the immature Pomarine Skua and Longtailed Skua except by size and shape, and from the latter by the greater extent of white on the primary base. With its very fast flight action the Arctic Skua appears falcon-like in motion, chasing terns and small gulls, twisting and jinking to make them disgorge. Usually silent at sea, it favours inshore waters. S

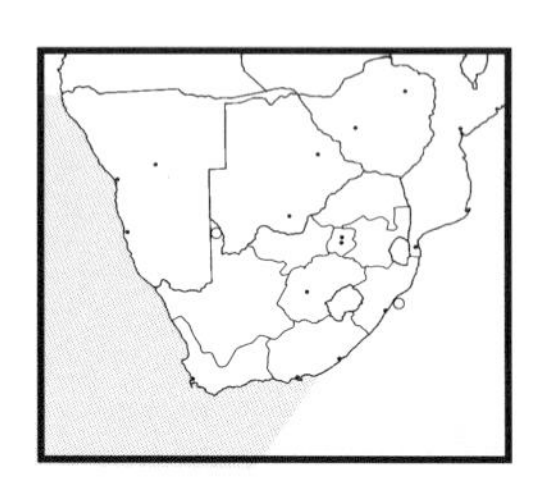

Longtailed Skua *Stercorarius longicaudus* (308) 50 cm

In breeding plumage this small-bodied skua is unmistakable with its exceptionally long central tail projections. Confusable only with the Arctic Skua in nonbreeding and immature plumage, it can be told apart from that species by its overall greyer appearance and little or no white at the primary base. Its flight is infinitely more agile, buoyant and tern-like, and it frequently hovers; it has very long, narrow, pointed wings. At sea it is usually silent. It feeds in a tern-like manner, dipping into the water's surface with its bill, and associates with Sabine's Gull (see page 110). S

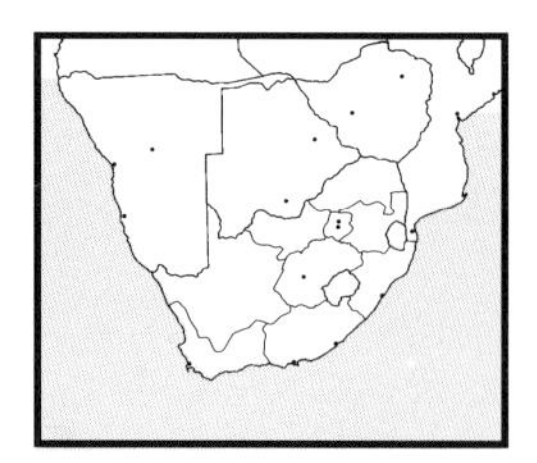

Pomarine Skua *Stercorarius pomarinus* (309) 50 cm

The long, blunt tail projections of this bird are diagnostic. When these are worn or absent, the Pomarine Skua is easily confused with the Arctic Skua but it differs in its larger size, broader-based wings and longer, broader-tailed appearance. Immatures are more heavily barred on the uppertail and undertail coverts than are immature Arctic Skuas. Size, shape and flight mode are the best means of identification at sea. This species is much larger than the Longtailed Skua and smaller and narrower than both the South Polar Skua and the Subantarctic Skua, both of which have more rounded wings. The pale phase of the Pomarine Skua is the most common. Usually silent at sea, it squawks and squeals when scavenging food behind trawlers in more tropical oceans. It harries terns, gulls and other seabirds. S

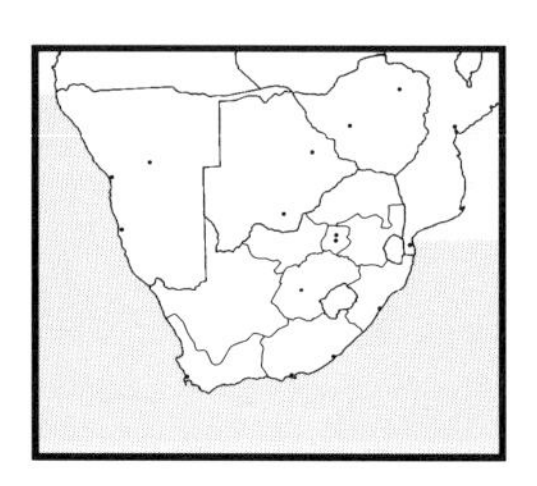

Subantarctic Skua *Catharacta antarctica* (310) 60 cm

The Subantarctic Skua resembles a first-year immature Kelp Gull (see page 110) but has large white patches at the base of the primaries and a dark, not pale, barred rump. It is much larger than other skuas, except for the rarer South Polar Skua from which it differs by being more robust and broader winged, having a larger and thicker-based bill, and lacking the contrasting appearance of the head and body with the darker wings. Usually silent at sea, Subantarctic Skuas utter a soft 'wek-wek' and 'yap-yap' when scavenging at trawlers. Normally found far out at sea, they do also venture closer inshore and scavenge around seal colonies. P, W, S

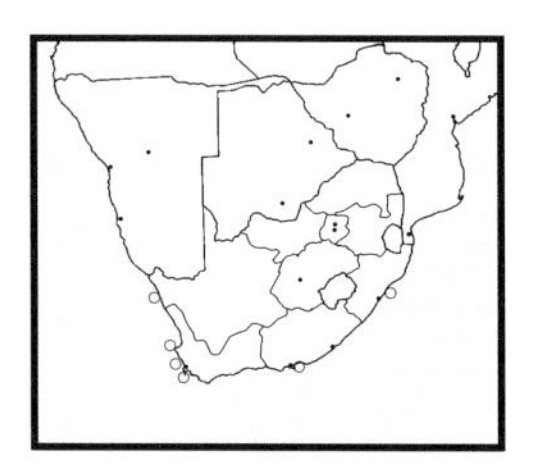

South Polar Skua *Catharacta maccormicki* (311) 53 cm

Very similar in appearance to the Subantarctic Skua but slightly smaller and more slender, the South Polar Skua has a paler head and body which contrast with the darker upperwing and underwing; the Subantarctic Skua can also show a contrasting paler head but this is not uniform with the breast and belly and therefore does not contrast with the underwings. At close range a paler, grizzled area is noticeable at the bill base of the South Polar Skua. Immatures have a very pale buff collar, which is diagnostic. Silent at sea, the South Polar Skua scavenges behind trawlers and harries birds more regularly than do Subantarctic Skuas. P, W

Adult Subantarctic Skua

Adult South Polar Skua

1. Adult Arctic Skua (pale phase, breeding)
2. Adult Arctic Skua (dark phase, breeding)
3. Adult Arctic Skua (pale phase, breeding)
4. Adult Longtailed Skua (breeding)
5. Adult Pomarine Skua (pale phase, non-breeding)
6. Adult Longtailed Skua (breeding)
7. Adult Subantarctic Skua
8. Immature Pomarine Skua
9. Adult South Polar Skua
10. Adult Subantarctic Skua

1		2
3	4	5
6		7
8	9	10

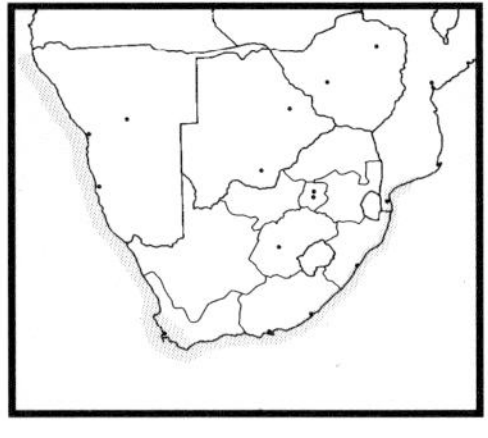
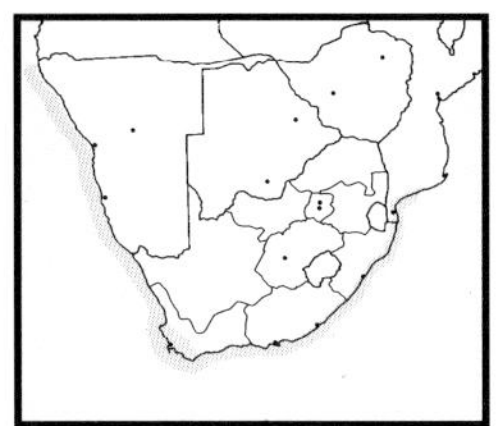

Kelp Gull *Larus dominicanus* (312) 60 cm

The Kelp Gull may be confused with the Lesser Blackbacked Gull but differs by its larger size, more robust and thicker bill, and olive, not yellow, legs and feet; the eye is dark brown, not pale yellow, but this is discernible only at close range. In profile the Kelp Gull has a less slender appearance and the wings do not project far beyond the tail tip. Immatures differ from immature Lesser Blackbacked Gulls only in size and shape and by their grey, not fleshy-pink, legs and toes. First-year immatures could be confused with the Subantarctic Skua (see page 108) or the South Polar Skua (see page 108) but lack white flashes at the primary base and have a pale barred rump. The call is a yelping 'ki-ook' and a short, repeated 'kwok' alarm. Most often seen on inshore waters, this bird also frequents deep-sea trawlers, the open coast, estuaries, harbours and dumps. R

Immature Kelp Gull

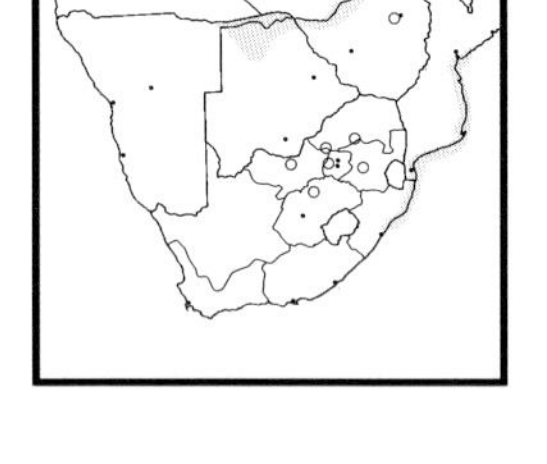

Lesser Blackbacked Gull *Larus fuscus* (313) 55 cm

The adult Lesser Blackbacked Gull closely resembles the adult Kelp Gull but is smaller and very much more slender in profile with the wings projecting well beyond the tail. The legs and feet are bright chrome-yellow, not dull olive-yellow, and the eyes are pale yellow in colour, not dark brown. Immatures differ in size and shape from the immature Kelp Gull and have noticeably thinner legs which are fleshy-pink, sometimes appearing white, not grey or dark grey as in the immature Kelp Gull. Silent in the southern African region, the Lesser Blackbacked Gull is the most frequently encountered large gull inland on freshwater lakes; it also occurs on the east coast. S

Immature Lesser Blackbacked Gull

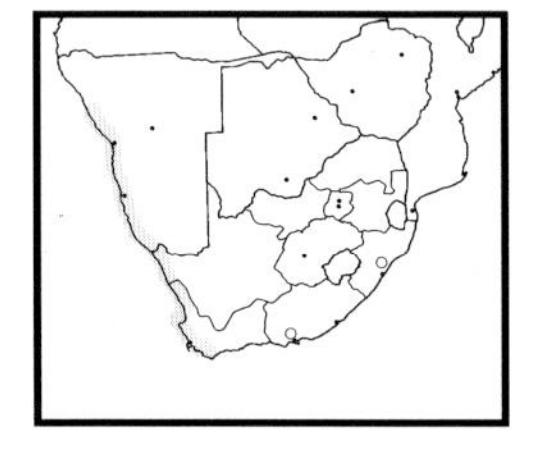

Hartlaub's Gull *Larus hartlaubii* (316) 38 cm

Although most easily confused with the Greyheaded Gull, Hartlaub's Gull never shows the deep grey hood of that species. Some individuals in breeding plumage show a faint grey hood but have dark, not silver-coloured, eyes. Immatures differ from immature Greyheaded Gulls by their smaller size, their more pigeon-chested appearance, all-dark, not dark-tipped pink, bill, and by lacking extensive dark markings on the head. Calls are a drawn-out, rattling 'kaaaarh' and a 'pok-pok'. This is the common small gull on the south and west coasts, frequenting rubbish dumps and fish factories and following machinery ploughing fields. It breeds on offshore islands. E

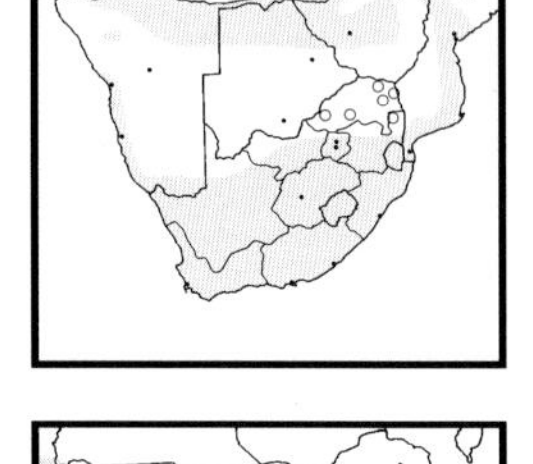

Greyheaded Gull *Larus cirrocephalus* (315) 42 cm

This common inland gull differs from the similar Hartlaub's Gull by its larger size; deep grey, not pale grey, head; silver, not dark-coloured, eyes; and bright red, not dull red, bill, legs and feet. Immatures differ by having extensive dark head markings, a dark-tipped pink (not all-dark) bill and a black tail tip. The call is similar to that of Hartlaub's Gull. This gull breeds in winter on inland wetlands and in some coastal areas, and visits the coast during summer. R

Sabine's Gull *Larus sabini* (318) 34 cm

This small seagoing gull has a diagnostic tri-coloured upperwing pattern and a shallowly forked tail; at close range the yellow tip of the black bill is visible. Its flight is very tern-like and buoyant. Immatures are darker on the upperparts and have a dark nape and neck. Adult birds in breeding plumage have an all-black head. The call has not been recorded in the southern African region. Sabine's Gull is not often seen close to shore and is rarely seen on land but occurs in small flocks far out to sea. S

1. Adult Kelp Gull
2. Immature Kelp Gull
3. Adult Kelp Gulls
4. Adult Hartlaub's Gull
5. Adult Greyheaded Gull
6. Immature Greyheaded Gull
7. Adult Lesser Blackbacked Gull
8. Immature Lesser Blackbacked Gull
9. Immature Sabine's Gull

1	2	
3	4	
5	6	
7	8	9

R *resident* • S *summer visitor* • E *endemic*

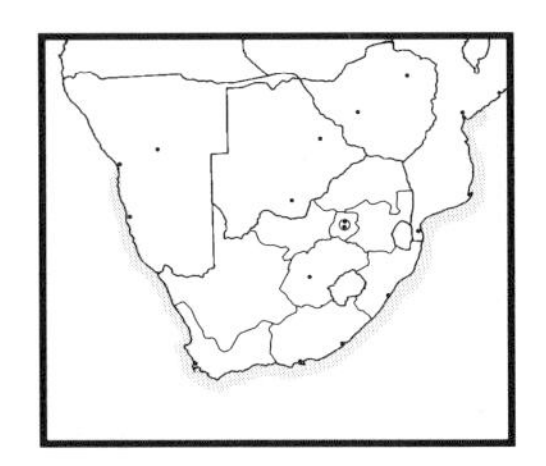

Swift Tern *Sterna bergii* (324) 46 cm

This large coastal and pelagic tern might be confused with the much larger Caspian Tern and the smaller Lesser Crested Tern. The main differences between it and the former is its yellow, thinner bill and the lack of black wing tips. It differs from the latter species also by its yellow, not orange, bill and by its darker mantle and upperwings. Immatures are much darker on the upperparts with barring and paler feather margins, and have a duskier yellow bill and sometimes yellow legs and feet. The flight is powerful with deep wing beats; these birds indulge in graceful, follow-my-leader display acrobatics. The call is a 'kree-aaak'; immatures give a thin, vibrating whistle. Frequenting coastal waters to sometimes well offshore, the Swift Tern breeds on offshore islands. R

Immature Swift Tern

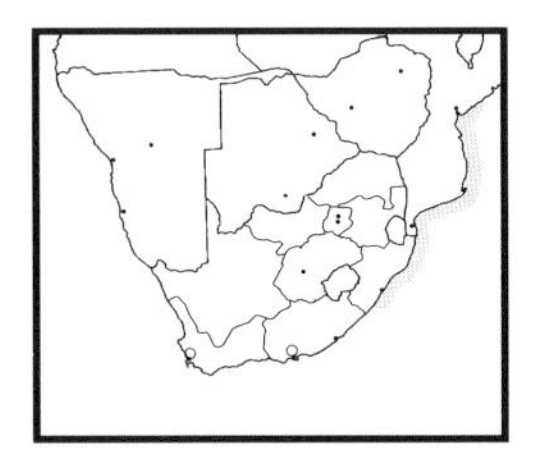

Lesser Crested Tern *Sterna bengalensis* (325) 38 cm

The bright orange to coral-orange bill, paler grey back and smaller size differentiates this species from the Swift Tern. It is very much smaller in size and build than the Caspian Tern and its bill is slender, not thick and chunky. Immatures resemble immature Swift Terns but can be distinguished by the bill which is orange-yellow, not dirty yellow. Silent in our area, the Lesser Crested Tern is a coastal and offshore bird, preferring large estuaries and coastal lagoons. It is usually seen in small numbers. S

Immature Caspian Tern

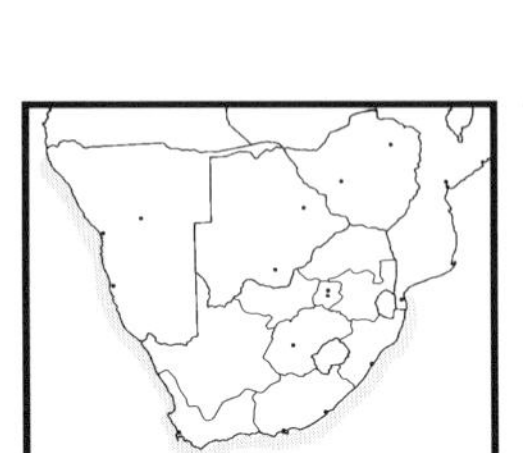

Sandwich Tern *Sterna sandvicensis* (326) 40 cm

Similar to the Lesser Crested Tern in size and shape, this bird has a black, not orange, bill and a paler back; in mixed flocks of terns it appears the whitest of all the birds. At closer range the diagnostic yellow tip of the bill can be discerned; beware of confusion with the Common Tern (see page 114), some of which have transparent bill tips. Larger than both the Common Tern and the Arctic Tern (see page 114), it also has a paler back than those two species. In breeding plumage the breast has a pinkish flush and the cap is all black with a shaggy crest. The call is a harsh 'kee-raaak', similar to that of the Swift Tern, although this tern is usually silent in the region. It is found along inshore waters, estuaries and bays in mixed flocks. S

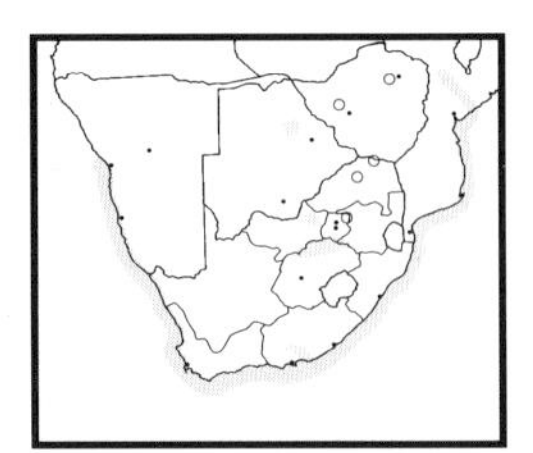

Caspian Tern *Hydroprogne caspia* (322) 50 cm

This very large, gull-sized tern is unmistakable with its large, bright red bill. In flight at long range it can be told apart from the Swift Tern by its black wing tips and slower, more leisurely flight action. Non-breeding adults and immatures have dark-tipped orange bills, and immatures have well-patterned backs. When feeding, the Caspian Tern dives for fish but also skims the water with its thick red bill. For this reason it is sometimes mistaken for the African Skimmer (see page 106), but that species may be differentiated by its black, not grey, upperparts. The call is a raucous, grating 'kraaaak'. Frequenting coastal and inland lakes, it is common in small numbers on the coast but is rare inland. R

1. Adult Swift Tern (breeding)
2. Adult Swift Tern (non-breeding)
3. Adult Lesser Crested Tern (non-breeding)
4. Adult Lesser Crested Tern (non-breeding)
5. Adult Sandwich Tern (non-breeding)
6. Adult Caspian Tern (breeding)
7. Adult Sandwich Tern (breeding)
8. Adult Caspian Tern (non-breeding)

1	2
3	4
5	6
7	8

R *resident* • S *summer visitor*

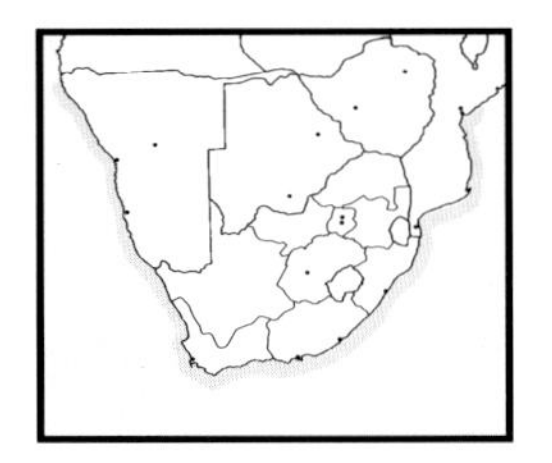

Common Tern *Sterna hirundo* (327) 33 cm

This is the most abundant tern in the large coastal gatherings of these birds. Most closely resembling the Arctic Tern and the Antarctic Tern, the Common Tern stands slightly taller than those two species, has longer legs, and a slightly longer and very slightly downcurved bill, quite unlike the short, pointy bills of the other two species. In flight it shows a grey, not white, rump and darker edges to the primary tips. The sexes are alike, and immatures resemble non-breeding adults but have dark carpal bars. Although rarely seen in breeding plumage in the region, the Common Tern then shows a red bill with a dark tip; the breeding Roseate Tern, which has a similar bill colour, is overall very much paler, has a longer and more deeply forked tail and a pinkish flush on the underparts. The call is a short, sharp 'kik-kik', given mostly in flight. It frequents open sea and coastal regions and is rarely seen inland. S

Arctic Tern *Sterna paradisaea* (328) 33 cm

This species can be told apart from the Common Tern by its much shorter legs; it appears almost legless at rest. Its bill is short and more pointed and has a distinctly spiky appearance. In flight it shows a white, not grey, rump, has fewer dark edges on the primary tips, and when seen from below the wings appear translucent. The Antarctic Tern also has short legs but has a thicker-based bill which is normally dull red and black, and it has much darker primary edgings. In flight the Arctic Tern is overall much paler than either the Common Tern or the Antarctic Tern. The call is a sharp 'kit-kit', higher pitched than that of the Common Tern. This bird frequents coastal regions but tends to be pelagic in range. P, S

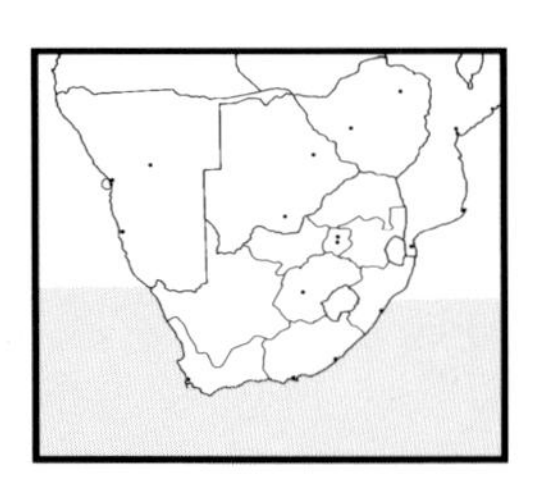

Antarctic Tern *Sterna vittata* (329) 34 cm

This bird differs from the Common Tern and the Arctic Tern by its thicker-based and more robust bill, heavier build and darker overall colouring. In breeding plumage it is dark grey with a black cap and a white line on the cheeks separating the cap from the underparts; in this plumage it could be mistaken for a Whiskered Tern (see page 116) but that is a freshwater species and has a dark, not white, rump and a less forked tail. The bill is normally black but many birds show variable red and black bills. In non-breeding plumage the Antarctic Tern has varying amounts of grey on the underparts and a grizzled forehead. The sexes are alike, and immatures are barred buff and brown on the back. This tern roosts ashore on beaches and rocky headlands and ranges far out to sea. W

Roseate Tern *Sterna dougallii* (330) 36 cm

Much paler than the similar-sized Common Tern, Arctic Tern and Antarctic Tern, the pinkish flush on the breast of this bird is diagnostic. When breeding it is pinker on the underparts and has an orange, dark-tipped bill and a long, white, forked tail. The Sandwich Tern (see page 112) is also very white on the back but is a larger bird and has an all-black bill with a yellow tip. The sexes are alike, and immatures are barred brown and buff on the back. In flight the wing beats of the Roseate Tern are more clipped and rapid than those of similar-sized terns, and the tail appears extra long. Calls are a harsh 'keraack' and a grating 'aaarh'. These birds favour open coastline, sandy shores and rocky offshore islands. R, S

Sooty Tern *Sterna fuscata* (332) 44 cm

This large tern is conspicuously black and white. The sexes are similar, and immatures are a sooty blackish brown with a white vent. At sea its flight is powerful yet graceful, and flocks wheeling over waves flicker white-black-white as they twist and turn. The call is a loud, far-carrying 'weka-wek', often heard at night as the birds fly over ships at sea. Sooty Terns are frequently found inshore after the passage of cyclones or far out to sea in more tropical waters. They are often harassed and chased by other seabirds. P, S, W

Adult Common Tern (non-breeding)

Adult Arctic Tern (non-breeding)

Immature Antarctic Tern

1. Adult Common Tern (non-breeding)
2. Adult Arctic Tern (breeding)
3. Adult Arctic Tern (breeding)
4. Adult Antarctic Tern (breeding)
5. Adult Roseate Tern (breeding)
6. Adult Antarctic Tern (non-breeding)
7. Adult Sooty Tern

1	2	
3	4	
5	6	7

S *summer visitor* • P *passage visitor* • W *winter visitor* • R *resident*

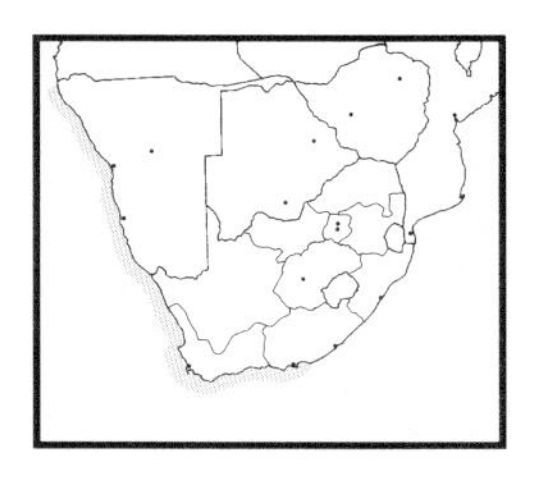

Damara Tern *Sterna balaenarum* (334) 23 cm

Similar in appearance to the Little Tern, the Damara Tern can be distinguished in breeding plumage by its complete black cap and black bill; the Little Tern has a dark-tipped yellow bill and a white forehead. The non-breeding bird can be recognized by its longer, very slightly decurved bill and uniformly darker upperparts; the Little Tern has a white rump and tail. The flight action of the Damara Tern is jinking with rapid wing beats and frequent hovering. It plunge-dives with speed and flies straight up to hover again if the prey item is missed. The calls are often the first sign of its presence in an area, and comprise a short, high-pitched 'tsit-tsit' and a harsher 'kidik kidik'. Occurring in small numbers and breeding in very loose colonies in desert regions, Damara Terns frequent open shorelines with a wide surf zone, salt pans and estuaries. S, BE

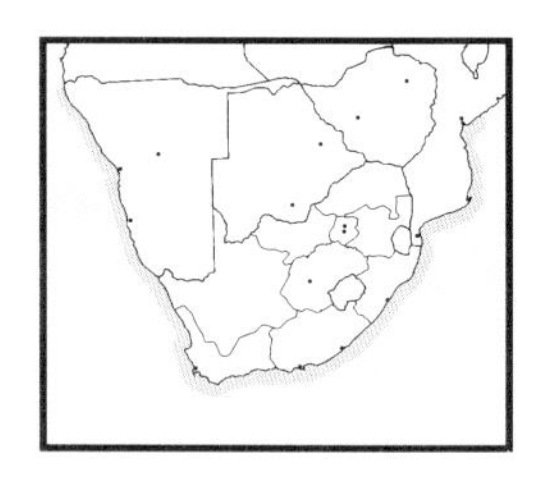

Little Tern *Sterna albifrons* (335) 23 cm

Easily identified when in breeding plumage by its white forehead, black-tipped yellow bill and yellow legs and feet, the Little Tern is similar in size to the tiny Damara Tern. In non-breeding plumage it can be told apart from that species by its grey back which contrasts with a white rump and tail; in this plumage the bill is black but shorter and straighter than that of the Damara Tern. The sexes are alike. The flight action is also similar to that of the Damara Tern but the Little Tern feeds well offshore and rarely in the surf zone. The call is a short 'eke-kek'. It roosts in sometimes large flocks but otherwise occurs in small numbers when feeding. S

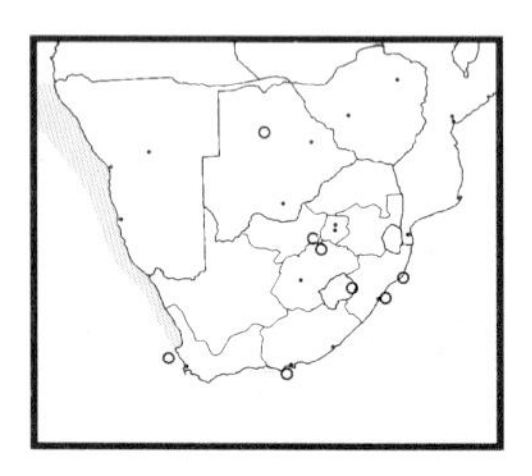

Black Tern *Chlidonias niger* (337) 22 cm

In breeding plumage the Black Tern is easily distinguished from the similar Whitewinged Tern by its sooty all-black body, dark grey, not white, wing coverts and whitish, not black, wing linings. It is seen in our region mainly in non-breeding plumage, when it differs from the Whitewinged Tern by being darker overall with a uniform dark mantle, rump and tail; the non-breeding Whitewinged Tern has a contrasting pale rump and paler tail. Further, the Black Tern has a dark 'thumb print' on the shoulder and a greater extent of black on the head. The call is a soft 'kik-kik' but the bird is usually silent when in the region. It occurs mostly at sea where, in flocks over the ocean, it appears like a small petrel (see page 16), and is rarely seen inland or on the coast. S

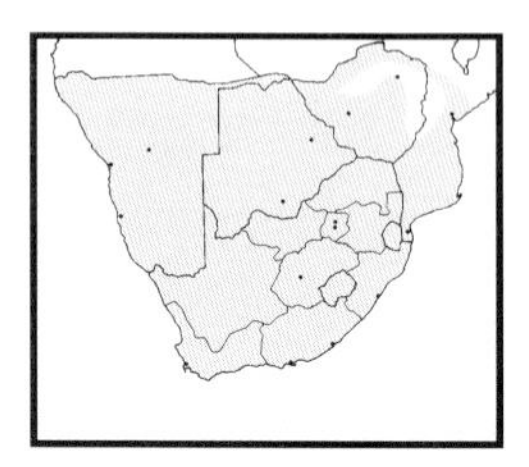

Whitewinged Tern *Chlidonias leucopterus* (339) 23 cm

The breeding plumage of this species is striking, the black underparts of the body and wing linings contrasting with the silver and grey upperparts. In non-breeding plumage it can be distinguished from the Black Tern by its lack of 'thumb prints' on the shoulders, its less uniform upperparts – the back contrasting with a pale grey rump and tail – and by the smaller amount of black on the head. It very often shows a black and white patterned underwing, which is never seen in the Black Tern. The sexes are alike, and immatures resemble the non-breeding adults. The flight is very agile and butterfly-like; the birds often dip their bills into water but never dive to retrieve food. The call is a short 'kek-kek'. Whitewinged Terns occur mostly over freshwater wetlands but occasionally may be found in estuaries. S

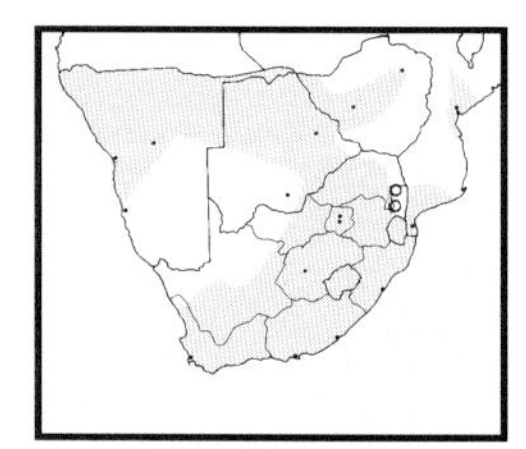

Whiskered Tern *Chlidonias hybridus* (338) 25 cm

The Whiskered Tern differs from other 'marsh' terns in breeding plumage by its conspicuous white cheeks which separate the black cap from the grey underparts. In non-breeding plumage it differs from the Whitewinged Tern by its thicker and heavier bill, its whiter head (with less black), and by lacking a white wedge behind the ear. It is larger and paler overall than either the Black Tern or the Whitewinged Tern. The flight action is also stronger and more powerful, and it frequently dives for food. The call is a harsh, nasal 'zzzezz'. The Whiskered Tern frequents varied freshwater areas, from small farm dams choked with floating weed to lakes and flooded grasslands, and is rarely seen on the coast. S, R

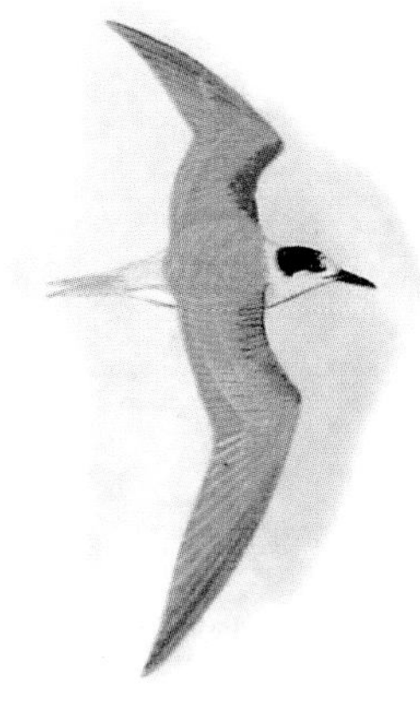

Adult Damara Tern (non-breeding)

Adult Little Tern (non-breeding)

1. Adult Damara Tern (breeding)
2. Adult Little Tern (non-breeding)
3. Adult Little Tern (breeding)
4. Adult Black Tern (breeding)
5. Adult Black Tern (non-breeding)
6. Adult Whitewinged Tern (breeding)
7. Adult Whitewinged Tern (non-breeding)
8. Adult Whiskered Tern (breeding)
9. Adult Whiskered Tern (non-breeding)

1		2
3	4	
5	6	
7	8	9

Sandgrouse Family Pteroclidae

Medium-sized, desert, semi-desert and dry savanna-dwelling birds with cryptically coloured plumage, sandgrouse fly considerable distances daily to reach their water sources (each species preferring different drinking times), sometimes gathering in thousands to drink. On the ground they look like very short-legged francolins (see pages 70-72) but in flight they resemble swiftly flying doves (see page 122).

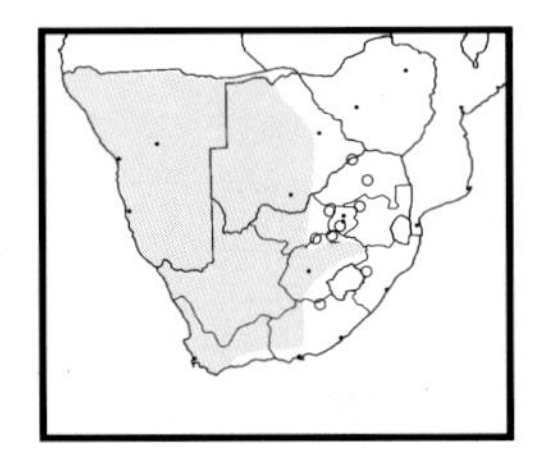

Namaqua Sandgrouse *Pterocles namaqua* (344) 25 cm

This bird flies overhead at great speed and is the only local sandgrouse that has a long pointed tail in this silhouette. When seen shuffling along on the ground the male has double, chestnut and white breast bands which might cause confusion with the male Doublebanded Sandgrouse, but it differs by lacking the white and black markings on the head and by its long, pointed tail. Females and immatures are barred and streaked buff and brown. In the morning the Namaqua Sandgrouse flies in tightly packed flocks to waterholes and alights some distance away before proceeding to drink. The diagnostic call is a clear 'kalke-ven' given in flight, and it utters various growling noises when at waterholes. It is found in very dry conditions in desert and semi-desert regions on gravel and stony plains and thinly grassed areas. It avoids wooded areas and feeds in loose groups or pairs. NE

Burchell's Sandgrouse *Pterocles burchelli* (345) 25 cm

The overall cinnamon-reddish colour, finely spotted with white both above and below, identifies this sandgrouse. The male and female are alike but the male has a grey face and the female a yellow face. In flight it has a dumpy appearance, lacks the long pointed tail of the Namaqua Sandgrouse and shows reddish wing linings. It flies to drink at waterholes in the mornings, sometimes with Namaqua Sandgrouse, and will also sometimes drink in the evenings with Doublebanded Sandgrouse. The call is a soft, mellow 'chup-chup or 'chooop-chooop' uttered in flight and at waterholes. Burchell's Sandgrouse is found in semi-desert areas, especially the Kalahari region. NE

Doublebanded Sandgrouse *Pterocles bicinctus* (347) 25 cm

This small, buffy sandgrouse has a double, black and white breast band and diagnostic black and white forehead markings. The female is similar to the female Namaqua Sandgrouse but is more vermiculated on the back and has a yellow patch around the eye. Most often encountered sitting on dust roads, these birds shuffle slowly away when approached; when flushed they spring straight up and utter their 'chuck-chuck' alarm call. Habitually they fly to drink just after sunset, whistling their quiet 'whee whee-chweelee' call. They occur in more wooded areas, from acacia savanna to mopane woodland. R

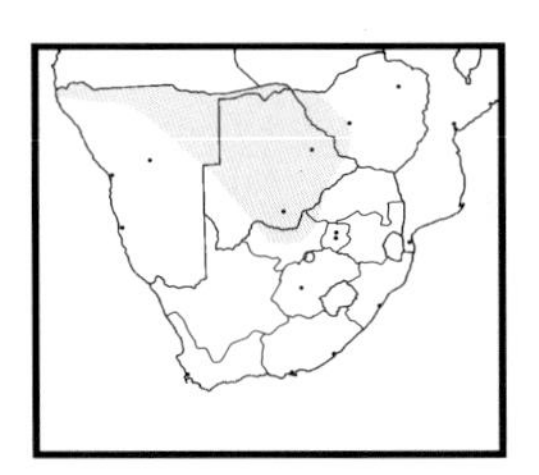

Yellowthroated Sandgrouse *Pterocles gutturalis* (346) 30 cm

This chunky sandgrouse, larger than any other sandgrouse in the region, has a diagnostic yellow throat with a black throat band. Females and immatures are very streaked and mottled black and buff above with a pale buffy face and throat. In flight Yellowthroated Sandgrouse are broad winged, have a powerful flight action and show much darker underparts than other, smaller sandgrouse. They habitually drink at waterholes in the afternoons. The call is a 'twee-twee' given in flight and a deeper 'aw-aw' with the first syllable higher pitched. These uncommon birds occur on wide-open grassy areas, more open grassed woodland and old agricultural lands. R

Male Namaqua Sandgrouse

Male Burchell's Sandgrouse

Male Doublebanded Sandgrouse

1. Male Namaqua Sandgrouse
2. Female Namaqua Sandgrouse
3. Male Burchell's Sandgrouse
4. Female Burchell's Sandgrouse
5. Male Doublebanded Sandgrouse
6. Female Doublebanded Sandgrouse
7. Male Yellowthroated Sandgrouse
8. Female Yellowthroated Sandgrouse

1	2
3	4
5	6
7	8

NE *near endemic* • R *resident*

Pigeons and doves Family Columbidae

The term 'pigeon' normally refers to the larger species and 'dove' to the smaller members of this large family. Most have distinctive calls and many are identifiable by their tail patterns. All domestic pigeons are descendants of the Rock Dove of the northern hemisphere. Most species are granivorous but some eat fruit.

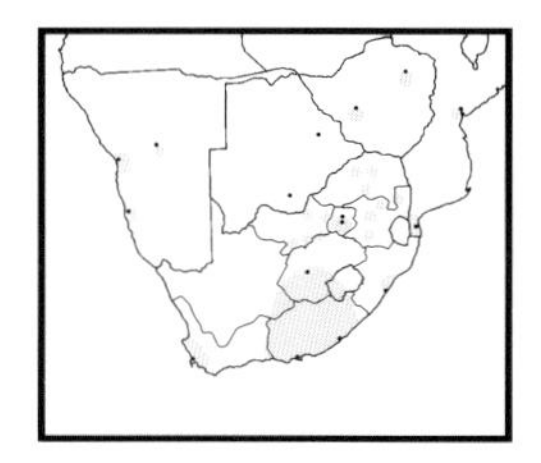

Feral Pigeon *Columba livia* (348) 33 cm

The Feral Pigeon has a wide variety of plumage types, the most common being grey and black with two black bars on the secondaries and a broad white rump, visible in flight. A green, oily sheen is visible on the neck. Males puff out their chests when displaying; females are duller than the males. Occurring in most cities but rarer in small towns, these birds are fearless, taking hand-proffered food, and will breed on man-made structures such as building ledges and bridges. Tight flocks seen away from cities are mostly racing pigeons, but these birds are also kept as a food source in rural areas. The call is a typical dove-like cooing. The Feral Pigeon is becoming a pest in larger cities. R

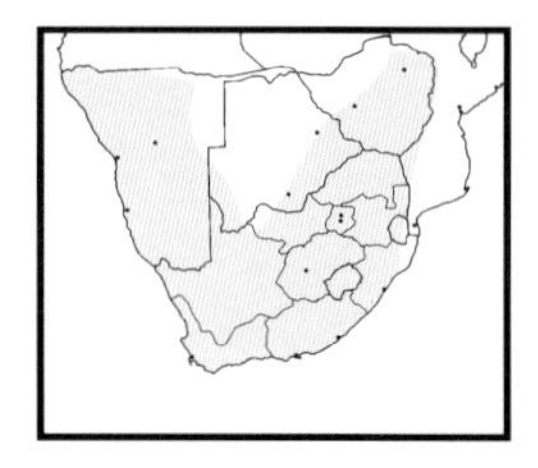

Rock Pigeon *Columba guinea* (349) 33 cm

Unlikely to be confused with the Feral Pigeon if seen clearly, this bird has a cinnamon to brownish back spotted with white, and a broad patch of bare red skin around the eye. The sexes are alike, and immatures lack the red on the face. In flight a flock is uniformly coloured, unlike flocks of Feral Pigeons which together appear in a range different greys, black and white. The Rock Pigeon could be confused with the Rameron Pigeon but is smaller and greyer and has red, not yellow, skin around eye and red, not yellow, legs and feet. Calls are a deep, almost owl-like 'hooo-hooo-hooo' and a softer 'cooo-cooo-cooo'. These birds frequent mountains, cliffs, gorges, and any suitable rocky area, and have adapted to towns and cities where they nest on building ledges alongside Feral Pigeons. R

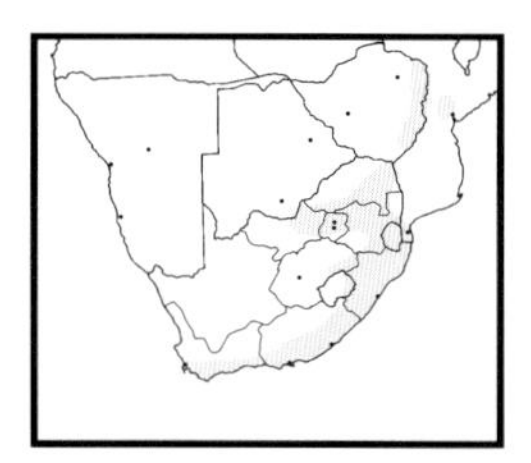

Rameron Pigeon *Columba arquatrix* (350) 42 cm

This very large pigeon shows a distinctive yellow bill, yellow bare skin around the eyes and yellow legs and feet. In flight the legs and toes, if not tucked under the vent feathers, show up well against the dark background. The general colour of the bird is a dark maroon with fine white spots concentrated on the wing coverts, breast and belly. Flocks seen over forests have a heavy, laboured flight with slower wing beats than those of smaller doves. The call is a low, harsh 'cooo'. Rameron Pigeons favour large tracts of evergreen forests, usually at higher altitudes, and sit conspicuously in the early morning on exposed dead trees above the forest canopy. R

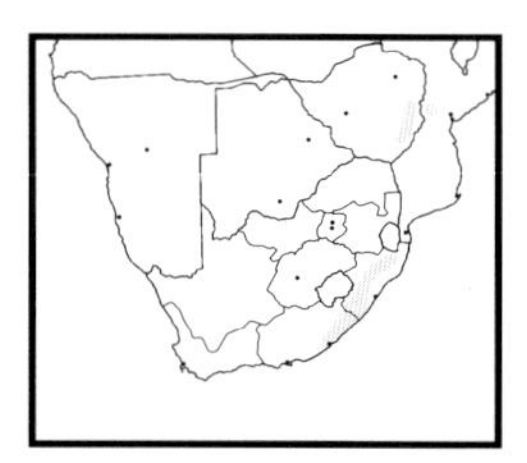

Delegorgue's Pigeon *Columba delegorguei* (351) 30 cm

In flight Delegorgue's Pigeon may be separated from the Rameron Pigeon by its very obvious smaller size and faster flight, by lacking the yellow bill and legs and by showing a faint, paler tail tip. The Redeyed Dove (see page 122) is paler and longer-tailed than this species and shows an obvious broad grey tip to the undertail. The broad white hind collar seen on male Delegorgue's Pigeons is diagnostic. Females and immatures lack the white hind collar and have a paler head and upper breast. Most often seen flying swiftly over the forest canopy, these pigeons also regularly sunbathe in the early mornings on exposed branches of the canopy. The call is a low, mournful 'glu-glu-glu-glu' which descends and quickens in tempo towards the end. They are seen singly or in small groups in evergreen forests. R

Adult Rock Pigeon

Adult Rameron Pigeon

Adult Delegorgue's Pigeon

1. Adult Rock Pigeon
2. Adult Rameron Pigeon
3. Adult Rameron Pigeon
4. Adult Feral Pigeon
5. Delagorgue's Pigeon

R *resident*

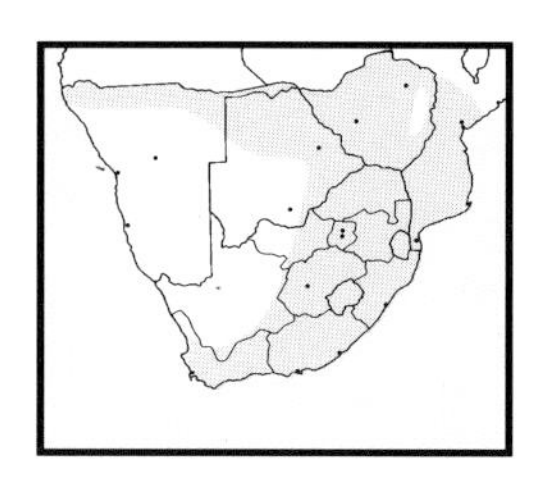

Redeyed Dove *Streptopelia semitorquata* (352) 35 cm

The largest and darkest of the 'ringneck' doves, the Redeyed Dove differs from the Cape Turtle Dove by its pinkish head, grey forehead and its red eye surrounded by bare red skin. In flight it has a dark band across the uppertail and a greyish-white tip to the undertail, but has no white outer tail tips. It differs from the Mourning Dove by lacking the grey head and yellow eye of that species. The sexes are alike, and immatures lack the black hind collar, have grey, not red, skin around the eyes and have buff barring on the mantle. The call is usually a dove-like 'coo-coo, kook-co-co'. Seen singly or in flocks, the Redeyed Dove has adapted well to suburbia from its normal forest and riverine forest habitats. R

Adult Redeyed Dove

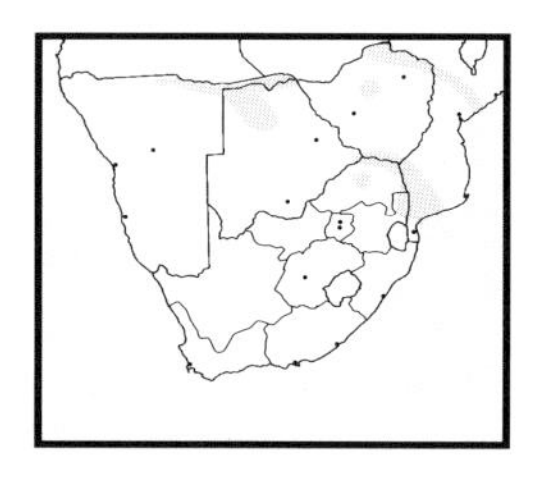

Mourning Dove *Streptopelia decipiens* (353) 30 cm

This species is much pinker than the Cape Turtle Dove and has an obviously grey head, and a yellow eye with bare red skin around it. It differs from the Redeyed Dove by its smaller size, generally much paler appearance, grey head and yellow, not red, eye. In flight it has a tail pattern similar to that of the Cape Turtle Dove but is much darker with less white on the outer tail tips. The sexes are alike, and immatures lack the hind collar and are greyer with buff barring on the mantle. The call is a soft 'krrrtt-cooooo'. Mourning Doves are found in moist habitats, often near water and usually along river courses. R

Adult Cape Turtle Dove

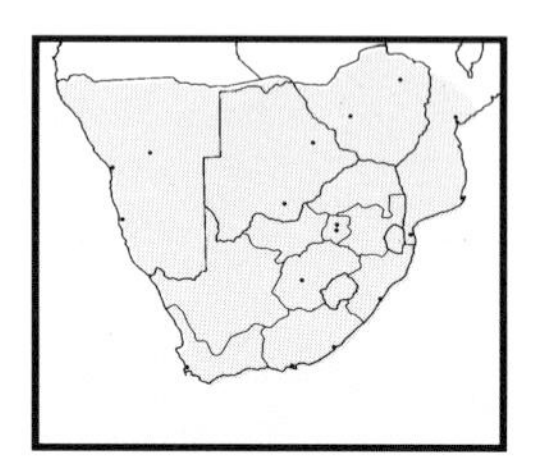

Cape Turtle Dove *Streptopelia capicola* (354) 28 cm

A smaller and overall greyer dove than either the Redeyed Dove or the Mourning Dove, this bird lacks the bare red skin around the eyes of those species and has brown, not red or yellow, eyes. In flight it shows white tips to the outer tail feathers from above and a broad white tip to the undertail. It is larger and greyer than the Laughing Dove and in flight has less extensive white on the uppertail. The sexes are alike, and immatures are duller than the adults. Large flocks gather at waterholes in more arid regions and adhere to regular flight paths and drinking times. The call is a well-known dove sound, 'kuk-cooo-kuk'. It occurs in virtually all habitats in the region except dense forests and coastal regions in the northeast. R

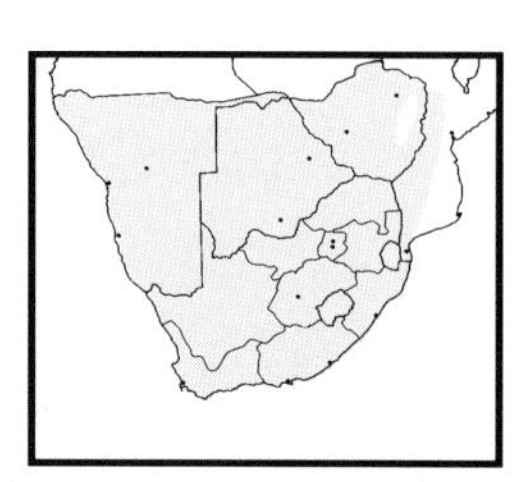

Laughing Dove *Streptopelia senegalensis* (355) 26 cm

The Laughing Dove differs from all the 'ringneck' doves by being smaller in size and lacking a black hind collar. Its general colour is reddish brown with contrasting blue-grey wing coverts. The pinkish breast is freckled with fine black spots and streaks although this is variable. It appears longer tailed and shorter winged than the other doves, and in flight shows white outer tail feathers and, except for the central feathers, white tips to the tail. The sexes are similar but females are smaller and duller than the males; immatures are duller than the adults. The call is a series of rising and falling, cooing notes, 'ooo-coooc-coooc-coo-coo'. It inhabits a variety of regions but avoids dense forests and true deserts. R

Adult Laughing Dove

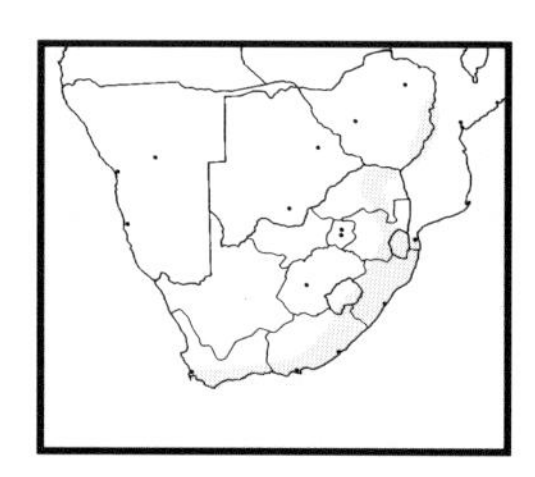

Cinnamon Dove *Aplopelia larvata* (360) 26 cm

The grey face, cinnamon body colour and darker back identify this species if seen clearly. The sexes are similar but females are duller than the males; immatures are drabber than the adults. The most furtive of all our doves, it usually explodes off the forest floor when disturbed and clatters away, managing to keep a tree trunk between itself and the watcher. The call is a deep, rough 'hooo-hoooo'; the calling male will respond to a recording of this. The Cinnamon Dove inhabits evergreen forests in coastal, montane and riverine areas; it also frequents exotic plantations. R

1. Adult Redeyed Dove
2. Adult Mourning Dove
3. Adult Cape Turtle Dove
4. Adult Laughing Dove
5. Adult Cape Turtle Dove
6. Adult Cinnamon Dove

1	2
3	4
5	6

R *resident*

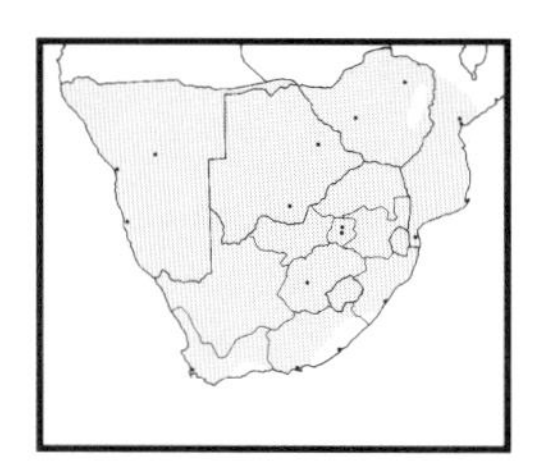

Namaqua Dove *Oena capensis* (356) 28 cm

Male Namaqua Doves differ from females and immatures by having a black face and throat and a yellow bill. In its rapid, twisting flight the extra-long tail of this species is very noticeable, as are the bright chestnut wings. It shuffles around on the ground when feeding, appearing almost legless, and the head is cocked back and forth. It attends waterholes, sometimes in large flocks. The call is a soft, two-syllabled hoot, the first syllable sharp and the second longer. The Namaqua Dove occurs in varied habitats from desert to grasslands and thornveld but avoids dense, evergreen forests. R

Male Namaqua Dove

Greenspotted Dove *Turtur chalcospilos* (358) 22 cm

This small greyish-brown dove has two lines of large iridescent green spots on the secondaries and tertials but these are not always obvious. Greenspotted Doves differ from the very similar Bluespotted Dove by having an all-brown, unmarked bill and green, not blue, spots on the wings. In flight both show russet wings and two bars on the rump but this species is paler and has more contrasting upperparts. The call is a series of descending 'du-du-du' notes which speed up towards the end and are higher pitched than those given by the Bluespotted Dove. The Greenspotted Dove occurs in varied woodland and savanna where its call is a familiar sound during the heat of the day; it normally avoids the evergreen forests frequented by the Bluespotted Dove. R

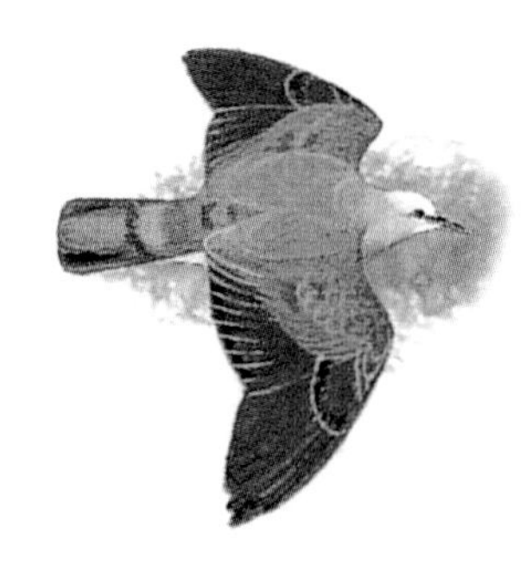

Adult Greenspotted Dove

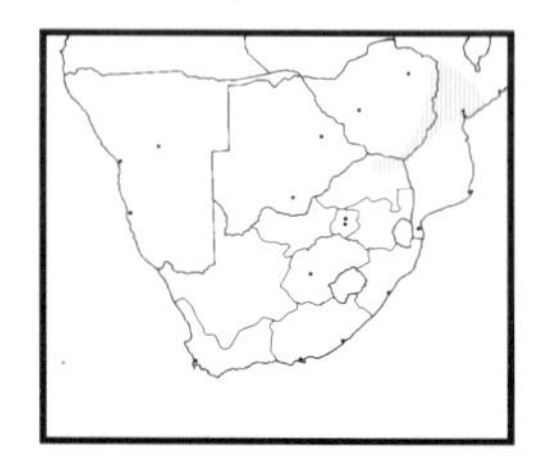

Bluespotted Dove *Turtur afer* (357) 22 cm

This small dove may be confused with the Greenspotted Dove but the two species rarely occur together and live in different habitats. The Bluespotted Dove has a yellow tip to its bill (although this is not always easy to see) and small, inconspicuous blue, not large and green, spots on the wings. In flight this species is darker overall and is more uniformly coloured on the upperparts. The sexes are alike. The call is a slower, lower-pitched series of descending 'du-du' notes than those given by the Greenspotted Dove. The Bluespotted Dove occurs in more moist evergreen forests than the Greenspotted Dove. R

Tambourine Dove *Turtur tympanistria* (359) 22 cm

Similar in size to the Greenspotted Dove and the Bluespotted Dove, the Tambourine Dove shares the russet wings and two-barred-rump characters of those two species, but differs by having a very obvious white face and white underparts. Females and immatures have darker underparts but still show the white face. These doves occur in thick tangles of riverine and evergreen forests where they are difficult to observe; they are seen mostly in flight. The call is a series of 'du-du' notes, similar to those given by the Greenspotted Dove and the Bluespotted Dove but the notes are evenly pitched and do not descend the scale. R

Adult Tambourine Dove

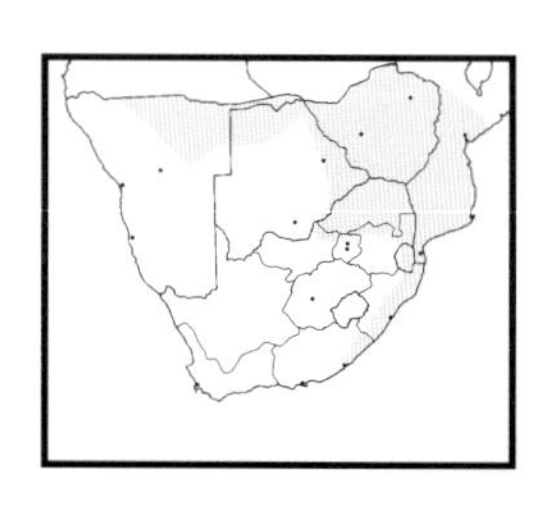

African Green Pigeon *Treron calva* (361) 30 cm

This is the only green pigeon in the region. Its flight is straight with rapid wing beats and it has a hunched shape and fat-bellied appearance. When a feeding flock is disturbed their wings clatter and whirr as they make a noisy departure. When seen clambering about fruiting trees, sometimes upside down, they appear very parrot-like with their bright chestnut vents and yellow 'trousers'. The call is an un-dove-like series of liquid, whistled 'thweeeloo-tleeeoo' notes. African Green Pigeons are found in forest, bushveld and savanna, mostly in fruiting trees, and commonly occur in small flocks although large numbers may gather in ripe fig trees. R

1. Male Namaqua Dove
2. Female Namaqua Dove
3. Adult Greenspotted Dove
4. Adult Bluespotted Dove
5. Adult (right) and immature (left) Tambourine Dove
6. Adult African Green Pigeon

R *resident*

Parrots and lovebirds Family Psittacidae

Small to medium-sized birds with vivid green, blue, brown and red coloration, members of this family have a short, stubby and deeply hooked beak, ideally adapted for cracking hard nuts and ripping open fruit. The flight is mostly rapid and direct. Calls consist of shrieks and screams.

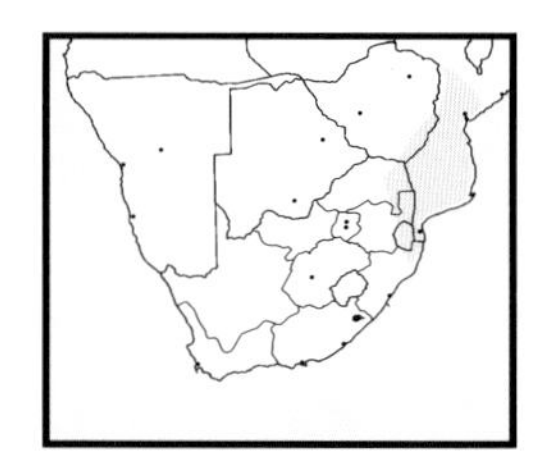

Brownheaded Parrot *Poicephalus cryptoxanthus* **(363) 24 cm**

This species with its bright yellow vent is much smaller than the Cape Parrot from which it differs further by lacking red in the plumage. Overall it is a very green parrot with a contrasting, unmarked brown head. In flight, on noticeably bowed wings, it shows bright yellow, not green, underwings. It is very vocal, emitting a typical parrot-like shriek. It is found in various woodland habitats, from thornveld to riverine forest and more open woodland, where it clambers around in the middle to upper canopy. R

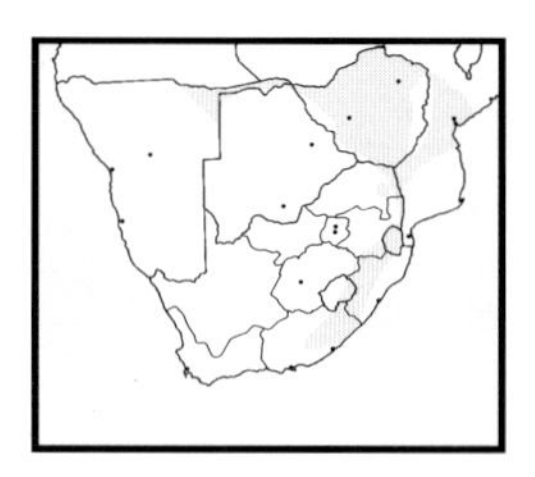

Cape Parrot *Poicephalus robustus* **(362) 35 cm**

The Cape Parrot is by far the largest parrot in the region. The slower wing beats of its broad wings differ from the more rapid flight of other parrots. When seen perched, the red on the forehead (if present), red shoulders and red shaggy 'trousers' are diagnostic; no other parrot in the region has red in its plumage. This species is most likely to be confused with the Brownheaded Parrot but lacks the bright yellow underwings and yellow vent of that species. The Cape Parrot is very vocal in flight but is usually silent when feeding. It frequents evergreen and riverine forests and is sometimes found in exotic plantations. R

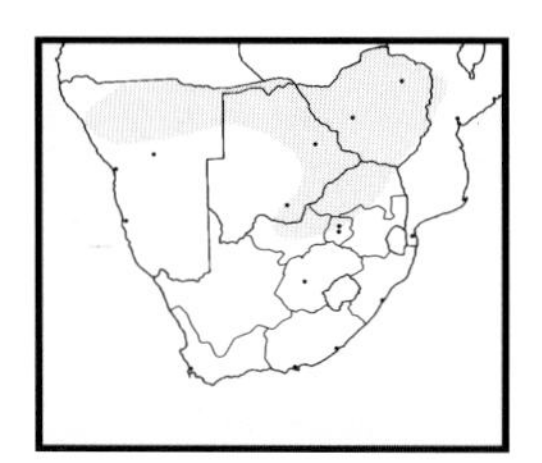

Meyer's Parrot *Poicephalus meyeri* **(364) 22 cm**

This species may be confused with Rüppell's Parrot. It sometimes shows yellow on the forehead which, if present, is diagnostic. Rüppell's Parrot, however, never shows a yellow forehead. Further, the head of Meyer's Parrot is brown, not grey, and the breast, belly and rump are more greenish than blue although they can appear very blue in some lights. In flight less extensive yellow is seen on the underwing but this is difficult to see due to the rapidity of the wing beats. The call is a loud, piercing 'chee-chee-chee-chee', and various other screeches and squawks. Meyer's Parrot favours various woodland types and savanna but avoids evergreen forests. R

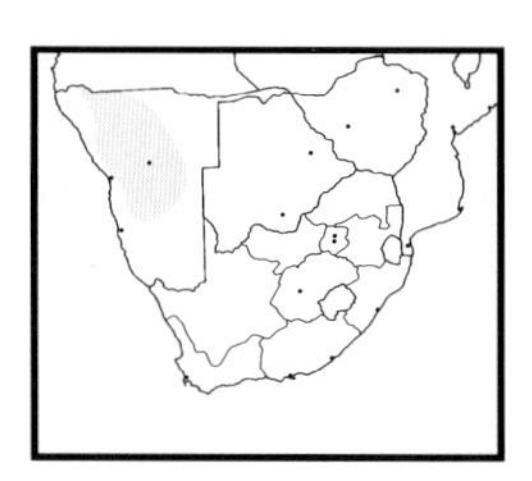

Rüppell's Parrot *Poicephalus rueppellii* **(365) 22 cm**

This is a much greyer bird than the similar Meyer's Parrot, never shows yellow on the forehead and has a blue, not bluish-green, vent and rump. This coloration encompasses the breast and belly on Meyer's Parrot; on Rüppell's Parrot it is confined to the lower belly and vent. In addition, Rüppell's Parrot has a red, not brown, eye and in flight the whole underwing lining, not just the carpals, is yellow. Found mostly in pairs and small family parties, Rüppell's Parrot gathers in tall trees in dry river courses, favouring dry thornveld and dry riverine forest, and stands of baobabs in the north. Its calls are similar to those uttered by Meyer's Parrot. NE

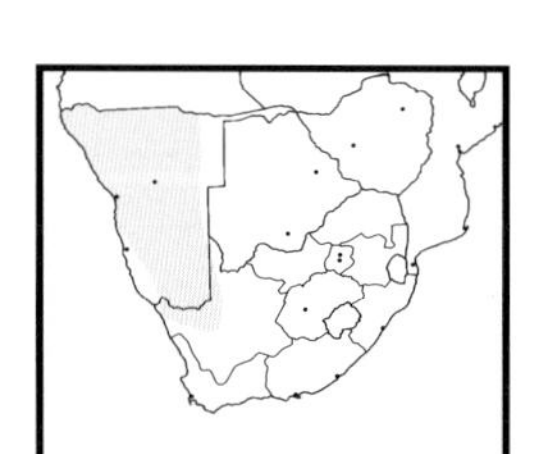

Rosyfaced Lovebird *Agapornis roseicollis* **(367) 18 cm**

The very small size of this bird alone should rule out confusion with other parrots in the region. It is usually detected by its parrot-like screeching calls and is then seen as it hurtles by in a flash of green, blue and pink. The blue rump is clearly seen against the green back. It is found in arid to semi-arid regions in riverine woodland, mountainous areas and savanna. An abundant cage bird, many escapees are seen in suburbia. NE

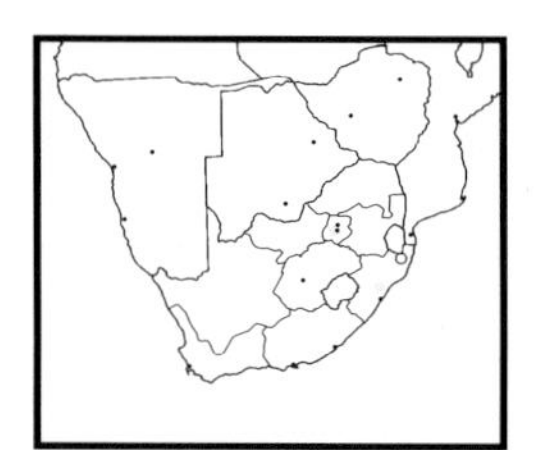

Roseringed Parakeet *Psittacula krameri* **(366) 40 cm**

The long, pointed tail of this parrot immediately identifies it. The bill is large and bright rosy-red in colour. The male has a black throat which continues as a thin, black collar. In flight, when it is very vocal, this parakeet shows yellow wing linings and a yellow undertail. Locally common in Durban and Johannesburg, it has established itself in suburban areas and is a frequent visitor to fruiting fig trees in gardens. It gives various shrieks and screams, and is especially vocal when going to roost. R

1. Adult Brownheaded Parrot
2. Adult Cape Parrot
3. Adult Rosyfaced Lovebird
4. Adult Cape Parrot
5. Female Meyer's Parrot
6. Male (left) and female (right) Rüppell's Parrot
7. Adult Roseringed Parakeet

1	2	3
4	5	
6	7	

R *resident* • NE *near endemic*

Louries Family Musophagidae

These are medium-sized, long-tailed birds which, except for the drab Grey Lourie, display bright green, red and blue plumage. Mostly forest dwellers, they have loud, raucous calls and a distinctive bounding action as they leap from branch to branch through the canopy. The flight is laboured, with fast wing beats interspersed with long glides. The diet consists mainly of fruit.

Adult Knysna Lourie

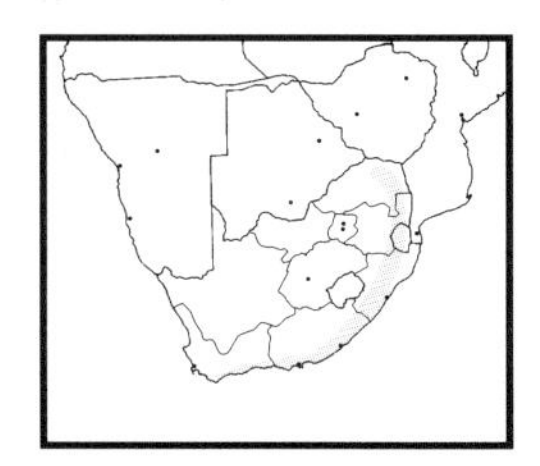

Knysna Lourie *Tauraco corythaix* **(370a) 46 cm**

The ranges of this species and the similar Livingstone's Lourie do not overlap so confusion between them should not arise. The Knysna Lourie differs from the Purplecrested Lourie in having a green head, a white-tipped crest and white stripes above and below the eye. In flight it shows bright red wing patches, and its fast wing beats are interspersed with short glides. A very restless bird, it bounds and bounces with twists and turns along large branches in evergreen forests. Its call is similar to that of Livingstone's Lourie but is higher pitched, a quicker 'kow-kow-kow'. E

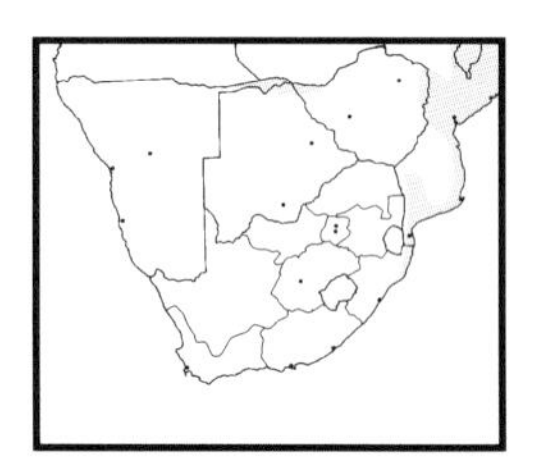

Livingstone's Lourie *Tauraco livingstonii* **(370b) 46 cm**

The very long, pointed, white-tipped crest separates this species from the Knysna Lourie; in addition, the back and mantle are darker in colour. The ranges of these two species do not overlap, however, so confusion should not arise. Livingstone's Lourie displays the same behaviour as the Knysna Lourie but is sometimes more furtive and retiring. It occurs in riverine, mountain and coastal forests. The call is a deeper, slower 'kow-kow-kow-kow' than that of the Knysna Lourie. R

Adult Purplecrested Lourie

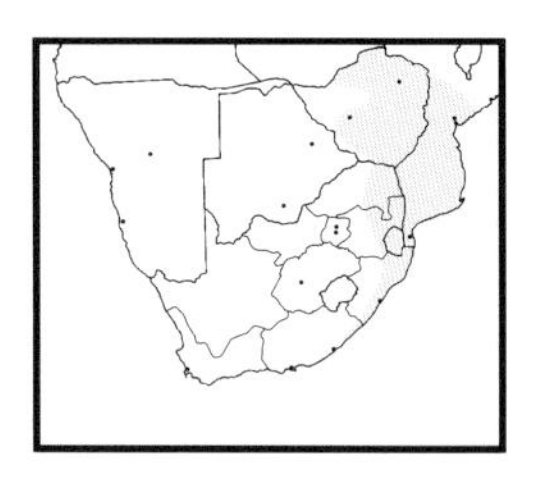

Purplecrested Lourie *Tauraco porphyreolophus* **(371) 46 cm**

A particularly noisy species, the call of this otherwise shy and furtive bird is most often the best way of detecting it. It differs from the Knysna Lourie and Livingstone's Lourie by being darker overall above and below and having an obvious dark blue, unmarked crest (at a distance this appears black). The call is a loud, far-carrying 'kok-kok-kok-kok', a faster version of which is given in flight or when the bird is alarmed. Preferring drier forests and more open woodland than either the Knysna Lourie or Livingstone's Lourie, the Purplecrested Lourie usually occurs in pairs or family parties but large numbers may gather at fruiting trees where they create a cacophony by all calling at once. R

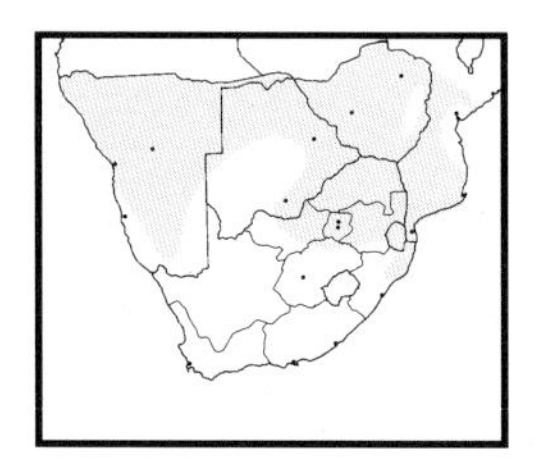

Grey Lourie *Corythaixoides concolor* **(373) 48 cm**

The Grey Lourie looks like a giant mousebird with its long erect crest and long tail. Its alarm call is a well-known sound in the bushveld. Its drab, overall grey colour is diagnostic and, unlike other louries, it lacks red patches in the wings. The sexes are alike and immature birds are buffier than the adults and have a shorter crest. It frequents dry thornveld and savanna, venturing into suburbia in some areas, and occurs in small parties, flying from one tree to the next in a follow-my-leader fashion. It does not bound and bounce around on large branches as much as other louries do. Its call is the well-known 'waaaaay' or 'kay-waaaay' from which it derives its vernacular name, 'Go-away Bird'. R

1. Adult Knysna Lourie
2. Adult Livingstone's Lourie
3. Adult Purplecrested Lourie
4. Adult Angola Pitta
5. Adult Grey Lourie

Pittas Family Pittidae

Brightly coloured, forest-dwelling birds, pittas forage on the ground but nest and display in trees. The males have distinctive calls and displays.

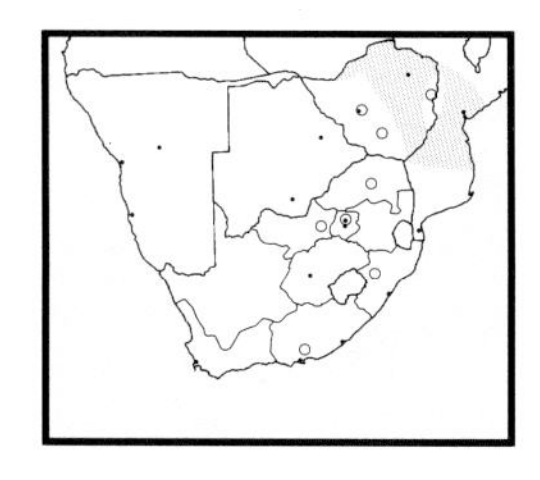

Angola Pitta *Pitta angolensis* **(491) 23 cm**

The sexes of this species are similar, both having a bright red belly and vent feathers, and a turquoise rump and upper covert spots. Immatures are similar to the adults but duller. Easily overlooked, this bird favours the undergrowth of lowland forest, riverine underbrush and thickets, and is most frequently seen as it rises off the forest floor in a bright flash of colour. The call, uttered when breeding, is a frog-like 'quoort'. I

Cuckoos Family Cuculidae

Variable in size, colour and appearance, all the cuckoos have zygodactylous feet and parasitic breeding habits. Some species are iridescently coloured, others are sombre coloured. In some the sexes are alike; others are highly dimorphic. Each species parasitizes either a single host species or a limited range of hosts. Most of the birds are seasonal visitors to the region.

Adult European Cuckoo

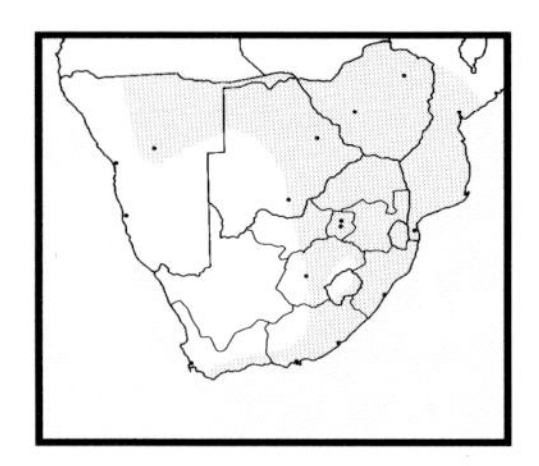

European Cuckoo *Cuculus canorus* (374) 33 cm

This bird may be mistaken for a small hawk in flight but its wings are normally held below the horizontal and its small head with its thin bill is always pointed upwards. This species and the African Cuckoo are very difficult to tell apart, and both are secretive. The mostly dark bill of this species differs from the black and yellow bill of the African Cuckoo, and the undertail pattern is spotted, not barred. The sexes are alike. Immatures may be brown, grey or chestnut, and have heavily barred underparts. A rare rufous morph occurs in the European Cuckoo, but this has never been recorded in the African Cuckoo. The European Cuckoo does not call in the region. These birds are usually found in thornveld but also occur in forest, open woodland and savanna. S

Adult African Cuckoo

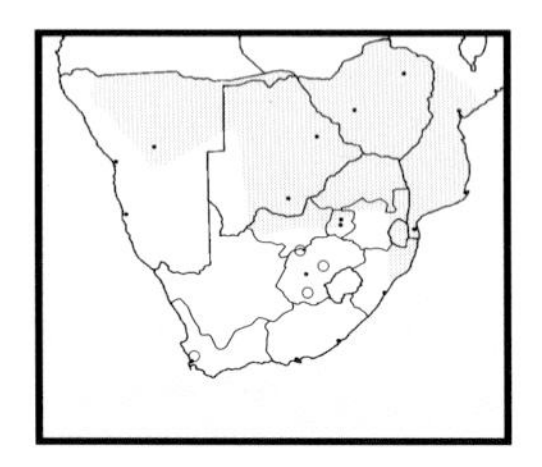

African Cuckoo *Cuculus gularis* (375) 33 cm

This species and the European Cuckoo are virtually indistinguishable in the field, and may be told apart at close range on bill colour and undertail pattern. Two thirds of the African Cuckoo's bill is dark-coloured and about one third, at the base, is yellow; the European Cuckoo has only a small amount of yellow at the base of its bill. The undertail of the African Cuckoo is barred, not spotted as in the European Cuckoo. Unlike the silent European Cuckoo, this bird gives a double-noted 'hoop-hoop' call which is diagnostic. It occurs in many types of woodland but is commonest in thornveld and broad-leaved types. I, S

Adult Redchested Cuckoo

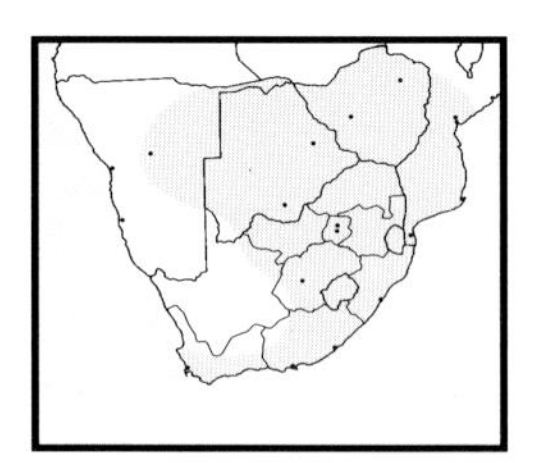

Redchested Cuckoo *Cuculus solitarius* (377) 30 cm

This cuckoo resembles both the African Cuckoo and the European Cuckoo but is darker above and has an obvious russet breast. Immatures are very different from the adults, being black with a white breast and having the belly heavily barred with black. As is the case with the European Cuckoo in Europe, the ringing call of this species heralds the onset of spring and continues right through summer. Calls, given from the canopy, are a ringing, whistled 'weeet-weeet-weeeeooo' and a shriller 'pipipipipi' note; it is usually the bird's call that betrays its presence, as it sits motionless in thick foliage. The Redchested Cuckoo occurs in a wide range of habitats from exotic plantations to thick forest and open woodland; it has adapted well to suburbia. I, S

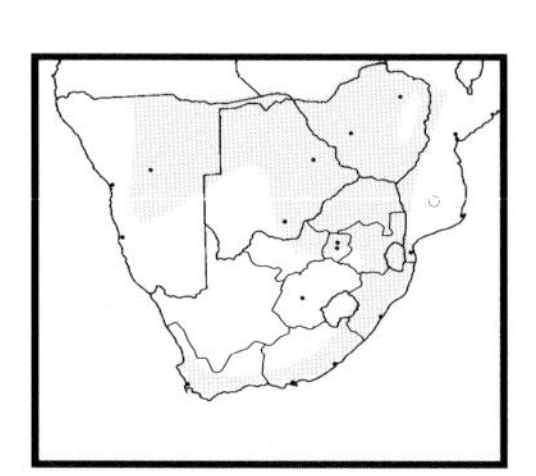

Black Cuckoo *Cuculus clamosus* (378) 30 cm

The only bird likely to be confused with the Black Cuckoo is the all-black form of the Jacobin Cuckoo (see page 132). The Black Cuckoo differs from that species by lacking any white patch on the wings and tail; the underwing shows a little white barring at the primary base but this is hardly visible in flight, and neither are the pale tips to the tail feathers. Immatures have a brown cast to their plumage. Rarely seen, the Black Cuckoo hides in thick tangles and tree canopies; the diagnostic call, a droning, four-noted, whistled 'whoo-wheee-whoo-whoo', is often the only indication of its presence. It also gives a yelping, rapid 'yow-yow-yow'. It is found in woodland, riverine forests, plantations and suburbia. I, S

1. Female European Cuckoo
2. Adult Redchested Cuckoo
3. Adult African Cuckoo
4. Adult Thickbilled Cuckoo
5. Adult Black Cuckoo

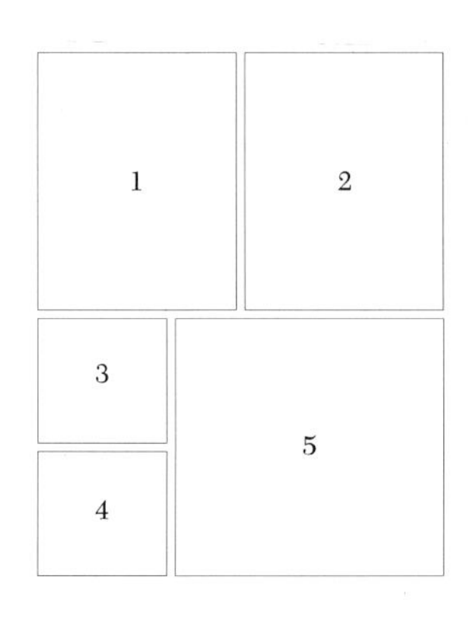

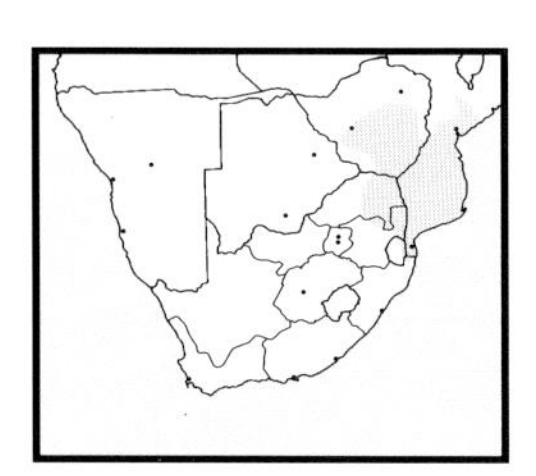

Thickbilled Cuckoo *Pachycoccyx audeberti* (383) 34 cm

This species most closely resembles the Great Spotted Cuckoo (see page 132) but has uniform dark grey upperparts and lacks a crest. The sexes are alike. Immatures have much more white on the head than the immature Great Spotted Cuckoo, lack a crest and do not show chestnut in the wings. The bill is noticeably thick based and heavy. Adults in flight appear very white when seen from below. Thickbilled Cuckoos display over forests on slowly flapping wings, giving their repeated 'were-wick' call; they also give a repeated, harsh, ringing 'wee-yes-yes' when perched. They favour riverine forests and open woodland. I, S, W

S *summer visitor* • I *intra-African migrant* • W *winter visitor*

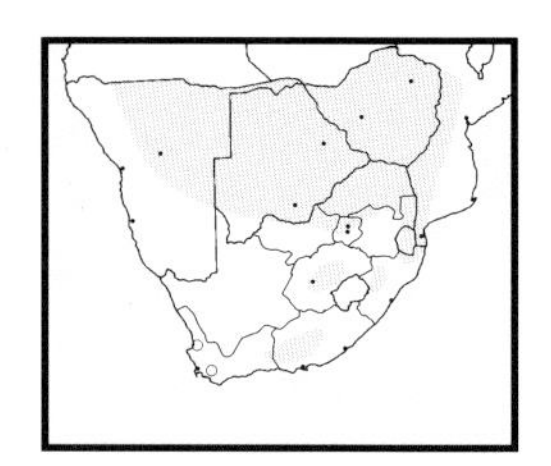

Great Spotted Cuckoo *Clamator glandarius* (380) 39 cm

The adult Great Spotted Cuckoo is unmistakable with its grey crest, white spotted back and creamy underparts. Immatures have a black cap and a slightly crested appearance, richer creamy underparts and obvious russet primaries in flight; confusion might arise with the immature Thickbilled Cuckoo (see page 130) but that bird has a blotched white and grey head. Great Spotted Cuckoos have an undulating flight action on bowed wings with quick, shallow wing beats. They forage freely on the ground in the open and in the heat of the day sit low down in the shade of thickets. They call from exposed perches, a loud and far-carrying 'keeeow-keeeow-keeeeow' and a shorter, crow-like 'kark'. They frequent open woodland, savanna and dry thornveld. I, S

Immature Great Spotted Cuckoo

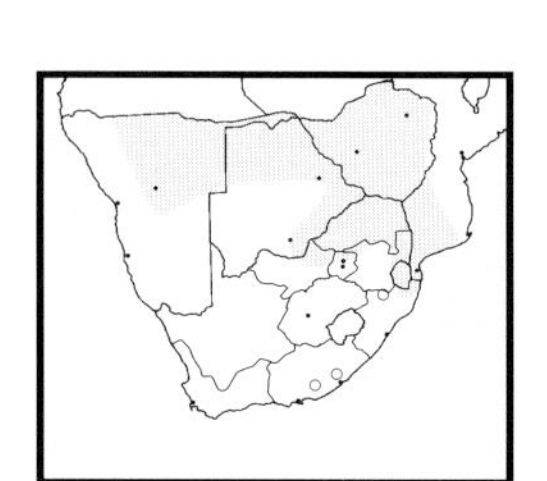

Striped Cuckoo *Clamator levaillantii* (381) 38 cm

The Striped Cuckoo is unlikely to be confused with any other cuckoo except the pale form of the Jacobin Cuckoo but differs by having its throat and flanks heavily striped black. In flight both species show white flashes in the wings and white spots on the undertail. The sexes are alike, and immatures are browner versions of the adults but still show the throat striping. Pairs may be seen chasing each other through woodland, calling loudly, a 'klee-klee-kleeuu' followed by a 'che-che-che', but otherwise these birds are secretive and shy. They prefer thornveld but also occur in other woodland types. I, S

Immature Klaas's Cuckoo

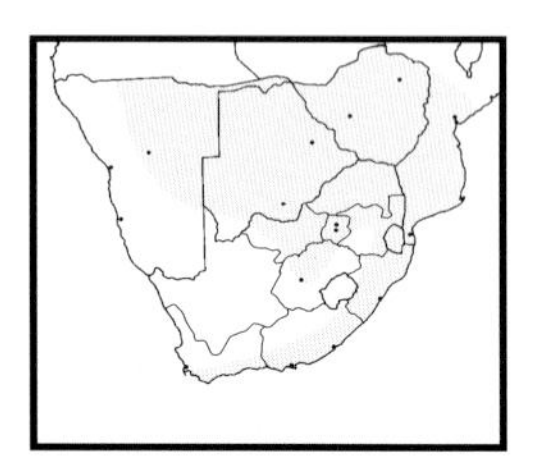

Jacobin Cuckoo *Clamator jacobinus* (382) 34 cm

The pale form of this bird may be confused with the Striped Cuckoo, but it lacks any markings on the underparts and, in flight, shows a greater extent of white in the wings and tail. The dark form is similar to the Black Cuckoo (see page 130) but has a crest and shows white flashes at the base of the primaries and obvious white spots on the tips of the tail feathers. Immatures are a browner version of the adults. The bird's call, similar to that of the Striped Cuckoo, is more staccato and higher pitched. The Jacobin Cuckoo is often seen flying about or sitting on exposed perches. It frequents a wide range of woodlands from open protea scrub in mountains to thornveld and open woodland. I, S

Immature Diederik Cuckoo

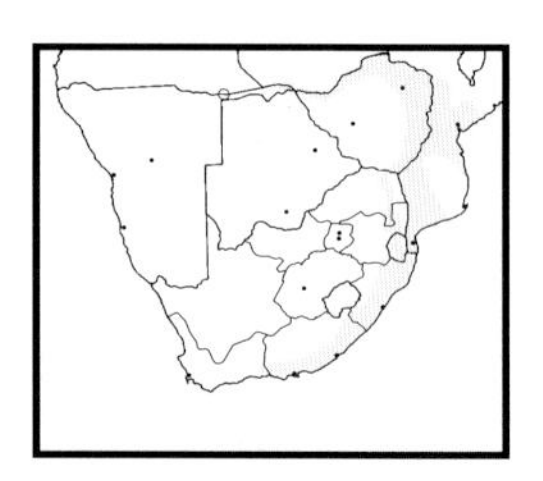

Emerald Cuckoo *Chrysococcyx cupreus* (384) 20 cm

The male Emerald Cuckoo is bright iridescent green and sulphur-yellow; females closely resemble the female Klaas's Cuckoo but lack the white markings behind the eye and are more densely barred on the underparts. Females and immature birds can be distinguished from the immature Diederik Cuckoo by their lack of white spotting on the wings. Males are extremely well camouflaged in the forest canopy, from where they call, a clear, ringing 'whee-cheet whee-chochee' often rendered as 'pretty georg-ee'. The Emerald Cuckoo is found in evergreen and riverine forests. I, S

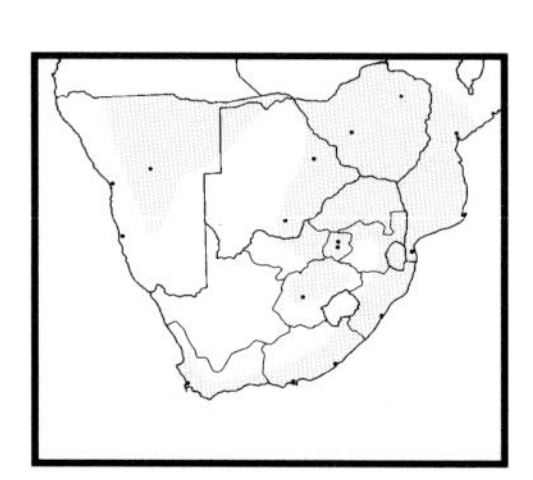

Klaas's Cuckoo *Chrysococcyx klaas* (385) 18 cm

This and the Diederik Cuckoo are very similar but Klaas's Cuckoo is very much greener on the upperparts, has no white spotting in the wings, and shows a single white stripe behind the eye. Also, the eyes of this species are brown, not red. Immatures and females differ from the immature and female Emerald Cuckoo by having a white flash behind the eye and not as heavily barred underparts; they differ from the similar immature and female Diederik Cuckoo by lacking the white wing spots. Secretive and furtive, its soft 'huee-jee' call most often reveals the bird's presence. It occurs in forests, open woodland, parks and gardens. I, S, W

1. Adult Great Spotted Cuckoo
2. Adult Great Spotted Cuckoo
3. Immature Striped Cuckoo
4. Adult Jacobin Cuckoo
5. Male Emerald Cuckoo
6. Male Klaas's Cuckoo
7. Male Diederik Cuckoo

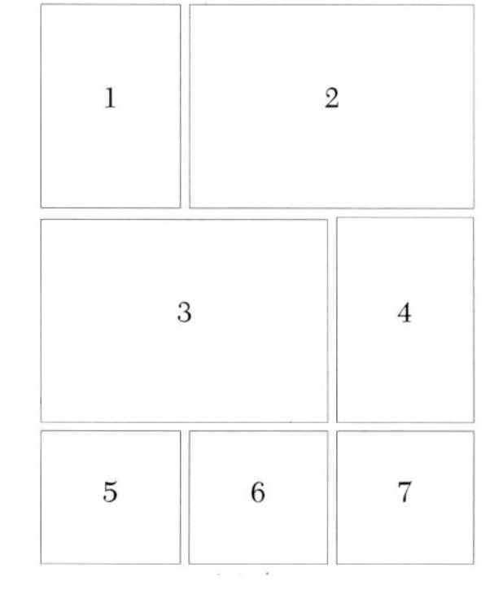

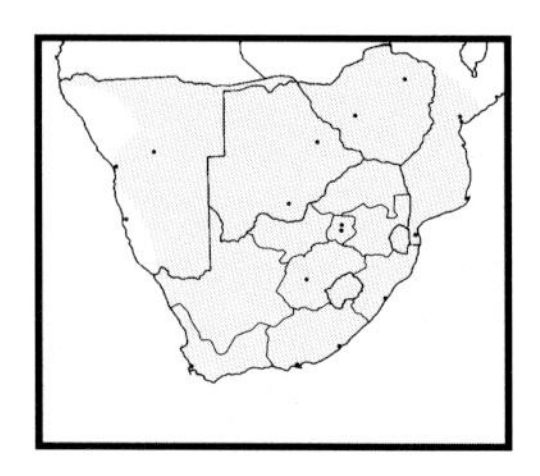

Diederik Cuckoo *Chrysococcyx caprius* (386) 18 cm

This small green cuckoo may be confused with Klaas's Cuckoo but is immediately identified when the very obvious white spotting in the wing is seen. It differs further from that species by having more extensive white behind the eye, a bronzy sheen to the iridescent green upperparts and red, not brown, eyes. The female differs from the female Klaas's Cuckoo and Emerald Cuckoo by having very broad, not fine, barring confined to the flanks, and by the white spotting on the wing. Immatures have a diagnostic red bill. The call is a clear 'dee-dee-dee-deedereek'. Often seen being chased by weavers, these cuckoos are found in a wide range of habitats from woodland, grasslands, reedbeds and riverine woodland to suburban gardens. I, S

I *intra-African migrant* • S *summer visitor* • W *winter visitor*

Coucals Family Centropodidae

Mainly rather large, long- and broad-tailed birds with strongly curved beaks, coucals utter liquid bubbling or hooting calls which rise and fall on the scale. They live solitarily or in pairs and most are sedentary. Unlike the closely related cuckoos, they build their own nests and raise their own young. They are largely insectivorous although some species also prey on the eggs and nestlings of other birds.

Immature Burchell's Coucal

Adult Whitebrowed Coucal

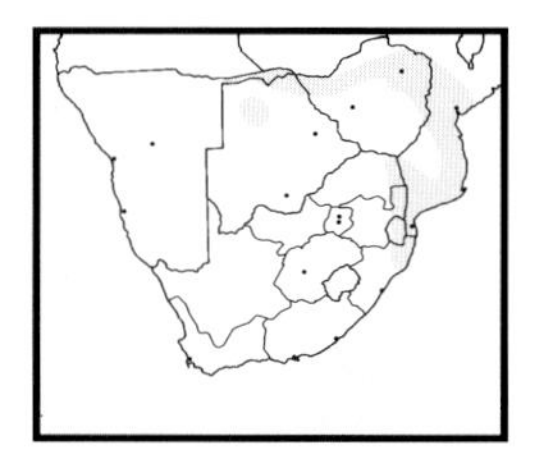

Black Coucal *Centropus bengalensis* (388) 35 cm

Smaller than other coucals in the region, the male in breeding plumage is unmistakable with its all-black body and contrasting chestnut-coloured wings. Immatures differ from the immature Burchell's Coucal by their finely barred tail and by the heavy black streaking on the head and back. The call is a frequently repeated 'poopoop' given by the female and a shorter 'ku-ku-ku' hooting note. These birds are most often seen in the early morning, sitting on the tops of reeds or grassy mounds, sunning and drying themselves. They creep around in grass and when flushed fly clumsily for a few metres before crashing back into cover. They frequent flooded grasslands and reedbeds. S

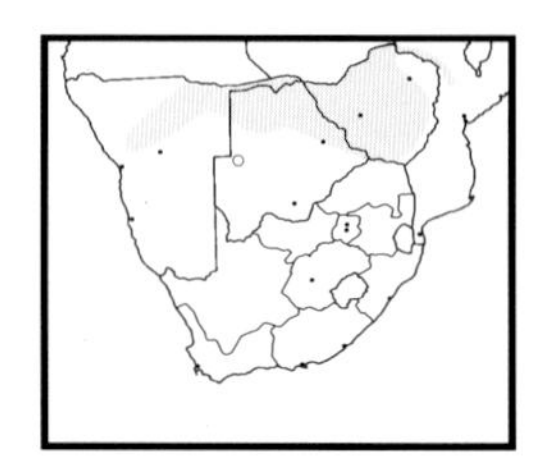

Senegal Coucal *Centropus senegalensis* (390) 40 cm

The Senegal Coucal might be confused with Burchell's Coucal but has a more chestnut mantle and wings, and lacks barring on the rump and uppertail coverts; immatures have less barring on the rump and uppertail coverts and less streaking on the head than the immature Burchell's Coucal. Senegal Coucals inhabit drier areas than do the Copperytailed Coucal and Burchell's Coucal, from thickets in savanna to the edge of woodland. R

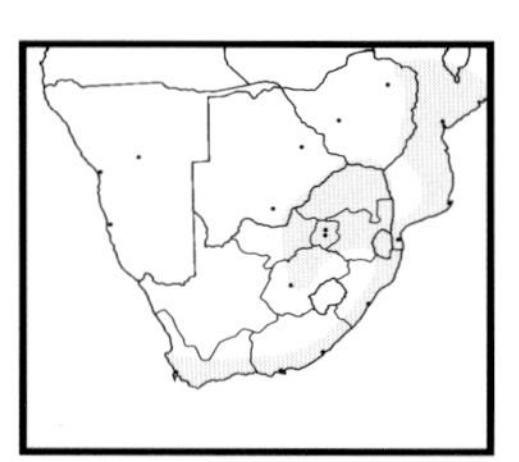

Burchell's Coucal *Centropus burchellii* (391a) 44 cm

Burchell's Coucal was once considered to be a race of the Whitebrowed Coucal and in immature plumage the two cannot be told apart in the field. The adult Burchell's Coucal has a black cap extending on to the nape and may be distinguished from the Senegal Coucal by the extensive barring on its rump and uppertail coverts, which the Senegal Coucal lacks. The Copperytailed Coucal is similar but is much larger and has a longer, floppier, broader tail. These birds creep about in tangled vegetation and sun themselves in the early mornings on exposed perches. Their flight is slow and laboured. They frequent thick tangles, thickets, creepers and riverine forest. R

Whitebrowed Coucal *Centropus superciliosus* (391b) 44 cm

This coucal can be told from all other coucals in the region by its white-flecked head, nape and mantle, and by its creamy-white eyebrow stripe. The immature Burchell's Coucal shows a very similar plumage pattern to the immature of this species. Whitebrowed Coucals climb awkwardly through vegetation but can run quickly on the ground. The flight is awkward and clumsy, and over short distances. Whitebrowed Coucals are found close to water in rank grass and thickets along streams and rivers but also occur in drier bush and on woodland edge. R

Copperytailed Coucal *Centropus cupreicaudus* (389) 48 cm

The largest coucal in the region, superficially the Copperytailed Coucal resembles the Senegal Coucal. Immatures have a streaked head and barred flight feathers. The call is a deep baritone version of typical coucal bubbling notes; when calling, the bird sits on exposed reed clumps, bows its head, puffs out its throat and lowers its bill on to its chest. It frequents flooded grasslands, papyrus swamps, reedbeds and adjoining bush. R

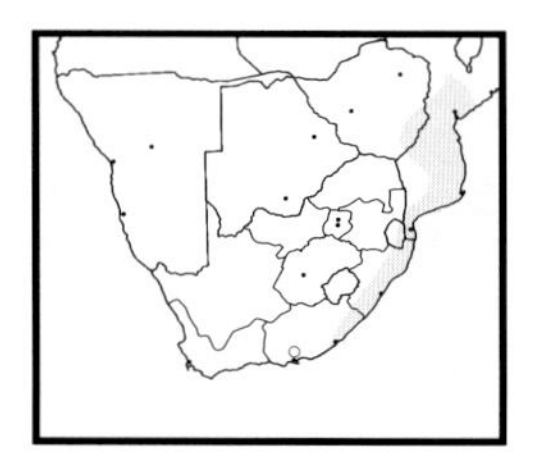

Green Coucal *Ceuthmochares aereus* (387) 33 cm

When seen, this shy species appears to be greyish and only in good light can the greenish upperparts be discerned. The bright yellow bill is diagnostic. The call, often the first sign of its presence, is a series of metallic 'tick-tick' notes run together and then speeded up to conclude with a yelping 'cher-cher-cher-cher' which trails off slowly. Green Coucals keep to lowland evergreen forest, remaining well concealed in the darkest recesses of thick tangles and creepers. They respond to a mimic of their call, approaching slowly and peering from the foliage, when sometimes only the bright yellow bill is seen. R

1. Adult Black Coucal
2. Adult Senegal Coucal
3. Adult Burchell's Coucal
4. Adult Copperytailed Coucal
5. Adult Whitebrowed Coucal
6. Adult Green Coucal

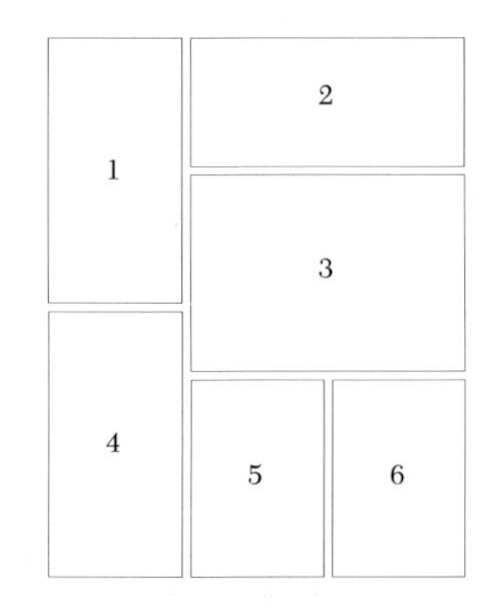

S *summer visitor* • R *resident*

Owls Families Tytonidae and Strigidae

These nocturnal birds of prey all have distinctive calls and are most vocal just after dusk and before dawn. The plumage is soft and fluffy, with brown, buff or grey colouring, and often with heavy barring or streaking. Owls are silent fliers and their prey ranges from insects to mammals and birds and, in one species, fish.

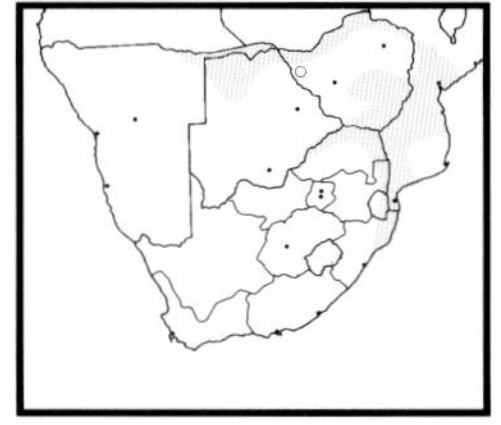

Pel's Fishing Owl *Scotopelia peli* (403) 63 cm

An unmistakable, tawny bird with dark brown eyes, this owl has no distinct facial disc. Immatures are similar to the adults. The tarsi are unfeathered and the feet are covered in rough, spiky scales that help it to grip its prey – mainly fish but also crabs and even small crocodiles. From a perch close to the water, the bird swoops down to snatch its prey from the water's surface, rarely immersing its body. The mournful, hooting call is uttered most often in the early hours of the morning. Found in riverine forest, it favours tall palms near permanent water in rivers or pans. R

Adult Cape Eagle Owl

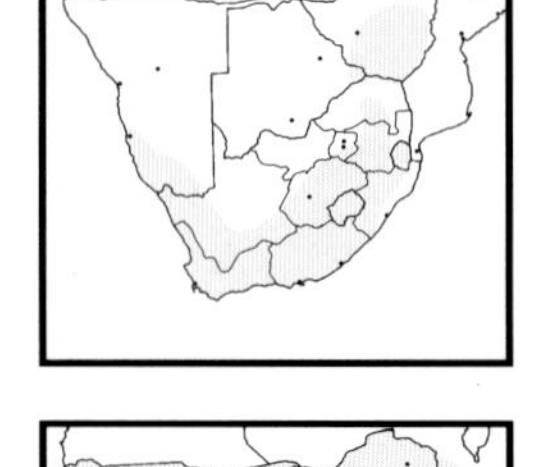

Cape Eagle Owl *Bubo capensis* (400) 48-54 cm

Slightly larger than the similar Spotted Eagle Owl, the bright orange eyes, heavy black and rufous blotching on the breast, and broad (not fine) bars on the belly of the Cape Eagle Owl differentiate it from that species. The call is a far-carrying and loud 'hu-hooo-hu' or 'hoo-hoo-hoo-hoo-hooh', and also a loud 'wak-wak-wak'. Inhabiting rocky and mountainous country and plateau edges, in the Cape these owls occur in fynbos. R

Adult Spotted Eagle Owl

Spotted Eagle Owl *Bubo africanus* (401) 43-50 cm

This, our commonest owl, a little smaller than the Cape Eagle Owl, is well adapted to the urban environment. The colour of the eyes varies from sulphur-yellow to orange-yellow but is never as orange as those of the Cape Eagle Owl; and the breast and belly are finely, not boldly, barred. The call is a two-syllabled 'hooo-hooe', distinct from the three-syllabled call of the Cape Eagle Owl. The Spotted Eagle Owl occurs in lightly wooded savanna areas but is absent from forest, dense woodland and open grasslands without trees. R

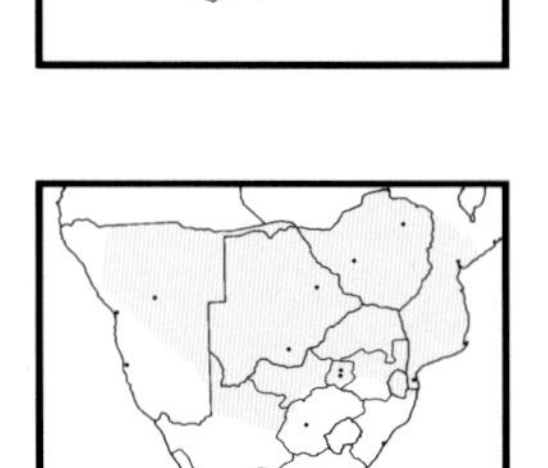

Giant Eagle Owl *Bubo lacteus* (402) 60-65 cm

This, our largest owl, has diagnostic large, dark brown eyes (appearing black) and distinctive pink eyelids. It is grey overall with fine barring and has a pale facial disc edged with black. An opportunist, it may hunt during the day if prey wanders beneath its roosting site but is usually active at dusk. It uses the old stick nests of eagles, vultures, crows and the Hamerkop (see page 30) to rear its two chicks. The grunting hoot can be heard up to five kilometres away. It roosts in very large, dense trees in mature woodland and riverine habitat. R

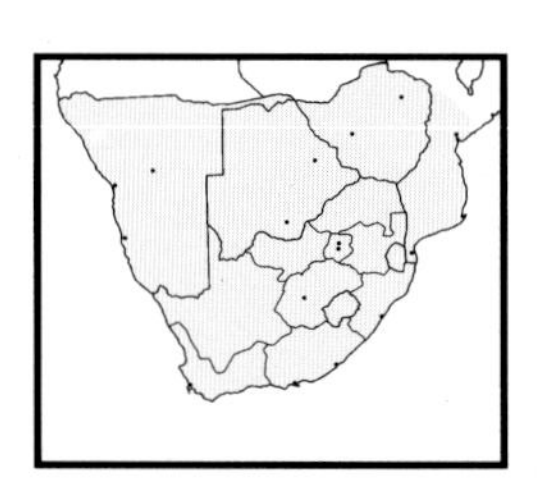

Barn Owl *Tyto alba* (392) 34 cm

This species and the Grass Owl both have heart-shaped facial discs, small eyes and long, bare legs. The Barn Owl appears predominantly orange or tawny and light grey on the back, not dark brown as does the Grass Owl. It roosts by day in hollow trees, wells, caves and in urban situations. Usually occurring in pairs, it hunts on the wing and swallows its prey whole. Its call is a thin, guttural 'schreeeu' and it will hiss when disturbed or alarmed. Hamerkop nests are favourite nest sites of this bird. R

Grass Owl *Tyto capensis* (393) 36 cm

Like the Barn Owl, this species has a white, heart-shaped facial disc but its upperparts are dark brown, not tawny. While its habitat preferences are similar to those of the Marsh Owl, it prefers long grasses in marshy conditions whereas the Marsh Owl tolerates much drier habitats. In flight it shows pale, almost white, outer tail feathers, an almost black, not yellowish-buff, underwing and an unbarred tail, and its feet extend beyond the tail. It roosts during the day in dense, marshy vegetation and reedbeds, and nests on the ground under and between large grass tufts. When flushed during daylight hours it may emit hissing sounds and typically flies only a short distance before dropping from view. Grass Owls are usually seen in pairs, but sometimes occur in groups of up to five individuals. R

1. Adult Pel's Fishing Owl
2. Adult Cape Eagle Owl
3. Adult Spotted Eagle Owl
4. Adult Spotted Eagle Owl
5. Adult Giant Eagle Owl
6. Adult Barn Owl
7. Adult Grass Owl

1	2	3 / 4
5	6	7

R *resident*

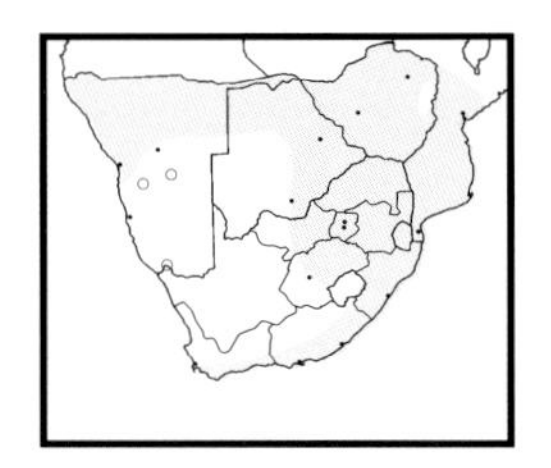

Marsh Owl *Asio capensis* (395) 36 cm

In flight the buff underwing with black wing tips and the barred tail separate this species from the Grass Owl (see page 136) which shows similar habitat preferences; the feet of the Marsh Owl do not extend beyond the tail in flight, as is the case with the Grass Owl. During the winter months the Marsh Owl may be seen in large groups, often hunting in the early morning and late afternoon, flying over grasslands, pastures and agricultural lands in search of rodents and insects; it also hunts from a perch. Nesting on the ground in dense grass which it bends over to form a bower, the Marsh Owl generally favours drier conditions than the Grass Owl. When breeding it occurs in pairs but thereafter may roost gregariously in groups of up to 40 individuals. The call is a peculiar, frog-like 'zzzzrk-zzzzrk'. R

Adult Marsh Owl

Wood Owl *Strix woodfordii* (394) 35 cm

This owl has a rounded head without 'ear' tufts, a dark face with prominent white eyebrows and dark brown eyes surrounded by white. The chest is spotted and the belly has broad white bars. The sexes are alike, and immatures resemble the adults. Two distinct races occur, one chocolate-brown and the other rufous in colour. The call is a rapid hoot sounding a little like a yapping dog. Strongly territorial, Wood Owls favour forest and mature woodland. They use the same nest year after year. R

Adult Pearlspotted Owl (back view)

Whitefaced Owl *Otus leucotis* (397) 28 cm

This little owl is light grey in colour, with dark streaks above and white with dark streaks below. It has 'ear' tufts, bright orange eyes and a white facial disc edged with black. It is both larger and a lighter grey in colour than the African Scops Owl, which also has 'ear' tufts but can be differentiated by its yellow, not orange, eyes. The Whitefaced Owl behaves in a similar fashion to the African Scops Owl when disturbed, elongating its body. Its call is a very soft 'whoooo', indiscernible from any great distance. R

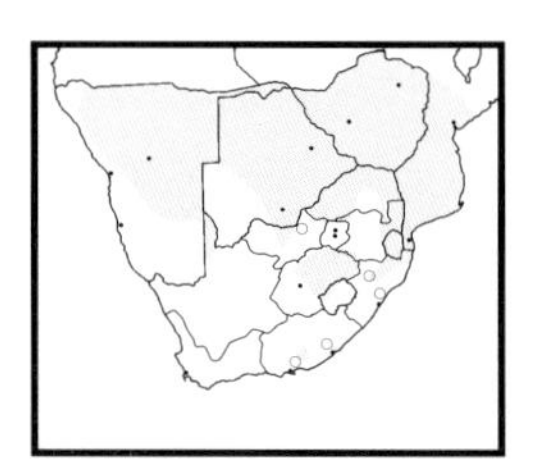

African Scops Owl *Otus senegalensis* (396) 20 cm

This species is slightly larger than the Pearlspotted Owl; its dark grey plumage with black streaks and prominent 'ear' tufts also help to differentiate it from that species. The Whitefaced Owl, like this species, has 'ear' tufts, but its orange, not yellow, eyes help to differentiate it. When alarmed, the African Scops Owl raises its 'ear' tufts and elongates its body by sitting very upright; its small size and habit of sitting very close to the trunk of a tree make it difficult to see. It nests in holes in trees and preys solely on insects. The call is a ventriloquial, insect-like 'prrrrpt'. African Scops Owls favour savanna and dry woodland habitat. R

Pearlspotted Owl *Glaucidium perlatum* (398) 18 cm

Our smallest and commonest owl, the Pearlspotted Owl has a rounded head without 'ear' tufts, yellow eyes, and two black 'eye spots' on the back of the head which separate it from both the African Scops Owl and the Whitefaced Owl. The sexes are alike, and immatures resemble the adults. The Pearlspotted Owl has a habit of flicking its tail when it is alarmed. Despite its size it is belligerent and when disturbed glares with hostility at the intruder. It hunts (quite often during the day in winter) from a perch, diving fast with whirring wings and short glides and striking its prey (insects, mice and small birds) with its legs. The call is a loud, penetrating whistle: 'tuu, tiuu, tiuu' ascending, and then followed by a descending 'teeu, teeeu, teeeu'. This bird is often mobbed by bird parties, a behaviour frequently initiated by bulbuls (see pages 196-98). Pearlspotted Owls favour thornveld and broad-leaved woodland. R

1. Adult Marsh Owl
2. Adult Wood Owl
3. Adult Whitefaced Owl
4. Adult African Scops Owl
5. Adult Pearlspotted Owl
6. Adult Barred Owl

1	2	3
4	5	6

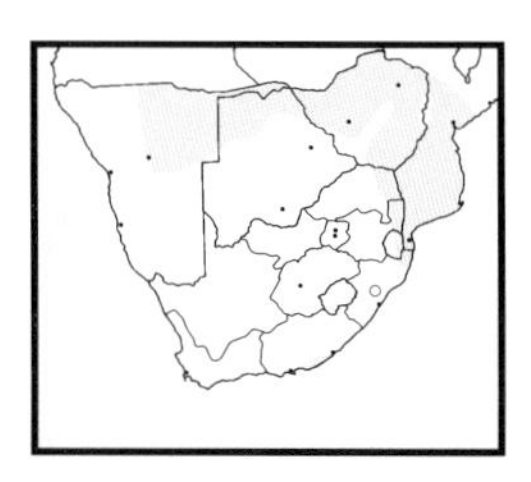

Barred Owl *Glaucidium capense* (399) 21 cm

The large, rounded head with fine concentric barring, the white scapulars and the lack of 'eye spots' on the nape differentiate this species from the slightly smaller but quite similar Pearlspotted Owl. The Barred Owl is white below, with dark brown, triangular spots. It hunts from a perch, dropping down on to its prey, which varies from insects to small birds, and it nests in holes in trees, laying two or three eggs. The Barred Owl is usually seen singly. Its call is a repeated, two syllabled 'prr-purr, prr-purr'. It prefers acacia bush, mature woodlands and riparian forest. R

R *resident*

Nightjars Family Caprimulgidae

Nocturnal, dove-sized birds with large heads and eyes, a wide gape for catching insects in flight, and very short, weak legs, nightjars are cryptically coloured and difficult to locate during the day because they are superbly camouflaged as they rest in leaf litter and stony areas. Although it is not easy to distinguish between the species, a combination of the extent or absence of white in the wings and tail differentiates species in the field. As with the owls, nightjars are best identified by their calls at night.

Natal Nightjar *Caprimulgus natalensis* (407) 22 cm

Male Natal Nightjars have the outer tail feathers entirely white and the penultimate outer tail feather white from the tip to half the way down its length; white spots occur on four of the primaries. Females and immatures resemble the male but have buff, not white, spots. This species has similar wing and tail markings to the Mozambique Nightjar but is brown rather than grey and lacks the white flecks on the folded wing of the Mozambique Nightjar. The call is a continuous, churring 'tchop, tchop, tchop, tchop'. R

European Nightjar *Caprimulgus europaeus* (404) 25-28 cm

Males of this species have the two outer tail feathers white for a quarter of the length from the tail tip. Females are plain without spots on the wings or markings in the tail but are greyer than female Pennantwinged Nightjars with which they could be confused. This nightjar is solitary and normally silent in Africa, and characteristically roosts during the day on a horizontal branch, rarely on the ground. Found in open woodland and in urban situations, it feeds at night over open ground. S

Fierynecked Nightjar *Caprimulgus pectoralis* (405) 24 cm

Male Fierynecked Nightjars are most likely to be confused with the Rufouscheeked Nightjar but have the outer two tail feathers white for half, not a quarter, of their length from the tip; four white spots show in the primaries. In females the outer two tail feathers are buffy-white for a quarter of their length from the tip, and the wing spots are buffy. The call, a characteristic song of the bushveld, sounds like 'Good Lord, deliver us', and is uttered from a perch on the branch of a tree. The commonest nightjar in our region, it favours woodland and open savannas. R

Rufouscheeked Nightjar *Caprimulgus rufigena* (406) 24 cm

Male birds have the two outer tail feathers white for a quarter of the length from the tip, and have four white spots in the primaries. Females have the two outer tail feathers buffy-white for a quarter of their length, and show buff wing spots. This species roosts mainly on the ground. The call is a prolonged, loud, churring sound, likened to a small-engined motorcycle preceded by a coughing 'chukoo, chukoo'. The Rufouscheeked Nightjar prefers thornveld, broad-leaved woodland and semi-arid scrub. I, S

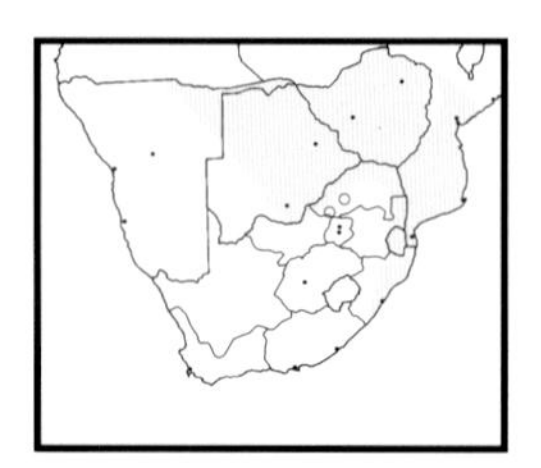

Mozambique Nightjar *Caprimulgus fossii* (409) 24 cm

Similar to the Natal Nightjar, which is smaller and browner than this species, male Mozambique Nightjars have the outer tail feathers entirely white, and have four white spots in the primaries. In females the outer tail feathers are whitish buff and the wing spots are buff. They have a churring 'rrrrrrr' call which changes in pitch at intervals and is likened to a motor changing gear. This species prefers savanna and riverine bush with a sandy substrate, and is often found near lakes and rivers. R

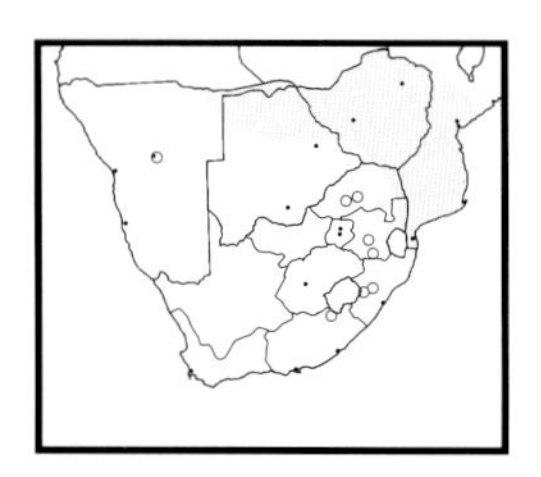

Pennantwinged Nightjar *Macrodipteryx vexillarius* (410) 28 cm

The breeding males of this large species have a diagnostic elongated primary feather. The white at the base of the primaries shows as a vertical white bar on the open wing (also in non-breeding condition), and its unmarked tail renders this nightjar unmistakable. Females are entirely plain, rather similar to the female European Nightjar, but are ginger-coloured, not grey. The call uttered by the male is a rather nondescript, high-pitched, bat-like twittering. The female is silent. These birds occur in open, broad-leaved woodland and adjacent grasslands. S

Male Natal Nightjar

Male Fierynecked Nightjar

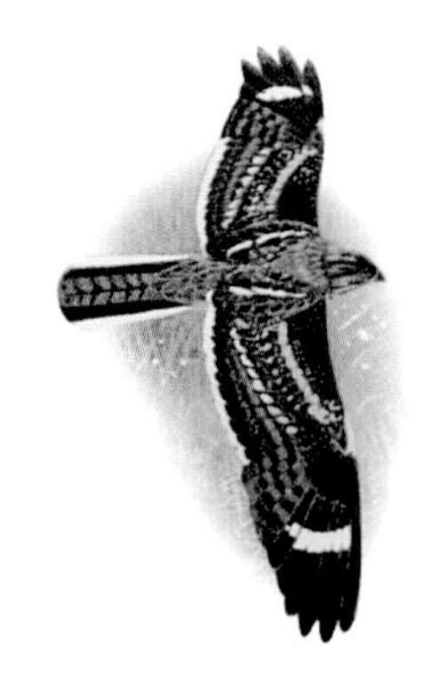

Male Mozambique Nightjar

1. Adult Fierynecked Nightjar
2. Adult Mozambique Nightjar
3. Adult Natal Nightjar
4. Adult European Nightjar
5. Adult Rufouscheeked Nightjar
6. Male Pennantwinged Nightjar

1	2
3	4
5	6

R *resident* • S *summer visitor* • I *intra-African migrant*

Swifts Family Apodidae

The long, sickle-shaped wings of these birds – which should not be mistaken for swallows – make their flight rapid and effortless. They do not perch, but feed on insects caught on the wing; some species roost in flight at great heights. Their legs are very short and the toes point forwards, an adaptation for clinging to their nest sites: rock faces, bark or palm fronds. Identification is based largely on size, rump pattern and tail shape.

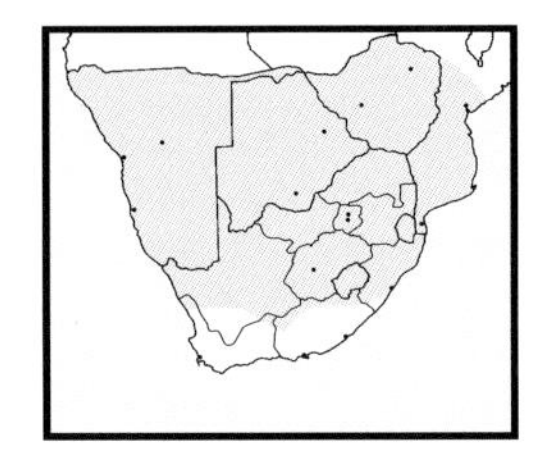

European Swift *Apus apus* (411) 17 cm

The European Swift, a Eurasian migrant that spends most of its life on the wing flying between Africa and the Palearctic where it breeds, is similar in size and colour to the resident Black Swift; however, the back and the upperside of the wings are a uniform brown whereas the Black Swift has greyish secondaries, paler than the rest of the upperwing, which provide a slight contrast. The European Swift occurs over a wide range of habitats. It is normally silent in the region and typically accumulates in very large flocks. S

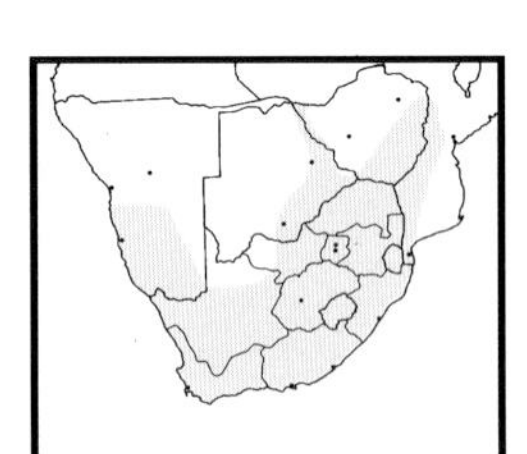

Black Swift *Apus barbatus* (412) 18 cm

The Black Swift closely resembles the European Swift, from which it can be separated in good light by the secondaries on its upperwing being paler grey in colour and contrasting with the darker primaries and with the body. The Black Swift breeds on inland cliffs. Its call is a high-pitched, screaming chitter made both in the air and while on the nest, but is normally heard only around the breeding sites. On feeding forays in search of aerial insects, the Black Swift may be seen far from its breeding grounds and over quite open, flat country. R, I

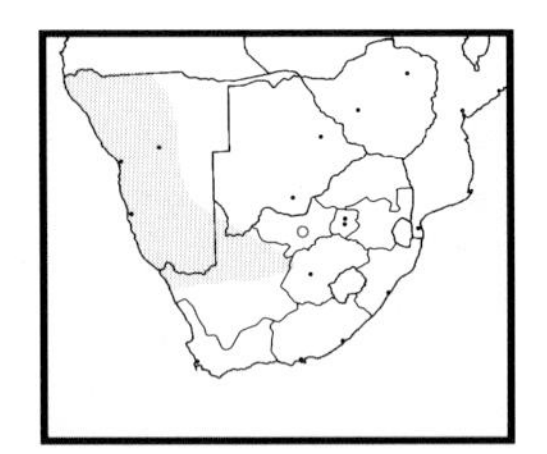

Bradfield's Swift *Apus bradfieldi* (413) 18 cm

Similar in size and build to the Black Swift, Bradfield's Swift differs by being grey-brown, like a Palm Swift (see page 144), but is more robust and lacks the long, slim, deeply forked tail of that species. It has much less white on the chin than either of the black swifts. It feeds aerially on insects and its call is typically swift-like, a high-pitched screaming given mostly around breeding sites on high, inaccessible cliff faces. It is often seen in mixed flocks with other swift species. NE

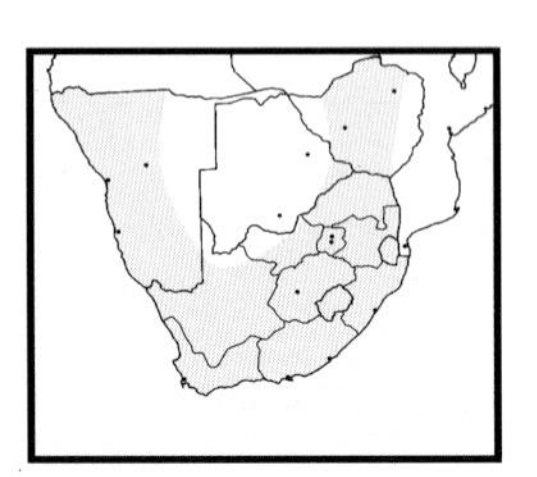

Alpine Swift *Apus melba* (418) 22 cm

This huge swift, with its white belly and throat separated by a broad grey-brown band, is unlikely to be mistaken for any other species. It occurs mostly at higher altitudes, near cliffs, plateau grasslands and mountain ranges and often in mixed flocks with other swift species. It is a high aerial feeder but, like other swifts, flies low prior to weather changes and storms. A wide-ranging species, it breeds on high inland cliffs in vertical clefts where it is most vocal, giving high-pitched chittering sounds. It moves northwards when not breeding. S

Mottled Swift *Apus aequatorialis* (419) 20 cm

This species is comparable in size to the Alpine Swift but is all-grey-brown in colour. It is similar in colour to, although a bit darker than, Bradfield's Swift, but their sizes and distributions differ. Mottled Swifts are gregarious and are frequently seen in association with other swift species. Feeding aerially on insects, they are vocal only in the vicinity of the breeding sites when their typically swift-like screaming calls may be heard. The Mottled Swift is generally a species of cliffs and high mountain ranges. R

Adult Alpine Swift

Adult Mottled Swift

1. Adult European Swift
2. Adult Black Swift
3. Adult Alpine Swift
4. Adult Alpine Swift
5. Adult Bradfield's Swift
6. Adult Mottled Swift

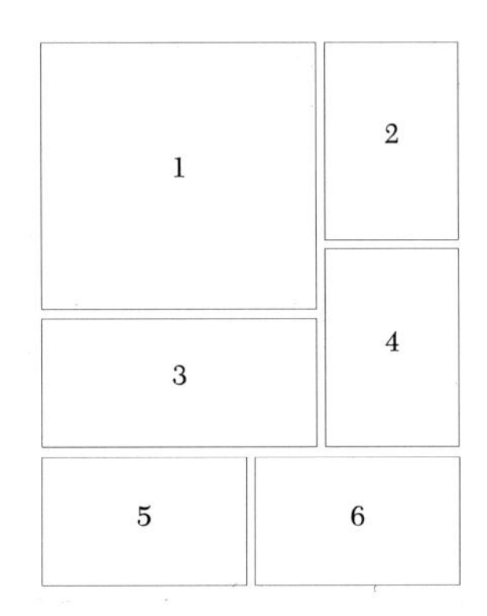

S *summer visitor* • R *resident* • I *intra-African migrant* • NE *near endemic*

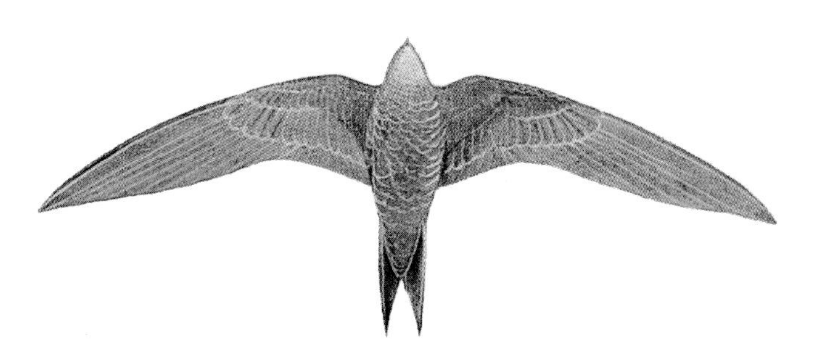

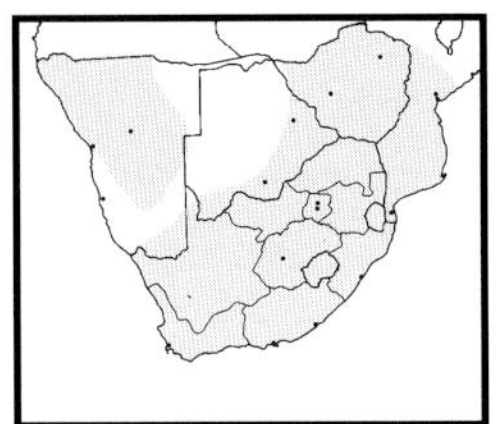
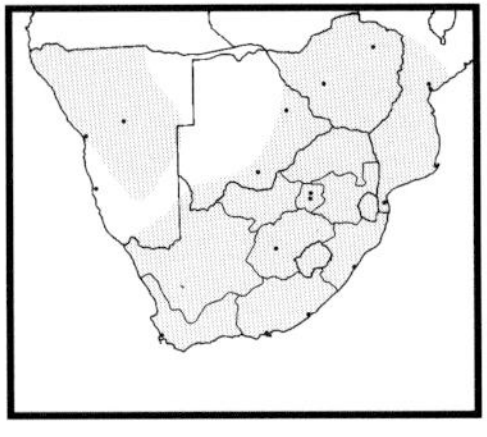

Whiterumped Swift *Apus caffer* (415) 15 cm

This medium-sized, black swift has a narrow 'U'-shaped white rump and a deeply forked tail which is diagnostic. The similar Little Swift is smaller, and can be further told apart by having a short, square to round-ended tail and a broad white rump. The similar Horus Swift is also smaller, and that species has a broad white rump extending to the sides of the body and a short, broad tail which is forked but not as elongate as that of the Whiterumped Swift. Gregarious, the Whiterumped Swift may be seen in large numbers and in mixed flocks around buildings and bridges in cities, and is also common over open country and in mountainous terrain. It is an aerial feeder and is vocal only around its nesting sites. I

Adult Whiterumped Swift

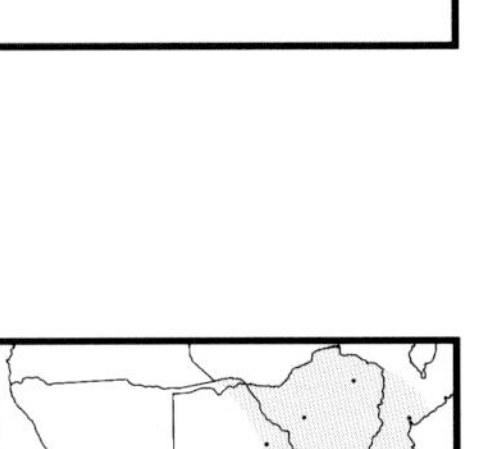

Horus Swift *Apus horus* (416) 16 cm

The Horus Swift has a shallowly forked tail which is not as elongate as that of the similar Whiterumped Swift. It differs further from that swift by its stockier build and by the size of its broad, white rump, which extends to the sides of the body. The smaller Little Swift can be separated from this species by its square to round-ended tail. The Horus Swift is an aerial bird, frequently found over mountainous terrain. It nests in burrows in deep vertical sandbanks along rivers and quarries, foraging for insects over adjacent areas. It is gregarious over much of its breeding range and is rarely seen far from its breeding grounds. R, I

Adult Palm Swift

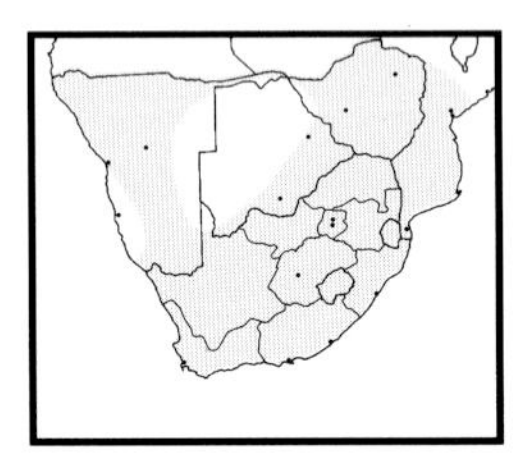

Little Swift *Apus affinis* (417) 14 cm

This small, dumpy, black swift has a square to round-ended tail and a broad, white rump which extends to the sides of the body. It may be confused with the Horus Swift but that species may be differentiated by its forked tail. In some localities these two swifts and the Whiterumped Swift might be seen flying together, hawking for insects. A gregarious and noisy species, the Little Swift is often seen wheeling around in cities, where it builds its nest, often colonially with adjacent nests touching, under bridges and ledges on buildings. This species is particularly vocal, screaming as it comes in to roost and when leaving in the early mornings. R, S

Palm Swift *Cypsiurus parvus* (421) 17 cm

This long, slender, grey-brown swift has long, narrow, pointed wings and a long, slender, deeply forked tail. Its colour is similar to that of Bradfield's Swift (see page 142) but it is a smaller bird, more streamlined in build and generally more slender than that species. The Palm Swift always occurs in association with palms, even in suburbia where the cultivation of many different species of palms in gardens and parks has encouraged it further. It roosts clinging to the underside of palm fronds at night and builds its nest by gluing feathers to the undersides of these leaves with its saliva. The call is a soft, high-pitched scream. R

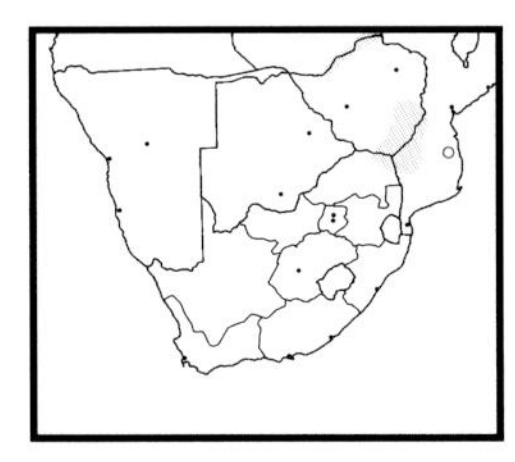

Mottled Spinetail *Telacanthura ussheri* (422) 14 cm

Similar in size, shape and colour to the Little Swift, the Mottled Spinetail has a more extensive white throat which extends on to the upper breast (where it appears mottled), and a narrow white bar across the vent, which is usually diagnostic. As with all spinetails, the feather shafts extend beyond the vanes, but this is virtually impossible to see other than if the bird is in the hand. This species occurs along well-wooded rivers and may nest in baobabs. It occurs in mixed groups with the Little Swift but may be differentiated from that species when on the wing by its slower flight action. The call is a soft twittering, unlike that of the swifts. R

1. Adult Whiterumped Swift
2. Adult Horus Swift
3. Adult Little Swift
4. Adult Palm Swift
5. Adult Mottled Spinetail
6. Adult Böhm's Spinetail

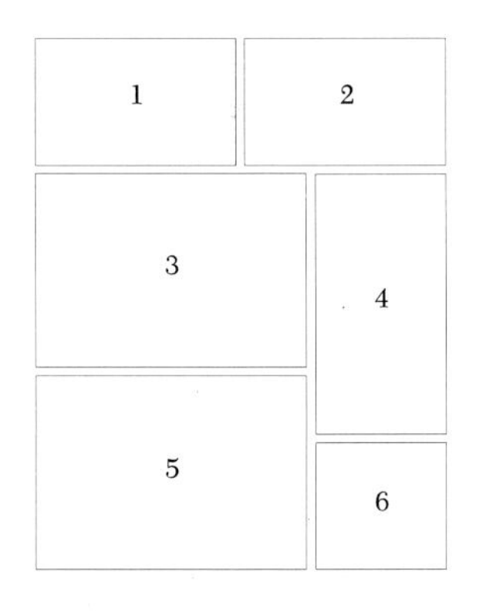

Böhm's Spinetail *Neafrapus boehmi* (423) 9 cm

This small, white-rumped bird with its white belly, brown throat and stumpy tail vaguely resembles a Brownthroated Martin (see page 182) but can be told apart from that species by its flight action and its broad white rump. It flits rather like a bat, its flight action being fast and erratic. As with all spinetails, the birds' spines – the elongations of the feather shafts – are visible only in the hand. Böhm's Spinetail occurs in thornveld and broad-leaved woodland wherever baobabs are to be found; it nests inside hollow baobabs. The call is a high-pitched 'tri-tri-tri-peep'. R

I *intra-African migrant* • R *resident* • S *summer visitor*

Mousebirds Family Coliidae

These are small, mouse-like, grey or brown birds with long, stiff tails, crests and bare faces. They live in trees and feed on fruit and vegetables, climbing dexterously about the branches. Flocks sleep huddled together.

Adult Speckled Mousebird

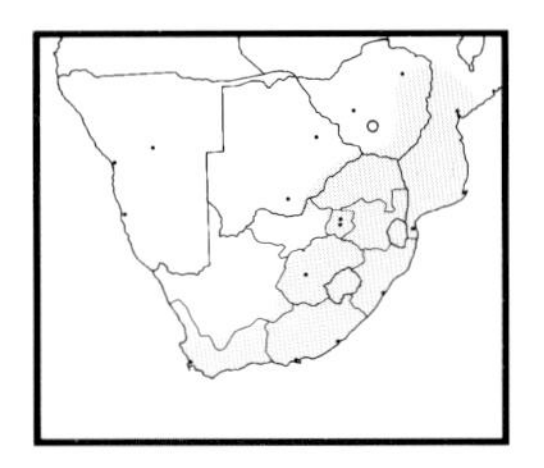

Speckled Mousebird *Colius striatus* (424) 35 cm

The Speckled Mousebird has dark, almost black legs, which separate it from the Redfaced and Whitebacked mousebirds, both of which have pink to red legs. The lower mandible is white, the upper black; the plumage on the underside is tawny, particularly on the vent, with some fine, black barring on the throat and chest. The tail is long and untidy. This mousebird frequents thick tangled bush, and is a common visitor to fruit trees in gardens and parks. Its call is a harsh 'krikk, krikk, krikk' series of notes. A clumsy and reluctant flier, it is often seen crashing into bushes on landing. R

Adult Redfaced Mousebird

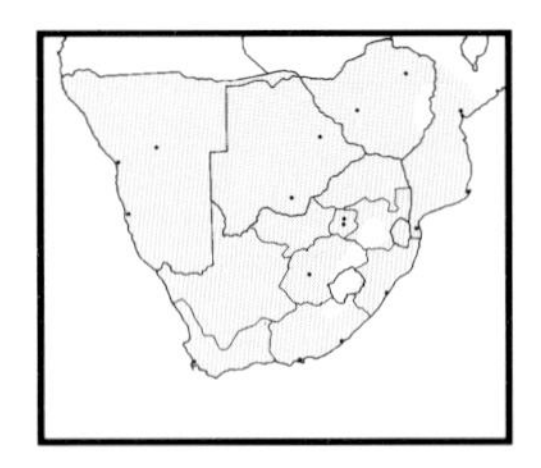

Redfaced Mousebird *Urocolius indicus* (426) 34 cm

The red facial skin, cere and legs readily identify this species. Both mandibles are black. The plumage is generally greyish to rusty-brown around the head, underwing and on the chest, and a darker grey on the back, tail and vent. It has a stiffer, narrower tail than the other two species. This species prefers riverine bush, gardens and thickets in savanna. The call is a series of notes, falling in pitch 'too weewee, too weeweewee'. R

Adult Whitebacked Mousebird

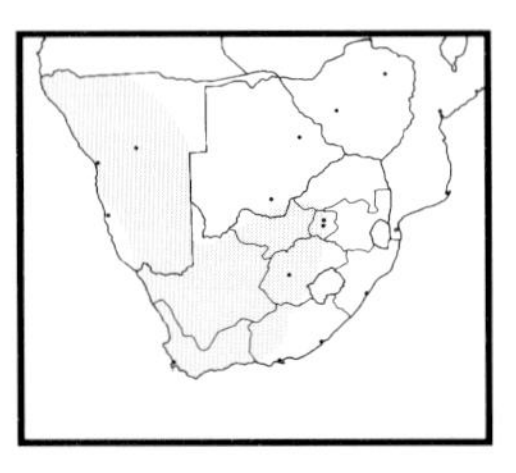

Whitebacked Mousebird *Colius colius* (425) 34 cm

The bill of this mousebird is light grey except for a black tip to the upper mandible, and the legs are red. It is generally grey in colour except for the rusty vent. In flight the back shows a white stripe bordered on either side by a black stripe. It frequents arid and semi-arid scrub-bush, riverine bush, kraals, gardens and orchards. The call of the Whitebacked Mousebird is a series of repeated 'zeee wewhit, zeee wewhit' notes. E

Trogons Family Trogonidae

Trogons are brilliantly coloured, forest-dwelling birds. They perch upright, and hawk aerial insects like a flycatcher. They nest in holes in trees.

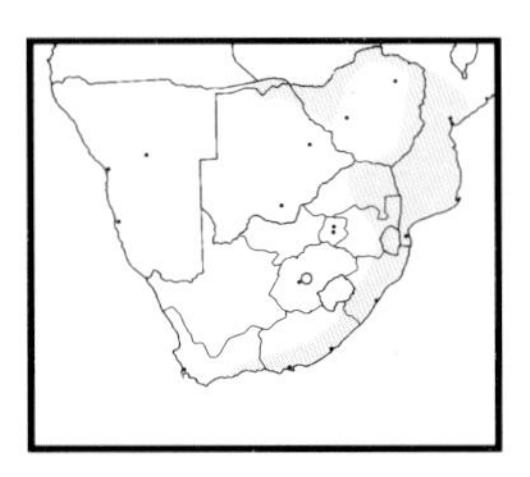

Narina Trogon *Apaloderma narina* (427) 34 cm

The bright yellow bill, emerald green upperparts and throat, and bright red breast and belly render the male of this species unmistakable; females are similar but the throat and facial area are brown. The call is reminiscent of an African Cuckoo: a series of soft 'hoo-hoo, hoo-hoo' notes, repeated up to ten times. Occurring singly or in pairs, this bird prefers the canopy of riverine and coastal forest, and moist, broad-leaved woodland. R, S

Broadbills Family Eurylaimidae

These small, rather nondescript forest-dwelling birds perform elaborate courtship displays when breeding. Insectivorous, they forage like a flycatcher.

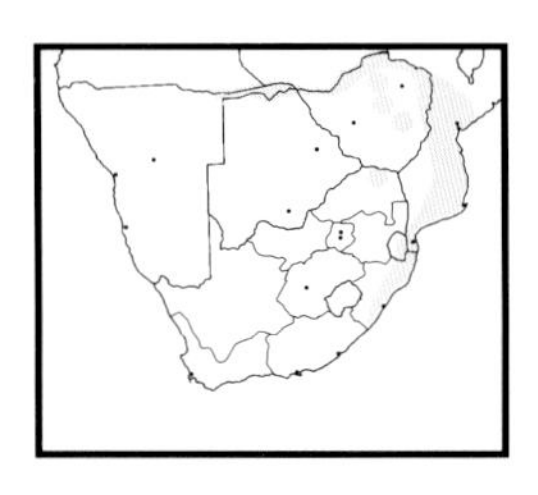

African Broadbill *Smithornis capensis* (490) 14 cm

These birds are easily overlooked and usually only seen when displaying. The male has a black cap and heavily streaked underparts; females are duller with grey streaks on the black cap and streaking below. Immatures are more yellow than adults and lack any obvious cap. African Broadbills usually occur in pairs, and frequent mixed broad-leaved woodland, thickets in sandveld terrain, and lowland evergreen forest. They call at dawn and dusk, a frog-like 'prrrrrrrruup' which is given in display flight. R

1. Adult Speckled Mousebird
2. Adult Speckled Mousebird
3. Adult Redfaced Mousebird
4. Adult Redfaced Mousebird
5. Male Narina Trogon
6. Adult Whitebacked Mousebird
7. Adult Whitebacked Mousebird
8. Female African Broadbill

1	2	3
4		5
6	7	8

R *resident* • E *endemic* • S *summer visitor*

Kingfishers Families Alcedinidae and Cerylidae

Very small to medium-sized birds, kingfishers are frequently dazzling blue and orange in colour, and have long, stout, pointed bills. They frequent water and woodland habitats, feeding on fish, insects and reptiles.

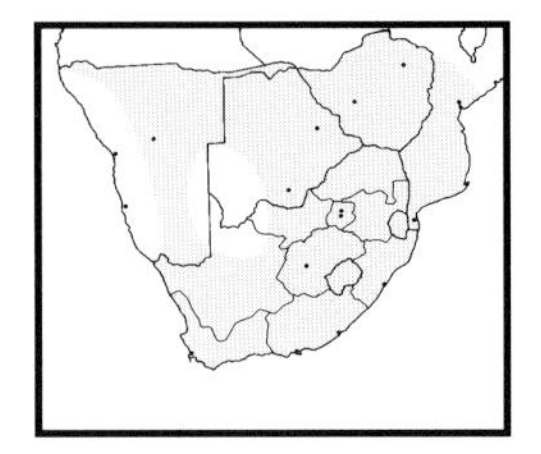

Pied Kingfisher *Ceryle rudis* (428) 28 cm

The only black and white kingfisher in our region, the Pied Kingfisher has a black, dagger-like bill, and black legs and feet. Males can be distinguished from females by their black double breast bands, which are sometimes incomplete; females and immatures show a single, incomplete band. The bird's chattering 'chik-chik' call often alerts the observer to its presence before it is seen. It fishes from perches but is also seen hovering with fast-beating wings while keeping its head motionless and pointed downwards, before diving to seize a fish. When perched it cocks its tail up and down and frequently raises the feathers on the hind crown. It nests in holes in sand banks which are excavated by both adults. The Pied Kingfisher is confined to larger inland slow-moving rivers, coastal estuaries, lagoons and dams. R

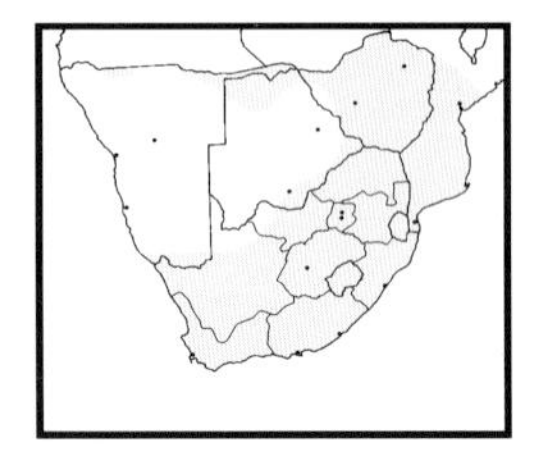

Giant Kingfisher *Ceryle maxima* (429) 46 cm

Africa's largest kingfisher, this species is unmistakable with its heavy black bill, black back speckled with white, and rufous underparts. Females are more extensively rufous below and show rufous underwing coverts in flight (white in the males) and an all-rufous underbody. Immature females are all white underneath and immature males have a speckled black breast band. Found on slow-moving rivers with overhanging vegetation, lakes, estuaries and mangroves, Giant Kingfishers fish from shady perches usually under cover of overhanging greenery. They nest in holes excavated in riverbanks. The bird's call is a harsh 'kahk-kahk-kahk'. R

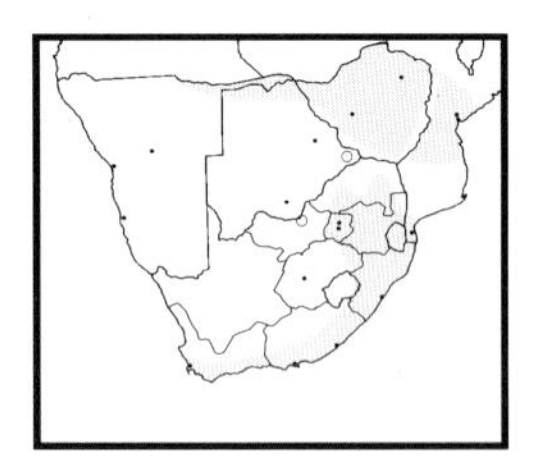

Halfcollared Kingfisher *Alcedo semitorquata* (430) 20 cm

Apart from its larger size, this species may be separated from the adult Malachite Kingfisher and Pygmy Kingfisher by its all-black, not red, bill and all-blue crown extending below the eye and on to the nape and back. The immature Halfcollared Kingfisher is separable from the immatures of those species by its larger size and all-blue crown which extends well below the eye. All three species show a clear white patch, of varying size, on the side of the neck. Quite often the Halfcollared Kingfisher is only seen as it flies away, fast, direct and low over the water. A bank-nesting species, it is found along fast-flowing, wooded streams with dense bank vegetation, along slow-moving, secluded waterways and occasionally in heavily vegetated estuaries. The call is a high-pitched 'chreep' or a softer 'peeek-peek'. R

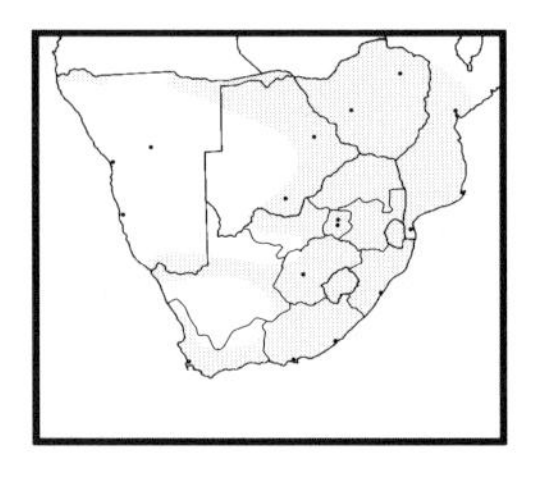

Malachite Kingfisher *Alcedo cristata* (431) 14 cm

Although similar in size to the Pygmy Kingfisher, the Malachite Kingfisher is an inhabitant of riverine habitat and is thus unlikely to be seen alongside that species. The Malachite Kingfisher has an iridescent red bill, blue upperparts and rufous cheeks and underparts. Immatures resemble the adults but have a black, not red, bill. The green to blue cap extends to the top of the eye and nape, and the rufous, not violet, ear coverts distinguish it from the Pygmy Kingfisher. It perches on reeds, sedges or sticks and plunges head first into the water, bringing its prey back to the perch to stun and swallow whole. It calls in flight, a high-pitched 'peep-peep'. R

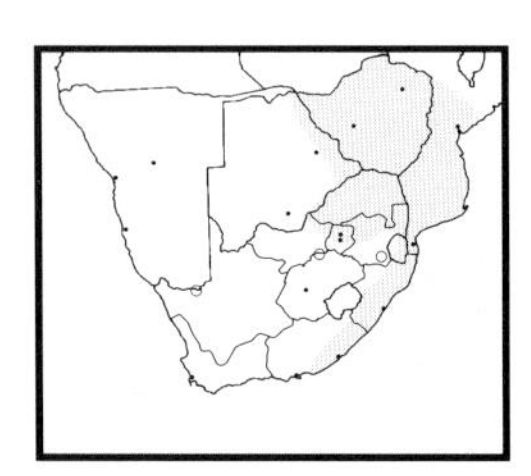

Pygmy Kingfisher *Ispidina picta* (432) 13 cm

This species is similar to the Malachite Kingfisher, but is smaller and not dependent on either fish or water. Like the Malachite Kingfisher it has a bright red bill (and, like that species, the bill is black in immatures) and a blue back but this species has a rufous nape and shows a violet ear patch and a narrow blue crown with a chestnut supercilium. The Pygmy Kingfisher may be found in open grassy woodland, coastal bush and forest, usually perching quite low down. It nests in tunnels in banks and often in the roof of a warthog or ant bear burrow near the entrance. The call, given in flight, is a high-pitched 'chip-chip' note. I

Female Pied Kingfisher

Male Giant Kingfisher

Female Giant Kingfisher

1. Female Pied Kingfisher
2. Male Pied Kingfisher
3. Adult Halfcollared Kingfisher
4. Male Giant Kingfisher
5. Immature Giant Kingfisher
6. Female Giant Kingfisher
7. Adult Malachite Kingfisher
8. Adult Pygmy Kingfisher

1	2	3 / 4
5	6	
7	8	

R *resident* • I *intra-African migrant*

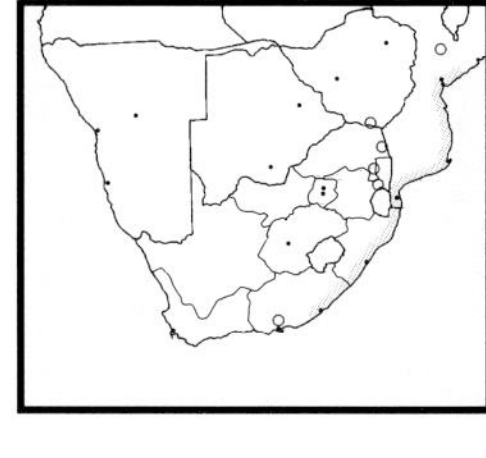

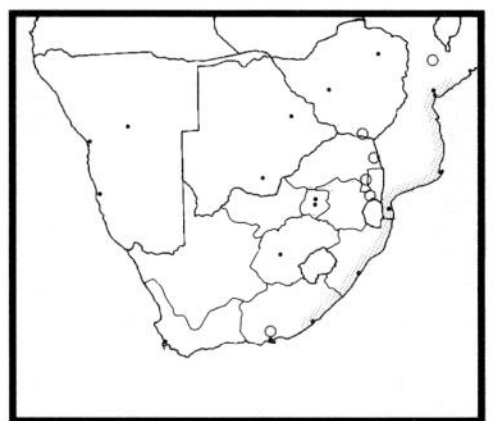

Mangrove Kingfisher *Halcyon senegaloides* (434) 24 cm

Although similar to the Woodland Kingfisher, this species is more aquatic. The all-red bill, light grey head and turquoise upperparts distinguish it from the Woodland Kingfisher, which has a black lower mandible and all-turquoise upperparts. Further, the Mangrove Kingfisher shows a black carpal patch on the otherwise white underwing coverts, while the Woodland Kingfisher has all-white underwing coverts. The sexes are alike, and immatures are similar to the adults but show a brownish bill and dark scaling on the breast. The Mangrove Kingfisher favours low-lying woodlands and well-wooded streams, moving into wooded estuaries and mangroves during the non-breeding season. It keeps close to the coast although it sometimes moves up river systems. A noisy species, it utters a loud ringing 'cheet choo-che che che', the latter part ending in a trill. R

Adult Mangrove Kingfisher

Brownhooded Kingfisher *Halcyon albiventris* (435) 24 cm

The all-red bill, brown hood and brown, not blue, back help to distinguish the Brownhooded Kingfisher from similar species. In addition, the upperwing coverts and back are seen to be brown in flight but are black in both the Mangrove Kingfisher and the Woodland Kingfisher. Immatures resemble the females, which may show a lighter-coloured back than the males. Occurring singly or in pairs, the Brownhooded Kingfisher is aggressively territorial when breeding. Courting birds sit alongside and facing each other, calling, and holding out and quivering their wings. They hunt from a perch, flying to the ground to pick up insects, scorpions, lizards, chameleons and small snakes. A common, noisy kingfisher, it gives a whistled 'tyi-ti-ti-ti', and favours woodland, savanna, and coastal and riverine bush. R

Adult Greyhooded Kingfisher

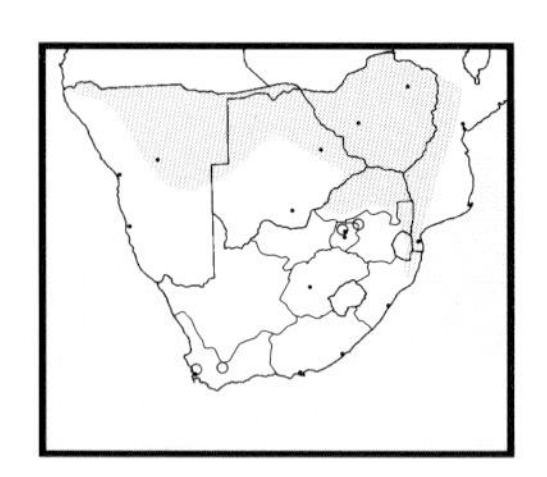

Greyhooded Kingfisher *Halcyon leucocephala* (436) 20 cm

Slightly smaller than the Brownhooded Kingfisher, the orange-red bill, silvery-grey head, nape and breast, and chestnut belly and vent further distinguish the Greyhooded Kingfisher from that species. Its lower back, secondaries and tail are navy blue, not turquoise. In flight the underwing coverts are seen to be chestnut, and at the base of the otherwise black primaries there is a large white patch. The sexes are alike; immatures have a blackish bill and dark barring on the breast and neck. This kingfisher feeds on insects, frogs and scorpions, and favours broad-leaved woodland and savanna habitats. The call, a whistled 'cheeo cheeo weecho-trrrr', is similar in pitch to that of the Brownhooded Kingfisher but much slower. I

Adult Woodland Kingfisher

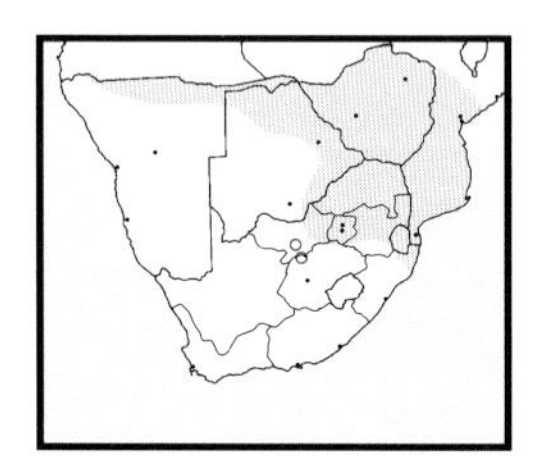

Woodland Kingfisher *Halcyon senegalensis* (433) 23 cm

Unlike similar kingfishers, this species has a black lower and a red upper mandible. The all-blue back separates it from all other *Halcyon* kingfishers except the less common Mangrove Kingfisher, which can be separated by its all-red bill. These two kingfishers are, however, unlikely to be found in the same habitat. In flight it shows all-white underwing coverts, and the wing is bright blue above with black upperwing coverts. Pairs are strongly territorial, and raucous disputes are frequently heard. Paired birds sing in duet and display facing each other, turning from side to side with outstretched wings. The call is a loud, piercing 'trrp-trrrrrrrr', the latter part descending. They inhabit woodlands and savanna with tall trees, and hunt from a perch, picking up prey from the ground, or in the air close to the ground. I

1. Adult Mangrove Kingfisher
2. Adult Brownhooded Kingfisher
3. Adult Woodland Kingfisher
4. Adult Greyhooded Kingfisher
5. Adult Woodland Kingfisher
6. Adult Striped Kingfisher

1	2
3	4
5	6

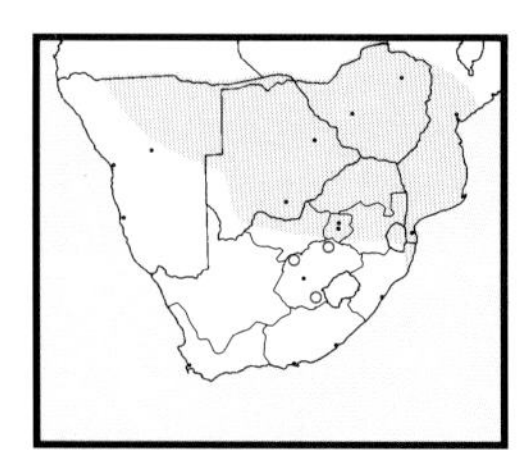

Striped Kingfisher *Halcyon chelicuti* (437) 18 cm

Smaller than the similar Brownhooded Kingfisher, the two species can further be separated on bill colour, the Striped Kingfisher having the upper mandible black and the lower one red. In the Brownhooded Kingfisher both mandibles are red; in the Woodland Kingfisher (which should not, in any case, be confused with this species on appearance) the upper mandible is red and the lower one black. The dark brown, streaky crown and mantle of the Striped Kingfisher are separated from a bright blue rump and tail by a broad white collar and, as the common name suggests, a well-striped belly and lores. Inhabiting dry woodlands and thornbush and most often seen singly, the Striped Kingfisher feeds on lizards and insects which it hunts from a perch. Its call is a high-pitched and piercing 'cheer-cherrrrr', the last notes running together. R

R *resident* • I *intra-African migrant*

Bee-eaters Family Meropidae

Bee-eaters are a group of brightly coloured, slender birds that usually occur in flocks and have distinctive contact calls. They have long, slightly decurved bills, long, pointed wings and, in some species, elongated central tail feathers. Insectivorous, they hawk their prey from the ground or from exposed perches and are attracted to veld fires, where they glean insects flushed by the heat. Some are colonial breeders, nesting at the end of long tunnels excavated in sandy banks. Most are identified by their brilliant plumage colour combinations and by their tail projections.

Adult European Bee-eater

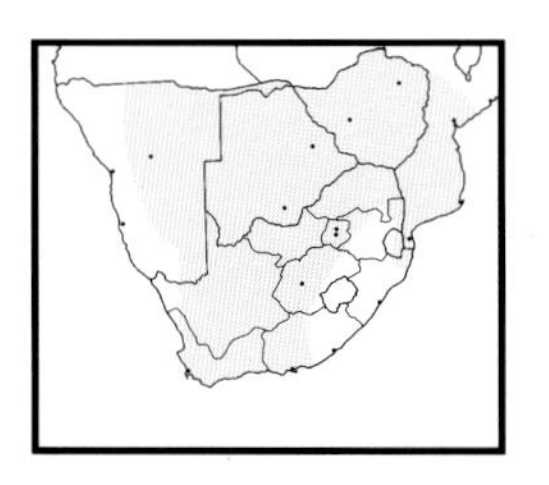

European Bee-eater *Merops apiaster* (438) 28 cm

The adults are the only bee-eaters in the region with an all-brown crown and back. Immatures have a greenish back but their blue underparts with a washed-out yellow throat separate them from the immature Bluecheeked Bee-eater. Occurring in large feeding flocks over wooded savannas, the far-reaching flight call, a frog-like 'prrrp', is often heard before the bird is seen. European Bee-eaters roost high up in the foliage of tall trees, packed together in small groups and all facing the same direction. I, S

Adult Swallowtailed Bee-eater

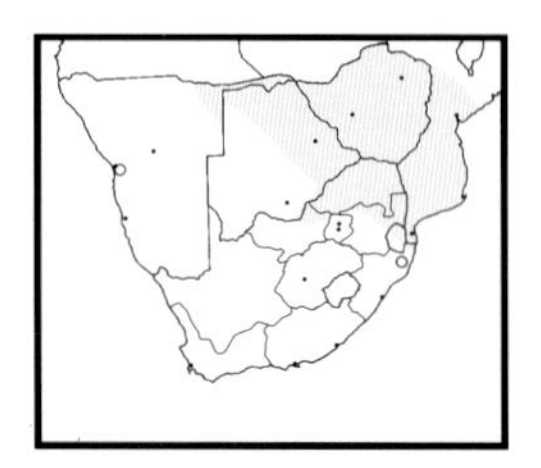

Carmine Bee-eater *Merops nubicoides* (441) 36 cm

The Carmine Bee-eater is unlikely to be misidentified as it is the only nearly all-red bee-eater in the region. Immatures are brown above, pinkish brown below and lack the elongated central tail feathers of the adults. They nest in burrows in vertical sandbanks but may also, in the absence of suitable banks, excavate burrows in level ground. They occur in wooded savannas and on grassy plains along wide, slow-moving rivers wherever large sandbanks occur. The call is a deep 'terk terk' which, given en masse, makes for a far-carrying clamour. I

Adult Bluecheeked Bee-eater

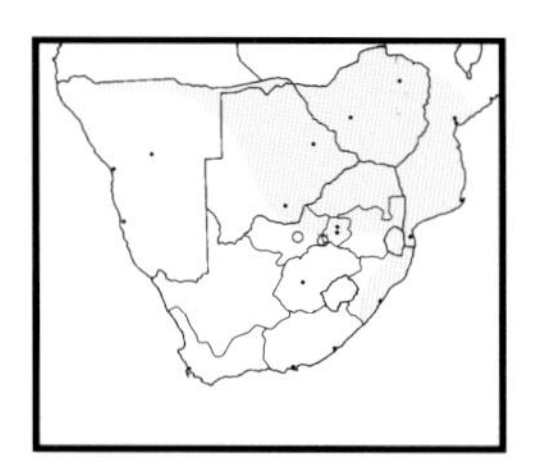

Little Bee-eater *Merops pusillus* (444) 17 cm

The smallest bee-eater in the region, this species differs from the Swallowtailed Bee-eater by its square to slightly notched, not forked, tail – which is yellowish, not blue, with a broad black subterminal band. It has a yellow throat with a black breast band (abesent in immatures). The upperparts are green and the underparts buffy yellow; in flight the bird shows russet underwings. It is found in woodland, forest margins and on the edges of thickets, and its call is a quiet 'sip' or 'chip' given from a perch. R

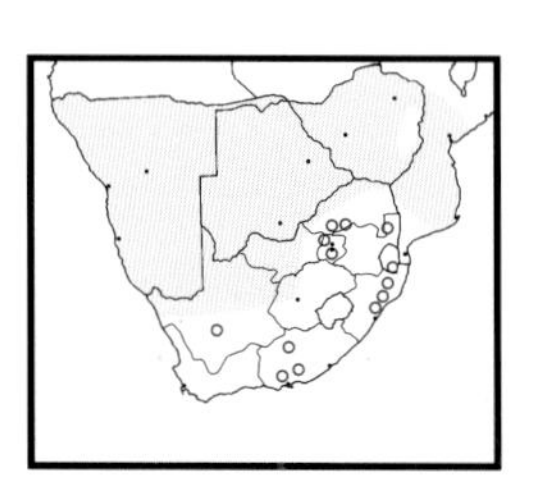

Swallowtailed Bee-eater *Merops hirundineus* (445) 22 cm

This is the only bee-eater in the region with a deeply forked, blue tail. It might be confused with the Little Bee-eater which at times also shows a slightly forked (but not blue) tail. The Swallowtailed Bee-eater's blue, not black, throat band, and greenish-blue, not buffy-yellow, underparts distinguish it further. Immatures lack the blue throat band. It is usually seen in pairs hawking for insects from a perch, and at night small groups roost huddled together. The Swallowtailed Bee-eater is found from thornveld and semi-desert scrub to forest margins and grassy miombo woodland. Its call includes soft twittering and short notes, and is similar to that of the Little Bee-eater. R

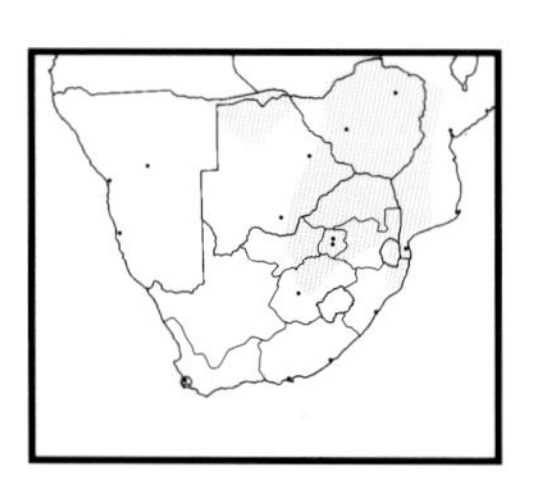

Whitefronted Bee-eater *Merops bullockoides* (443) 24 cm

This square-tailed bee-eater has a white chin and forehead and a red throat. It is a gregarious, vocal species, buffy below and dark green above and with a navy blue vent. In flight the broad black trailing edge to the wing is diagnostic. It occurs along larger rivers wherever large sand banks or erosion gullies occur, and there may nest in dense colonies. Its voice is a nasal 'kwaa', similar to that of the Greater Blue-eared Starling. R

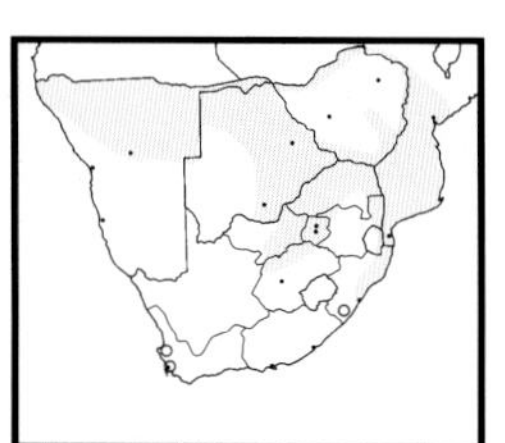

Bluecheeked Bee-eater *Merops persicus* (440) 31 cm

Adult birds are green above, including the crown, and show broad blue stripes above and below the eye and a broad black bar through the eye. From below, the turquoise-blue vent and greenish breast contrast with the yellow throat. Long tail streamers separate the adults from the immature birds. Highly gregarious, the Bluecheeked Bee-eater normally occurs in grassland and open woodland, seldom far from water, along reeded and papyrus-edged lakes and rivers. Its call is very like that of the European Bee-eater but more mellow. S

1. Adult European Bee-eater
2. Adult Carmine Bee-eater
3. Adult Little Bee-eater
4. Adult Swallowtailed Bee-eater
5. Adult Whitefronted Bee-eater
6. Adult Bluecheeked Bee-eater

1	2	3
4	5	6

I *intra-African migrant* • S *summer visitor* • R *resident*

Rollers Family Coraciidae

These stocky perching birds derive their common name from their acrobatic, noisy display flights, during which they tumble through the air. Most species have a plumage combination of bright blues, greens, violets and browns. All nest in holes in trees. Although mostly insectivorous, they also eat reptiles and small rodents.

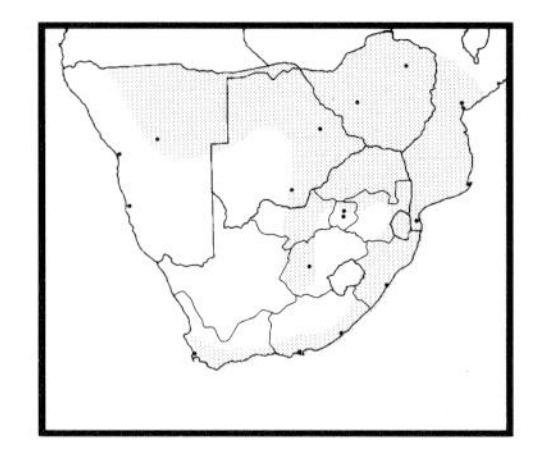

European Roller *Coracias garrulus* (446) 31 cm

This species lacks the tail streamers of the Racket-tailed Roller and the Lilacbreasted Roller. At a glance immatures might be confused with the adult Lilacbreasted Roller without tail streamers; also with the immatures of that species and the immature Racket-tailed Roller, but the bluish head and forehead should identify it. In flight this species shows all-blue upperwings in contrast with the Racket-tailed Roller's brown upperwing coverts. European Rollers forage from a perch, dropping to the ground to grab an insect, lizard or small rodent. They occur in open woodland and savannas, where they are attracted to bush fires and termite swarms. Normally silent, when alarmed the birds may utter a 'krack-krack' call. S

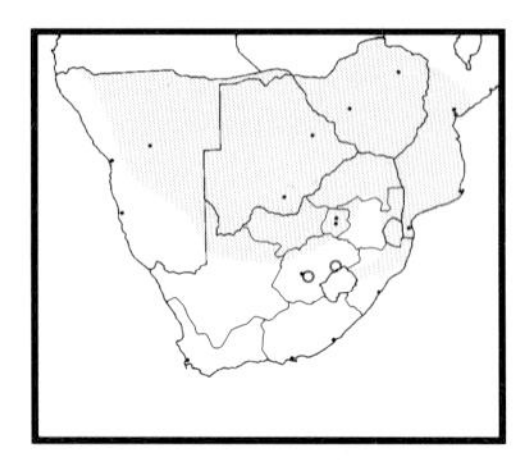

Lilacbreasted Roller *Coracias caudata* (447) 36 cm

The distinctive lilac (not blue) breast differentiates both adult and immature Lilacbreasted Rollers from the European Roller and the Racket-tailed Roller; adults lose their outer tail streamers in the non-breeding season and then resemble the immatures. A noisy species with its harsh 'rak-rak-raak' shrieks, it always perches conspicuously in the open on telephone poles, dead branches or tree stumps. In display, it flies strongly upwards, then falls, gathering speed with folded wings, before levelling out and rocking from side to side. This and the Purple Roller are the commonest rollers in the region and of the two this species is the more aggressive. Like the Purple Roller, it favours open woodland and savanna habitats. R

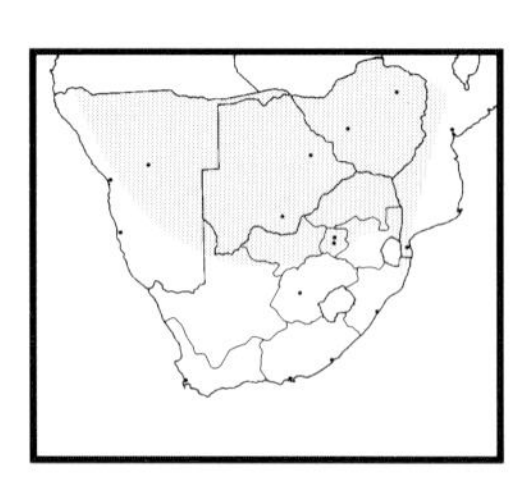

Purple Roller *Coracias naevia* (449) 38 cm

The Purple Roller has a heavy white eyebrow, a brownish-green crown and back, and lilac-brown underparts heavily streaked with white. The tail is square and lacks any tail streamers. The European Roller, which also lacks tail streamers, is brown on the back, with the blue confined to the wings and the head. The Purple Roller is the largest and least noisy roller in our region, perching in one place for long periods of time. It displays in flight, calling 'chik-kaaa, chik-kaaa, kakakaka' while rocking from side to side. It normally occurs solitarily in thornveld and open woodland. R

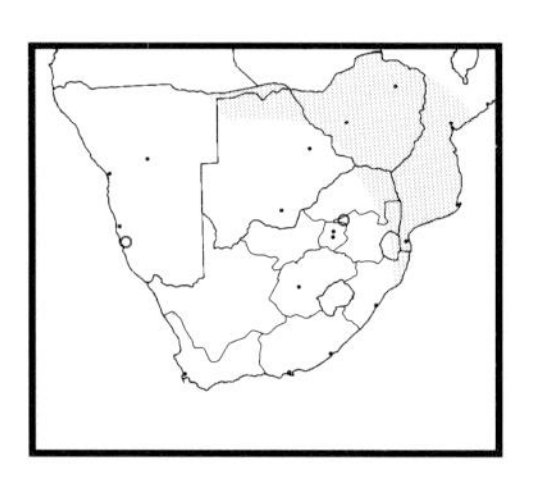

Broadbilled Roller *Eurystomus glaucurus* (450) 27 cm

This, our smallest roller, has a generally dark plumage and a bright yellow bill. The sexes are alike, and immatures are duller versions of the adults and have greenish underparts streaked with black, but also have the bright yellow bill. Despite its size it is an aggressive bird and is strongly territorial, chasing any larger bird that ventures near to it. It has a raucous call, 'karaa-karaa', and is normally seen singly on a high, open perch, usually a dead branch. It feeds on flying ants and termites, hunting in groups in the late afternoon. The Broadbilled Roller prefers large, open clearings that border thick woodland with tall trees, and it is often associated with water, miombo woodland, mopane and mixed thornveld. I

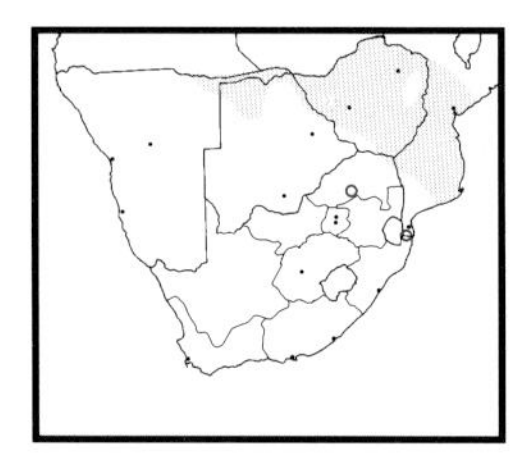

Racket-tailed Roller *Coracias spatulata* (448) 36 cm

This species is similar in size to the Lilacbreasted Roller, but appears slimmer and is bluer with no lilac on the breast. It is very similar to the European Roller but has elongated outer tail feathers the tips of which are spoon-shaped, and a brown, not blue, crown with a white, not blue, forehead. Immatures lack tail streamers, but can be identified by the brown crown, white forehead and blue breast which differ from the Lilacbreasted Roller's green crown and lilac breast, and the European Roller's all-blue head. The Racket-tailed Roller inhabits mature mopane, miombo and teak woodland and perches under the canopy on open branches. Its call is similar to the harsh screams and squawks of the Lilacbreasted Roller. R

Adult European Roller

Adult Lilacbreasted Roller

Adult Racket-tailed Roller

1. Adult European Roller
2. Adult Lilacbreasted Roller
3. Adult Purple Roller
4. Adult Broadbilled Roller
5. Adult Racket-tailed Roller

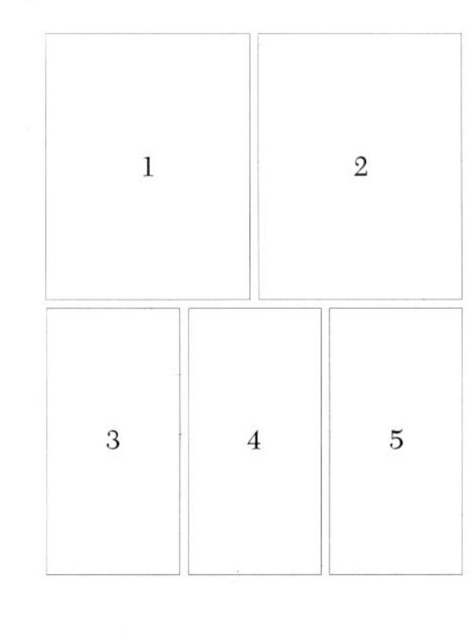

S *summer visitor* • R *resident* • I *intra-African migrant*

Hoopoe, woodhoopoes and scimitarbills
Families Upupidae, Phoeniculidae and Rhinopomastidae

The four species in this group share little in common apart from their long, thin, decurved bills. The African Hoopoe is largely terrestrial, even nesting in holes in the ground, whereas woodhoopoes and scimitarbills are arboreal, gleaning insects from the bark of trees and nesting and roosting in tree cavities. Woodhoopoes are gregarious and co-operative breeders whereas the other two species are solitary or live in pairs.

Adult Redbilled Woodhoopoe

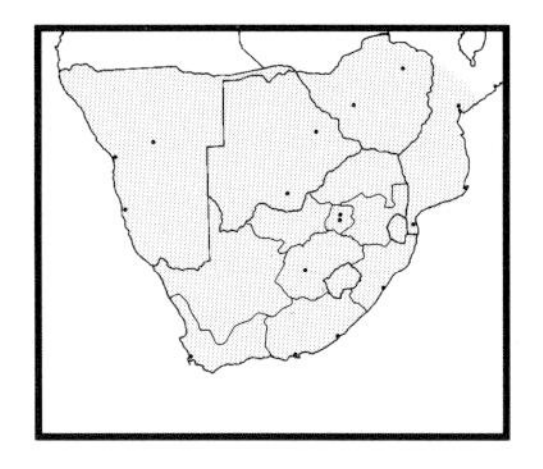

African Hoopoe *Upupa africana* (451) 28 cm

An unmistakable cinnamon-coloured species, the African Hoopoe has an erectile, black-edged crest that it raises when alarmed. It flies with shallow and abrupt wing beats, interspersed with glides, showing its conspicuous black and white wing pattern. When seen flying in pairs, the male can be seen to show more white in the wing than the female. Males at times call continuously: 'hoop-hoop-hoop' or 'hoop-hoop'. African Hoopoes feed on the ground, probing with their bills for crickets, insect larvae and earthworms. Territorial in the breeding season, they use old woodpecker holes, crevices in trees and cracks in old walls as nest sites; outside the breeding season they form loose groups. African Hoopoes frequent gardens, open woodland and thornveld. R

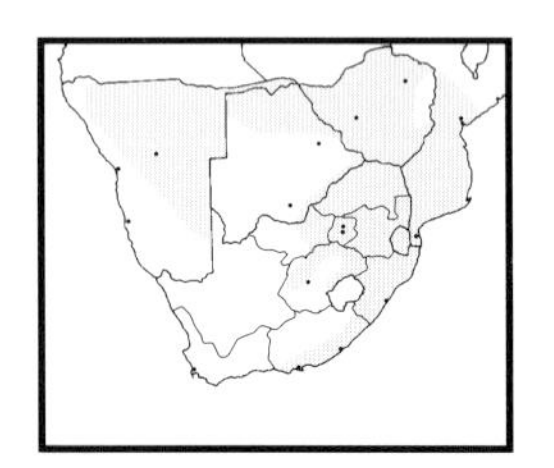

Redbilled Woodhoopoe *Phoeniculus purpureus* (452) 36 cm

Usually heard before being seen, the noisy babble of this bird is similar to that of the Arrowmarked Babbler (see page 194) and its Zulu name translates as 'the cackle of women'. It has a bright red bill, red legs, iridescent green on the mantle and underparts, and a long dark tail with white tips. Immatures have a black bill, which may cause confusion with the Greater Scimitarbill, but the bill in this species is far less decurved. The Redbilled Woodhoopoe may be mistaken for the Violet Woodhoopoe in areas of distribution overlap but that species has iridescent violet, not green, on the mantle and underparts. The Redbilled Woodhoopoe occurs in small family parties and babbles a contact call while flying from tree to tree or when feeding. They display as a group, the birds rocking back and forth with lowered heads. Typically co-operative breeders, with the offspring of previous years assisting in the collection of food for the fledglings, they roost in tree cavities and use these or old barbet holes as nest sites. They occur in savanna, open woodland and in gardens. R

Adult Greater Scimitarbill

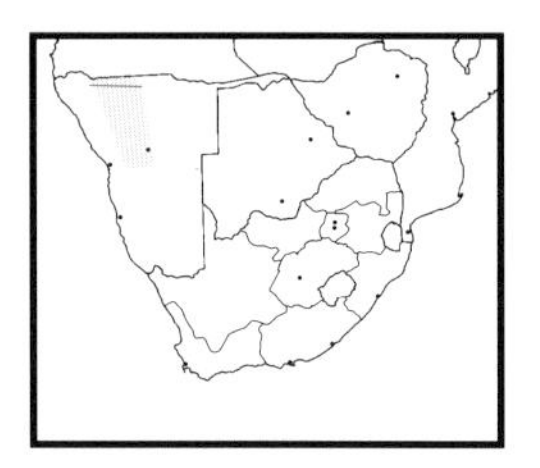

Violet Woodhoopoe *Phoeniculus damarensis* (453) 40 cm

Similar in behaviour to the Redbilled Woodhoopoe, the Violet Woodhoopoe can be separated from that species by its violet or dark purple (not iridescent green) back, mantle and underparts. It is also larger than that species and has a floppier flight action. Immatures have a black bill, and are extremely difficult to separate in the field from the immature Redbilled Woodhoopoe. All members of the family group help to raise the youngsters. The call is very similar to the cackle of the Redbilled Woodhoopoe but a little slower. The Violet Woodhoopoe occurs in drier thornveld and mopane habitat. R

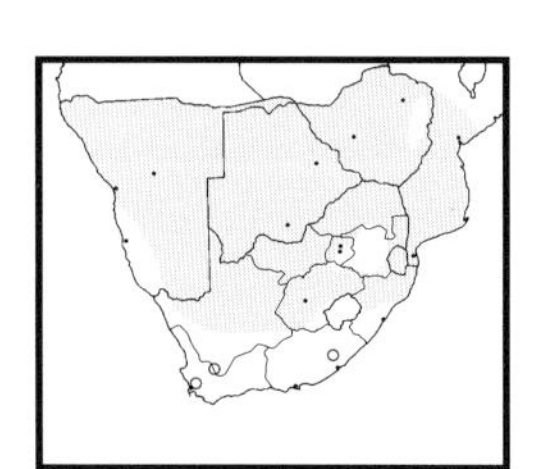

Greater Scimitarbill *Rhinopomastus cyanomelas* (454) 26 cm

This species is usually recorded singly. It is smaller and has a black, sharply decurved and much finer bill than the Redbilled Hoopoe and black, not red, legs. Males have a black body with a metallic blue or greenish sheen, depending on the light conditions; females and immature birds are browner with a markedly shorter bill than the male. All plumages show a white bar at the base of the primaries in flight, appearing as a white spot on the folded wing. Normally silent when feeding, the Greater Scimitarbill scrambles along branches probing into crevices and holes with its fine bill. Its call is a mournful, penetrating 'wheep, whoop, wheep, whoop'. It nests in natural cavities or in old hole nests and the youngsters are fed by both parents. This is a widespread species of thornveld and broad-leaved woodland. R

1. Adult African Hoopoe
2. Adult Redbilled Woodhoopoe
3. Adult Violet Woodhoopoe
4. Female Greater Scimitarbill
5. Adult Redbilled Woodhoopoe

1	2	
3	4	5

R *resident*

Hornbills Families Bucerotidae and Bucorvidae

Medium-sized to very large birds with long, heavy, decurved bills, some species of hornbill have a casque on the upper mandible. Most are identifiable by bill and body coloration. While incubating the eggs, the female is typically sealed inside the nest cavity by the male (except in the case of the Ground Hornbill, see page 160), and during this period moults the flight feathers. Most hornbills are woodland inhabitants and their diet consists mainly of fruit and berries. The huge Ground Hornbill is unusual in its diet, feeding not on fruit and berries but on insects, reptiles and small rodents.

Adult Trumpeter Hornbill

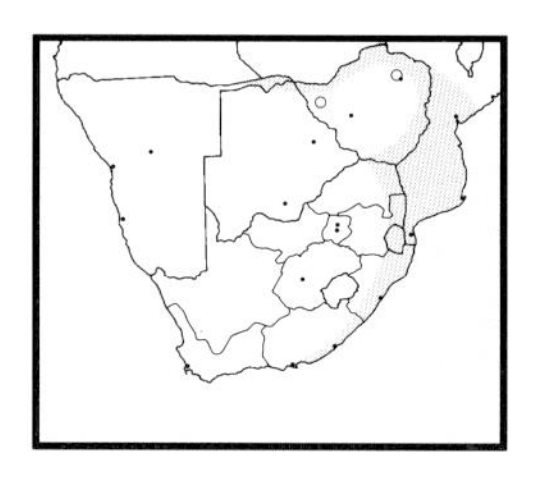

Trumpeter Hornbill *Bycanistes bucinator* (455) 58 cm

This species is similar to the Silverycheeked Hornbill but is smaller in all proportions. In flight it shows a white trailing edge to the wing, white underwing coverts, and a white belly and vent, but is otherwise black in colour. The bill has a large, dark casque on the upper mandible. The bare skin around the eye is red. This hornbill gives a prolonged, wailing, baby-like cry. It nests in holes in trees and the female seals itself in with mud pellets brought by the male; the female undergoes a wing and tail feather moult during the incubation period. This hornbill favours lowland forests, and riverine and coastal bush. R

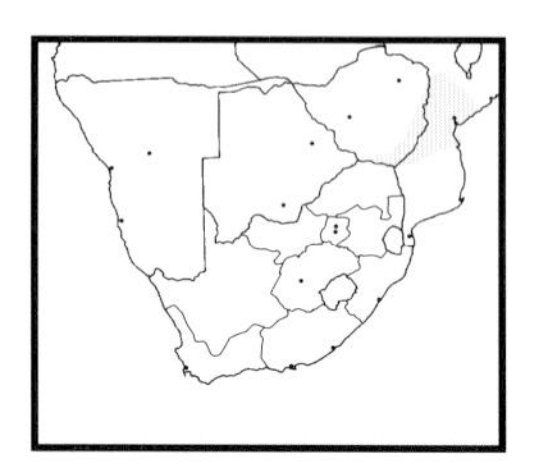

Silverycheeked Hornbill *Bycanistes brevis* (456) 75 cm

Larger and darker in all respects than the Trumpeter Hornbill, this species has an all-black belly and a white vent; in flight it shows all-black wings with a white carpal patch and an extensive white back. It has a very large, cream-coloured casque on the bill, and a black face. The Silverycheeked Hornbill feeds on fruits and insects and may at times take fruit bats. The female seals itself into the nest hole. In our region this species is rare, and is confined to the forests of the eastern highlands of Zimbabwe and eastwards. R

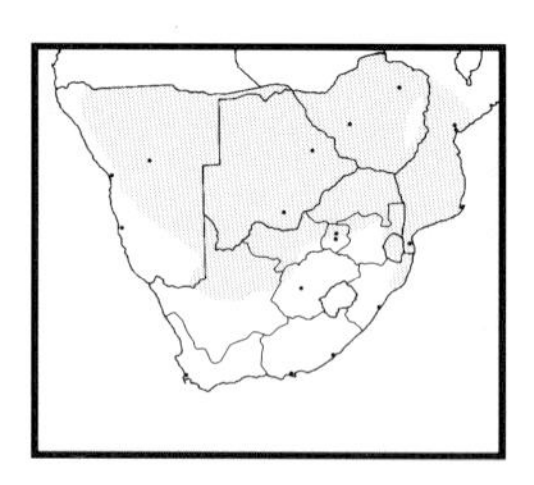

Grey Hornbill *Tockus nasutus* (457) 46 cm

The male of this species has a cream-coloured wedge at the base of the upper mandible and a few cream diagonal streaks on the lower mandible which is otherwise all black; females have a reddish end to both mandibles, the base of the upper mandible creamy white and, as in the male, diagonal streaks of cream along the base of the lower mandible. Both sexes have a brown to red-brown eye. These hornbills feed mostly on insects caught in flight, tree frogs and chameleons collected off leaves and branches, and fruit when available. The call is a mournful, wailing 'phee pheeoo, phee pheeoo'; the head is thrown back and the wings flicked open on each note. These birds are found predominantly in thornveld and dry broad-leaved woodland. R

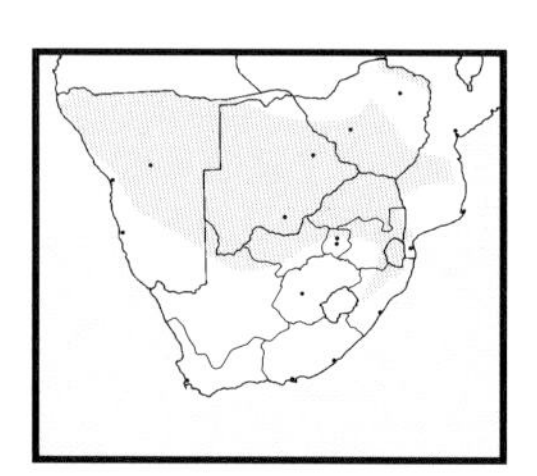

Southern Yellowbilled Hornbill *Tockus flavirostris* (459) 55 cm

The flight action and call of the Southern Yellowbilled Hornbill are virtually indistinguishable.from those of the Redbilled Hornbill. The deep-yellow eye surrounded by bare red skin, the red throat patch and the large yellow bill of the Southern Yellowbilled Hornbill separate it from the Redbilled Hornbill, however. Immatures are similar to the adults, with a washed-out yellow bill and a greyish eye. Omnivores foraging mostly on the ground where ground cover is sparse, they take termites, grasshoppers and caterpillars; they also hawk for insects, and will eat fruits and seeds. The call is a 'kok-kok-kok-kok', changing to a scrambled, continuous 'wokawokawokawoka'. These birds are widespread residents of thornveld and drier broad-leaved woodland. R

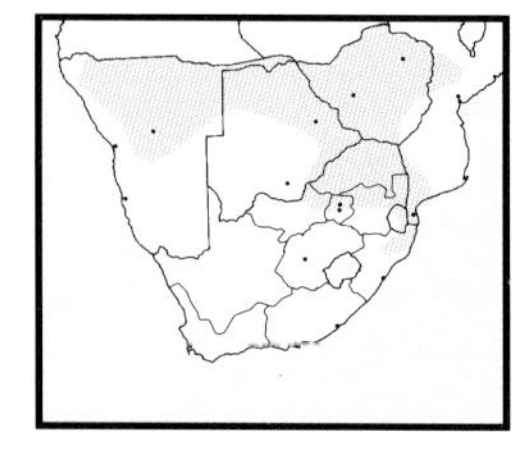

Redbilled Hornbill *Tockus erythrorhynchus* (458) 46 cm

The flight and call of this species could be mistaken for that of the more common Southern Yellowbilled Hornbill but the Redbilled Hornbill is smaller in size, has a more slender red, not yellow, bill and less extensive, yellowish naked skin around the eyes and on the throat. Males have a black base to the lower mandible and immatures have an all-dark bill. Where its range overlaps with that of Monteiro's Hornbill (see page 160), the Redbilled Hornbill can be distinguished by its white breast, white sides to the neck and face, and yellow eye. The Redbilled Hornbill searches on the ground for grasshoppers, ground beetles and termites. An open woodland and thornveld resident, its call is a rapid 'wha wha wha' followed by 'kukwe kukwe'. R

1. Adult Trumpeter Hornbill
2. Adult Silverycheeked Hornbill
3. Male Grey Hornbill
4. Female Grey Hornbill
5. Adult Silverycheeked Hornbill
6. Adult Southern Yellowbilled Hornbill
7. Adult Redbilled Hornbill

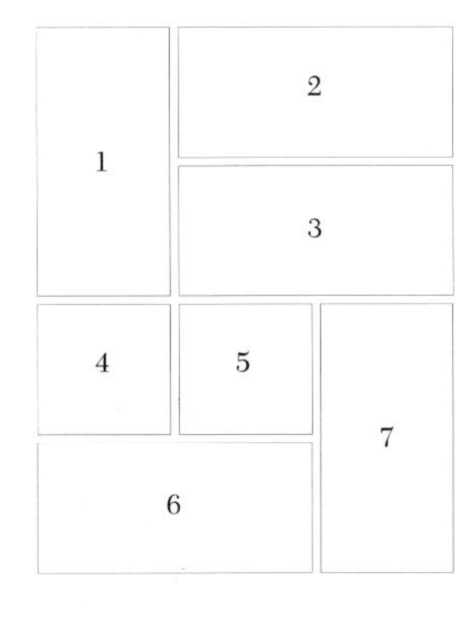

R *resident*

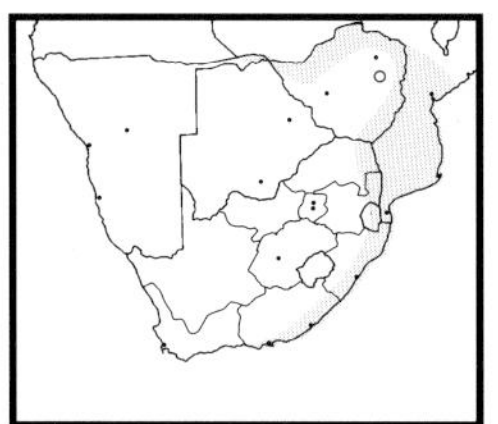

Crowned Hornbill *Tockus alboterminatus* (460) 54 cm

This species, Bradfield's Hornbill and Monteiro's Hornbill all have orange-red bills, but the Crowned Hornbill has a narrow yellow base to its bill which matches its bright yellow eye. It also shows a deeper casque than the other two species. In flight it has a dark, unmarked back and wings, and shows white tips to the outer tail feathers; below it has a white belly and a dark grey breast and throat. Immatures have a greyish eye and a plain tail. A tree-loving species, the Crowned Hornbill searches for food in the foliage and sometimes catches insects in the air. It is readily identified by its whistling 'pi-pi-pi-pi-pi' call. It frequents riverine bush, lowland savanna, coastal bush and forest edges. R

Adult Bradfield's Hornbill

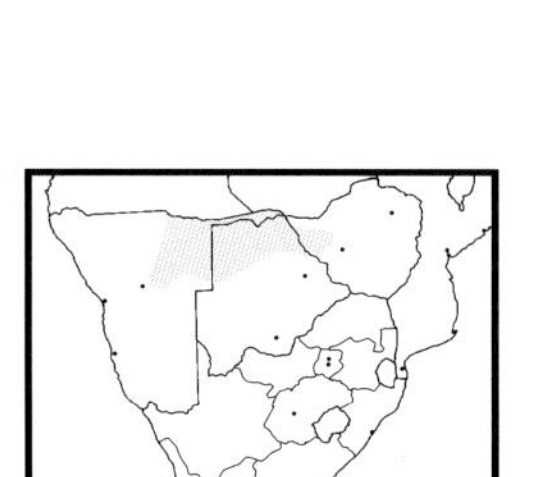

Bradfield's Hornbill *Tockus bradfieldi* (461) 56 cm

The range of this species hardly overlaps with that of the similar Monteiro's Hornbill; confusion is therefore more likely with the Crowned Hornbill. Bradfield's Hornbill has all-dark wings and white tips to the otherwise dark, unmarked tail feathers; Monteiro's Hornbill has all-white outer tail feathers and white secondaries showing as an extensive white patch. Bradfield's Hornbill has a yellow-orange eye and Monteiro's Hornbill a dark reddish-brown eye, while that of the Crowned Hornbill is bright yellow. Immatures resemble the adults. These birds search for food in trees, as well as on the ground, taking insects, locusts, termites and the occasional lizard. The call is a plaintive, whistled 'pleeeoo, pleeoo', almost identical to that of the Crowned Hornbill. They are found in teak and mopane woodland. NE

Adult Monteiro's Hornbill

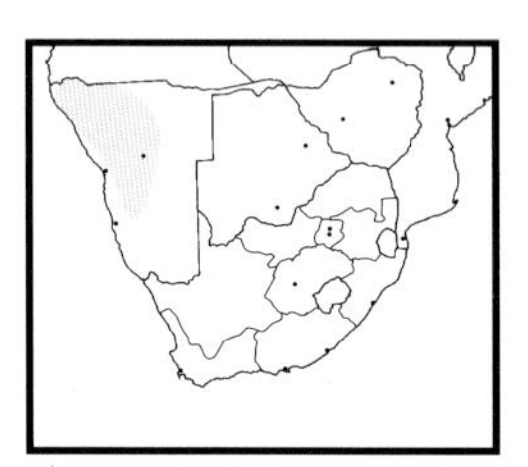

Monteiro's Hornbill *Tockus monteiri* (462) 56 cm

Monteiro's Hornbill is similar to Bradfield's Hornbill, but is readily identifiable in flight by its all-white outer tail feathers (it has dark central feathers) and all-white secondaries. Its upperwing coverts are heavily spotted with white and the eye is a dark reddish brown. Immatures are similar to the adults but have a paler bill. Monteiro's Hornbill spends much of its time foraging on the ground, digging for bulbs with its bill and searching for berries, insects, lizards and large crickets. The call is a hollow-sounding 'tooaak-tooaak', and in display it lowers its head and closes its wings. These birds prefer semi-arid desert, mopane and thornveld, in hilly country with a stony substrate. R

Adult Ground Hornbill

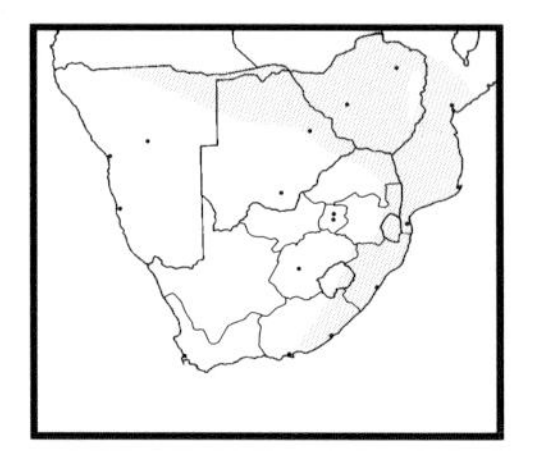

Ground Hornbill *Bucorvus leadbeateri* (463) 90 cm

Most unlike the usual tree-dwelling hornbills, the conspicuous unfeathered red face and red inflated throat sacs, black plumage and very long, deep black bill easily identify this species. The female is distinguished from the male by its blue, not red, throat patch, and the immature bird differs from the adults by having a yellow, not red, face and throat patch. In flight these birds show broad white wing patches. The Ground Hornbill is not often found outside national parks and reserves. Its call, a duetted, booming 'ooomph, ooomph, ooomph' is uttered in the early morning. R

1. Adult Monteiro's Hornbill
2. Adult Bradfield's Hornbill
3. Immature Ground Hornbill
4. Male Crowned Hornbill
5. Adult Ground Hornbill

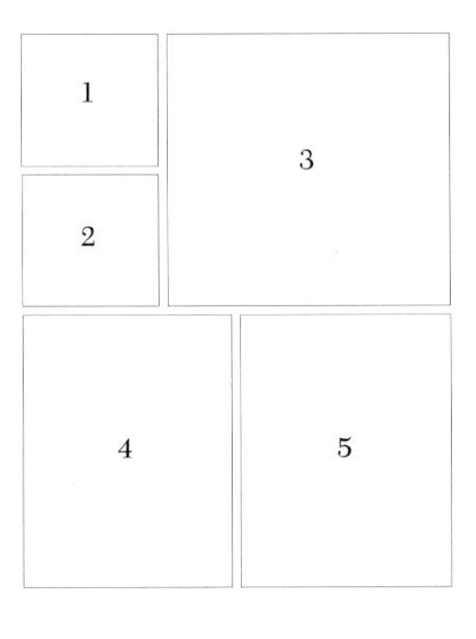

R *resident* • NE *near endemic*

Barbets Family Capitonidae

These are small birds with stout bodies and large heads and bills. They have an unusual toe arrangement in that two toes point forwards and two backwards. All have distinctive calls, the tinker barbets (see page 164) having clinking call notes. Frugivorous and insectivorous forest- and bush-dwellers, they excavate nesting holes in dead trees; their nests are regularly parasitized by honeyguides (see pag 166).

Adult Blackcollared Barbet (yellowheaded form)

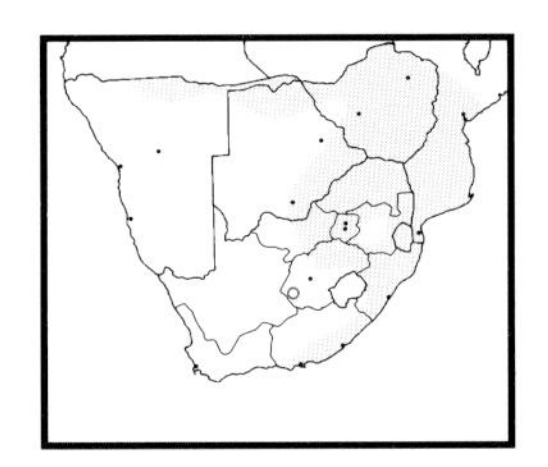

Blackcollared Barbet *Lybius torquatus* (464) 20 cm

The bright red face surrounded by a black collar of this bird is diagnostic, although a rare yellow-faced morph does occur. The sexes are alike; immatures have a dark brown head and throat streaked with orange and red. Its flight is heavy and fast on whirring wings. An omnivorous forager, it feeds on soft fruits such as papaya, figs and berries, and also takes insects. The youngsters are fed by both adults and up to two other adult helpers. The call is a far-reaching duet beginning 'krrr krrr' and exploding into a 'too puddly too puddly', repeated seven to eight times. Blackcollared Barbets frequent thornveld, coastal forest, savanna and broad-leaved woodland, and are also common in suburban gardens where can become quite confiding. R

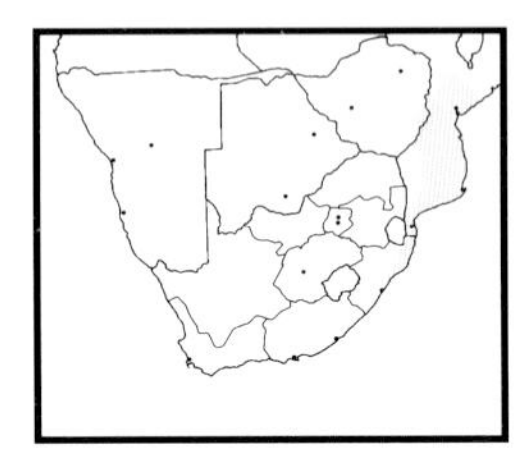

White-eared Barbet *Stactolaema leucotis* (466) 17 cm

This all-dark-brown bird, slightly darker on the head, has a prominent broad white stripe behind the eye. It also has a white belly. It feeds on fruit, with a predilection for figs, and insects, and in miombo woodland on *Uapaca* fruits. It roosts communally in tree holes. The youngsters are fed by both adults and up to two adult helpers. White-eared Barbets are parasitized by Greater Honeyguides (see page 166), Lesser Honeyguides (see page 166) and Scalythroated Honeyguides (see page 166). Occurring in pairs and small groups, these barbets favour lowland and coastal evergreen forests, especially fig forests and, in Zimbabwe, miombo woodland. The call is a high-pitched 'kreep-kreep-kreep' changing in pitch to 'krip-krip-krip'. R

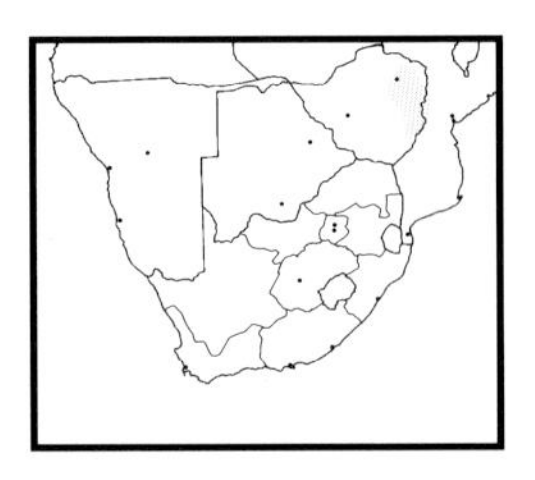

Whyte's Barbet *Stactolaema whytii* (467) 18 cm

Whyte's Barbet is superficially similar to the White-eared Barbet. It is a paler brown, however, and lacks the white ear patches of that species. It can be further distinguished by its white to yellow forehead, white patch in the wing formed at the base of the inner primaries, and its white vent. Immatures have a black forehead speckled with white. An inconspicuous barbet with low-key 'coo-coo' vocalization, it may roost communally in holes at night. It is often parasitized by the Lesser Honeyguide (see page 166) and is most likely to be encountered in miombo woodland. R

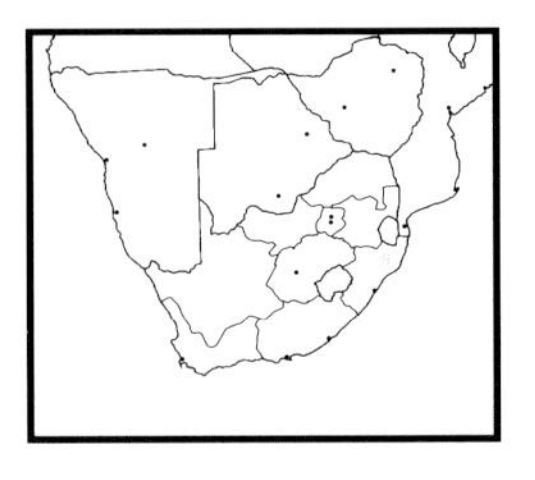

Woodwards' Barbet *Cryptolybia woodwardi* (468) 17 cm

Clothed in a uniform, drab dark green except for a pale, yellow-green patch behind the eye, this barbet has one of the most restricted ranges of any species in southern Africa, being confined to the Ngoye forest in KwaZulu/Natal. The sexes are alike, and immatures are similar to yet duller than the adults. Woodward's Barbet feeds on fruit and insects but little is known about its breeding habits. Its call is a monotonous, hollow-sounding 'pok pok pok pok' or 'chop chop chop' continuing for 10 to 15 seconds at intervals of about one second. E

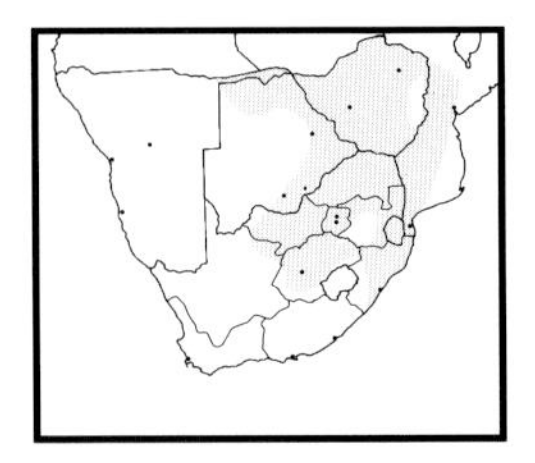

Crested Barbet *Trachyphonus vaillantii* (473) 23 cm

One of a group of superficially similar-looking barbets belonging to the genus *Trachyphonus*, the Crested Barbet is the only representative of its genus in southern Africa. Its yellow underparts streaked with red and separated by a black breast band are diagnostic, as are its yellow face and short, straggly crest. The sexes are similar but the females are usually less vividly coloured than the males; immatures resemble the adults. It is found either solitarily or in pairs and can become quite confiding in sub-urban gardens. Territorial in the breeding season, it aggressively defends its nest hole against other hole-nesting species. The Crested Barbet feeds on insects, fruit and worms. The call is a sustained, trilling 'trrrr'. It frequents thornveld, suburbia, broad-leaved woodland and savanna. R

1. Adult Blackcollared Barbet
2. Adult White-eared Barbet
3. Adult Whyte's Barbet
4. Adult Woodward's Barbet
5. Adult Crested Barbet

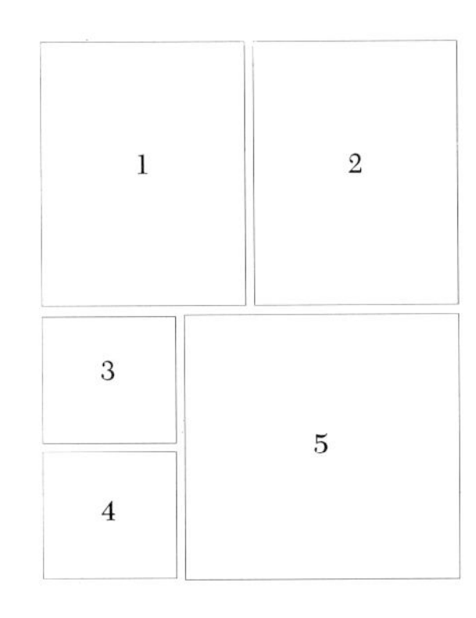

R *resident* • E *endemic*

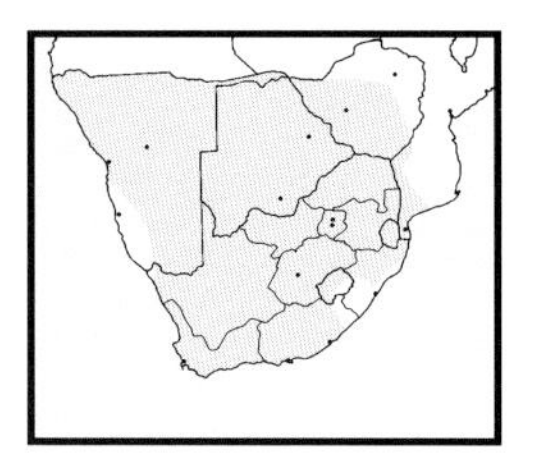

Acacia Pied Barbet *Tricholaema leucomelas* (465) 18 cm

This barbet has a red forehead like the Redfronted Tinker Barbet but it is a much larger bird and has a black throat and white underparts; these are all cream in the Redfronted Tinker Barbet. A broad white supercilium, with yellow in front of the eye, separates the black crown from a heavy black stripe running from the base of the bill through the eye to the nape. The call is a distinctive, nasal 'nehh, nehh, nehh', sometimes likened to the noise made by a tinny toy trumpet. This barbet is found in arid semi-desert scrub, thornveld and woodland on Kalahari sandveld, and in gardens, but is especially common in arid thornveld. R

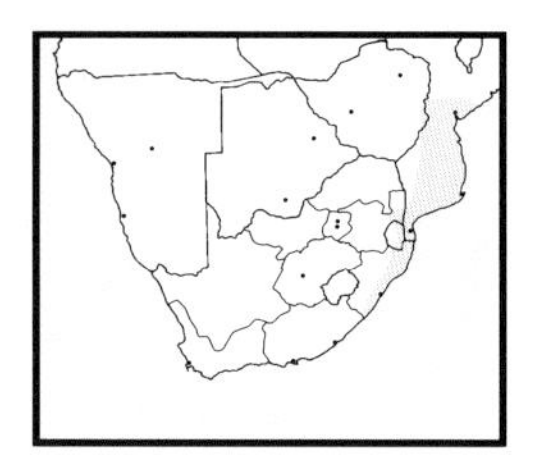

Goldenrumped Tinker Barbet *Pogoniulus bilineatus* (471) 10 cm

The black back and crown and the two white neck stripes of the Goldenrumped Tinker Barbet are diagnostic and contrast with its greyish-yellow underparts. Its yellow rump is seen more easily in flight than when the bird is perched. It calls from the tops of trees, giving five or six 'tonk-tonk' notes before a break. The calls of the Yellowfronted Tinker Barbet and the Redfronted Tinker Barbet are similar to those given by this species but are continuous. The Goldenrumped Tinker Barbet feeds on fruit and actively searches for insects. It nests in holes in trees in coastal and evergreen forests, and may be parasitized by honeyguides (see page 166). R

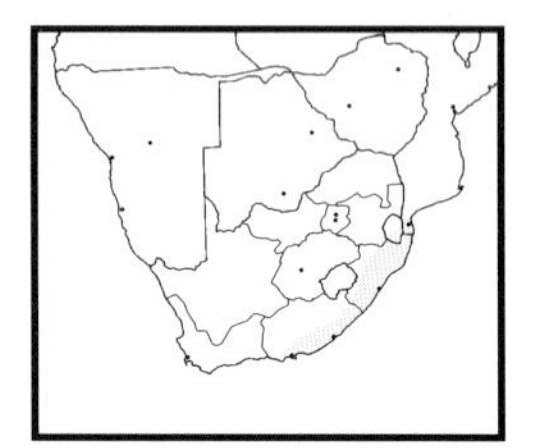

Redfronted Tinker Barbet *Pogoniulus pusillus* (469) 11 cm

The Redfronted Tinker Barbet is similar to the Yellowfronted Tinker Barbet – particularly the orange-fronted form – but the ranges of the two species do not overlap, the Yellowfronted Tinker Barbet preferring a drier habitat. As the name suggests, this bird has a bright red forehead. The diagnostic golden-yellow patch on the wing also separates this species from the Yellowfronted Tinker Barbet, which has pale yellowish edges to the wing feathers instead. The call, a continuous 'pop-pop-pop-pop' or 'tink-tink-tink-tink', is almost indistinguishable from that of the Yellowfronted Tinker Barbet but it is slightly faster and higher pitched. The Redfronted Tinker Barbet occurs in coastal and lowland riparian forest and feeds along branches and in foliage. It takes insects and also berries, especially those of the parasitic mistletoes. R

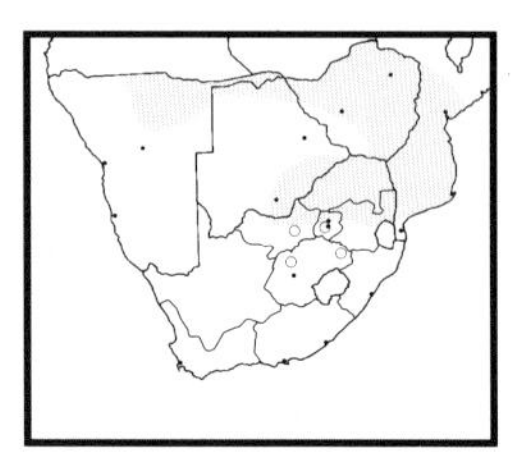

Yellowfronted Tinker Barbet *Pogoniulus chrysoconus* (470) 11 cm

This species is very similar to the Redfronted Tinker Barbet, but the ranges of the two do not overlap. The forehead varies in colour from yellow to orange but is never red as in the Redfronted Tinker Barbet. The Yellowfronted Tinker Barbet also lacks the golden wing patch of that species, having pale edging to the wing feathers instead. The immature bird lacks the yellow forehead. The call is a continuous 'tonk tonk tonk' but is slower and lower pitched than that of the Redfronted Tinker Barbet. The Yellowfronted Tinker Barbet feeds on mistletoe fruits, beetles and other insects; the stones of the fruits are regurgitated and rejected. This is a widespread species of thornveld, open woodland and savanna. R

1. Adult Acacia Pied Barbet
2. Adult Goldenrumped Tinker Barbet
3. Adult Redfronted Tinker Barbet
4. Adult Yellowfronted Tinker Barbet

1	2
3	4

R *resident*

Honeyguides Family Indicatoridae

Small, short-legged birds, honeyguides are usually drab in coloration and have short, stubby or pointed bills. Species identification is usually based on call, shape of bill and habits. These birds are unique in that they eat beeswax. Brood parasites, some lay their eggs in the nests of barbets and woodpeckers, others in the nests of cisticolas and white-eyes.

Adult Sharpbilled Honeyguide

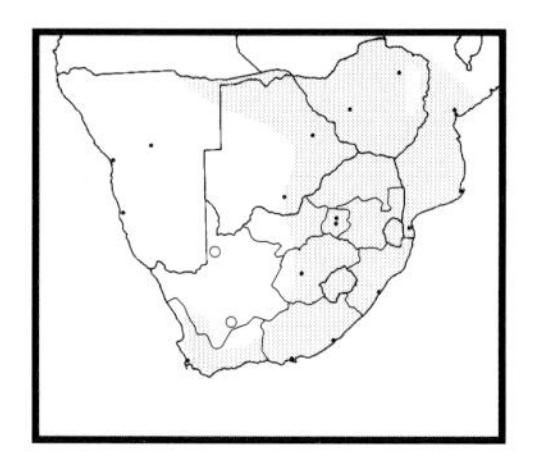

Greater Honeyguide *Indicator indicator* (474) 20 cm

Similar in size to a Blackeyed Bulbul (see page 196), the male Greater Honeyguide is unmistakable with its pink bill and white cheek patches contrasting with the black throat and dark crown. Females are plainer, being grey above, with a horn-coloured bill and a plain, pale, unmarked throat and breast, differing in this respect from the similar Scalythroated Honeyguide which has a well-mottled throat and breast. Immatures are creamy yellow below and have a dark brown back. Males have a fixed call site and will guide man to beehives. The call is far reaching and sounds like 'victor, vic-tor'. As a brood parasite, this bird uses a wide range of hole-nesting hosts, including kingfishers (see page 148), barbets (see page 162), bee-eaters (see page 152) and hoopoes (see page 156). It is found in a variety of habitats including broad-leaved woodland, forest edges and exotic plantations, but tends to avoid forests. R

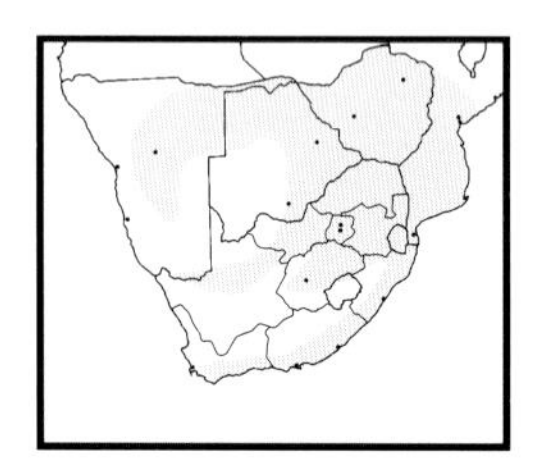

Lesser Honeyguide *Indicator minor* (476) 15 cm

Resembling a Greyheaded Sparrow (see page 268) in size and shape, the Lesser Honeyguide can be told apart from that species by its white outer tail feathers, a feature of all the honeyguides in our region. Smaller in size than the Scalythroated Honeyguide, its dark grey head and grey, unmarked throat and breast further separate it from that species. The sexes are alike. Immatures are similar to but darker than the adults, and lack a moustachial stripe. Usually solitary, the Lesser Honeyguide makes use of a favourite call site but does not guide man to bees' nests, as does the Greater Honeyguide. The call is a trilling, far-reaching 'krrr, krrr', repeated many times; the bird can usually be located by its call. Lesser Honeyguides occur in woodland, forest and thornveld, and have adapted to urban gardens. They feed on beeswax, bees, ants, termites and caterpillars. They are known to parasitize Blackcollared Barbets, Crested Barbets and White-eared Barbets (see page 162). R

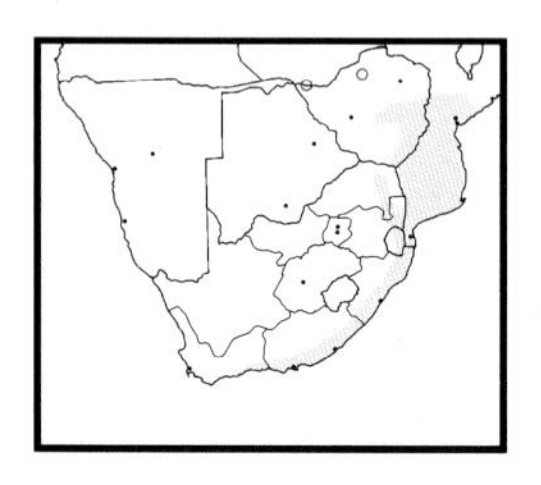

Scalythroated Honeyguide *Indicator variegatus* (475) 19 cm

This species is larger than the Lesser Honeyguide and appears a uniform olive-green in colour with a streaked head and lores, and a mottled chin and breast – it is the only honeyguide in the region to show this mottling. The sexes are alike but the male is larger than the female. Immatures have the front washed with green and spotted with black. Its dipping flight is rather like that of a woodpecker. Its call is a frog-like 'prrrrp', rising towards the end and repeated every minute or so. It feeds on beeswax, honey, bee larvae, flies and occasionally fruit. A brood parasite, its hosts are the Goldentailed Woodpecker (see page 168) and the Cardinal Woodpecker (see page 170) and also, rarely, tinker barbets (see page 164). The Scalythroated Honeyguide is found in the canopy areas of coastal and riverine forests. R

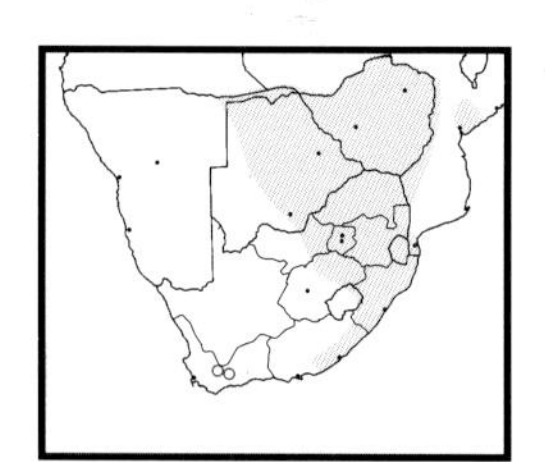

Sharpbilled Honeyguide *Prodotiscus regulus* (478) 13 cm

Similar in colour to a Spotted Flycatcher (see page 234) and in shape and appearance to a Dusky Flycatcher (see page 234), the white outer tail feathers (conspicuous in flight) of this species separate it from the flycatchers. When perched, the tail appears white below and brown above. The bill is slender and pointed, rather warbler-like, unlike those of other honeyguide species, which have short, stout bills. The sexes are alike. Immatures are paler than the adults and the outer tail feathers are entirely white; these are brown-tipped in the adults. Sharpbilled Honeyguides are usually seen singly, foraging from a perch and hawking for insects in the manner of a flycatcher. This honeyguide parasitizes the Neddicky (see page 228) and both bleating warblers (see page 222). It gives a rapid, churring call and a metallic 'zwick' during its dipping display flight. It favours woodland, savanna, coastal forests and exotic plantations. R

1. Female Greater Honeyguide
2. Male Greater Honeyguide
3. Adult Lesser Honeyguide
4. Adult Sharpbilled Honeyguide
5. Adult Scalythroated Honeyguide

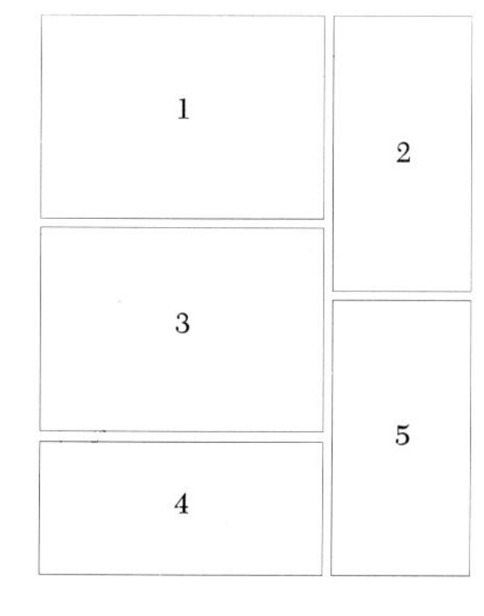

R *resident*

Woodpeckers and wrynecks

Families Picidae and Jyngidae

These small to medium-sized birds have stout, pointed bills which are used to hammer and bore into wood to reach grubs and insects, and also to excavate nest holes. The tails are stiff and brace the birds as they cling to branches and move jerkily up tree trunks.

Immature Goldentailed Woodpecker

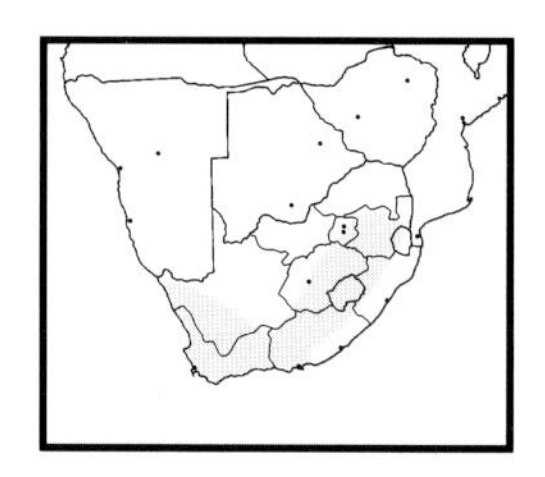

Ground Woodpecker *Geocolaptes olivaceus* (480) 25 cm

An aberrant woodpecker in being entirely terrestrial, the Ground Woodpecker nests in burrows in earth banks. Our largest woodpecker, it is a little larger than a Cape Rock Thrush (see page 202), which occurs in similar habitat, and is easily identifiable by its white eye, rosy-pink breast, bright pink uppertail coverts and by its yellow-spotted wings. Unlike other woodpeckers, it lacks any distinctive facial markings although it does have reddish moutachial stripes. Females and immatures are less brightly coloured than the males, and lack the moustachial stripes. The call is a far-reaching, screamed 'peeeaaargh'. These birds hop on the ground and forage among boulders. When disturbed they fly close to the ground, often for quite a distance. They occur in family groups of three to five individuals, preferring boulder-strewn, grassy hill slopes and rocky gorges; they occur to sea level in the southwestern Cape. E

Immature Knysna Woodpecker

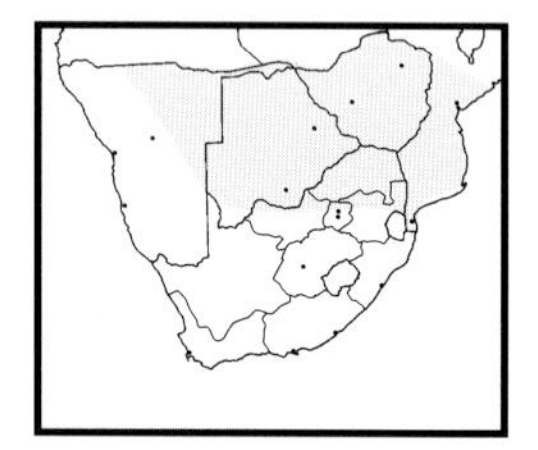

Bennett's Woodpecker *Campethera bennettii* (481) 24 cm

A fairly large woodpecker, the male Bennett's Woodpecker is the only woodpecker in our region with a red forehead and crown and a broad, red moustache. Females have a brown throat and broad, brown streaks below and behind the eye but, unlike the males, have a black forehead flecked with white. Immatures resemble the females. All plumage stages show the heavily spotted, black on cream breast and belly. The call is a high-pitched chattering, 'whirr-it-whirrr-it', offered in duet. Bennett's Woodpeckers feed on the ground, taking mostly ants and their pupae, and prefer mature, broad-leaved woodland and savanna habitats. R

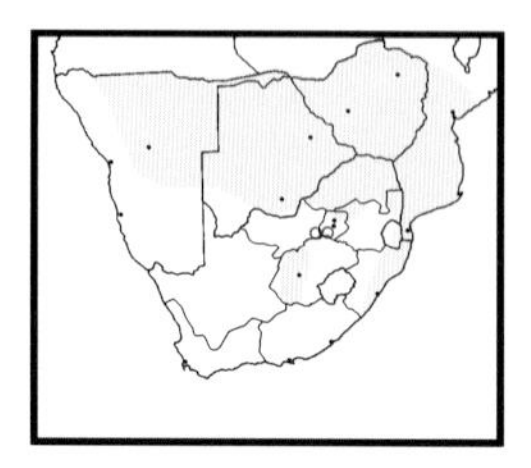

Goldentailed Woodpecker *Campethera abingoni* (483) 23 cm

This species is similar to Bennett's Woodpecker but is smaller, and at all plumage stages shows a streaked rather than spotted breast and belly. The male has a red nape and a grey to black forehead and crown flecked with red; the moustachial stripe is short, red stippled with black; the throat is white with heavy black streaks and spots; and the breast is streaked with black, not with large brown to black spots as in Bennett's Woodpecker. Females are similar to males but the forehead and crown are black with white speckling; the moustachial stripe is broad and black with white flecks. Immatures resemble the females. The Goldentailed Woodpecker may also be confused with the Cardinal Woodpecker (see page 170) but the smaller size and the brown forehead and black nape of the latter readily separate the two species. The presence of this bird is often announced by its characteristic 'whehh' vocalization. It forages in trees in a wide variety of habitats, tapping away at dead wood in search of insect larvae. R

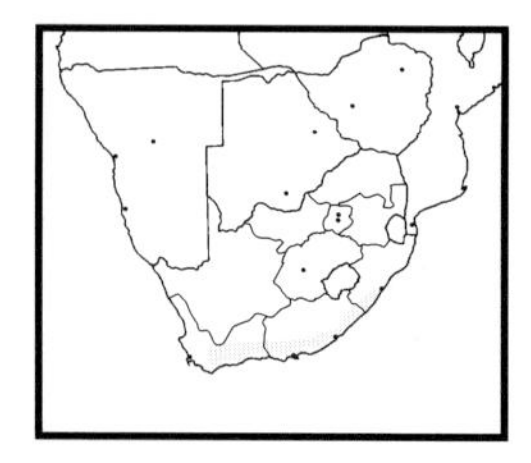

Knysna Woodpecker *Campethera notata* (484) 20 cm

This is a very dark woodpecker and the only one within its range that is very heavily spotted. In males the forehead, crown and moustachial stripe are red, heavily streaked with black; the nape is red. Females have a black forehead and crown lightly stippled with white, and a red nape. In both sexes the back is dark green and almost unmarked, save for some spotting. The call is a high-pitched, shreaked 'kreee-kreee', similar to that of the Goldentailed Woodpecker. Restricted to mature coastal forest, *Euphorbia* scrub and mature thickets, this is a mid-canopy species that feeds mainly along larger branches. E

1. Female Ground Woodpecker
2. Male Bennett's Woodpecker
3. Female Bennett's Woodpecker
4. Male Goldentailed Woodpecker
5. Female Goldentailed Woodpecker
6. Female Knysna Woodpecker

1	2	3
4	5	6

E *endemic* • R *resident*

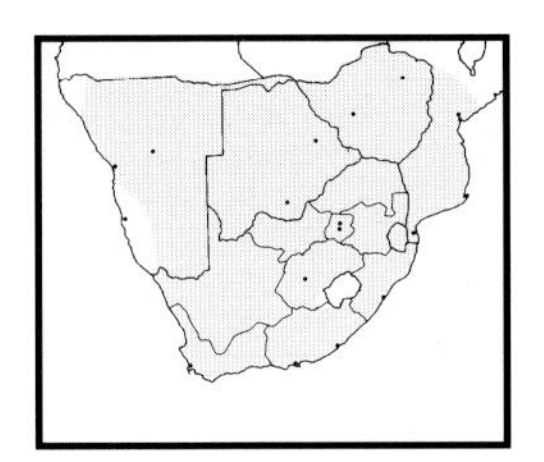

Cardinal Woodpecker *Dendropicos fuscescens* (486) 15 cm

A common species found in a range of habitats, from forest to dry thornveld, this is the smallest woodpecker. From the rear the Cardinal Woodpecker resembles the Goldentailed Woodpecker (see page 168), having similar back and tail markings and coloration, but its size and the head and facial markings differentiate it. In males the forehead and crown are unmarked brown and the nape is red; females have an all-brown crown and forehead and a black nape, not black speckled with white spots. Both sexes have a narrow black moustache, and immatures resemble the females but may show a red crown. As with many woodpecker species, the Cardinal Woodpecker may first be located by the sound of a continuous tapping as it forages for food. It feeds on insect larvae which it digs out of dead twigs, and along small dead branches. The call is a high-pitched 'kree kree kree'. R

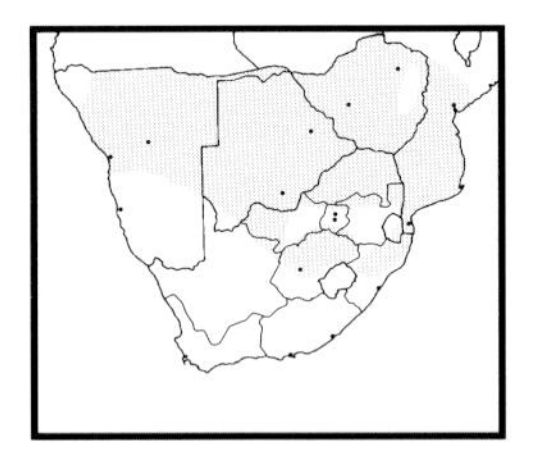

Bearded Woodpecker *Thripias namaquus* (487) 25 cm

One of our larger woodpeckers, the Bearded Woodpecker is also the only one that is barred on the breast and belly. The broad black moustache and stripe through and behind the eye, and the white throat are common to both sexes. Males have a black forehead flecked with white, a red crown and a black nape. Females have an all-black forehead, crown and nape with white flecking on the forehead. Both sexes drum very loudly, often on resonant wood, and may be heard up to a kilometre away. The call is a loud, rapid 'wik-wik-wik', consisting of six to eight notes. These woodpeckers prefer open dry savanna and woodland, foraging high up on the dead branches of large trees. They excavate nest holes in dead or living trees, using the same nest site each year. R

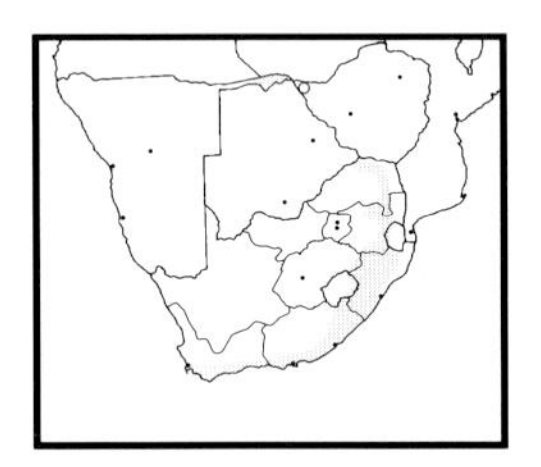

Olive Woodpecker *Mesopicos griseocephalus* (488) 20 cm

Both sexes of the Olive Woodpecker lack any distinctive facial markings. They have grey heads (with a red cap in the male), unmarked olive-green wings and underparts, and a distinctive red rump, seen most clearly as the bird flies away. Immatures are a duller olive-green, and immature males have a reduced red crown spotted with black. The call is a whistled 'whee-whee-whee'. The bird's coloration makes it difficult to see in the poor light of the forest where it lives, and as with most woodpeckers it is most often located by following the sound of its tapping as it probes for insects in rotting tree boughs. It forages in the mid to upper stratum of forests. R

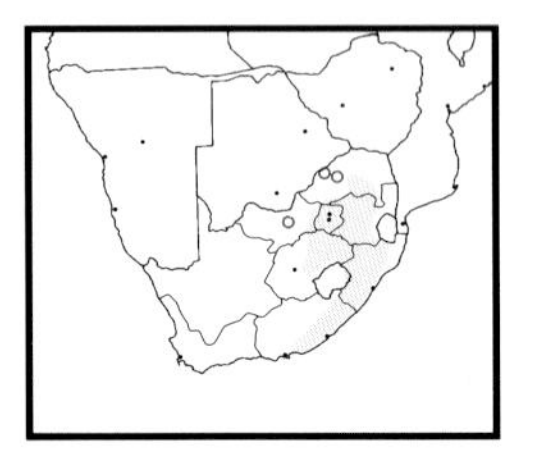

Redthroated Wryneck *Jynx ruficollis* (489) 19 cm

This woodpecker-like bird is a little bigger than a Cape Sparrow (see page 266) and, with its brown, rather scaly plumage, is reminiscent of a nightjar (see page 140). It has a dark chestnut throat patch. Immatures are similar but paler than the adults. The call is a series of squeaky 'kweek-kweek' notes. It feeds on the ground, predominantly on ants, and nests in old barbet and woodpecker holes and also in artificial hollows such as hollow steel fence posts. The Redthroated Wryneck favours highveld grasslands, thornveld, open bushveld and suburban gardens. R

1. Male Cardinal Woodpecker
2. Female Bearded Woodpecker
3. Female Cardinal Woodpecker
4. Male Olive Woodpecker
5. Adult Redthroated Wryneck

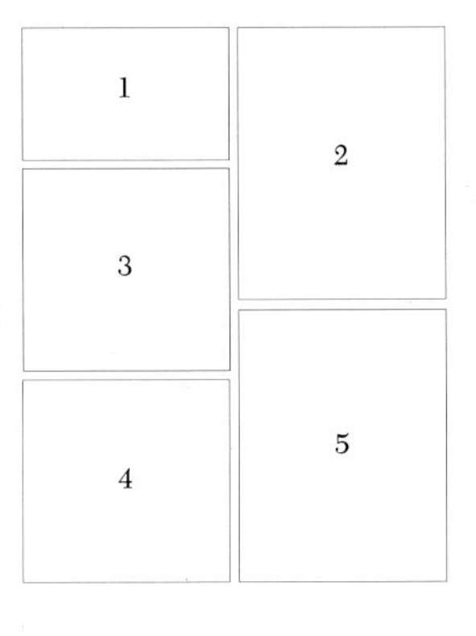

R *resident*

Larks and finchlarks Family Alaudidae

Small, usually drab terrestrial birds, larks and finchlarks resemble pipits (see pages 242-44) but have shorter tails, stouter bills and much dumpier bodies. Identification is based on subtleties of plumage coloration, as well as bill shape and song. All build their nests on the ground.

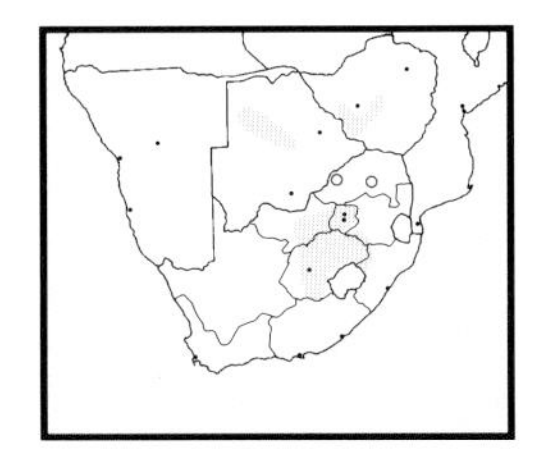

Melodious Lark *Mirafra cheniana* (492) 12 cm

A small lark, the Melodious Lark has a white supercilium, a well-marked white collar and a white throat. It has buffy underparts separated by a well-marked, speckled breast. It feeds on the ground on seeds, ants and termites. In display, it rises on whirring wings and then circles the nest site for long periods, up to 20 minutes at a time. Masters at imitating other bird species, these larks call a repetitive 'chuk-chuk-chuker'. They are confined to mature grasslands dominated by *Themeda* and in some cases cultivated *Eragrostis* grasses. E

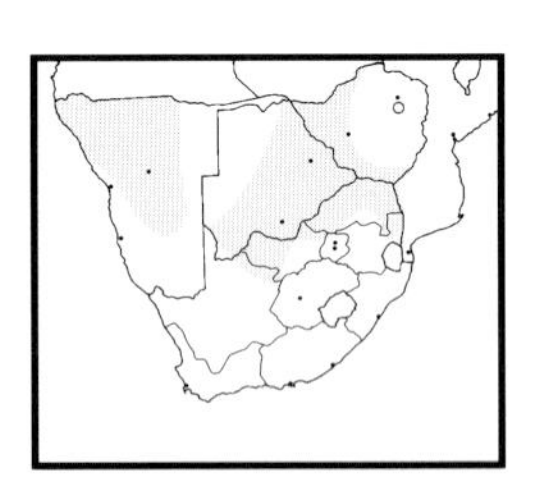

Monotonous Lark *Mirafra passerina* (493) 14 cm

The Monotonous Lark is short tailed and has a white throat which contrasts strongly with the poorly marked facial area (unlike that of the Melodious Lark which is well marked) and dark, slightly streaky breast. In areas of overlap with Stark's Lark (see page 176), this species shows chestnut wing patches in flight. It sings from a high perch, with its throat puffed up, uttering its monotonous call, 'trrp, chirp, chip, choop' over and over again, often day and night. Its habitat preferences include mopane and *Combretum* woodland and open acacia savanna with stony soils and sparse grass cover. NE

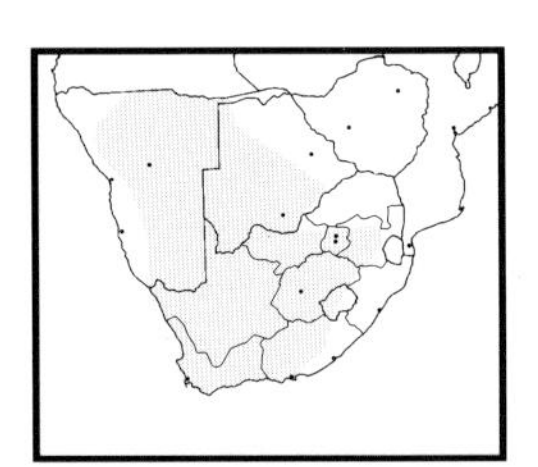

Clapper Lark *Mirafra apiata* (495) 15 cm

Clapper Larks and Flappet Larks are difficult to separate in the field; their ranges, however, rarely overlap. Clapper Larks are shorter tailed than Flappet Larks and the outer tail feathers are buffy-white, not buffy to rufous. They climb steeply into the sky, clapping their wings like a rattle at the top, and then drop earthwards while giving a thin, whistling 'peeeooo' note. They occur in rocky areas where tall grasses predominate as well as in semi-arid grassland and densely grassed interdune valleys in Kalahari sandveld. E

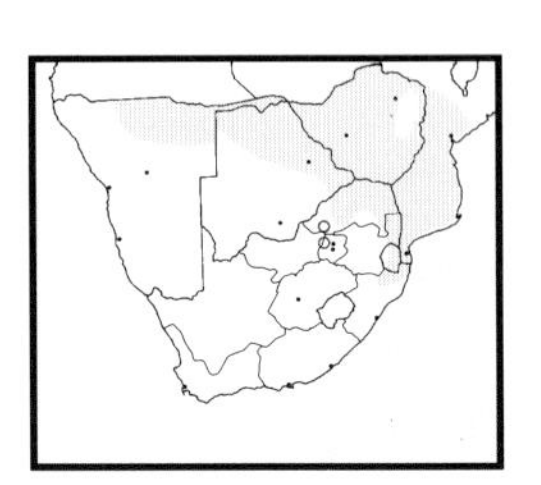

Flappet Lark *Mirafra rufocinnamomea* (496) 15 cm

Flappet Larks characteristically fly upwards with short clapping spells and on reaching the top of their climb clap their wings in a 'prrrr-prrr' fashion at intervals before dropping silently to the ground like a stone. Unless displaying it is difficult to separate this species from the Clapper Lark; the Flappet Lark is usually darker, longer tailed with more rufous outer tail feathers than the Clapper Lark. Flappet Larks are found where grassland predominates, including in clearings in woodland areas and open savanna. R

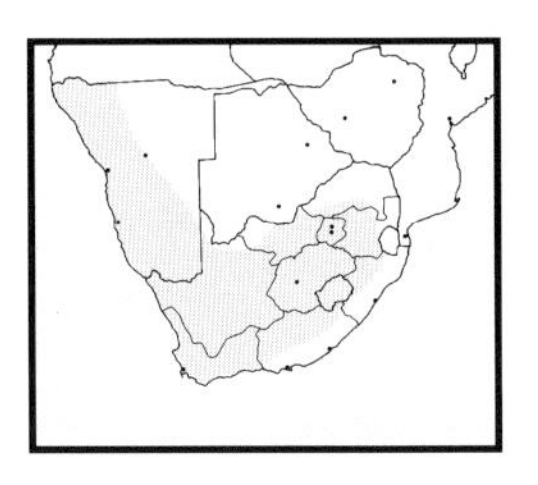

Longbilled Lark *Certhilauda curvirostris* (500) 20 cm

This is a large lark, generally reddish brown or greyish brown in colour and with a clear white eyebrow. The bill, a diagnostic feature, is long (longest in western races) and slightly decurved; females have shorter bills than do the males. The breast is finely streaked with dark brown on buff. In display it rises vertically from the ground, gives its despondent, ventriloquial 'peeeeou' whistle at the peak of its climb and then drops earthwards with its wings folded, opening them at the last minute. When foraging it turns over stones looking for invertebrates; it also digs in termite tunnels. It favours arid, semi-arid and highveld grassland areas dominated by rocky and stony substrates. NE

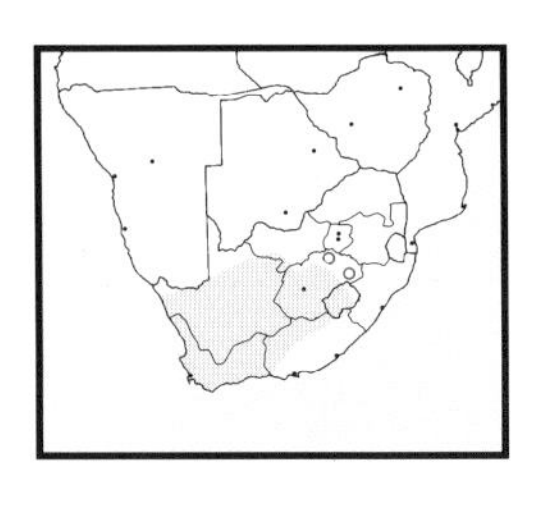

Thickbilled Lark *Galerida magnirostris* (512) 18 cm

A stocky lark, this species has a heavy, thick-base bill that is yellow in colour at the base of the lower mandible. The upperparts are light brown, strongly mottled with black, and the underparts are whitish with bold black streaking. When alarmed or when singing the bird typically raises its crest. The Thickbilled Lark searches the ground for food, using its bill to dig for seeds and bulbs, and also eats fruit. It climbs into the sky on fluttering wings, calling at the top of the climb, 'treeeleeeleee treeleetreelee'. It is common in coastal and montane fynbos, succulent Karoo shrublands and semi-arid grasslands. E

Adult Clapper Lark (western form)

Adult Clapper Lark (eastern form)

Adult Longbilled Lark (southwestern form)

Adult Longbilled Lark (northwestern form)

1. Adult Melodious Lark
2. Adult Monotonous Lark
3. Adult Clapper Lark
4. Adult Flappet Lark
5. Adult Longbilled Lark
6. Adult Thickbilled Lark
7. Immature Thickbilled Lark

1	2	3
4	5	
6	7	

E *endemic* • NE *near endemic* • R *resident*

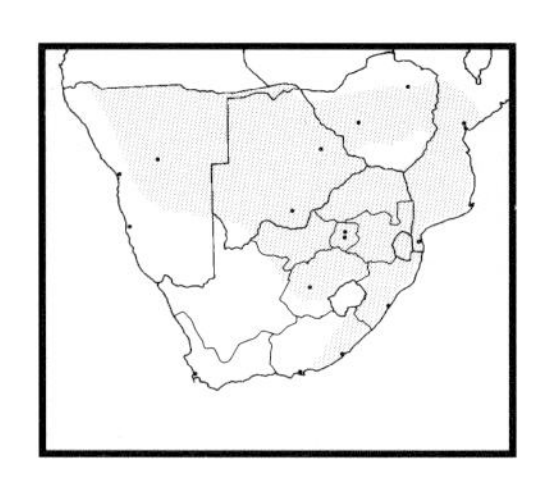

Rufousnaped Lark *Mirafra africana* (494) 18 cm

This chunky, heavy-billed lark shows a rufous wing panel (in flight) and belly, a clearly spotted breast and an erectile crest. The sexes are alike. Immatures are more scaly on the upperparts and less spotted on the breast than the adults. This species is most easily recognized by its call, a two-noted 'tiree-tiroo', given from a prominent perch; at this time it often flaps its wings. In display flight it gives a jumbled mixture of imitated calls. The Rufousnaped Lark forages around grass tufts for insects and grass seeds. It is found in grasslands with termite mounds and scrubby bushes, and in open scrubby thornveld. R

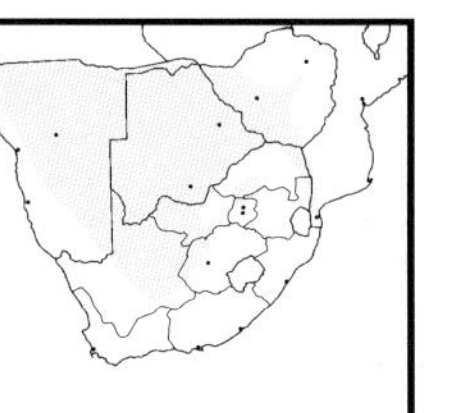

Fawncoloured Lark *Mirafra africanoides* (497) 14 cm

The Fawncoloured Lark generally shows very pale underparts with a lightly streaked brown breast and rufous to paler brown upperparts. Its prominent white eyebrow stripe and the white stripe below the dark eye-stripe are useful identification characters. The outer edge to the tail feathers is light buffy to white, and a reddish wing patch is visible in flight. The sexes are alike. Immatures are generally more mottled than the adults. It occurs in thornveld and mixed broad-leaved woodland on Kalahari sandveld. This bird sings from the top of a tree, a series of harsh 'chips' ending in a slurred 'chweeer'. R

Sabota Lark *Mirafra sabota* (498) 15 cm

The Sabota Lark forages for insects and seeds by digging with its bill, the size of which varies in response to local conditions. The lower mandible is, however, always lighter than the upper. The upperparts are scaly and boldly marked dark brown, reddish brown, greyish brown or buffy grey (varying in colour according to region), and a prominent eyebrow imparts a capped appearance. The underparts are white, and the bird has a well-marked speckled breast band. The sexes are alike. Immatures are tawnier than the adults, and have more mottled upperparts. The song of the Sabota Lark is a mixed jumble of fluty notes, and it is a master at imitating other birds' calls. It frequents thornveld and mixed broad-leaved woodland growing on stony terrain. R

Dusky Lark *Pinarocorys nigricans* (505) 19 cm

This large lark superficially resembles the Groundscraper Thrush (see page 200). Both species have a heavily spotted breast, but the Dusky Lark has a more crouched stance, whitish, not yellow, legs and feet, and a short and stout bill which is darkish, not yellow. Its habit of stopping and flicking its wings while walking, its all-dark upperwing and white underwing coverts (seen in flight), and its lack of a pale yellowish wing panel, further separate it from the Groundscraper Thrush. The sexes are alike, and immatures have heavily mottled underparts. When flushed it utters some soft 'chrrp, chrrp' notes. The Dusky Lark prefers short grass in wooded savanna and newly burnt grasslands. I

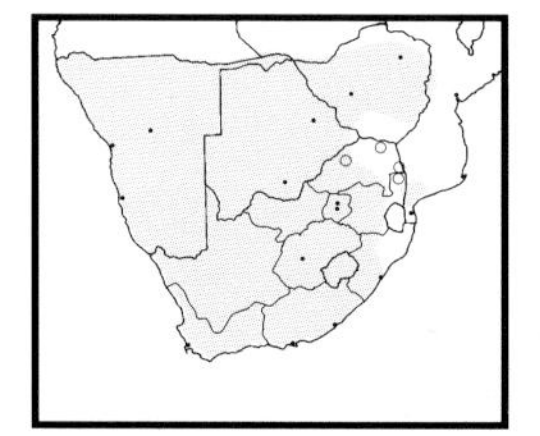

Redcapped Lark *Calandrella cinerea* (507) 16 cm

Although the coloration of this bird is variable, the rufous cap and shoulder patches, clear white eyebrow and its unmarked white underparts should render it unmistakable. The crest (longer in the male) is raised when the bird is stressed or hot. In flight it appears pipit-like and shows a dark, slightly forked tail and white outer tail feathers. Immatures are dark brown above with whitish spots, and below are whitish with a strongly spotted breast. The bird's song is a sparrow-like 'tchweerp' and a mixed jumble of melodious notes given during display flight. Gregarious out of the breeding season, the Redcapped Lark is found in open country, including semi-desert, on bare ground and in cultivated fields. R

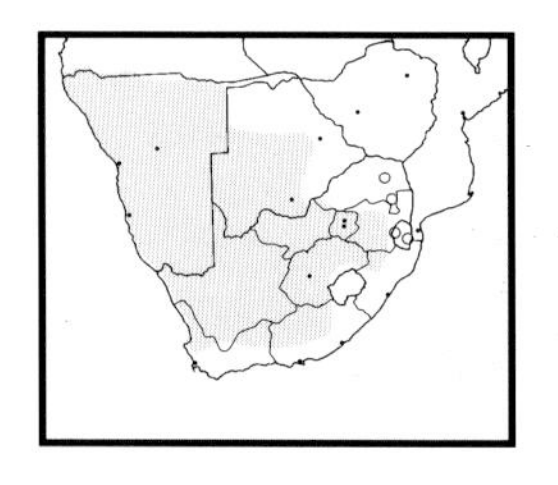

Spikeheeled Lark *Chersomanes albofasciata* (506) 15 cm

The Spikeheeled Lark has a decurved bill that varies in length according to region, a very upright stance, a diagnostic very short, white-tipped, dark tail, and a white throat which contrasts with the buffy to rufous underparts. The sexes are alike but the males are larger than the females. Immatures are more mottled with white (above and below) than are the adults. These larks forage on the ground, digging with their bills, or jump up to take food from shrubs. They may be seen taking shelter from the midday sun in larger rodent burrows. They favour drier savanna and desert plains. The song is a trill 'piree-piree-piree', usually given in flight. R

Adult Sabota Lark (large-billed form)

Adult Sabota Lark (small-billed form)

Adult Spikeheeled Lark (southeastern form)

Adult Spikeheeled Lark (northwestern form)

1. Immature Sabota Lark
2. Adult Fawncoloured Lark
3. Adult Rufousnaped Lark
4. Adult Rufousnaped Lark
5. Adult Dusky Lark
6. Immature Dusky Lark
7. Adult Redcapped Lark
8. Adult Spikeheeled Lark

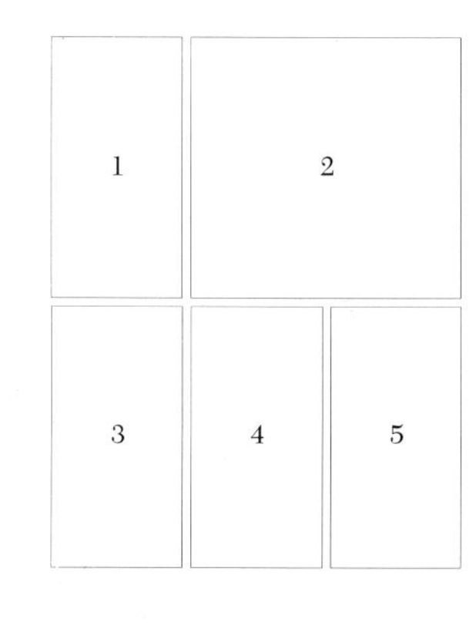

R *resident* • I *intra-African migrant*

Rudd's Lark *Heteromirafra ruddi* (499) 14 cm

On the ground Rudd's Lark has an erect stance and appears long legged with a wispy tail, an oversized head with a prominent eye, and a pinkish bill. It has a white supercilium and a whitish line – seen at close range – down the centre of the otherwise dark crown. In flight display it climbs steeply into the sky and flies in a circular pattern, singing 'is it wireee, is it wirree' before descending sharply to the ground. Rudd's Lark forages for insects around grass tufts. It prefers hill-tops and ridges and does not frequent fallow lands; burning, and winter grazing by cattle and sheep, help to maintain optimum conditions for this bird. E

Adult Botha's Lark

Pinkbilled Lark *Spizocorys conirostris* (508) 13 cm

The Pinkbilled Lark may be separated from the similar Botha's Lark by its conical pink bill (this is more slender and elongate in Botha's Lark); its all-buffy underparts; its buffy, not whitish, outer tail feathers; and the lack of a distinct eyebrow. Although similar to Stark's Lark, the Pinkbilled Lark lacks a crest, is less grey and has a stumpier, more conical and much pinker bill than that species. Immatures resemble the adults but are speckled with buff; the bill is greyish and the legs and feet are pink. The call is a series of 'si-si-si' notes. The Pinkbilled Lark occurs in small flocks in the non-breeding season. It is found in open, short to heavily grazed grasslands in the more arid parts of the region, where it forages for seeds and insects close to the ground. E

Adult Pinkbilled Lark

Botha's Lark *Spizocorys fringillaris* (509) 12 cm

Botha's Lark could be mistaken for the Pinkbilled Lark but has whitish, not buff, outer tail feathers, a buffy breast contrasting with a white belly, throat and vent, a more slender pink bill with a dark tip, and a distinct white supercilium or eyebrow; black streaks on the upper flanks further differentiate it. Immatures are similar to the adults but are more spotted with buff above, and have a greyish bill and pink legs and feet. The call is a melodious 'chiree chiree chiree', repeated a number of times. Found singly and in small groups, it forages on the ground. Botha's Lark prefers short grass, such as heavily grazed grassland areas. E

Sclater's Lark *Spizocorys sclateri* (510) 14 cm

Like Stark's Lark, this species has a large head but can be distinguished by its lack of an erectile crest and by the black teardrop-shaped patch in front of and below the eye. Sclater's Lark is a light buffy colour, streaked with grey above; below it is white to buffy, with the breast lightly streaked with brown. The bill is strong and whitish, and the eye is surrounded by a white eye-ring. Immatures are paler, greyer and more spotted than streaked above. The call is a 'trrrt trrt trrrt', uttered in flight. It feeds on the ground, searching for insects and seeds, and in the non-breeding season may be recorded in groups of more than 20 birds. Sclater's Lark prefers arid stony plains with grassy tufts on clayey soils which are susceptible to flooding during rain. E

Stark's Lark *Eremalauda starki* (511) 14 cm

The large, seemingly bulging eyes surrounded by a white ring, together with the upright stance and erectile crest of this species, are diagnostic. It is paler than the Pinkbilled or Sclater's larks. The bill is pinkish white with a diagnostic black tip and is more slender than that of the Pinkbilled Lark. Immatures are similar to the adults except for white speckling on the upperparts. It does occur singly but is more often seen in very large flocks on arid stony and calcrete soils on flat, thinly grassed plains. The flight call is an irregular 'treee', and the song, given during display, is a medley of notes, 'prrr-prrr-preee-preee-prrr'. E

1. Adult Rudd's Lark
2. Adult Pinkbilled Lark
3. Adult Sclater's Lark
4. Adult Botha's Lark
5. Adult Stark's Lark
6. Adult Gray's Lark

Gray's Lark *Ammomanes grayi* (514) 14 cm

Two races of Gray's Lark occur: *hoeschi* is darker with a greyer mantle and redder wings; and *grayi* has pale pinkish upperparts, including the sides of the face and central tail feathers, and white underparts. Both races have a thin, dark, black-tipped bill, and the outer web of the outer tail feather is white; except for the central tail feathers, the base of the tail is white. Calls comprise high-pitched, tinkling notes and whistles, given mainly at night. Gray's Lark shelters in rodent burrows and on low branches of shrubs in the heat of the day. It is usually seen in small groups, and is confined to gravel plains along the northern Namibian coast. NE

E *endemic* • NE *near endemic*

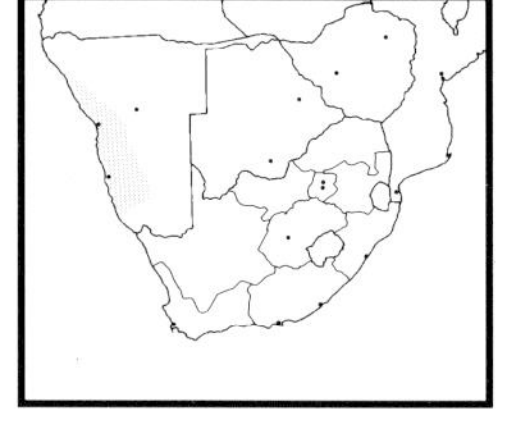
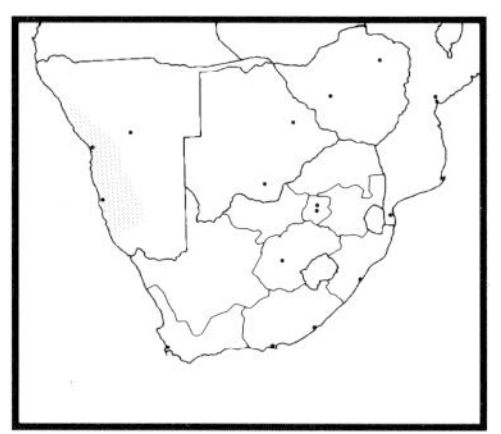

Dune Lark *Certhilauda erythrochlamys* (503) 17 cm

A large pale lark with a sandy-coloured back and a lightly streaked, whitish breast, the Dune Lark runs between vegetation, foraging at the base of grass tufts, digging with its bill for seeds and taking insects; youngsters are raised on invertebrates. It does not need to drink. It roosts in grass tufts at night and in the heat of the day. It differs from the Red Lark in having a more slender, longer bill, and by being paler and more sandy coloured above and having a lightly streaked breast below. It differs from the Karoo Lark in being plain to very lightly streaked above, not heavily streaked above and below. Its call, similar to that of the Karoo Lark, is a mellow series of bubbling notes. E

Karoo Lark *Certhilauda albescens* (502) 17 cm

Closely related to the Dune Lark and the Red Lark, this bird has boldly streaked upperparts that vary from brown (in the south) to red (in the north) and which differentiate it from the other two species. Like the Red Lark, the Karoo Lark has a boldly marked face but the upperparts are more extensively streaked than those of the Red Lark. In flight the tail looks very dark. Seen singly or in pairs, Karoo Larks forage on the ground using their bills to dig for seeds, and searching grass tufts for insects and seeds. Calling from a perch or in flight, the song is a short 'chleep-chleep-chrr-chrrp'. They occur on coastal dunes, in Karoo scrub on sandy and clayey soils, and on fallow land. E

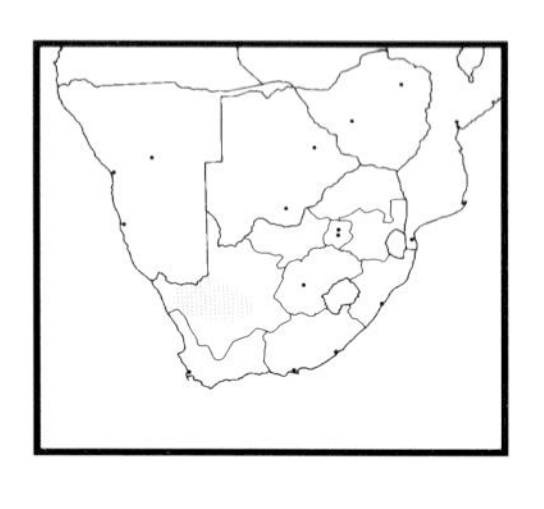

Red Lark *Certhilauda burra* (504) 19 cm

The Red Lark has a very upright stance and in flight shows an unmarked rich rufous back, and rufous and black wings and tail. The underparts are white, the breast heavily streaked, and the face is boldly marked with a broad white eyebrow and stripe below the eye, split by a dark line from gape to ear coverts. The bill is heavier than in either the Dune Lark or the Karoo Lark. Red Larks forage on the ground, pecking but rarely digging with the bill, and gleaning insects from grasses. They are found on red vegetated Kalahari dunes and surrounding karroid shrublands, especially when *Rhigozum* shrubs predominate. The call is a short 'chrrk' given when flushed, otherwise a whistled 'toodly-woo-tu-wee'. E

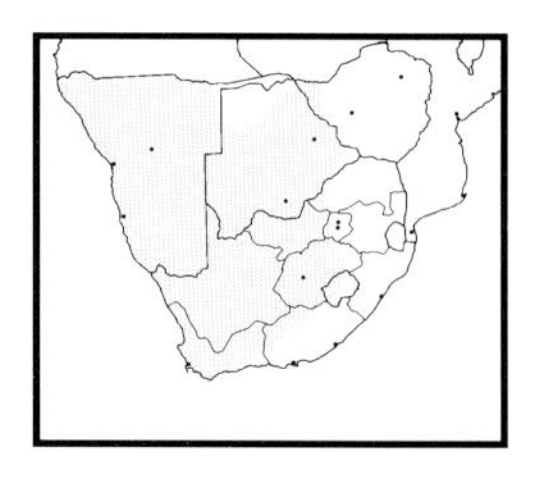

Greybacked Finchlark *Eremopterix verticalis* (516) 13 cm

Male Greybacked Finchlarks have a light grey back, all-black underparts and head, and a clear white cheek patch joining a white shoulder patch and a nape patch. The females are much less colourful with a streaky breast, a black patch on the belly and a grey back (rufous in the female Chestnutbacked Finchlark). Immatures are similar to the females. During courtship flights the male birds dangle their legs; the flight call is a sharp chirping 'chruk, chruk'. They occur in large flocks out of the breeding season and favour open, short grasslands to grassless gravel plains. NE

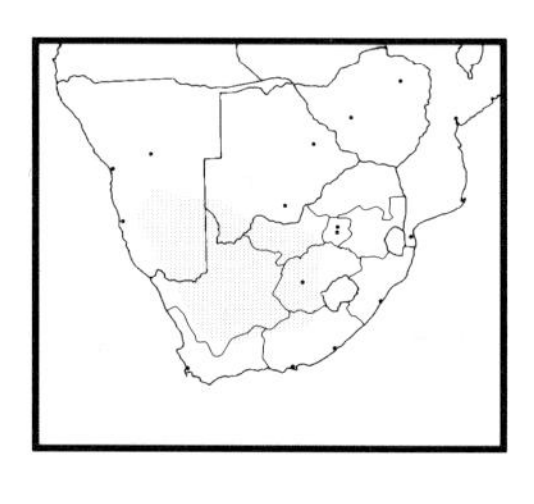

Blackeared Finchlark *Eremopterix australis* (517) 13 cm

The male of this species is all black on the head and underbelly, with dark chestnut upperparts and all-black underwings (seen in flight). The female is heavily streaked black below and lacks the black belly patch of female Chestnutbacked Finchlarks and Greybacked Finchlarks; the underwings are black with a chestnut to yellowish panel at the base of the primaries. Blackeared Finchlarks form flocks in the non-breeding season, often with other species. When disturbed, a short 'preep' alarm note is uttered; otherwise they give a buzz-like flight call. They occur in shrub Karoo vegetation and red Kalahari sandveld, especially where *Rhigozum* shrubs occur. E

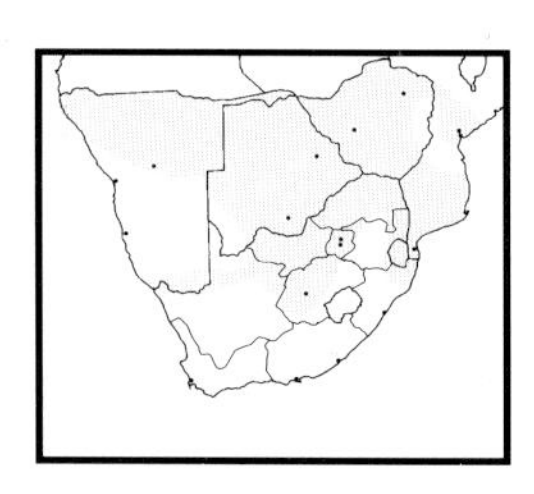

Chestnutbacked Finchlark *Eremopterix leucotis* (515) 12 cm

The male Chestnutbacked Finchlark has a rich chestnut back, a black breast and belly with a pale vent, and a black head with unjoined, clear white cheek, nape and shoulder patches (joined in the Greybacked Finchlark). The female is much less colourful with a streaky breast, a thin white collar, a black patch on the belly and a chestnut back (grey in the female Greybacked Finchlark). Immatures are similar to the females. Chestnutbacked Finchlarks usually occur in large flocks out of the breeding season and, like the Greybacked Finchlark and Blackeared Finchlark, are highly nomadic. They favour open, short grasslands, grassless gravel plains, fallow lands and grassy patches in open woodland. The call is a 'chip-chwep' uttered in flight. R

Female Greybacked Finchlark

Male Greybacked Finchlark

Female Blackeared Finchlark

Male Blackeared Finchlark

1. Adult Dune Lark
2. Adult Karoo Larks
3. Adult Karoo Lark (red form)
4. Female Chestnutbacked Finchlark
5. Male Greybacked Finchlark
6. Female Greybacked Finchlark
7. Male Chestnutbacked Finchlark
8. Adult Red Lark
9. Female Blackeared Finchlark
10. Male Blackeared Finchlark

1	2	3
4	5	6
7	8	
9	10	

E *endemic* • NE *near endemic* • R *resident*

Swallows and martins Family Hirundinidae

Shorter- and less stiff-winged than swifts, swallows and martins are frequently seen perched on telephone wires. Plumage colours range from glossy blues to reds and dull browns. All are aerial and insectivorous and have dorsoventrally flattened bills with a wide gape. Some are colonial breeders, nesting in holes in riverbanks or using mud pellets to build elaborate nests on man-made structures. Their calls, unless otherwise stressed, comprise soft warbles and twittering notes, normally uttered in flight or at communal roosts at night.

Adult Eastern Saw-wing Swallow

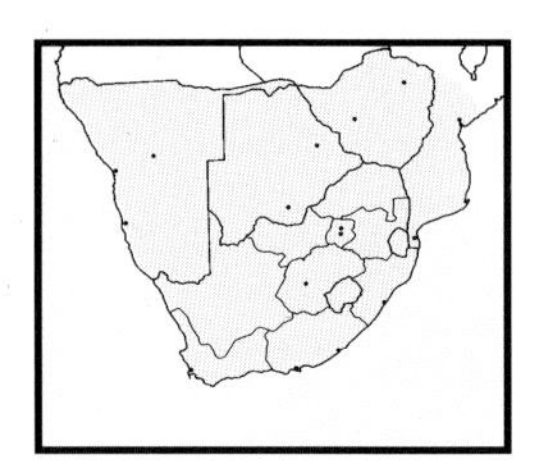

European Swallow *Hirundo rustica* (518) 18 cm

Adults are metallic blue to black with a rufous forehead and throat. The rest of the underparts are buffy, separated from the throat by a broad metallic blue-black breast band. The length of the tail streamers varies. Immatures are browner on the back, and have a browner, broad collar, a dirty-white forehead and throat, and an off-white belly. These swallows forage on the wing, often being seen in mixed flocks, and in the evenings congregate in their hundreds – and sometimes hundreds of thousands – roosting in reedbeds and at times in maize fields. S

Adult Black Saw-wing Swallow

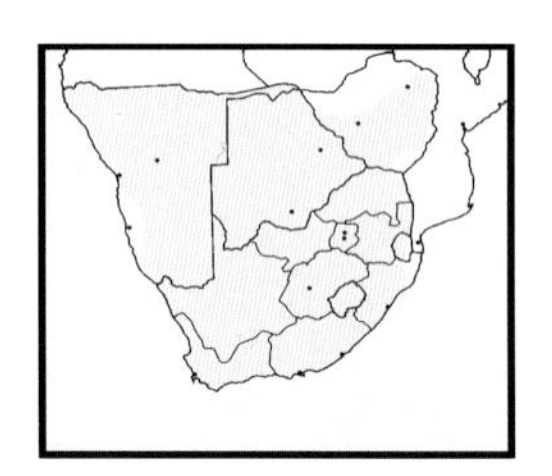

Whitethroated Swallow *Hirundo albigularis* (520) 17 cm

The pure white underparts of this swallow contrast with its metallic-blue back and narrow blue breast band. The orange forehead is not always easy to see but the white spots in the tail, tail streamers and white underwing coverts help to separate this from other species. The Whitethroated Swallow nests under bridges and in culverts. It is closely associated with water – streams, rivers and dams – but may also be found over damp grasslands. I

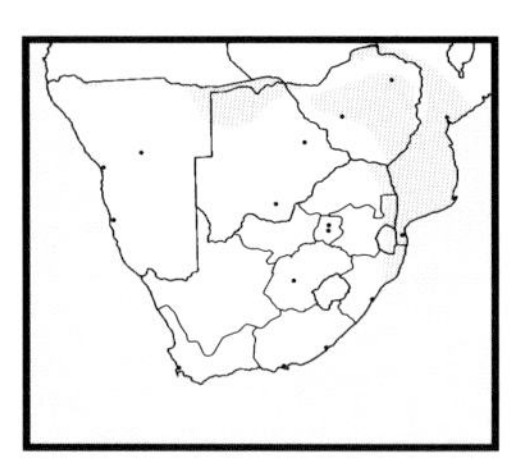

Greyrumped Swallow *Pseudhirundo griseopyga* (531) 14 cm

The Greyrumped Swallow has a grey-brown crown and rump, dirty-grey underparts and blue-black wings and back. It may be told from the House Martin by its dirty-grey, not white, underparts and greyish, not white, rump; and also by its more deeply forked tail. It occurs in pairs and in small flocks (often with other swallows), foraging over grasslands, open thornveld, cultivated lands, at the edges of marshes and over airstrips. R, S

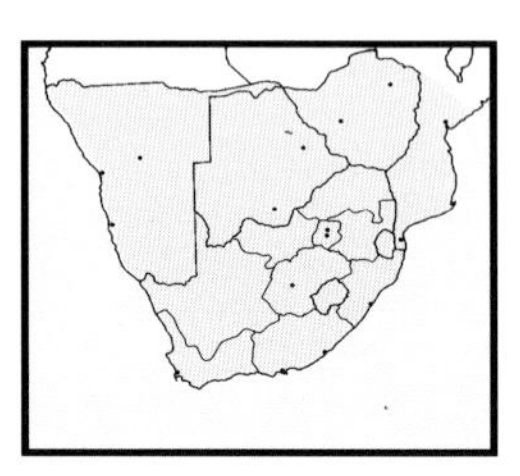

House Martin *Delichon urbica* (530) 14 cm

This bird may easily be mistaken for a Greyrumped Swallow but its pure white, not dirty-grey, underparts, the broad white, not greyish, rump, and its less deeply forked tail should prevent any confusion. The wings appear triangulate and the underwing coverts are grey. Foraging up high with a flap-and-glide-type flight pattern, the House Martin is found singly and in large flocks throughout the region. It may be seen foraging over mountainous terrain, dry broad-leaved woodlands and thornveld. R, S

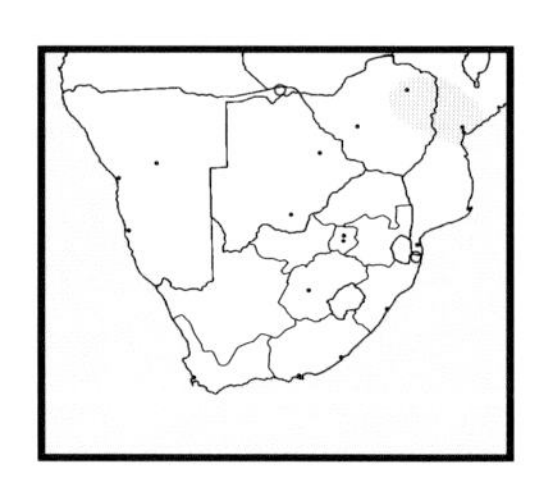

Eastern Saw-wing Swallow *Psalidoprocne orientalis* (537) 15 cm

Other than the silver-grey to white underwing coverts, this bird appears black although good light will suggest a dark green gloss. It has a deeply forked tail. It is very similar to the Black Saw-wing Swallow but the ranges of the two do not overlap so confusion should not arise. Immatures are similar to the adults, lacking any sheen, and have very dirty-white underwing coverts. The name 'saw-wing' is derived from the barbs on the outer edge of the outer primaries which give these birds' wings a jagged appearance. The Eastern Saw-wing Swallow may be seen flitting over and close to the canopy, and in clearings of evergreen forest and miombo woodland. R

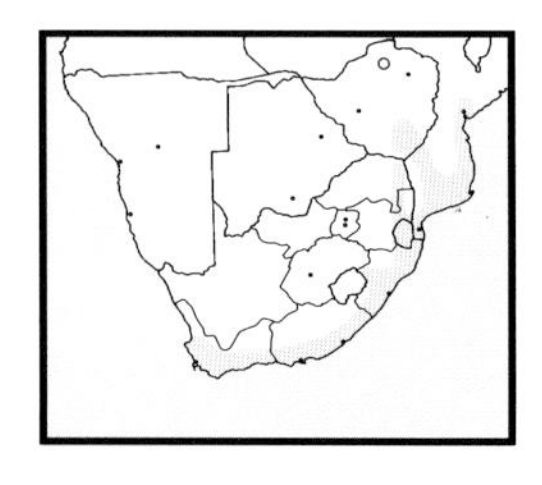

Black Saw-wing Swallow *Psalidoprocne holomelas* (536) 15 cm

Although this species closely resembles the Eastern Saw-wing Swallow, their ranges in our region are allopatric and therefore confusion should not arise. The Black Saw-wing Swallow is all glossy-green to black with dark underwing coverts. Its short, triangular, not long, narrow and bow-like, wings should eliminate confusion with any of the swifts (see pages 142-44). Immatures are similar to the adults but are very dark brown and lack any gloss. The flight is graceful and the bird skims between trees and along forest paths and streams in forested and dense woodland habitats, and also in plantations. R

1. Adult European Swallow
2. Adult Whitethroated Swallow
3. Adult Eastern Saw-wing Swallow
4. Adult Greyrumped Swallow
5. Adult Black Saw-wing Swallow
6. Adult House Martin

1	2
3	4
5	6

S *summer visitor* • I *intra-African migrant* • R *resident*

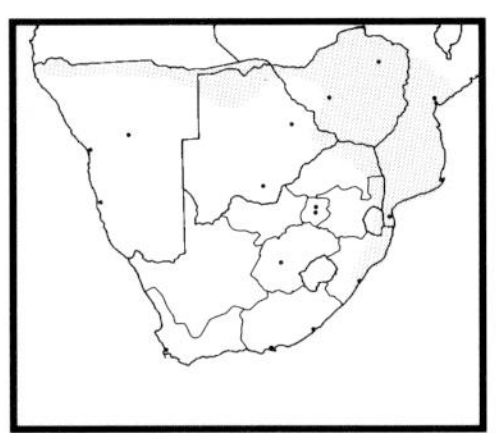

Wiretailed Swallow *Hirundo smithii* (522) 13 cm

This fast-flying, rufous-crowned swallow is most easily distinguished by its thin, dark vent band and by the hint of a breast band on the sides of the otherwise all-white underparts. Its long, needle-like tail streamers are often difficult to see but these, along with its white underwing coverts and white tail spots, help to separate it from the similar Pearlbreasted Swallow. The sexes are alike. Immatures have a brown crown and are less glossy blue above; the throat and breast have a pinkish tinge. Nearly always found near water, this bird often nests under bridges. Its call is a sharp metallic 'tchik'. R

Adult Rock Martin

Pearlbreasted Swallow *Hirundo dimidiata* (523) 14 cm

Like the Wiretailed Swallow, the Pearlbreasted Swallow is glossy blue above and white below, but it has an all-blue, not rufous, crown, and lacks the fine tail streamers of the Wiretailed Swallow as well as the faint breast band and darker vent band. It differs from the Greyrumped Swallow (see page 180) and the House Martin (see page 180) in having the underwing coverts mostly white, not dark. The sexes are alike. Immatures are similar to the adults but are less glossy blue. These agile fliers favour the edges of clearings in open woodland, grasslands and semi-arid scrub bush. They utter a subdued chipping note in flight. R, S

Adult Brownthroated Martin (dark form)

Rock Martin *Hirundo fuligula* (529) 15 cm

This all-brown martin is greyish brown on the back and cinnamon coloured on the throat and belly. The short, square, brown tail shows distinct white spots, visible in the spread tail in flight. The Rock Martin differs from dark forms of the Brownthroated Martin by being larger, and light brown, not dark brown, on the throat and belly. The sexes are alike. Immatures are similar to the adults but the feathers on their upperparts are edged buff. Rock Martins give soft, indistinct twitterings. They are found in all habitat types but most often in association with rocky crags, cliffs and gorges, and may be encountered around human dwellings. R

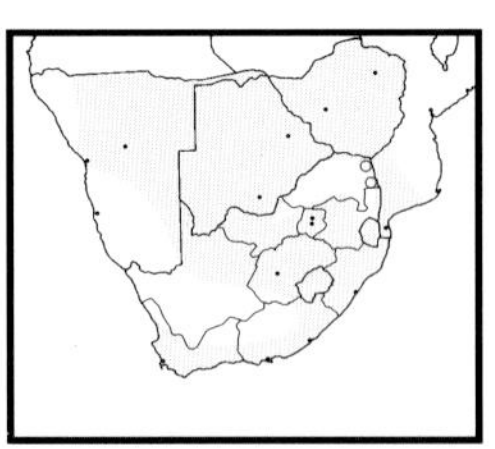
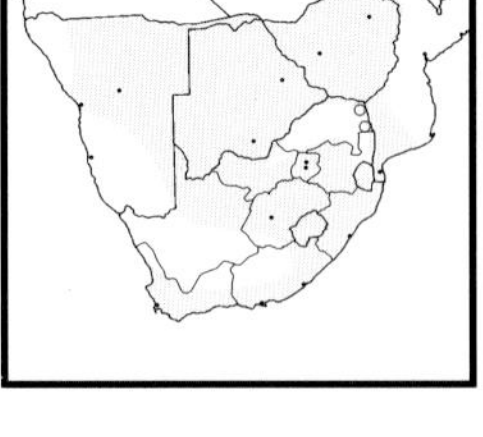

Banded Martin *Riparia cincta* (534) 17 cm

The largest of the brown martins, the Banded Martin has a wide brown throat band separating its white throat and belly and, sometimes, a thin brown band across the vent. Its white underwing coverts and white eyebrow separate it from other brown martins, including the Sand Martin – which has a similar breast band but dark brown underwing coverts. The sexes are alike. Immature birds lack the white eyebrow and the feathers of their upperparts are edged buffy. Frequenting grassland areas, the Banded Martin forages low over the tops of the grass, snapping at insects as it goes. Its flight call is a 'che-che-che'. I

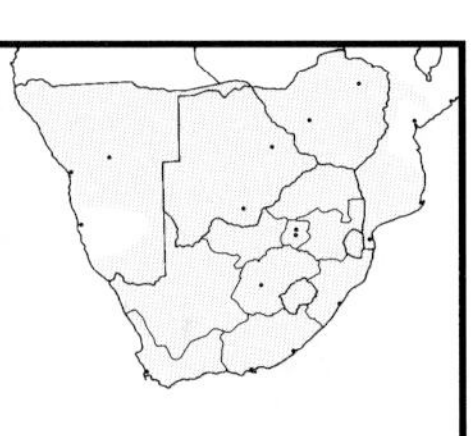
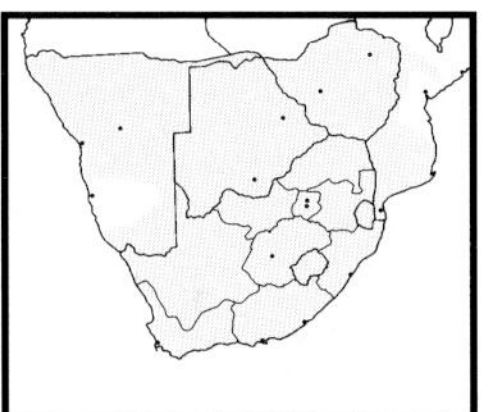

Brownthroated Martin *Riparia paludicola* (533) 12 cm

One of the smaller brown martins, this species appears in two colour morphs, one with a brown throat and a white belly and the other, less common, all dark brown above and below. Dark morphs may be separated from the similar Rock Martin by being smaller in size with dark brown underparts, by having a notched, not square, tail and by lacking white tail spots. The sexes are alike. The immature Brownthroated Martin is scaled buffy above and the belly is tinged with buff. Often gathering in large groups, these birds may be seen fluttering over water and open grasslands, uttering their soft, twittering call. R

1. Adult Wiretailed Swallow
2. Adult Rock Martin
3. Adult Sand Martin
4. Adult Pearlbreasted Swallow
5. Adult Banded Martin
6. Adult Brownthroated Martin

1	2
3	4
5	6

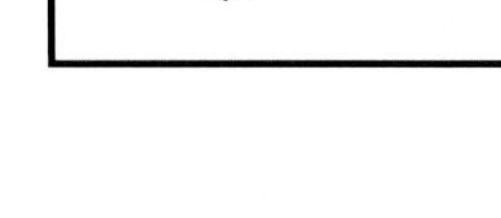

Sand Martin *Riparia riparia* (532) 12 cm

The Sand Martin is similar to the Banded Martin in that it is grey-brown above and white below, but the brown breast band is narrower and its underwing coverts are brown, not white. It has a forked, not square, tail, seen in flight, and it lacks any white flecks in the tail. It is similar in size to the Brownthroated Martin, but can be distinguished from that species by its white, not brown, throat. The immatures resemble the adults except for the pale edging to their upperpart feathers. The Sand Martin roosts gregariously at night in reedbeds, and may be seen in large flocks over open waters, reedbeds, swamps, lakes and open grasslands. Its call is a grating 'chrrr', and it also utters a single, harsh 'ret'. S

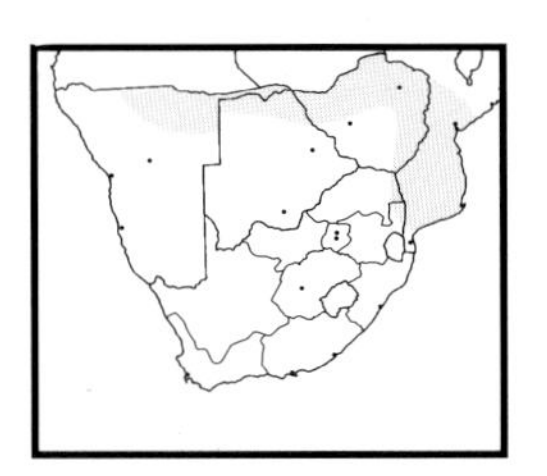

Mosque Swallow *Hirundo senegalensis* (525) 24 cm

One of the largest African swallows, this species with its glossy-blue back and rufous underparts may be mistaken for the similar-sized Redbreasted Swallow but can be told from that species by its white, not rufous, throat and ear coverts, and by its whitish, not buffy, underwing coverts. Immatures are paler below and less glossy above. The bowl-shaped nest is made of mud pellets, has a long tunnel, and is most often constructed inside a baobab tree. The Mosque Swallow is found singly or in small flocks in open woodland, especially where baobab trees predominate, and its call is a nasal 'harrrrp' and guttural chuckling. R

Adult Mosque Swallow

Redbreasted Swallow *Hirundo semirufa* (524) 24 cm

Resembling the Mosque Swallow, this species differs by having all-rufous underparts, including the throat and sides of the face, and buffy, not whitish, underwing coverts. The blue on the crown extends below the eye and on to the ear coverts whereas the Mosque Swallow has white ear coverts and an orange eyebrow. Immatures are paler on the throat and breast than the adults and are less glossy above. The Redbreasted Swallow uses rock overhangs, culverts and bridges as shelters under which to build its bowl-shaped nest which incorporates a long tunnel. It occurs in pairs in open woodland and savanna and also over grasslands, and utters various twittering notes in flight, and a soft warbling song. S

Adult Redbreasted Swallow

Greater Striped Swallow *Hirundo cucullata* (526) 20 cm

This medium-sized swallow is lightly streaked on the breast, the streaking being visible only at close range. Overall, it appears paler than the smaller Lesser Striped Swallow, with a paler orange crown and rump, finely streaked ear coverts and slightly buffy underparts. Immatures are similar to the adults but are a less metallic blue above and have short outer tail feathers. The choice of nest site and method of construction are similar to those favoured by the Lesser Striped Swallow. A widespread species, it occurs in treeless country, and its call is twittering 'chissick'. I

Adult Greater Striped Swallow

Adult Lesser Striped Swallow

Lesser Striped Swallow *Hirundo abyssinica* (527) 16 cm

The Lesser Striped Swallow may be told from the Greater Striped Swallow by the bold black streaks on its white breast (light buffy and finely streaked in the Greater Striped Swallow), and its orange ear coverts. The crown, nape, rump and underwing coverts are a deeper orange than in the Greater Striped Swallow. Immatures have a brown crown, shorter outer tail feathers and are duller overall than the adults. The Lesser Striped Swallow builds a bowl-shaped nest with a tunnel under culverts, bridges and rock overhangs on cliff faces. This species may be found in open savannas, woodland and grassland areas. Its call is a series of squeaky, nasal 'zeh-zeh-zeh-zeh' notes. S, R

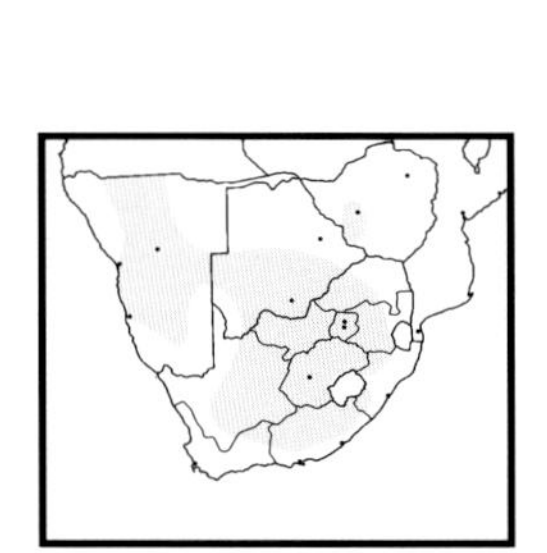

South African Cliff Swallow *Hirundo spilodera* (528) 15 cm

At a glance this bird might be mistaken for one of the striped swallows but its dumpy profile (House Martin-like), short, black, square tail (without white windows), dark brown crown, light buffy underparts with heavy spotting on the throat and breast (appearing as a throat band), and rufous vent distinguish it from those two species. It can be told from the European Swallow (see page 180) by its pale rufous, not blue-black, rump and square, not deeply forked, tail. Immatures are less glossy above and show a brownish throat. The call of this swallow is a twittering 'chooerp-chooerp'. It nests mainly under road bridges and may be seen over highveld grasslands and sparsely wooded savannas. I

Blue Swallow *Hirundo atrocaerulea* (521) 25 cm

A glossy blue-black swallow with exceptionally long and fine tail streamers in breeding plumage, the Blue Swallow may be mistaken for the Black Saw-wing Swallow (see page 180) but the different flight actions and the blue-black colour of the Blue Swallow should render it unmistakable. The Blue Swallow has a purposeful flight, very close to the ground, while the Black Saw-wing Swallow has a fluttery, higher flight. The Blue Swallow is severely endangered in South Africa as a breeding species due to continued agro-forestry policies which threaten its habitat. This bird nests in old mine shafts, potholes and antbear holes, plastering its cup-shaped nest to the side of the site. It utters a musical 'bee-bee-bee-bee' in flight. I

1. Adult Mosque Swallow
2. Adult Mosque Swallow
3. Adult Redbreasted Swallow
4. Adult Lesser Striped Swallow
5. Adult Greater Striped Swallow
6. Adult South African Cliff Swallow
7. Adult Blue Swallow

R *resident* • S *summer visitor* • I *intra-African migrant*

Cuckooshrikes Family Campephagidae

Cuckooshrikes are slow-moving, arboreal birds which superficially resemble cuckoos. Primarily insectivorous, they glean insects from the canopy in the evergreen forests they frequent. They have soft calls.

Male Black Cuckooshrike (showing yellow shoulder)

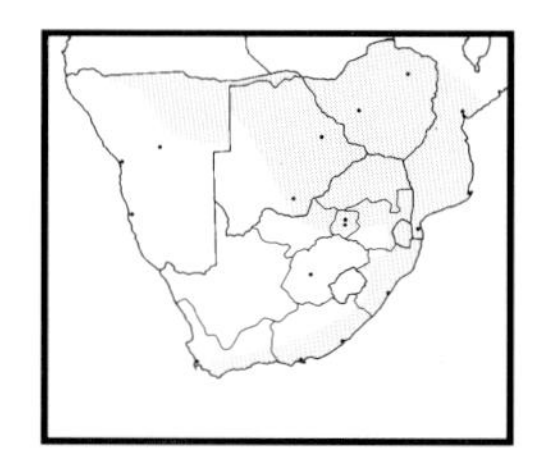

Black Cuckooshrike *Campephaga flava* (538) 22 cm

The male is all black with an orange-yellow gape and often (not always) a yellow shoulder patch visible on the folded wing. Females are quite different, being brown above with yellow edging to the median coverts and secondaries, and having yellow outer tail feathers; below they are white with brown edging to the feather tips, giving a banded appearance, and in flight the underwing is seen to be almost all yellow (black in males). Black Cuckooshrikes inhabit mature woodland and forest edges, and may move to drier areas after rain and to lower altitudes in the winter months. The call is a high-pitched 'trrrrr'. R

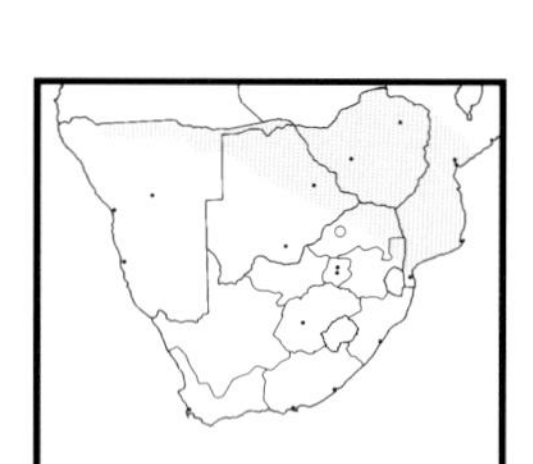

Whitebreasted Cuckooshrike *Coracina pectoralis* (539) 27 cm

This species is lighter smokey-grey in colour than the Grey Cuckooshrike, and has a white breast and belly. Males have a grey throat (sometimes present in the females). In flight they show white underwing coverts (all-grey in the Grey Cuckooshrike). Immatures are barred black and white on grey above, and below are white with dark brown spots. The male's call is a soft 'duid-duid', and the female's is a trilled 'tehee-ee-ee-ee'. They are usually seen in pairs, in the canopy of mature, tall miombo woodland. R

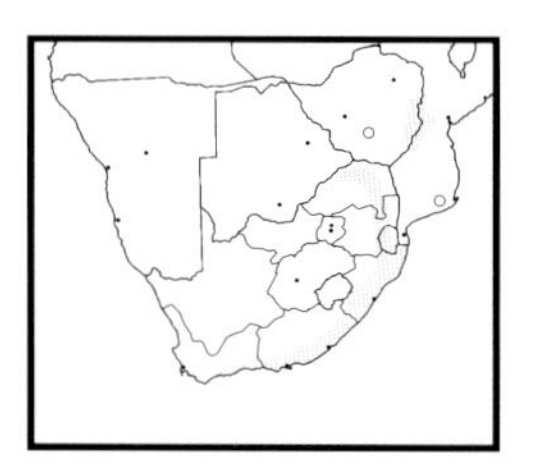

Grey Cuckooshrike *Coracina caesia* (540) 27 cm

This bird is all-dark-grey with a lighter grey head and a distinctive white eye-ring. The sexes are separable on the colour of the lores: black in the male and plain grey in the female; generally, females are paler than the males. Immatures are similar but have finely barred, buffy underparts. This species can be told from the Whitebreasted Cuckooshrike by being dark grey, not white, on the underparts, and having grey, not white, underwing coverts. Grey Cuckooshrikes are restricted to the canopy of evergreen forest and coastal bush, moving to lower elevations in the winter months. The call is a soft, drawn-out whistle. R

Drongos Family Dicruridae

Noisy insectivores, drongos are bold and conspicuous, and fearless when harassing large birds of prey, chasing and diving at them in flight. They have stout, slightly hooked bills with prominent rictal bristles. They catch insects on the wing, darting from an exposed perch in wooded and open country habitats.

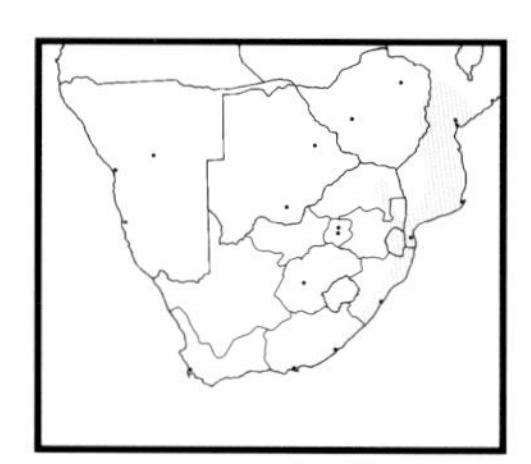

Squaretailed Drongo *Dicrurus ludwigii* (542) 19 cm

This species is very similar to the Forktailed Drongo but is smaller and the tail is not as deeply forked. It could also be mistaken for the Southern Black Flycatcher (see page 236), but can be separated by its red, not brown, eye and the shallow fork to the tail (the tail of the Southern Black Flycatcher has a rounded end). Females are duller than the males, which have a green to blue sheen, and immatures are similar to the females but are speckled light grey below. A resident of evergreen forest and coastal bush, the Squaretailed Drongo rarely perches out in the open as does the Forktailed Drongo. It is a noisy species with various strident whistled and twanging phrases. R

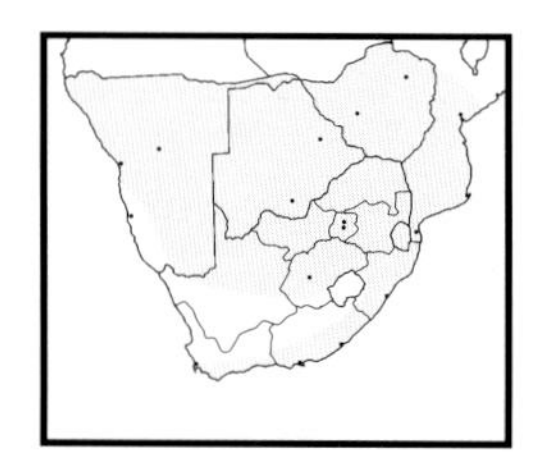

Forktailed Drongo *Dicrurus adsimilis* (541) 25 cm

This all-black species shows a deeply forked tail and a deep red eye. When moulting, the fork in the tail may not be so obvious and then the bird could be mistaken for a Squaretailed Drongo or a Southern Black Flycatcher (see page 236); the latter is distinguishable by the rounded end to its tail, its brown eye and its bill which lacks a hook. Immatures are grey brown with buffy-tipped feathers below and a yellowish gape. Noisy with a multitude of rasping and twanging phrases, this bird is a master at imitating the calls of other species. It occurs in open woodland and thornveld, and along forest edges. R

1. Male Black Cuckooshrike
2. Adult Squaretailed Drongo
3. Adult Whitebreasted Cuckooshrike
4. Adult Grey Cuckooshrike
5. Adult Forktailed Drongo
6. Female Black Cuckooshrike

1	2
3	4
5	6

R *resident*

Orioles Family Oriolidae

Resembling starlings in size and shape, these brightly coloured birds of forest and bushveld all give similar clear, liquid, piping and bubbling notes. They feed on a variety of fruits and insects and, occasionally, on nectar.

Adult Pied Crow

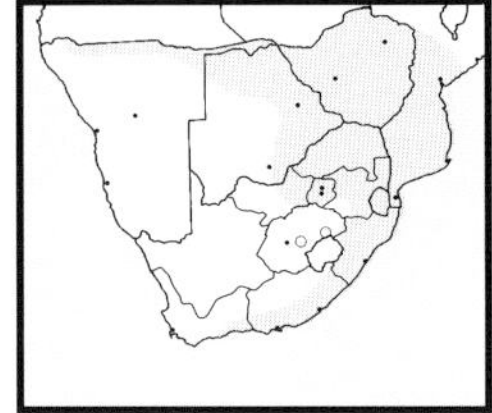

Blackheaded Oriole *Oriolus larvatus* (545) 24 cm

This golden-yellow bird has a diagnostic all-black head and throat extending to the breast and, as with all the orioles, a red bill and a red eye. Immatures are similar to the adults except for the head and throat, which are mottled black on yellow, and the bill, which is blackish. Blackheaded Orioles are found in all types of woodland but are more common in mature broad-leaved woodland; they also occur in exotic plantations and on forest edges. R

Adult Whitenecked Raven

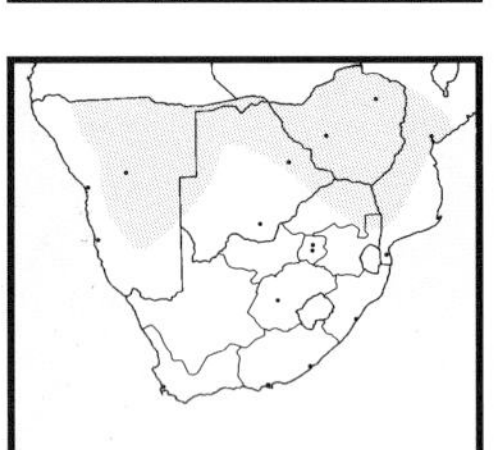

African Golden Oriole *Oriolus auratus* (544) 24 cm

The male African Golden Oriole is golden-yellow with yellowish upperwing coverts, black lores which extend over and behind the eye, all-yellow outer tail feathers and black central tail feathers. Females and immatures are similar to the males, being greenish yellow above and dull yellow below with olive streaks. This species prefers the canopy of mature miombo woodland, riverine forest and, occasionally, savanna. I

Crows and ravens Family Corvidae

Fairly large, apparently black or black and white birds with strong bills, at close range the seemingly black parts of the plumage can be seen to be glossy purple and green. Crows and ravens are found in a variety of habitats, and are very vocal species, with a variety of harsh 'kraaks' or caws and liquid bubbling and snorting repertoires.

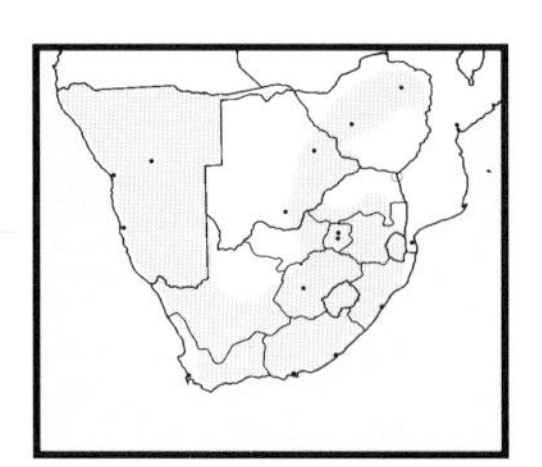

Black Crow *Corvus capensis* (547) 50 cm

The only entirely black crow in the region, this bird has a long, slender, slightly decurved, black bill. It is larger than the House Crow and has a glossy black, not grey, collar and breast. Immature birds are browner than the adults, lacking the glossy plumage of the adult. Black Crows feed on grains, insects and frogs. They are found in savanna, open grasslands and cultivated lands, and also occur in dry desert regions. R

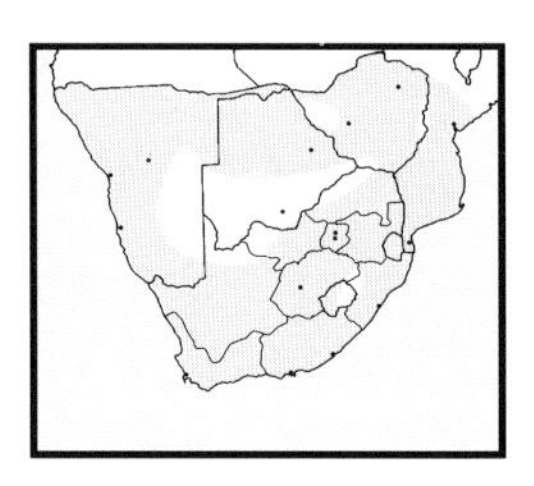

Pied Crow *Corvus albus* (548) 50 cm

An abundant and widespread species and the only white-bellied crow in the region, the Pied Crow has successfully adapted to urban situations. The white belly and smaller bill distinguish it from the Whitenecked Raven, and the white, not grey, underparts distinguish it from the House Crow. The Pied Crow performs aerial acrobatics and may be seen in flocks of up to 50 individuals. It is an opportunist and a scavenger, feeding on road kills and at rubbish dumps. It occurs in agricultural lands, grassland, open woodland and on roadsides. R

1. Male Blackheaded Oriole
2. Immature Blackheaded Oriole
3. Male African Golden Oriole
4. Adult Pied Crow
5. Adult Black Crow
6. Adult Pied Crow
7. Adult House Crow
8. Adult Whitenecked Raven

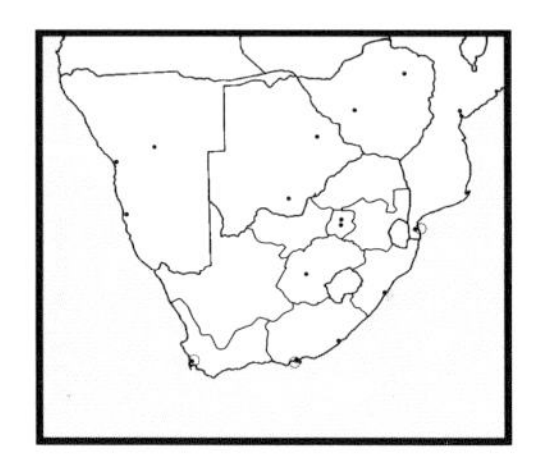

House Crow *Corvus splendens* (549) 42 cm

This unwelcome, alien species was introduced to Durban as a stowaway on ships from the east. A purely urban species and the only grey-bodied crow in the region, the House Crow may be told from the Black Crow and Pied Crow by its smaller size and broad grey collar extending around the hind neck and on to the breast. Immatures resemble the adults but are greyish brown in colour. Omnivorous and gregarious, House Crows are often seen in large groups. R

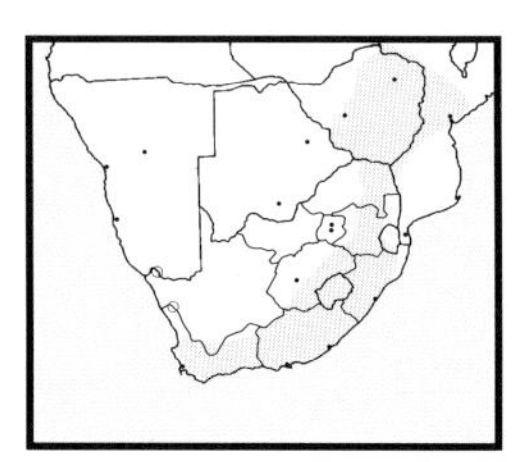

Whitenecked Raven *Corvus albicollis* (550) 54 cm

The Whitenecked Raven is a very large corvid with a huge bill and an all-black body, except for a broad white collar on the back of the neck. Its broad wings, broad tail and heavy head should help to identify it at a distance from the similar Pied Crow. Immatures are browner than the adults, with the white hind collar flecked with brown. The Whitenecked Raven is most often recorded in pairs, and feeds on grain, birds' eggs, reptiles and fruit, as well as on carrion at roadsides. It inhabits mountainous and hilly terrain and gorges. R

R *resident* • I *intra-African migrant*

Tits and penduline tits

Families Paridae and Remizidae

These small, highly active arboreal birds have short, robust bills. Some have black, white and grey plumages, others are yellow or grey. Usually encountered in pairs or small groups of four to six, they are prominent and noisy members of mixed bird parties. The tits nest in holes whereas the penduline tits build elaborate, suspended, felted nests.

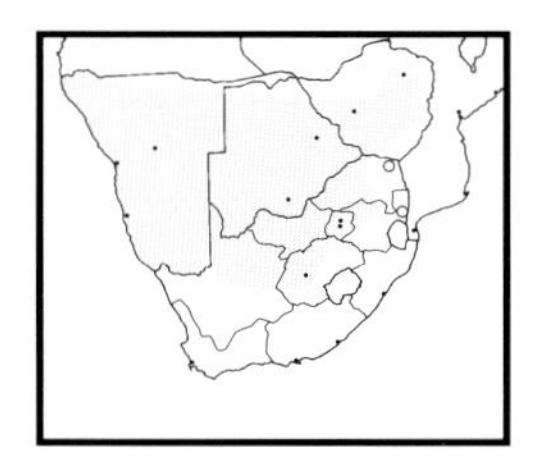

Ashy Tit *Parus cinerascens* (552) 13 cm

This species could be mistaken for the Northern Grey Tit or the Southern Grey Tit. It is separable from the former by its white, not buff, outer tail feathers and grey, not off-white, flanks, and from the latter by its white, not pinkish-buff, hind neck and by its blue-grey, not buffy, back and flanks. The sexes are alike, and immatures are duller versions of the adults. An active and restless feeder along branches and in the foliage of trees and bushes, it takes caterpillars and other insects. It may often be seen hanging upside down. It utters a series of ringing 'tseeu, tseeu, tseeu' notes and musical 'chu-weeeeou' sounds. It prefers dry Karoo bush, acacia thornveld and dry savannas. NE

Northern Grey Tit *Parus griseiventris* (553) 13 cm

As with the Ashy Tit, this species has a black crown and a triangular bib extending down the belly to a point. It appears whiter than the Ashy Tit and is separable from that species by its off-white, not grey, flanks and buffy, not white, outer tail feathers. The sexes are alike, and immatures are duller versions of the adults. The Northern Grey Tit feeds along large, dead branches in the canopy, digging with its bill under bark flakes and in lichens, as well as gleaning from leaves. The call is a series of harsh churring notes and also includes scolding 'tjou-tjou-tjou-tjou' sounds. This species is virtually confined to mature miombo woodland. R

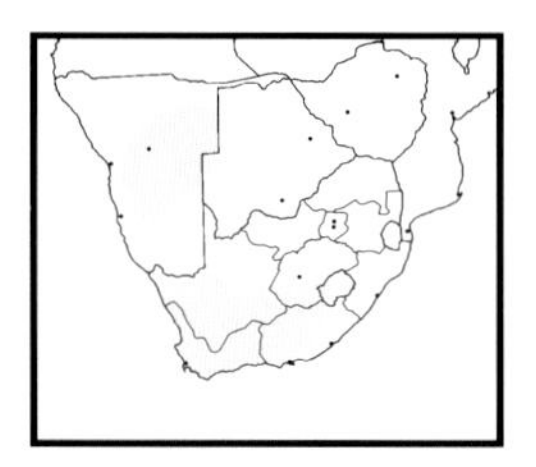

Southern Grey Tit *Parus afer* (551) 13 cm

This, the Ashy Tit and the Northern Grey Tit have very similar plumage patterning, being separable from each other on colour differences and habitat preferences. It can be told from both species by its pinkish-buff, not white, hindneck and further by its dull brown, not blue-grey, back and buffy, not grey or pinkish-white, flanks and belly. The sexes are alike, and immatures are browner than the adults. This bird utters a series of churring notes and musical 'kleee-kleee-kleee-kleep' sounds. A restless forager, the Southern Grey Tit searches for insects, especially caterpillars, in the foliage of shrubs, small trees and bushes. As with the other species, it nests in a hole in a tree, favouring fynbos and Karoo scrub bush. E

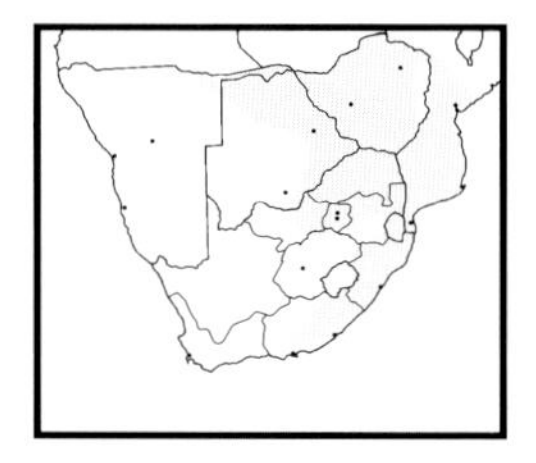

Southern Black Tit *Parus niger* (554) 16 cm

This species and Carp's Tit are similar, but since their ranges are allopatric no confusion should arise. The male is all-glossy-black with a white wing stripe; the female is a little greyer on the underparts. Immatures resemble the females. The Southern Black Tit is an active feeder, searching under bark and in leaves for insects, and it has a penchant for *Combretum* seedpods, which it holds in one foot while probing for insects with its bill. As with the other *Parus* tits, it is commonly found in feeding parties, in almost any moist woodland in the east or northeast of the region. The call is a harsh chattering 'chrr-chrr-chrrr-chrrr'. R

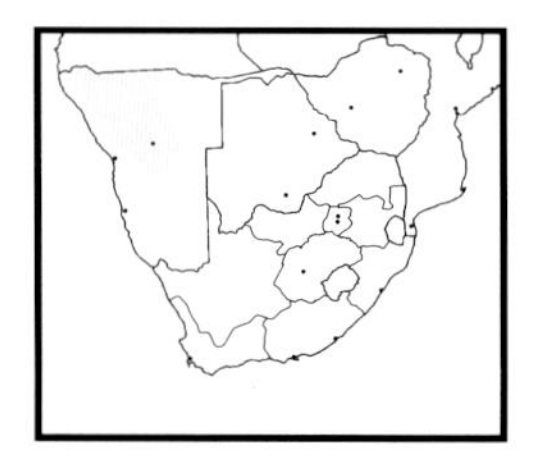

Carp's Tit *Parus carpi* (555) 14 cm

Generally black like the Southern Black Tit, this species has much more white in the wing and all-black, not grey-barred, undertail coverts. The sexes are alike, although females are slightly duller than the males. This bird is unlikely to be mistaken for the Southern Black Tit in our region, however, as the distributions of the two species do not overlap. It is a restless feeder in bushes and small trees along dry watercourses, as well as on scrubby hillside bushes in thornveld and arid savanna. It utters harsh, chattering, trilling and rasping notes, similar to those given by the Southern Black Tit. NE

1. Adult Ashy Tit
2. Male Southern Black Tit
3. Female Southern Black Tit
4. Adult Northern Grey Tit
5. Adult Carp's Tit
6. Adult Southern Grey Tit

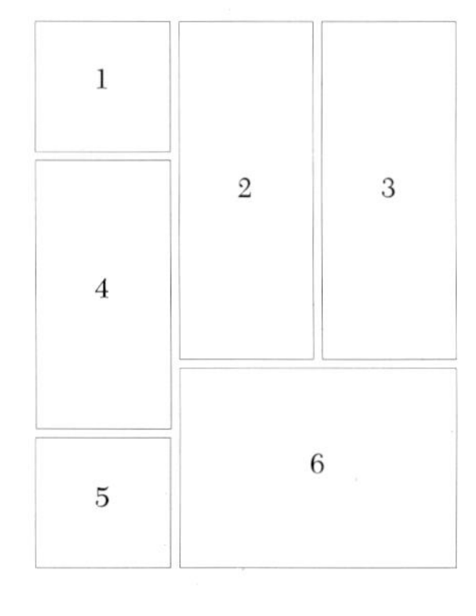

NE *near endemic* • R *resident* • E *endemic*

Rufousbellied Tit *Parus rufiventris* (556) 15 cm

The orange belly, all-black head and throat and cream-coloured eye of this species are diagnostic, and are unlike those of any other *Parus* species in the region; the eastern race is much paler on the belly and has a light brown eye. Males and females are similar; immatures are duller with a light brown eye. Like the Northern Grey Tit (see page 190), this species is confined to miombo woodland and is often seen in feeding parties with that species. A restless feeder, it can be seen foraging in the canopy and canopy edge along fairly thin branches. Its call is a series of harsh churring notes and a clear 'chick-wee, chick-wee, chick-wee'. R

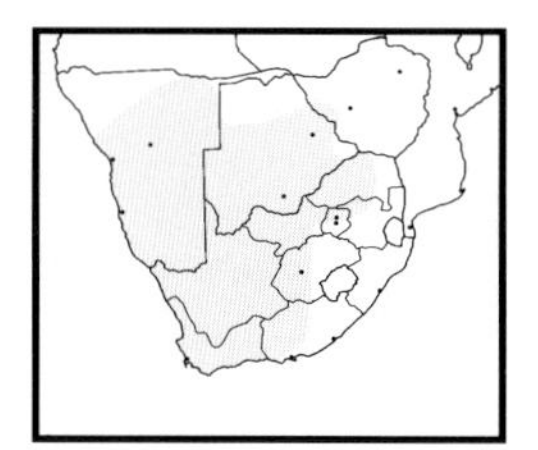

Cape Penduline Tit *Anthoscopus minutus* (557) 8 cm

A tiny bird, warbler-like in appearance and a little smaller than an eremomela (see page 222), the Cape Penduline Tit occurs in small parties of about five individuals. It is very easy to mistake this species for the Yellowbellied Eremomela (see page 222). Diagnostically, the Cape Penduline Tit has a black forehead speckled with white, whereas the Yellowbellied Eremomela has a plain grey forehead. Both species have a dark streak through the eye, and the yellow belly and vent of the Yellowbellied Eremomela fades to almost white in the arid west, there appearing very similar to the underpart coloration of the Cape Penduline Tit. The Cape Penduline Tit can be told from the Grey Penduline Tit on forehead colour: black and white in the Cape Penduline Tit and an unmarked buffy colour in the Grey Penduline Tit. The Cape Penduline Tit builds a characteristic nest out of woolly plant and animal fibres. It favours thornveld, semi-arid scrub and fynbos, and gives a soft, thin 'tseeep tseeep tseeep' call. R, NE

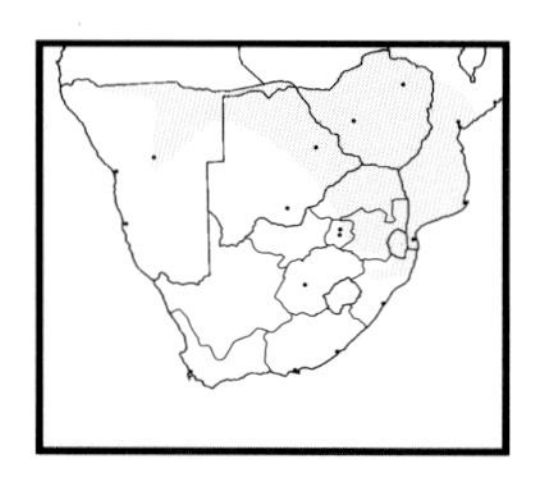

Grey Penduline Tit *Anthoscopus caroli* (558) 8 cm

Although similar in appearance to the Cape Penduline Tit, the Grey Penduline Tit can be told from that species by its buff, not black and white, forehead, and by its buffy cheeks, flanks and vent. The call is a soft, continuous 'tseep tseep tseep', higher pitched than that of the Cape Penduline Tit. Like that species, the Grey Penduline Tit builds a characteristic oval nest with a false entrance tube near the top, and uses woolly plant and animal fibres in its construction. The nest is usually a conspicuous dirty white but is darker in areas where Dorper and Karakul sheep occur. The Grey Penduline Tit forages for small insects and shows a preference for miombo woodland and acacia savannas. R

Spotted Creeper Family Salpornithidae

Small, cryptically marked, brown birds with long, decurved beaks, Spotted Creepers forage by clambering about tree surfaces like woodpeckers. They are easily overlooked. Sedentary and insectivorous, they are confined to well-wooded habitats.

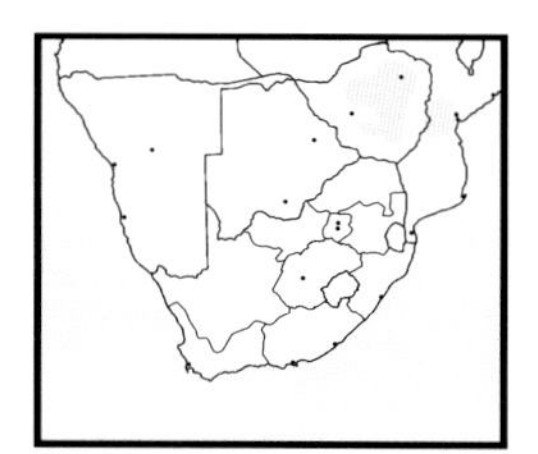

Spotted Creeper *Salpornis spilonotus* (559) 15 cm

This species with its decurved, sunbird-like bill and undulating woodpecker-like flight is placed in its own family. Its brown upperparts spotted with white, its short barred tail and its buffy white underparts barred with black are diagnostic. It is often seen on its own but does occur in mixed bird parties – in larger numbers but not necessarily as a group. It has a habit of sneaking to the back side of a branch or tree when disturbed. Its call is a very weak, soft and thin 'sweepy-tseep-tseep-tseep' and is unlikely to attract the attention of the casual observer. A well-camouflaged species, it creeps around and up trunks and along the branches in lichen-covered miombo woodland. R

1. Adult Rufousbellied Tit (eastern race – above; western race – below)
2. Adult Cape Penduline Tit
3. Adult Spotted Creeper
4. Adult Grey Penduline Tit

1	2
3	4

Babblers Family Timaliidae

Medium-sized black, white, brown and grey birds inhabiting reedbeds, woodland and forest fringes, most babblers are highly vocal and gregarious. They feed on fruit, insects and on small reptiles. Some, perhaps all, southern African species are co-operative breeders.

Adult Hartlaub's Babbler

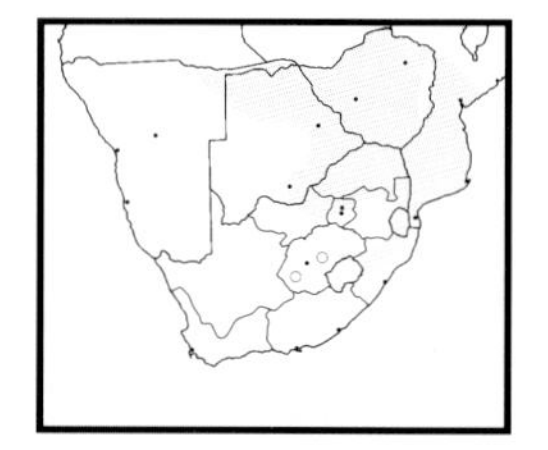

Arrowmarked Babbler *Turdoides jardineii* (560) 24 cm

A very noisy species, this bird's call – a nasal whirring crescendo with many birds calling at once a 'ra-ra-ra-ra-ra-ra-ra' – is often the first sign of its presence. Through most of its range it is unlikely to be mistaken for anything else; where its distribution overlaps with those of Hartlaub's Babbler and the Blackfaced Babbler confusion may arise. At close range the Arrowmarked Babbler can be seen to have a yellow to orange eye with a red orbital ring, differing in this respect from the other two species; Hartlaub's Babbler has a white rump which both the Arrowmarked Babbler and the Blackfaced Babbler lack, and the Arrowmarked Babbler has white arrow-like streaks on the head and throat whereas the other two species are scaled with white. Immatures lack the white streaks of the adults and have a brown eye. Babblers forage on the ground in family groups of up to 12 individuals, noisily scratching and overturning dead leaves beneath thick undergrowth. The Arrowmarked Babbler is found in thick grass, thickets in scrub savanna, bushveld and thornveld. R

Barecheeked Babbler *Turdoides gymnogenys* (564) 24 cm

The patches of bare black skin below and behind the eye, the tawny feathers of the nape and the brown back distinguish this species from the similar Southern Pied Babbler. Immatures are whitish, flecked with brown and tawny feathers, and may easily be confused with the immature Southern Pied Babbler; immatures of both species are always found in the company of the adults of the same species, however. The call is a typical babbler-like chatter of 'kerra-kerra-chuka-chuka-chuka'. Barecheeked Babblers are found along dry watercourses and on rocky wooded hills. NE

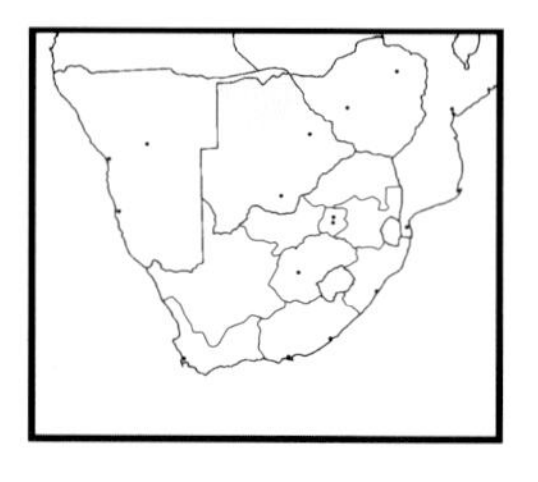

Hartlaub's Babbler *Turdoides hartlaubii* (562) 26 cm

This species closely resembles the Arrowmarked Babbler but is separable from that species in flight by its diagnostic white rump. When perched, the red eye with its yellow rim, and the scaly appearance of the head and belly, rather than the arrow-like streaking of the Arrowmarked Babbler, distinguish the two species. Immatures are lighter on the throat than the adults. These noisy birds, with their nasal, rolling 'papapapapaa' sounds, feed on the ground; as with most babblers in the region, their flight is direct with an alternate flutter-and-glide pattern. They favour dense riverine forest, areas of papyrus and reedbeds, and nearby woodland. R

Blackfaced Babbler *Turdoides melanops* (561) 28 cm

More secretive and less noisy than other babblers, when perched this bird can be seen to have a light yellow eye and the scaly appearance of Hartlaub's Babbler, but it is much browner and lacks the white rump of that species. In flight the back and rump are brown, like those of the Arrowmarked Babbler, but the underwing is blackish, not tawny-coloured. Immatures are less well marked and have a brown eye. The bird's call is composed of short, nasal, cat-like yells 'wha-u wha-u' and chattering 'pa-pa-pa-pa' notes. The Blackfaced Babbler prefers dense thickets and in particular *Commiphora* woodland. R

Southern Pied Babbler *Turdoides bicolor* (563) 26 cm

The only black-and-white babbler in the region, the Southern Pied Babbler is unlikely to be mistaken for any other bird except perhaps as an immature, when it may be confused with a Barecheeked Babbler. However, it is unlikely for immature birds not to be found in the company of adults so, providing careful observation is undertaken, confusion with the immature Barecheeked Babbler should not occur. An uncommon but noisy species, the Southern Pied Babbler makes its presence known by its cackling contact and alarm calls: 'kwee kwee kwee kwee' notes, higher in pitch than other babblers. It frequents arid thornveld savannas, semi-arid woodland and dry watercourses. E

1. Adult Arrowmarked Babbler
2. Adult Arrowmarked Babbler
3. Adult Barecheeked Babbler
4. Adult Hartlaub's Babbler
5. Adult Blackfaced Babbler
6. Adult Southern Pied Babbler

1	2
3	4
5	6

R *resident* • NE *near endemic* • E *endemic*

Bulbuls Family Pycnonotidae

Bulbuls are small to medium-sized brown, green and yellow birds with fairly short bills – hooked in some species. They occur in a wide range of habitats from desert fringes to montane forests. Found solitarily or in small groups, they feed on fruit and insects, and occasionally on nectar.

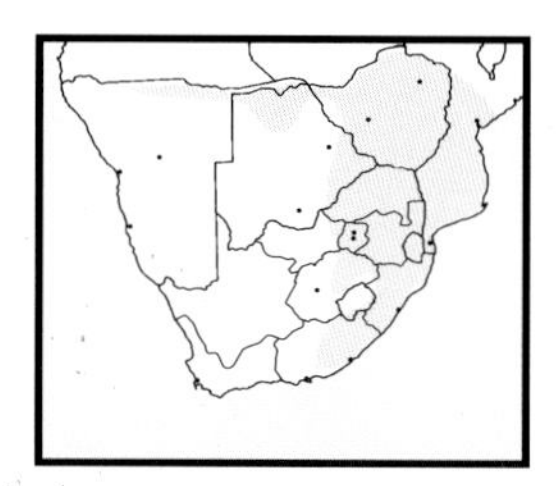

Blackeyed Bulbul *Pycnonotus barbatus* (568) 22 cm

There is virtually no overlap in the distributions of this species, the Cape Bulbul and the Redeyed Bulbul so, although the three are very similar, confusion should not arise. The Blackeyed Bulbul has a dark eye wattle, the same colour as the eye and head plumage, but the black on the head is less extensive than it is in the Redeyed Bulbul. The sexes are alike, and immatures resemble the adults. The Blackeyed Bulbul is a noisy species, always the first to make a fuss with its sharp 'kwit-kwit-kwit' alarm call when it comes across a predator such as a snake or an owl. It also gives a lively, liquid 'cheloop chreep choop' song. It forages in trees for fruit and insects and also hawks insects in flight. It frequents a wide variety of habitats but tends to favour suburban parks and gardens, thornveld and forest edges. R

Redeyed Bulbul *Pycnonotus nigricans* (567) 21 cm

The bright red eye wattle surrounding a dark eye is diagnostic of this species, and its black cap extends to the mantle, being more extensive than in the similar Blackeyed Bulbul. (The ranges of these species seldom overlap, however, so confusion should not arise.) Immatures have a pale pink, not bright red, eye wattle. The Redeyed Bulbul forages for fruit, nectar and insects arboreally and on the ground. It is as noisy as the Blackeyed Bulbul, with similar liquid whistles and harsh alarm calls, and is common in gardens, thornveld and dry riverine bush. NE

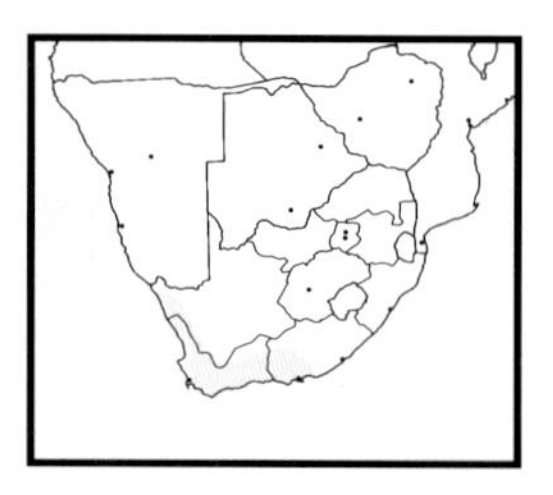

Cape Bulbul *Pycnonotus capensis* (566) 21 cm

Although similar in shape, size and behaviour to the Redeyed Bulbul and the Blackeyed Bulbul, the Cape Bulbul generally lacks the darker head of those two species, and its white eye wattle is diagnostic; further, there is virtually no overlap in the distributions of these three species, so confusion should not arise. The immature Cape Bulbul lacks the distinct eye-ring of the adult bird but is darker brown below than immatures of either of the other two species. A noisy, conspicuous species with its liquid series of 'peet-peet-patata' notes, the Cape Bulbul perches on top of bushes or trees, feeding on fruit and nectar; at these times its forehead often takes on a yellowish hue as it becomes covered in pollen. The Cape Bulbul is found in fynbos, coastal and riverine bush, gardens, and exotic plantations. E

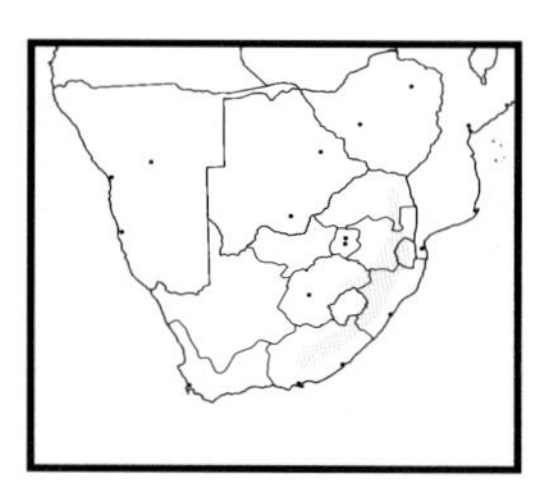

Bush Blackcap *Lioptilus nigricapillus* (565) 17 cm

A shy yet unmistakable species, the Bush Blackcap has a coral-pink bill contrasting with a black chin, and a black crown which extends below the eye and as far as the mantle. The underparts are light grey and the legs pale pink. Immatures are more pallid in colour, with a pink bill and a brown crown. The call of this bird is rather similar to that of the Blackeyed Bulbul but is more melodious and more variable. The Bush Blackcap forages in thick undergrowth, searching for fruit and berries, within temperate forest or in forest margins in the mist belt and adjacent scrubby bush on hillsides, especially in *Leucosidea* scrub. E

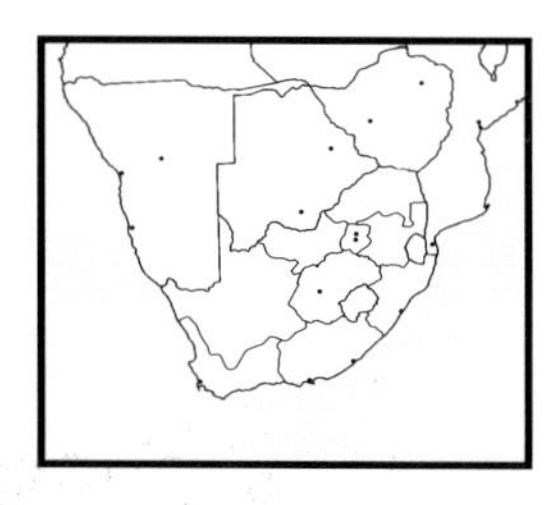

Yellowspotted Nicator *Nicator gularis* (575) 23 cm

A skulker, the Yellowspotted Nicator is easily overlooked unless it is heard calling and then it is not easy to find as it sings from a concealed perch. Its bill is heavy and shrike-like. It has large white to yellow spots on the upperwing coverts and a yellow tip to the tail on otherwise olive-green upperparts. Its underparts are buffy-white shading to yellow on the vent and undertail. The sexes are alike, and immatures are duller than the adults. The Yellowspotted Nicator forages on the ground in among leaf litter, searching for insects, in riverine forest and thickets. Its call is a rich, liquid jumble of penetrating notes: 'wip chip chop rrrup chop chop chop chirrup'. R

1. Adult Blackeyed Bulbul
2. Adult Redeyed Bulbul
3. Adult Cape Bulbul
4. Adult Yellowspotted Nicator
5. Immature (left) and adult (right) Bush Blackcap

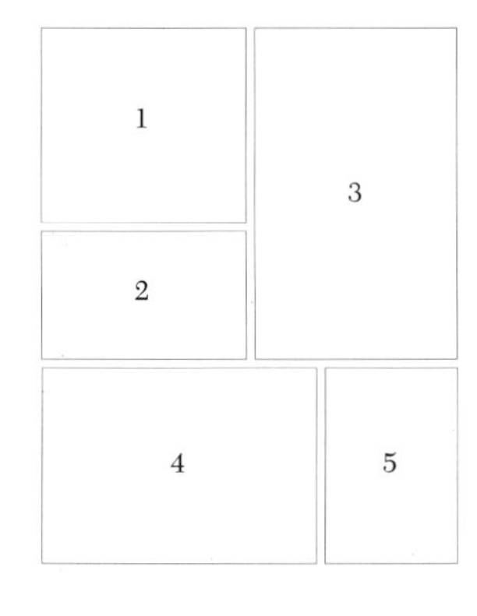

R *resident* • NE *near endemic* • E *endemic*

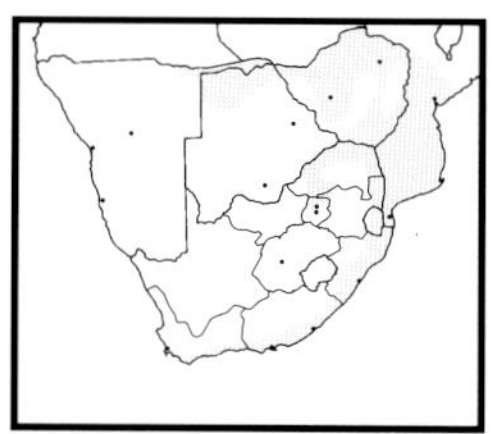

Terrestrial Bulbul *Phyllastrephus terrestris* (569) 21 cm

The red eye and white throat contrasting with the reddish-brown upperparts of this bird are good field characters. The sexes are alike and immatures resemble the adults. A ground-feeding species, it is often seen in small parties, scratching in among leaf litter on the forest floor or in riverine undergrowth. Feeding parties of four or five birds chatter to one another, a soft, chattering 'trrup cherrup trrup', as they scatter leaves and earth, alerting the observer to their presence. The Terrestrial Bulbul is found in coastal forest along the east coast, in riverine thickets and in the understorey of evergreen forest. R

Adult Yellowbellied Bulbul

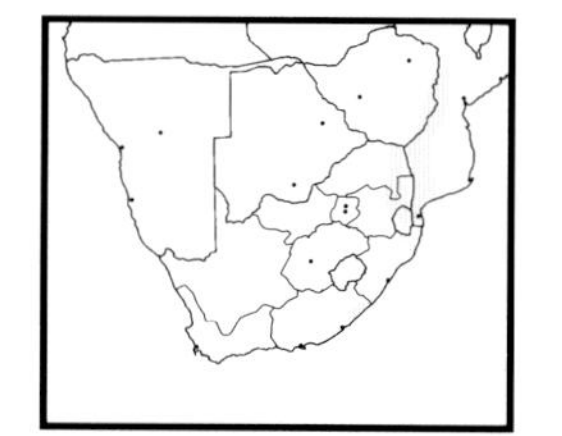

Yellowstreaked Bulbul *Phyllastrephus flavostriatus* (570) 20 cm

This is a small bulbul with a grey crown and olive-green upperparts; the underparts are off-white, streaked with yellow on the belly but this streaking is often indistinct and is not a good field character. The Yellowstreaked Bulbul favours the mid-stratum and upper-canopy levels of evergreen forest. The best field character for differentiating this species from others in this habitat is its habit of flicking one wing at a time while it clambers along branches or in among creepers in search of food. Usually seen singly or in pairs it chatters noisily, a penetrating 'weeteweeti' and nasal 'winky-wink winky-wink-chink sounds'. R

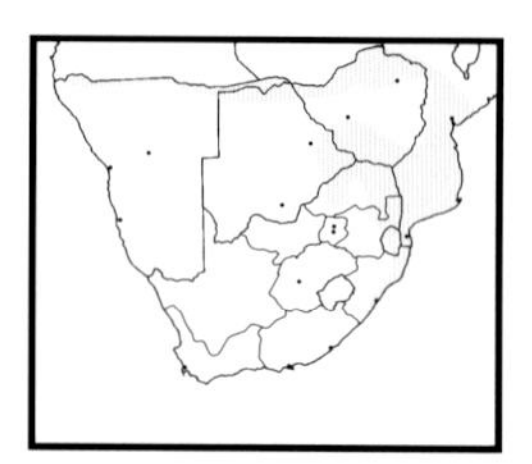

Yellowbellied Bulbul *Chlorocichla flaviventris* (574) 23 cm

While superficially similar to the Sombre Bulbul, this species has a red (not white) eye, bright yellow underparts including the underwing, and is olive-brown above. Like the Terrestrial Bulbul it forages in small groups, keeping to dense tangled undergrowth at the lower levels of the forest, as well as scuffling on the ground in search of food. Feeding parties chatter to one another, a nasal, 'nah, nah, nah, nah' increasing in tempo when alarmed. The Yellowbellied Bulbul prefers coastal forest, riverine thickets and inland evergreen forest. R

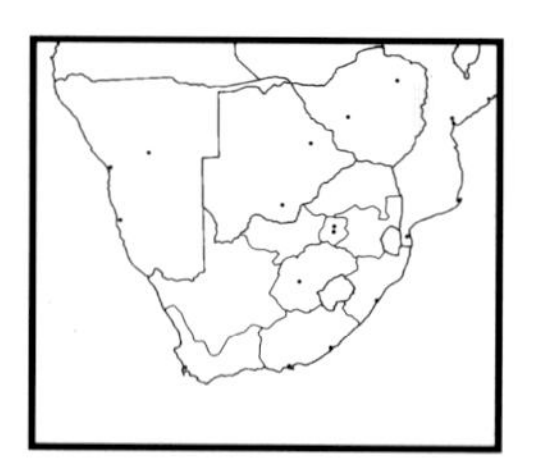

Stripecheeked Bulbul *Andropadus milanjensis* (573) 21 cm

This bulbul has a grey head and cheeks, and dark eyes with contrasting white eyelids, the upper eyelid more pronounced and diagnostic than the lower (which may be indistinct). The white streaks on the grey cheeks are not readily visible in all light conditions. The underparts are greenish yellow and the upperparts olive-brown. Foraging at all levels of the forest, this resident of montane evergreen forest and forest margins is usually difficult to locate due to its shy and skulking behaviour. Its call is a throaty 'chrrp chrrp chrrp chrrp'. R

Sombre Bulbul *Andropadus importunus* (572) 23 cm

The commonest of the dull olive-green bulbuls, the Sombre Bulbul is most easily distinguished by its white eye; the race to the northeast is much yellower below and could readily be mistaken for a Yellowbellied Bulbul were it not for its white eye. Immatures have a light grey eye and are yellower below. The Sombre Bulbul frequently perches on top of a bush, giving its characteristic call, 'willie', sometimes followed by a jumble of notes interpreted as 'come on out and fight ... sca-a-ared?' Sombre Bulbuls forage in the upper parts of trees and low down in thick undergrowth, making them difficult to see. They frequent thick bush, riverine habitat, coastal bush and evergreen forest. R

1. Adult Terrestrial Bulbul
2. Adult Yellowstreaked Bulbul
3. Adult Yellowbellied Bulbul
4. Adult Stripecheeked Bulbul
5. Adult Sombre Bulbul

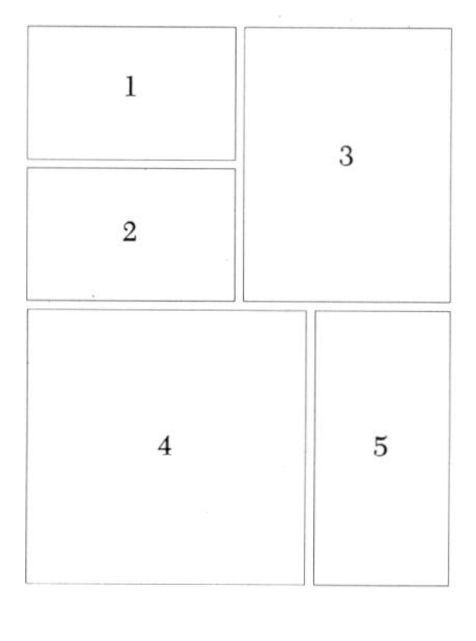

R *resident*

Thrushes, rockjumpers, chats and robins Family Turdidae

These are small to medium-sized birds. Thrushes are generally found in well-wooded or forested habitats, as are some robins. Chats inhabit open areas from deserts to savannas, and rockjumpers are found in montane grassland and fynbos. Most species feed on invertebrates, and some include fruits and seeds in their diet.

Immature Southern Olive Thrush

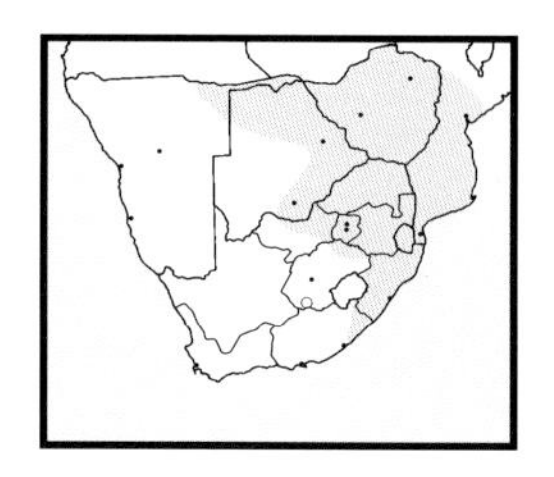

Kurrichane Thrush *Turdus libonyana* (576) 22 cm

The Kurrichane Thrush is separable from the Southern Olive Thrush by its dark malar stripes, white, slightly speckled throat, orange eye-ring and bright orange bill. It shows a white belly with orange flanks and plain, unmarked grey-brown upperparts. In immatures the wing coverts are tipped russet and the underparts are orangey-buff mottled with black. This thrush favours open woodland, including miombo woodland, and also thornveld and gardens where it may occur alongside the Southern Olive Thrush. The call is a loud whistled 'peet-peeou' or 'sweety-weet-weet' usually given from a perch, and a 'witeet witeet' when flushed from the ground. R

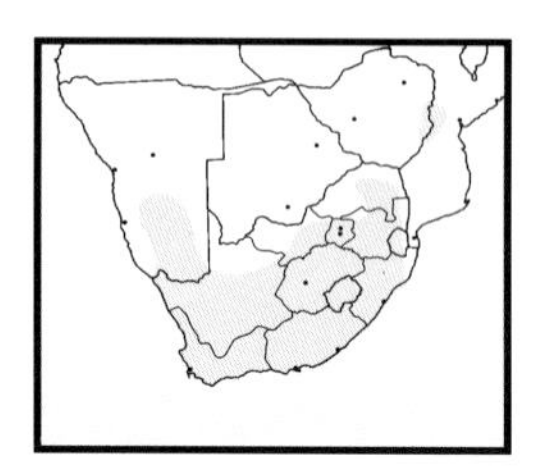

Southern Olive Thrush *Turdus olivaceus* (577) 24 cm

The absence of malar stripes, the dark speckled throat, dark eye-ring and orange-coloured underparts distinguish this species from the Kurrichane Thrush. Its belly ranges from pale orange to dark orange whereas in the Kurrichane Thrush the belly is white and the flanks are orange. Immatures are streaked buffy above and spotted blackish below. In suburbia this thrush is most active at dusk and dawn and prefers well wooded, shady areas. It is a common resident of gardens, plantations and montane forests. It gives a thin 'tseep' on take-off when alarmed, otherwise a fluty 'wheeeet-tooo-wheeeet'. R

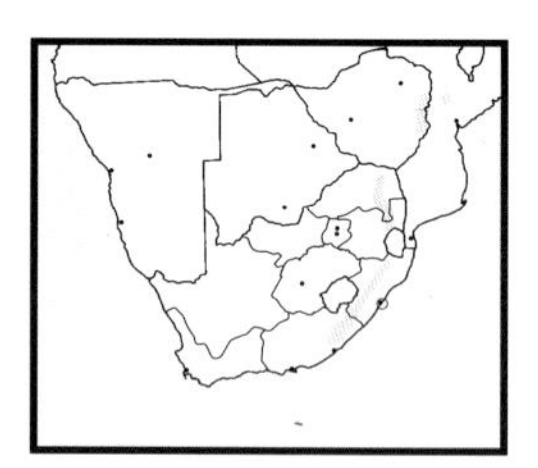

Orange Ground Thrush *Zoothera gurneyi* (579) 23 cm

Similar in size to the Kurrichane Thrush and the Southern Olive Thrush, this species differs from the other two orange-coloured thrushes by having a dark bill, a deep orange throat and breast, and dark brown upperparts with two clear white bars on the wing coverts. Immatures are spotted with buff above and mottled with black and orange below, but show the clear white wing stripes. Elusive and scarce, the Orange Ground Thrush has a penchant for forest streams, and is most active during the twilight hours. It is confined to montane evergreen forest, moving to coastal lowland forests in the winter. The call is a melodious song of whistled phrases like 'chee-cheeteeroo-chirrup'. R

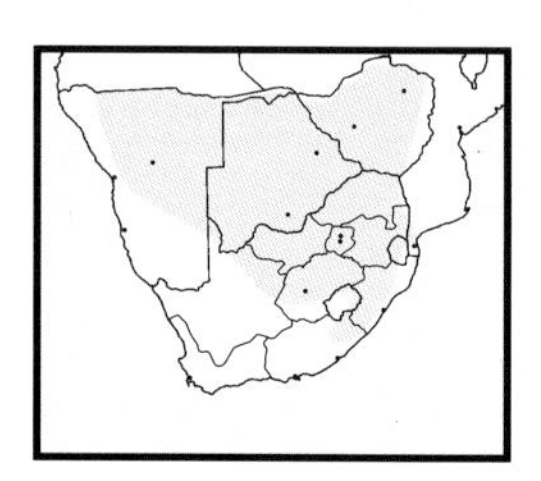

Groundscraper Thrush *Turdus litsitsirupa* (580) 22 cm

While similar to the Spotted Ground Thrush, the Groundscraper Thrush is unlikely to be confused with that species due to their different habitat preferences: the Groundscraper Thrush favours dry thornveld and open broad-leaved woodland while the Spotted Ground Thrush prefers the understorey of evergreen forests. Confusion may, however, arise with the Dusky Lark (see page 174). All three species have boldly marked underparts but the Dusky Lark is much smaller than the other two, its facial pattern is not as bold and it lacks the vertical black mark through the eye. The Groundscraper Thrush shows large yellowish patches in the wing in flight. Immature birds have reduced spotting on the belly, and the wing coverts are speckled with white above. The Groundscraper Thrush is a ground-living species, found in savanna woodland and thornveld. Its call sounds somewhat like 'litsitsirupa' as in its specific name. R

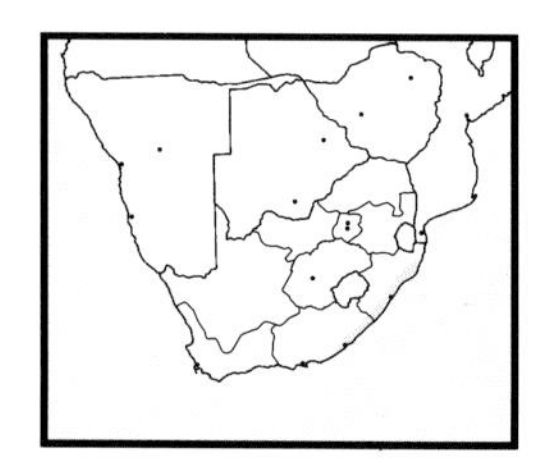

Spotted Ground Thrush *Zoothera guttata* (578) 23 cm

This species is unlikely to be confused with either the Groundscraper Thrush or the Dusky Lark (see page 174) due to differences in habitat preferences. It has a similar facial pattern to the Groundscraper Thrush but its upperparts are brown, not grey, and its upperwings show two distinct white wing bars. Immatures are more finely spotted below, and above are spotted with buff. Occurring singly, the Spotted Ground Thrush forages on the forest floor and is most active at dusk and dawn. It is confined to coastal and lowland evergreen forests, and has a quiet 'tseep tseep' call as well as fluty, whistled phrases. R, W

1. Adult Kurrichane Thrush
2. Adult Kurrichane Thrush
3. Adult Southern Olive Thrush
4. Adult Groundscraper Thrush
5. Adult Spotted Ground Thrush
6. Adult Orange Ground Thrush

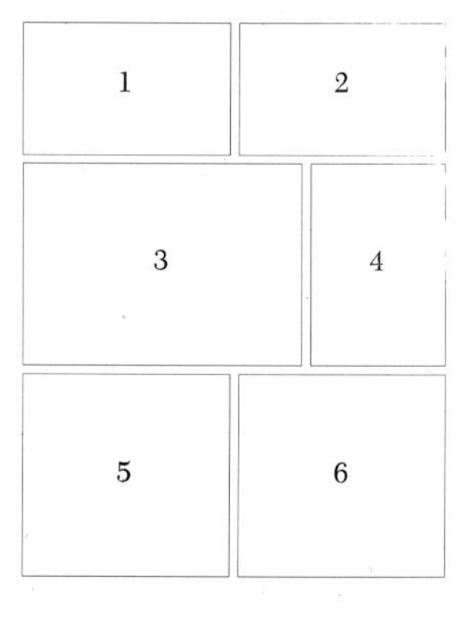

R *resident* • W *winter visitor*

Sentinel Rock Thrush *Monticola explorator* (582) 18 cm

The male Sentinel Rock Thrush can be told from the male Cape Rock Thrush by having a blue-grey, not brown, back; and from the Short-toed Rock Thrush by lacking a pale crown. Females have all-brown upperparts and buffy to white underparts which are streaked with brown; the female Cape Rock Thrush and Short-toed Rock Thrush have bright rufous bellies. Immatures are spotted white above and scaled brown below. A conspicuous species, it frequents rolling grasslands and rocky slopes, and is often seen together with the Cape Rock Thrush. At higher altitudes it is subject to altitudinal movements, moving lower during the winter months. Its call is a whistled song of short phrases, 'teeu-teeu-teeu-preet', similar to that of the Cape Rock Thrush. E

Cape Rock Thrush *Monticola rupestris* (581) 21 cm

Males have a blue-grey head and throat, an orange breast and underparts, and brown upperparts. Females are paler orange below, rather than the mottled brown and white shown in the female Sentinel Rock Thrush, with a brown head and wings and a speckled throat. In areas where the distribution of this species overlaps with that of the Short-toed Rock Thrush, the colour of the back and extent of grey on the throat (in males) are important field characters. The Cape Rock Thrush forages on the ground and usually sings its whistled song, similar to that of the Sentinel Rock Thrush, while perched on a rock. It frequents rocky slopes, gorges and rock-strewn hillsides with bushes. E

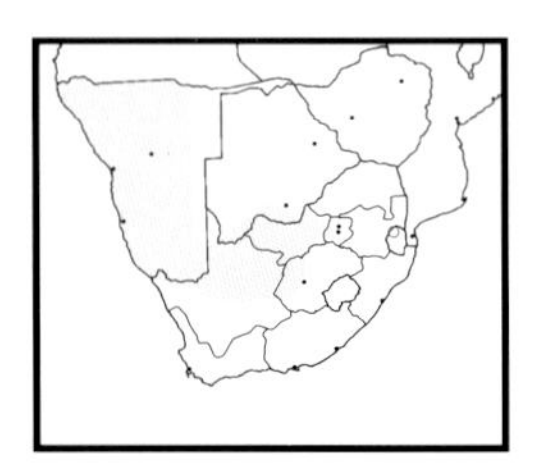

Short-toed Rock Thrush *Monticola brevipes* (583) 18 cm

Where the distributions of this, the Cape Rock Thrush and the Sentinel Rock Thrush overlap, caution is required to avoid misidentification. The males of this species have a pale blue-grey to almost white crown (dark blue-grey in both other species) contrasting with a dark blue-grey back (brown in the Cape Rock Thrush) and throat; the rest of the underparts are orange. Females are all-brown above and show an extensive white throat (more so than in other female rock thrushes) and rufous underparts. The song is a series of whistled phrases, similar to those of other rock thrushes. Short-toed Rock Thrushes are found on arid rocky hillsides, koppies and escarpments, and are often seen perched on telegraph poles and lines along roads. E

Miombo Rock Thrush *Monticola angolensis* (584) 18 cm

The range of this species does not overlap with the ranges of the other rock thrushes in our region, so confusion should not arise. Males have a blue-grey head, throat and back, wings speckled with black, and a pale orange breast fading to white at the vent. Females are similar to the males but are much paler and more mottled on the upperparts; they show distinct malar stripes, unlike other female rock thrushes. Immatures resemble the females but are mottled with black on white on the underparts. The Miombo Rock Thrush is the only rock thrush that is confined to miombo woodland and it is usually associated with hilly, but not necessarily, rocky terrain. Its call is a varied high-pitched whistled song, 'peeu-pweet-weet-wheet'. E

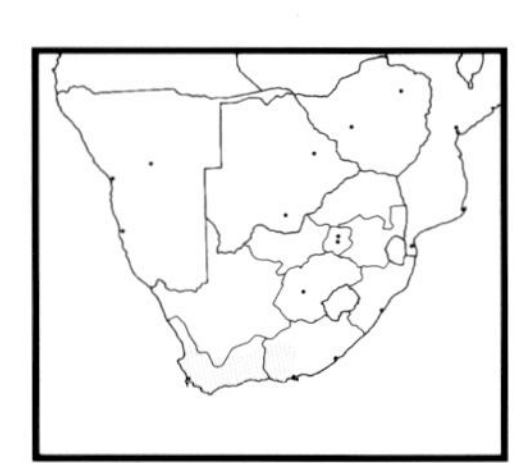

Cape Rockjumper *Chaetops frenatus* (611) 25 cm

Similar to the Orangebreasted Rockjumper but much more brightly coloured, the male Cape Rockjumper has a chestnut belly contrasting with a black throat, and a broad white malar stripe. Females are duller, more rufous than chestnut on the belly, with the malar stripe streaked with black and the throat grey in colour. Immatures are similar to the females. These birds forage by digging in the soil and among leaf litter. They occur on rocky mountain slopes from sea level up to mountain peaks. The call is a clear piping 'wheeeo' and 'pee-pee-pee-pee' notes. E

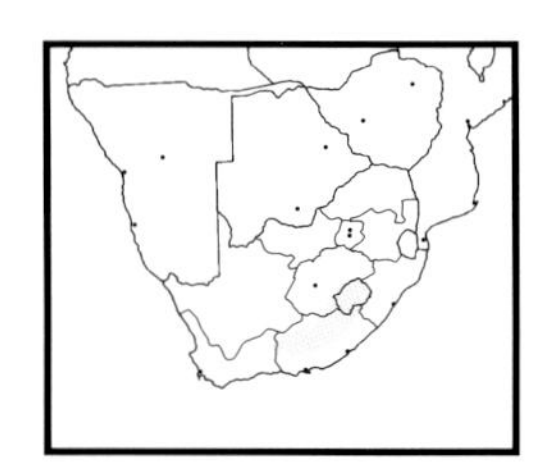

Orangebreasted Rockjumper *Chaetops aurantius* (612) 21 cm

Smaller and less colourful than the Cape Rockjumper, the male Orangebreasted Rockjumper has a pale orange belly, a black throat and a white malar stripe. Females and immatures are paler with a buffy belly and indistinct malar stripes. The Orangebreasted Rockjumper behaves in a similar manner to the Cape Rockjumper. It occurs at higher altitudes than does the Cape Rockjumper, on rocky mountain slopes and on grassy scree slopes. Its call, a rapidly repeated piping whistle is similar to that of the Cape Rockjumper. E

1. Male Sentinel Rock Thrush
2. Female Sentinel Rock Thrush
3. Female Cape Rock Thrush
4. Male Short-toed Rock Thrush
5. Male Cape Rock Thrush
6. Female Short-toed Rock Thrush
7. Female Miombo Rock Thrush
8. Male Miombo Rock Thrush
9. Male Cape Rockjumper
10. Male Orangebreasted Rockjumper
11. Female Orangebreasted Rockjumper

1	2	3
4		5
6	7	8
9	10	11

E *endemic*

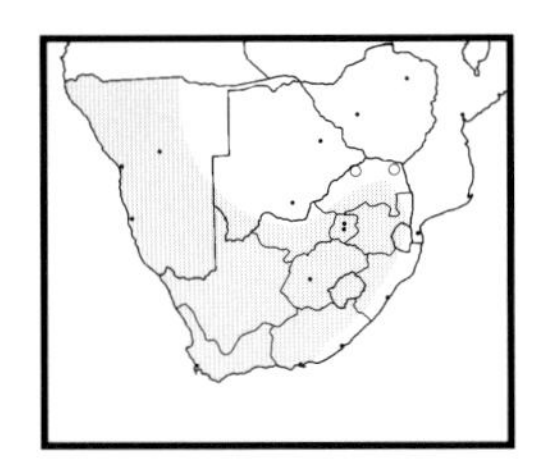

Mountain Chat *Oenanthe monticola* (586) 20 cm

This is a variable species, but males are generally either black or grey. In the dark form they have a white to grey crown (sometimes all black or grey), a white shoulder patch (sometimes absent) and white outer tail feathers; the underparts are either wholly black or show a white throat and, sometimes, a white throat and belly. Pale forms are grey with a white rump, white outer tail feathers, white shoulder patches and black flight feathers. Females and immatures are usually an overall dark brown, darker on the back than the underparts, with a white rump and white outer tail feathers tipped with black. The grey morphs resemble the Karoo Chat, but the white shoulder patch and white rump, lacking in the Karoo Chat, will separate the two species. The Mountain Chat is found in mountainous and rocky terrain, rocky outcrops and hillsides with scrubby bushes, and also in gardens and kraals. It calls with a clear thrush-like whistle and various harsh scolding 'churrs'. NE

Male Mountain Chat (pale form)

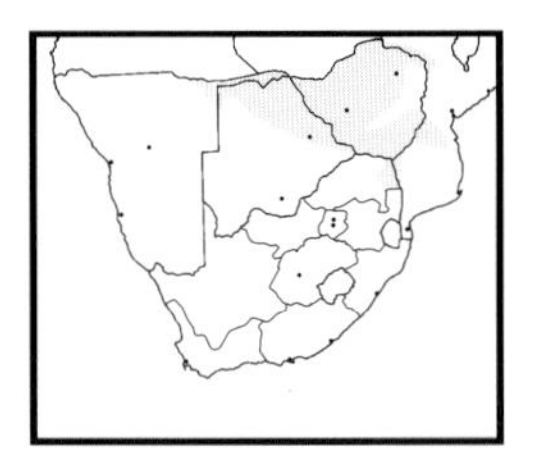

Arnot's Chat *Thamnolaea arnoti* (594) 18 cm

Similar to the dark form of the Mountain Chat in that males are all-black with a white cap and shoulder patch, Arnot's Chat can be distinguished from that species by its rump, vent and tail which are entirely black. Females are also black but lack the white cap of the male and show an extensive white throat and upper breast. Immatures are all black with a white wing patch and a white-speckled throat or crown depending on the sex. Arnot's Chat occurs in well-developed mature mopane, miombo and teak woodland. Its call is a quiet musical 'fik' or 'feee-feee'. R

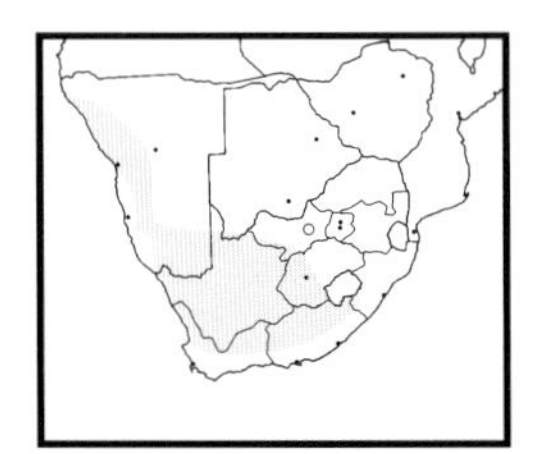

Karoo Chat *Cercomela schlegelii* (592) 18 cm

Similar in size to and resembling the grey morph of the Mountain Chat, this species can be told apart by having a grey, not white, rump, white outer tail feathers and no white shoulder patch. It is darker grey in colour than the Tractrac Chat, from which it can further be differentiated by its brownish ear coverts and white outer tail feathers for the entire length of its tail. Immatures are spotted buff above and scaled blackish below. The Karoo Chat occurs on scrubby semi-desert plateaus and stony arid hillsides, and the call is a harsh 'chak-chak' and 'trrat-trrat'. E

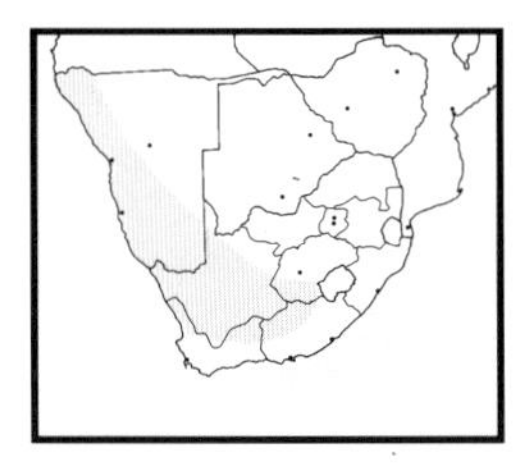

Tractrac Chat *Cercomela tractrac* (590) 15 cm

This small, round-bodied, long-legged chat varies in coloration from light grey to brownish grey. The rump and upper two-thirds of the tail are white, the central tail feathers and lower third being all black and forming a pointed triangle. The similar Karoo Chat can be separated from this species by its white outer tail feathers and greyer rump. Immatures are speckled buff above and spotted black below. The Tractrac Chat is found on gravel plains, in Karoo scrub, on coastal sand dunes with some vegetation and on desert golf courses. Its call is a soft, sharp 'tchak-tchak' given when disturbed. E

Sicklewinged Chat *Cercomela sinuata* (591) 15 cm

Similar to the Familiar Chat, the contrast between the darker upperparts and lighter underparts of this species should distinguish it from the overall grey-brown plumage of the Familiar Chat. The rump and uppertail are buffy, not chestnut, and the tail shows a black triangular, not a 'T' shape. This species also twitches its wings on landing but this behaviour is less obvious than (and not as frequent as) the deep bowing and flicking action of the Familiar Chat. The Sicklewinged Chat is found in short lowland and montane vegetation, Karoo scrubland and stony pastures. It is often silent other than quiet 'chak-chak-chak-chak' notes that it utters. E

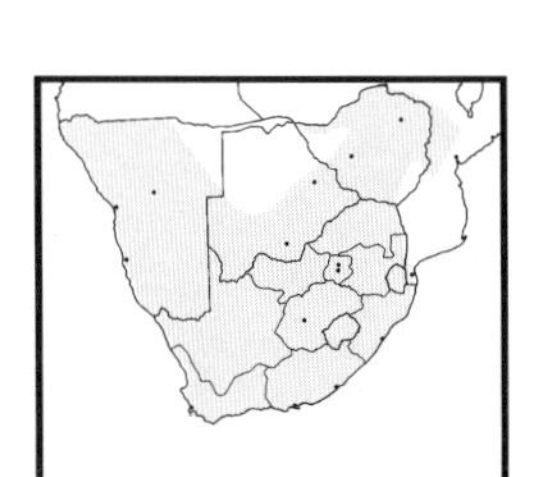

Familiar Chat *Cercomela familiaris* (589) 15 cm

This ubiquitous chat is uniformly grey in colour and habitually bows and flicks its wings on landing, often more than once, showing its chestnut rump and chestnut outer tail feathers, and the black 'T'-shaped tail pattern. It can be distinguished from the Sicklewinged and Tractrac chats by its darker grey-brown underparts. Immatures are flecked buff above and scaled below. This bird is most common in drier areas but occurs in all habitat types, from arid stony hills to moister hilly woodland. It utters harsh 'chak-chak' noises when alarmed, otherwise gives a warbled series of trills and churrs. R

1. Male Mountain Chat
2. Female Mountain Chat
3. Male Arnot's Chat
4. Female Arnot's Chat
5. Adult Karoo Chat
6. Adult Tractrac Chat
7. Adult Familiar Chat
8. Adult Tractrac Chat
9. Adult Sicklewinged Chat

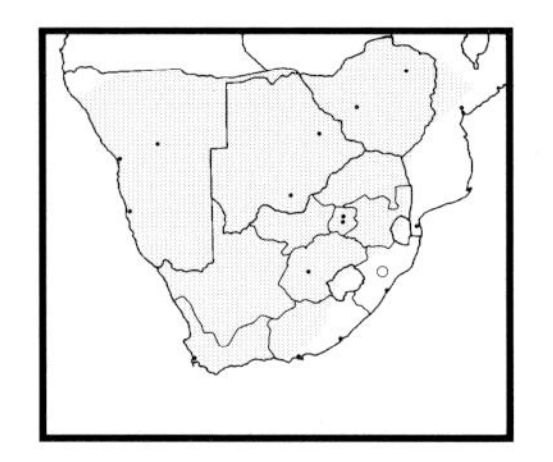

Capped Wheatear *Oenanthe pileata* (587) 18 cm

The adult Capped Wheatear is conspicuous with its prominent white forehead and eyebrow which separate the black cap and ear coverts. A broad black bib separates the white throat and underparts. The basal half of the tail is white and the central tail feathers are all black; the rump is white. Immatures are brown above with some buff spotting, and below are dirty-white with a mottled buffy-brown breast and flanks. This species stands perched very upright and flies down to the ground after prey; on landing it bows, swinging its tail up and down. It utters loud and melodious warbling noises and 'chik-chik' alarm notes. It prefers stony plains, flat, short grassland and airstrips. R

Immature Capped Wheatear

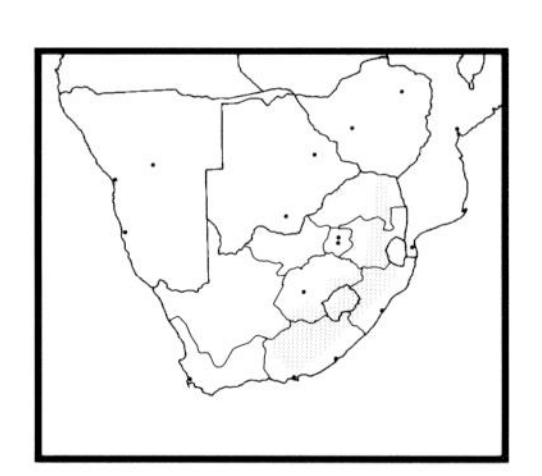

Buffstreaked Chat *Oenanthe bifasciata* (588) 17 cm

Males of this species have a black throat and upper breast with a white supercilium extending as an edging to the ear coverts. The underparts and rump are buff. Females are buffy, lighter below, and show a weak white supercilium. They differ from the similar immature Capped Wheatear in having a buff, not white, rump. The immature Buffstreaked Chat is similar to the female but is spotted with buff above and scaled below. An active species, the Buffstreaked Chat forages on the ground in among grass tufts and boulders. It occurs on rock-strewn, grassy slopes along the eastern escarpment, and has a loud and rich whistling song, and is also known to mimic other birds. E

Female Buffstreaked Chat

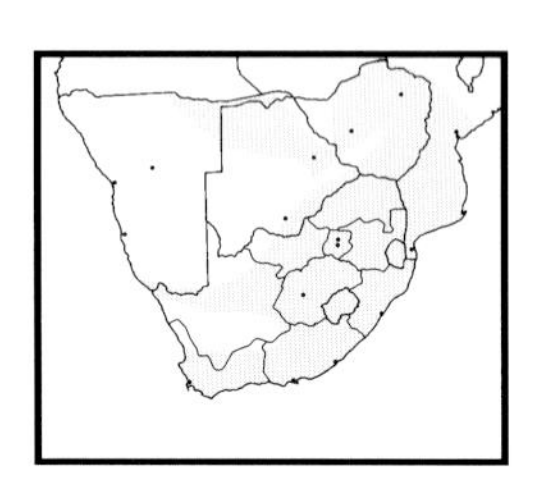

Stonechat *Saxicola torquata* (596) 14 cm

Males of this ubiquitous, cosmopolitan species have an all-black head with a conspicuous white neck patch and chestnut flanks and breast. Females have a mottled brown to grey head, dark brown upperparts streaked with black, and buffy underparts. Both sexes have a distinct white rump and wing patches, visible in flight. They perch conspicuously and are nearly always seen in pairs. Stonechats are widespread in upland grasslands, on the edges of vleis, in tall grass along roadsides, in irrigated fields and in riverine bush. The call is a sharp 'weet chak chak' given when alarmed; it also utters canary-like piping and trilling notes. R

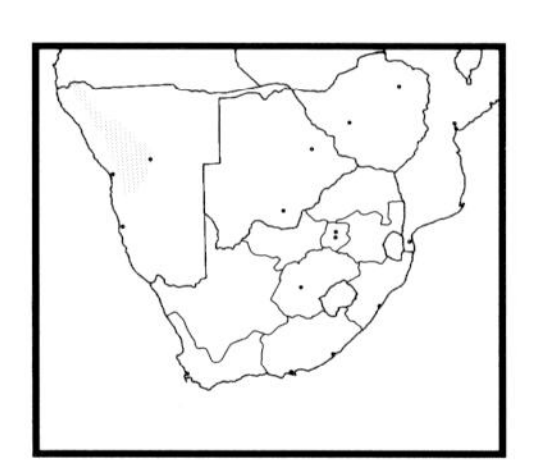

Herero Chat *Namibornis herero* (618) 17 cm

At a distance this species could be mistaken for the Familiar Chat with its chestnut rump and outer tail feathers and its wing-flicking habits, but closer views show a prominent white supercilium and white throat contrasting with a solid black line through the eye. The diagnostic dark streaking on the breast on the otherwise white underparts is indistinct from a distance. The Herero Chat frequents arid stony plateaus and stony hillsides with scrub vegetation, especially in association with *Euphorbia* species. It is mostly silent but when breeding utters a melodious warbling 'twi-tedeelee-doo' song. NE

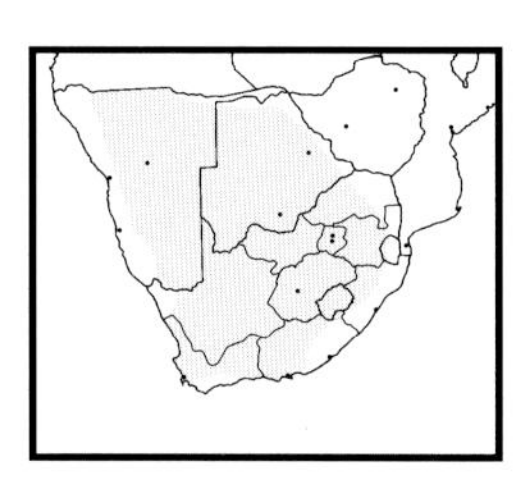

Southern Anteating Chat *Myrmecocichla formicivora* (595) 18 cm

On the ground the male Southern Anteating Chat is darker brown (almost black in some light) than the female bird, with a white patch on the shoulder, although this is often inconspicuous. In flight the conspicuous white primaries, seen in both sexes, show as a white patch in the wing. At rest, this bird appears plump and short tailed. Immatures are similar to the females but are more mottled. In habit these birds may be seen to bounce off the ground with fast, whirring wings; on landing they bow forwards, cocking the tail up. They forage on the ground for ants, termites and other small insects. They favour rolling grasslands interspersed with termite mounds, and open, sandy or stony areas, and their call is a short sharp whistled 'peek'. E

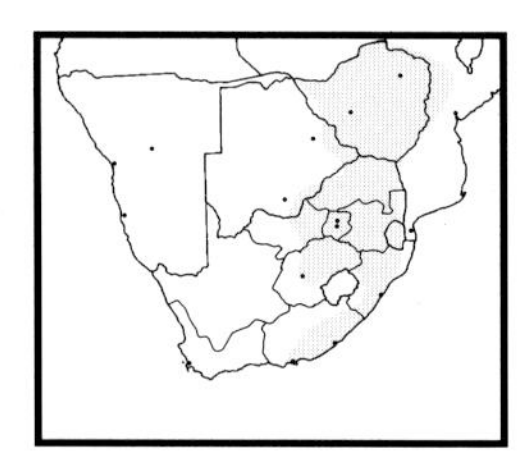

Mocking Chat *Thamnolaea cinnamomeiventris* (593) 23 cm

The male Mocking Chat is unmistakable with its chestnut belly and rump, and its black upperparts with a white shoulder patch, although when perched the shoulder patch is sometimes hidden by the black covert feathers. Females are dark grey above with a chestnut belly and rump and lack any white in the wing; a lone female might be mistaken for a rock thrush but Mocking Chat females are rounder, have shorter legs and do not stand as upright as do rock thrushes. Immatures are similar to the adults but are paler in colour. The song is loud and melodious and it also gives a jumble of imitated calls. These birds are invariably seen in pairs, on cliffs, boulder-strewn hillsides and wooded gullies. R

1. Adult Capped Wheatear
2. Female Buffstreaked Chat
3. Male Buffstreaked Chat
4. Female Stonechat
5. Adult Herero Chat
6. Female Southern Anteating Chat
7. Male Southern Anteating Chat
8. Male Stonechat
9. Male Mocking Chat
10. Female Mocking Chat

R *resident* • E *endemic* • NE *near endemic*

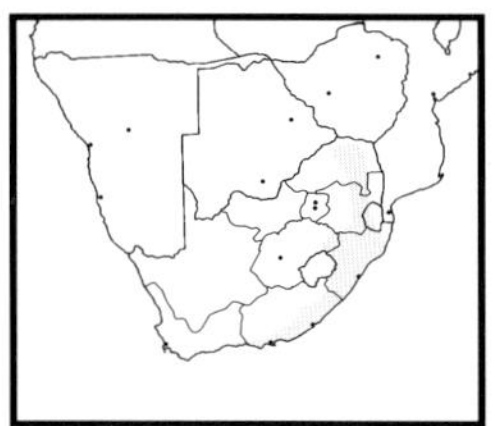

Chorister Robin *Cossypha dichroa* (598) 20 cm

This robin is larger and much darker than the Natal Robin, with a dark grey head and face (mostly orange in the Natal Robin) but is similar in size and coloration to Heuglin's Robin. It can be distinguished from the latter by the lack of a prominent white supercilium. The all-dark-grey, not powder-blue, upperparts, further separate the two species. Immatures are sooty, mottled buff above and below. The Chorister Robin is normally solitary, and is restricted to evergreen forest and forest patches, keeping to the forest canopy. It gives a ratchet-like 'chrrr-chrrr' as well as a medley of melodious notes, including mimicry of other birds. E

Immature Cape Robin

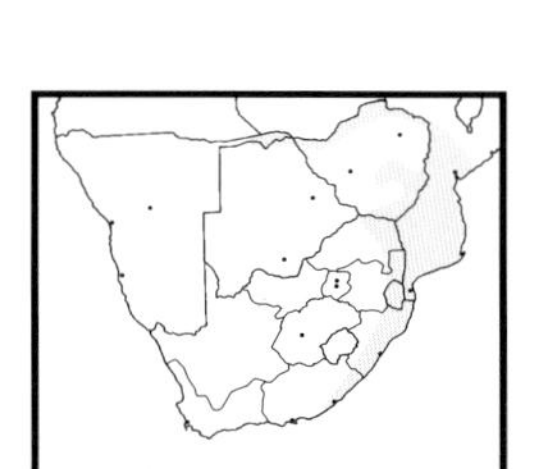

Natal Robin *Cossypha natalensis* (600) 18 cm

The smaller size, powder-blue wings, brownish mantle and otherwise orange head, face and underparts distinguish this species from the Chorister Robin which occurs in similar habitat. Immatures are spotted dark brown above and below. It calls from a low branch, a soft 'seee-saw, seee-saw', and it is an accomplished mimic, imitating the calls of as many as 30 other species. A shy and retiring robin, it is difficult to see, foraging mostly on the ground and moving to higher strata when trees are fruiting. It frequents thickets and tangles in the undergrowth of evergreen forests. R

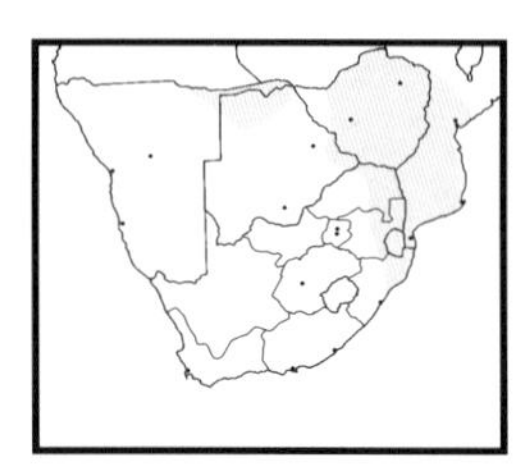

Heuglin's Robin *Cossypha heuglini* (599) 20 cm

The head and the sides of the face of this species are black separated by a prominent white supercilium which extends from the top of the bill to well behind the eye. Similar in size and plumage to the Chorister Robin, it can be told from that species by its white eyebrow stripe. Immatures are scaled brown on buff below and mottled buff on brown above. The bird's call, given from a low perch, is a loud crescendo of phrases, repeated again and again, and this species, like the Natal Robin, is a very good mimic. Heuglin's Robin feeds on the ground and frequents dense riverine thickets, evergreen thickets and lowveld gardens. R

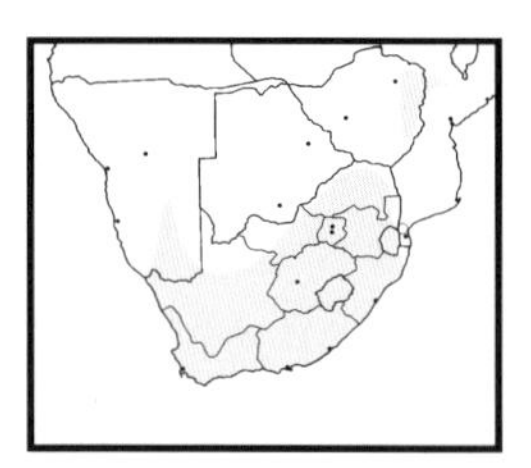

Cape Robin *Cossypha caffra* (601) 18 cm

Considerably smaller than Heuglin's Robin, the Cape Robin shows a white eyebrow and an orange throat and vent separated by a greyish belly. Immatures are brown mottled with buff and black, and the tail is orange with a dark centre. The Cape Robin is most often seen feeding at dusk and dawn out in the open on the edge of thick undergrowth (which provides refuge when the bird is threatened). It calls from a low perch, 'teeu teeu teeu', and is easier to see than are many of the other robins. It hops about on the ground, jerking up its tail and flexing its wings on landing. It is found on the edges of forest, and in riverine bush, fynbos scrub, along drainage lines in Karoo scrub, and in forest clearings and gardens. R

African Whitethroated Robin *Cossypha humeralis* (602) 17 cm

The adults of this ground-feeding, black-and-white robin have a prominent white wing bar, a broad white eyebrow, and all-white underparts – other than the pale orange flanks. Immatures are brown with the feather tips on the upperparts edged with buff and those below edged with black; the tail is rufous and black as in the adults. A solitary species, it feeds on the ground and is most active during twilight hours. It favours thornveld thickets and riverine bush. It gives an attractive medley of whistled phrases and is a good mimic of many other bird calls. E

1. Adult Heuglin's Robin
2. Adult Chorister Robin
3. Adult African Whitethroated Robin
4. Adult Cape Robin
5. Adult Natal Robin

1	3
2	
4	5

E *endemic* • R *resident*

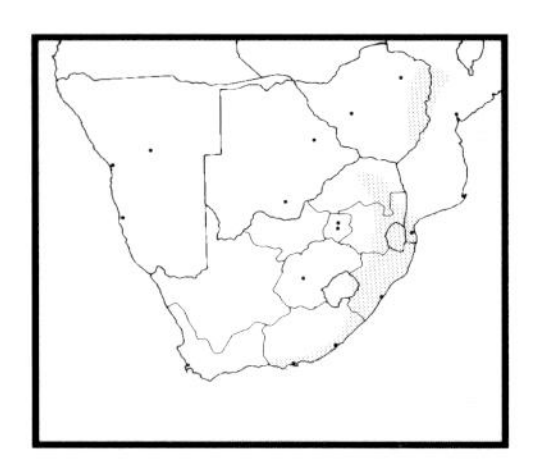

Starred Robin *Pogonocichla stellata* (606) 16 cm

The 'starred' of this robin's name hails from the inconspicuous white spots in front of its eyes and on its throat. Generally yellow and dark blue in colour, its most obvious identification feature is the flash of yellow seen on the tail as it flits through the forest tangle. Immatures are quite different: when they leave the nest they are spotted black and brown above, and below are yellow mottled with black; as subadults they have the same tail pattern as the adults but are olive-green above and light yellow below. The Starred Robin frequents montane evergreen forest, moving to lower coastal and evergreen forest in the cooler months of the year. Its call is a piping whistled 'too-twee' contact call, which is frequently repeated. R

Immature Starred Robin

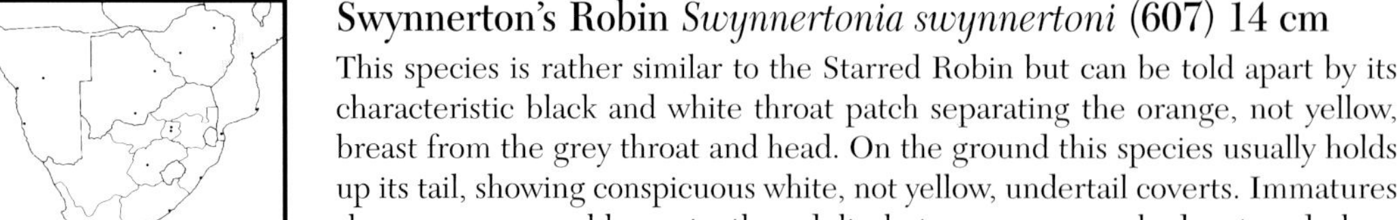

Swynnerton's Robin *Swynnertonia swynnertoni* (607) 14 cm

This species is rather similar to the Starred Robin but can be told apart by its characteristic black and white throat patch separating the orange, not yellow, breast from the grey throat and head. On the ground this species usually holds up its tail, showing conspicuous white, not yellow, undertail coverts. Immatures show some resemblance to the adults but are more washed out and show extensive white speckling. Restricted to isolated evergreen-forest patches, these birds forage on the forest floor in open areas with deep leaf cover, and are attracted to ant columns, where they feed on insects flushed by the column. The song, uttered by the male bird, is a high-pitched, frequently repeated 'pee-pee, sweet-swee'. R

Immature Swynnerton's Robin

Gunning's Robin *Sheppardia gunningi* (608) 14 cm

Gunning's Robin, similar in size to Swynnerton's Robin and the Starred Robin, has a pale orange throat and breast fading to white on the belly, an orange vent and a rusty-coloured tail. Its powder-blue forewings and indistinct short white eyebrow – which does not extend beyond the eye – are diagnostic. Immatures are olive-brown spotted with buff above, and the underparts are buffy-scaled rufous-brown. The cryptic plumage coloration of this species and its furtive nature in the lower stratum of dark forest undergrowth make it difficult to see. It favours low-lying evergreen and broad-leaved coastal forest. It gives a high-pitched but soft song 'titu widdle-titu, widdle-titu'. R

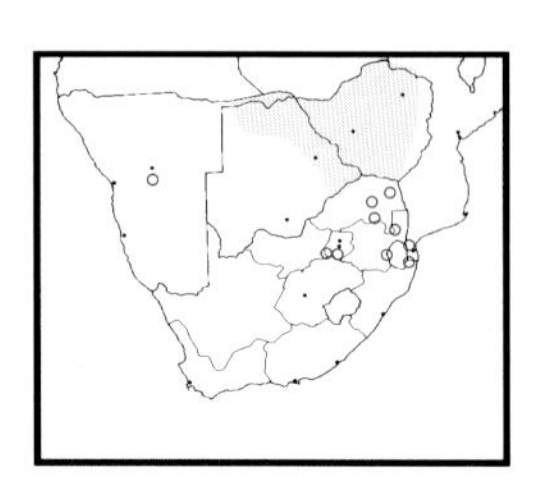

Thrush Nightingale *Luscinia luscinia* (609) 16 cm

Equivalent in size to a large brown warbler, this species has a russet tail, a speckled throat and a habit of cocking and flicking its tail when it is excited. The sexes are alike, but immatures are more mottled on the head, back and breast. The Thrush Nightingale feeds on the ground. Territorial in its wintering area and a master skulker, it is more often heard than seen. The bird's call is a rich, warbling song interspersed with harsh, grating sounds. It frequents thornveld thickets and other scrub, usually near to rivers and flooded or damp areas. S

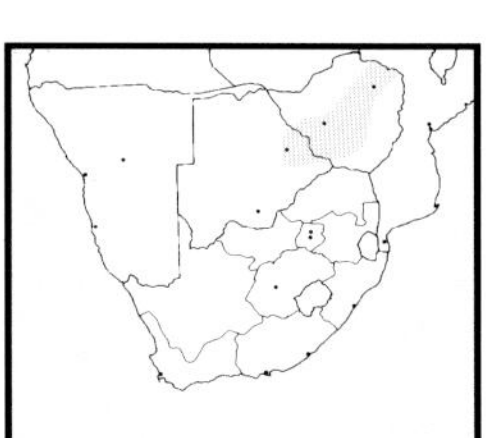

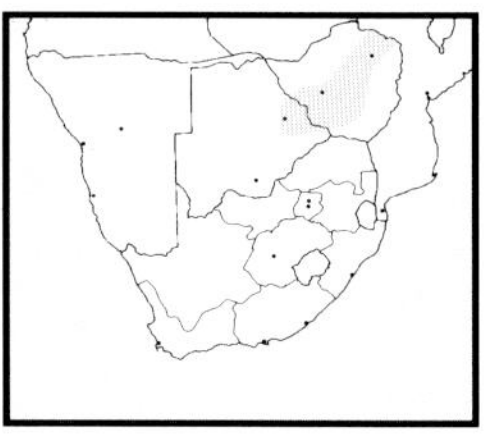

Boulder Chat *Pinarornis plumosus* (610) 25 cm

This uncommon, sooty-brown, thrush-like species has white tips to the outer tail feathers, and white spots along the covert edge of the wing, noticeable only in flight. Females are duller than the males. This species is normally recorded in pairs and in small family parties as it runs and bounds in search of insects and small lizards. On landing on a boulder it appears unable to control the motion of its tail, which appears to fall on to its back before being lowered to a normal position. The whistled call of this bird has been likened to a squeaky wheel. The Boulder Chat has a restricted habitat, being confined to the lower slopes of granitic, boulder-strewn, wooded hills. R

Collared Palm Thrush *Cichladusa arquata* (603) 19 cm

Similar in size and shape to a robin, the Collared Palm Thrush is by no means as secretive as those birds, and is immediately recognizable by its cream-coloured throat with a black border, and by its greyish underparts, neck and ear coverts. The sexes are alike. On the ground it hops about in the open with its tail raised. It calls from high up in thickets and palms, where it perches on open branches, flicking and fanning its tail. Its voice is similar to that of Heuglin's Robin (see page 208). The Collared Palm Thrush favours palm savanna and associated riverine bush and thickets. R

1. Adult Starred Robin
2. Adult Gunning's Robin
3. Adult Thrush Nightingale
4. Adult Swynnerton's Robin
5. Adult Boulder Chat
6. Adult Collared Palm Thrush

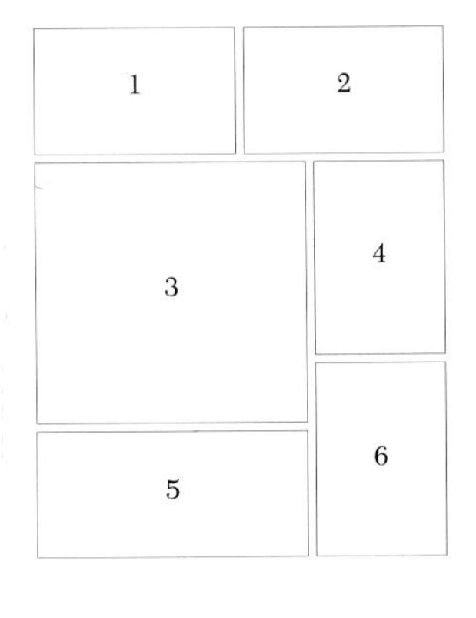

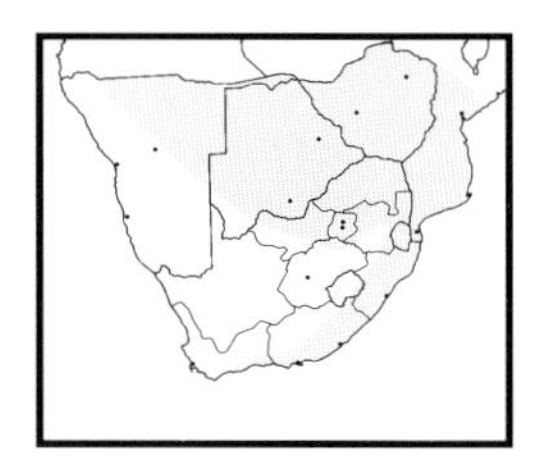

Whitebrowed Robin *Erythropygia leucophrys* (613) 15 cm

The streaked breast and the white edging to the upperwing coverts forming two white wing bars differentiate this species from the Kalahari Robin; both species have rufous uppertail coverts but the basal section of the tail in the Kalahari Robin is rufous, not blackish as in this species. The sexes are alike, and immatures are speckled with buff and brown above, and below are whitish heavily scaled with brown on the breast; the tail of immature birds resembles that of the adults. The Whitebrowed Robin is sometimes difficult to see as it keeps to the lower levels of thickets and scrub. It hops around on the ground with its tail held erect. When it flits from bush to bush it does so with a spread tail, showing the white corners to the tail that are characteristic of this genus. This bird favours dry thornveld, open woodland, thickets, drier riverine margins and savanna. Its song is very variable, yet repetitive: a series of plaintive and penetrating phrases. R

Adult Whitebrowed Robin

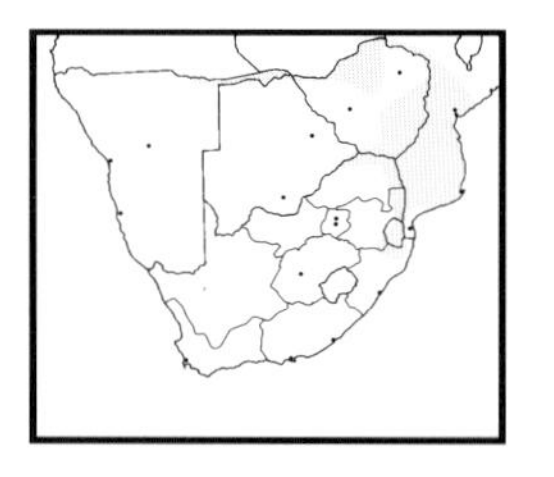

Eastern Bearded Robin *Erythropygia quadrivirgata* (617) 18 cm

The Eastern Bearded Robin, while similar to the Brown Robin with its white supercilium and throat, is readily distinguishable from that species by its richer range of colours. The orange flanks and upper breast as well as the pale rufous rump are diagnostic field characters. The sexes are alike, and immatures are scaled and speckled with buff and dark brown above and below; the tail, like that of the adult, is black, tipped white. This robin walks on the ground with its tail raised, scratching among leaf litter. It mimics other birds and gives a clear and penetrating song of mixed, repeated phrases, and has a greater preference for drier forest undergrowth and thickets than does the Brown Robin. R

Adult Eastern Bearded Robin

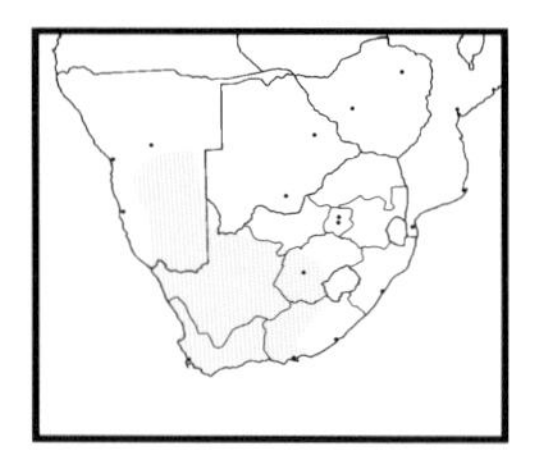

Karoo Robin *Erythropygia coryphoeus* (614) 17 cm

The Karoo Robin and the Brown Robin are quite similar, both lacking the rufous rump that their generic name implies. This robin is, however, characteristically noisy and outgoing compared to the reclusive Brown Robin, which displays quite the opposite behaviour. The Karoo Robin perches out in the open and scolds at any intruder; when frightened it flies low, with its tail fanned, to the seclusion of a bush. It has weak facial markings and is generally grey-brown in colour with a pale throat. It has white tips to the outer tail feathers, characteristic of the genus. The sexes are alike, and immatures are sooty brown, mottled with buff, and have an indistinct eyebrow. The Karoo Robin is found in Karoo scrub bush and fynbos thickets. Its song is a mixture of whistles and harsh grating notes; its alarm call is a prolonged churring and hissing noise. E

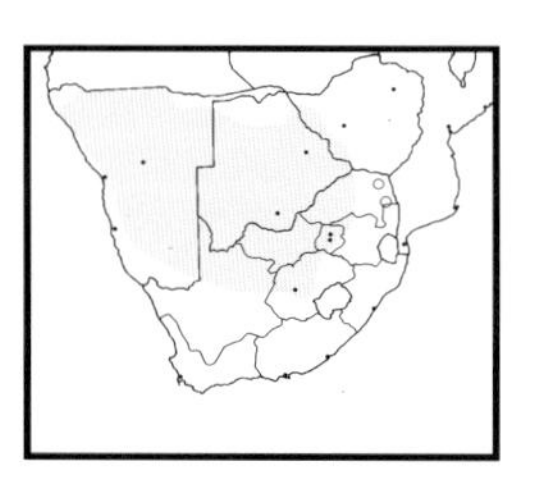

Kalahari Robin *Erythropygia paena* (615) 17 cm

The plain, unmarked underparts with a pinkish flush, the unmarked, cinnamon-coloured back and the rufous tail with its broad subterminal bar help to differentiate this species from the Whitebrowed Robin. The sexes are alike, and immatures are mottled above and below but have similar tail markings to the adults. Kalahari Robins run on the ground, foraging for termites, ants, spiders and some fruits, cocking their tails every now and then. They sing a lively, sustained song of mixed whistles and chirps from the midst of a bush, usually perched low down; this musical song is much more varied than those given by the Karoo Robin and the Whitebrowed Robin. This species prefers a drier, more open habitat than does the Whitebrowed Robin, which it replaces in the very arid west. NE

1. Adult Whitebrowed Robin
2. Adult Eastern Bearded Robin
3. Adult Karoo Robin
4. Adult Kalahari Robin
5. Adult Brown Robin

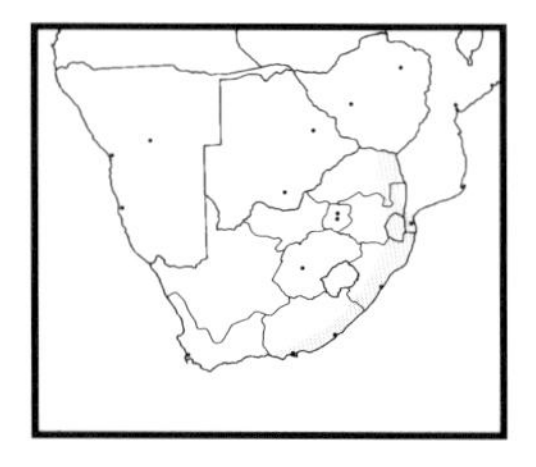

Brown Robin *Erythropygia signata* (616) 18 cm

Identified by its white eyebrow edged with black above and by the spots of white on the bend of the wing, this robin is generally brown above and white below. It has facial markings that are similar to but less distinct than those of the Eastern Bearded Robin. The sexes are alike, and immatures are similar to the adults but are spotted above and scaled below. Easily missed, the Brown Robin forages about in the darkest patches of shadow, usually where undergrowth is minimal, flicking leaves aside with its bill and picking up insects. The call is a loud and rapid 'tritritritritri' series of notes; also a 'sweet-twee-too-twit-twit-treeep'. It prefers danker habitat with deeper shade than does the Eastern Bearded Robin. E

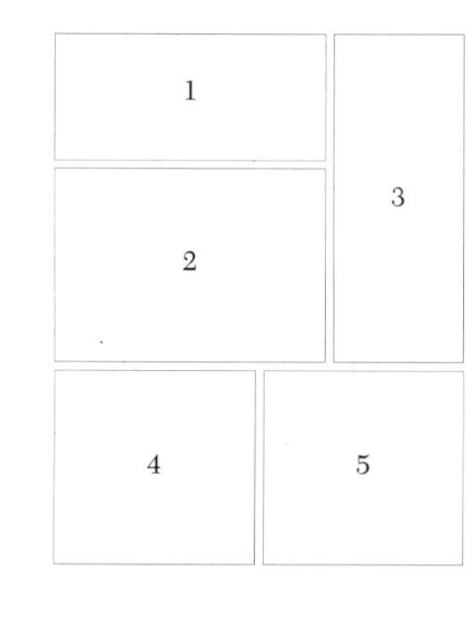

R *resident* • E *endemic* • NE *near endemic*

Warblers, apalises, crombecs, eremomelas, Grassbird, Rockrunner, prinias, titbabblers and cisticolas Family Sylviidae

A diverse group of mostly small birds, members of this family are usually dull-coloured and lack any marked sexual dimorphism. Cisticolas in particular can present identification problems, and are best identified by call.

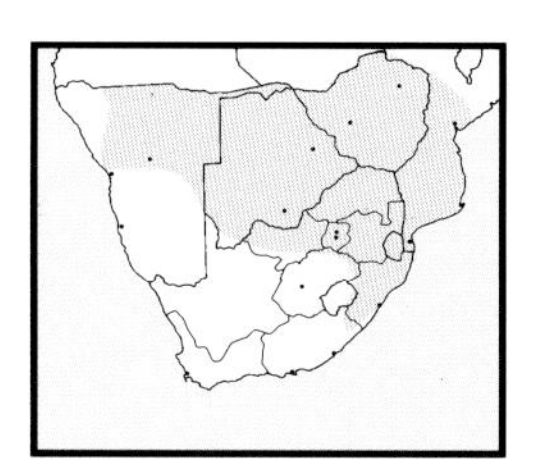

Garden Warbler *Sylvia borin* (619) 14 cm

The Garden Warbler is olive-brown to grey above and white below suffused with brownish buff. It has an inconspicuous pale eyebrow and an indistinct white ring around the eye; the tail is square or slightly rounded at the tip. In keeping with other *Sylvia* warblers, it has a rounded head and a short, stubby bill. It frequents thick subcanopy vegetation in mixed woodland and forest edges. Its call is a monotonous jumble of chirps and a grating alarm call. S

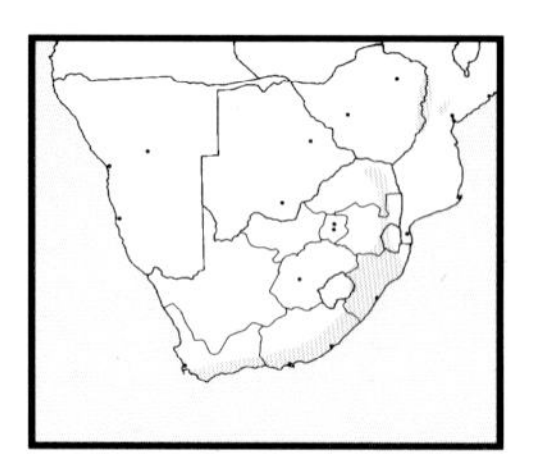

Yellowthroated Warbler *Phylloscopus ruficapillus* (644) 11 cm

A small, energetic warbler, the Yellowthroated Warbler has a yellow eyebrow contrasting with a rufous crown and eye-stripe, and a grey belly contrasting with a yellow throat and vent. Immatures are greener on the breast. Active, restless birds, usually seen in ones and twos and sometimes in mixed bird parties, gleaning insects from leaves and branches, they forage in the middle to upper layers of their evergreen, mainly montane forest habitat. The call is a high-pitched 'wittee' and also includes 'tweety-tweety-twit' notes. R

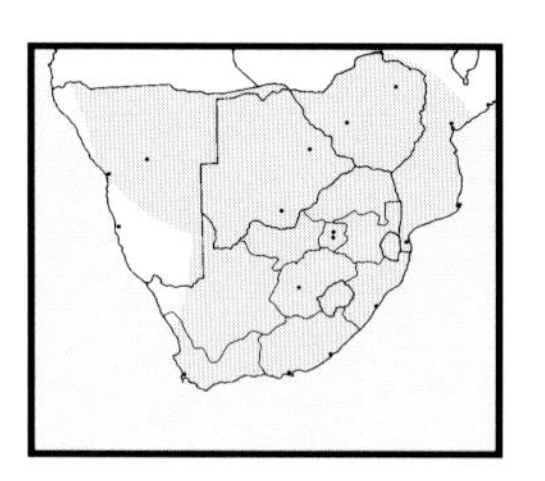

Willow Warbler *Phylloscopus trochilus* (643) 11 cm

The upperparts of the Willow Warbler are olive-brown with a yellowish-green tinge; the underparts are whitish suffused with yellow which is brightest on the breast. The supercilium is pale white to yellowish and the shoulder shows a yellow edge. The tail is notched at the tip. The bill is small compared to that of the similar Icterine Warbler, which is also larger and a brighter yellow below. The Willow Warbler has pink legs while those of the Icterine Warbler are blue-black. The Willow Warbler occurs in a range of woodland and savanna habitats. The call comprises a soft 'wheeeet wheeet' and a melodious song. S

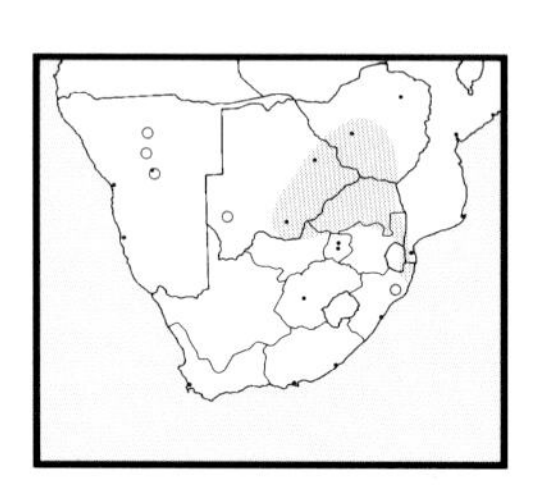

Olivetree Warbler *Hippolais olivetorum* (626) 16 cm

This bird gives the impression of a very large, grey warbler with a large bill and a pale panel in the wing, rather like the Icterine Warbler. It is brownish grey above with a slight white supercilium and eye-ring; the underparts are greyish white to yellowish. The bill is long and bayonet-like, and the lower mandible is pinkish orange in colour. The Olivetree Warbler forages above head height in thick, tangled vegetation. Its song, reminiscent of a Great Reed Warbler (see page 216), is a series of churring and grating notes. S

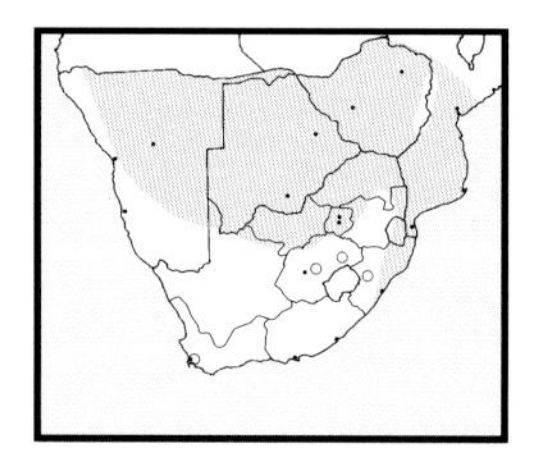

Icterine Warbler *Hippolais icterina* (625) 13 cm

The bill of this warbler is long, pointed and appears orange in the field, and is generally more robust than that of the similar Willow Warbler. The bird is greenish yellow to olive-grey above and bright yellow to pale yellow below. The upperwing coverts and secondaries are edged white to yellow, showing as a distinct pale panel in the folded wing, and the legs are blue-black (pink in the Willow Warbler). The frequent loud songs, a sustained jumble of melodious and jarring notes, announce its presence but it is easily overlooked when not calling. It frequents acacia bush, savanna, mixed woodland and exotic plantations. S

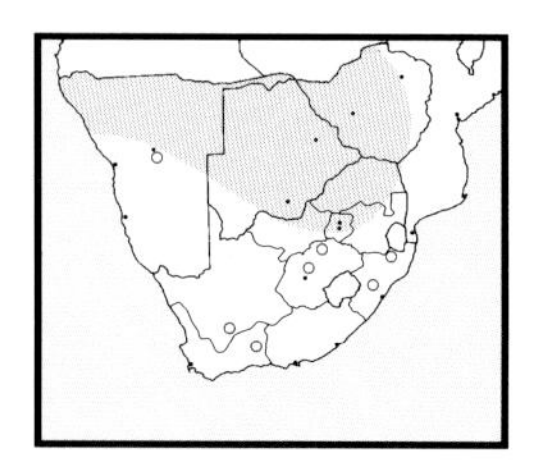

Whitethroat *Sylvia communis* (620) 14 cm

The short, stubby bill and rounded head of this bird are characteristic of *Sylvia* warblers. Males have a grey head which contrasts with the white throat, pinkish breast and reddish-brown edges (showing as a distinct panel) to the coverts and secondaries of the folded wing. The tail is black and the outer tail feathers are edged white. Females are similar but have a light brown head and a buff-coloured breast. Whitethroats frequent dry thornveld thickets. A mixture of grating and melodious notes make up the bird's call. S

1. Adult Garden Warbler
2. Adult Yellowthroated Warbler
3. Adult Willow Warbler
4. Adult Whitethroat
5. Adult Olivetree Warbler
6. Adult Olivetree Warbler
7. Adult Icterine Warbler

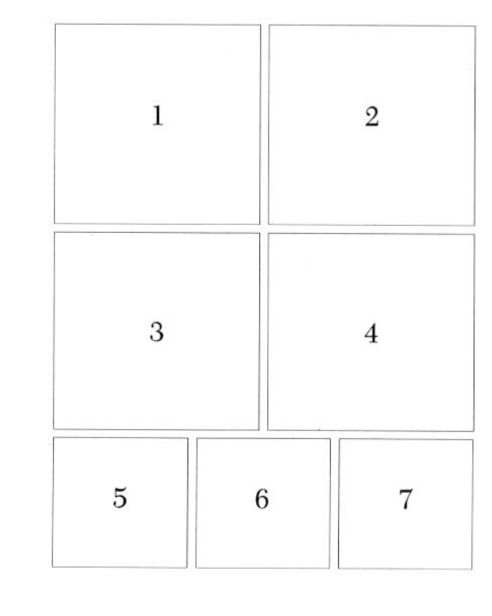

S *summer visitor* • R *resident*

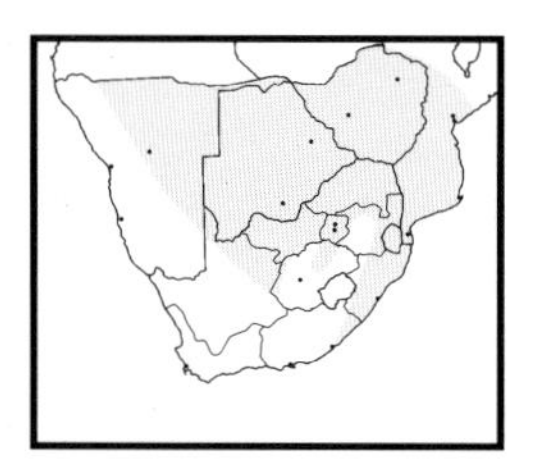

Great Reed Warbler *Acrocephalus arundinaceus* (628) 19 cm

A very large, stocky warbler, this species is similar in size to the Whitebrowed Sparrow-weaver (see page 266). As with all *Acrocephalus* warblers, it has a large, heavy bill and a sloping forehead. Its general coloration is rusty-brown above with a clear white supercilium, and buffy-white below with, in some individuals, faint grey streaks on the throat. In flight it fans its tail. The Great Reed Warbler keeps close to the ground while foraging for insects. Its song is a series of harsh creaking and grating sounds: 'chee-chee-chaak-chaak'. It frequents reedbeds and long, rank grass near watercourses. S

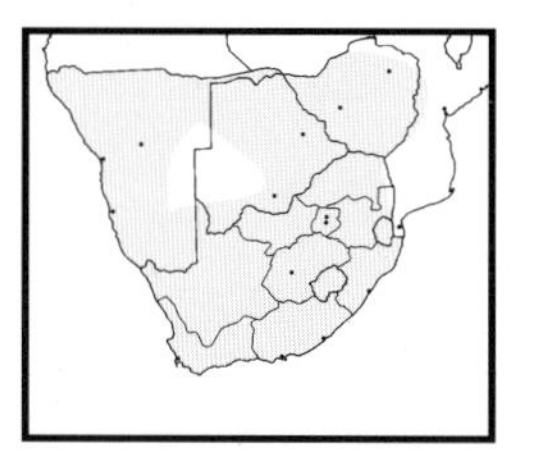

African Marsh Warbler *Acrocephalus baeticatus* (631) 13 cm

Light brown above with an indistinct eyebrow, and white below with a cinnamon wash across the breast and flanks, this species differs from the European Marsh Warbler on call. It also has shorter primaries – noticeable in the folded wing – which do not extend beyond the rump as in the European Marsh Warbler, is more rufous brown above, and has different habitat preferences. The sexes are alike, and immatures resemble the adults. This bird skulks and forages low down in vegetation, rustling the reeds or sedges as it goes. Its song is more repetitive than that of the European Marsh Warbler. The African Marsh Warbler prefers extensive reedbeds, marshy areas with rank growth, and willow growth along rivers and streams, quite different to the type of vegetation favoured by the European Marsh Warbler. I

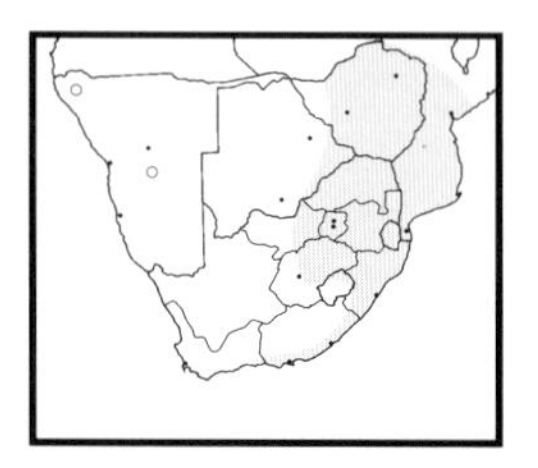

European Marsh Warbler *Acrocephalus palustris* (633) 13 cm

The European Marsh Warbler is very similar to the African Marsh Warbler. At close range it can be seen that the primaries on the folded wing extend beyond the rump whereas in the African Marsh Warbler the feathers extend only as far as the rump. The sexes are alike, and immatures resemble the adults. The European Marsh Warbler has different habitat preferences, tending to frequent non-aquatic habitats such as bracken-briar on the edges of forest, thickets, rank grass and gardens with dense undergrowth. Its song is more melodious than that of the African Marsh Warbler, consisting of musical canary-like trills; it also mimics other bird calls. S

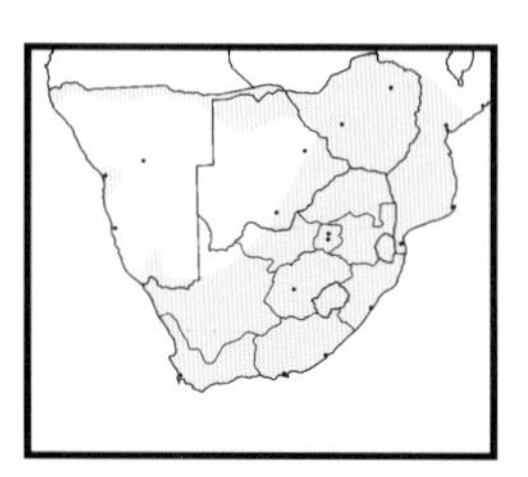

Cape Reed Warbler *Acrocephalus gracilirostris* (635) 17 cm

A little larger than the African Marsh Warbler and the most easily seen of all the reed warblers, this species shows a distinct white supercilium (this character is poorly visible in both the European Marsh Warbler and the African Marsh Warbler). The Cape Reed Warbler is dark brown above and white below except for the rufous wash to its flanks and the very dark legs (these are paler in many other *Acrocephalus* warblers). The sexes are alike, and immatures resemble the adults. It feeds low down in reeds, deftly climbing up and down reed stems. Its song is a rich, fluty 'cheerup-chee-trooreeee'. It constructs a nest of reed blades and grasses, strapped to vertical reed stems. R

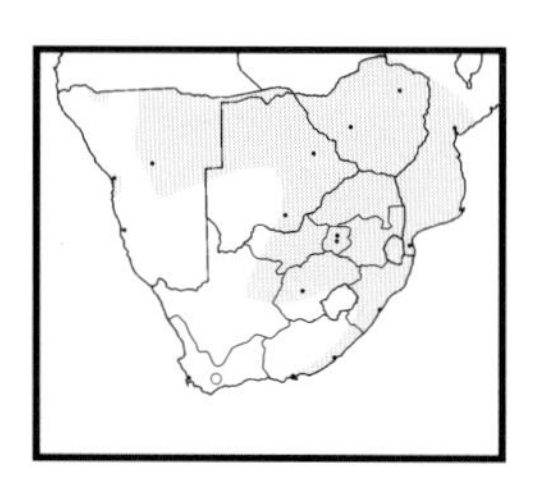

European Sedge Warbler *Acrocephalus schoenobaenus* (634) 13 cm

This is the only streaky-backed *Acrocephalus* warbler in the region, a characteristic which, together with the short tail and rufous rump, renders it rather cisticola-like. The broad creamy-white eyebrow is diagnostic. The crown is streaked and the underparts are creamy-white with rufous flanks. The tail is plain, unlike that of any similar cisticola species (see pages 228-32), all of which have black sub-terminal bands to their tails. The sexes are alike; immatures tend to be yellower than the adults. Its call is a harsh series of churring and chattering notes interspersed with a sharp 'tak' sound. The European Sedge Warbler inhabits reedbeds, swampy areas with sedges, rank weedy areas and, sometimes, fallow lands far from water. S

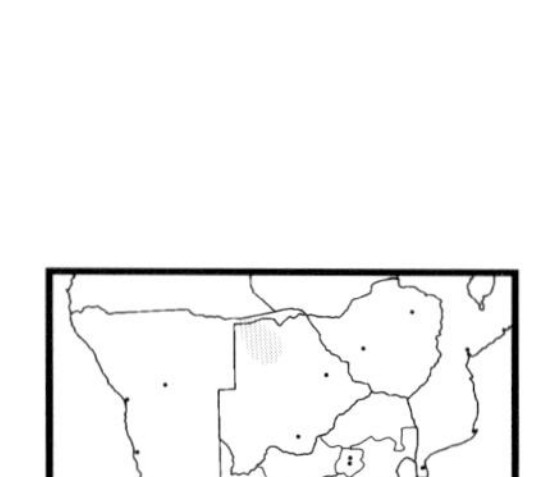

Greater Swamp Warbler *Acrocephalus rufescens* (636) 18 cm

This species is very similar to the Great Reed Warbler, being slightly smaller and dark olive-brown above, but it lacks a thin, well-defined supercilium. Below it has a whitish throat and greyish flanks and belly. The sexes are alike, and immatures resemble the adults. This species should not be confused with the Cape Reed Warbler which, although similar in size, has a prominent white eyebrow. The Greater Swamp Warbler is a resident of papyrus swamps and extensive reedbeds. Its call is a loud 'churrup-churrp, churr-churr'. R

1. Adult Great Reed Warbler
2. Adult African Marsh Warbler
3. Adult European Marsh Warbler
4. Adult Cape Reed Warbler
5. Adult European Sedge Warbler
6. Adult Greater Swamp Warbler

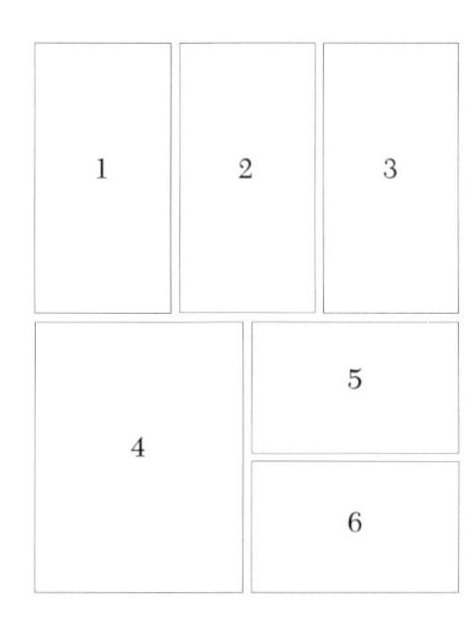

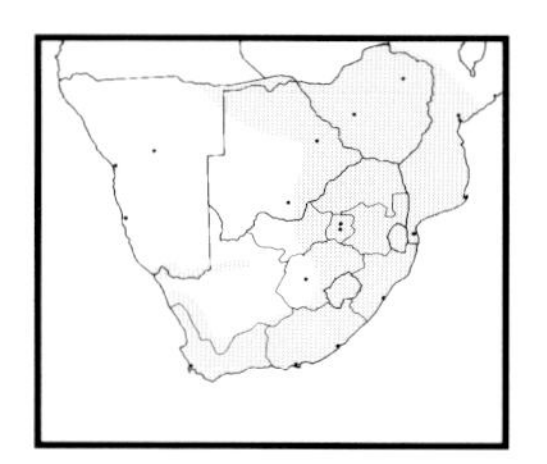

African Sedge Warbler *Bradypterus baboecala* (638) 17 cm

The African Sedge Warbler is separable from other reed-dwelling warblers by its dark brown upperparts with a rusty tinge to the rump, and by its buffy eyebrow. Below it is greyish white with a streaky throat and slightly rufous flanks and tail. The tail is long and rounded at the tip. The sexes are alike, and immatures resemble the adults. Although skulking and secretive, the African Sedge Warbler has a loud and strident song, beginning with some deliberate 'tirrup, tirrup' noises and gathering momentum before ending abruptly. Habitat preference is important, the African Sedge Warbler favouring extensive reedbeds, and heavily reeded streams and rivers with large areas of bulrushes and sedges. R

Adult African Sedge Warbler

Victorin's Warbler *Bradypterus victorini* (641) 16 cm

The most colourful of the region's *Bradypterus* warblers, Victorin's Warbler has buffy-orange underparts contrasting with dark brown upperparts, and has a broad, wedge-shaped tail. Its orange eyes are diagnostic and contrast with the grey face mask. The sexes are alike; immatures tend to be paler below than the adults and slightly more rufous above. The bird's song, a clear, repeated 'weet-weet-weeeooo' accelerating at the end, is diagnostic. A secretive species, Victorin's Warbler is confined to short, dense, montane fynbos, especially along gullies and streams. E

Adult Broadtailed Warbler

Barratt's Warbler *Bradypterus barratti* (639) 15 cm

Although similar to the African Sedge Warbler, this species is more streaked on the throat and lacks any rufous towards the vent. It habitually keeps very close to the ground. At the southern tip of its range its more heavily spotted breast and longer, rounded tail separate it from the Knysna Warbler. The sexes are alike; immatures tend to show slightly warmer coloration. The call is a loud, warbling series of high-pitched 'tsip-tsip-tsip-tsip' notes, speeding up to a confused 'trill-trrrrl'. Barratt's Warbler prefers dense, tangled undergrowth at the edge of forests, along streams and kloofs, so confusion with the African Sedge Warbler, which frequents reeds and sedge beds, is unlikely. R

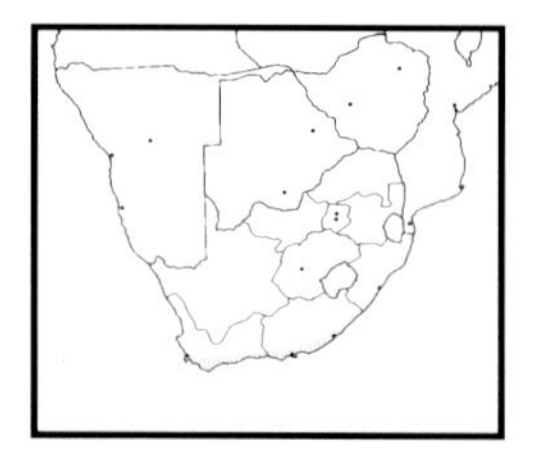

Knysna Warbler *Bradypterus sylvaticus* (640) 14 cm

This all-olive-brown bird has a slightly speckled throat, and a shorter, more square-ended tail than does the similar Barratt's Warbler. It is also smaller than that species, paler and more secretive, foraging on the ground in the undergrowth and flicking over leaf litter with its bill. The sexes are alike, and immatures resemble the adults. It builds its nest into a bush just above the ground, using dry plant material and grasses. The call is a loud 'tseep-tseep-tseeep' building up to end in a rattling 'churrr'; because it is so retiring, this bird is best located by its song. The Knysna Warbler is restricted to lowland and coastal wooded gullies and bracken briar-thickets. E

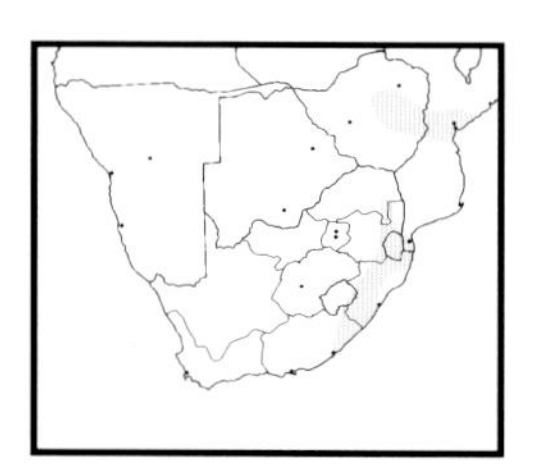

Broadtailed Warbler *Schoenicola brevirostris* (642) 17 cm

The Broadtailed Warbler is a dark brown bird with an exceptionally long, broad tail and a flat forehead; in profile the bill and forehead form an almost straight line. From close range it can be seen that the feathers on the underside of the tail have buffy edges. The tail is conspicuous and seems to weigh down the bird in flight. The sexes are alike; immatures are yellower below than the adults. Its favourite habitat includes dense, grassy and shrubby vegetation and grassy vleis. The bird is more visible in damp conditions when it comes out into the open to dry itself off. It utters a slow and purposeful 'zeenk zeenk zeenk' song and a clear, high-pitched 'peee-peee'. R, S

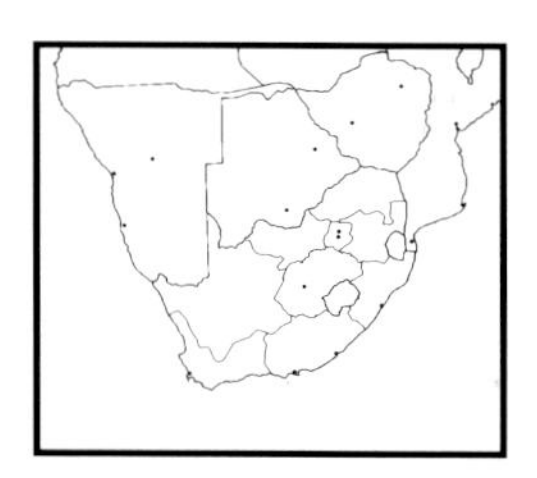

African Moustached Warbler *Melocichla mentalis* (663) 19 cm

In some respects showing resemblances to the Grassbird (see page 224), the African Moustached Warbler can be told apart from that species by its smaller size and its plain rufous, not striped, crown and back. Immatures lack the rufous forehead. The wing feathers, noticeable on the folded wing, are rusty coloured, compared with the Grassbird's heavily streaked wing, and it has a single black malar stripe compared to the two malar stripes of the Grassbird. It occurs in dense, long, rank grass along drainage lines, on the edges of evergreen forests and in association with dense palm vegetation. Its song is a melodious bubbling 'tip-tiptwiddle-iddle-eeee'. R

1. Adult Broadtailed Warbler
2. Adult African Sedge Warbler
3. Adult Knysna Warbler
4. Adult Barratt's Warbler
5. Adult Victorin's Warbler
6. Adult African Moustached Warbler

1	2
3	4
5	6

R *resident* • E *endemic* • S *summer visitor*

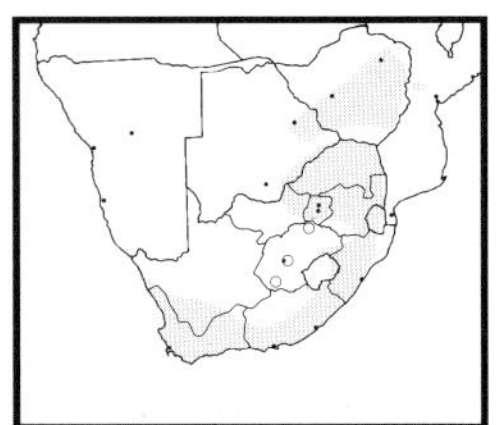

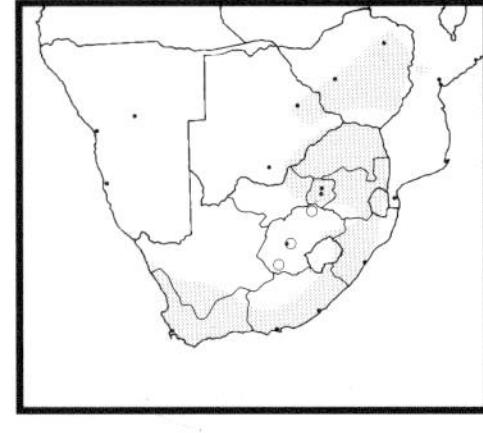

Barthroated Apalis *Apalis thoracica* (645) 13 cm

One of the long-tailed warblers, the Barthroated Apalis is very variable and a number of recognized subspecies occur. It is, however, readily distinguished from the similar Yellowbreasted Apalis and Rudd's Apalis. The eye colour is important in apalis identification, and this species always has a pale yellow eye, not dark brown as in Rudd's Apalis or light brown with a red eye-ring as in the Yellowbreasted Apalis. Both Rudd's Apalis and the Barthroated Apalis have a black breast band, which the Yellowbreasted Apalis often lacks or shows as only a small central spot on the breast. The upperparts vary from grey-brown to grey and, while the throat is always white, the belly and vent vary from light yellow to almost white. The Barthroated Apalis forages at all levels in tangled vegetation in evergreen forest, forested kloofs and gullies, gleaning insects from leaves, flowers and stems. Its call is a sharp, rapid, often repeated 'pillip-pillip-pillip'. R

Adult Barthroated Apalis (dark form)

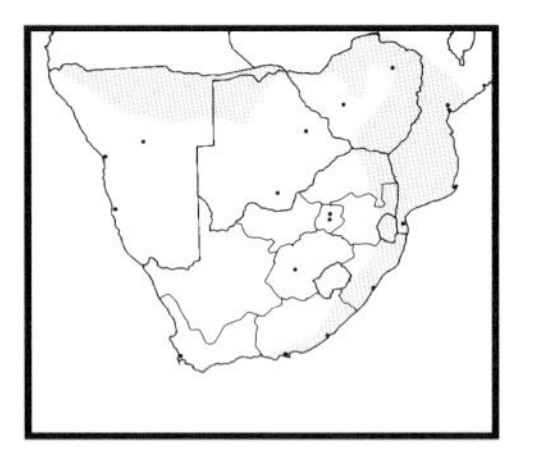

Yellowbreasted Apalis *Apalis flavida* (648) 13 cm

A noisy, sociable species, the Yellowbreasted Apalis is smaller than the similar Barthroated Apalis. It is best identified by its grey head and ear coverts, its white throat, broad yellow breast band (sometimes with a small black, central breast spot in males), and white belly. It has a light brown eye with a reddish eye-ring. When alarmed it flicks its tail up and down and crouches with drooping wings. A fast 'chirrup-chirrup-chirrup' song is given, often as a duet. Its nest is oval and made of moss and lichens held together with spider web, with the entrance close to the top. The Yellowbreasted Apalis occurs in a wide range of woodland habitats, other than the evergreen forests found in the northeast of the region. R

Male Rudd's Apalis

Rudd's Apalis *Apalis ruddi* (649) 13 cm

This species is remarkably similar to the Barthroated Apalis. The important field characters separating it from that species are its eyes, which are dark brown, not yellow as in the Barthroated Apalis, and the small white stripe above the eye. The tail is olive-green, not grey, and this species also lacks the white outer tail feathers of the Barthroated Apalis. Its olive-green back and grey head contrast strongly. Rudd's Apalis creeps about in tangled undergrowth and occasionally takes insects in flight. It frequents coastal bush, forest patches and woodland. Its call is a fast 'tuttuttuttut', somewhat like tapping on wood, and also includes slower tinker barbet-like 'clink-clink' sounds. E

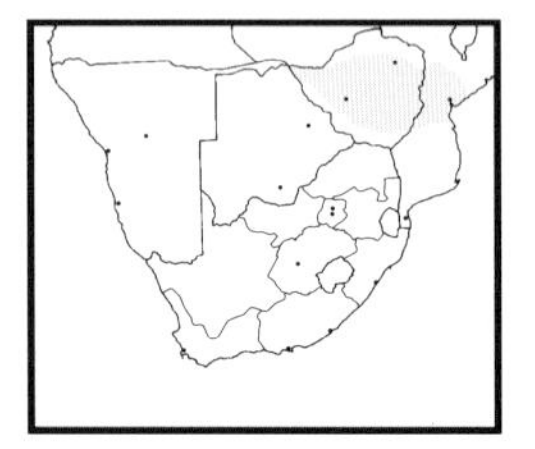

Redfaced Crombec *Sylvietta whytii* (650) 11 cm

While similar to the Longbilled Crombec in appearing almost tailless, this species has a shorter bill, a rich buffy face and underparts, and lacks the whitish eyebrow of that species. The sexes are alike and the immature is brownish-grey, rather than ashy-grey, above. The call of the Redfaced Crombec is a repeated trill, 'wit-wit-wit-wit', and also includes a 'chik' contact call. It prefers a moister climate and tends to stay in the canopy of miombo woodland and along the edges of evergreen and riverine woodland. R

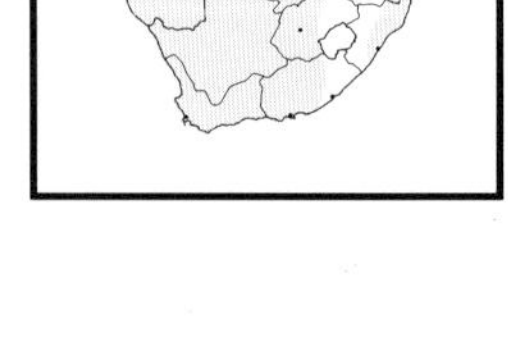

Longbilled Crombec *Sylvietta rufescens* (651) 12 cm

This small, squat warbler appears almost tailless and could be mistaken only for the Redfaced Crombec. Its long, slightly decurved bill (much longer than in Redfaced Crombec), white eyebrow and pale buffy to light tawny underparts separate it from that species. It occurs in a wide range of habitats but prefers dry savanna, arid scrub bush in dry watercourses, thornveld, and undergrowth in moister broad-leaved woodland. A high-pitched, trilled 'preee-prip', repeated several times, or a short 'prrttt' call is given. R

1. Adult Barthroated Apalis
2. Male Yellowbreasted Apalis
3. Adult Rudd's Apalis
4. Adult Redfaced Crombec
5. Adult Longbilled Crombec

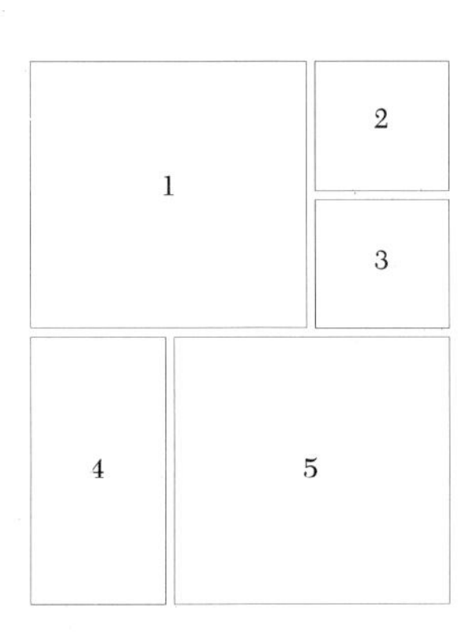

R *resident* • E *endemic*

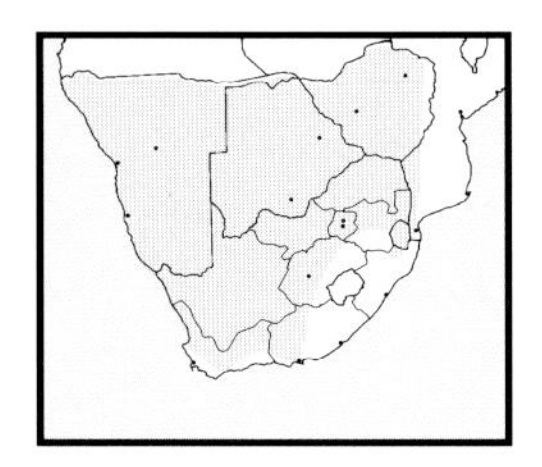

Yellowbellied Eremomela *Eremomela icteropygialis* (653) 10 cm

This short-tailed warbler has a brighter yellow belly and vent in the east than in the west of its range. A dark line through the eye contrasts with a pale eye-stripe above and with the grey to whitish underparts. It can be distinguished from the similar Cape Penduline Tit (see page 192) by its longer bill, the absence of black lores and by the lack of a black-speckled forehead. It occurs singly, in pairs and in mixed bird parties, foraging restlessly from twig to twig, in almost any woodland, from bushveld to scrub bush in arid areas. Its call is a quick, high-pitched 'klee-tchee-tchuu', repeated over and over again. R

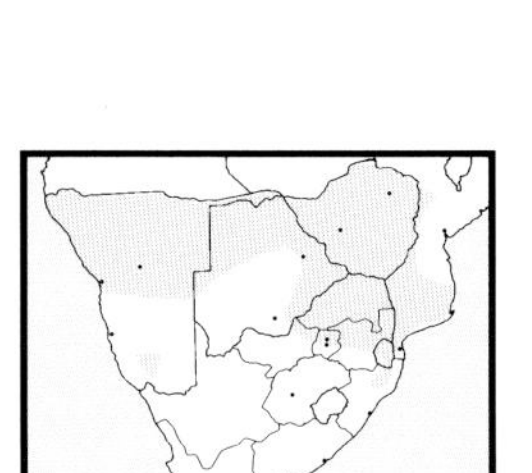

Burntnecked Eremomela *Eremomela usticollis* (656) 10 cm

The yellow eye and russet cheeks together with the contrasting blue-grey upperparts and buffy underparts identify this bird. The narrow brown bar or mark on the throat is often indistinct, and in immatures the russet patch behind the eye and on the throat is absent. This highly active, restless species forages for insects in the canopy of acacia savanna and thornveld. Its call is a high-pitched 'chii-cheee-cheee', sometimes ending as a trilled 'trrrrrrr'. R

Immature Burntnecked Eremomela

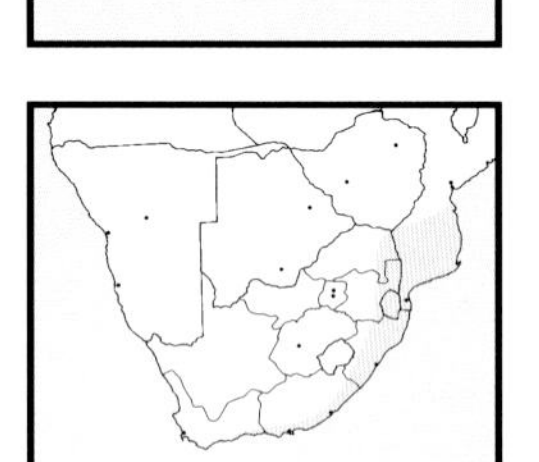

Greenbacked Bleating Warbler *Camaroptera brachyura* (657a) 12 cm

The call – consisting of a nasal 'neeehhh' and loud snapping sounds – and habits of this species are inseparable from those of the Greybacked Bleating Warbler; at one time they were considered a single species. The bird's olive-green crown, mantle and back separate it from that species, although the green wings are common to both. The Greenbacked Bleating Warbler has a habit of cocking its tail. Its goat-like, bleating alarm call, given from the midst of a bush or forest tangle, often indicates its presence. It frequents low-altitude, coastal and inland forest undergrowth, thick riparian undergrowth and thornveld brush. R

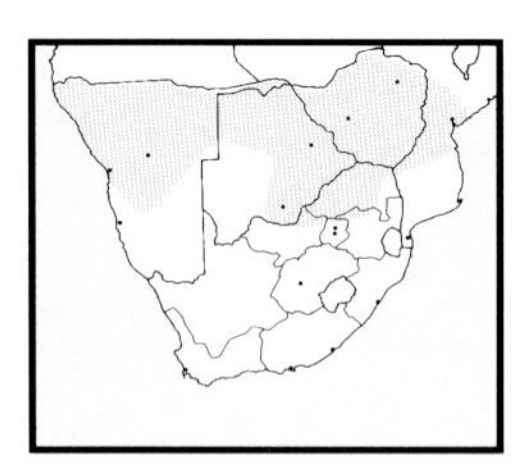

Greybacked Bleating Warbler *Camaroptera brevicaudata* (657b) 12 cm

Identical in behavioural characteristics to the Greenbacked Bleating Warbler, this species is adapted to drier environmental conditions than is its congener. It may be further separated by its grey, not green, head, mantle and back. It occurs singly or in pairs and prefers tangles and thickets in dry woodland, thornveld thickets and dry riverine bush. Its call is indiscernible from that of the Greenbacked Bleating Warbler. R

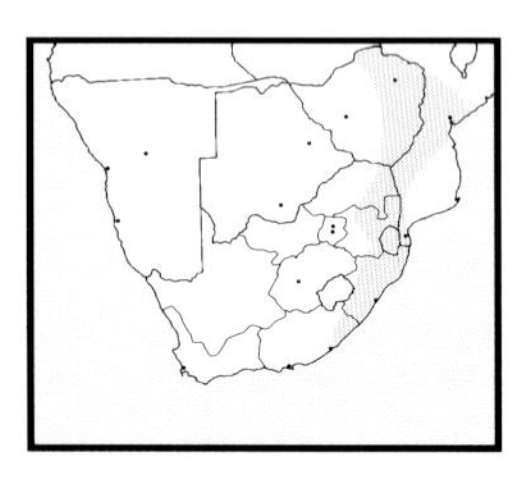

Yellow Warbler *Chloropeta natalensis* (637) 14 cm

The Yellow Warbler is sulphur-yellow below and olive-green above, with a yellow rump. Its long bill, sloping forehead and habit of foraging low down liken it to an *Acrocephalus* warbler (see page 216). It is quite secretive but sings from a prominent perch, a soft yet guttural 'chip-chip-cheezee-cheezee' and a 'chirupp-chirupp-chirup'. Unmistakable, it adds colour to the rank grass along streams and at forest edges, to bracken and to the grasses in vleis that are its chosen home. R

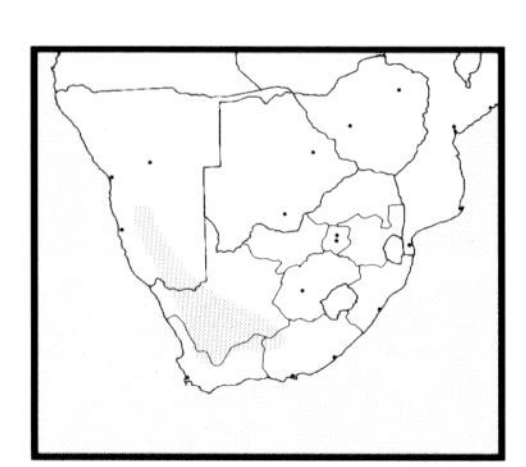

Cinnamonbreasted Warbler *Euryptila subcinnamomea* (660) 14 cm

This small, rock-loving warbler is reminiscent of a prinia (see page 226) in its manner of cocking and flicking its tail. It is a warm russet-brown above, with a chestnut breast band, flanks and rump. The eyebrow and face are speckled white and black; the throat and breast are grey, and the lower belly and tail are black. The call is a shrill, short, whistled 'peeee' or 'chreeee' and a burst of melodious phrases. While foraging it runs, creeps or hops from boulder to boulder, even clinging to the sides of rocks, in boulder-strewn hillsides with scattered bushes, canyons and gullies. E

1. Adult Yellowbellied Eremomela
2. Adult Greenbacked Bleating Warbler
3. Adult Burntnecked Eremomela
4. Adult Yellow Warbler
5. Adult Greybacked Bleating Warbler
6. Adult Cinnamonbreasted Warbler

1	2
3	4
5	6

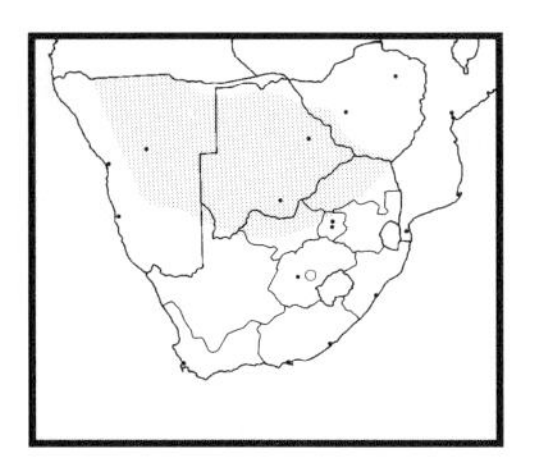

African Barred Warbler *Calamonastes fasciolata* (658) 14 cm

This small warbler is dark brown above and buffy below, females and non-breeding males having fine, dusky barring from throat to tail. Breeding males are dark brown on the throat with some scalloping to the edges of the throat and flank feathers; the rest of the underparts are buffy to white. Immatures are more rufous than the adults, and have a yellowish wash to the breast. The call is a distinctive 'preep-preep-preep'. African Barred Warblers forage from the bottom to the top of thick bushes, favouring drier habitat than do Stierling's Barred Warblers, and are found in thornveld thickets, mixed broad-leaved woodland and mixed savanna. R

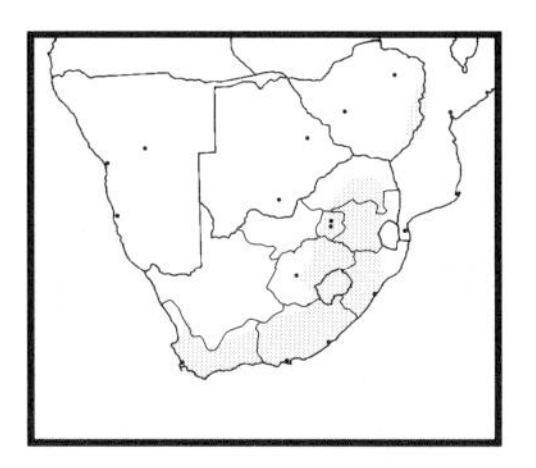

Grassbird *Sphenoeacus afer* (661) 19 cm

This large, russet-capped warbler is separated from the similar African Moustached Warbler (see page 218) by its two malar stripes, heavily streaked back, and long, straggly tail. The sexes are alike; immatures have a streaked cap and are generally duller than the adults. Its flight is heavy on short, rounded wings, and it prefers to clamber from grass tuft to grass tuft than to fly. It is a bird of long, rank grass along streams, and also favours the thickets and bracken-briar in montane and coastal fynbos. Its call is a nasal 'pheeeoo' and a jumbled series of musical notes ending in a whistle. E

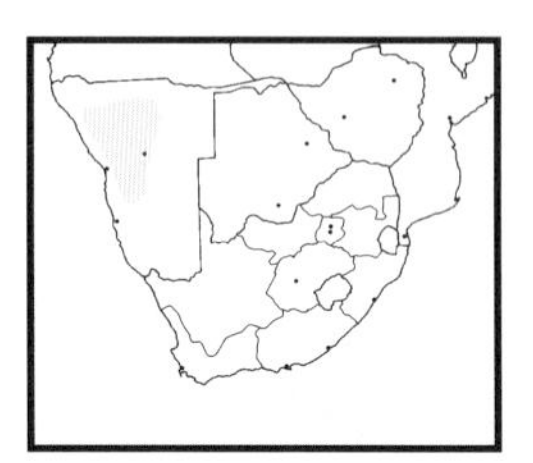

Rockrunner *Achaetops pycnopygius* (662) 17 cm

This unmistakable bird has a rich chestnut belly and vent, a white throat with a dark malar stripe and a white breast streaked with black. The sexes are alike; immatures are less distinctly marked than the adults. The Rockrunner stands on prominent boulders, rendering its melodious, warbling song. When alarmed it becomes secretive, scrambling around in thick bushes and sneaking behind boulders. Its nest is a cup of grass, well hidden in the midst of a grass tuft. It favours arid, boulder-strewn, grassy hillsides and ridges. E

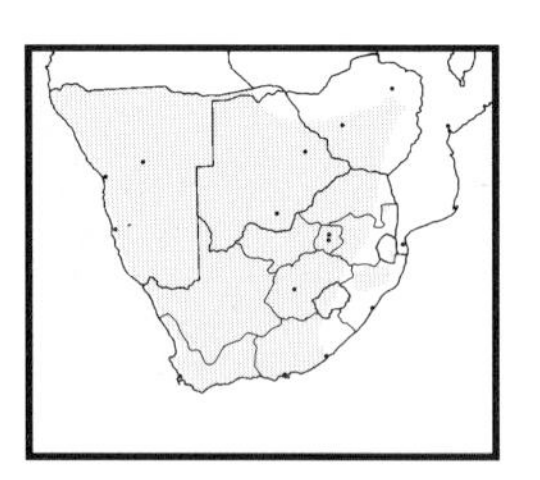

Titbabbler *Parisoma subcaeruleum* (621) 15 cm

This species is dark grey overall with a well-marked, streaky throat, a distinctive rufous vent, and a whitish eye (seen most clearly at close range). The sexes are alike. Immatures are uniform grey below and lack black streaking on the throat. A restless species, it moves through the foliage, gleaning insects from branches and flying low from bush to bush. Its loud fluty 'cheruup-chee-chee' call is characteristic, and it is also a good mimic of other species in the area. The Titbabbler occurs in thornveld, Karoo scrub and semi-arid scrub bush. R

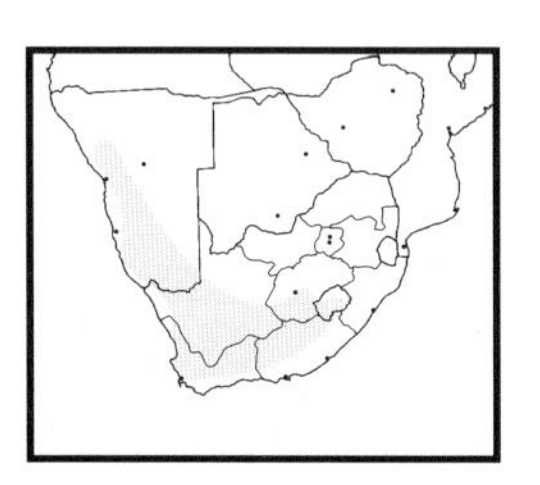

Layard's Titbabbler *Parisoma layardi* (622) 15 cm

Similar to the Titbabbler in appearance, this species is lighter grey overall and has a white, not rufous, vent and white undertail feathers. The silvery-white eye contrasts with the dark head, and the throat streaking is less pronounced than in the Titbabbler. More of a skulker than the Titbabbler, Layard's Titbabbler forages low down in scrubby bushes. It occurs in mountainous fynbos, thorn-veld and Karoo scrub, especially in hilly and stony areas. Its call is a clear 'pee-pee-cheeri-cheeri', similar in quality to that of the Titbabbler but with different phrasing. E

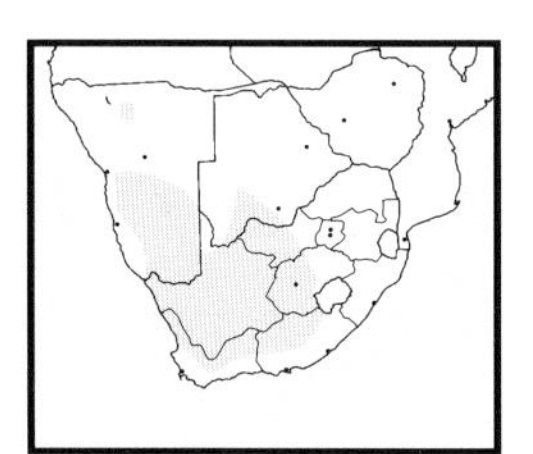

Rufouseared Warbler *Malcorus pectoralis* (688) 15 cm

Adults of this prinia-like species have orange ear coverts and a narrow black breast band. They are brown above and heavily streaked, unlike the *Prinia* species (see page 226), which all have plain, unmarked backs. Immatures are similar to the adults but lack the narrow breast band; they may be confused with the Blackchested Prinia (see page 226), but the buffy back with dark brown streaks and the lack of any supercilium should help separate the two. The Rufouseared Warbler forages mostly on the ground, running, hopping and bounding with the long tail held high. Its call is a monotonous and scolding, repeated 'teee, teee, teee, teee'. It frequents fynbos, Karoo scrub, and thick, short, semi-desert scrub. E

1. Adult African Barred Warbler
2. Adult Grassbird
3. Adult Titbabbler
4. Adult Layards' Titbabbler
5. Adult Rockrunner
6. Adult Rufouseared Warbler
7. Adult Rufouseared Warbler

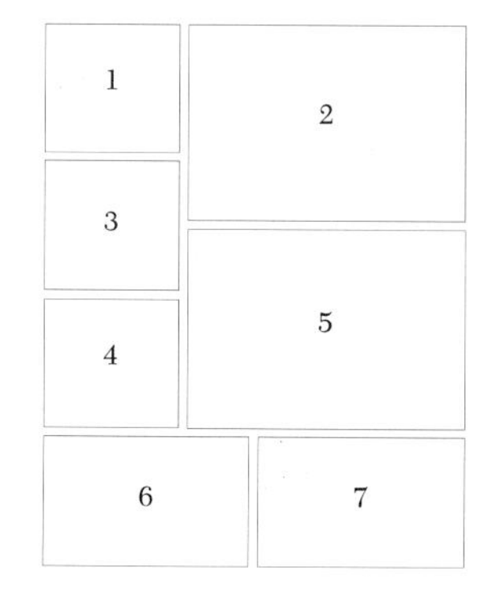

R *resident* • E *endemic*

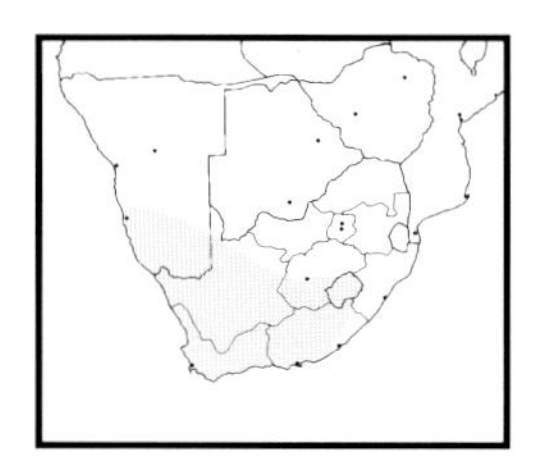

Spotted Prinia *Prinia maculosa* (686a) 14 cm

This species until recently was considered sympatric with the Drakensberg Prinia. It can be told from that species by being dark brown above and heavily and extensively streaked below (only the throat is streaked in the Drakensberg Prinia). Immatures are yellower below than are the adults. The Spotted Prinia forages at the base of bushes and long grass and commonly occurs in Karoo scrub bush, fynbos and mountainous scrub, in rank grass along streams and in exotic plantations. The bird's call is a sharp 'chleet-chleet-chleet' and a faster 'tit-tit-tit-tit'. E

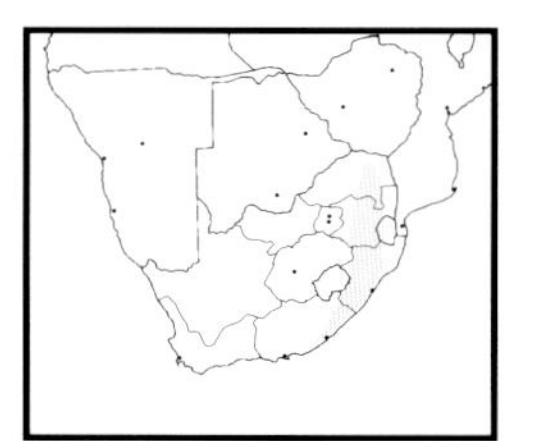

Drakensberg Prinia *Prinia hypoxantha* (686b) 14 cm

Although closely allied to the Spotted Prinia, the ranges of these two species are allopatric. The Drakensberg Prinia can be differentiated from that prinia by the light streaking on its throat only, and the yellowish wash to its plumage which is brighter than in the Spotted Prinia. Immatures are paler than the adults. The bird's habits and call are very similar to those of the Spotted Prinia. It is resident in long grass along the edges of forest, and in wooded gullies and bracken-briar thickets. E

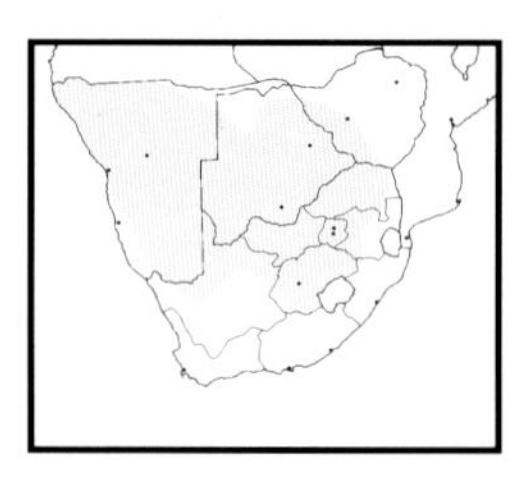

Blackchested Prinia *Prinia flavicans* (685) 15 cm

In non-breeding plumage this bird might be mistaken for the Tawnyflanked Prinia as at this time the black breast band is usually absent, but its yellowish throat and breast and all-brown wings should separate it from that species. Both species have a prominent white supercilium. In breeding plumage the Blackchested Prinia has a prominent broad black breast band. Females have a narrower breast band than the males; juveniles resemble the non-breeding adults but are yellower below. This is an inquisitive bird which forages in bushes and sometimes on the ground, with its tail held high. It can be found in shrubs along dry watercourses, in Kalahari sandveld scrub, thornveld savanna and neglected farmlands. Its call is a loud and repetitive 'zzzrt, zzzrt'. R

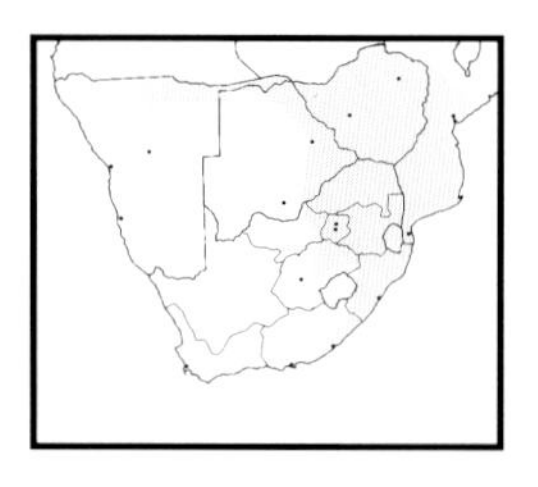

Tawnyflanked Prinia *Prinia subflava* (683) 11 cm

This species could be mistaken for a non-breeding Blackchested Prinia but the Tawnyflanked Prinia has a white throat and breast (as opposed to the yellowish chest of the Blackchested Prinia), an orange to buffy undertail and vent, and russet edges to the wings. The sexes are alike, and immatures resemble the adults. Normally recorded in pairs, it forages low down at the base of grass tufts. It is inquisitive and will clamber to the top of tall grass stems when its curiosity is aroused, and will scold, its tail wagging and swinging from side to side, attracting others in the party. Its call is a series of rapidly repeated 'przzt-przzt-przzt' and harsh 'chrzzzt' notes. The Tawnyflanked Prinia is the common prinia seen among rank grass along streams, or tall grass among trees. R

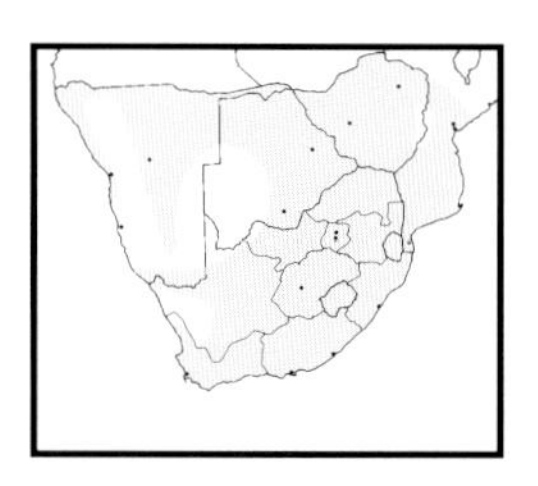

Fantailed Cisticola *Cisticola juncidis* (664) 10 cm

This is one of the small, so-called 'short-tailed' cisticolas. It is readily identifiable by its call, a 'zit, zit, zit' sound, uttered five to 20 metres above the ground during the undulating flight, with a 'zit' given at the peak of each rise. It is similar to the Desert Cisticola (see page 228) but can be told from that species by having a black subterminal band in its tail. It breeds when grasses are green, and its nest is shaped like an upright bottle, made by binding together upright grasses and adding spider web and plant down. This cisticola frequents damp grasslands, marshes, rank grasses in cultivated and fallow fields and open grasslands. R

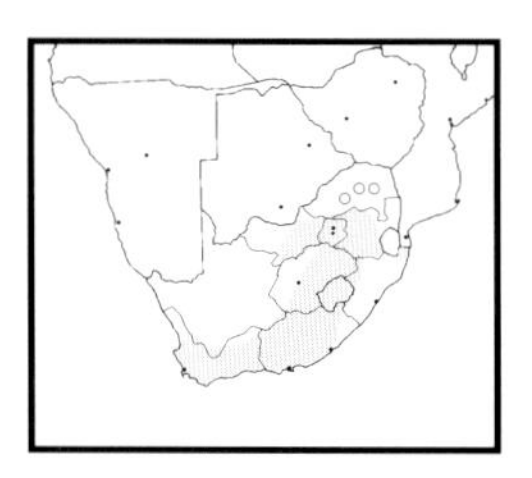

Cloud Cisticola *Cisticola textrix* (666) 10 cm

This small, short-tailed cisticola is indistinguishable from Ayres' Cisticola (see page 228) and the Desert Cisticola (see page 228) except on call. Birds in the southern Cape are easier to recognize, however, because they have streaking on the breast. The Cloud Cisticola rises from the ground when disturbed, uttering its familiar 'tsee-tsee-tsee-chick-chick-chick' call before descending and skimming over the grasslands with a 'chick-chick-chick'. Unlike Ayres' Cisticola (see page 335) it does not snap its wings prior to landing. It forages in grasses and on the ground, and builds its nest – an untidy ball of dry grass, lined with plant downs and with a side entrance on or just above ground level. The Cloud Cisticola occurs in short grasslands above 500 metres in altitude. R

Adult Cloud Cisticola (southern Cape)

1. Adult Spotted Prinia
2. Adult Drakensberg Prinia
3. Adult Fantailed Cisticola
4. Adult Spotted Prinia
5. Adult Cloud Cisticola
6. Adult Blackchested Prinia (breeding)
7. Adult Tawnyflanked Prinia

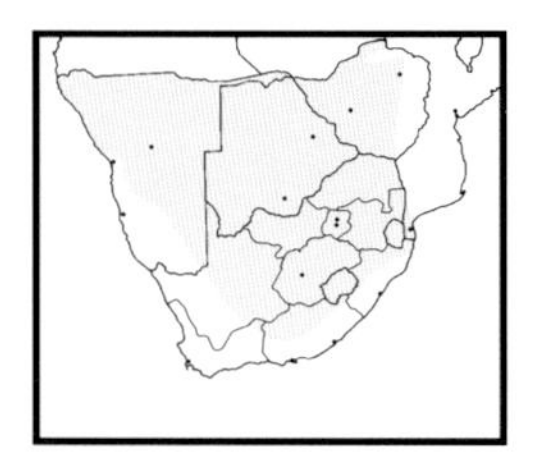

Desert Cisticola *Cisticola aridulus* (665) 10 cm

The Desert Cisticola can be told apart from the similar Fantailed Cisticola (see page 226) by its shorter, white-tipped tail and lack of a black subterminal tail bar; further, it frequents a different habitat to that species. It also resembles Ayres' Cisticola and the Cloud Cisticola (see page 226) but the male's display flight distinguishes it. In aerial display the Desert Cisticola calls 'tsing-tsing-tsing-tsing'; it also makes clicking noises, with wing snaps at the peak of each bounce, and swoops down low over grasslands. The sexes are alike, but the female has a shorter tail; immatures are paler below. The nest, an untidy ball of woven grass with the entrance on the side and close to the top, is usually placed in a grass tuft well above ground level. These birds live in short grasslands, desert and semi-desert scrub above 1 200 metres in altitude. R

Adult Neddicky (northern race, non-breeding)

Palecrowned Cisticola *Cisticola brunnescens* (668) 10 cm

The non-breeding Palecrowned Cisticola is indistinguishable from the Cloud Cisticola (see page 226) and Ayres' Cisticola, but males in breeding plumage can be identified by their dark lores, the pale buffy to whitish-buff, unstreaked crown and the tawny rump which is most conspicuous in flight. The call is an indistinct, faint 'tsee-tsee-tsee' and no wing-snapping behaviour is shown. The nest is similar to that of the Fantailed Cisticola (see page 226). Palecrowned Cisticolas forage low down in wet grasslands and along moist drainage lines below 1 200 metres in altitude. R

Adult Greybacked Cisticola (northern form)

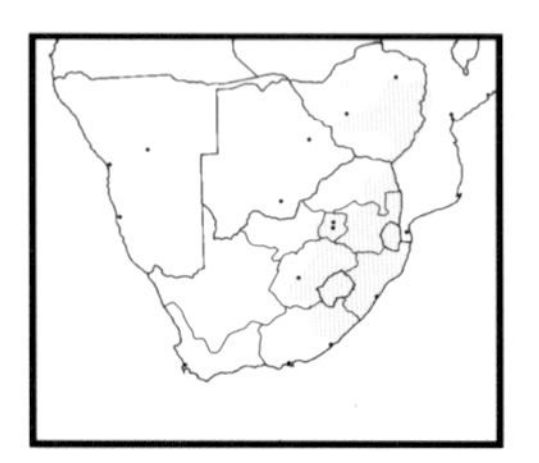

Ayres' Cisticola *Cisticola ayresii* (667) 10 cm

Virtually indistinguishable from the Desert Cisticola and the Cloud Cisticola (see page 226), the call of this bird readily identifies it. It can be heard up high, often out of sight, giving its familiar 'see-see-see' call for many minutes before descending steeply to skim over the grasslands with fast 'tiktiktiktiktik' notes accompanied with wing snaps prior to jinking or landing. The sexes are alike, and the immatures are paler than the adults. The nest – placed either on the ground or just above it – is a ball of woven grass material with a side entrance. This species favours short, high-lying grasslands, usually above 1 200 metres in altitude. R

Adult Wailing Cisticola

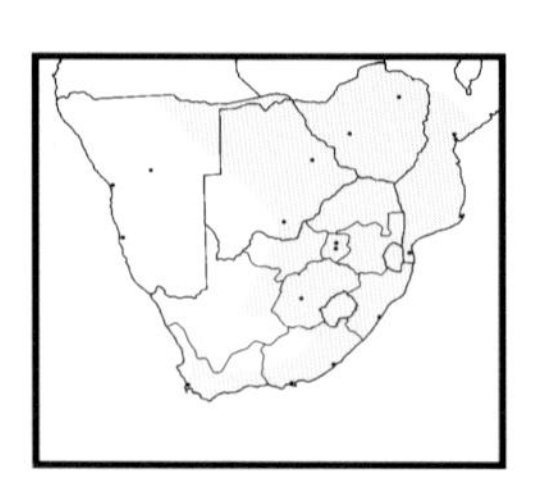

Neddicky *Cisticola fulvicapillus* (681) 11 cm

The pale greyish, unmarked underparts and grey-brown back, rufous crown and short, narrow, plain tail render this cisticola easy to identify. The sexes are alike; the immatures are yellower than the adults. Its call is a thin 'seep-seep-seep', given as it forages in undergrowth. When alarmed it hops to an exposed perch and utters a fast 'tictictictic' series of alarm notes, flicking its tail from side to side. The nest is a ball of dry grass built in low, thick scrub or thorny scrub beneath a tree or in tangled weeds and grasses. This bird is found in bushveld, grassy woodland and scrubby vegetation. R

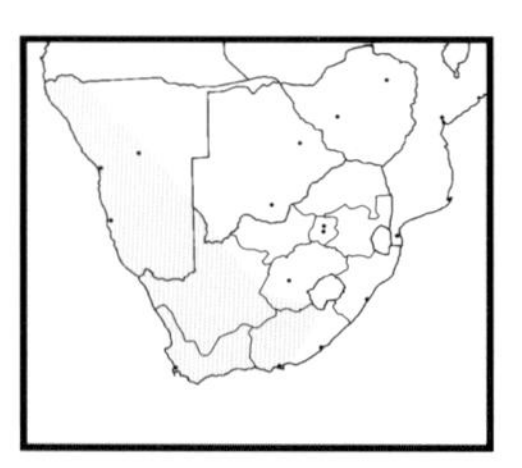

Greybacked Cisticola *Cisticola subruficapillus* (669) 13 cm

This species is difficult to separate from the Wailing Cisticola; even the calls are similar, but at close range the Greybacked Cisticola can be seen to be greyer (rather than buffy) below than the Wailing Cisticola. The sexes are alike; the immatures are duller than the adults. The Greybacked Cisticola forages low down in bushes and grasses and often perches up high in the open. It sings from a high perch, in the breeding season only, giving a series of wailing, high-pitched 'phwree-tee-tee-tee' notes. The nest is ball shaped, made of woven grasses and built on or close to the ground in a grass tuft or low shrub. These birds occur in montane grassland, fynbos and Karoo scrub in rocky terrain above 1 200 metres in altitude. NE

1. Adult Desert Cisticola
2. Adult Palecrowned Cisticola (breeding – top; non-breeding – bottom)
3. Adult Ayres' Cisticola
4. Adult Neddicky
5. Adult Wailing Cisticola
6. Adult Greybacked Cisticola

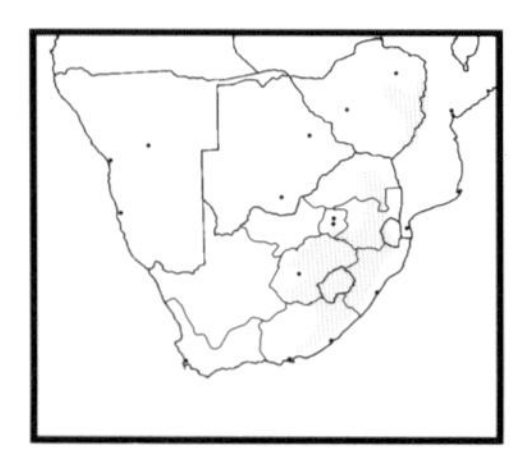

Wailing Cisticola *Cisticola lais* (670) 13 cm

This species closely resembles the Greybacked Cisticola. Both have a reddish crown, a grey back with black streaks, and a rufous wing patch visible on the folded wing; however, the Wailing Cisticola has warmer buffy, not greyish, underparts. The sexes are alike; the immatures are washed with yellow below. It occurs in pairs and small groups when not breeding, foraging low down in thick grass and shrubs. The call, rendered only in the breeding season, is a plaintive 'wheee-tee-tee-tee' with some other shorter notes. It frequents rocky montane grasslands, bracken and scrub vegetation on rocky slopes. R

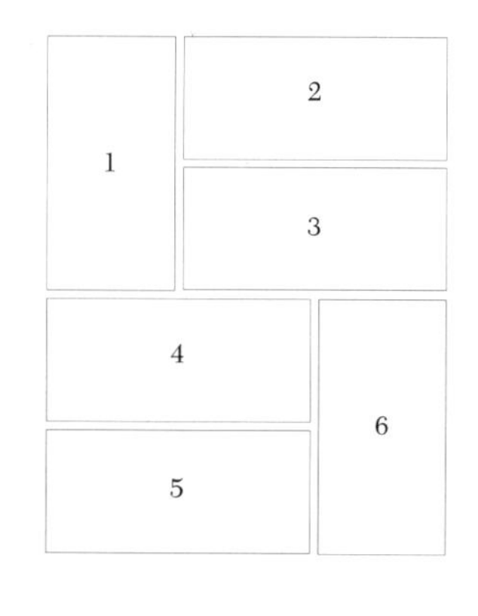

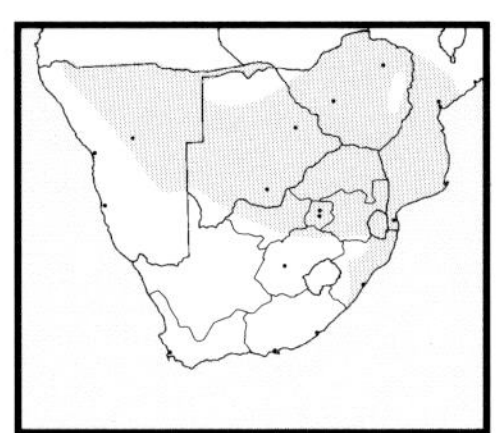

Rattling Cisticola *Cisticola chiniana* (672) 13 cm

The noisiest and most inquisitive cisticola, the Rattling Cisticola has a plain rufous crown, a greyish-brown back, a brownish tail and whitish underparts. It is separable from the Tinkling Cisticola (see page 232) by its greyish-brown, not rufous, tail, and by its harsh scolding, not bell-like, call. Its call, a series of high-pitched notes, 'cher, cher, cher, tsee, tsee, tsee', is most often given from the top of a bush. The nest, built in a grass tuft or scrubby thornbush, is a dry ball of grass, bound with spider web and lined with downy plant material. Rattling Cisticolas are found in dry woodland and acacia savanna. R

Adult Levaillant's Cisticola (breeding)

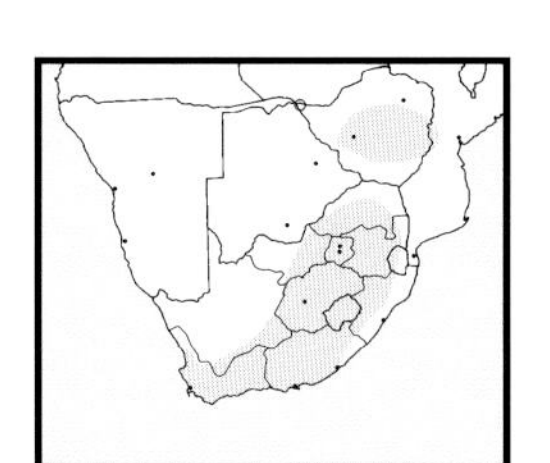

Levaillant's Cisticola *Cisticola tinniens* (677) 14 cm

This large cisticola with its rufous crown and longish tail might be mistaken for the Blackbacked Cisticola (both have streaky black backs) but can be separated from that species by the black feathers on the back edged with buff, not grey, by the olive-brown rump streaked with black and, in breeding condition, by the reddish-buff, not grey, tail. Its call is a warbling, bubbling 'chrip-trrrup-treee' and includes loud 'tee-tee-tee-tee' notes. Levaillant's Cisticola forages low down on grass stems; when disturbed it habitually clambers to near the top of a grass stalk and flicks its tail from side to side, calling noisily. Its nest, an oval ball of grass with a side entrance and lined with soft plant material, is built in grass tufts in flooded terrain or in grasses overhanging streams and vleis. R

Adult Blackbacked Cisticola (breeding)

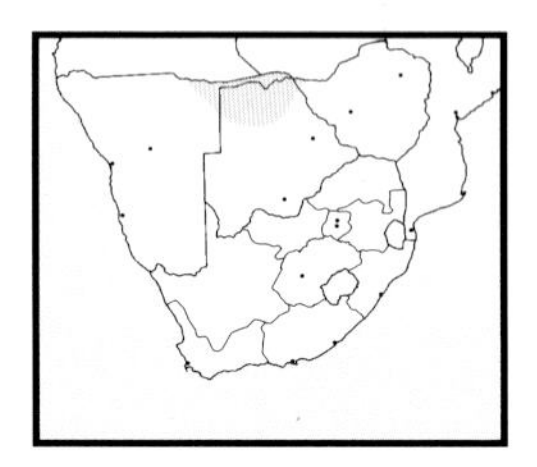

Chirping Cisticola *Cisticola pipiens* (676) 15 cm

This large cisticola has a rufous crown, black back feathers edged with grey-brown and a dark reddish-brown tail. It might be mistaken for the similar Blackbacked Cisticola but has a broad brown, not grey, tail with subterminal black spots and indistinct terminal pale edges; the faint rufous, not buff, eye-stripe also separates it. The most reliable identification feature is its call, a twanging 'trreeet-trreet-terrr' uttered in flight or from a perch. During the zigzag display flight its broad tail flops from side to side. The oval nest of dry grasses is typically well hidden in the dense reed or papyrus undergrowth that this bird frequents. R

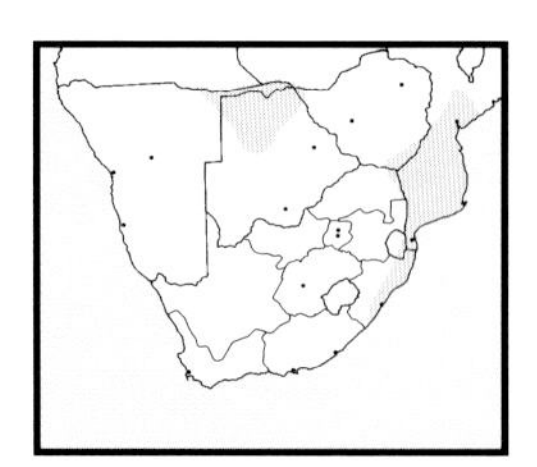

Blackbacked Cisticola *Cisticola galactotes* (675) 13 cm

This fairly large, long-tailed cisticola is similar to Levaillant's Cisticola and the Chirping Cisticola. Breeding males have a reddish crown and a black back streaked with grey; in non-breeding plumage the back is black streaked with brown. In breeding plumage the feathers of the grey tail have obvious creamy tips which are almost absent in the Chirping Cisticola, while in Levaillant's Cisticola the tail is reddish buff. Breeding males sing from an open perch or in the air during a low circular flight above the nest site. Their song is a long, harsh 'tzzzrp' and a louder whistled alarm, 'prrrrt'. The woven nest is ball shaped and built into growing grasses; it has a side entrance and is lined with various plant materials. Blackbacked cisticolas occur below 500 metres in altitude, in marshy grasslands and sedges. R

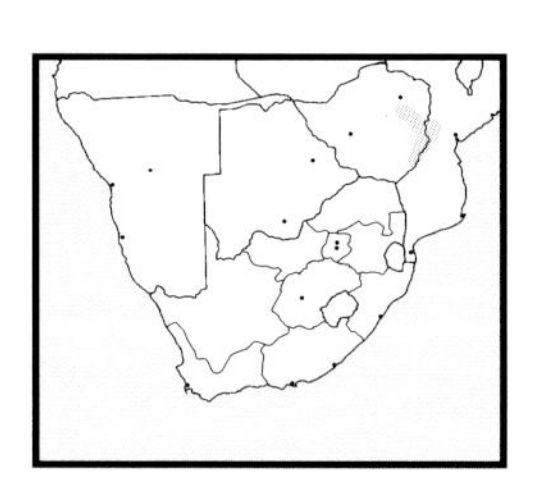

Singing Cisticola *Cisticola cantans* (673) 13 cm

This smallish, long-tailed cisticola has a rufous crown graduating to a grey, unmarked back, and reddish primaries. The clear white eyebrow, black lores and the grey back, breast and flanks separate it from the similar Redfaced Cisticola. The Singing Cisticola is secretive, but when breeding the males are quite vocal and call a two-syllabled 'jhu-jee' or 'wheecho' from a prominent perch. In building the nest the birds make use of large, broad leaves which they weave together from dry grasses to form an oval ball with a side entrance. They frequent long grasses in open woodland. R

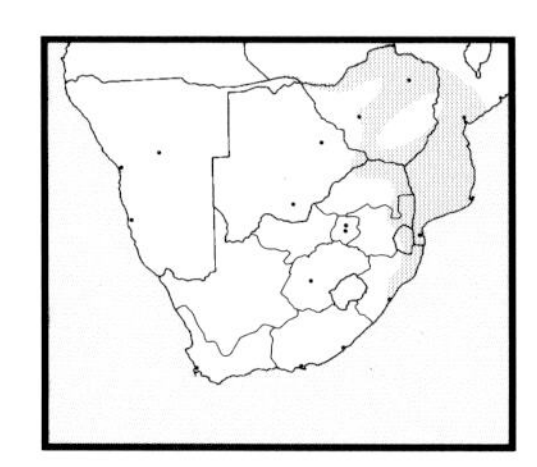

Redfaced Cisticola *Cisticola erythrops* (674) 13 cm

This long-tailed, plain-backed cisticola has a reddish crown graduating to an unstreaked, greenish-grey back. Its mantle and facial area are always red. It differs from the Singing Cisticola by lacking rufous edges to the primaries. It is more common to hear the males singing than to see them. The call is a 'weet-weet-weet' which quickly rises in pitch. The Redfaced Cisticola constructs its nest by sewing together the large leaves of a shrub with dry grasses, to form an oval structure with a side entrance. It occurs at low altitudes in rank grasslands, reeds, scattered bushes and grasses along drainage lines. R

1. Adult Rattling Cisticola
2. Adult Levaillant's Cisticola
3. Adult Chirping Cisticola
4. Adult Singing Cisticola
5. Adult Blackbacked Cisticola
6. Adult Redfaced Cisticola

1	2
3	4
5	6

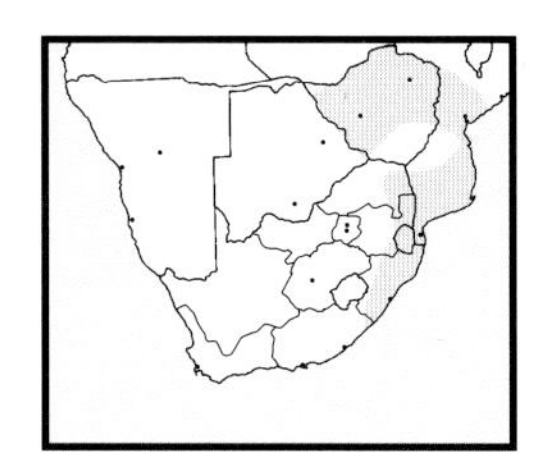

Croaking Cisticola *Cisticola natalensis* (678) 13-17 cm

This, the largest of our cisticolas, is bulky in build and has a shortish tail and a heavy bill. Generally buffy-grey, it lacks any hint of rufous colouring. The crown is streaky brown and black, the underparts buff. In breeding plumage the back is greyer and the underparts are white becoming yellowish on the breast. The call is a loud croaking 'trrrrp' sound, given from a conspicuous perch on top of a bush. Its display is an erratic, circular flight just above head height over the grass. Living grasses are woven into the roof of the ball-shaped, dry grass nest, forming a sheltering bower. Croaking Cisticolas are usually found below 1 200 metres in altitude, in tall, wet grasslands and on the edge of marshes surrounded by bushes. R

Adult Croaking Cisticola

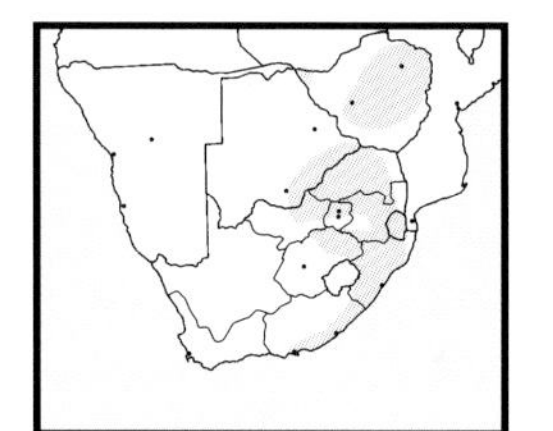

Lazy Cisticola *Cisticola aberrans* (679) 14 cm

This species is prinia-like in behaviour. Its plumage, however, does not resemble that of a prinia as it has a rufous crown and nape graduating to brownish-grey on the back, and buffy underparts. It is quite similar to the smaller Neddicky (see page 228) but can be told from that species by its much longer tail. It forages low down in vegetation as well as on the ground and may often be seen running, mouse-like, between grass tufts and bouncing over rocks, cocking its tail like a prinia. Males sing from a prominent perch a scolding 'tzeeeee-tzeeeeh-cheeee-cheeee', but do not display in flight. The nest, a ball of grass, is built near to the ground in a grass tuft, on grassy and rock-strewn hillsides and plateaus. R

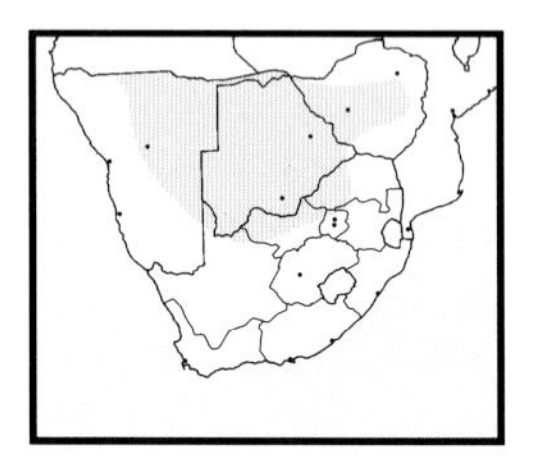

Tinkling Cisticola *Cisticola rufilatus* (671) 14 cm

This species is similar to the Rattling Cisticola (see page 230), but is redder in colour with a more rufous tail and crown. The sexes are alike but females have shorter tails; immatures resemble the adults. A secretive, skulking species, the Tinkling Cisticola keeps low down and sometimes runs, mouse-like, on the ground. It is less vocal than the Rattling Cisticola, its song having been likened to the tinkling of a bell. The nest of dry grasses is well hidden in dense grass or in a shrub. This bird is found in open savannas and dry broad-leaved woodland, including the edges of miombo and teak woodland. R

White-eyes Family Zosteropidae

These are small arboreal birds. Gregarious, they behave like tiny babblers (see page 194), gathering in small parties and continually calling to keep contact. They are insectivorous and frugivorous, and occasionally feed on nectar too.

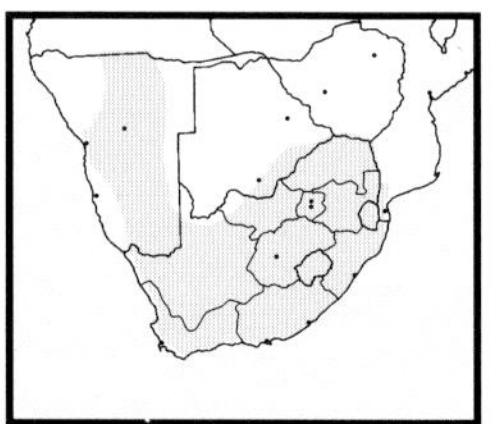

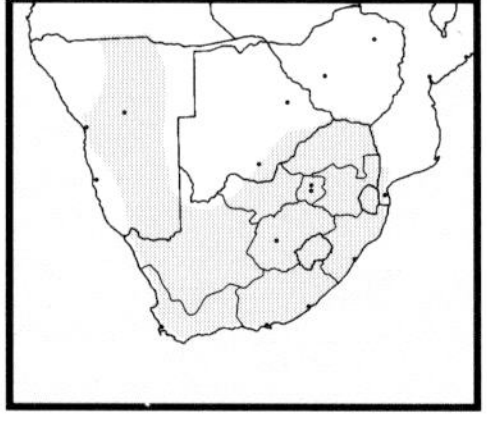

Cape White-eye *Zosterops pallidus* (796) 12 cm

The Cape White-eye varies in plumage from the west to the east of its range. The eastern race has a pale green, almost yellow, back and is separable from the Yellow White-eye by its greyish-green vent and greenish, not yellow, head. The western race has a yellow throat, upper breast and vent separated by a dull grey belly. The arid western race has a pinkish flush to the flanks and a buffy belly. The call of this species and that of the Yellow White-eye are inseparable: a series of 'pirrup-pirrup' notes; the contact call is a continuous 'pee, prreee, pirree'. The Cape White-eye occurs in evergreen forest, thornveld, woodland and savanna, in dry vegetated riverbeds and in suburban gardens. E

Yellow White-eye *Zosterops senegalensis* (797) 11 cm

Like the Cape White-eye, this very small, sociable, leaf-gleaning warbler is an active forager. The bright sulphur-yellow underparts and very pale green, almost yellow, upperparts separate this species from the Cape White-eye, but it is distinguished with difficulty from the eastern race of the Cape White-eye. The head is almost completely yellow, not greenish. The sexes are alike. Immatures are much paler yellow and green than immature Cape White-eyes. The Yellow White-eye feeds on aphids and other small insects, as well as on nectar from flowers. It frequents a variety of woodland habitats, such as evergreen forest and tangles of vegetation in riverine woodland. Its call is very similar to that of the Cape White-eye. R

1. Adult Croaking Cisticola
2. Adult Lazy Cisticola
3. Adult Tinkling Cisticola
4. Adult Cape White-eye
5. Adult Yellow White-eye
6. Adult Cape White-eye

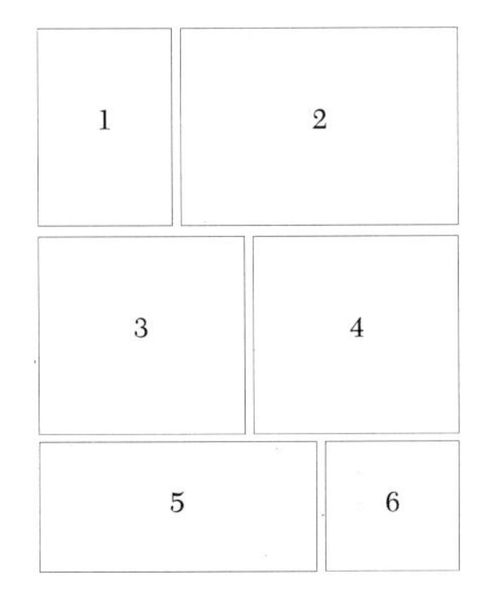

R *resident* • E *endemic*

Flycatchers and batises Family Muscicapidae

Generally small passerines, these birds typically have short, rounded wings and short, dorsoventrally compressed bills. Flycatchers hunt from perches, taking insects either in the air or on the ground. Batises and Wattle-eyed Flycatchers are short-tailed, with the plumage a combination of black, white, grey and orange. These birds hunt by gleaning insects, mostly from leaves or bark, as well as in aerial pursuit. The nests are typically neat, cup-shaped structures, positioned on a branch or ledge.

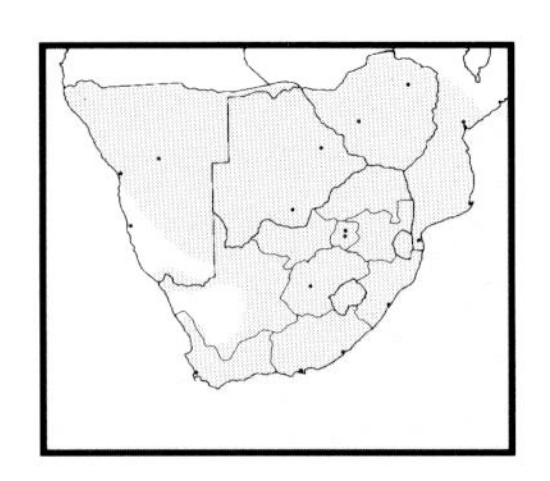

Spotted Flycatcher *Muscicapa striata* (689) 14 cm

This species is similar to the Dusky Flycatcher but is larger, has a streaky crown, pale underparts with streaking on the breast only, and lacks an eye-ring. Immatures are mottled brown and buff but are unlikely to be encountered in our region. The Spotted Flycatcher occurs in almost any woodland and savanna habitat, sometimes flying to the ground, and flicking its wings on returning to its perch. Its song is a soft 'tzeep'; it also utters a 'tjek-tjek' alarm. S

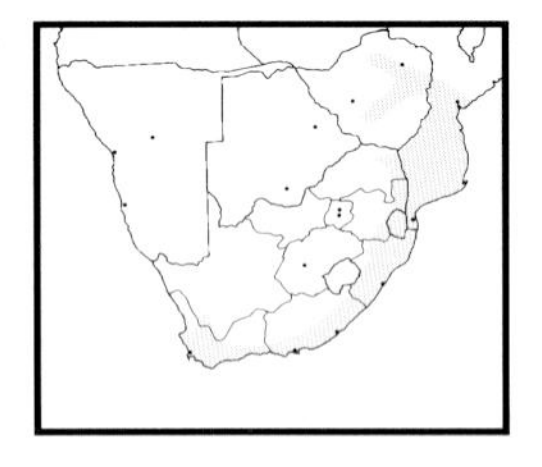

Dusky Flycatcher *Muscicapa adusta* (690) 12 cm

A smaller version of the Spotted Flycatcher, the Dusky Flycatcher is generally darker brown with almost no spotting on the crown. It also has a pale eye-ring, lacking in the other species. Aside from the white chin, it is generally washed with brown, and shows extensive but indistinct streaking on the breast. The basal third of its bill is yellowish. Immatures are spotted with buff above and are white below with brown spots. This bird occurs in evergreen forest, coastal forest and riverine scrub. Its call is a soft, high, repeated 'tzeet'. R

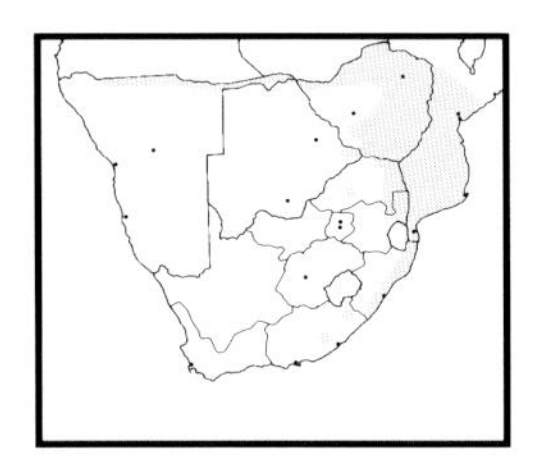

Bluegrey Flycatcher *Muscicapa caerulescens* (691) 15 cm

The Bluegrey Flycatcher differs from the grey variant of the Dusky Flycatcher by its all-dark bill. Although generally blue-grey in colour, this species is lighter below than the Dusky Flycatcher, shading to white on the belly and vent, with black lores and a white eye-ring. It differs from the Fantailed Flycatcher by its plain, dark grey tail, including the outer tail feathers. Immatures are speckled dark brown and buff above and below. The Bluegrey Flycatcher hawks insects from a perch and flicks its wings on returning to the perch. It favours evergreen forest edges, and riverine and moist broad-leaved woodland, including miombo woodland. The call is a soft 'sszzit-sszzit-sreee-sree', descending in scale. R

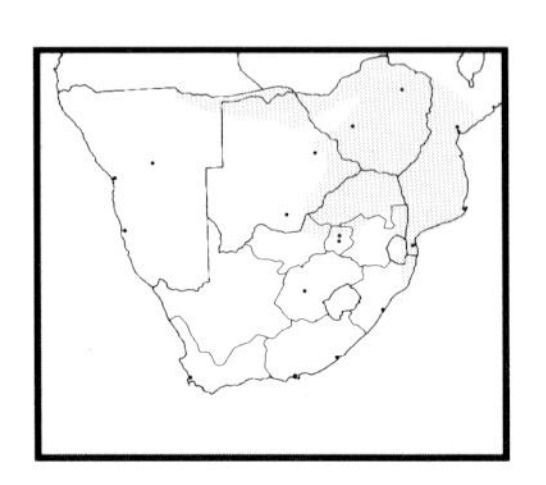

Fantailed Flycatcher *Myioparus plumbeus* (693) 14 cm

Like the Bluegrey Flycatcher, the Fantailed Flycatcher is dark blue-grey in colour and is similar in size but can be separated from that species by its black tail with diagnostic white outer tail feathers. It feeds in the canopy, gleaning insects from branches like a warbler, and has a habit of spreading its tail and twisting it from side to side, exposing the white tail feathers. Its song is a characteristic whistled 'treeee-trooo', repeated several times. Unlike the flycatchers which construct their own grass nests, this species nests in old barbet or woodpecker holes or in natural tree holes. The Fantailed Flycatcher frequents moist riverine woodland and broad-leaved woodland and savanna. R

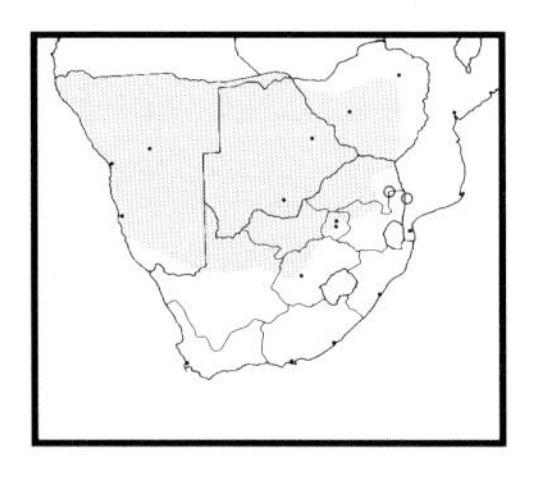

Marico Flycatcher *Melaenornis mariquensis* (695) 18 cm

This species and the Mousecoloured Flycatcher are approximately the same size, but the Marico Flycatcher is clean white, not mousy-brown, below with uniform brown upperparts. Immatures are spotted with buff above and streaked below. It occurs in thornveld habitat and feeds from an outer branch of a bush or a tree, flying to the ground to catch prey. A soft 'chreeep-cheruk-tukk' call is given. R

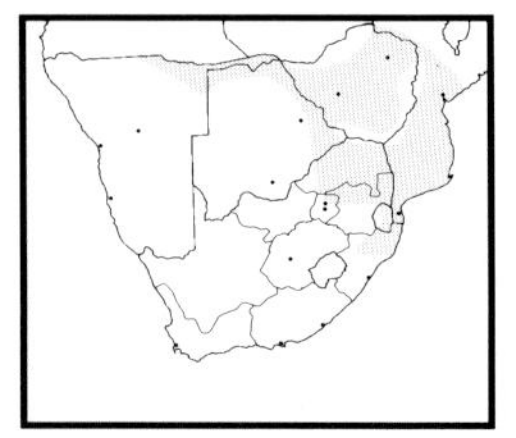

Mousecoloured Flycatcher *Melaenornis pallidus* (696) 17 cm

This species differs from the Marico Flycatcher by its buffy-brown, not pure white, underparts and its different habitat preferences. While similar to the larger Chat Flycatcher (see page 236), it lacks that species' pale panel visible on the folded wing. Immatures are paler than the adults, mottled with grey and scaled with black. It utters a melodious jumble of notes interspersed with harsh chitters and a soft 'chrrrr' alarm note. This flycatcher occurs in moist, broad-leaved woodland, avoiding montane, evergreen and riverine forests. R

1. Adult Spotted Flycatcher
2. Adult Dusky Flycatcher
3. Adult Bluegrey Flycatcher
4. Adult Marico Flycatcher
5. Adult Fantailed Flycatcher
6. Adult Mousecoloured Flycatcher

1	2
3	4
5	6

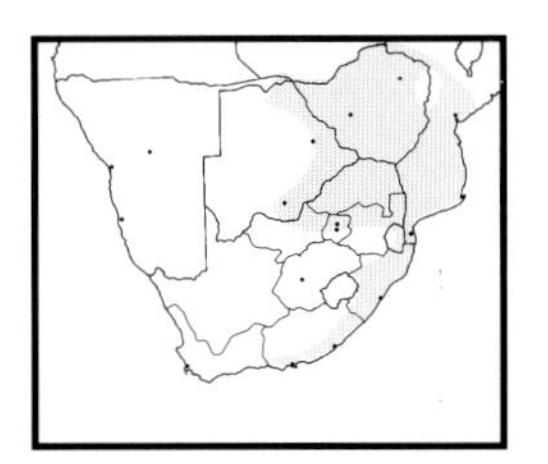

Southern Black Flycatcher *Melaenornis pammelaina* (694) 22 cm

This all-black flycatcher with its shallowly notched tail closely resembles the Squaretailed Drongo (see page 186) but has different habitat preferences and a brown, not deep red, eye; further, this flycatcher has a slender bill and a high, rounded forehead while the bill of the Squaretailed Drongo is wide based and the forehead sloping. Both the Southern Black Flycatcher and the all-black Black Cuckooshrike (see page 186) have dark brown eyes but the Black Cuckooshrike has a yellow gape, a rounded, not square, tail, and its behaviour differs. Immatures are dull black scalloped with brown below. The Southern Black Flycatcher occurs in woodland and savannas. Its song is a high-pitched 'tseep-tseep-terra-loora-loo'. R

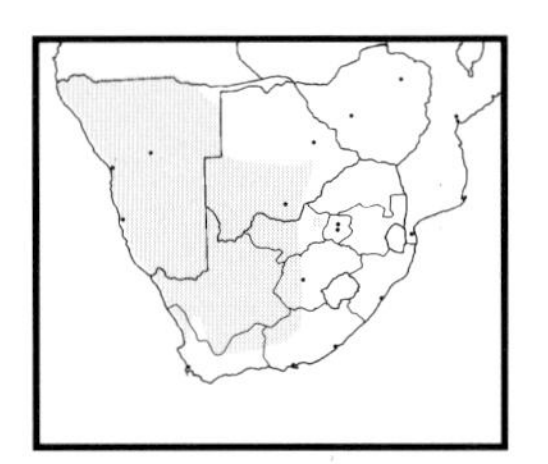

Chat Flycatcher *Melaenornis infuscatus* (697) 20 cm

This large flycatcher, similar in general coloration to the Mousecoloured Flycatcher (see page 234), exhibits chat-like behaviour. It is brown above and paler below with a distinct pale panel on the secondaries of the folded wing. It hops around on the ground with wings slightly spread, often eating from the ground. The call is a rich warbled 'cher-cher-cherip'. Immatures are strongly streaked brown and white above and below, unlike most other immature flycatchers, which are spotted. The Chat Flycatcher is confined to Karoo scrub, semi-desert scrub and open areas with scrubby bushes. R

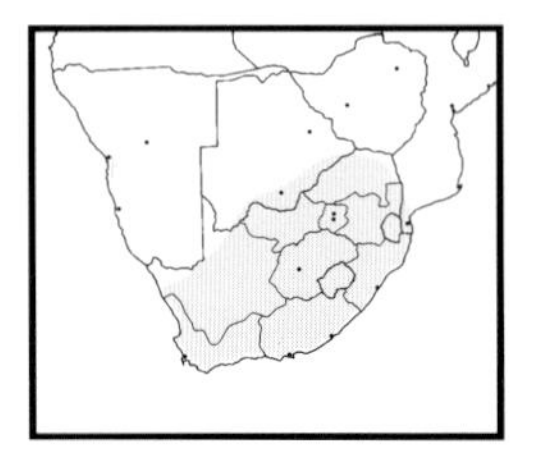

Fiscal Flycatcher *Sigelus silens* (698) 17-20 cm

The Fiscal Flycatcher might be mistaken for the Fiscal Shrike (see page 246) with its black upperparts and pale underparts but differs by having a white throat and the rest of the underparts greyish. Other identification features are the small white wing flashes in the secondaries, the short tail with the basal part of the outer tail feathers white, and the thin (not stubby and hooked) flycatcher bill. Females are browner than males, and immatures are brown above with pale specks and below are scalloped brown on creamy white. The call is a soft chittering mixture of notes and a sharp 'tssisk' given when alarmed; they also imitate other bird calls. These birds favour Karoo scrub, bush in grassland areas, thornveld, exotic plantations and suburban gardens. E

Wattle-eyed Flycatcher *Platysteira peltata* (705) 13 cm

A very small flycatcher, this bird is similar in size to members of the batis family. Both sexes have conspicuous red wattles above the eyes and both are black above, including the tail which is tipped with white. Males are white below with a narrow black breast band. Females have a black throat and upper breast with a small white chin patch; the belly and vent are white as in the male. Immatures resemble the females. The call of the Wattled-eyed Flycatcher is a repeated 'whichee, whichee, whichee, whichee'. This is a secretive species, keeping to secondary lowland forest undergrowth and riverine thickets, often near to water. R

Mashona Hyliota *Hyliota australis* (624) 14 cm

Males of this species have matt blue-black upperparts and a short but broad white wing bar; below they are creamy white to yellowish. Female birds are browner above with white edgings to the secondary wing coverts but show white edgings to the outer tail feathers, as do the males. Immatures are similar to but duller than the females and lack any streaking on their underparts. The call is a high-pitched 'tree trreet trrreet'. This very active, warbler-like bird is found in the canopy of *Brachystegia* woodland throughout the year and is commonly seen in bird parties foraging through the upper canopy. R

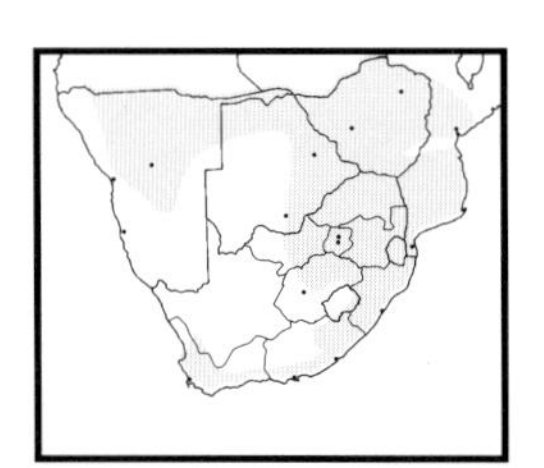

Paradise Flycatcher *Terpsiphone viridis* (710) m=23-41 cm (including tail); f=16-18 cm (including tail)

Male and female Paradise Flycatchers both have a blue-black head and throat with a blue bill, broad blue eye wattles, a chestnut back and tail, and light grey underparts. In the male the tail is twice the body length while the tail of the female is as long as the body; the male loses its long tail out of the breeding season. Immatures are similar to females but are duller. The song is a loud and characteristic 'tweee-tiddly-te-te', and the alarm call a harsh 'zweeeet-zweeet-zwayt'. These birds occur in riverine and coastal bush, thornveld and broad-leaved woodland. R, S

1. Adult Southern Black Flycatcher
2. Adult Chat Flycatcher
3. Adult Fiscal Flycatcher
4. Adult Fiscal Flycatcher
5. Male Wattle-eyed Flycatcher
6. Female Wattle-eyed Flycatcher
7. Male Paradise Flycatcher
8. Adult Mashona Hyliota
9. Adult Paradise Flycatcher

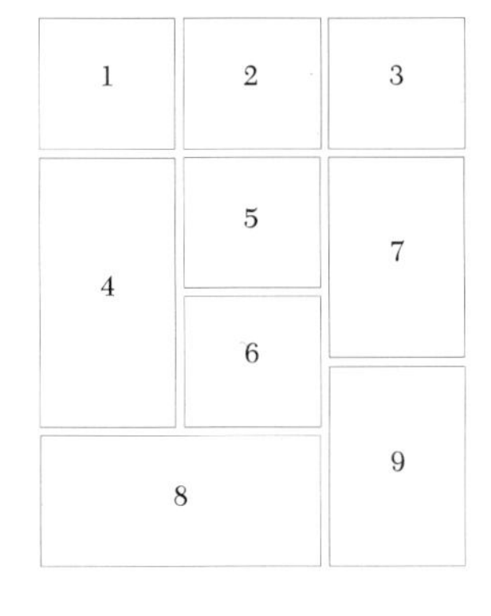

R *resident* • E *endemic* • S *summer visitor*

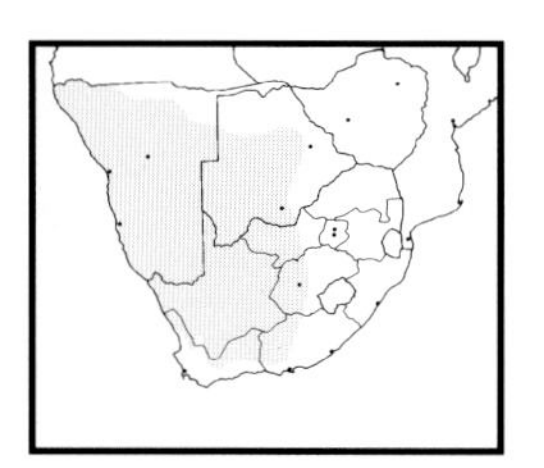

Pririt Batis *Batis pririt* (703) 12 cm

The male Pririt Batis is similar to the Chinspot Batis but the calls of the two species are different and their ranges rarely coincide. The male Pririt Batis has a broad black breast band and white underparts with some black flecking on the flanks. Females differ from the female Chinspot Batis by having a buffy to rufous wash on the throat and breast. Immatures are similar to the females although their upperparts are washed with rufous. The call is a series of 'teuu, teuu, teuu, teuu' notes descending in scale. This confiding yet active species forages for insects in the lower strata of bushes. Usually seen in pairs, it occurs in thornveld thickets and dry riverine bush. NE

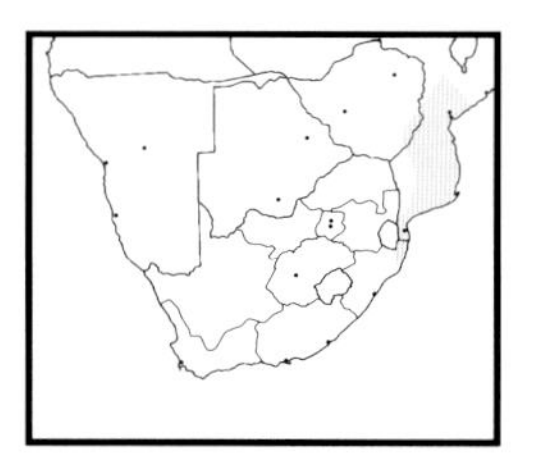

Woodward's Batis *Batis fratrum* (704) 11 cm

Males of this species have a tawny breast band (not black as in all other male batises) which extends to the flanks. They resemble the Pririt Batis but the ranges of the two species are mutually exclusive. The female is similar to the female Chinspot Batis but lacks the chestnut chin spot and has a tawny wing bar. Females are separable from the female Cape Batis by their narrow white eyebrow which extends from the bill to the sides of the neck; and by their tawny, not chestnut, throat, breast and flanks. A clear penetrating whistle 'teh-teh-pheeeooo' is uttered. Immatures resemble the females but have a buff, not white, eyebrow, and the face mask is indistinct. This batis frequents coastal forest and scrubby thickets. R

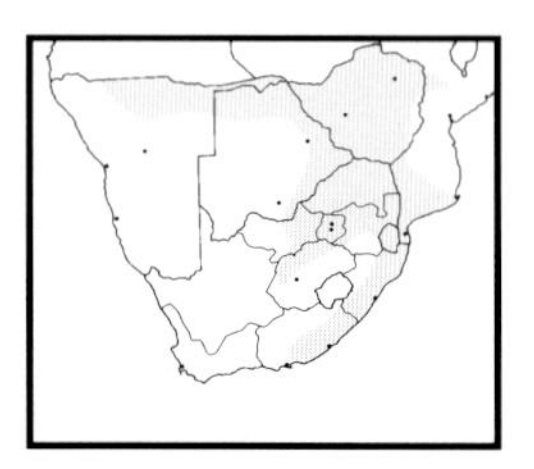

Chinspot Batis *Batis molitor* (701) 13 cm

This batis might be confused with the Cape Batis but its white wing bar, flanks and belly distinguish it. The pure white underparts of the males separate them from the Pririt Batis which has black flecking on the flanks. Females have a distinctive chestnut spot on the chin and a chestnut breast band; the remaining underparts are white. Both sexes have a white wing bar. Females show an extensive white eyebrow like that of Woodward's Batis, but that species has a tawny wing bar and a buffy-yellow throat and breast which helps to separate the two. Immatures are similar to the females but have a brownish wash to the upperparts, and males have a buff chin spot and breast band. The call is a descending 'teuu-teuu-teuu', likened to 'three blind mice'. The Chinspot Batis occurs in dry thornveld, savanna and broad-leaved woodland. R

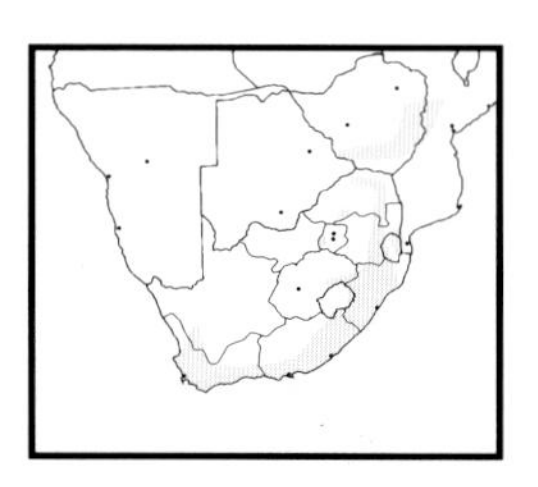

Cape Batis *Batis capensis* (700) 13 cm

The male Cape Batis resembles the male Chinspot Batis, both showing a broad black breast band, but the breast band of the Cape Batis is broader than in any other male batis, and the chestnut flanks, wing coverts and secondaries further distinguish it. Females resemble the female Chinspot Batis but have chestnut, not white, flanks and broad chestnut, not white, wing patches. Females differ from the female Woodward's Batis by having a very short eyebrow stripe and rufous, not buff, underparts. Immatures lack the black face mask of the adult females but otherwise are similar. The call, a soft 'chewrra-warrra-warrra', is characteristic. It is common in evergreen forests and heavily wooded gorges. E

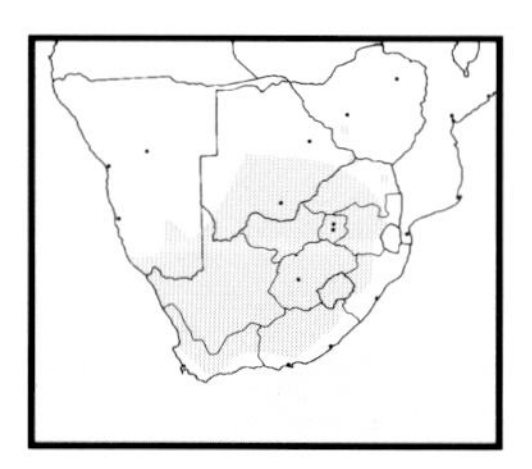

Fairy Flycatcher *Stenostira scita* (706) 12 cm

In some respects similar to a slim batis, having a white wing bar and a black face mask, the Fairy Flycatcher has much longer legs than the batises and a longer tail with white outer tail feathers. The throat is white and the breast is grey fading to a pink flush on the belly. When breeding it occurs in fynbos and Karoo scrub; outside of the breeding season the bird moves into thornveld, savanna and riverine bush. Its song is a thin squeaky 'tisee-tchee-tchee'. E

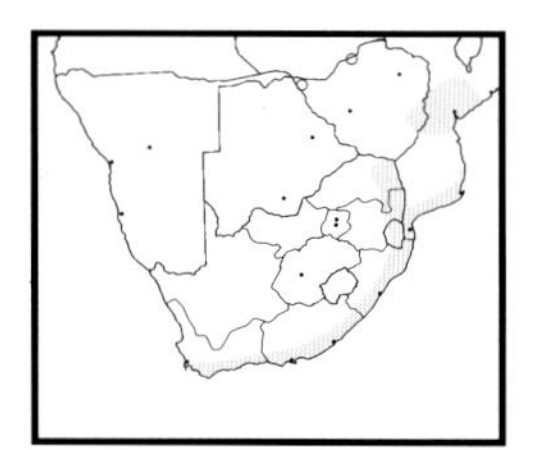

Bluemantled Flycatcher *Trochocercus cyanomelas* (708) 18 cm

Found in the mid to lower strata of forest growth, this species is often quite difficult to see but its characteristic 'zweet-zwa' call, somewhat like that of a Paradise Flycatcher (see page 236), is a giveaway. Bluemantled Flycatchers are active foragers, hopping from branch to branch, frequently fanning their tail feathers and moving their bodies from side to side. Males have a dark blue-black head, a shaggy crest and a black breast which contrasts with a white belly. Females are duller with a blue-grey head and back, and white underparts. Both sexes have white wing bars, like the batises, and all-grey tails. The Bluemantled Flycatcher is found in montane evergreen forest and riverine forest. R

1. Male (right) and female (left) Pririt Batis
2. Male Woodward's Batis
3. Male Chinspot Batis
4. Female Chinspot Batis
5. Male Cape Batis
6. Female Cape Batis
7. Adult Fairy Flycatcher
8. Female Bluemantled Flycatcher

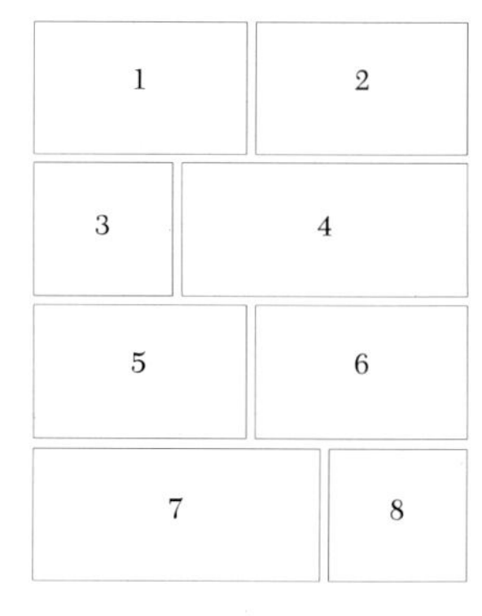

Wagtails, pipits and longclaws
Family Motacillidae

Long-tailed, ground-living birds, the wagtails and pipits have the habit of wagging their tails up and down while walking. Pipits are confusingly similar-looking and are best identified by call and habitat choice. Longclaws have brightly coloured underparts, show diagnostic white-tipped outer tail feathers in flight, and have exceptionally long hind claws. All species are insectivorous, and most nest on the ground and live in grassland.

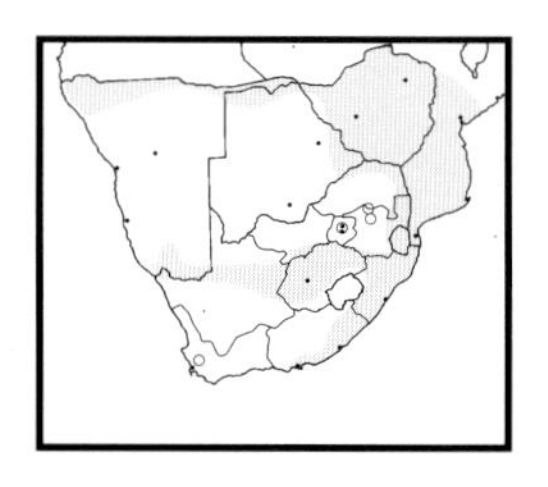

African Pied Wagtail *Motacilla aguimp* (711) 20 cm

Adults of this species have white underparts except for a black bib. The upperparts are black except for a broad white eyebrow and the coverts and secondaries, which are white on the folded wing. The sexes are alike. Immatures are duller and might be confused with the immature Cape Wagtail but the extensive white colouring on the wing should separate the two. The African Pied Wagtail forages mostly on the ground, striding about, or flies to catch moving prey. It occurs along river systems, at sewage-disposal works, on school fields and in gardens. Its call is a loud, shrill 'chee-chee-cheree-cheeroo'. R

Longtailed Wagtail *Motacilla clara* (712) 20 cm

The clean, pale blue to grey upperparts and pure white underparts of this species help to separate it from the similar-sized Cape Wagtail; also, it appears slimmer than that species, and has pinkish-grey, not black, legs and a much longer tail. The sexes are alike. The nest is built in a hollow in a stream bank, concealed by overhanging vegetation. It is a cup-shaped structure of roots and hair with a base of leaves, mosses and grass. The call is a sharp, high-pitched 'cheeerup' or 'chissuk'. The Longtailed Wagtail is found along fast-flowing, rocky mountain streams, and quieter streams in forested areas. R

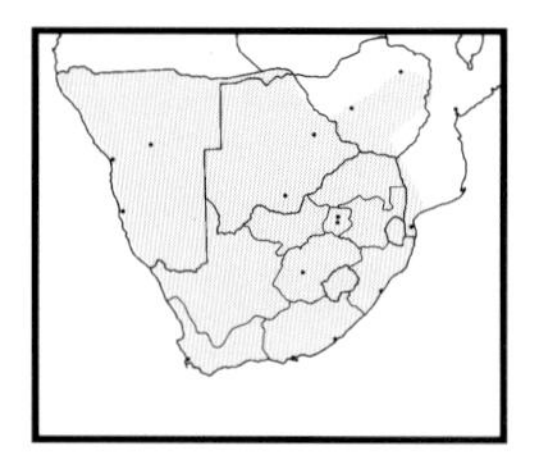

Cape Wagtail *Motacilla capensis* (713) 18 cm

The adult Cape Wagtail is olive-grey above and dirty-white below with a narrow, greyish chest band. It can be told from the Longtailed Wagtail by being olive-grey, not pale blue-grey, above; by having black, not pinkish-grey, legs; by lacking black lores; and by having less white in the wing. Immatures are browner than the adults and are separable from the immature Longtailed Wagtail by the absence of a white wing patch. The nest is similar to that of the Longtailed Wagtail. Its call is a clear ringing 'tseee-chee-chee' and includes some whistled trills. The Cape Wagtail is commonly found in city parks and gardens, along coastal lagoons and slow-moving streams and dams. R

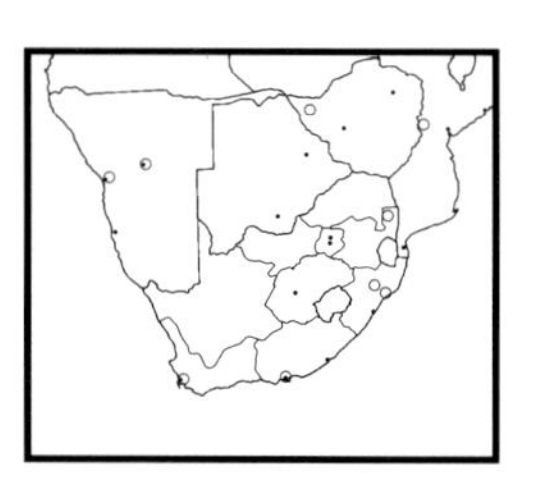

Grey Wagtail *Motacilla cinerea* (715) 18 cm

The breeding male has a black throat but in non-breeding plumage resembles the female, which always has a white throat. The head and back of the male are grey, like those of the Longtailed Wagtail, but the bright yellow underparts and rump are diagnostic. The female has a grey back, an ochre to yellow breast and a yellow vent and rump, the remaining underparts being pure white. Non-breeding birds are very similar to some races of the Yellow Wagtail in non-breeding plumage, but the Grey Wagtail has a longer tail and a grey, not olive-yellow, back. This species is attracted to swift-flowing mountain streams. Its call is a metallic 'tsillip' and a mixtures of trilled and piped notes. S

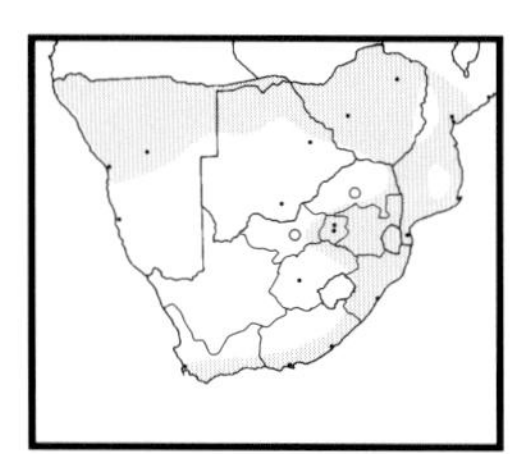

Yellow Wagtail *Motacilla flava* (714) 16 cm

There are innumerable subspecies of this bird; most birds recorded in the region belong to the race *M.f. flava*. All races may be confused with the Grey Wagtail but all have a shorter tail and a greenish, not dark grey, back with variable head patterns, and in flight they do not show a pale wing bar. Breeding males differ widely from race to race on the amount of yellow on the throat and most are identifiable on a diagnostic head pattern. Non-breeding males and females are greenish grey above with a white throat and yellow underparts. Immatures are yellowish brown above and dull white below with a blackish breast band. Yellow Wagtails usually occur in small groups, foraging on the ground, and are most likely to be seen in open, short grasslands, on the edges of pans and at sewage works. The call is a pleasing 'tsee-e' or 'tsree-e'. S

Male Grey Wagtail (breeding)

Male Yellow Wagtail
M.f. feldegg *(breeding)*

Male Yellow Wagtail
M.f. thunbergi *(breeding)*

Male Yellow Wagtail (breeding)

1. Adult African Pied Wagtail
2. Adult Longtailed Wagtail
3. Male Grey Wagtail (breeding)
4. Adult Cape Wagtail
5. Male Grey Wagtail (non-breeding)
6. Adult Yellow Wagtail (breeding)
7. Adult Yellow Wagtail (non-breeding)

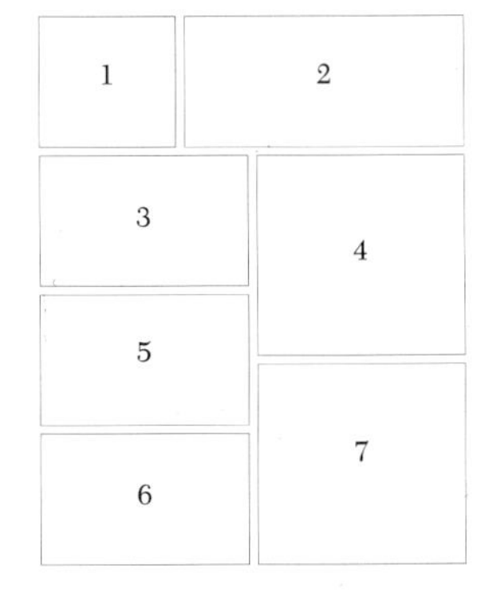

R *resident* • S *summer visitor*

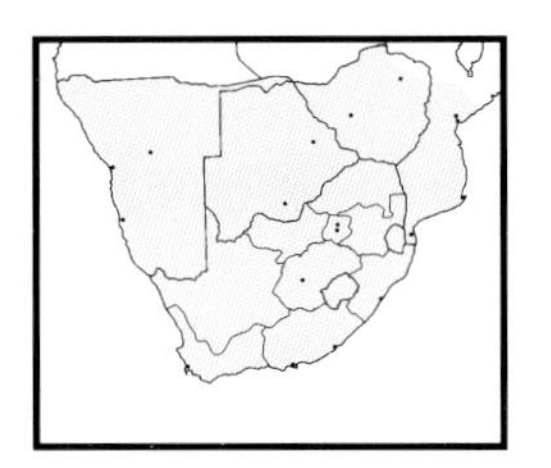

Grassveld Pipit *Anthus cinnamomeus* (716) 16 cm

This species is similar to the Longbilled Pipit, the Buffy Pipit and the Plainbacked Pipit. It is, however, the only grassland pipit that shows white, not buffy, outer tail feathers in flight. It is brown above with a strongly streaked back; underneath, the breast and malar stripes are spotted, the throat is white and the base of the bill is yellowish (the base of the bill is pinkish in many other pipits); the breast and flanks are tawny fading to white on the belly. In display flight the Grassveld Pipit climbs to about 30 metres and calls before dropping steeply earthwards and calling again before alighting. The song of three to five 'trrt-trrt-trrt' notes readily separates it from the other pipits. It occurs in open grasslands, on airstrips and on playing fields. R

Mountain Pipit *Anthus hoeschi* (901) 18 cm

It is difficult to separate this species from the Grassveld Pipit but its larger size, more heavily streaked breast, pinkish base to the bill, and buff, not white, outer tail feathers should aid identification. It is brown above with dark streaks and below is buffy with heavy, dark brown spotting on the breast. The bird's habits and display flight are similar to those of the Grassveld Pipit. Its grass nest is cup shaped and is typically built on the ground underneath a grass tuft. The Mountain Pipit breeds in montane grasslands above 2 000 metres in altitude. Its call is similar to that of the Grassveld Pipit but is deeper in pitch and slower in tempo. I, S

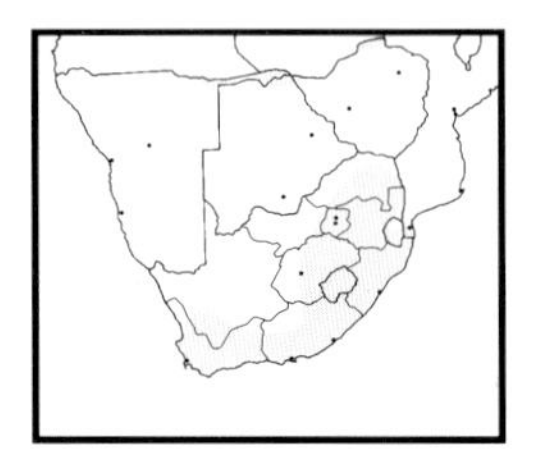

Plainbacked Pipit *Anthus leucophrys* (718) 17 cm

This pipit closely resembles the Buffy Pipit, but it lacks the tail-bobbing habit of that species. It is separable from the Grassveld Pipit and the Longbilled Pipit by its plain, unmarked back. It is dark brown above with a buffy eyebrow, an indistinct malar stripe, and a yellowish base to the bill, and has buffy outer tail feathers. Below it is buffy, being darkest on the breast, where it is faintly streaked, and fading to off-white at the vent. Its call is a loud clear 'chrrp-chereeoo'. It prefers short grassland in hilly country, especially overgrazed or burnt pastures, and when not breeding may be seen in flocks of up to 20 birds in cultivated fields. R

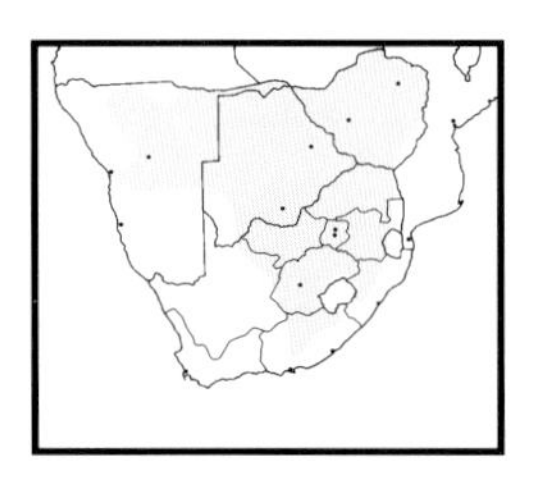

Buffy Pipit *Anthus vaalensis* (719) 18 cm

The Buffy Pipit is slightly larger than the Grassveld Pipit and the Plainbacked Pipit. It may be separated from the Grassveld Pipit and the Longbilled Pipit by its unmarked, not streaky, back. It is light brown above with a buffy eyebrow and buff outer tail feathers. Below it is buffy, darker on the breast and with indistinct streaking; the base of the bill is pinkish. Behaviourly, this pipit is more like a wagtail, stopping frequently and bobbing its tail up and down. Its call is a soft, repeated, two-noted song 'tchreep-churup' and a short 'sshik' given when disturbed. It occurs in similar habitat to the Plainbacked Pipit. R

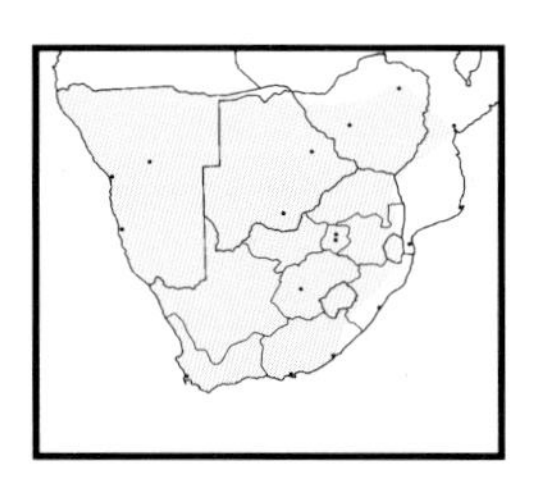

Longbilled Pipit *Anthus similis* (717) 18 cm

This species is similar to the Wood Pipit but differs in habitat preference, bill length and tail length (both are longer in this species). The Longbilled Pipit is dark brown above, lightly streaked on the back and has a whitish eye-stripe; the base of the bill is yellowish to pink. Below it is buffy with distinct malar stripes and brown spotting on the breast. It is usually seen singly, foraging on the ground, and readily perches on rocks and mounds; it does not wag its tail like the Buffy Pipit or the Grassveld Pipit. It may be told apart from the Grassveld Pipit by its buffy, not white, outer tail feathers. The Longbilled Pipit is attracted to recently burnt areas of grassland, and boulder-strewn, grassy hillsides with some scrubby bushes. It has a three-noted call 'tchreep-tritit-churup'. R

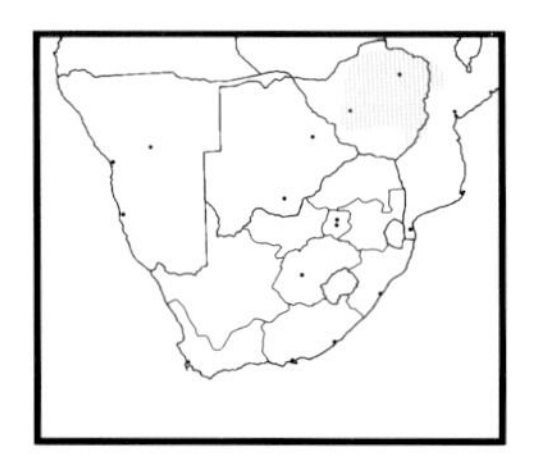

Wood Pipit *Anthus nyassae* (909) 18 cm

This species is very similar to the Longbilled Pipit, from which it has recently been separated. It is distinguished from that species by its shorter bill and tail. It is dark brown above with a whitish eye-stripe. Below it is buffy with distinct malar stripes and brown spotting on the breast. It forages on the ground and flies on to a low branch of a tree when disturbed or alarmed; it also walks along tree branches. Its call is similar to that of the Longbilled Pipit but is more variable and high pitched. The Wood Pipit is confined to open miombo woodland where it forages in rocky clearings. R

1. Adult Grassveld Pipit
2. Adult Mountain Pipit
3. Adult Buffy Pipit
4. Adult Plainbacked Pipit
5. Adult Buffy Pipit
6. Adult Wood Pipit
7. Adult Longbilled Pipit

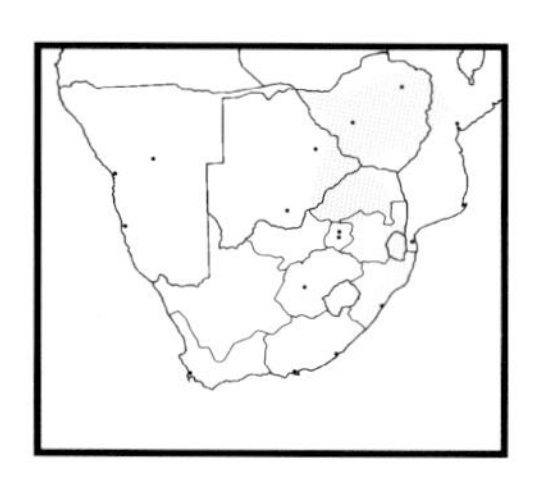

Striped Pipit *Anthus lineiventris* (720) 18 cm

This species is buffy above with heavy, dark streaking and a white eyebrow. Below it is very heavily streaked on the breast and the flanks. Its wing and tail feathers are edged with yellow, and the outer tail feathers are white. The Striped Pipit is seen singly or in pairs, foraging on the ground, and may also walk along branches of trees, as does the Wood Pipit (see page 242). It builds a cup-shaped nest of grass and roots on the ground under a rock or grass tuft, and favours grassy and wooded boulder-strewn hillsides. Its call is a loud and penetrating thrush-like song uttered from a rock or tree. R

Male Yellowbreasted Pipit (non-breeding)

Yellowbreasted Pipit *Hemimacronyx chloris* (725) 17 cm

In breeding plumage both sexes are bright yellow below and in flight show yellow underwing coverts; above they are buffy brown with dark brown streaks, and show a whitish eyebrow. In display the males call a rapid 'chip-chip-chip' during a circular flight about 20 metres in height before dropping sharply earthwards. In non-breeding plumage the birds are buffy below and brown above, with the feather tips scaled with a light edging. Extremely shy, the Yellowbreasted Pipit sneaks behind tufts of grass and keeps low when approached. It breeds above 1 500 metres in altitude and prefers thick, tufty grasses in rolling montane grasslands; it moves to lower altitudes in the non-breeding season. E

Adult Pinkthroated Longclaw

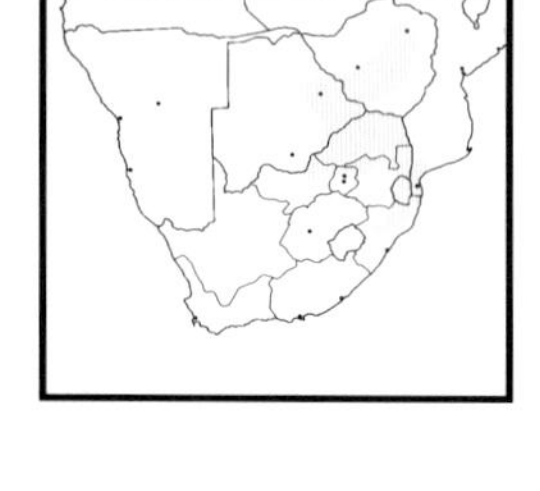

Bushveld Pipit *Anthus caffer* (723) 14 cm

This small pipit with its short tail and brown and black streaked upperparts is reminiscent of a non-breeding bishop or widow species. Below it is buffy white and the throat is washed brown and faintly streaked; the breast and flanks are boldly streaked blackish. The sexes are alike and immatures are paler than the adults. Its call is a characteristic 'zeet', given as it flies from the ground into a tree, otherwise a 'zrrrt-zrrree' or 'zweep-tseeer' song, alternating higher and lower notes. It is usually seen singly in thornveld and savanna woodland. R

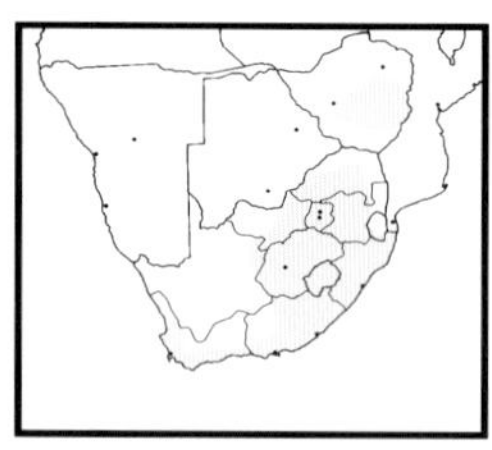

Orangethroated Longclaw *Macronyx capensis* (727) 20 cm

The underparts and eyebrow of this species are bright orange-yellow and a strong black collar separates the throat and belly. Immatures have a yellowish throat and a vestigial black collar and are otherwise buffy below and, like the adults, have brown and scaled upperparts. Immatures may be differentiated from the immature Yellowthroated Longclaw by having buff to orange underparts and buff, not yellow, edgings to the wing feathers. Orangethroated Longclaws have long legs and stand erect when motionless. They normally keep close to the ground when disturbed, flying off at the last moment if flushed. The call can be likened to the mew of a cat. This longclaw prefers coastal and montane grasslands and marshy grounds. E

Yellowthroated Longclaw *Macronyx croceus* (728) 20 cm

This species differs from the Orangethroated Longclaw by having a yellow throat, belly and eyebrow. It has a broader, heavier black breast band, with some black streaking on the breast below the band. Females are duller than the males. Immatures are distinguished from immature Orangethroated Longclaws by being buff-yellow below. The Yellowthroated Longclaw occurs in pairs and small groups, foraging among tufts of grass. It frequents coastal grasslands around estuaries and lagoons, and along drainage lines, favouring a more treed habitat than does the Orangethroated Longclaw. Its call is a loud whistled 'phoooooeeet', or a series of loud whistles, uttered from the top of a bush. R

Pinkthroated Longclaw *Macronyx ameliae* (730) 20 cm

Similar in size to the other two longclaws, this species is more pipit-like in shape and behaviour. Its call is a pipit-like 'chiteeet'. Above it is more grey-brown than brown, scaled with light edgings to the feather tips. The bright pink throat is diagnostic, and is separated from the pinkish breast by a broad black breast band. Females and immatures lack the breast band and are duller overall with a pinkish hue to the underparts. The Pinkthroated Longclaw is usually seen singly or in pairs, running through the grass or taking flight reluctantly when flushed. The flight is pipit-like and not stiff winged like that of the other two species. This longclaw prefers wetter, more waterlogged grasslands than either of the other two longclaws. R

1. Adult Striped Pipit
2. Adult Yellowbreasted Pipit
3. Adult Bushveld Pipit
4. Adult Orangethroated Longclaw
5. Adult Yellowthroated Longclaw
6. Adult Pinkthroated Longclaw

1	2
3	4
5	6

Shrikes Family Laniidae

These small to medium-sized birds have medium to very long tails. The plumage of the southern African species is predominantly grey, black and white. The bills are short, stout and hooked, and the feet are strong and sharp-clawed. The birds are found in semi-desert, woodland and savanna.

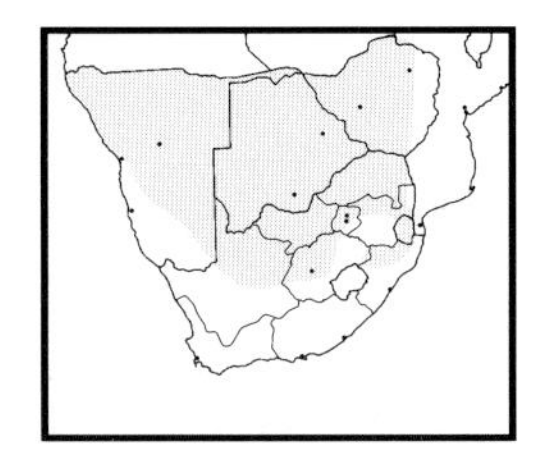

Lesser Grey Shrike *Lanius minor* (731) 21 cm

This species is a little smaller than the Fiscal Shrike, has a shorter tail, and is more dumpy in appearance. It has a black forehead and face mask, and a grey crown, back and rump. Its underparts are pure white. Females and immatures are lighter in colour, and immatures have some buff edging to the underpart feathers. The birds are usually seen singly, perched on a prominent bush or post, from which they drop to the ground to catch their insect prey, which they impale on thorns and other useful spikes. The Lesser Grey Shrike occurs in thornveld, savanna and grasslands with scrubby bushes. The call, given from a perch, is a harsh 'chek' note and a warbled song usually heard prior to the birds' migration nothwards. S

Immature Fiscal Shrike

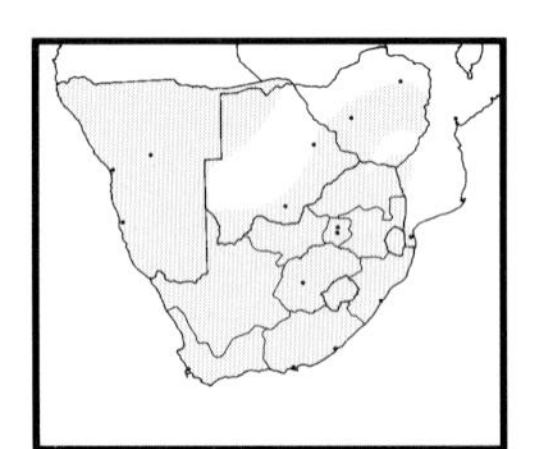

Fiscal Shrike *Lanius collaris* (732) 23 cm

The black upperparts and white underparts of this bird may cause confusion with the Fiscal Flycatcher (see page 236), but the Fiscal Shrike has a longer tail, whiter underparts and a 'V'-shaped white patch on the back; the western subspecies has a prominent white eyebrow. While males are all white below, females have a small chestnut patch on the lower flank. Immatures are greyish brown, darker above than below, and finely barred with crescent-shaped marks on each feather. The Fiscal Shrike impales its prey on thorns, barbed wire or sharp twigs; this behaviour gave rise to the bird's colloquial name, 'jackie hangman'. An opportunist, it takes doves, small birds, insects, frogs, lizards and small snakes. It calls from a perch, a melodious whistled song, and a harsh 'ghree, ghree, ghree' alarm call, and it mimics other bird calls. It frequents grasslands with some trees and bushes, thornveld, gardens and semi-arid scrub. R

Adult Fiscal Shrike (western form)

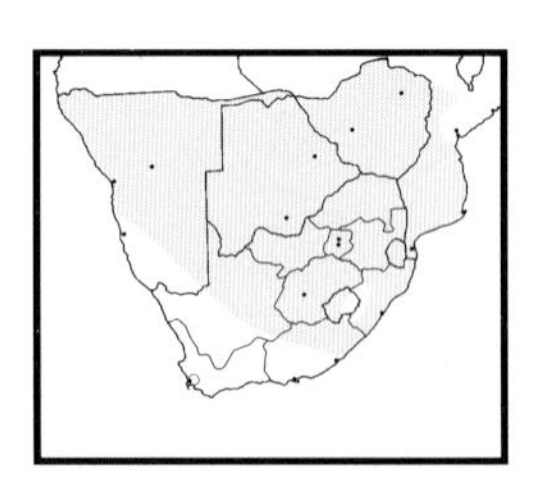

Redbacked Shrike *Lanius collurio* (733) 17 cm

This shrike has a grey crown and rump and a chestnut back. Males have a dark grey head with a black face mask; the underparts are white with a pinkish flush. Females and immatures have a brown face mask, a lighter chestnut back and lightly scalloped underparts with brown edges to the feathers. Usually seen alone, perching on branches sticking out of the side of a bush, these birds drop to the ground to pick up insects and lizards. They impale their prey on thorns or barbed-wire fences. Redbacked Shrikes occur in thornveld and wooded savannas, and utter a harsh 'chak-chak' alarm note and a soft warbled song. S

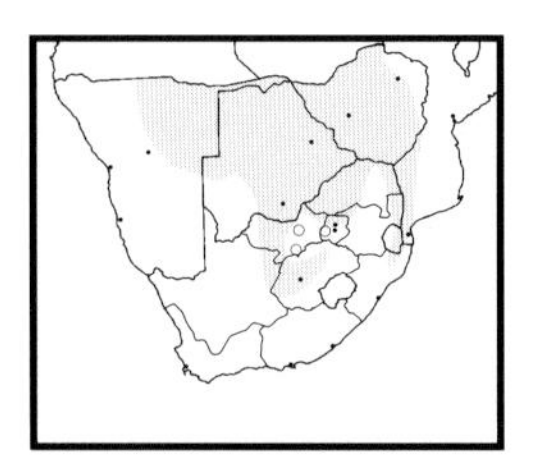

Longtailed Shrike *Corvinella melanoleuca* (735) 40-50 cm

This species is mostly black; the wing covert feathers on the folded wing are edged with white and show as a 'V'-shaped white mark on the back. The white tips to the primaries and the grey rump are noticeable in flight. It has an exceptionally long, wispy tail which it jerks as it calls. The female has a shorter tail than the male and has white patches on the flanks. Albino specimens have been recorded. Immatures are browner than the adults and show some barring. Foraging from a perch, this shrike drops to the ground to pick up food. Nestlings are fed by the parents and up to two adult helpers. This species occurs in small groups in acacia thornveld, and its call is a liquid, whistled 'peeeeeo'. R

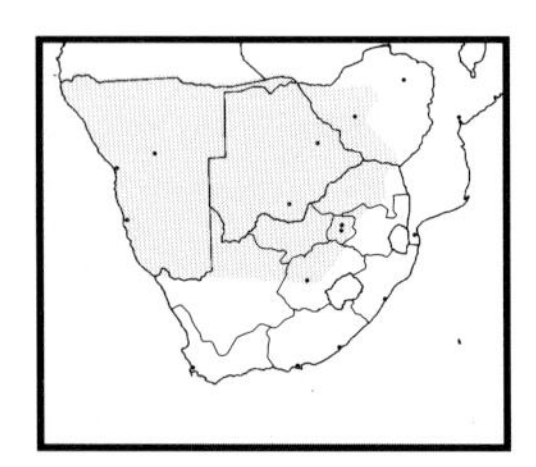

Crimsonbreasted Shrike *Laniarius atrococcineus* (739) 23 cm

A member of the *Laniarius* genus, which includes the boubous (see page 248), this species differs from its congeners in that it has crimson underparts. Its all-black upperparts with a white line through the wing are, however, identical to the plumage of others in its group. A rare yellow-orange-bellied morph occurs. The female resembles the male, and immatures are barred greyish brown with varying amounts of crimson on the underparts. The Crimsonbreasted Shrike forages for insects on the ground. The call, a clear, liquid, whistled 'quip quip', uttered in duet, is a characteristic sound of the bushveld. These birds occur in thornveld and semi-arid scrub. NE

1. Adult Lesser Grey Shrike
2. Male Redbacked Shrike
3. Adult Longtailed Shrike
4. Male Fiscal Shrike
5. Female Redbacked Shrike
6. Adult Longtailed Shrike
7. Female Fiscal Shrike
8. Adult Crimsonbreasted Shrike

1	2	3
4	5	6
7	8	

S *summer visitor* • R *resident* • NE *near endemic*

Boubous, tchagras, bush shrikes, puffbacks, brubrus and the White-tailed Shrike Family Malaconotidae

This is a family of small to medium-sized shrikes, most with heavy, hooked bills. Most are highly vocal. They inhabit a range of habitats from semi-desert to forest, many favouring dense thickets and tangled vegetation.

Adult Threestreaked Tchagra

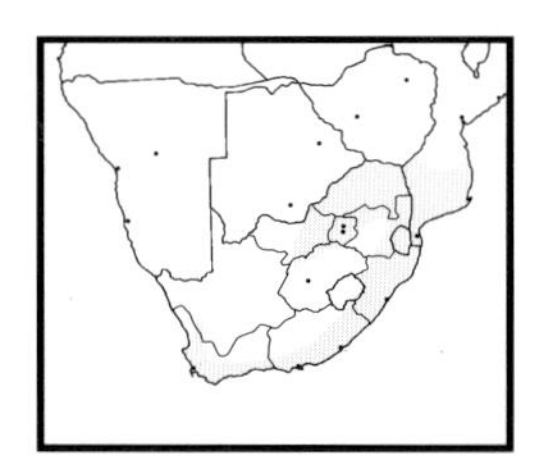

Southern Boubou *Laniarius ferrugineus* (736) 23 cm

This shrike has all-black upperparts except for a white line on the wing, and an off-white throat and breast graduating to buffy-orange around the vent. Immatures are mottled buff-brown above and barred below. A shy and secretive species, it forages through the undergrowth close to the ground. It usually occurs in pairs which are very vocal, the loud duet 'boo-boo, whee-ooo' being initiated by either sex. The Southern Boubou is found in riverine and bushveld thickets, fynbos and evergreen forest. E

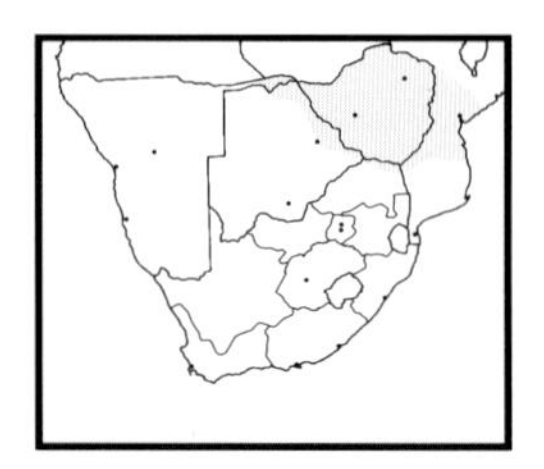

Tropical Boubou *Laniarius aethiopicus* (737) 23 cm

This species is similar to the Swamp Boubou, from which it differs by having off-white underparts with a tinge of buff to the vent (all white in the Swamp Boubou). The immature is duller than the adults, and is spotted buffy above and below. This boubou produces a similar duetting call to that of the Southern Boubou, but harsher, with a croaking 'haw' and scraping 'weer-weer' notes. Like that species, it is secretive, but may be seen hopping on the ground with its tail raised. It frequents bushveld thickets, riverine thickets and forest edges. R

Swamp Boubou *Laniarius bicolor* (738) 23 cm

This species is similar to the Southern Boubou and Tropical Boubou in having black upperparts and a white line through the wing, but its pure white underparts distinguish it, as does its habitat preferences. Immatures are buff spotted above and barred below. This bird is comparable in habits to the other two boubous and its duetting call is also very similar – only less variable with more clicking and harsh rattling noises. The Swamp Boubou prefers papyrus swamps and surrounding bush, and reeded thickets along rivers. R

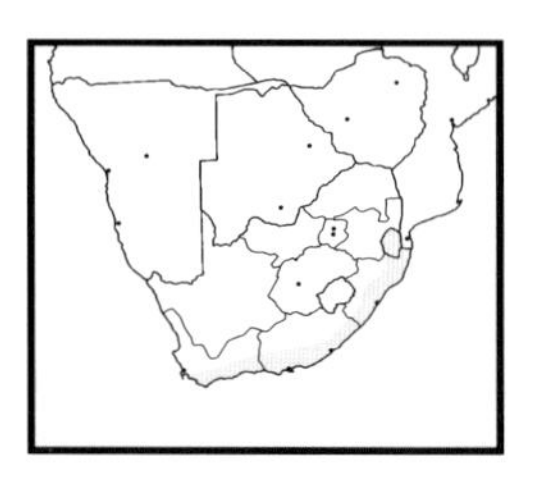

Southern Tchagra *Tchagra tchagra* (742) 21 cm

This species is larger and darker than the Threestreaked Tchagra, and differs further by having a rusty-brown, not dull brown, crown without any black edging above the broad white eyebrow stripe (as in the Threestreaked Tchagra). It is also greyer below, with chestnut wings and a black line through the eye. A secretive species, it keeps near to the ground. It favours thick coastal bush, riverine thickets and coastal dune forests. A 'prrr-prrr-prrr-prrr' and loud whistled 'tew-tew-tew-tew', descending in pitch, is given in a low aerial display. E

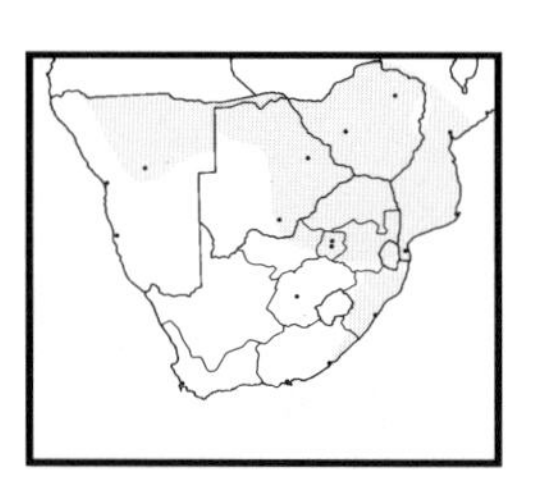

Blackcrowned Tchagra *Tchagra senegala* (744) 23 cm

The brown back, chestnut wings (black towards the centre) and finely barred, brown tail with white outer tips resemble the plumages of other tchagras, but this species can be separated by its all-black, not brown, crown and forehead. Immatures have a mottled crown and buff, not white, tips to the tail. It is less secretive than the other tchagras. The call is a distinctive 'whee-cheree, cheroo, cheree-cheroo', on a descending scale. This bird favours mixed thornveld and riverine scrub but avoids arid areas. R

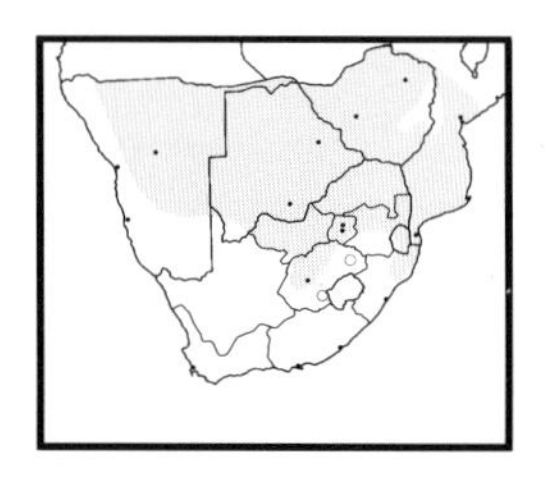

Threestreaked Tchagra *Tchagra australis* (743) 19 cm

Very similar to the Southern Tchagra, with its black eye-stripe, chestnut wings and brown back, this tchagra is smaller than that species and is further distinguished by the dull brown, not reddish-brown, crown which is edged with black where it meets the white eyebrow stripe. Immatures are duller and have buff, not white, tips to the tail. In display it flies steeply into the sky with bursts of wing claps before dropping with its tail spread and giving a series of melodious whistles, similar to the display flight and call of the Southern Tchagra. The Threestreaked Tchagra occurs in thornveld thickets in the bushveld. R

1. Male Southern Boubou
2. Female Southern Boubou
3. Male Tropical Boubou
4. Adult Swamp Boubou
5. Adult Southern Tchagra
6. Adult Blackcrowned Tchagra
7. Adult Threestreaked Tchagra

1	2
3	4
	5
6	7

E *endemic* • R *resident*

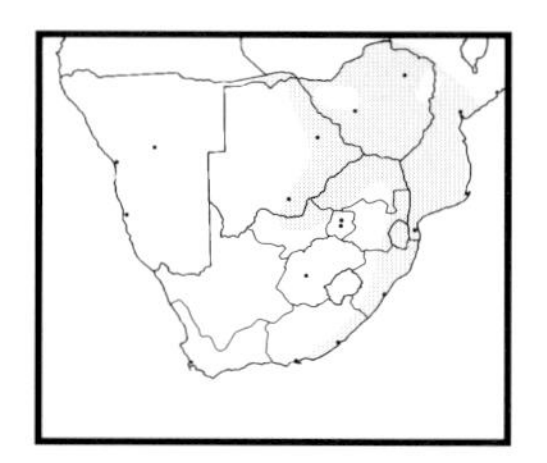

Greyheaded Bush Shrike *Malaconotus blanchoti* (751) 26 cm

This species and the Bokmakierie show some resemblances but they occur in completely different habitats, so confusion should not arise. Both have a grey head, olive-green upperparts and yellow underparts, but the Grey-headed Bush Shrike has a bright yellow, not dark brown, eye and has yellow underparts flushed with orange on the breast. A very large shrike, it has a distinctive, mournful call, 'oooooooop', that sounds much like a foghorn and accounts for its Afrikaans name, *Spookvoël* (Ghostbird). The sexes are alike. Immatures are pale yellow below, and grey on the head with some fine brown barring. The Greyheaded Bush Shrike feeds on insects, frogs, lizards and birds, and forages at all levels in vegetation. It is found in woodland and riverine thickets. R

Immature Orangebreasted Bush Shrike

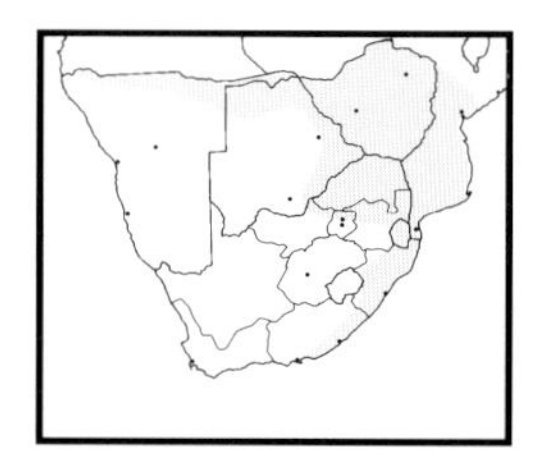

Orangebreasted Bush Shrike *Telophorus sulfureopectus* (748) 19 cm

This species superficially resembles a very small Greyheaded Bush Shrike, the yellow underparts showing an orange tinge on the breast, but its yellow forehead and eyebrow and its dark eye distinguish it from that species. Immatures are duller than the adults, lacking the yellow on the face and the orange flush on the breast. The Orangebreasted Bush Shrike is easily recognizable by its song, a repeated 'poo-poo-poo-pooooo', but it is often difficult to locate because of its skulking nature. It frequents riverine acacia scrub and thornveld thickets where it feeds in the upper strata of trees and bushes, searching for insects. R

Immature Gorgeous Bush Shrike

Olive Bush Shrike *Telophorus olivaceus* (750) 18 cm

This species occurs in two colour morphs. The olive morph is the duller of the two; it has an olive head and back, and a yellow eyebrow above the black face mask which extends through the eye to the ear coverts; the underparts are yellow suffused with orange. The ruddy form has a distinctive white eyebrow above the black face mask, a dark grey cap and an olive back while the underparts are a pinkish buff. Females of both morphs lack the black face mask. Immatures of both morphs are similar to the females, lacking the male's head markings, and show faint brown barring on the breast. Olive Bush Shrikes feed on insects and fruit, figs in particular. Their call is variable and includes a whistled 'teeoo-teeoo-teeoo-teeoo' and a call similar to the Orangebreasted Bush Shrike's 'poo-poo-poo-pooooo'. The Olive Bush Shrike is found on the edges of evergreen forest and in dense riverine bush. R

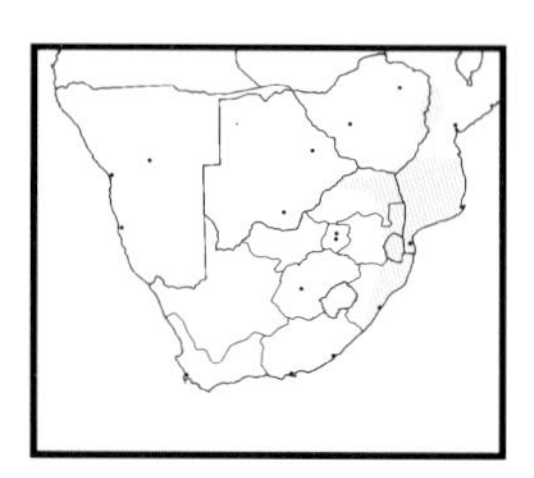

Gorgeous Bush Shrike *Telophorus quadricolor* (747) 19 cm

This species has olive-green upperparts, including the head, which immediately distinguishes it from the Bokmakierie and the Orangebreasted Bush Shrike, both of which have grey heads. On the underside the throat is bright red and bordered by a black breast band, and the belly is yellowish orange contrasting with a red flush to the vent. Females are duller than the males. Immatures are yellow below and olive above, separable from the immature Orangebreasted Bush Shrike and Olive Bush Shrike, which have grey heads. The Gorgeous Bush Shrike may be seen in thornveld, coastal and evergreen forest thickets, foraging low down in vegetation but also on the ground flicking over leaves with its bill in the same manner as a thrush (see page 200). Its call is a bell-like 'kong-kong-kooit' and a harsh, guttural 'graak-graak' alarm note; this species is more often heard than seen. R

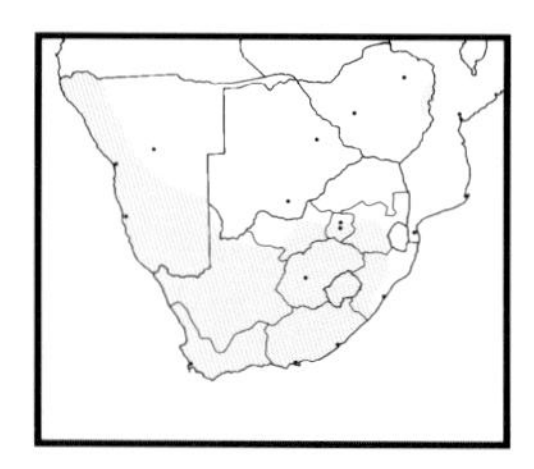

Bokmakierie *Telophorus zeylonus* (746) 23 cm

The Bokmakierie has a grey head and olive-green upperparts and differs from the Greyheaded Bush Shrike in having a broad yellow eyebrow over a dark, not yellow, eye and by its yellow underparts with a broad black bib (which is diagnostic) across the breast. It flies with fast wing beats and shows a bright yellow tip to its otherwise green tail (seen as it fans its tail on landing) which readily identifies it. The sexes are alike. Immatures are duller than the adults, lacking the black breast band, and are a greyish yellow with fine bars below. Bokmakieries feed mostly on the ground in arid areas and low down in vegetation in other areas. They take insects, birds, lizards, snakes and frogs. These birds occur in thornveld, *Euphorbia* scrub and scrub bushes; they are not uncommon in suburban gardens. They call a variable ringing song, 'bokmakiri, bokmakiri, koki-koki-koki', and harsh alarm notes, 'krrr'. E

1. Adult Greyheaded Bush Shrike
2. Adult Orangebreasted Bush Shrike
3. Male Olive Bush Shrike
4. Adult Gorgeous Bush Shrike
5. Immature Gorgeous Bush Shrike
6. Adult Bokmakierie

1	2
3	4
5	6

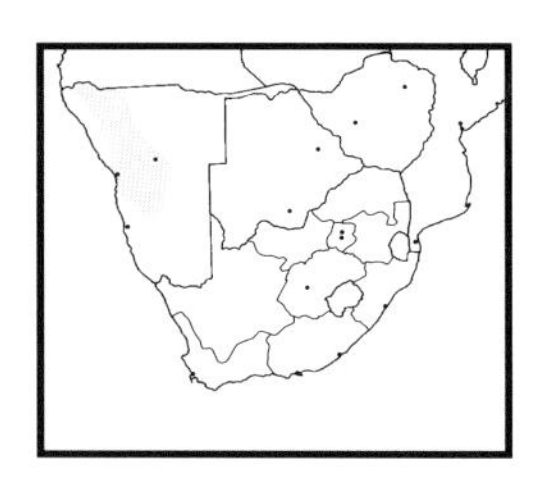

Whitetailed Shrike *Lanioturdus torquatus* (752) 15 cm

This short-tailed shrike has a large head with a white forehead, a black crown, a black face mask contrasting with a bright yellow eye, a grey back and a tail that is all white except for the black tip. Below, a black breast band separates the pure white throat and the underparts. Immatures have a light brown eye and a narrower breast band. The call is made up of loud drawn-out whistles and harsh cackling. This shrike spends a lot of its time foraging on the ground, but also forages in trees and bushes. It occurs in bushveld and in thornveld. NE

Southern Whitecrowned Shrike *Eurocephalus anguitimens* (756) 24 cm

The adult bird has a pure white crown and nape, dark brown ear coverts, a greyish-brown back and tail, and in flight shows a conspicuous white rump. Immatures are browner with a mottled crown and whitish ear coverts. These birds forage from a perch, flying to the ground to walk about. Their call is a shrill whistled 'kree, kree, kree', often given in chorus. Frequently seen in pairs and sometimes in groups of five or six, they occur in mixed dry woodland and savannas, and when not breeding become nomadic. R

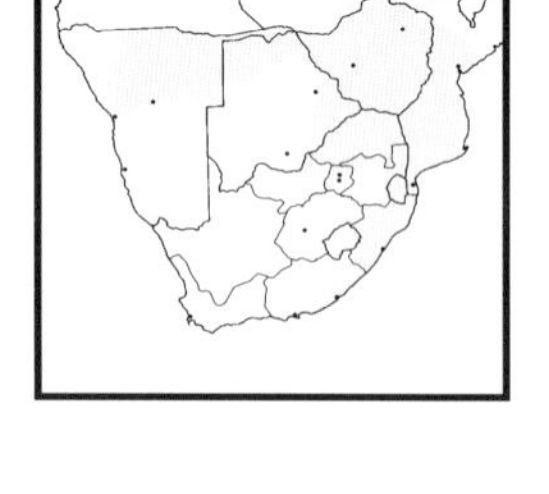

Puffback *Dryoscopus cubla* (740) 18 cm

The male has a white rump that is conspicuous and puffed up during courtship displays when the bird beats its wings and flits around with its tail cocked. It has an all-black crown, forehead and eyebrow. The eye colour varies depending on range: yellow in the south and red in the north. Females are duller above with a white forehead and eyebrow. Immatures have a brown eye and are buffy where adults are white. When not calling its repeated, two-syllabled 'chick-weeo' it is easily overlooked as it forages in the upper strata of forests. This is a ubiquitous shrike of the bushveld, evergreen forests and coastal bush. R

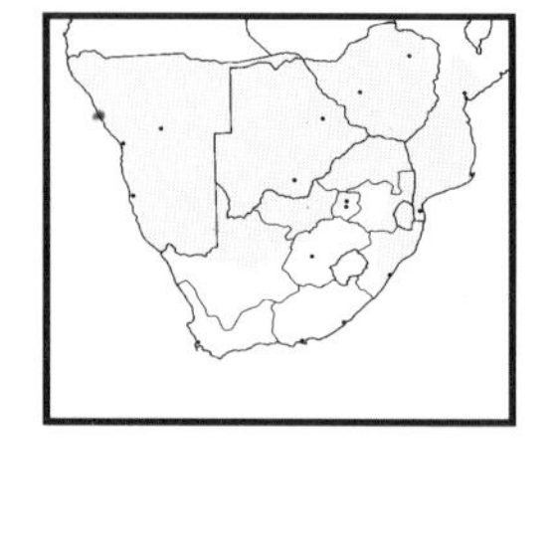

Brubru *Nilaus afer* (741) 15 cm

Also known as the 'telephone bird' because of the male's shrill trilling 'prrr' call, this species can be likened to a very large batis, but its heavy bill and size distinguish it. Males have a black crown, a black eye-stripe, and an extensive white forehead and eyebrow stripe extending to almost encircle the crown. Females are similar but have a brown crown, a brown line through the eye, and paler chestnut flanks. The race to the northeast of the region tends to lack the black stripe through the eye. Brubrus frequent acacia bush and riverine woodland. R

Helmetshrikes Family Prionopidae

Small to medium-sized birds with short, hooked bills and bristled foreheads, all southern African species are gregarious, occurring in groups, usually of four to ten birds. All breed co-operatively.

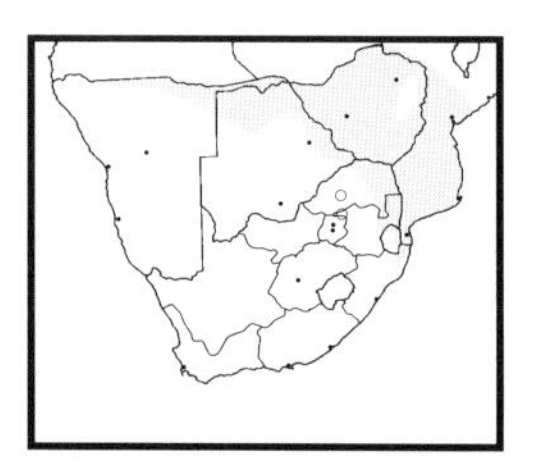

Redbilled Helmetshrike *Prionops retzii* (754) 22 cm

Adults are glossy black with an obvious white vent and white tip to the tail. They have a red bill and a red eye wattle surrounding a yellow iris. Immatures are brown where the adult is black, have a dull bill and no eye wattle. The Redbilled Helmetshrike mobs predators such as snakes and owls, making loud grating and bill-clicking sounds. Favouring deciduous broad-leaved woodland, mopane and miombo woodland, it feeds along branches in the upper canopy and moves from tree to tree with a fairly fast, low and slightly undulating flight. R

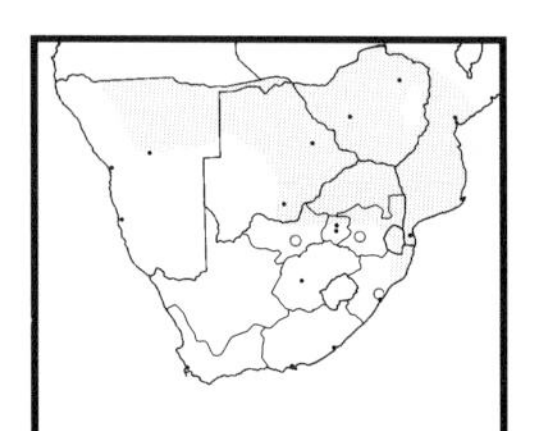

White Helmetshrike *Prionops plumatus* (753) 20 cm

An unmistakable species, this bird displays similar behaviour to the Redbilled Helmetshrike. Its bright yellow eye-ring surrounding a yellow iris contrasts with the grey mantle and crown. The underparts are pure white extending around the neck as a complete collar. Immatures lack the eye wattle and are tinged with brown above. In flight the white lines in the wings and the white outer tail feathers contrast with the otherwise black wings and back. The call is a series of loud clicks, given as the bird flies quickly from bush to bush. It favours mixed woodland and thornveld where it forages along branches of trees and on the ground, keeping in touch with others through contact calls. R

1. Adult Whitetailed Shrike
2. Male Puffback
3. Adult Southern Whitecrowned Shrike
4. Female Puffback
5. Female Brubru
6. Adult Redbilled Helmetshrike
7. Adult White Helmetshrike

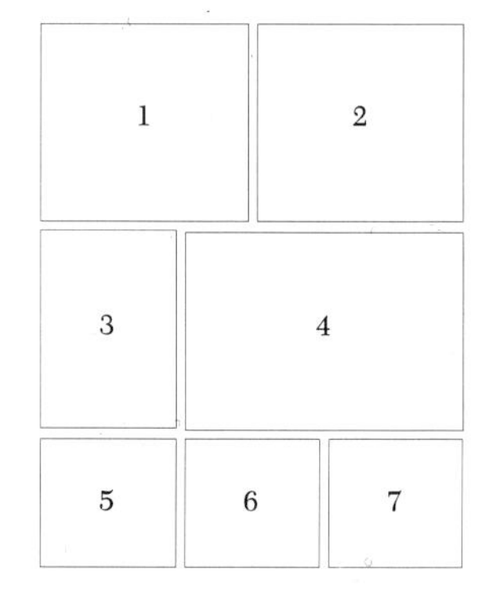

NE *near endemic* • R *resident*

Starlings Family Sturnidae

Starlings are mostly small to medium-sized birds with strong, pointed bills. The *Lamprotornis* starlings are mostly iridescent blue and green in colour; the others are variable. These birds eat insects and fruit and most feed on the ground. They occur across the habitat spectrum. Some species are commensal with man. Many form flocks outside the breeding season.

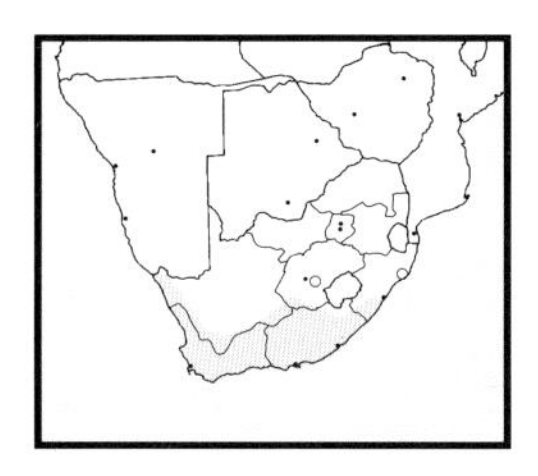

European Starling *Sturnus vulgaris* (757) 21 cm

This alien species was introduced to the Cape from Europe towards the end of the nineteenth century by Cecil John Rhodes and is now resident throughout the eastern and western Cape. Its bright yellow bill (dark in non-breeding plumage) and its black and iridescent green plumage with buff speckling above and below readily identify it. The flight is fast with rapid wing beats, and when in flocks the birds' flight is highly synchronized. A gregarious species, it occurs in rural, urban and suburban situations. Its call is a mixture of high-pitched squeaks and whistles. R

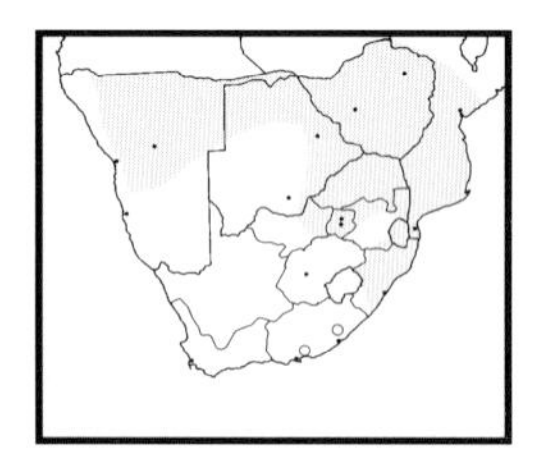

Plumcoloured Starling *Cinnyricinclus leucogaster* (761) 19 cm

Although in some light conditions this small starling may appear black above and white below, it has an iridescent purple or violet head and upperparts. Females and immatures are quite different from the males, being mottled brown above and white below, with heavy dark streaks on the throat, breast and flanks. Plumcoloured Starlings nest in holes in trees and when not breeding often occur in flocks of only males or only females. They also tend to associate in winter-feeding flocks with Wattled Starlings and Glossy Starlings (see page 256). The call is a series of short, buzzy whistles, somewhat thrush-like. A conspicuous species, this bird perches at the tops of trees, commonly in savannas, bushveld, and miombo and teak woodland. S, R

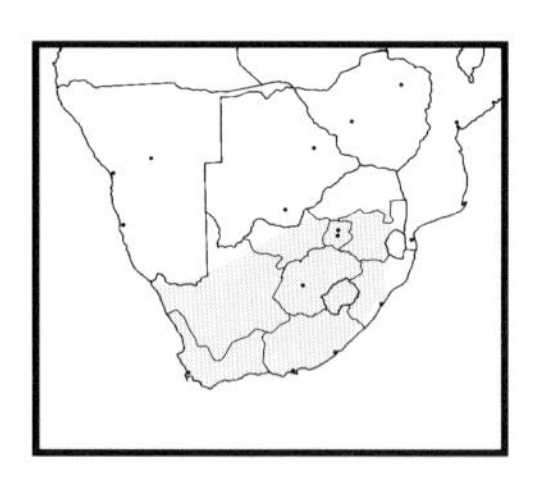

Pied Starling *Spreo bicolor* (759) 27 cm

The yellow gape of this bird contrasts with its black bill; its white eye and black legs differentiate it from the Indian Myna. Otherwise it is overall dark brown, tinged greenish on the tail and with a white vent. It is a gregarious species, feeding and roosting in large flocks in trees and reedbeds. It nests in a burrow in a river bank, donga or quarry, usually colonially. Immatures are dull black and lack any sheen; the eye is dark brown and the gape is white. The Pied Starling may be seen in open grasslands, farmyards, and on the moister eastern edge of the Karoo in fynbos and scrub bush. The call is a series of squeaky 'skeeeeo, skeeeo, skeeeo' notes. E

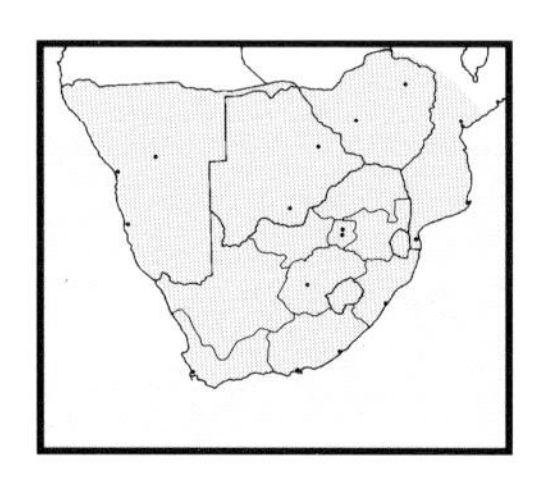

Wattled Starling *Creatophora cinerea* (760) 21 cm

In flight this starling is similar in shape to the European Starling, but shows a whitish rump with a grey back and grey upper wing coverts. Breeding males are distinctive with their black crown and facial wattle, and extensive yellow hind crown; otherwise the plumage is greyish except for the flight feathers and tail which are black. Non-breeding males do not have the wattle, and have a greyish crown (uniform with the remaining upperparts), a small yellow patch below and behind the eye, and black lores. Females are similar to non-breeding males but may show black wing coverts, and immatures resemble the females but are browner. Wattled Starlings roost and nest communally in trees. This nomadic species occurs in large flocks at all times and may occur anywhere in the region. Its call is a series of thin squeaky whistles and warbles. R

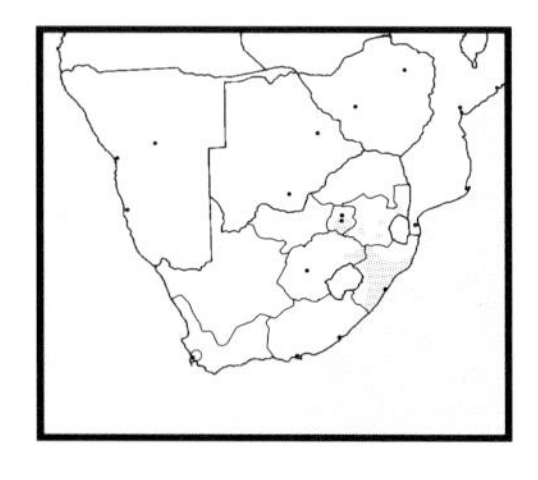

Indian Myna *Acridotheres tristis* (758) 25 cm

This species from India and eastern Asia was introduced into the region at Durban around the end of the nineteenth century. An aggressive yet wary bird, it has displaced indigenous starlings in suburbia. It has a bright yellow bill, a bare yellow patch behind the eye, yellow legs, a black head, chestnut underparts and a white vent. In flight it may be identified by its white wing patches and the white tips to the tail. Showing a penchant for cultivated kikuyu lawns, it is rarely seen outside cities and their urban sprawls. It feeds mainly on insects but will also take fruit and most food scraps. The bird's call is a mixture of loud whistles, gurglings and croaks. R

1. Adult European Starling
2. Female Plumcoloured Starling
3. Male Plumcoloured Starling
4. Male and female Wattled Starlings (non-breeding)
5. Adult Pied Starling
6. Male (breeding) and female Wattled Starlings
7. Adult Pied Starling
8. Adult Indian Myna

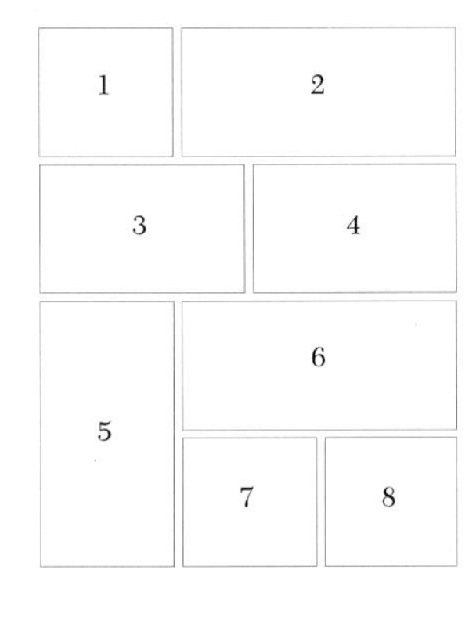

R *resident* • S *summer visitor* • E *endemic*

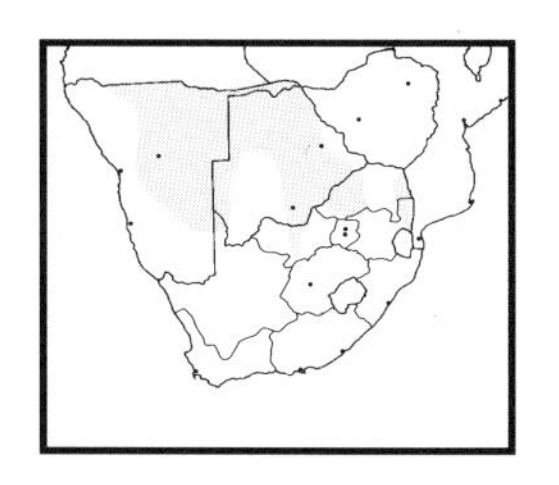

Burchell's Starling *Lamprotornis australis* (762) 34 cm

This large, black and glossy green starling with a long, broad, tapered tail could be mistaken for the Longtailed Starling but is much heavier and in its laboured flight shows a much broader, shorter and rounded tail and broader wings. It is usually seen in pairs or small groups and is not gregarious like the Longtailed Starling. Burchell's Starling nests in a natural hole in a tree, usually quite high up, in thornveld and dry broad-leaved woodland. Its call is a mixture of throaty chortles and chuckles. R

Longtailed Starling *Lamprotornis mevesii* (763) 34 cm

The adult Longtailed Starling and adult Burchell's Starling are the only glossy starlings with dark brown eyes and both have a dark face and black ear coverts. This species is smaller and slimmer than Burchell's Starling, and has a longer, narrower and graduated tail. It roosts colonially, performing aerial manoeuvres before settling for the night. It chooses natural holes in trees for nesting, or females may excavate their own holes in soft-wooded branches. The Longtailed Starling prefers semi-arid savanna, especially tall mopane and riverine woodland habitat. The call is a churring 'chwirr-chwirr' and a harsh 'keeeaa' note. R

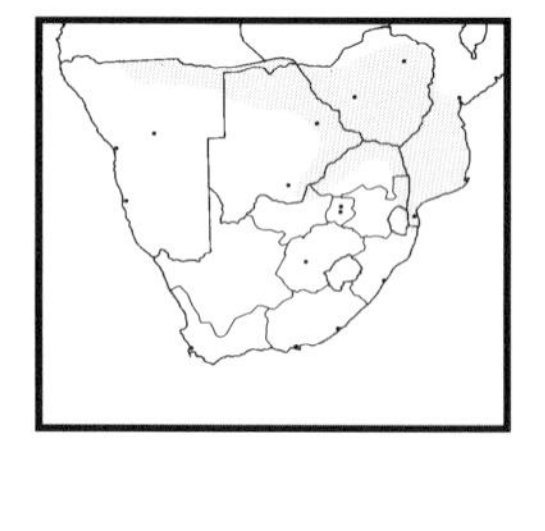

Greater Blue-eared Starling *Lamprotornis chalybaeus* (765) 23 cm

This species, the Lesser Blue-eared Starling, the Glossy Starling and the Blackbellied Starling all have yellow-orange eyes as adults and differ from one another on ear-covert size, belly colour, jizz and call. Adults of this species are shinier than the Glossy Starling and have a dark-blue to black ear patch and a blue-black belly and flanks; the ear coverts contrast more strongly with the head colouring than in the Glossy Starling. The Greater Blue-eared Starling has a larger ear patch than does the Lesser Blue-eared Starling. Immatures are brownish black with a greyish eye. The 'skwee-aaar' call is quite different to those of the Glossy Starling and the Lesser Blue-eared Starling. This species occurs in miombo and teak woodland, riverine forest and in savannas. R

Lesser Blue-eared Starling *Lamprotornis chloropterus* (766) 20 cm

Smaller and with a finer bill than the Greater Blue-eared Starling, this species has a less extensive dark blue ear patch, appearing more as a dark line through the eye, and its belly and flanks are purplish. In flight, the wing beat is deeper than in the Greater Blue-eared Starling. Immatures are chestnut-brown below (other 'glossy' starling immatures are always blue-black in colour) and therefore serve as an aid to identification when seen with the adults. They feed in the tree canopy as well as on the ground and nest in tree holes built by woodpeckers, or behind loose bark in the forks of large trees. The call is a more musical, higher-pitched 'cheeu-cheeu-chirrup' than that of the Greater Blue-eared Starling. It also utters a clear 'wirri-girri' flight call on take-off. This species occurs predominantly in *Brachystegia* woodland. R

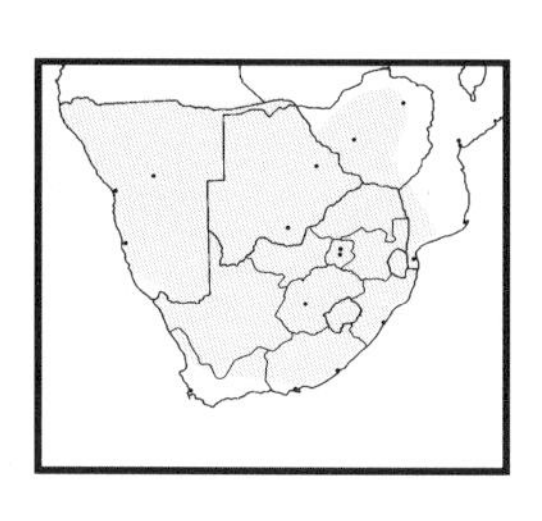

Glossy Starling *Lamprotornis nitens* (764) 25 cm

This species resembles both the Greater Blue-eared Starling and the Lesser Blue-eared Starling but is distinguished from those species by being uniformly dull glossy green, including the ear coverts and belly. All three of these species have one or two rows of black spots along the covert edges of the folded wing and the Glossy Starling often shows a purplish-brown patch (although this is not diagnostic) on the shoulder of the folded wing. Adults have a yellow-orange eye and indistinct ear coverts. Immatures are similar to the adults but are blacker and less iridescent, and have a brownish eye. The call is a slurred 'trrr-chree-chrrr'. Glossy Starlings nest in natural holes in trees, under eaves of buildings and in hollow fence posts. R

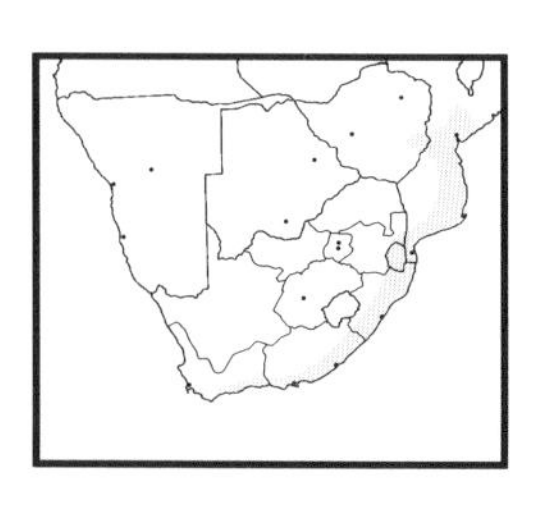

Blackbellied Starling *Lamprotornis corruscus* (768) 21 cm

The smallest, darkest and least glossy of the glossy starlings, the Blackbellied Starling lacks distinct ear coverts, and has a black belly. The adults may be separated from immature glossy starlings on size, by their yellow-orange, not brown, eyes and by habitat preference. The immature Blackbellied Starling is dark brown with a dark grey eye. This species feeds mainly on fruit and flowers, and nests in old barbet or woodpecker holes fairly high up in the canopy. Its call is a jumble of harsh trill and shrill whistles. It forages in the canopy of evergreen and coastal forests. R

Immature Lesser Blue-eared Starling

1. Adult Burchell's Starling
2. Adult Blackbellied Starling
3. Adult Longtailed Starling
4. Adult Greater Blue-eared Starling
5. Adult Lesser Blue-eared Starling
6. Adult Glossy Starling

1	2
3	4
5	6

R *resident*

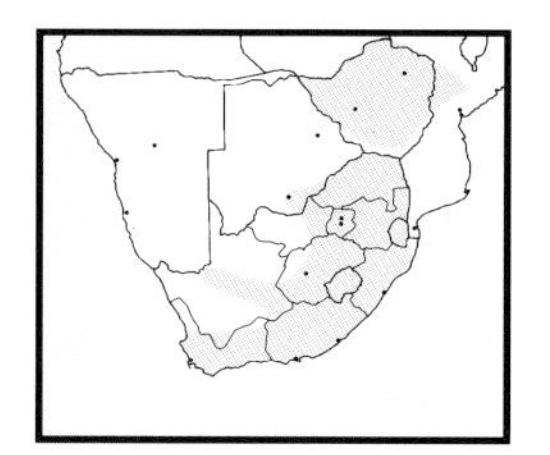

Redwinged Starling *Onychognathus morio* (769) 27 cm

A large, blue-black starling, this species has chestnut to pale russet primaries that show as an extensive russet wing patch in flight. Females differ from the males, having the head, mantle and upper breast dark grey. Where its range overlaps with that of the Palewinged Starling, the russet wing patch and dark red (appearing dark brown), not orange-red, eye separate the two species. Immatures are similar to the adult males. The Redwinged Starling nests in rock holes, crevices or on a ledge under an overhang. Out of the breeding season it is gregarious, although it is usually seen in small groups, even during the breeding season. It may be seen hopping on the ground foraging for insects but prefers fruits and berries. Its call, a whistled 'tcheew' or 'wheeooo', is different from that of the Palewinged Starling. The Redwinged Starling frequents rocky cliffs, gorges, forested cliffs and mountain ranges; and is not uncommon in suburbia. R

Adult Redwinged Starling

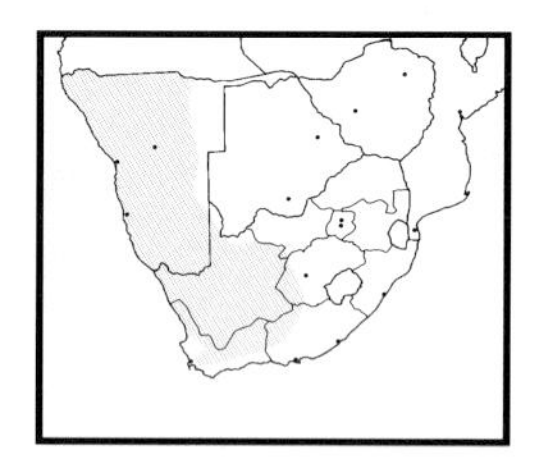

Palewinged Starling *Onychognathus nabouroup* (770) 26 cm

A large, entirely glossy blue-black starling, this bird could be confused with the Redwinged Starling but it has white to pale buffy primaries that show as an extensive creamy-white wing patch in flight; when the wing is folded, this patch appears russet because of the rusty edging to the primaries. The eye is yellow to orange, whereas that of the Redwinged Starling is dark. The sexes are alike, and the immatures are duller than the adults. This is a gregarious species even when breeding. It hops on the ground, feeding on insects, sometimes collected off Klipspringers, and on fruit. In flight it utters a harsh chatter and gives warbling Glossy Starling-like 'preeoo' noises; it's call is quite unlike that of the Redwinged Starling. Like the Redwinged Starling, it occurs in gorges, and on cliffs and mountain ranges. NE

Adult Palewinged Starling

Oxpeckers Family Buphagidae

These brown and buff-coloured birds have short, heavy bills which are laterally flattened. They are highly specialized feeders, spending much of their time perched on large wild and domestic animals from which they remove ectoparasites and loose skin with scissoring movements of the bill. This unusual feeding technique is aided by the birds' sharp, curved claws, and by the stiff tail feathers which are used for support. Oxpeckers are gregarious birds and breed co-operatively.

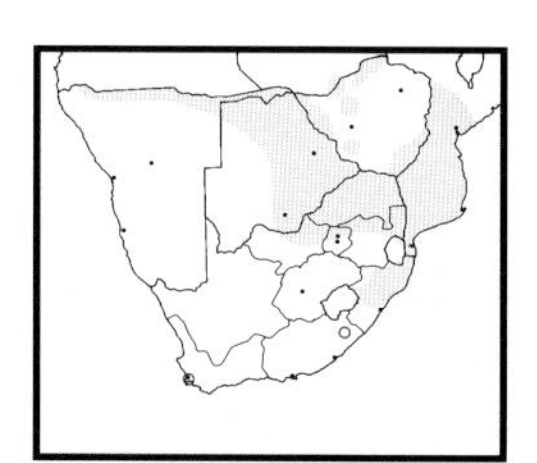

Redbilled Oxpecker *Buphagus erythrorhynchus* (772) 22 cm

Similar in size to a starling, the Redbilled Oxpecker may be distinguished from the Yellowbilled Oxpecker by its all-red bill, the bright yellow eye wattle surrounding its red eye and, in flight from above, by its uniform brown colour with a dark, not pale, rump. The sexes are alike. Immatures are similar in colour to the adults but have a brown bill and a dark brown eye. This bird is likely to be seen mostly on antelope, giraffe and cattle. Its cup-shaped nest is placed in a hole in a tree and consists largely of grasses and animal hair. A common resident in reserves and national parks, it is uncommon elsewhere, especially in stock-farming areas where the use of toxic insecticides and dips has significantly reduced its numbers. The call comprises sharp hisses, 'zzzzzzist, zzzzzist', and scolding 'churrr' notes. R

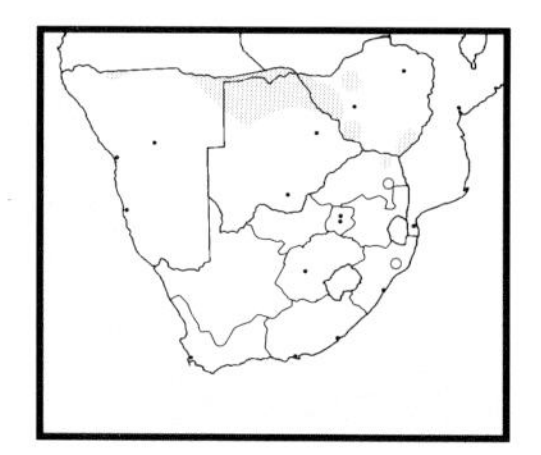

Yellowbilled Oxpecker *Buphagus africanus* (771) 22 cm

This species differs from the Redbilled Oxpecker by having the basal half of the bill yellow (and the remainder red, whereas the bill of the Redbilled Oxpecker is entirely red), and by having an orange to red eye without an obvious eye wattle. The sexes are alike. Immatures of this species are similar to the immature Redbilled Oxpecker. In flight the Yellowbilled Oxpecker shows a pale rump which readily separates it from the Redbilled Oxpecker, which shows a dark rump. These birds tend to favour thinner-haired animals such as hippopotamus, buffalo and rhinoceros, but are just as likely to be found on antelope and cattle. They feed by plucking, not combing, at ectoparasites and wound tissues. When disturbed they fly off with a noisy, chittering 'kriss, kriss' sound. They make their nests in natural holes in trees and line them with grass and animal fur. R

1. Female Redwinged Starling
2. Adult Palewinged Starling
3. Adult Palewinged Starling
4. Adult Yellowbilled Oxpecker
5. Adult Yellowbilled Oxpecker
6. Adult Redbilled Oxpecker

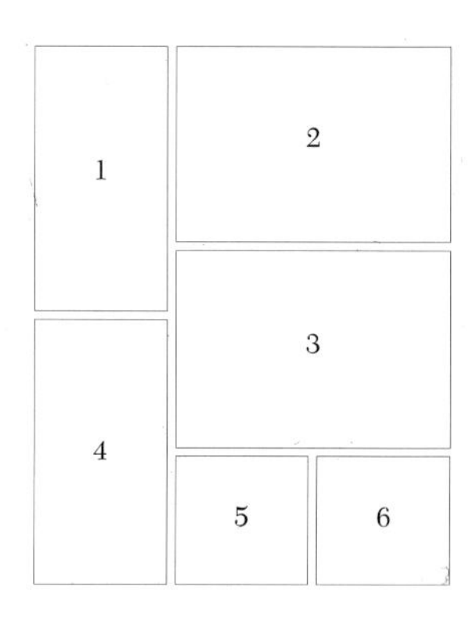

R *resident* • NE *near endemic*

Sugarbirds and sunbirds

Families Promeropidae and Nectariniidae

Most male sunbirds have brilliant plumage and are easily identifiable. Females are drabber and can be confusingly similar. The long, decurved bills are ideal for probing flowers for nectar, but the birds also eat insects to supplement their diets. When probing flowers, they usually perch and, contrary to popular belief, rarely hover. Their flight is fast and dashing. Sugarbirds are larger and longer-tailed than sunbirds, with long, decurved bills, and are less brightly coloured. They are closely associated with proteas and are seasonal migrants.

Female Bronze Sunbird

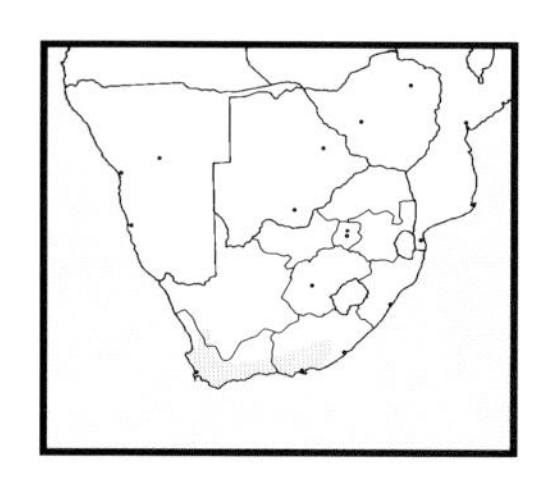

Cape Sugarbird *Promerops cafer* (773) m=34-44 cm; f=25-29 cm

The Cape Sugarbird is easily distinguished from Gurney's Sugarbird by its very long, wispy tail and distinct malar stripes; otherwise, it is brown above with a white belly heavily streaked with brown and a bright yellow vent. Immatures lack the yellow vent and dark flank streaks. During territorial displays the males often perch at the top of an open bush from which they fly with rapidly beating wings and a flicking tail action. A noisy and conspicuous species, its song is a complex jumble of starling-like chirps and whistles. It occurs especially where proteas abound, from the coast to the foothills of mountain slopes. E

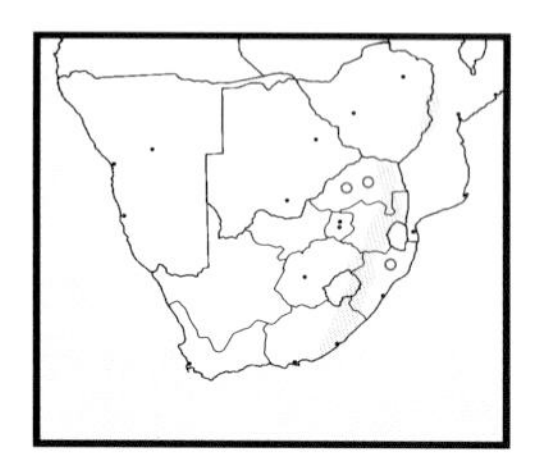

Gurney's Sugarbird *Promerops gurneyi* (774) m=29 cm; f=23 cm

This species can be distinguished from the Cape Sugarbird by its shorter tail, white throat which lacks malar stripes, broad russet breast band and reddish crown. The sexes are similar; immatures resemble the females. In display, males perch conspicuously, then fly up steeply and dive steeply down again. Gurney's Sugarbird occurs in mountainous terrain and undergoes some altitudinal movements dependent on flowering shrubs. Its song is a higher-pitched, more melodious mixture of twanging and rattling notes than that of the Cape Sugarbird. E

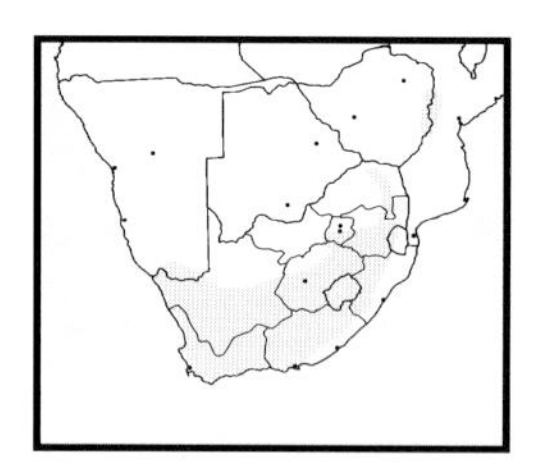

Malachite Sunbird *Nectarinia famosa* (775) m=25 cm; f=15 cm

The breeding male is metallic-green with elongated central tail feathers and yellow pectoral tufts, although these are often not visible. The females and immatures are yellowish grey above and yellow green below, with a yellow malar stripe and some indistinct brown streaks on the breast; they lack the elongated tail feathers of the breeding male. Non-breeding males may or may not have elongated tail feathers. The Malachite Sunbird is subject to seasonal movements from higher altitudes and occurs in fynbos. Its call is a loud 'tseep-tseep' and a series of twittering notes. R

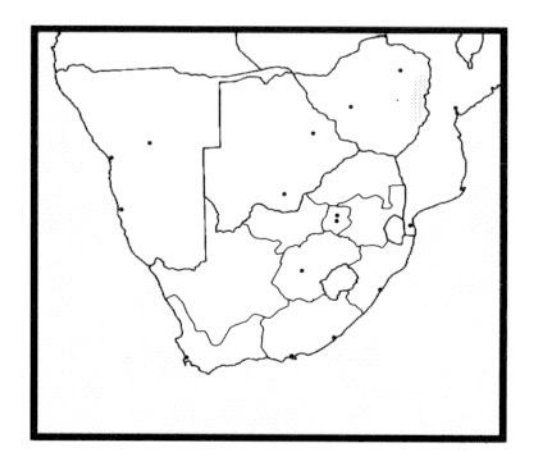

Bronze Sunbird *Nectarinia kilimensis* (776) m=21 cm; f=14 cm

Males are iridescent bronze to metallic purple in colour, appearing black under some light conditions. Unlike the Malachite Sunbird, male Bronze Sunbirds do not pass through a non-breeding or eclipse plumage. Females are smaller than the males, and differ from female Malachite Sunbirds by having a dark face mask, a grey throat, and brighter yellow underparts streaked with grey. The bird frequents evergreen forest edges, rank grasses and scrubby vegetation. Its call comprises a repeated 'chee-wit' and high-pitched twittering notes. R

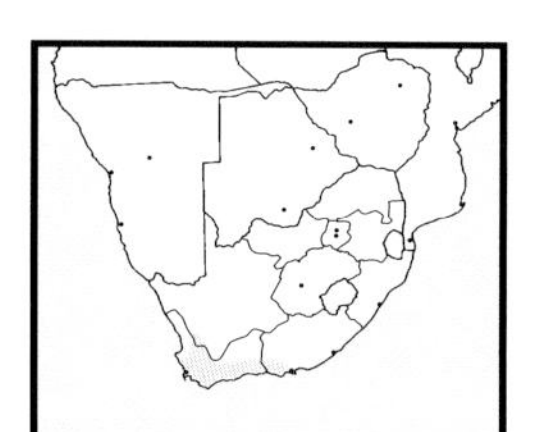

Orangebreasted Sunbird *Nectarinia violacea* (777) m=15 cm; f=12 cm

This a small, exquisitely coloured sunbird. Males have a metallic-green head, a purple throat patch, a bright orange breast fading to yellow on the vent, and elongated central tail feathers. Females and immatures lack the elongated tail feathers and are duller, being olive-grey above and yellow-green below. This sunbird occurs in the winter-rainfall area, among fynbos with *Protea* and *Erica* species. Its call is a metallic twanging, and also rapid 'ticks', given in flight. E

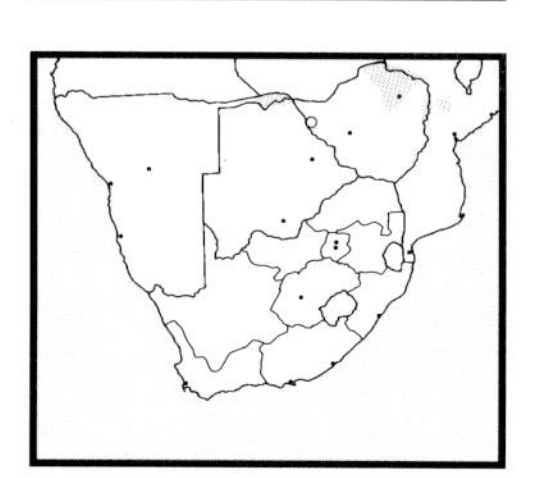

Coppery Sunbird *Nectarinia cuprea* (778) 12 cm

In poor light this bird could be mistaken for a very small Bronze Sunbird or a Black Sunbird. Males are a metallic golden-coppery colour and have a short, square tail, lacking the elongated tail feathers of the male Bronze Sunbird. Immatures resemble the females, being drab olive-green above, and yellow below. This species occurs in a variety of woodland habitats. Its call is harsh 'chit-chat', and a soft warbling song. S

1. Adult Cape Sugarbird
2. Adult Cape Sugarbird
3. Adult Gurney's Sugarbird
4. Adult Malachite Sunbird
5. Male Bronze Sunbird
6. Female Bronze Sunbird
7. Adult Orangebreasted Sunbird
8. Adult Orangebreasted Sunbird
9. Male (left) and female (right) Coppery Sunbird

1		2
3	4	
	5	6
7	8	9

E *endemic* • R *resident* • S *summer visitor*

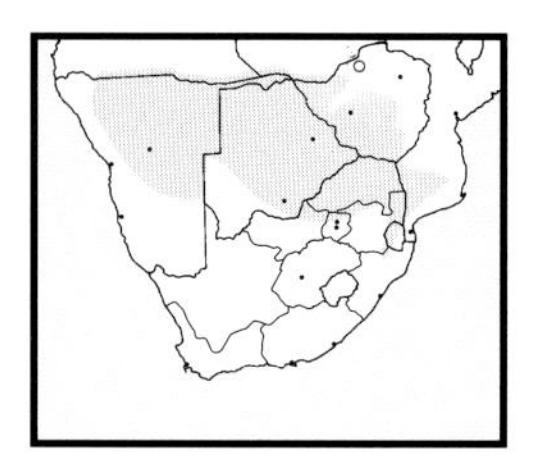

Marico Sunbird *Nectarinia mariquensis* (779) 14 cm

This species and the Purplebanded Sunbird both have black bellies and red-hued breast bands. The Marico Sunbird can be differentiated from the Purplebanded Sunbird, however, by being larger overall and having a longer, thicker and more decurved bill. Further, in bright sunlight the green sheen on the upperparts of the Marico Sunbird shows a distinct coppery iridescence which is absent in the Purplebanded Sunbird. Females, males in eclipse and immatures are exceedingly difficult to tell apart from other similar sunbirds unless the shape and voice are well known. The call is a long series of short 'tsips' and the song is a fast warbling. Very active and aggressive, the Marico Sunbird will not hesitate to chase other birds away from a food source or breeding area. This species occurs in dry woodland and semi-desert scrub. R

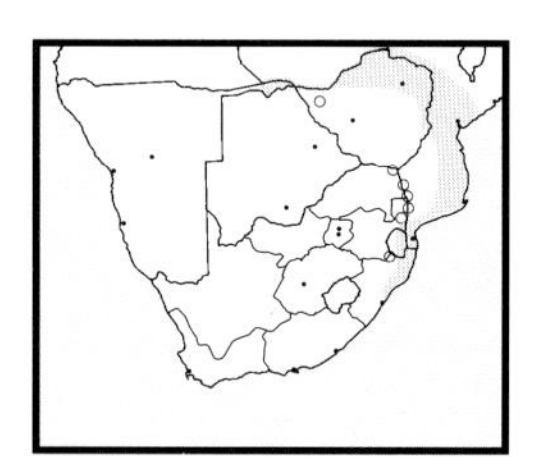

Purplebanded Sunbird *Nectarinia bifasciata* (780) 12 cm

This sunbird appears to be an overall smaller version of the Marico Sunbird. It has a smaller, thinner, shorter and less decurved bill than that species. The female and immature birds are also smaller versions of the female and immature Marico Sunbird, being grey-brown above with very pale yellow underparts, and having a shorter bill. The song is a high-pitched 'teet-teet-tit-tit', accelerating at the end and never sustained as is the call of the Marico Sunbird. This species prefers moist woodland and is found in mangrove swamps and coastal forests. R

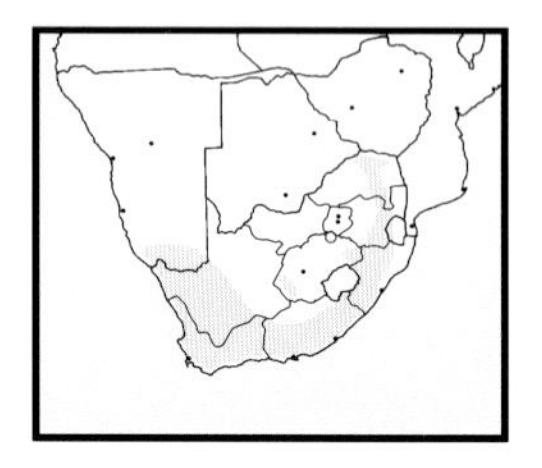

Lesser Doublecollared Sunbird *Nectarinia chalybea* (783) 12 cm

This is a scaled-down version of the Greater Doublecollared Sunbird and where they occur together the two species are easily told apart by a direct comparison in size. The male of the species has a narrow red breast band and a short, thin bill. Females and immatures are overall greyer in tone than the female and immature Greater Doublecollared Sunbird. The call is a harsh 'chee-chee' and the song is fast and variable, rising and falling in pitch. This is the common sunbird in fynbos but also occurs in evergreen forests, protea scrub and even in suburban gardens. E

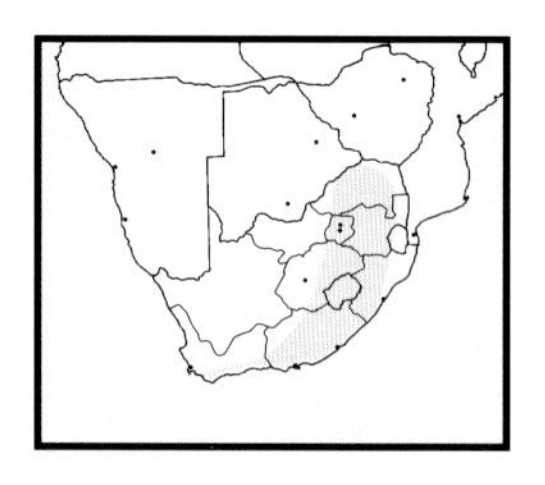

Greater Doublecollared Sunbird *Nectarinia afra* (785) 14 cm

This species can be differentiated from the Lesser Doublecollared Sunbird by its overall larger size, obvious if the two species are seen in close proximity to each other. Further, the Greater Doublecollared Sunbird has a broad red breast band which extends on to the belly, and its bill is long, decurved and thick at the base. The female has grey-brown upperparts and is yellow-grey below, and differs from the female Lesser Doublecollared Sunbird by its longer, heavier bill. Immatures resemble the female. The call is a harsh 'tchut-tchut-tchut' and the song is a fast, twittering 'chipping'. This sunbird occurs in montane scrub, fynbos, forest edges and parks and gardens. R

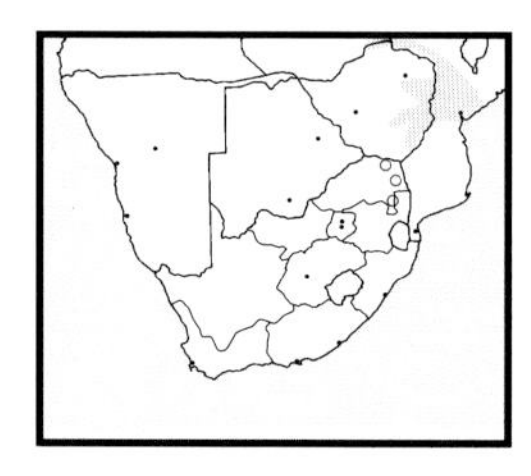

Yellowbellied Sunbird *Nectarinia venusta* (786) 11 cm

Adult male Yellowbellied Sunbirds are unmistakable with their dazzling blue and green upperparts and sulphur-yellow underparts. Females of this species resemble female Whitebellied Sunbirds, that is, being dull brown above and paler below, but have a distinctive yellow wash across the underparts. The immatures resemble the females. The call is a 'tsui-tse-tse' and a trilling song. They favour forest edges in mountainous areas and riverine forest edges. R

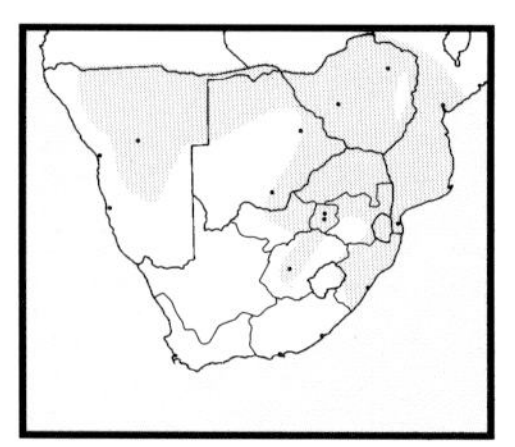

Whitebellied Sunbird *Nectarinia talatala* (787) 11 cm

The male Whitebellied Sunbird is the only sunbird in the region to have a bottle-green head and breast, and a white belly. The female is very similar to females of other sunbird species: uniform dull brown above, and off-white below with indistinct streaking. The immature resembles the female. The call is a loud 'pichee-pichee' and the song a jumble of tinkling notes. This sunbird inhabits a wide range of woodland from dry thornveld to suburbia. R

1. Male Marico Sunbird
2. Female Marico Sunbird
3. Female (top) and male (bottom) Purplebanded Sunbirds
4. Male Lesser Doublecollared Sunbird
5. Female Lesser Doublecollared Sunbird
6. Male Greater Doublecollared Sunbird
7. Female Greater Doublecollared Sunbird
8. Male Yellowbellied Sunbird
9. Male Whitebellied Sunbird
10. Female Whitebellied Sunbird

1	2	3
4	5	6
	7	8
9	10	

R *resident* • E *endemic*

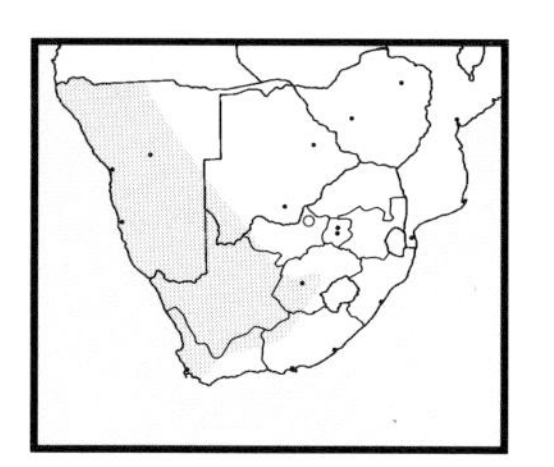

Dusky Sunbird *Nectarinia fusca* (788) 10 cm

The male Dusky Sunbird is variable in colour: some have an all-black head, back and breast and a contrasting white lower belly and vent; others are more mottled black and brown or have black on the throat extending on to the breast in a black stripe. The upperparts rarely show iridescence except for a slight metallic black on the head. When excited or in display the male shows brilliant orange pectoral tufts. The females are the only small sunbirds to show all-white underparts. Immatures resemble the females but have a blackish throat. The call is a scolding 'chrrrr-chrrrr', and this bird also utters a 'chipping' song. This dry-country sunbird is found from desert edge to scrub and thornveld. NE

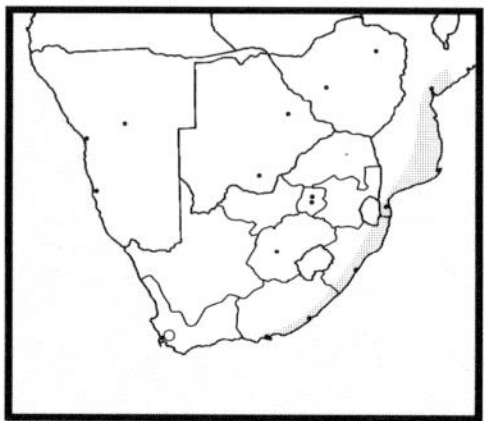

Grey Sunbird *Nectarinia veroxii* (789) 14 cm

Both the males and females of this nondescript sunbird might be overlooked as the female of another sunbird species unless it is seen displaying, when its diagnostic red pectoral tufts are seen. The sexes are similar, and immatures resemble the adults but are more olive below. The call, a harsh and grating 'tzzik-tzzik', is diagnostic. The song is a series of 'chip-chop-chop' notes. The Grey Sunbird is mainly a bird of coastal forest, riverine forest and dune scrub. R

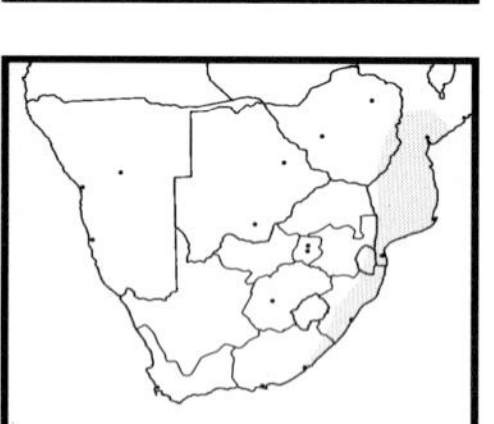

Olive Sunbird *Nectarinia olivacea* (790) 14 cm

This is a dull, unmarked, greenish sunbird which lacks any remarkable field characters, and both the males and females could be overlooked as a drab female sunbird of another species. It could be confused with the Grey Sunbird, which occurs in the same habitat, but this species is distinctly olive, not grey. When displaying and alarmed it erects its sulphur-yellow pectoral tufts. It calls continually, giving a sharp 'tuk-tuk' and an accelerating, descending 'chip-chip-chuup-chupp-cheep'; the flight call is a fast 'tuk-tuk'. It frequents all levels of coastal and montane evergreen forests. R

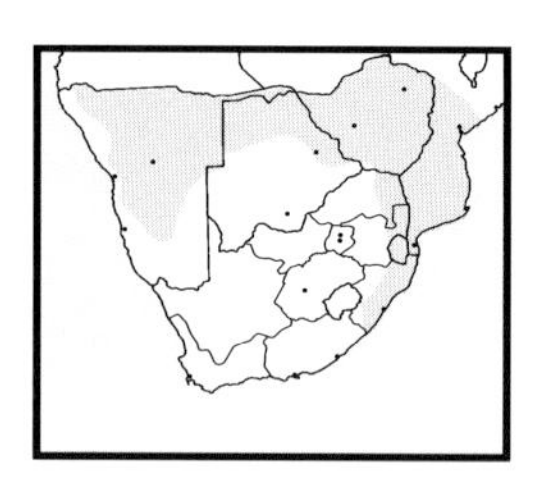

Scarletchested Sunbird *Nectarinia senegalensis* (791) 15 cm

Adult males of this species are unmistakable with their matt black plumage and bright scarlet breast and, seen at closer range, the iridescent green and blue forehead. Females are browner than the similar female Black Sunbird and may be further differentiated from that species by having mottled brown, not streaked, underparts and broad, buffy malar stripes. Immatures resemble the females. The call is a loud, whistled 'cheeup, chup, tooop, toop, toop' song and a harsher 'sship' or 'sshup'. This is a large, aggressive sunbird, chasing all comers to a flowering tree and continually dashing around. It is found in a variety of woodland and parkland habitats. R

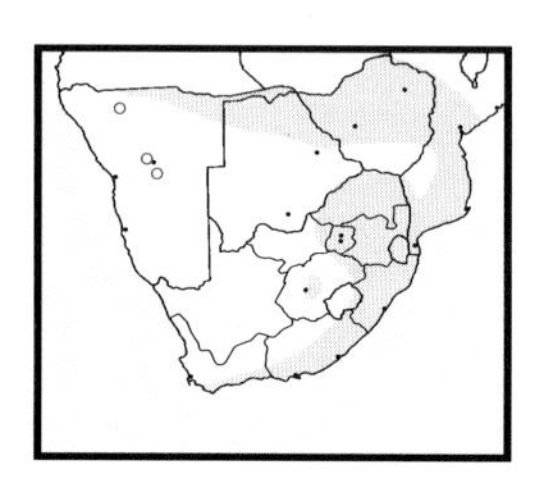

Black Sunbird *Nectarinia amethystina* (792) 15 cm

The only apparently all-black sunbird in the region, when seen at close range the iridescent purple throat, shoulder and rump of this species are evident; the forehead and crown are iridescent emerald-green and black although this is not always obvious as they can be discoloured by yellow or orange pollen. Females are similar to the female Scarletchested Sunbird but are overall very much greyer in appearance and have streaked, not mottled, underparts. The call is a mixture of 'tschiek' flight notes; they give a 'tit-tit-tit' alarm call and have a fast, twittering song. Black Sunbirds frequent forest and forest edges, drier woodland and savanna, and suburbia. R

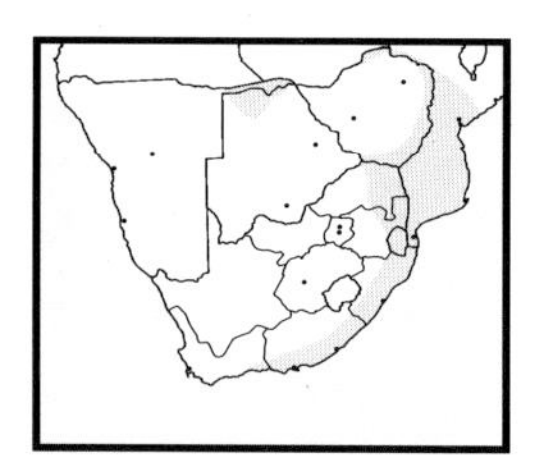

Collared Sunbird *Anthreptes collaris* (793) 10 cm

The smallest sunbird in the region, this species shows iridescent emerald-green upperparts, bright yellow underparts and a very short, almost warbler-like bill. It vaguely resembles the larger Yellowbellied Sunbird (see page 262). The females and immatures are metallic green above and uniformly yellow below, and behave and look like small warblers (see pages 214-18) but can be distinguished by their iridescent green upperparts. The call is a soft 'tswee' and the bird also gives a harsh, chirpy song. This species favours various woodland types from evergreen forests, scrub and riverine forest to dry woodland. R

1. Female Dusky Sunbird
2. Adult Grey Sunbird
3. Adult Olive Sunbird
4. Female Scarletchested Sunbird
5. Male Scarletchested Sunbird
6. Male Black Sunbird
7. Female Black Sunbird
8. Male Collared Sunbird
9. Female Collared Sunbird

1 2 3
4 5
6 7
8 9

NE *near endemic* • R *resident*

Weavers, sparrows, queleas, bishops, widows and Cuckoo Finch Family Ploceidae

Except for sparrows, the males of the species in this group are brightly coloured in summer (some with long tails), and drab in winter. Most are polygamous, males weaving the nests but females performing all parental duties. Sparrows are mainly brown coloured; some exhibit sexual dimorphism and all are monogamous. All are partly or wholly granivorous and live in grassland, marshy habitats or savanna.

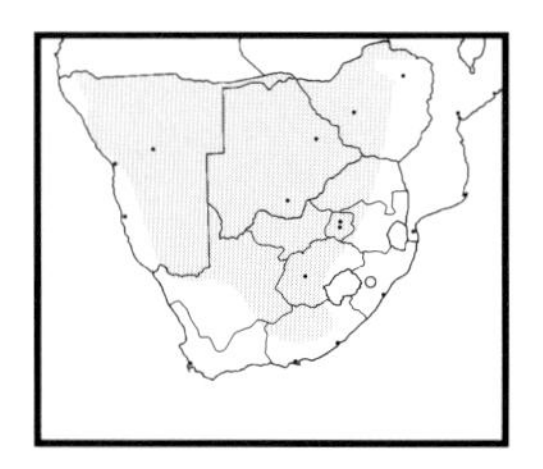

Whitebrowed Sparrow-weaver *Plocepasser mahali* (799) 19 cm

The broad, white eyebrow extending well behind the eye and on to the nape of this bird is vaguely reminiscent of the same feature in the Yellowthroated Sparrow (see page 268). However, the Whitebrowed Sparrow-weaver is a much larger bird, more robust and plumper, shorter tailed and shows a broad white rump in flight. The sexes are similar except for the bill colour, which is black in the male and buff in the female. Immatures resemble the adults but have a pinkish-brown bill. Calls are a loud, liquid 'cheeoop-preeoo-choop' and a harsher 'tweek-tweek' flight chatter. This bird feeds on the ground and on road verges. The large, untidy straw nests do not hang like those of other weavers but are built into the thorny ends of branches. Whitebrowed Sparrow-weavers frequent dry acacia and mopane woodland. R

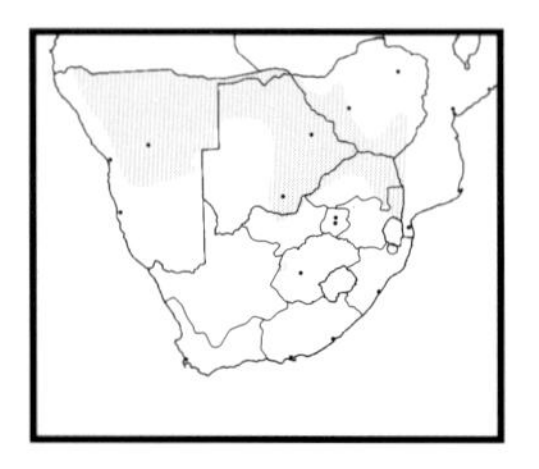

Redbilled Buffalo Weaver *Bubalornis niger* (798) 24 cm

The male Redbilled Buffalo Weaver is large and black with a bright red bill; females are greyish brown but also show a reddish bill. Males could be confused with the Palewinged Starling (see page 258) in flight but this species shows only a small amount of white on the primaries. At rest it shows white edges to the breast feathers near the shoulder. Immatures resemble the females but have whitish or buff edges to the breast feathers which impart a scaled effect. The calls are a mixture of squeaks and chips and the song is a warbled 'chip-chip-doodley-doodley-dooo'. Redbilled Buffalo Weavers are found in dry thornveld and savanna and in mixed dry woodland. R

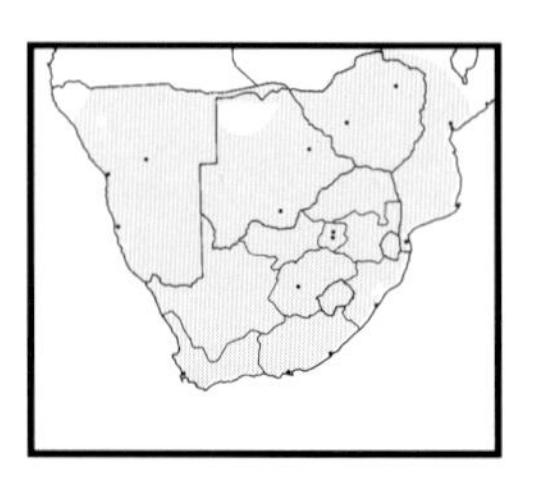

House Sparrow *Passer domesticus* (801) 14 cm

If seen away from human habitation in drier regions the House Sparrow could be confused with the Great Sparrow but it is much drabber than that species, and the black bib extends on to the throat and breast. The female is easily distinguished from the female Great Sparrow, being grey, not the rich chestnut of that bird; it also lacks the bright chestnut rump of that species. Immatures resemble the female. The calls include the familiar chirps and 'chissick' notes. This bird is common around human habitation, and also occurs in more remote areas and in farm buildings. R

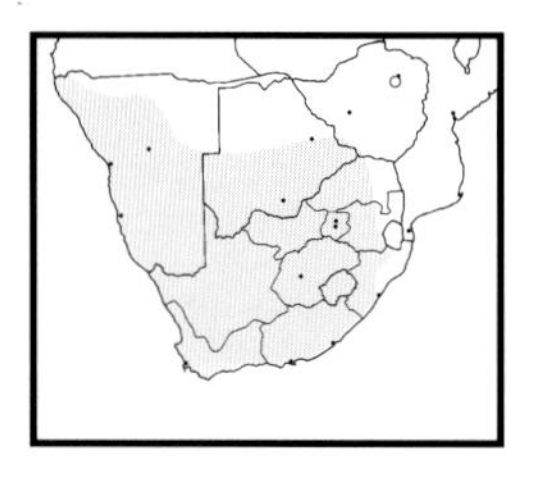

Cape Sparrow *Passer melanurus* (803) 15 cm

This species with its black and white head pattern is more bunting-like than it is sparrow-like. The male is unmistakable: the only sparrow in the region to have a pied head. The female shows a shadow pattern of the male's head pattern, and the immature resembles the female. The call is a more melodic series of 'cheeps' and 'chirps' than that of the House Sparrow. Like the House Sparrow, this species has adapted well to human habitation and is seen around towns and cities, often alongside House Sparrows. However, it can also be found in wild and remote areas far from human habitation where the birds are shy and unapproachable, flying off at the least disturbance. NE

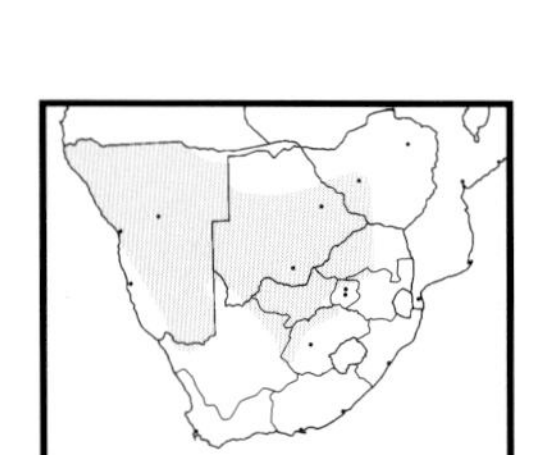

Great Sparrow *Passer motitensis* (802) 15 cm

The Great Sparrow resembles the House Sparrow but is much brighter than that species, with richer chestnut coloration on its back and on the sides of the head, whiter cheeks, and a small black bib confined to the chin. Females differ from the female House Sparrow by being chestnut, not greyish-brown in colour. The bird's call is a typical sparrow-like 'cheereep' or 'chissick'. Usually encountered well away from habitation in dry bushveld and savanna, it occurs in pairs or small groups, and often in company with canaries and waxbills. It nests around old farm buildings and water-pump windmills. R

1. Adult Whitebrowed Sparrow-weavers
2. Male Redbilled Buffalo Weaver
3. Female Redbilled Buffalo Weaver
4. Male House Sparrow
5. Female House Sparrow
6. Male Cape Sparrow
7. Female Cape Sparrow
8. Male Great Sparrow
9. Female Great Sparrow

1 2
3 4
5 6 7
8 9

R *resident* • NE *near endemic*

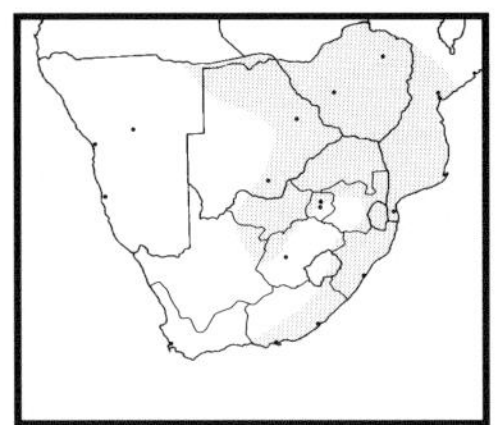

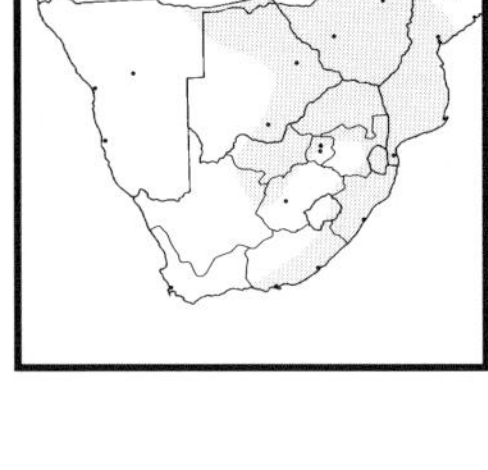

Yellowthroated Sparrow *Petronia superciliaris* (805) 15 cm

The name of this bird should not be used as a clue to its identity in the field, as the yellow throat spot is virtually invisible except at close range; the buffy or off-white eyebrow stripe which broadens behind the eye and runs on to the nape is the best field character. The sexes are alike, and the immature resembles the adults but lacks the yellow throat spot. The Yellowthroated Sparrow might be confused with the Whitebrowed Sparrow-weaver (see page 266) but is much smaller, has a less robust bill and lacks a white rump. The call is a sparrow-like chipping. This bird is found in various woodland types but is very common in mopane and other broad-leaved stands. It feeds on the ground and when disturbed will fly into the canopy or on to dead branches where it runs back and forth. R

Adult Yellowthroated Sparrow

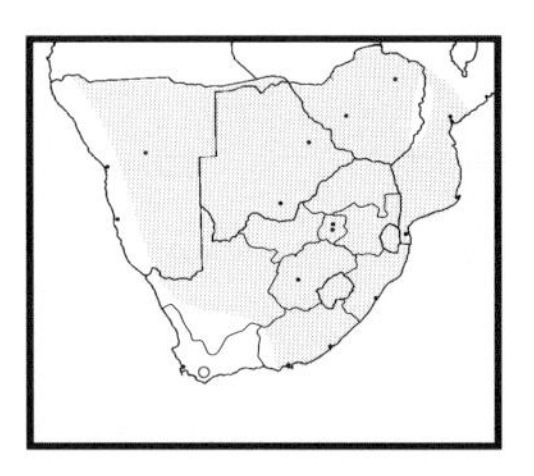

Greyheaded Sparrow *Passer griseus* (804) 15 cm

This small, greyish sparrow could be confused with the female Cape Sparrow (see page 266) but lacks any pale markings on its uniformly grey head. It forages on the ground and when disturbed takes off in small groups, clearly showing the chestnut tail, rump and back as it goes. The sexes are alike, and the immatures are duller than the adults. The call is the usual 'chipping' song of sparrows. The Greyheaded Sparrow is found in a wide range of habitats but most commonly in woodland of various types. It has adapted well to human habitation and frequents farmhouses and gardens but avoids larger cities. R

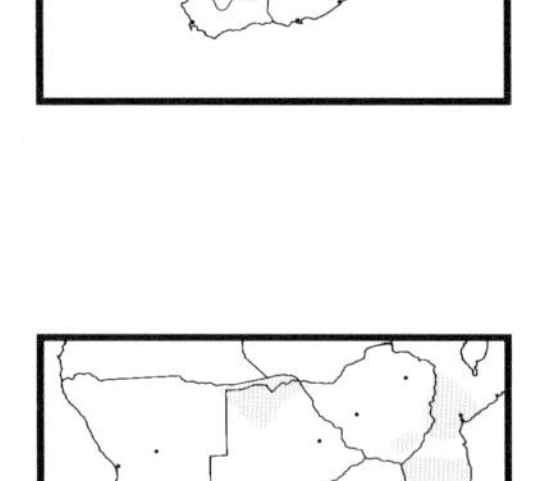

Scalyfeathered Finch *Sporopipes squamifrons* (806) 10 cm

This tiny finch resembles a small sparrow in general coloration but at close range can be seen to have broad black and white malar stripes and the forehead and wing feathers edged with white, imparting a scaled appearance. The tiny bill is pink. The sexes are alike. Immatures resemble the adults but lack both the scaling on the forehead and the black malar stripes. The call is a soft 'chizz-chizz-chizz' given in flight or by restless, roosting groups. The Scalyfeathered Finch frequents dry bushveld, woodland and semi-arid regions. Common around human habitation, it rarely visits waterbutts or the drinking pools so often visited by waxbills (see page 284) and sparrows. NE

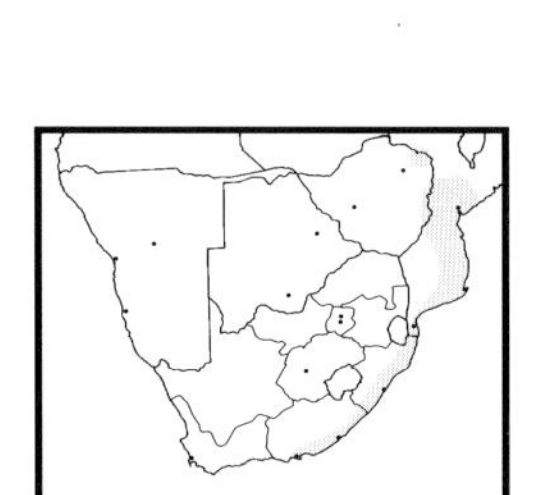

Thickbilled Weaver *Amblyospiza albifrons* (807) 18 cm

The largest weaver in the region, the dark male of this species is unmistakable with its oversized conical bill and white spot on the forehead. In flight it shows a white flash at the primary base. Female and immature Thickbilled Weavers are sometimes mistaken for an entirely different species, having heavily spotted underparts but retaining the huge bill. The calls are various 'chipping' and twittering sounds made by the male within a breeding colony; the flight call is a 'tweek-tweek'. Essentially a forest species, the Thickbilled Weaver forages on the ground among leaf litter but roosts and breeds in reedbeds. R

Forest Weaver *Ploceus bicolor* (808) 16 cm

The only weaver in the region to have all-black upperparts and bright yellow underparts, this species should be easy to identify. The sexes are alike. Immatures have a brown cast to the dark upperparts and show a black and white grizzled throat and forehead. The yellow on the underparts in fresh plumage can be so intense as to appear orange and then, in the same habitat, the bird might be confused with the Chorister Robin (see page 208), but its weaver-like habits and calls should prevent confusion. The calls are a musical duet of 'coooeee-coooee' notes and a harsher 'squizzzz' note. The Forest Weaver occurs in pairs or in family groups and bird parties, poking around in lichens and mosses and hanging upside-down to glean from under leaves. This bird favours evergreen, coastal and riverine forests. R

1. Adult Yellowthroated Sparrow
2. Adult Greyheaded Sparrow
3. Adult Scalyfeathered Finch
4. Adult Scalyfeathered Finch
5. Female Thickbilled Weaver
6. Male Thickbilled Weaver
7. Adult Forest Weaver

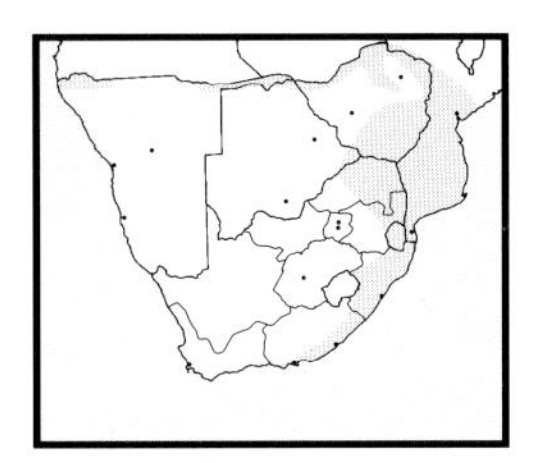

Spectacled Weaver *Ploceus ocularis* (810) 15 cm

This bird has unmarked olive upperparts and a yellow head and underparts. Diagnostic are the thin black mask through the yellow eye, the black bib, and the sharp, pointed, black bill. Females are similar to the males but lack the black bib, and immatures resemble the females but have a brown bill. The calls are a descending 'dee-dee-dee' and also a softer chattering. Occurring in pairs and bird parties, Spectacled Weavers are more furtive than most weavers, spending most of their time in deep cover, and gleaning food, warbler-like, from leaves. The nest has a very long tunnel entrance and hangs on a single, long branch. Chiefly a forest species, this bird does occur in riverine and thicker woodland and has adapted to suburbia. R

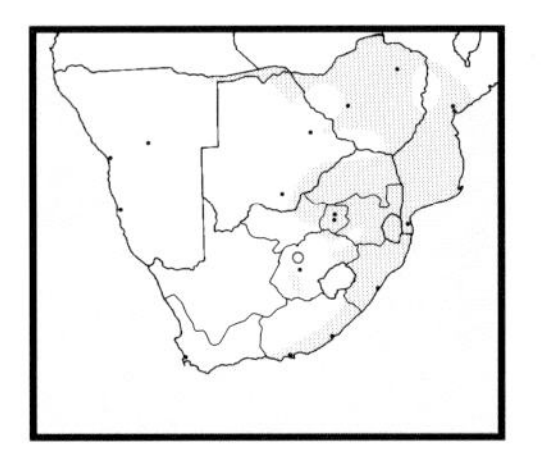

Spottedbacked Weaver *Ploceus cucullatus* (811) 17 cm

The male Spottedbacked Weaver in breeding plumage differs from all other weavers with black heads by having the back spangled with black and yellow. The amount of black on the head varies from region to region, with those in the north showing the greatest extent of black. Non-breeding males, females and immatures are drab, olive and yellow birds and are virtually indistinguishable from other, similar-plumaged weavers. The contact call is the usual weaver 'chuck', with chattering and wheezy notes given in display. The Spottedbacked Weaver forms large flocks outside of the breeding season. It frequents grasslands and roosts in reedbeds, and breeds in colonies, in trees overhanging water, in reedbeds and, often, in trees far from water and around human habitation. The birds can become garden pests. R

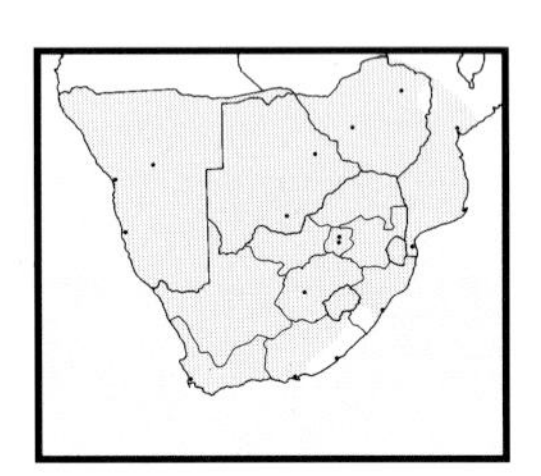

Southern Masked Weaver *Ploceus velatus* (814) 15 cm

The breeding male Southern Masked Weaver differs from the breeding male Spottedbacked Weaver by having a more uniformly olive, unmarked back and by its smaller size, and from the Lesser Masked Weaver by having a red eye and brown legs. It differs further from both of those species by having less black on the crown, and by the fact that the black on the breast is not rounded off but developed into a point. Non-breeding males resemble the females but retain their red eyes; females have brown eyes. Females and immatures are unlikely to be separated from the similar-plumaged Spottedbacked Weaver unless they are seen together, when the size difference is apparent. Calls are the typical weaver 'squizzel' and 'chuck' notes. The Southern Masked Weaver is found in a wide range of habitats, from desert edges to moister wooded areas and suburbia, and colonies consist of only a dozen or fewer nests. R

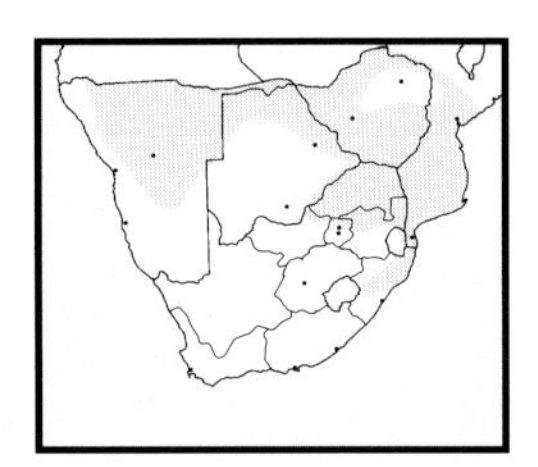

Lesser Masked Weaver *Ploceus intermedius* (815) 15 cm

This is the only black-headed weaver in the region with a white eye. Both sexes show this diagnostic feature. In breeding plumage the male is distinguished by the shape of the black mask, which extends well on to the crown and comes to a rounded (not pointed, as is the case with the Southern Masked Weaver) end on the throat. The Golden Weaver (see page 272) and Cape Weaver also have pale irises but they lack the black head and are much larger than this species. Female and immature Lesser Masked Weavers are much brighter yellow than the female and immature Spottedbacked Weaver and female and immature Southern Masked Weaver. Calls are typical weaver 'chuck' and 'squizzel' notes. Found in a wide range of habitats, these birds normally form larger colonies than do Southern Masked Weavers. R

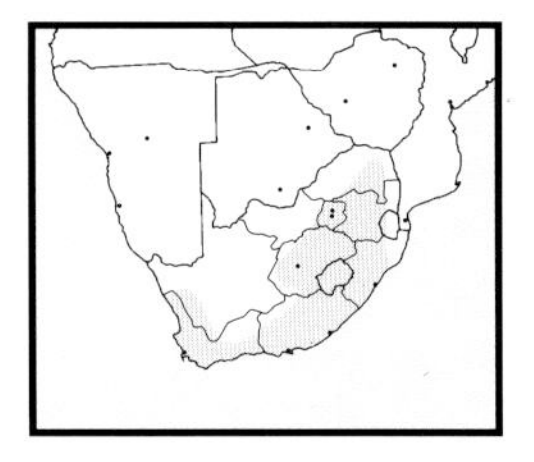

Cape Weaver *Ploceus capensis* (813) 17 cm

Most often confused with the smaller Yellow Weaver (see page 272), this bird has a yellow, not red, eye, a heavier, more pointed bill, and an olive, not yellow, back. The orange face in the breeding male can be so intense in some individuals as to cause confusion with the Southern Brownthroated Weaver (see page 272), but this species has a darker back, a yellow, not brown, eye, and a less well-defined brown bib. The larger Golden Weaver (see page 272) has a much chunkier bill and does not show any orange in the face. Females and non-breeding males are olive brown above. Females differ from the female Golden Weaver by having a smaller, more pointed bill and less robust and chunky proportions. The calls are typical weaver notes and display chatterings. The Cape Weaver breeds in reedbeds and trees, mostly near water, in western coastal regions and mountainous areas. E

1. Male Spectacled Weaver
2. Female Spectacled Weaver
3. Male Spottedbacked Weaver
4. Female Spottedbacked Weaver
5. Male Southern Masked Weaver
6. Female Southern Masked Weaver
7. Male Spottedbacked Weaver
8. Male Lesser Masked Weaver
9. Male Cape Weaver

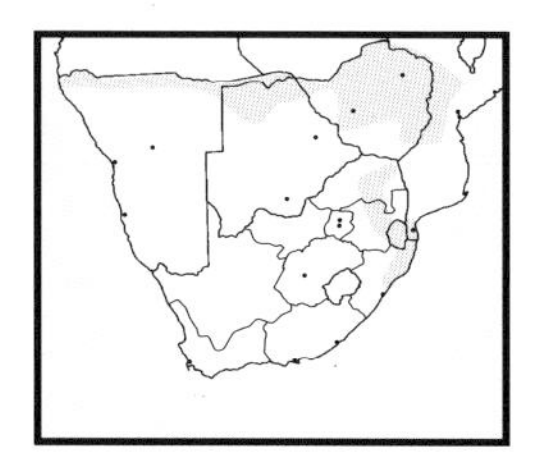

Golden Weaver *Ploceus xanthops* (816) 18 cm

The Golden Weaver differs from the Yellow Weaver by being much larger and more robust, and by having a larger, thicker-based bill and a pale yellow, not red, eye. Also, it is slightly darker on the mantle and has less yellow on the wings and tail. The non-breeding male is duller overall and resembles the female but retains the black bill; females have a brown bill. Females differ from female Yellow Weavers by their larger size and pale eye. The female Lesser Masked Weaver (see page 270) is very similar to this species but is very much smaller and has blue, not brown, legs. The call is a harsh 'chuk', harsher and more raucous than other typical weaver-like calls. The Golden Weaver is usually found in small groups or in pairs, but not in large colonies. It frequents woodland and savanna and nests in trees and thickets close to water. R

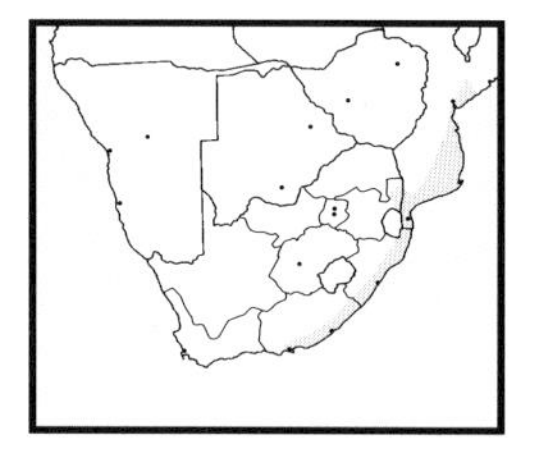

Yellow Weaver *Ploceus subaureus* (817) 15 cm

Breeding males of this species might be confused with the larger Golden Weaver which has a pale, not red, eye. Some males show deep orange on the face and may then be confused with the Southern Brownthroated Weaver but do not have the clearly defined chestnut bib of that species. The Yellow Weaver differs from the breeding male Cape Weaver (see page 270) by its yellow, not olive, back and shorter, less pointed bill. Non-breeding males and females differ from other weavers by being brighter yellow and having a red eye. The calls are typical weaver 'chuck' sounds and 'squizzing' notes. In display the male hangs from its nest, bill pointing to the chest, wings outstretched and flapping, and the body swaying from side to side. The Yellow Weaver breeds in trees overhanging rivers and in large stands of reedbeds, and it typically forages in coastal and riverine forests. R

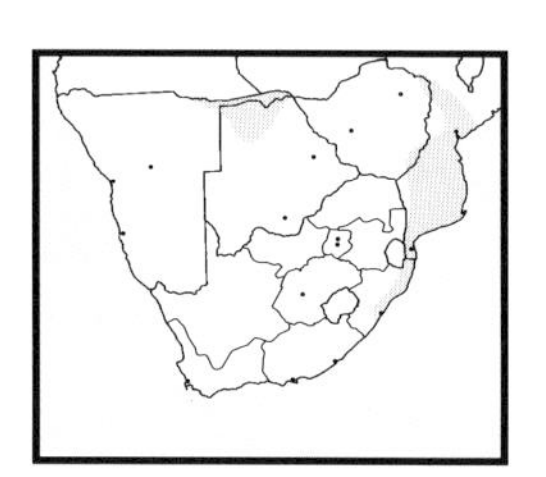

Southern Brownthroated Weaver *Ploceus xanthopterus* (818) 15 cm

The neat and clearly defined chestnut bib of the male of this species is diagnostic. In general colour, it is a vivid canary-yellow and may resemble the Cape Weaver (see page 270). Females are very similar to female Golden Weavers and Yellow Weavers but have a brown, not pale yellow, or red, eye. The calls are similar to those of other weavers. Confined to reedbeds and adjoining bush near water, the Southern Brownthroated Weaver forms small colonies in reedbeds, sometimes close to Yellow Weaver colonies. R

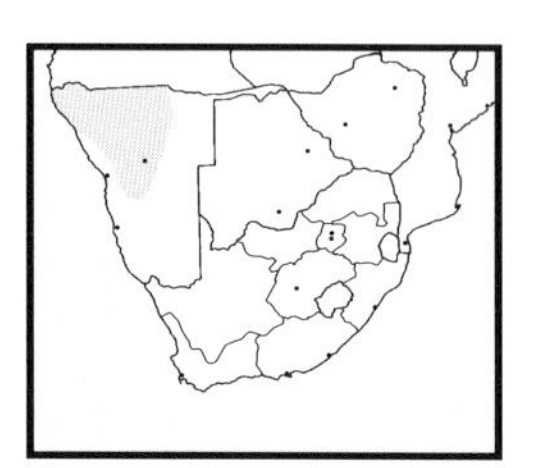

Chestnut Weaver *Ploceus rubiginosus* (812) 15 cm

The chestnut body colour of the breeding male Chestnut Weaver is diagnostic. Females and non-breeding males are drab greyish birds, rather than olive as in other non-breeding and female weavers, and have a clearly defined yellowish throat and a greyish-brown breast band. The calls do not differ appreciably from those of other weavers. When breeding, Chestnut Weavers form large colonies in trees, sometimes in dry river beds extending well into the desert. This species frequents dry thornveld and woodland to semi-desert. R

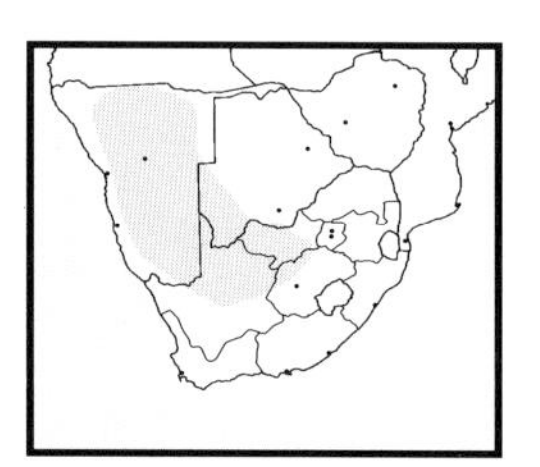

Sociable Weaver *Philetairus socius* (800) 14 cm

The most sparrow-like of our weavers and easily recognized by its black bib, the Sociable Weaver has a finely scaled mantle and a scaly patch on the flanks. The similar Scalyfeathered Finch (see page 268) is very much smaller and has a scaly pattern on the forehead, not on the mantle, and lacks the scaled pattern on the flanks. Immature Sociable Weavers resemble the adults but lack the black bib. The calls are a harsh, clipped 'tek-tek' and a 'chicker-chicker' given in flight. Sociable Weavers are usually found in the vicinity of their enormous 'thatched' nests where many pairs gather to breed, or in foraging flocks feeding on the ground in semi-arid areas. They frequent a mixture of habitats, from open acacia savanna to desert edge. NE

1. Male Golden Weaver
2. Male Southern Brownthroated Weaver
3. Male Yellow Weaver
4. Female Golden Weaver
5. Immature Sociable Weaver
6. Adult Chestnut Weaver
7. Female Yellow Weaver
8. Adult Sociable Weavers

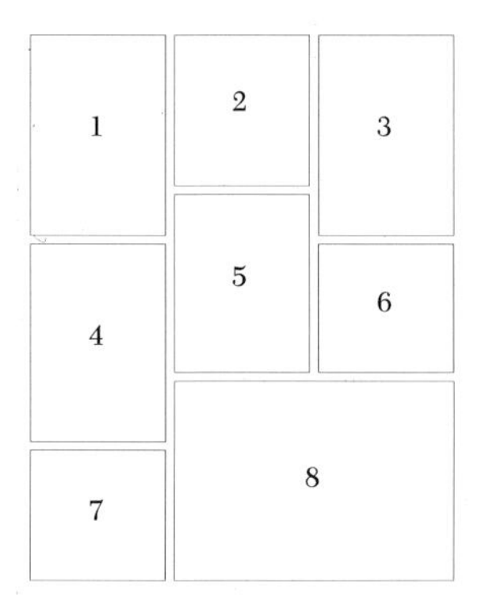

R *resident* • NE *near endemic*

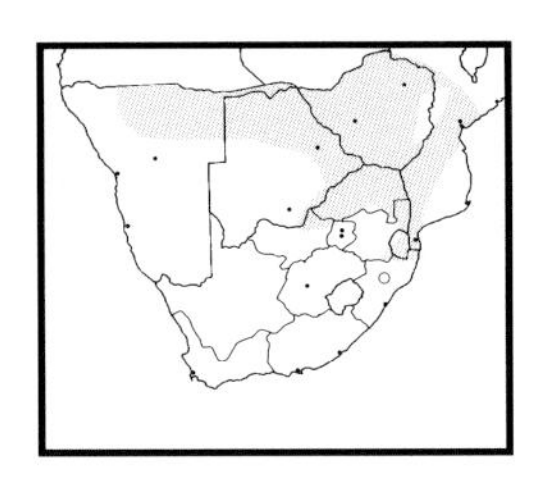

Redheaded Weaver *Anaplectes rubriceps* (819) 15 cm

The vivid red head and throat of the breeding male Redheaded Weaver are diagnostic. Non-breeding males and females have a bright yellow head which contrasts with a clear white belly and orange bill, and with this combination should not be confused with any other weaver. The call is a squeaky chatter, 'cherrra-cherrra', and a high-pitched 'swizzling'. The nests are often attached in small groups, hanging from telephone wires. Redheaded Weavers are found mainly in miombo woodland but also frequent drier broad-leaved woodland and thornveld habitats. R

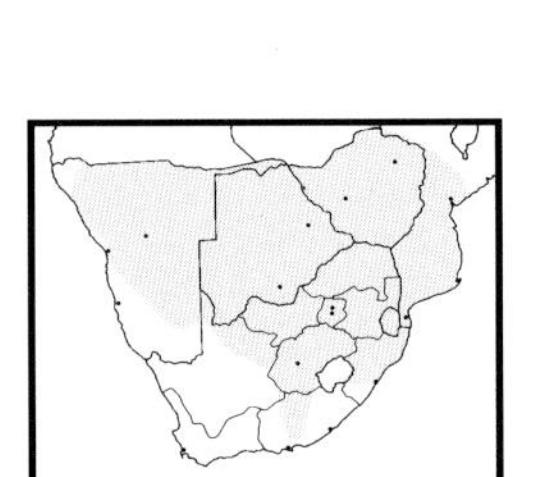

Redbilled Quelea *Quelea quelea* (821) 13 cm

In breeding plumage this small, finch-like bird has a variable head pattern. The normal breeding plumage features a diagnostic bright red bill, a black face and a pinkish-red nape and throat; other variations lack the pinkish wash to the nape and throat or have less black on the face, or even a totally white face. Females and non-breeding males have a red bill, which helps to distinguish them from female and non-breeding male bishops (see page 276). Immatures have a horn-coloured bill and resemble female bishops and other quelea species in non-breeding plumage. The call is a high-pitched chittering given by flocks in flight and at roost. The Redbilled Quelea can be encountered in flocks of countless thousands; otherwise they occur in small groups in mixed flocks of bishops and weavers. They inhabit savanna, especially thornveld, but also other woodland types and agricultural lands. R

Redbilled Quelea (breeding males)

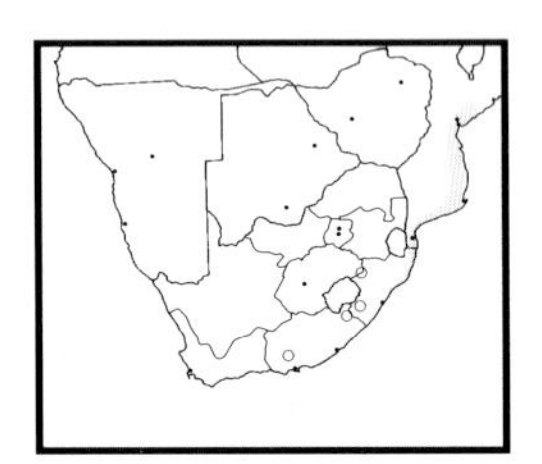

Redheaded Quelea *Quelea erythrops* (822) 12 cm

In breeding plumage this species differs from the Redbilled Quelea by lacking any black on the face and by having a grey, not red, bill. Breeding females have a pinkish wash across the face and a grey, not red, bill, thus distinguishing them from the female Redbilled Quelea. Immatures, non-breeding males and females are very similar to the immature Redbilled Quelea but are suffused with a more yellowish-buffy wash across the face and breast. The call is a soft twittering. This species does not occur in vast swarms as does the Redbilled Quelea but rather in small groups and colonies, in reedbeds and tall grasses. The birds are found in flooded grasslands, reedbeds and surrounding bush. S

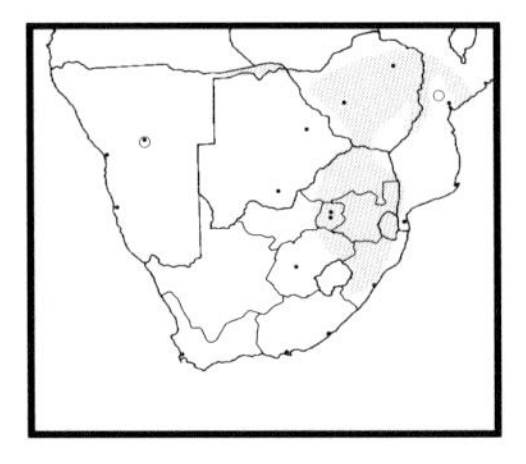

Cuckoo Finch *Anomalospiza imberbis* (820) 13 cm

Smaller than any similar-plumaged weaver, the Cuckoo Finch differs mainly by it short, black, conical bill. It has proportionately very large legs and toes. In fresh plumage it is dull greenish brown but the plumage wears to reveal bright yellow underfeathers. Females and immatures resemble similar-plumaged female and immature bishops (see page 276) but have reduced streaking on the breast, very fine streaking on the upperparts and a very short, stubby, conical bill. The call is a fast, staccato 'tssiddk' given in flight; the song is a series of warbled, harsh notes given from a fence post or from the top of a bush. Single males are most commonly seen although the birds gather in large flocks when roosting. They favour open grasslands, marshy areas and adjoining savanna. R, S

1. Male Redbilled Quelea
2. Adult Cuckoo Finch
3. Male Redheaded Quelea
4. Male Redheaded Weaver
5. Female Redbilled Quelea

1	2
3	4
	5

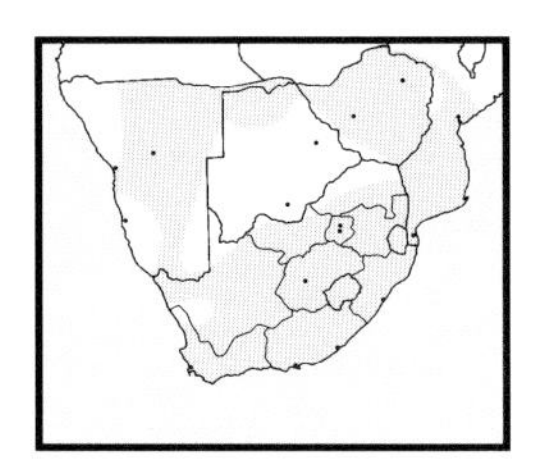

Red Bishop *Euplectes orix* (824) 14 cm

The Red Bishop might be confused with the Firecrowned Bishop only in breeding plumage but can then be distinguished from that species by having a black face which extends on to the forehead and by lacking black in the wings and tail. Females and immatures differ by having browner, not blackish, wings. Non-breeding males, females and immature Red Bishops resemble the Golden Bishop but are larger, generally darker overall and have more extensive, heavier streaking on the underparts. The flight call is a sharp 'cheet-cheet'. The male in display flies over the reedbeds like a large, orange bumblebee, with puffed-up back and breast feathers and an upright flight style, while it utters hissing and buzzing calls. The Red Bishop breeds in colonies in reedbeds over water, and gathers in large flocks when not breeding, at these times frequenting grasslands and agricultural lands. R

Male Golden Bishop (transitional)

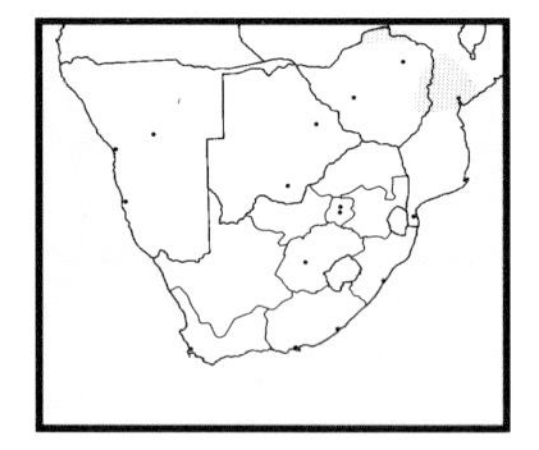

Firecrowned Bishop *Euplectes hordeaceus* (825) 14 cm

Similar in size to the Red Bishop, the Firecrowned Bishop is easily confused with that species, especially in breeding plumage. It differs by having a red, not black, forehead and by its wings and tail which are more black than brown in colour. Non-breeding males and females closely resemble non-breeding male and female Red Bishops but have a heavier bill and the male retains the black primaries. The call and display are very similar to those of the Red Bishop, but this bird flies shorter distances and prefers to puff itself up and sing a buzzing chatter from a perch. It is found in flooded grasslands, reedbeds and sugarcane fields. R

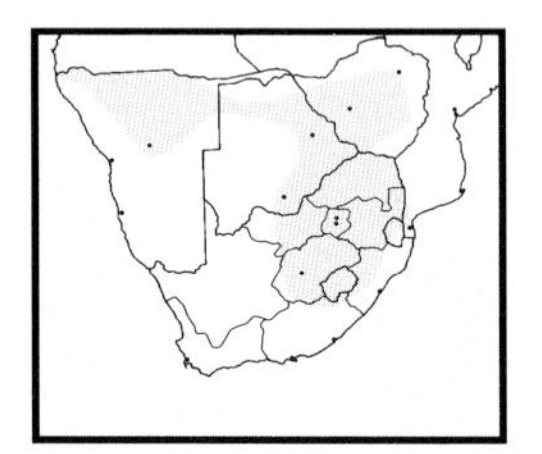

Golden Bishop *Euplectes afer* (826) 12 cm

The male bird's bright yellow and black breeding plumage is diagnostic; breeding male Yellowrumped Widows, with which this species may be confused, lack the yellow crown and nape of the Golden Bishop, and are much larger. Non-breeding males, females and immatures are very difficult to separate from the similar-plumaged Red Bishop, and direct comparison is normally necessary to make a positive identification of either of these two species in this drab, sparrow-like plumage. The call and display of the male are similar to those of the Red Bishop. The Golden Bishop breeds in reedbeds or, more often, in flooded grasslands and thick stands of weeds. It forms small flocks when not breeding and feeds on the ground in agricultural lands. R

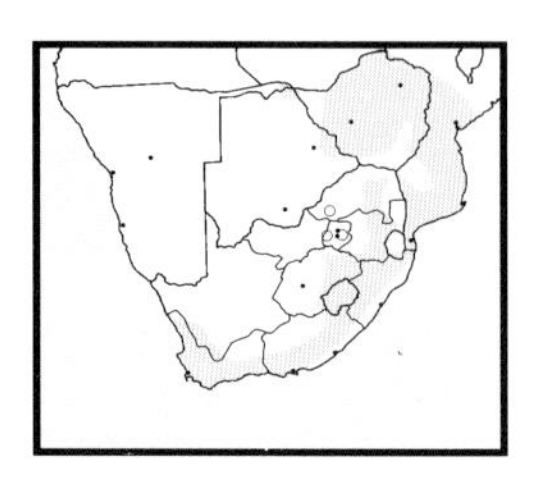

Yellowrumped Widow *Euplectes capensis* (827) 15 cm

The breeding male Yellowrumped Widow is a black bird with a bright yellow rump and shoulder patch. The similar Whitewinged Widow (see page 278) also has a yellow shoulder patch and white edgings to the wings but lacks the yellow rump. The non-breeding male of this species shows the yellow rump and shoulder patch which contrasts with the streaky buff and black head and body. Females are smaller and drabber than the males but also show a yellowish wash across the rump; immatures resemble the females. Calls are a 'zeeet-zeeeet' given in display and a harsh 'zzzzzzz' in flight; the male gives a bishop-like, buzzing display flight. These widows are found in damp, grassy areas, bracken-covered mountain valleys and fynbos. R

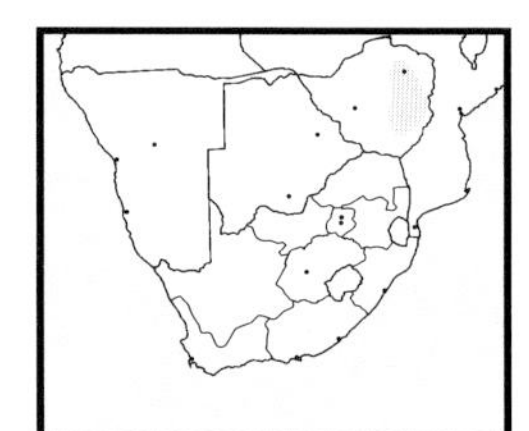

Yellowbacked Widow *Euplectes macrourus* (830) 15-22 cm

This is a black bird with a long tail, and conspicuous yellow on the mantle and shoulders which appears as a broad yellow band across the upper back when the bird is seen at rest. Non-breeding males closely resemble the similar-plumaged Yellowrumped Widow but lack the bright yellow rump of that species. Females and immatures are very difficult to tell apart from other female and immature widows if not accompanied by the easier-to-identify males, although they do have much reduced streaking on the breast and lack the dull yellow rump of the female Yellowrumped Widow. Calls include a 'tsweep' sound and a buzzing 'zzzzt' given in flight. Displaying males bounce along in flight and perch on tall grass stems to sing. The Yellowbacked Widow is found in damp grasslands and marshy areas when breeding and in flocks over agricultural lands when not breeding. R

1. Male Red Bishop
2. Female Red Bishop
3. Male Firecrowned Bishop
4. Male Yellowrumped Widow
5. Male Yellowbacked Widow
6. Male Golden Bishop
7. Female Golden Bishop

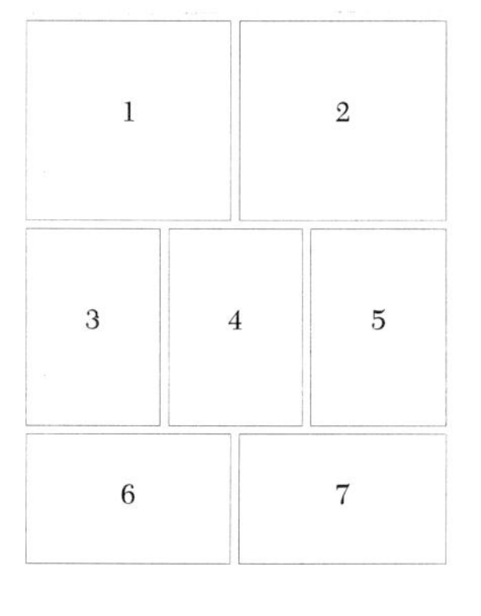

R *resident*

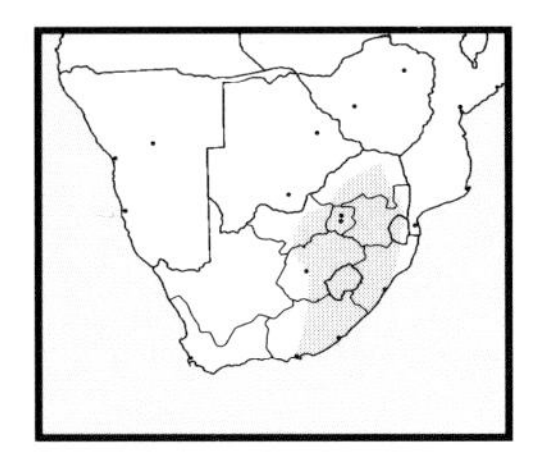

Longtailed Widow *Euplectes progne* (832)
m=19 cm (plus 40 cm tail in breeding plumage); f=16 cm

Breeding male Longtailed Widows are unmistakable. The smaller Redcollared Widow at long range resembles this species but lacks the conspicuous red shoulder edged with buff. Males in non-breeding plumage resemble the similar-plumaged Redshouldered Widow but are very much larger, broader winged and have a wide buff edge to the red shoulder. Females and immatures are much larger than other such plumaged widows, appear to have a pointed tail, and have dark underwings. The displaying male flies just above the grass with its tail held downwards and spread, and its wings beating in jerky slow motion. Calls are 'cheet-cheet' and a harsher 'zzt-zzt', given when the bird is perched. These birds are found over grasslands, and roost communally in reedbeds. R

Male Longtailed Widow (breeding)

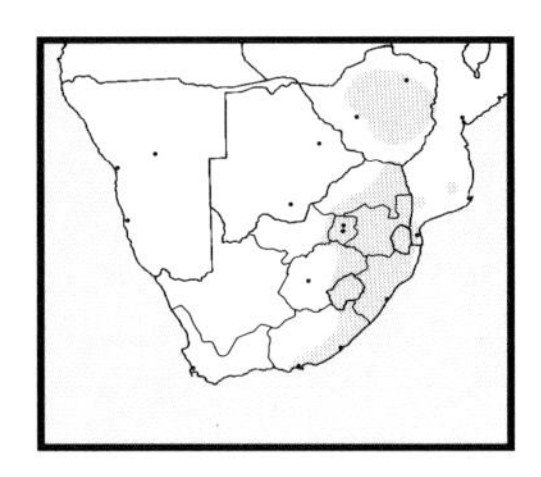

Redcollared Widow *Euplectes ardens* (831)
15 cm (plus 25 cm tail in breeding male)

Breeding males might be confused with the much larger Longtailed Widow, but this species lacks the conspicuous red shoulder patches of that species. Only at close range is the red collar visible, and it may be totally absent in some individuals. Non-breeding males, females and immatures differ from other widows and weavers by having broad, dark stripes on the head and buffy, unmarked underparts, and the males retain the black primaries. The call is a fast, high-pitched 'tee-tee-tee-tee' given by the male in display; the flight call of flocks is a soft twitter. Males in display fly upwards from a perch and then drift down with flicking wings before repeating the performance. The Redcollared Widow gathers in flocks outside the breeding season and roosts communally. It is found over upland grasslands, bracken-covered valleys in mountains and in sugar-cane plantations. R

Male Whitewinged Widow (non-breeding)

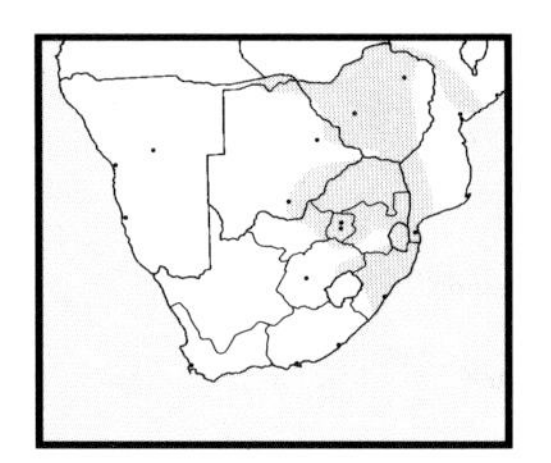

Whitewinged Widow *Euplectes albonotatus* (829) 15-19 cm

The conspicuous combination of white and yellow on the wings of this widow renders it unmistakable. Males in non-breeding plumage retain the white and yellow wing pattern and are easily identified. Females and immatures are overall paler below and less streaked than other widows in similar plumage but are nonetheless not easy to tell apart. Calls are a repeated, nasal 'zeh-zeh-zeh' and a buzzing 'witz-witz-witz'. The Whitewinged Widow occurs in a wide range of grassy and marshy areas and roosts communally in reedbeds with other widows and weaver species. R

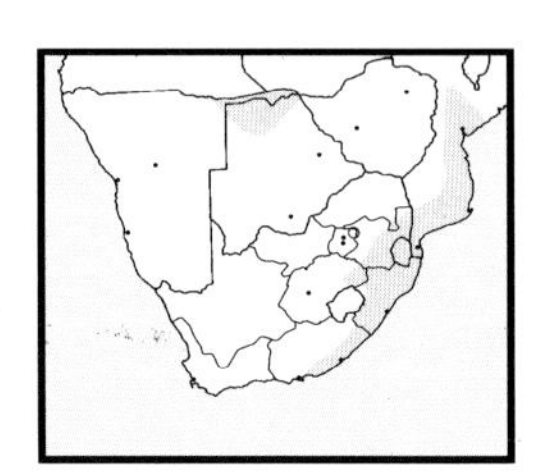

Redshouldered Widow *Euplectes axillaris* (828) 19 cm

This is a smaller, shorter-tailed version of the Longtailed Widow, and is further distinguished by its red shoulder patch which does not have a broad buff edging. Females and immatures resemble most other similar-plumaged widows and are extremely difficult to tell apart. The call, given in flight, is a short 'chit-chit', and displaying males utter a warbling, buzzing song and a metallic 'zing-zing'. In display the male flies in slow-motion over its territory with the tail fanned. These birds are found over damp grasslands and marshy areas and roost in large numbers in reedbeds, often with weavers. R

1. Male Longtailed Widow (breeding)
2. Male Redcollared Widow (breeding)
3. Male Whitewinged Widow (breeding)
4. Female Longtailed Widow
5. Female Redcollared Widow
6. Male Whitewinged Widow (breeding)
7. Male Redshouldered Widow (breeding)
8. Female Redshouldered Widow

1	2	3
4	5	6
7	8	

R *resident*

Pytilias, twinspots, crimsonwings, firefinches, waxbills and mannikins

Family Estrildidae

Small, mostly brightly coloured birds, all the members of this family are sexually dimorphic. All have short, conical bills, primarily adapted for eating seeds, but some species include insects in their diet. Most forage on the ground or low in the vegetation, often in small flocks.

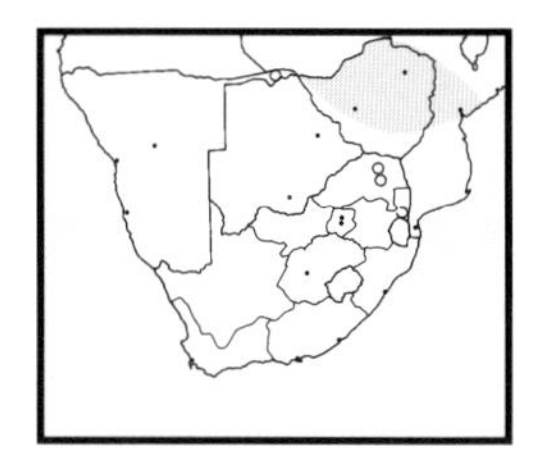

Goldenbacked Pytilia *Pytilia afra* (833) 11 cm

At a glance this bird could easily be mistaken for a Melba Finch but it is drabber and less brightly coloured and differs further in having orange wing panels and a barred green and white, not black and white, belly. The red patch on the face is less extensive and does not encompass the upper breast. Females lack red on the face and are very dull, lacking the contrasting, pale grey head and green back of the Melba Finch. Immatures are similar to the females but show more orange on the rump. Calls are a 'seee' and a double-whistled, widely spaced song. This species keeps to long grass and tangles in miombo and teak woodland, and is rarely seen in dry acacia thornveld. R

Melba Finch *Pytilia melba* (834) 12 cm

Very similar to the Goldenbacked Pytilia, this species differs mainly by the greater extent of red on the throat, the barred black and white breast and belly, and the green, not orange, on the wings. Females lack red on the face, as seen in the males, and differ from the female Goldenbacked Pytilia by their obvious black and white barred underparts. Immatures resemble the females but are more olive above. Overall a more strikingly coloured bird than the pytilia, the Melba Finch is also bolder and less skulking than that species. The call is a soft 'wick, wick', and it gives a tinkling song with wheezy notes. It occurs in dry acacia bush and thicket. R

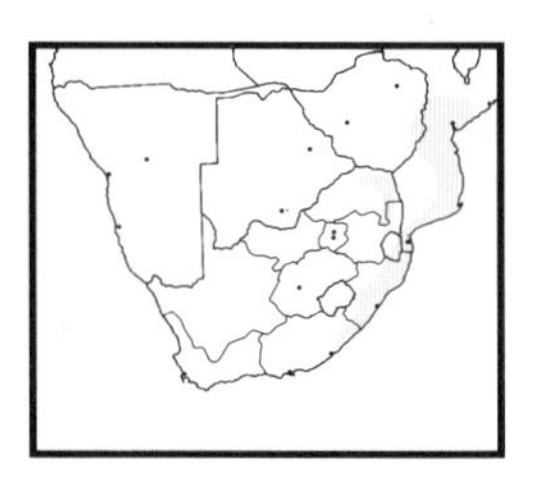

Green Twinspot *Mandingoa nitidula* (835) 10 cm

The overall green coloration of this tiny finch, combined with the small white spots on the black belly and flanks, is diagnostic. Males have a red face and rump, and females have a yellowish face. Immatures are duller than the females, lacking any red in the plumage and being a dull green and grey with a small area of white spotting on the flanks. The call is the best way of detecting this bird: it is a soft, rolling, insect-like 'zrrreeet', and the song is a soft tinkling sound. It feeds freely in the open in coastal areas under *Casuarina* trees. R

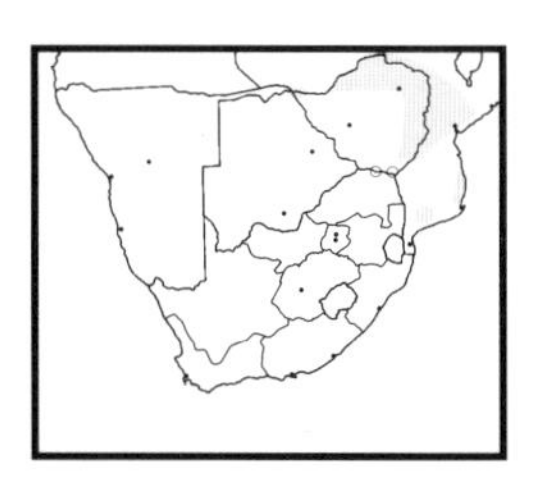

Redthroated Twinspot *Hypargos niveoguttatus* (839) 12 cm

The red on the face and throat of this species is generally (but not always) more intense than that on the face of the Pinkthroated Twinspot. Further, the crown of the Redthroated Twinspot is grey, not brown. Females have a pinkish, not grey, flush on the breast which immediately separates them from the female Pinkthroated Twinspot. Immatures lack any red in the plumage and are greyish-brown versions of the adults, and as such are barely distinguishable from the Pinkthroated Twinspot. The call is a soft, clicking, reedy trill. The Redthroated Twinspot is found on the edges of evergreen forests and riverine thicket and, rarely, in dry woodland and scrub. R

Pinkthroated Twinspot *Hypargos margaritatus* (838) 12 cm

The calls of this species and the Redthroated Twinspot are very similar, as is their behaviour, but this is an overall paler bird and has a brown, not grey, crown. Females, unlike the female Redthroated Twinspot, have no flush of pink to the breast, but immatures are barely distinguishable from immature Redthroated Twinspots. The Pinkthroated Twinspot forages on the ground and when disturbed flies into thickets, perching low down and giving a clicking, trilling contact call. It frequents dry woodland and thickets. E

Female Goldenbacked Pytilia

Female Melba Finch

1. Male Goldenbacked Pytilia
2. Female Goldenbacked Pytilia
3. Male Melba Finch
4. Male Green Twinspot
5. Female Green Twinspot
6. Male Redthroated Twinspot
7. Female Melba Finch
8. Male Pinkthroated Twinspot
9. Female Pinkthroated Twinspot

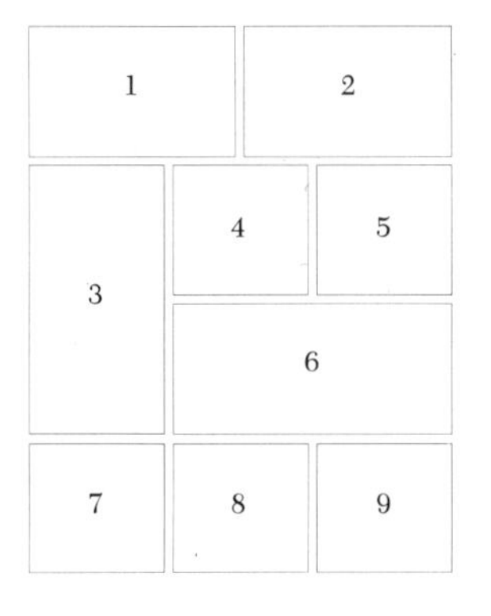

R *resident* • E *endemic*

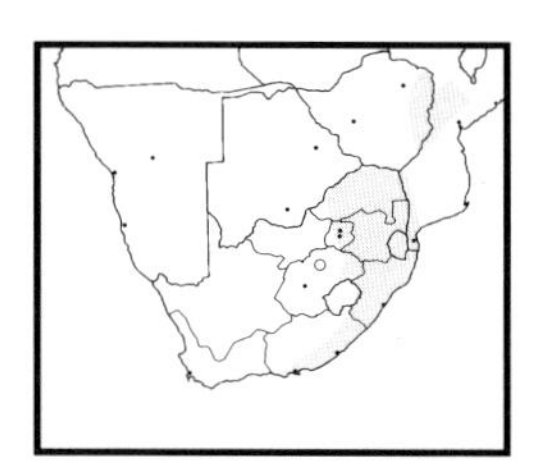

Bluebilled Firefinch *Lagonosticta rubricata* (840) 10 cm

Like Jameson's Firefinch, this species has a bluish bill but there are no further resemblances between the species. The Bluebilled Firefinch is very much darker than that bird and has a distinct greyish nape and a brown back; in the north it has a pinkish wash across the head but still shows the dark brown back. Females are darker on the back than the female Jameson's Firefinch. Usually found in pairs or family parties, they are most easily detected by their clicking contact calls, a metallic, fishing-reel-type 'trrt-trrt-trrrt-trrrt' and a 'wink-wink-wink'. This species frequents evergreen forests and adjoining scrub, riverine thickets and suburbia in some areas. R

Adult Quail Finch

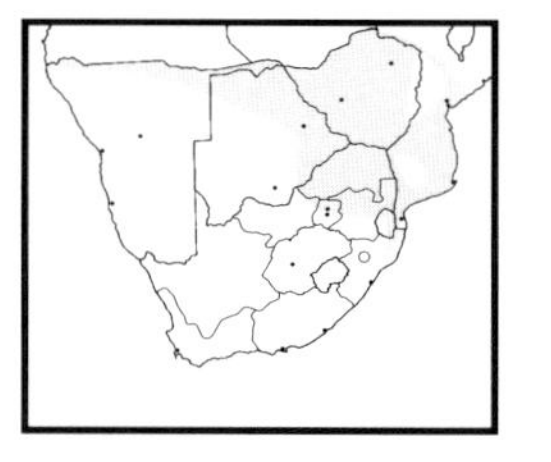

Jameson's Firefinch *Lagonosticta rhodopareia* (841) 10 cm

This is the brightest and pinkest of all the firefinches and differs from the very pink Redbilled Firefinch by having a blue bill, brown legs and a black vent and undertail. The Bluebilled Firefinch is a very much darker, deeper red below than this species and has a dark brown, not pink, back. Jameson's Firefinch females are paler and pinker on the back than females of that species. The call is a 'wink-wink', similar to that given by the Bluebilled Firefinch, and also a 'vit-vit-vit' contact call. Jameson's Firefinch feeds in small groups or in pairs, on the ground, and often with waxbills. When flushed they fly off weakly into the nearest tangle where they sit motionless until the threat has passed. They are found in grasslands and thickets in dry acacia thornveld and disturbed arable lands. R

Adult Locust Finch

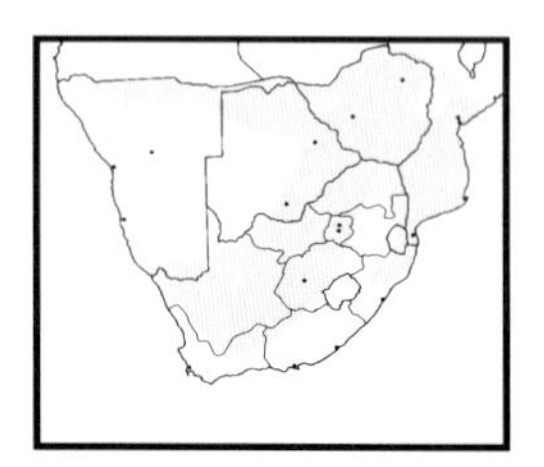

Redbilled Firefinch *Lagonosticta senegala* (842) 10 cm

Most closely resembling Jameson's Firefinch, this species is paler and differs further by having a red bill and a brown back, and by lacking the black vent and undertail. At close range the pale yellow eye-ring can be seen. Females are the least pink or red of all female firefinches and could be confused with the female Brown Firefinch but are paler and buffy, not brown, below and have red on the rump which the Brown Firefinch lacks. Immatures are similar to females but lack the white freckling on the breast and the yellow eye-ring. Calls are a short, fast 'vut-vut-vut-vut' and a soft 'sweeep'. This species occurs in a variety of woodland habitats and in suburbia in many areas. R

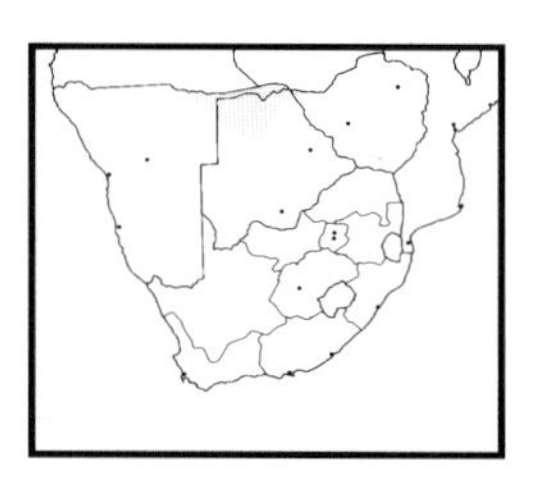

Brown Firefinch *Lagonosticta nitidula* (843) 10 cm

This species is easily told apart from other firefinches by having no red on the rump or uppertail. Males have a reddish blush confined to the face and upper breast with fine white speckles on the sides of the breast; they most closely resemble the Redbilled Firefinch because of the red bill but are overall drabber and darker and have no red on the rump. Females of this species are the drabbest of all firefinches, resembling the immature Jameson's Firefinch, but have a reddish, not blue, bill and lack any red on the rump. Calls are a 'tsiep-tsiep, tsiep-tsiep' flight call and a drawn-out trill. The Brown Firefinch is found on the edges of teak and miombo woodland, very often in disturbed and overgrazed areas, and in riverine thicket. R

1. Male Bluebilled Firefinch
2. Male Bluebilled Firefinch
3. Male Redbilled Firefinch
4. Male Redbilled Firefinch
5. Female Jameson's Firefinch
6. Female Redbilled Firefinch
7. Male Brown Firefinch
8. Female (left) and male (right) Quail Finch
9. Female (top) and male (bottom) Locust Finch

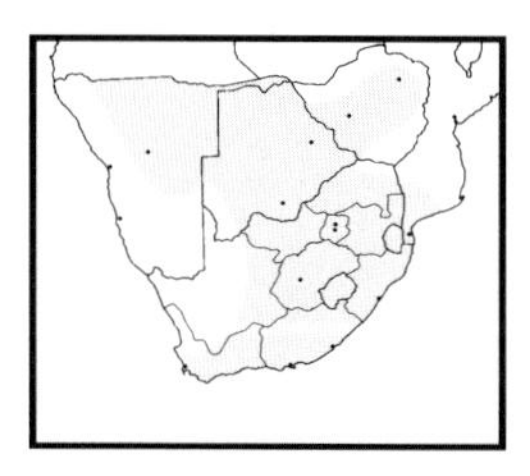

Quail Finch *Ortygospiza atricollis* (852) 9 cm

Most often seen in flight as they rise from the grass at one's feet, the black face (in the male), the eyes encircled with white and the heavily barred black and white breast and flanks are diagnostic of this species. Females lack the black face but have similar barred underparts. The call, uttered mostly in flight, is a two-noted, tinny 'streaky-streak' with the second note lower than the first. These birds gather in large flocks in suitable areas but occur mostly in small groups or pairs in short, stubbly grasslands. R

Locust Finch *Ortygospiza locustella* (853) 9 cm

This tiny black finch has orange wings and rump, and an orange-red face and throat. Females vaguely resemble the female Quail Finch but the wings and rump, both obvious in flight, are orange. Very like the Quail Finch in habits and behaviour, and often found in close proximity to that species, the Locust Finch prefers wetter grassy areas and muddy pools in grassy areas. When flushed they fly off in a similar manner to the Quail Finch but their flight is more direct and faster with a blur of wings and a soft 'tee-tee-tee' call more reminiscent of that of a firefinch. They are best seen when they hover and bounce for a few seconds before finally settling. R

R *resident*

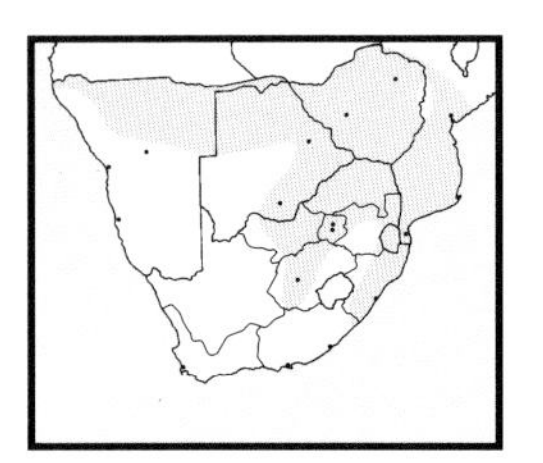

Blue Waxbill *Uraeginthus angolensis* (844) 13 cm

The only blue and brown finch-like bird in the region, this species should be unmistakable. Males have a blue face, underparts, rump and tail which contrast with the brown upperparts. Females and immatures are duller, having paler brown upperparts and the blue confined to the face and throat. The Blue Waxbill has a pointed-tailed appearance in flight, which is when it gives its typical waxbill 'tswee-tswee' call; the song is a jumbled mixture of these and other notes. They feed on the ground in small groups and pairs, and are confiding and approachable, but may fly off swiftly to dash into cover. They occur in dry thornveld and savanna but avoid moister woodland. R

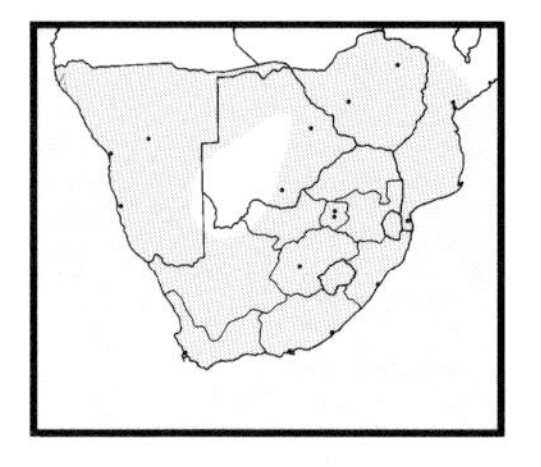

Common Waxbill *Estrilda astrild* (846) 13 cm

This fairly nondescript, small finch has lozenge-shaped red naked skin around the eyes, very fine, delicate barring on the breast and flanks, and a red stripe down the centre of the belly, all of which help to identify it at close range. The sexes are alike. Immatures are duller versions of the adults and have a black bill. Calls are a nasal 'cher-cher-cher' flight call and a 'ping-ping' bell-like note. The flight is direct and fast, just above grass level, and it is then that the dark, pointed tail can be seen. The Common Waxbill occurs in small groups and feeds on the ground or by clinging to grass stems and picking at seed heads. It frequents rank grass, reedbeds and thickets near water. R

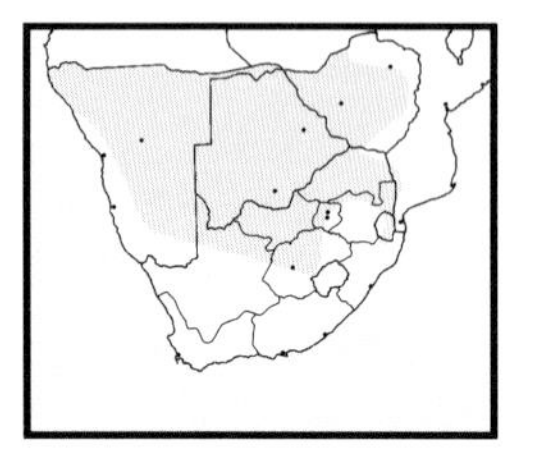

Violeteared Waxbill *Uraeginthus granatinus* (845) 15 cm

The male and female birds share the diagnostic features of violet cheeks, a royal-blue rump and a black tail. The male's body colour is a deep chocolate brown and it has a black chin; the female's body plumage is buffy brown in colour. The tail is long and pointed. Immatures resemble the females but are duller and lack the violet cheeks. The call is a thin, trilling 'tiu-woooee', the song a canary-like twitter. Violeteared Waxbills feed in company with other waxbills and firefinches and regularly drink at livestock waterbutts in the heat of the day. They occur in the drier regions in acacia thicket and scrub. NE

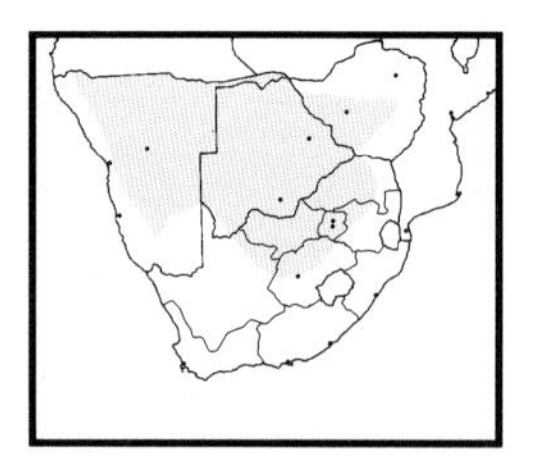

Blackcheeked Waxbill *Estrilda erythronotos* (847) 13 cm

This is an unobtrusive, small waxbill but nonetheless can easily be identified by the black on its face which extends to the ear coverts. The belly and rump are dark red and the wings have broad, black and grey barring but there is less bold, greyish barring on the mantle and head. The tail is black and is shorter and less pointed than that of the Violeteared Waxbill. The female and immature are duller than the male. Calls are a high-pitched 'chuloweee' and a short, sharp 'tzhik' alarm note. The Blackcheeked Waxbill is found mostly in small flocks which feed on the ground or on grass-seed heads and are frequent visitors to water sources. They occur in dry acacia thornveld and savanna, along dry water courses and in thicket. R

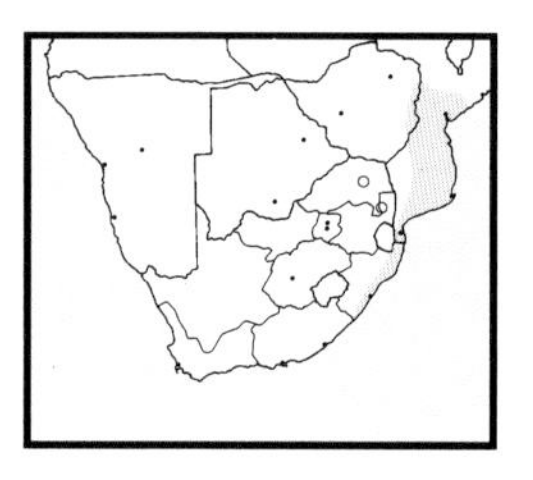

Grey Waxbill *Estrilda perreini* (848) 11 cm

This is a small, dark grey bird with a conspicuous red rump and lower back. The head is sometimes a slightly paler grey in female birds. Immatures are duller versions of the adults and lack the black eye-stripe. The call of the Grey Waxbill is a soft, high-pitched, whistled 'pseeu-pseeu'. Quiet and furtive, these waxbills feed on grass-seed heads in the shade of forest glades. Grey Waxbills usually occur in small groups of four to six, but sometimes may be seen in pairs. They frequent the edges of evergreen forests, riverine thicket in drier woodland, and coastal forests. R

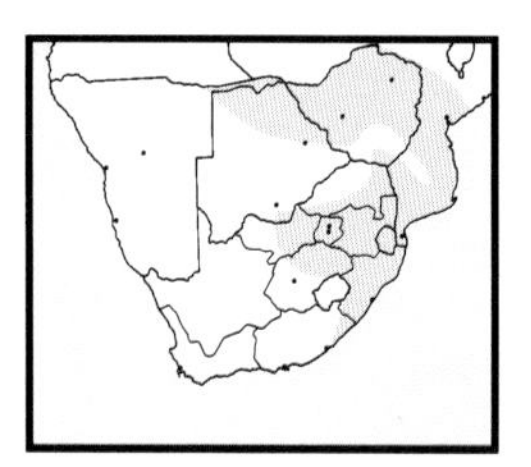

Orangebreasted Waxbill *Sporaeginthus subflavus* (854) 10 cm

The male Orangebreasted Waxbill is bright orange to golden-yellow below, with faded grey barring on the flanks. At close range the red bill and lozenge-shaped naked red eye patches can be seen. Females and immatures are dowdier versions of the male, and lack the red around the eyes. Orangebreasted Waxbills are distinguished from the Quail Finch (see page 282) by having a red, not dark, rump. The call in flight is a 'zink-zink' contact note and this bird also gives a rapid 'trip-trip' take-off call. Flocks fly rapidly, bunched together, giving their contact calls and showing the yellow underparts which contrast with the darker upperparts and red rumps. Orangebreasted Waxbills occur in flocks in damp, grassy areas and in sedges and reeds around water. R

1. Male Blue Waxbills
2. Male Violeteared Waxbill
3. Female Blue Waxbill
4. Adult Common Waxbill
5. Female Violeteared Waxbill
6. Adult Blackcheeked Waxbill
7. Adult Grey Waxbill
8. Male Orangebreasted Waxbill

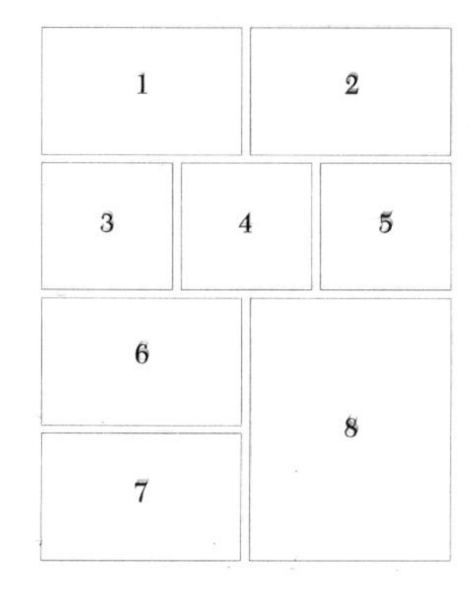

R *resident* • NE *near endemic*

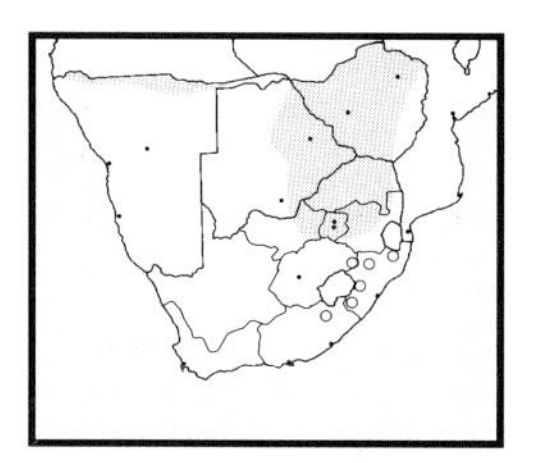

Cut-throat Finch *Amadina fasciata* (855) 12 cm

The males of this small, mottled, brown and white finch have a diagnostic red band across the throat, from ear to ear. Females resemble the female Redheaded Finch but can be distinguished from that species by having a barred head and a mottled, not uniform, back. Immatures resemble the females but have less barring on the head, and immature males have the red on the throat replaced with a pale creamy band. The call is a high-pitched 'eee-eee-eee' given in flight. The Cut-throat Finch sometimes occurs in mixed flocks with weavers (see pages 268-72) and queleas (see page 274) but more commonly associates with the Redheaded Finch. It forages on bare, stony ground and in short-grass areas, and drinks in flocks at waterholes and pans. It frequents acacia scrub and woodland. R

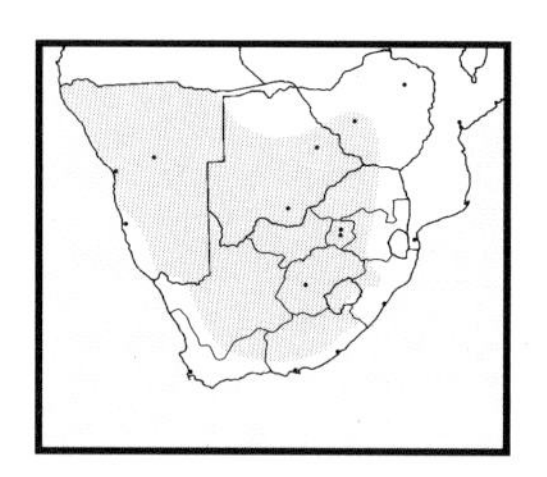

Redheaded Finch *Amadina erythrocephala* (856) 13 cm

Similar to the Redheaded Quelea (see page 274), this species can be told apart by its very obvious scalloped underparts. The male has a diagnostic bright red head. Females lack the red colouring on the head and have more uniform upperparts than the similar female Cut-throat Finch and a more barred, not mottled, pattern on the underparts. Immatures resemble the females. Calls are a soft 'chuk-chuk' and, in flight, a 'zree-zree'. The male displays with a puffed-out breast, bouncing up and down on a branch next to the female. Redheaded Finches frequent dry woodland, grasslands and acacia scrub and often frequent Sociable Weaver (see page 272) colonies and the old nests of other weavers. NE

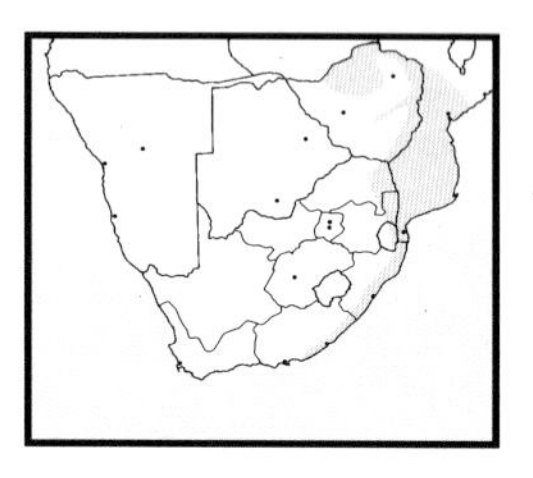

Redbacked Mannikin *Spermestes bicolor* (858) 9 cm

Easily told apart from the other mannikins by its chestnut back, this bird also shows black and white spangling on the folded primaries and on the flanks, and has a pale grey bill. The sexes are alike. Immatures may be confused with the immature Bronze Mannikin but have a warmer brown back with a chestnut wash and are paler below. The call is a soft, thin 'seeet-seeeet' given in flight. The Redbacked Mannikin occurs in small groups and feeds either on the ground or perched on grass heads. The male display has this tiny bird puffing up its breast feathers in a very upright position and singing its short, chippy song. These birds are found in rank grasses on the edges of evergreen forest and adjoining scrub, and in thickets along rivers. R

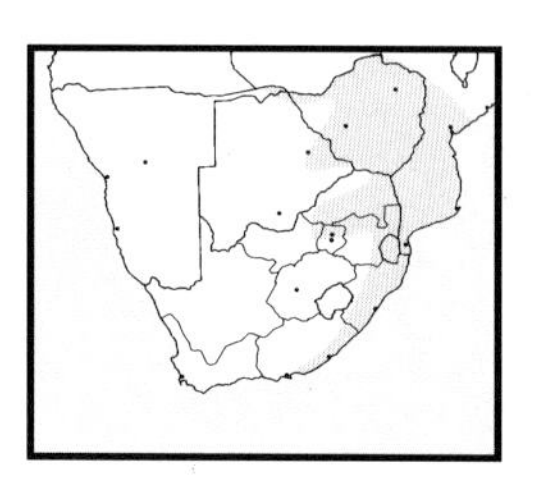

Bronze Mannikin *Spermestes cucullatus* (857) 9 cm

This species differs from the much larger Pied Mannikin by having fine barring on the flanks, lower back and rump and a greenish-bronze sheen to its wing coverts. Immatures resemble the immature Redbacked Mannikin but have no trace of chestnut on the back, being uniformly dun brown above and below and having a paler belly and vent; the immature Pied Mannikin is larger and has clear white underparts. The call is a soft, buzzy 'chizza-chizza'. Very restless and active, whole flocks will perch shoulder to shoulder on a branch or telephone wire. Bronze Mannikins frequent a wide variety of habitats, from forest edges to open woodland, marshy and grassy areas and suburbia. R

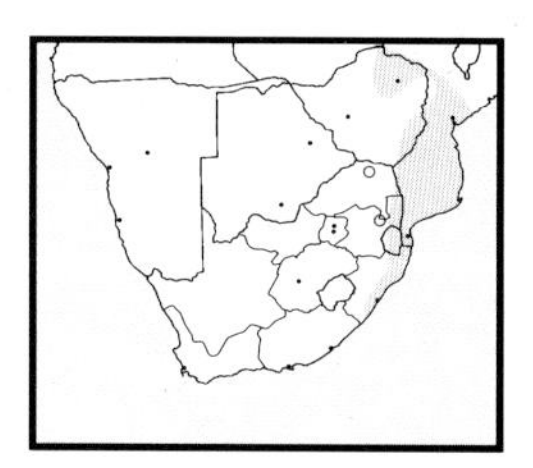

Pied Mannikin *Spermestes fringilloides* (859) 13 cm

The largest of the mannikins, this species is bulkier than the Bronze Mannikin and has a larger, more powerful bill and overall a more black-and-white contrasting appearance. It lacks the fine barring on the rump and flanks of the Bronze Mannikin, having instead broad black barring on the sides of the breast and flanks. Immatures are similar to the immature Bronze Mannikin but are much paler below. The flight call is a 'pee-oo, pee-oo' and these birds also give a harsher 'chuk-chuk' contact call. Pied Mannikins occur in small groups and fly in compact, tight flocks. They frequent grass-encroached tangles and thickets, reedbeds and stands of bamboo. R

1. Male Cut-throat Finch
2. Female (back) and male Redheaded Finch
3. Female Cut-throat Finch
4. Immature male Redheaded Finch
5. Female Redheaded Finch
6. Adult (back) and immature Redbacked Mannikins
7. Adult Bronze Mannikins
8. Adult Redbacked Mannikin
9. Adult Pied Mannikin

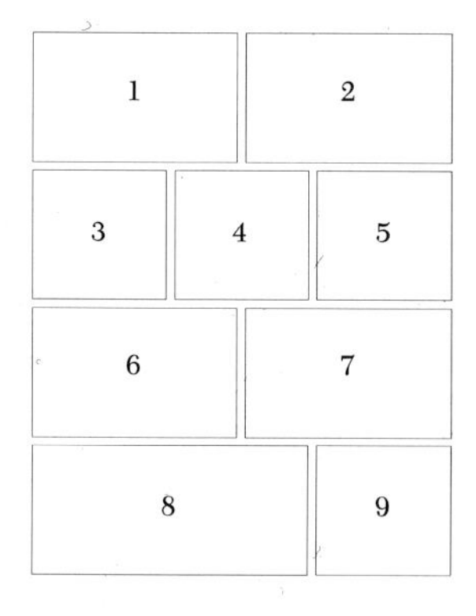

R *resident* • NE *near endemic*

Widowfinches and whydahs
Family Viduidae

These small birds have short, conical bills adapted for seed-eating. When breeding both groups exhibit extreme sexual dimorphism. Females and non-breeding males are short-tailed with dull, mottled brown, black and buff plumages. Widowfinches and whydahs are parasitic, with distributions matching those of their hosts.

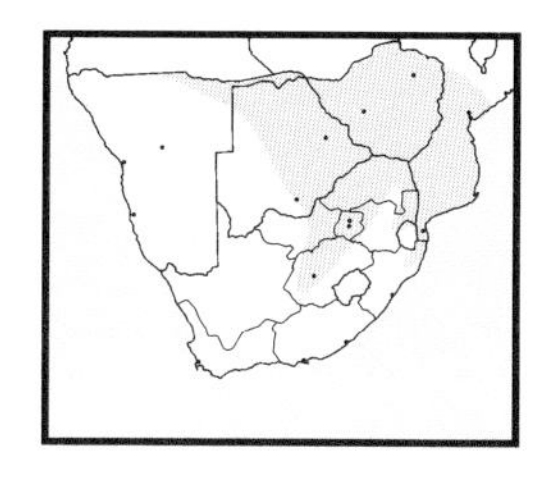

Steelblue Widowfinch *Vidua chalybeata* (867) 11 cm

This species is easily identified by the combination of a red bill and red legs and feet; the bill is a paler pink or whitish in the northwest of its range. All plumage stages are distinguished from other widowfinches by the red bill and legs. The male sings from an exposed perch, and mimics the song of its host, the Redbilled Firefinch (see page 282). The male display consists of a bouncing flight in front of the perched females, with continual twittering and calling, in the manner of a Pintailed Whydah. This widowfinch is found in a variety of habitats, from woodland to grasslands and old lands. R

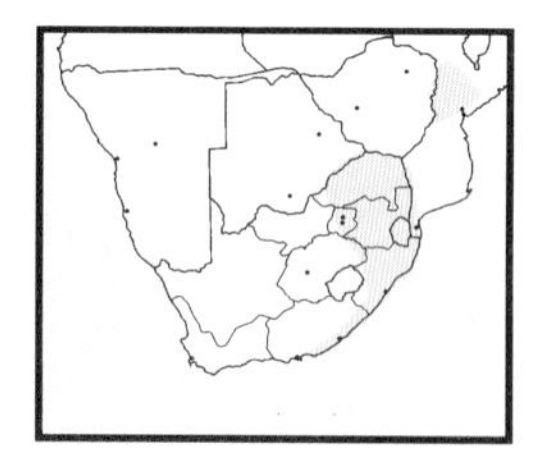

Black Widowfinch *Vidua funerea* (864) 11 cm

This widowfinch is readily recognizable in all its plumages, except immature, by having a white bill and deep red legs and toes. Non-breeding males, females and immatures are mottled black and buff above, and pale below. The call is a short 'chit-chit' and the song a jumbled mixture of chirps and warbles, as well as mimicry of its host, the Bluebilled Firefinch (see page 282). The Black Widowfinch is found in forest edges, thornveld and riverine thicket. R

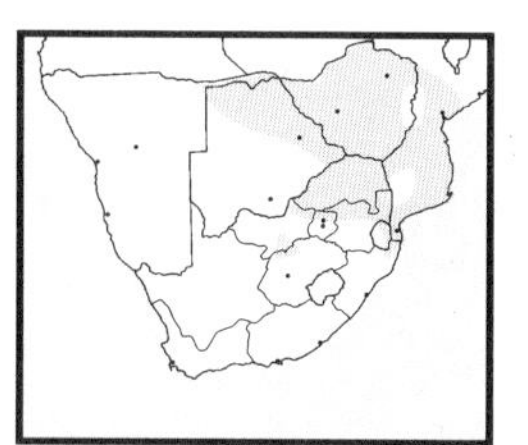

Purple Widowfinch *Vidua purpurascens* (865) 11 cm

Both the bill and legs of this widowfinch are whitish in colour. In non-breeding plumage the male and female retain the white bill, legs and toes; these are horn coloured in the immatures. The song is a jumbled mixture of chipping notes and it also mimics Jameson's Firefinch (see page 282), the host of this species. The Purple Widowfinch has a similar dancing, bounding flight display to those of other widowfinches. It occurs in savanna and thornveld. R

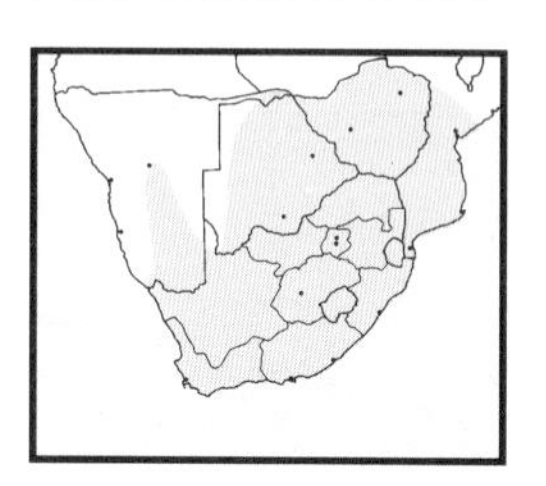

Pintailed Whydah *Vidua macroura* (860) 12 cm (plus 22 cm tail in breeding male)

The breeding male is unmistakable and a familiar bird in the region. Females are very similar to the female Shaft-tailed Whydah but have bolder head markings and a horn-coloured, not red, bill and legs. Immatures resemble the immature Pied Mannikin (see page 286) but are smaller and have a tiny bill. Non-breeding males, females and immatures in flight show white outer feathers and white tips to the tail. The male's display call is a 'tseet-tseet' and a jumbled mixture of twittering. The Pintailed Whydah frequents a wide range of habitats but favours moist grasslands, agricultural fields, parks and gardens. R

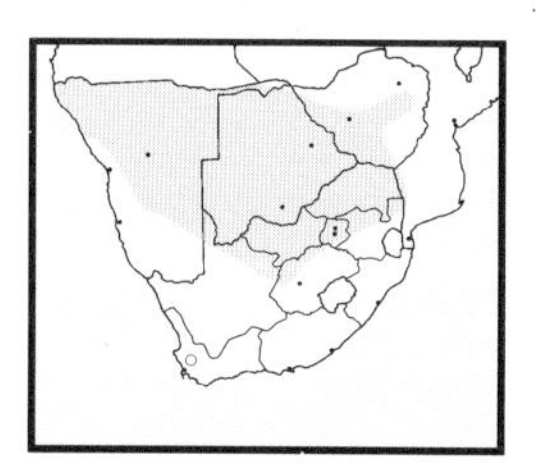

Shaft-tailed Whydah *Vidua regia* (861) 12 cm (plus 22 cm tail in breeding male)

Breeding males are easy to identify, differing from the Pintailed Whydah by having buffy orange in place of the white of that bird, and a long, thin tail with spatulate tips. Females have a less bold head pattern and a red, not brown, bill and legs. Paradise Whydahs in similar plumage are larger and have black or dark brown bills. Immatures resemble immature Bronze Mannikins (see page 286) but are larger and have a different shape. In flight the call is a short 'teet-teet'. These birds frequent dry acacia bush, savanna and dry grassy regions. NE

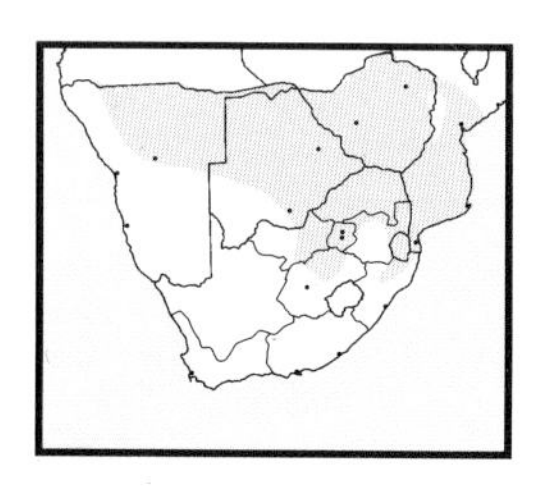

Paradise Whydah *Vidua paradisaea* (862) 15 cm (plus 23 cm tail in breeding male)

The breeding male has black upperparts and head with a yellow hind collar and belly, and a chestnut breast. Females, immatures and non-breeding males are grey-brown above with an off-white head striped black. The call is a short 'chip-chip' uttered in flight and the bird also mimics the song of its host, the Melba Finch (see page 280). The Paradise Whydah frequents mixed woodland, preferring drier thornveld and avoiding moister forests. R

Male Steelblue Widowfinch (transitional)

Female Black Widowfinch

1. Male Steelblue Widowfinch
2. Male Black Widowfinch
3. Female Shaft-tailed Whydah
4. Male Purple Widowfinch
5. Female Pintailed Whydah
6. Male Paradise Whydah (breeding)
7. Male Shaft-tailed Whydah (breeding)
8. Male Pintailed Whydah (breeding)
9. Male Pintailed Whydah (non-breeding)

1 2 3 4 5 6 7 8 9

R *resident* • NE *near endemic*

Canaries, siskins, finches and buntings
Family Fringillidae

Small birds, the members of this family range from the brilliantly coloured to the drab and dowdy. Most are seed- and insect-eaters and are terrestrial in habits, but do use trees and scrub for nesting. They are highly prized by the cagebird industry for their fine, buzzy songs.

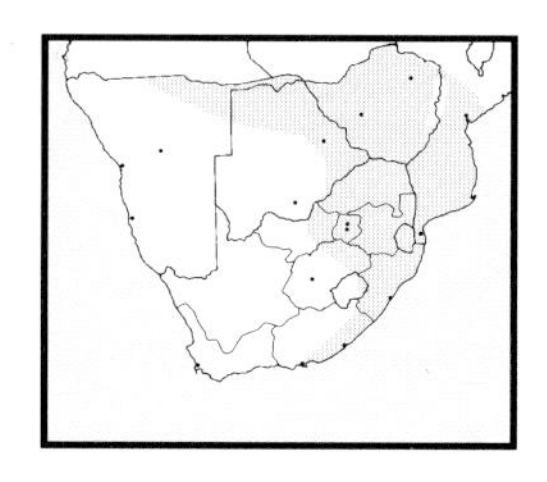

Yelloweyed Canary *Serinus mozambicus* (869) 12 cm

Adults of this species are most easily confused with the Bully Canary but have a more clearly defined facial pattern with black malar and eye stripes, which in the Bully Canary are suffused green and yellow. In flight the Yelloweyed Canary shows a yellow rump and contrasting white tail tips. Females are very similar to males, only slightly duller. The call is a 'zeee-zeree-chereeeo' and variations of this. The flight is markedly bounding and undulating. Yelloweyed Canaries feed on the ground and frequent a wide range of woodlands, grasslands, forest fringes and riverine forests in drier areas. R

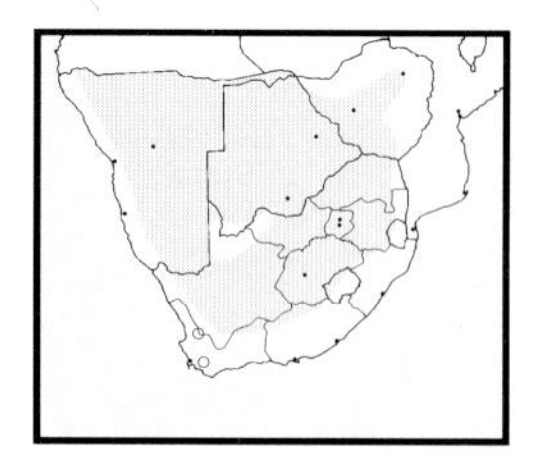

Blackthroated Canary *Serinus atrogularis* (870) 11 cm

This small, greyish canary is distinguishable by its brilliant lemon-yellow rump and white tips to the tail, both of which are obvious only in flight. The black on the throat is very variable and may appear as only a grizzled patch on the chin although in some individuals it is a clear black bib. The song is a prolonged series of wheezy whistles and chirrups given from an exposed perch; in flight it utters a 'tseeue'. The Blackthroated Canary prefers dry thornveld and moister savanna and avoids wetter areas. R

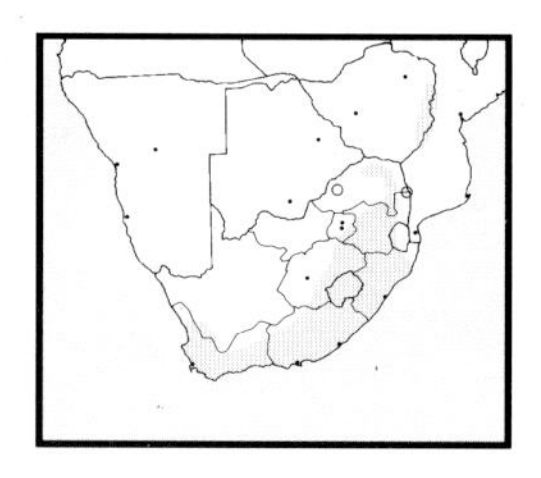

Cape Canary *Serinus canicollis* (872) 13 cm

This species is unlike other 'yellow' canaries in that it lacks bold facial markings. Instead, the face is greenish-yellow, brighter on the forehead and contrasting with a blue-grey nape and collar. Females are duller, with a streaked mantle and a greater extent of grey on the breast. Immatures are heavily streaked above and below, with a pale yellow tail and vent. The call is a 'sweet-sweet', and a warbled song is given from a high perch or, sometimes, in a slow, butterfly-like flight display. The Cape Canary occurs in fynbos, exotic plantations, open grasslands, suburbia and mountainous regions. R

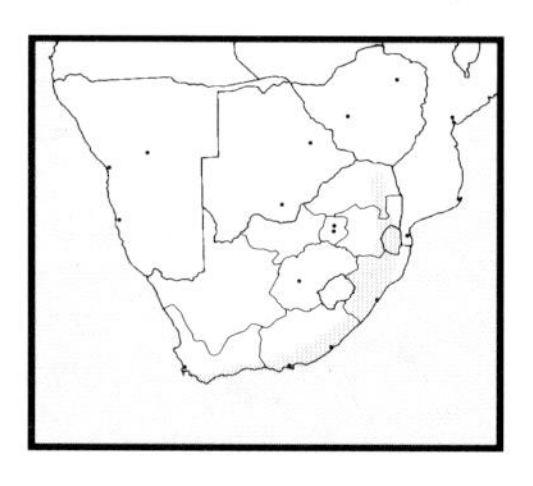

Forest Canary *Serinus scotops* (873) 13 cm

At close range this very dark, dull canary reveals heavily streaked underparts, a small, yellow eyebrow stripe and greyish cheeks; the black chin is a constant character. Females and immatures are slightly duller. The call is a high-pitched 'tseek', the song brisk but not far carrying. Much more skulking than are other canaries, the Forest Canary keeps low down and is heard more often than seen. It is found in evergreen forest edges and clearings and in mountain gullies. E

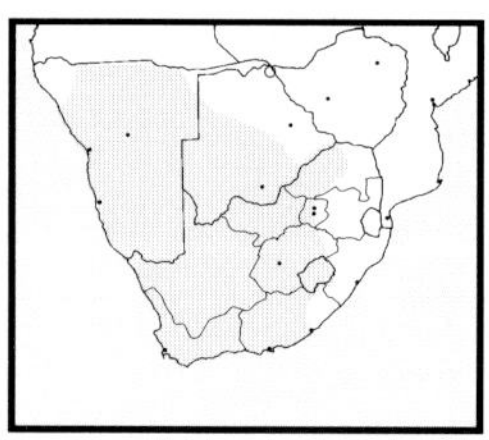

Yellow Canary *Serinus flaviventris* (878) 13 cm

This canary varies considerably in colour from region to region. In the west it is by far the brightest yellow of all canaries, the male an overall brilliant primrose-yellow with only slightly darker wings and tail; farther east the bird becomes progressively darker yellow with olive upperparts, and then resembles the Bully Canary. Females are greyish-brown with streaked underparts. Immatures are duller versions of the females. The song is a typical canary jumble of notes, the call a 'chissick' or 'cheree' notes. Yellow Canaries prefer drier areas from thornveld to fynbos and mountainous regions. NE

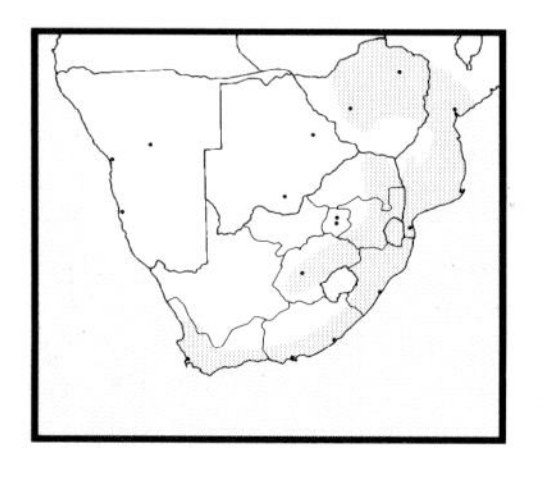

Bully Canary *Serinus sulphuratus* (877) 15 cm

The largest and most robust of the 'yellow' canaries, this species occurs as a dark and a pale form and as intermediates between these. It may, however, be told from the Yellow Canary by its much larger size and more massive bill. Immatures resemble the adults but are dowdier, with faint streaking on the breast. The contact call is harsher than that of most canaries, a 'chrruup'. The song is lower pitched and slower than those of other canaries. The Bully Canary frequents forest edges and coastal scrub to mountainous regions. R

Male Blackthroated Canary

Immature Yellow Canary

1. Adult Yelloweyed Canary
2. Adult Blackthroated Canary
3. Male Cape Canary
4. Female Cape Canary
5. Male Yellow Canary
6. Adult Forest Canary
7. Adult Bully Canary (yellow form)
8. Female Yellow Canary
9. Adult Bully Canary (green form)

1	2
3	4
5	6	7
8	9

R *resident* • E *endemic* • NE *near endemic*

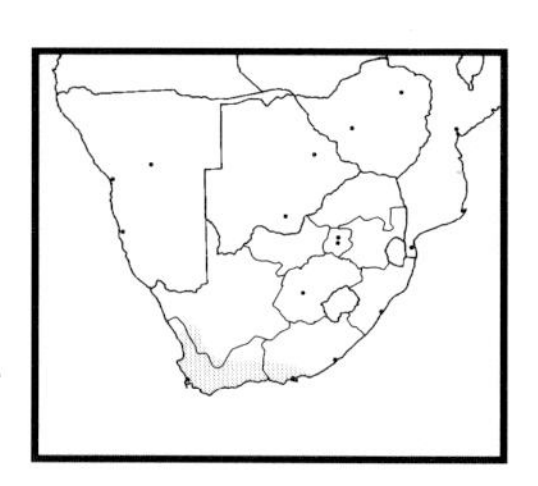

Cape Siskin *Pseudochloroptila totta* (874) 12 cm

A largely olive-brown bird, the Cape Siskin shows white tips to the primaries and tail feathers. Females are duller versions of the males, with less extensive white tips to the primaries; these may not be visible in the field. Immatures are heavily streaked on the head and breast. The flight call and contact note is a 'pee-chee', the song a jumbled canary-like mixture of twitters and 'pee-chee' notes. The Cape Siskin occurs in fynbos from coastal regions to arid scrub, and in mountainous terrain; it also frequents exotic pine plantations. E

Male Blackheaded Canary (white-headed race)

Blackheaded Canary *Serinus alario* (876) 12 cm

This small canary superficially resembles the Redbacked Mannikin (see page 286). The head is black as is the breast, the black dividing into two stripes which run on to the sides of the breast. The back and tail are chestnut in colour. Females and immatures lack the black on the head and breast but do show the diagnostic chestnut back and tail. The subspecies *S.a. leucolaema* has a white head with black stripes. The call is a short 'tswee-tswee'; the song is canary-like. The Blackheaded Canary favours drier regions, in particular Karoo scrub, arid fynbos and mountainous regions. E

Male Blackeared Canary

Whitethroated Canary *Serinus albogularis* (879) 15 cm

A drab greyish-brown canary, the Whitethroated Canary might be confused with the Protea Canary which also shows a white throat patch. However, this species has a greenish or yellow rump which the Protea Canary lacks. The female Yellow Canary (see page 290) is similar to but smaller than the male Whitethroated Canary, and also has a smaller bill and streaking on the breast which the Whitethroated Canary lacks. The call is a 'chissick' contact note and the song typically canary-like. The Whitethroated Canary is a dry-country canary, being found in arid to semi-desert areas, Karoo scrub, and in thornbelts on dry river courses. E

Adult Streakyheaded Canary (dark-cheeked race)

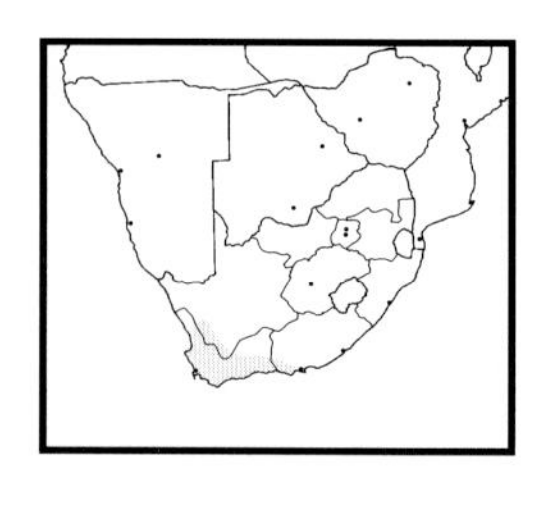

Protea Canary *Serinus leucopterus* (880) 15 cm

This very drab canary lacks any yellow in the plumage and most closely resembles the Whitethroated Canary but has a dark, not yellow, rump. It may be further differentiated from that species by its small black or grizzled chin. The Protea Canary has a large, pinkish-grey bill which contrasts with its dark face. The sexes are similar and immatures are even dowdier than the adults. The call is a clearly whistled 'tree-lee-leeoo' and the song a typically canary-like jumble of warblings and chirps. The Protea Canary is very shy and skulking, preferring to keep low down in scrub. Its thick bill is used to crack open protea seeds taken directly from the flowers or off the ground. This species is found in dense stands of proteas on hillsides, on mountains and in thick valley scrub. E

1. Adult Cape Siskin
2. Male Blackheaded Canary
3. Male Blackheaded Canary (white-headed form)
4. Female Blackheaded Canary
5. Adult Whitethroated Canary
6. Adult Protea Canary
7. Adult Streakyheaded Canary
8. Female (left) and male (right) Blackeared Canary

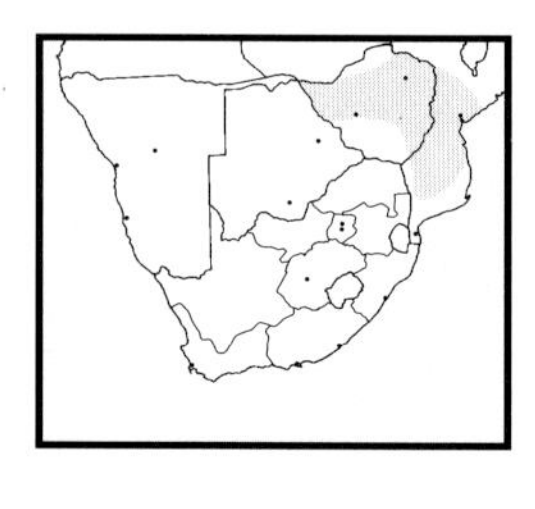

Blackeared Canary *Serinus mennelli* (882) 14 cm

The Blackeared Canary is similar to the Streakyheaded Canary, both species showing a broad white eyebrow stripe, but this species has very obvious black cheeks and streaking on the breast, which distinguish it. Females and immatures have brownish, not black, cheeks but also show the streaking on the breast. The call is a soft 'tuuee', the song typically canary-like and given in fluttering display over woodland canopy. The Blackeared Canary frequents miombo and teak woodland, and usually occurs in small groups and often in mixed parties. R

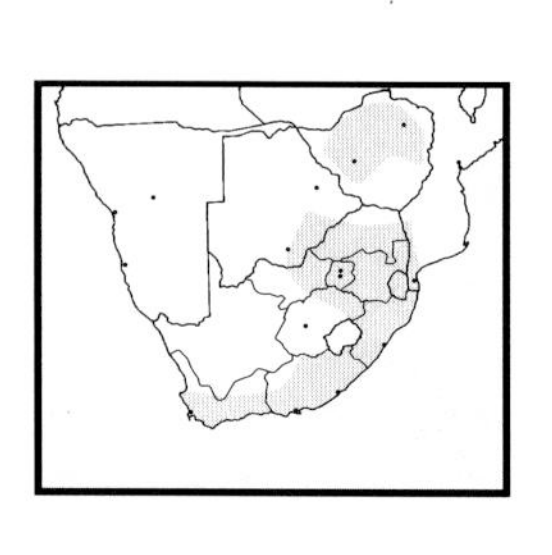

Streakyheaded Canary *Serinus gularis* (881) 15 cm

This species, the most distinctive feature of which is its broad whitish eyebrow-stripe, differs from the Blackeared Canary by lacking the black cheeks of that species, having a streaked grey-and-white forehead and crown, and lacking streaking on the breast. Females and immatures resemble the female and immature Blackeared Canary but do not show any streaking on the breast. The Streakyheaded Canary might be mistaken for the Whitethroated Canary but that species is very much larger, and has a more massive bill and a greenish rump. The call is a soft, weak 'trrreet', the song a quiet canary-like jumble of 'tsee-ch-che-swy' notes given when the bird is perched or in a display flight. Streakyheaded Canaries are found in a wide variety of woodland and scrub habitats. R

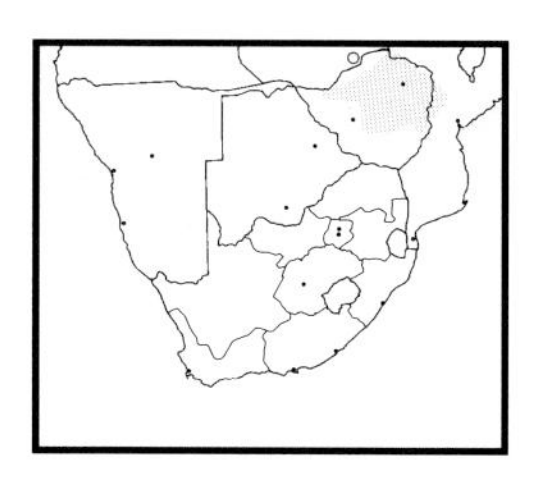

Cabanis's Bunting *Emberiza cabanisi* (883) 16 cm

Cabanis's Bunting is very similar to the Goldenbreasted Bunting but the head pattern in this species differs slightly, showing only a white eyebrow stripe and not the white stripe below the eye. Cabanis's Bunting also lacks the chestnut back of the Goldenbreasted Bunting; and the breast is clear yellow, not suffused with orange. Females and immatures are duller versions of the males. The call is a clearly whistled 'tsseeeoo', the song a whistled 'wee-chidder-chidder-weee' and variations of this. An unobtrusive bird, Cabanis's Bunting is confined to miombo and teak woodland and adjoining scrub. R

Male Cabanis's Bunting

Goldenbreasted Bunting *Emberiza flaviventris* (884) 16 cm

More brightly coloured and generally more active and conspicuous than the rarer Cabanis's Bunting, the Goldenbreasted Bunting differs from that species by having a white stripe below the eye, a chestnut mantle and an orange breast. Females and immatures have the same field characters that separate the males of these two similar species but are paler and have washed-out yellow underparts. The call is a nasal, buzzy 'zzhrrrr', the song a repeated 'weechee-weechee-weechee' given from the tops of trees. This bird occurs in dry thornveld, open woodland, secondary growth and exotic plantations. R

Male Goldenbreasted Bunting

Rock Bunting *Emberiza tahapisi* (886) 14 cm

This small, very dark bunting has a black and white striped head. It vaguely resembles the Cape Bunting but has cinnamon underparts and a black throat, and it lacks chestnut on the wings. Females and immatures are duller, paler versions of the males with less obvious black and white head stripes. Normally fairly quiet, the contact call is a soft 'pee-pee-wee' and the song is short and rattling, given from an exposed perch or vantage point. The display consists of vigorous flight chases, the birds twisting and turning through woodland and over rocky faces. The Rock Bunting is most frequently seen on gravel road verges in rocky or hilly terrain and on rocky ridges in woodland. R

Cape Bunting *Emberiza capensis* (885) 16 cm

In some regions this is a familiar and common bird, easily recognized by its black and white striped head and chestnut wing coverts. It might be confused with the Rock Bunting, which also has a black and white striped head, but the grey underparts and white throat distinguish it. Immatures and females are duller versions of the males. The call is a nasal, ascending, three- to four-note 'zzoo-zeh-zee-zee', the song a loud, chirping series of 'chip-chip-chop-cheep-chireee' notes. This confiding species feeds on the ground, shuffling around and scratching for seeds. It occurs in coastal fynbos and mountainous regions. R

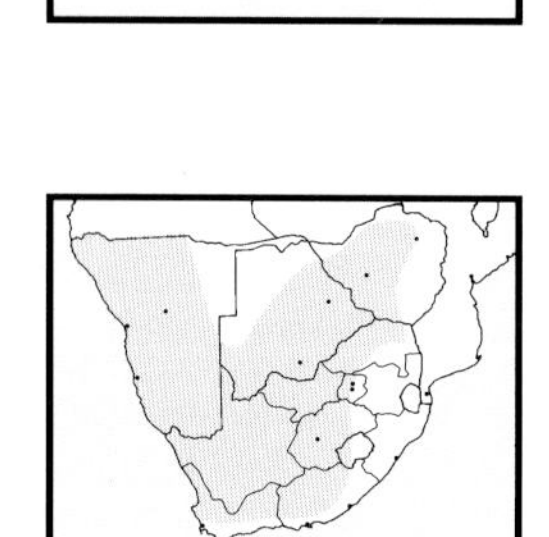

Larklike Bunting *Emberiza impetuani* (887) 14 cm

This bird has no diagnostic features, looking like a dowdy lark but behaving like a bunting with its upright posture, and hopping, not walking, over stones and bare ground in search of seeds. The pale, washed-out, cinnamon head and breast, buffy eyebrow and malar stripes, and chestnut-fringed wing feathers all aid in its identification. The call is a short 'tuk-tuk' given in flight and it sings a series of similar but more melodic notes. In drought years it erupts into moister regions in the east. Encountered in usually small groups, large concentrations of these birds occur around water points and, during the breeding season, in the desert after rains. The Larklike Bunting frequents the arid west from true desert to desert edge and Karoo. NE

1. Female (top) and male (bottom) Cabanis's Bunting
2. Male Goldenbreasted Bunting
3. Male Rock Bunting
4. Female Goldenbreasted Bunting
5. Female Rock Bunting
6. Female Cape Bunting
7. Adult Larklike Bunting
8. Male Cape Bunting

1	2
3	4
5	6
7	8

R *resident* • NE *near endemic*

Bird societies and clubs

Societies and clubs play an important role in communication and co-ordination between birders. Most also hold regular meetings and outings, and produce a newsletter. Bird clubs in South Africa and Namibia, with the exception of the Diaz Cross Bird Club, are affiliated to the Southern African Ornithological Society.

Southern African Ornithological Society
P.O. Box 84394, Greenside, Johannesburg 2034.
The Wildlife Society of Southern Africa
P.O. Box 44189, Linden 2104.

Transvaal
Lowveld Bird Club
P.O. Box 4113, Nelspruit 1200.
North-eastern Bird Club
P.O. Box 6007, Pietersburg Noord 0750.
Northern Transvaal Ornithological Society
P.O. Box 4158, Pretoria 0001.
Rand Barbets Bird Club
2 Flint Rd, Parkwood 2193.
Sandton Bird Club
P.O. Box 650890, Benmore 2010.
Vaal Reefs Bird Club
P.O. Box 5129, Vaal Reefs 2621.
Wesvaal Bird Club
P.O. Box 2413, Potchefstroom 2520.
Witwatersrand Bird Club
P.O. Box 72091, Parkview 2122.

Cape
Cape Bird Club
P.O. Box 5022, Cape Town 8000.
Eastern Cape Wild Bird Society
P.O. Box 27454, Greenacres 6057.
Diaz Cross Bird Club
39 African St, Grahamstown 6140.

Natal
Natal Bird Club
P.O. Box 1218, Durban 4000.
Natal Midlands Bird Club
P.O. Box 2772, Pietermaritzburg 3200.

Orange Free State
Goldfields Bird Club
P.O. Box 580, Virginia 9430.
Orange Free State Ornithological Society
P.O. Box 6614, Bloemfontein 9300.

Zimbabwe
Ornithological Association of Zimbabwe
P.O. Box 8382, Causeway, Zimbabwe.

Namibia
Namibian Bird Club
P.O. Box 67, Windhoek, Namibia.

Botswana
Botswana Bird Club
P.O. Box 71, Gaborone, Botswana.

Specialist Interest Groups
Vulture Study Group
P.O. Box 72334, Parkview 2122.
African Raptor Information Centre
P.O. Box 4035, Halfway House 1685.
Southern African Crane Foundation
P.O. Box 2310, Durban 4000.
African Seabird Group
P.O. Box 341113, Rhodes Gift 7707.

Further reading

Clancey, P.A. 1967. *Gamebirds of Southern Africa*. Purnell, Cape Town.

Clancey, P.A. (ed) 1980. SAOS Checklist of Southern African Birds. Southern African Ornithological Society, Johannesburg.

Clancey, P.A. 1985. *The Rare Birds of Southern Africa*. Winchester Press, Johannesburg.

Ginn, P.J., McIlleron, W.G. & Milstein, P.le S. 1989. *The Complete Book of Southern African Birds*. Struik, Winchester, Cape Town.

Hockey, P.A.R. 1994. *Sasol Birds of Southern Africa – Checklist and Alternative Names*. Struik Publishers (Pty) Ltd, Cape Town.

Maclean, G.L. 1984. *Roberts' Birds of Southern Africa*. John Voelcker Bird Book Fund, Cape Town.

Newman, K.B. 1983. *Birds of Southern Africa*. Southern Book Publishers, Johannesburg.

Newman, K.B. 1987. *Birds of the Kruger National Park*. Southern Book Publishers, Johannesburg.

Sinclair, J.C. 1987. *Field Guide to the Birds of Southern Africa*. Struik Publishers (Pty) Ltd, Cape Town.

Sinclair, J.C., Hockey, P. & Tarboton, W. 1993. *Sasol Birds of Southern Africa*. Struik Publishers (Pty) Ltd, Cape Town.

Skead, C.J. 1967. *The Sunbirds of Southern Africa; also Sugarbirds, White-eyes and Spotted Creeper*. A.A. Balkema, Cape Town.

Solomon, D. & Williams, J.1992.*Birds of a Feather*. Birdwatch Zimbabwe, Harare.

Steyn, P. 1982. *Birds of Prey of Southern Africa*. David Philip, Cape Town.

Tarboton, W.R., Kemp, M.I. & Kemp, A.C. 1987. *Birds of the Transvaal*. Transvaal Museum, Pretoria.

Urban, E.K., Fry, C.H. & Keith, S. 1986. *The Birds of Africa*, Vol. 2. Academic Press, London.

Index to common names

The numbers refer to the page on which the species account appears.

F

G

H

I

J

K

L

M

N

Index to scientific names

The numbers refer to the page on which the species' account appears.

Picture credits

Ardea London/D Avon p263:3 **Ardea London/A Greensmith** p223:6 **Ardea London/Peter Steyn** p237:5,6 **ABPL** p119:1 **ABPL/Daryl Balfour** p107:5; p169:4 **ABPL/Anthony Bannister** p13:1; p45:7; p47:6; p111:3; p137:1; p155:2 **ABPL/Daphne Carew** p175:3 **ABPL/Roger de la Harpe** p25:8; p47:1; p59:1; p75:3; p87:3; p139:2; p213:1 **ABPL/Nigel J Dennis** contents page; p23:5; p27:7,9; p29:2,6; p33:3; p39:8; p41:4; p43:8; p45:1,3; p47:11; p 49:5,7; p51:4; p53:2; p55:2; 61:2; p63:1; p85:2; p89:4; p95:2; p97:4,5; p123:3; p127:5; p129:3; p149:1,8; p153:2; p161:5; p163:2; p165:2; p167:2,3; p197:4; p199:3; p207:3; p255:6; p257:1,3; p271:3,9; p273:3; p277:1; p279:1 **ABPL/Aaron Frankental** p105:6 **ABPL/Paul Funston** p107:3; p195:1 **ABPL/Kerstin Geier** p119:2 **ABPL/Clem Haagner** p23:9; p27:11; p31:7; p39:1; p47:8; p49:6; p53:8; p69:6; p83:2; p95:5; p105:2; p115:4; p117:1; p125:6; p127:4; p135:2; p159:4; p163:1; p173:2; p175:5; p193:2; p201:1; p205:6; p221:5; p239:4; p251:2; p259:6; p269:1; p273:7; p283:7 **ABPL/Beverley Joubert** p27:10; p59:4 **ABPL/Tim Liversedge** p31:4; p59:9; p139:6; p149:2 **ABPL/Eliot Lyons** p203:4 **ABPL/Norman Mann** p71:1 **ABPL/Robert C Nunnington** p29:9 **ABPL/Rob Ponte** p255:5 **ABPL/Eric Reisinger** p137:5; p151:5; p155:1 **ABPL/Phillip Richardson** p39:3; p85:5 **ABPL/Brendan Ryan** p39:5; p43:5; p63:5; p65:6,7; p69:5; p71:4; p73:5; p79:3; p99:8; p103:4 ; p111:2,7; p115:1; p119:5; p121:3; p131:1; p133:3; p141:2,4,5; p145:3; p151:4; p153:6; p157:2; p161:2; p173:7; p175:2,6,8; p177:5; p179:4; p189:3; p195:6; p199:4,5; p201:3; p203:2; p215:2; p217:1,2; p223:5; p225:5; p237:1,2,3; p241:7; p243:6; p245:1; p247:3,5; p249:3,4; p253:6; p255:2; p259:3; p261:5,6; p263:5; p265:3,4; p273:1; p287:4; p289:3,5; p291:6,7; p295:4,6 **ABPL/Joan Ryder** p153:4 **ABPL/Wayne Saunders** p71:3; p139:3 **ABPL/Lorna Stanton** half-title page; p37:4; p51:3; p59:3; p69:7; p139:4; p185:2; p273:8 **ABPL/Gavin Thomson** p245:6 **ABPL/Prof. Rudi van Aarde** p15:4 **ABPL/Johann van Jaarsveld** p133:2; p255:4; p285:3; p291:9; p295:5 **ABPL/Hein von Hörsten** p61:4; p147:6; p153:1; p169:5; p207:4; p227:4; p233:4; p261:8 **Aquila/N J Bean** p23:1 **Aquila/J J Brooks** p181:5 **Aquila/G D Dean** p217:6 **Aquila/Nigel Ede** p241:6 **Aquila/Hanne & Jens Eriksen** p99:5 **Aquila/Darren Frost** p143:4 **Aquila/Hans Gebuis** p117:4; p215:1,7 **Aquila/R Glover** p101:5,7 **Aquila/Conrad Greaves** p61:3; p67:1; p91:3; p93:8; p101:6; p103:1; p105:1; p109:5; p117:5,9; p241:5 **Aquila/H Kinloch** p181:6 **Aquila/Mike Lane** p101:4; p111:8; p117:3p205:3; p241:3 **Aquila/Wayne Lankmen** p93:6 **Aquila/Tom Leach** p93:7 **Aquila/K A Linnard** p215:4 **Aquila/David Owen** p183:3 **Aquila/Ray Tipper** p91:4; p99:4 **Daryl Balfour** p99:6; p173:3 **Anthony Bannister** p111:1; p149:4; p253:4; p265:1 **K Begg** p27:8; p45:6,9; p85:1; p87:4; p105:3 **R M Bloomfield** p61:1; p171:5; p175:7; p187:6; p207:1; p223:1; p227:7; p243:7; p251:6 **N Brickell** p41:2; p43:4,6; p75:2,7; p121:4; p125:4,5; p179:7; p209:5; p275:3; p279:3; p281:3,6,8,9; p283:1; p289:6; p291:1; p295:1 **Theo H Buchholz** p89:2; p201:4; p235:6; p241:1; p261:3 **Terry Carew** p75:8 **R Cassidy** p173:1 **Derek Coley** p251:4 **May Craig-Cooper FPSSA** p35:1; p37:3; p65:4; p77:5; p113:8; p235:4; p255:3,8; **Peter Craig-Cooper FPSSA** p23:6; p27:1,5; p39:6; p41:3; p45:2; p47:2,7; p51:6; p55: 3; p59:5,10; p67:5; p75:4; p77:6; p81:10; p83:1; p99:7; p101:8 ; p103:5; p113:2; p119:3,4; p123:5; p125:1; p127:3; p135:3; p139:5; p153:3; p155:3; p175:4; p179:6; p203:6; p207:9; p231:2; p247:8; p2 53:1; p263:7; p265:5; p267:1,2; p269:6; p271:1,8; p279:2,7,8; p281:4,5,7; p283:2,4; p285:1,6,7; p287:6-9; p289:1,2,7,8; p291:2,3,4; p293:1,2,4,5,8; p295:3,8 **Gerald Cubitt** p19:9; p159:1; p161:3,4; p263:2 **R S Daniell FRPS** p159:5; p187:4; p209:2; p219:6; p231:4 **Bruce Coleman Ltd/Peter Davey** p159:2 **Ian Davidson** p47:10; p55:4; p113:1; p133:5; p157:3; p205:8; p211:6 **Nigel J Dennis** back cover: bottom; p13:2,6; p25:2,7; p27:2,4,6; p29:5,7; p31:1,2; p33:2; p35:2,5,7; p37:1,2,6; p39:7; p41:1,5; p43:2,9,10; p45:5,8; p51:7; p59:6,7; p63:2,7; p71:2; p79:1; p81:6,8; p89:7; p91:2; p93:3; p99:2; p101:2,9; p107:7; p111:4; p117:6,7; p135:4; p151:6; p159:7; p163:5; p165:3; p167:2,3; p197:1; p217:4; p241:2; p245:5; p253:7; p295:2; **Paul Doherty** p53:1 **J Enticott** p19:1,4,6; p21:2,3; p87:6; p153:5 **FLPA** p15:2,3 **FLPA/S C Brown** p105:4; p107:4 **FLPA/Michael Callan** p105:5 **FLPA/Christiana F Carvalho** p15:2,3; p17:1; **FLPA/S Clark** p21:7 **FLPA/Hans Dieter Brandl** p61:5; p189:3 **FLPA/T & P Gardner** p113:4 **FLPA/Michael Gore** p99:3 **FLPA/H Hautala** p65:1 **FLPA/Peggy Heard** p51:1 **FLPA/David Hosking** p17:6; p31:6; p217:3 **FLPA/E & D Hosking** p85:3; p109:7,9; p127:6; p143:1; p189:7; p273:6; p277:3 **FLPA/W T Miller** p239:8 **FLPA/Philip Perry** p19:5; p55:7; p67:3; p93:5; p95:3 **FLPA/Fritz Polking** p49:2; p259:4,5 **FLPA/H Schrempp** p69:4; p211:3 **FLPA/Silvestris** p143:3 **FLPA/Roger Tidman** p21:6,8; p109:8; p113:7 **FLPA/L West** p101:1 **FLPA/Roger Wilmshurst** p109:1,2 **FLPA/W Wisniewski** p91:6; p109:6 **FLPA/Martin Withers** p109:10 **P J Ginn** p49:9; p55:6; p57:2; p65:5; p75:6; p79:2,4; p81:7; p83:5,6; p87:10; p125:2; p129:2,4; p133:6; p147:7,8; p155:5; p157:4; p163:3; p169:2; p1 81:4; p187:2,3; p189:1; p191:3,4; p193:3,4; p195:2; p199:1,2; p201:6; p211:4,5; p219:2; p221:4; p223:2,4; p233:2,5; p243:1,5; p249:1; p251:1,3,5; p257:2; p263:8; p265:6; p273:4; p275:2; p277:5; p281:1,2 **M Goetz** p131:2; p265:2; p269:7 **André Goetz** p169:6 **B H Harper** p73:3; p271:7 **T Harris** p177:6 **R R Hartley** p49:8; p67:6 **Raymonde Johannesson FPSSA** p273:5 **Roy Johannesson FPSSA** p69:8; p147:2; p149:5; p181:2; p203:3; p241:4; p249:2; p257:6; p261:2,4; p277:2,4; p295:7 **M P Kahl** p15:1 **A C Kemp** p161:1 **Joris Komen** p273:2 **Gordon Langsbury** p35:8; p59:2; p61:8; p89:6; p91:5; p97:3; p101:3; p109:4; p111:9; p113:5; p115:3; p133:1; p135:5; p215:3; p217:5; p235:1 **T D Longrigg** p25:1; p29:1,p37:5; p65:3; p73:2; p83:8; p99:1; p113:6; p191:6; p203:5 ,9; p205:2,7; p219:1,3,5; p225:2,4; p227:5; p231:3; p247:4,7; p255:1; p257:5; p259:1; p267:8; p271:4; p285:4; p291:5,8; p293:3,7 **John Marchant** p61:7 **Geoff McIlleron** p143:2; p145:5; p229:5 **J M Mendelsohn** p19:8; p243:2 **Richard T Mills** p79:5 **Nico Myburgh** p57:5; p79:6; p81:3,5; p145:1; p167:4; p171:4; p173:6; 177:4; p179:3,8,9,10; p187:1; p205:9; p211:1; p293:6 **Will Nichol** p43:7; p55:1; p73:4 **G R Nichols** p215:5,6; p221:3; p231:5; p239:2 **J C Paterson-Jones** p31:9; p189:8; p213:4 **Photo Access** p53:3; p57:6 **Photo Access/C F Bartlett** p235:3 **Photo Access/J J Brooks** p57:6; p81:4; p147:5; p179:2 **Photo Access/G P L du Plessis** p207:7; p279:6 **Photo Access/HPH Photography** p53:3; p169:1; p201:5; 207:2; p213:5 **Photo Access/J&B Photography** p97:1 **Photo Access/David Steele** p229:6 **Photo Access/Peter Steyn** p65:2; p75:1; p81:1,2; p87:1; p225:7 **Peter Pickford** p51:2,5; p53:5; p57:4; p63:4 **Kim Prochazka** p87:7 **Dr and Mrs Manfried Reichardt** p23:7; p25:9; p27:3; p29:3; p31:5; p39:4; p43:3; p83:4; p173:4; p175:1; p181:1; p183:2; p189:2; p191:1; p205:5; p227:3; p229:4; p231:1,6; p233:1; p243:3; p265:8; p269:3; p277:7; p279:4,5; p287:5 **H Schrempp** p69:3 **SIL/Wendy Dennis** front cover: inset centre **SIL/Nigel J Dennis** front cover: main pic and inset right; back cover: top and centre right; title page; p13:5; p33:1,4-6; p35:3,6; p37:8; p39:9,10; p55:5; p63:3; p73:6; p75:5;p83:3; p87:6; p91:7; p93:1,2; p95:1,4,6; p97:2; p107:1; p119:6; p125:3; p127:1; p129:5; p137:4; p151:2; p153:5; p197:1; p247:6 **SIL/Peter Pickford** p67:2 **Ian Sinclair** p15:5-10; p17:2-5,7,8; p19:2,3,7; p21:1,4,5; p23:2,3; p25:6; p63:6; p 85:4; p87:2; p107:6; p113:3; p115:2,5-7; p117:2; p123:6; p141:3; p183: 4; p207:5; p211:2 **Peter Steyn** p57:3; p67:4; p189:4 **W R Tarboton** p13:4; p23:8; p59:8; p69:1; p71:5; p73:1; p81:9; p99:9; p103:2; p107:2; p109:3; p111:5; p117:8; p119:7,8; p121:1; p123:4; p131:5; p147:1,4; p149:3; p157:5; p159:3,6; p165:4; p167:1; p173:5; 177:1,3; p185:7; p187:5; p201:2; p203:1,10,11; p203:10,11; p209:3; p213:2; p223:3; p225:1,3; p227:2,6; p229:1; p233:3; p239:6; p245:2,3; p249:7; p253:5; p263:1; p267:6,7; p269:2; p271:5,6; p275:1,5; p277:6; p283:6; p285:2,5; p287:1,2,3; p289:9 **J J Theron** p25:3,4; p35:4; p43:1; p71:7; p83:9; p87:5,9; p131:3; p133:4,7; p145:4; p171:2; p169:3; p183:1,5,6; p185:4; p189:5,6; p195:4; p197:2,3; p207:6,10; p209:4; p229:3; p237:4; p243:4; p247:2; p253:2,3; p255:7; p257:4; p259:2; p263:6,9,10; p265:7; **Colin Urquhart** p13:3; p39:2; p45:4; p53:4; p123:1,2; p185:5; p221:1; p267:4,5 **Hein von Hörsten** p23:4; p165:1; p191:2; p207:8; p235:2; p237:9; p239:5,7; p261:7; p263:4 **Lanz von Hörsten** front cover, inset left; p147:3; p149:7; p249:5 **Johan van Jaarsveld** p47:3-5,9; p49:1; p57:1; p137:2,6,7; 139:1; p155:4; p179:5; p185:6; p205:4; p233:6; p239:3; p265:9; p267:9; p269:4,5; p283:5,8; p285:8; p289:4 **Zelda Wahl** spine; p25:5; p37:7; p77:2,3; p103:3; p121:2; p127:2; p129:1; p245:4; **Dave Wallis** p31:3 **Alan Weaving** p25:10; p29:4,8; p31:8; p35:9; p49:3,4; p53:6,7; p67:7; 69:2; p77:1,4; p83:7; p87:8; p89:1,3,5; p91:1; p93:4; p111:6; p135:1,6; p137:3; p141: 6; p149:6; p151:1; p157:1; p171:1,3; p185:1,3; p195:3,5; p203:7,8; p205: 1; p209:1; p213:3; p221:2; p225:6; p227:1; p237:7,8; p247:1; p249:6; p261:1 **MC Wilkes** p61:6 **Joe Williams** p179:1

Illustrations appearing on righthand pages **Peter Hayman** p71:6; p121:5; p131:4; p143:5,6; p145:2,6; p177:2; p181:3; p229:2; p261:9 **Norman Arlott** p163:4; p167:5; p191:5; p193:1; p197:5; 219:4; p235:5; p239:1; p283:9

Illustrations appearing on lefthand pages (right margin) **Peter Hayman** pp12-160; pp172-188; pp226-232; p260 **Norman Arlott** pp162-168; pp194-224; pp240-258; pp274-294 **Simon Barlow** p268